D1786468

Database Machines

Modern Trends and Applications

NATO ASI Series

Advanced Science Institutes Series

A series presenting the results of activities sponsored by the NATO Science Committee, which aims at the dissemination of advanced scientific and technological knowledge, with a view to strengthening links between scientific communities.

The Series is published by an international board of publishers in conjunction with the NATO Scientific Affairs Division

A Life Sciences B Physics	Plenum Publishing Corporation London and New York
C Mathematical and Physical Sciences	D. Reidel Publishing Company Dordrecht, Boston, Lancaster and Tokyo
D Behavioural and Social Sciences E Applied Sciences	Martinus Nijhoff Publishers Boston, The Hague, Dordrecht and Lancaster
F Computer and Systems Sciences G Ecological Sciences H Cell Biology	Springer-Verlag Berlin Heidelberg New York London Paris Tokyo

Series F: Computer and Systems Sciences Vol. 24

Database Machines

Modern Trends and Applications

Edited by

A. K. Sood and A. H. Qureshi

Department of Electrical and Computer Engineering
Wayne State University, Detroit, MI 48202/USA

Springer-Verlag
Berlin Heidelberg New York London Paris Tokyo
Published in cooperation with NATO Scientific Affairs Divison

Proceedings of the NATO Advanced Study Institute on Relational Database Machine Architecture held at Les Arcs, France, July 14–27, 1985

ISBN 3-540-17164-9 Springer-Verlag Berlin Heidelberg New York
ISBN 0-387-17164-9 Springer-Verlag New York Berlin Heidelberg

Library of Congress Cataloging in Publication Data. NATO Advanced Study Institute on Relational Database Machine Architecture (1986 : Les Arcs, France) Database machines. (NATO ASI series. Series F, Computer and systems sciences ; no. 24) "Published in cooperation with NATO Scientific Affairs Division." 1. Data Base management—Congresses. 2. Electronic digital computers—Congresses. I. Sood, A. K. II. Qureshi, A. H. III. Series. QA76.9.D3N38 1986 004 86-26302
ISBN 0-387-17164-9 (U.S.)

Printed in Germany

Printing: Druckhaus Beltz, Hemsbach; Bookbinding: J. Schäffer GmbH & Co. KG., Grünstadt
2145/3140-543210

Preface

This volume consists of a collection of 28 papers presented at the NATO Advanced Study Institute held July 14–27, 1985 in the beautiful resort at Les Arcs, France. The director of this ASI was A. K. Sood and A. H. Qureshi was the co-director.

Since its introduction in the early 1970s the relational data model has been widely accepted. Several research and industrial efforts are being undertaken to develop special purpose database machines to implement the relational model. In addition, database machines are being explored for applications such as image processing and information retrieval. In this NATO-ASI the lecturers discussed special purpose database machine architectures from the viewpoint of architecture and hardware detail, software, user needs, theoretical framework and applications. The papers presented were of two types – regular papers and short papers. The research in database machines is being conducted in several countries. This fact is underscored when it is noted that papers in this volume are authored by researchers in France, Germany, Italy, Japan, Portugal, Turkey, U.K. and U.S.A.

The first paper discusses the experience and applications of users with a commercially available database machine. In the following eight papers the characteristics of six database machines are discussed. The second, third and fourth papers deal with the RDBM project at the Technical University of Braunschweig (Germany). Zeidler discusses the design objectives, architecture and system design of RDBM. Teich presents the hardware utilized for sorting. Stiege discusses the RDBM control software and issues in performance modeling and evaluation.

Missikoff et al. present DBMAC with particular emphasis on data organization and logical and physical architectural considerations. Tanaka has suggested the Massive Parallel Database Computer (MPDC). MPDC architecture and the control schemes to exploit the parallelism of this computer have been presented. As part of Japan's Fifth Generation Computer project a relational database machine called Delta is being developed. Sakai et al. discuss Delta with special focus on the relational database engine, and also discuss an approach to knowledge base machine development. Next, Inoue and Kawazu present ADAM – a relational database machine – and discuss issues of data organization, and methods for performing selection and join operations. Gardarin and Pasquer report on the architecture and design of INRIA's parallel database machine called SABRE. This MIMD machine is being enhanced by the addition of rule management functions.

Childs has developed a theoretical framework within which systems development can be treated. The approach is based on the concept of Function Space Architecture. In the next paper Van Buer et al. present the results of a comparative study of several relational systems. In this study similar queries were implemented in different combinations of DBMSs and computer systems. Forker and Riechmann's study is based on their experience in integrating the Braunschweig RDBM and Britton Lee's IDM. They present a database-application protocol to support communication needs.

An important consideration in database machines is the implementation of the basic operations. Menon presents multiple processor based sorting and join algorithms and compares these approaches. Gonzalez-Rubio and Rohmer discuss the similarities between artificial intelligence and database systems and show that similar specialized hardware could be utilized in both environments. Sood et al. discuss two hardware implementations of relational algebra operations and aggregate functions. Boorman presents a search engine – CAFS-ISP – which is associated with the disk controllers. The operations, application and performance of CAFS are discussed.

Quick presents a parallel access cellular system which would have use in fifth generation systems. The next paper explores bus arbitration issues for an intelligent memory system employing massive parallelism. McPhee et al. outline some features of current knowledge base systems and discuss an alternative input/output architecture. The Flexible Deductive Engine (FDE) discussed by Van Buer et al. was motivated by the need to provide an experimental environment to evaluate alternative search strategies in support of logic programming and knowledge management.

The evolution of database machines has led to an interest in the study of multi-media databases. Tanaka and Takahashi present a transmedia machine which integrates the functions of a database manager and the electronic filing system. Grosky discusses a framework for integrating image and textual data in the database environment. Ataman analyzes the requirements for the database created using satellite imaging techniques. Can explores fact/document retrieval based on the database machine.

Caviglia et al. suggest a VLSI based array processor for parallel computation of list intersections. METU-GDBMS presented by Dogac supports network, hierarchical and relational data models. Pseudo-associative memories, built using random access memories and some additional hardware, are discussed by da Silva et al. Reynolds presents an expert database interface to simplify users' access of the database.

This NATO-ASI was a lively, informative and stimulating experience. It is hoped that the publication of this volume will aid in providing wider dissemination of the technical content of the ASI. This ASI was co-sponsored and supported by Ford Motor Company and Wayne State University. Finally, I would like to acknowledge and thank the lecturers, authors and participants and the Institute organizing committee members – S. Fujisaki, G. Gardarin, A.H. Qureshi and B. Yormark.

A.K. Sood

Table of Contents

User Experience with the Britton Lee IDM 500

Robert W. Taylor
Vice President, Engineering
Britton Lee, Inc.
14600 Winchester Blvd.
Los Gatos, CA 95030

1. Introduction

Well over 350 Britton Lee Intelligent Database Machines have been shipped to over 100 customers during the past four years. They are used, in some cases, seven days a week, 24 hours per day in a number of application areas. During the purchasing cycle, they are compared against more conventional, "software-only" relational systems. The customers usually return and purchase more IDMs as their applications proliferate through their organizations. And they ask for new features. All of this gives an excellent basis for evaluating database machine approaches, how the customers are using the IDM, how they compare it to other approaches, and what they want to see next. This direct experience also gives system developers insight into both hardware and software architectural issues, which in turn allows conclusions about what has been learned and where the field is going.

2. Review of the IDM

The basic structure of the IDM has been described in detail elsewhere [1,2,3]. We will summarize it briefly here for completeness. Like all database machines, the IDM attaches to one or more "host" computers using some sort of communication network (figure 1). Software in the host communicates with software in the IDM, with requests coming from the host as a collection of encoded packets, and collections of responses (data tuples, status, etc.) flowing back to the host. In addition to offering a database machine, Britton Lee offers software to run in a variety of host/operating system combinations. While not the main subject of this paper, the host software capabilities have turned out to be quite important in practice, as they are part of the database service that a user expects, and most users are not interested in writing this package themselves. It has turned out that portability of this software package is a major consideration as the connectability of the IDM to a variety of hosts allows usage of the machine in a variety of environments. Also, it is important to provide a rich set of application-building tools in the host package, including parsers, pre-compilers, fourth generation languages, screen formatters, and data conversion utilities. Britton Lee provides this package in a number of minicomputer, mainframe, and personal computer environments, and a number of third party capabilities have extended the range of capabilities using their own host software.

The basic structure of the IDM is shown in figure 2. The hardware is a collection of boards which plug into a proprietary bus running at 20 MByte/sec. Boards

NATO ASI Series, Vol. F 24
Database Machines. Edited by A. K. Sood and A. H. Qureshi

HOST STRUCTURE

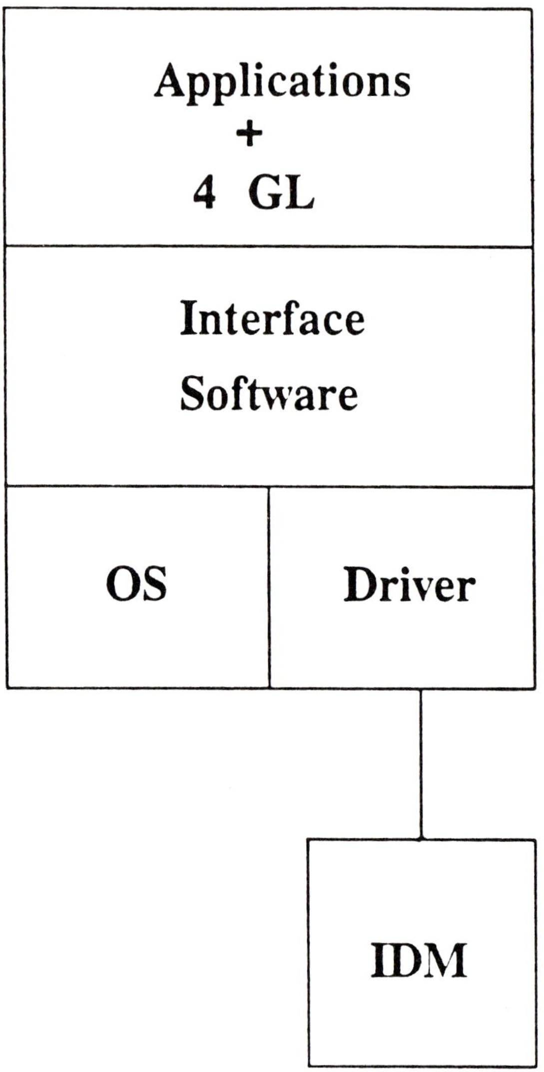

FIGURE 1

IDM STRUCTURE

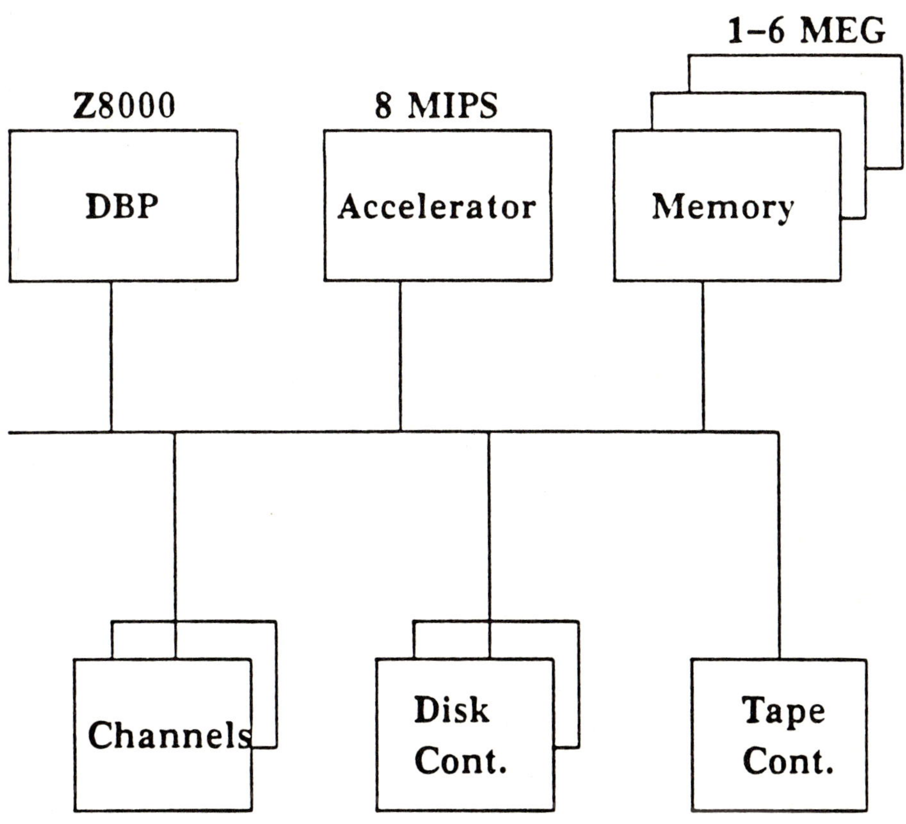

RS232

IEEE 488

Ethernet XNS

IBM BLK MUX

Z8000

1-16 Spindles

SMD

FIGURE 2

interfacing the host network to the IDM have been developed for RS232, IEEE 488, Ethernet (XNS), and IBM Block Multiplexer protocols. Each of these boards contains an on-board Z8000 microcomputer to offload network interrupt and protocol handling. Communication with the rest of the system is through a shared memory, queued interface.

The heart of the database processing is done on two boards working as co-processors. The Database Processor (DBP) contains a Z8000 microcomputer plus a remote dial-in and operator's console capability. The bulk of the database system runs on this board. In concert with the DBP, the Database Accelerator (DAC) is a special purpose 8 Million Instructions Per Second (MIPs) processor which, if present, runs certain key subroutines within the system. The DAC is optional, and the corresponding subroutines run in the DBP when the DAC is not present.

Up to 6 Megabytes of storage can be included in the machine, with the bulk of it being used for data buffering; especially in multi-user systems.

Up to 4 disk controllers, each supporting up to 4 spindles of SMD industry standard disks can be attached. At the present time, this allows up to about 10 Gigabytes of on-line storage. A mirrored-disk capability is also offered, though this must be included in the sixteen spindle limit.

A tape controller allows database dumps and loads without burdening the host and communication network.

In summary, the IDM hardware architecture is that of a bus-oriented minicomputer, allowing field upgradable capability and a wide variety of attachment strategies.

The software running on this hardware is a full function relational database management system supporting multiple users, transactions, a full relational language including views, authorization, stored commands, optimization, recovery - in short a state-of-the-art data management capability. The system is fully integrated with a customized operating system to take maximum advantage of the hardware. Much of the power of the IDM comes from this close coupling hardware and software. Because there is only one program that runs inside the IDM (excepting certain utilities and diagnostics) the hardware can be customized for this one problem and the operating environment can be tuned for it. We will return to this point in Section 4.

3. User Experiences with the IDM

Users are enthusiastic about the IDM and are finding a variety of uses for it. These uses are not for the most part in the traditional Data Processing departments offloading large mainframes. Rather, IDMs are being used in situations that exploit the power of workstations and minicomputers, which are noted for their excellent interactive and real-time capabilities, while adding high performance, shared database. We illustrate with several examples from our user base.

3.1. Metaphor

Metaphor Corporation markets an advanced, iconic, bit mapped graphic workstation to analysts and planners in Fortune 500 companies. These analysts need high performance access to large databases of census, demographic, financial and sales data to analyze market trends, explain market movements and recommend strategies. Typically they need access to this data for input into spread sheets which in turn can be embedded in reports and converted to charts and graphs. The particulars of the queries are unknown and much "what if" analysis takes place, both within the spread sheets and in accessing the data.

To accommodate this kind of use, Metaphor has constructed an advanced user interface which allows users to draw a picture of the query they would like run (see figure 3). The results can then be placed into a spread sheet which in turn can drive production of reports, memos, etc. Collections of operations can be built using data flow techniques and saved for later use. The system can also be programmed and queries can be written in SQL(TM).

A database machine is natural in this kind of application. It functions as a server to a variety of workstations, none of which could hold the data (they are diskless). The size of the database and response time that can be supported by a database machine is a sine-qua-non for this kind of application. The processing power in the workstation itself is devoted, as it properly should be, to more and more advanced user interface functions. Tying up the workstations with database processing, even if it were possible, would ultimately be self-defeating.

3.2. German Post Office

The German Post Office (Bundespost) offers a directory assistance service whereby users can phone an operator to determine a number or they can phone a computer directly and get audio response from inputs via the touch-tone keys.

An application such as this is a fairly traditional one from a technology viewpoint. There are a large number of inquiries of a predictable kind. Multi-indexing must be available. There are a large number of updates, but many can be processed in off hours. In this particular case, a 39 Gigabyte database is spread over multiple IDMs supporting 400 queries/minute and 50,000 updates per day.

One might ask with an application like this why the relational approach was used at all. This is the kind of system that has always in the past been the province of the highly structured transaction systems.

The reason the IDM was chosen is a combination of cost effectiveness, ease of application development, and adequacy of throughput. While it may be true that relational systems generally do not outperform more conventional systems in structured applications such as this, that does not mean relational systems perform badly. The ease of programming and overall cost effectiveness of using a database machine proved a special point - the day is gone (if it ever was) when relational technology needs to be restricted to non-production applications. Relational systems can compete when all the costs, including software and maintenance costs, are counted.

METAPHOR

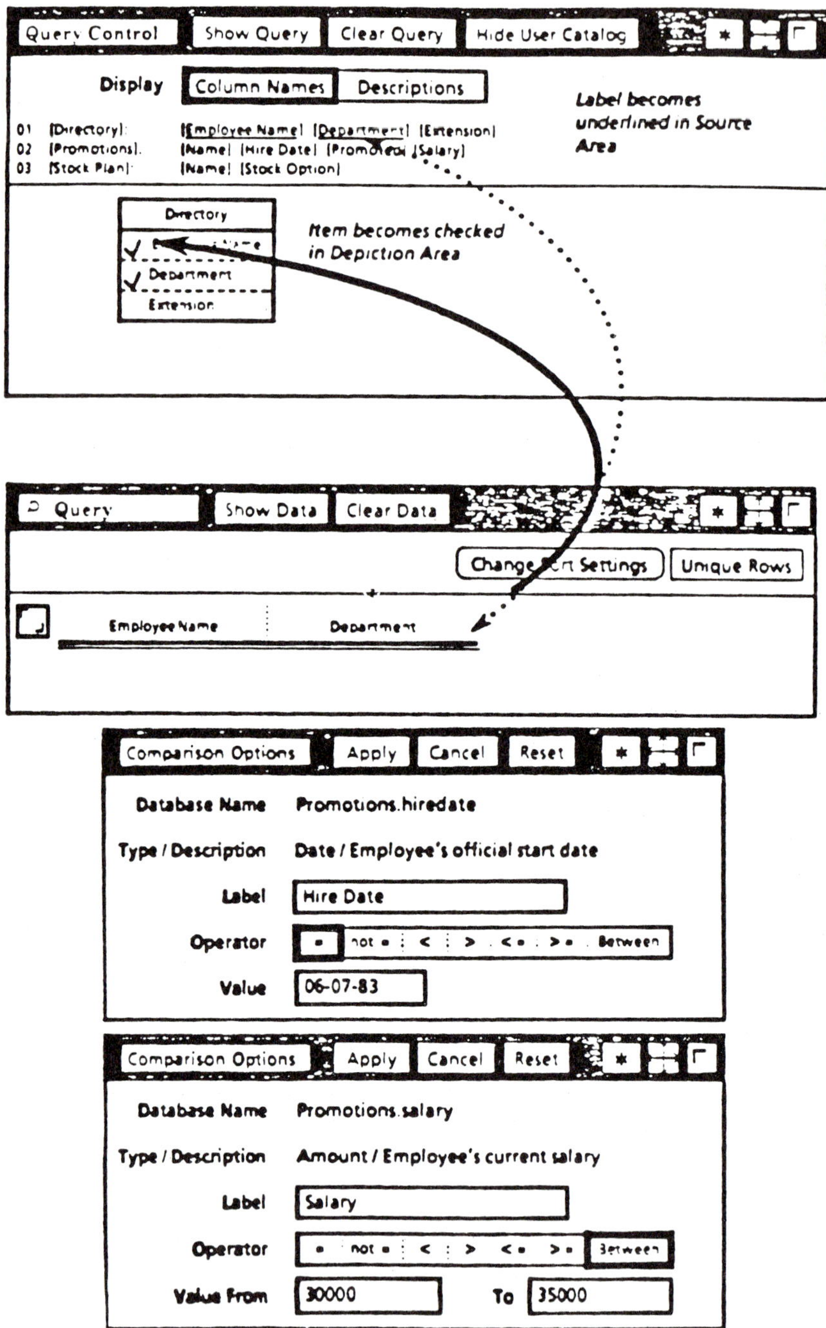

FIGURE 3

3.3. 3M Company

Minnesota Mining and Manufacturing (3M) provides a wide range of products in a number of areas. In one project, engineers are doing printed circuit layout using a computer aided engineering workstation connected to a minicomputer. They needed to share data with mechanical designers, running on a different mini, and with purchasing, whose system runs on a mainframe. The solution is an IDM holding a common database but accessible to all three groups (see figure 4). (The IBM to IDM link is indirect for pragmatic reasons; the link could be direct in today's environment.)

This kind of interconnectability with data sharing across diverse hosts has been realized since the earliest database machines [4]. It brings with it a number of problems in handling diverse character sets and a variety of numeric representations, which are handled jointly in the IDM and the host software package. But increasingly our users have found the value of this kind of sharing. It opens up a new set of applications not possible before. In the past, shared data meant applications on the same host. This was inconvenient and sometimes impossible. Now users can access shared data without having to abandon a familiar terminal/operating system just to get sharing. They don't have to give up access to a collection of other applications that may not be available on another host.

We have found that this new dimension of sharing generally comes later in the life cycle of an IDM in an installation. First, an application gets installed. After it works, others find a use for this new data resource. It is surprising how much can be saved using this approach. In the 3M case, product design time was shortened by as much as 50%, just by allowing all three functions (printed circuit, mechanical design and purchasing) to have up-to-date, accurate, consistent information.

3.4. Summary

These three examples were chosen for their diversity and uniqueness; there are many other examples today. But from the three examples certain key characteristics can be extracted. First, a database machine is a server, not just a back end. A back end off-loads cycles from a host and replaces them with more cost effective cycles inside the database machine. This allows application cycles to be devoted to applications. But as the trend widens to put application cycles on a users desk, the trend to the database machine as a server will become even more apparent. Second, the database machine is capable of high performance, even up to production levels. This level of performance and database capacity is unusual if not unique in relational systems today. Third, the dimension of sharing offered by database machines opens up totally new application areas which can have a dramatic impact on productivity. The results are real. The concept works.

3.5. Additional lessons

In our experiences with users, we have learned several other lessons. The relational model was put forth to free uses from "representational details" of earlier models and to give a model of "Spartan simplicity", both for ease of use and ease of understanding. The relational approach has succeeded in this, and has succeeded to such an extent that

3M Company

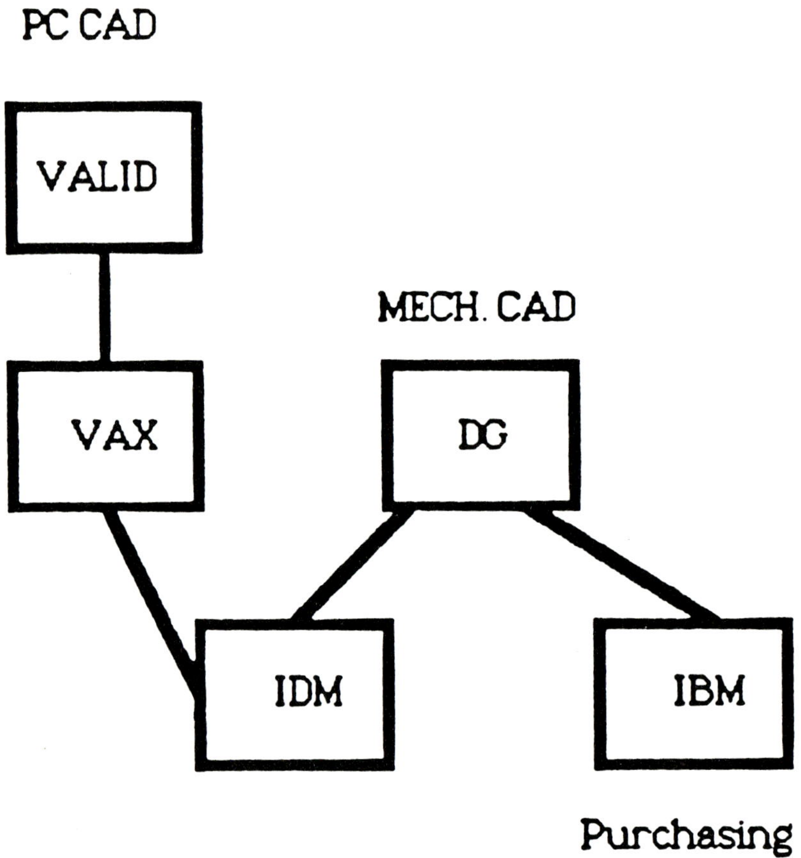

- Up to Date Bill of Materials
- Stable Inventory

FIGURE 4

database technology is now available to a whole new class of users. This is ultimately a benefit, but it brings with it a requirement for education, support, and patience. For example:

* Users often do not appreciate the subtleties of level 2 and level 3 [5] locking protocols. Thus, for example, users complain when a long running, read transaction blocks a short running update transaction at level 3 consistency.

* Users expect that multi-way joins (6 to 12 way) will always execute efficiently. Normalization theory suggests that splitting relations is a good idea under certain conditions. Reconstitution of data is not looked upon as a problem - it isn't a problem of function, only of efficiency. Consequently, users are surprised when an eight way join is slow, sometimes because the access path strategy chosen by the access path selector is incorrect. Our approach has been to let users select the access path strategy if they wish to. While one can look forward to the day when access path selectors always do better than humans, the fact today is that the heuristics used and the amount of skew in the data can easily fool the best access path selectors.

* As the user base widens, database administration tools, together with design tools, performance tools, and application development tools become even more important. When databases were the realm of specialists, people tolerated awkward tools and word-of-mouth transmission of techniques. When databases are widespread, this is not a viable way to operate.

All the above lessons are symptoms of success and confirm our belief that the future will see even more widespread use of this technology. However, eventually these seemingly peripheral issues limit the growth and/or competitiveness of a product or technology. Hence they must be addressed.

4. Database Machine Technology

As a vendor of database machines, we frequently have encountered arguments from database vendors, usually running a software system on a conventional mainframe/mini regarding the viability of database machines as a technology. At a conference on database machines, it makes sense to review these arguments against database machines, and it certainly has been part of our and our users' experience.

4.1. In two years . . .

This argument purports that in two (or four or some small number of years) conventional mainframes/minis will run twice as fast as today, hence any performance problems today will be cured by the next release of the software plus the next generation of general purpose hardware.

It is clearly true that general purpose mainframes/minis will speed up. Does this spell the end of database machines? I don't think so. For one thing, the argument presumes database machines will not speed up. This is counter to their history so far, and the silicon inside database machines will run faster as well. If we stopped development, the argument would hold. But there is no reason to stop development.

Further, general purpose mainframes/minis have a level of compatibility requirement that limits the uses to which the faster silicon can be put. Instruction set compatibility, virtual memory support, invisibility of a cache and preservation of I/O architecture are all problems which will cost chips and board space to the designer of the next generation. A database machine designer has a much different problem. The level of compatibility that must be maintained is at the network interface, a much more machine independent level. Consequently the instruction set of the processor, the memory architecture and the I/O configurations can be changed drastically to take advantage of new technology. Pieces of software can be rewritten if this is warranted - all without impacting user applications. The silicon works for everyone; it ought to work better for the special purpose machine designer.

On a more philosophical note, it is curious that people who profess great enthusiasm for specialized architectures for array processing have exactly the opposite opinion on database machine processing. Presumably this is because they feel the benefits for array processing are sufficient to justify the investment but do not feel the same for database processing. It is never quantified what the benefits have to be before specialized architectures are justified. Sometimes a factor of ten is used. While we have not found that users require a factor of ten difference before buying our machine, it is not unusual for us to achieve a factor of 10 in price/performance over conventional approaches. In many cases, database machine technology was the only cost effective solution; it seems inappropriate to argue about hypothetical factors in such cases.

4.2. Why the IDM runs fast

Rather than argue about what might happen in the future, it is instructive to understand why the current technology succeeds. As will be seen, it is not the result of "magic architectures"; it is entirely explainable in terms of engineering trade-offs that can be made when only one program (the dbms) needs to be run and this can be done in a totally controlled environment. A number of these trade-offs can be made. They compound and reinforce one another when done properly.

A hardware machine that needs to run only one program can be configured in ways that a general purpose computer could never be configured. For example:

* It is possible to use different kinds of memory in different parts of the address space, since which parts of the address space will be used for what is completely known.

* It is possible to employ specialized co-processors for sorting, searching, text processing. The usefulness of specialized co-processors is much easier to predict, because the instruction mix is completely known.

* Every decision can be approached from the point of view of whether changing the hardware is appropriate (in the long term) and what features should be incorporated for maximum performance. There is not a cacophony of conflicting needs. While this point is qualitative, it is important to making progress quickly.

On the software side:

* Operating system and dbms can be more closely tied with respect to buffering, dispatching, and process communication.

* Since there is only one workload to be understood, and it is described at a high level rather than only reference patterns, the balancing of resources is much easier.

* Queued I/O interfaces can be employed throughout the system, allowing high MIP processors to be employed with known cache miss characteristics.

The IDM outperforms the competition because these advantages reinforce one another. No single reason would make a large difference. Together they do. It is also encouraging from a technological point of view that most of these advantages are not easily duplicated in the environment of conventional systems. The advantages of a controlled environment will only increase as more advanced chips and algorithms become commercially available.

5. The Future

Database machines are now a routine part of many computer operations. Of course, users ask for new features. Many of these features are common to relational systems everywhere; in some cases, database machines have a special advantage.

5.1. Continuous operation

Data is a resource, and a database server should never go away. We feel this is a most important aspect of database machines and perhaps one where the quite loose coupling between the application and the database can be beneficial. So long as the server on the network gives the appearance of always being available, it is not necessary to build a system which can tolerate arbitrary faults. This greatly simplifies the problem. It is possible for a backup machine to take over processing of a transaction by synthesizing a message to the host forcing a transaction restart. This is far easier than having a processor which must pick up a computation in mid-stream.

5.2. Data types

The demand is increasing for morc data types, particularly those where "large" data objects can be incorporated in the system. This at least means the ability to coordinate database objects and file objects in a single transaction. But much more could be done. The database machine is the natural place for additional filtering of large data objects using specialized hardware. It also offers an environment where small programs could be introduced into the database environment in a controlled way. This would also allow enhanced integrity enforcement.

5.3. Federation

A database machine is a server, but the model which assumes all data resides in the server is too simplistic. The database machine should support protocols which span machines and data models. This implies participation in distributed commit protocols.

5.4. And of course

performance, more tools, easier to use interfaces, . . .

All these are reasonable requests and are symptomatic of a technology which the users are accepting enthusiastically. They indicate that database machines have a bright future so long as we exploit their inherent performance and functional advantages.

6. References

(1) Ubell, M., "The IDM", in *Query Processing in Database Systems*, W. Kim, ed., Springer-Verlag, 1985, pp. 237-247

(2) Epstein, R. and Hawthorn, P., "Design Decisions for the Intelligent Database Machine", Proc. 1980 NCC, AFIPS Press, Montvale, NJ, pp. 237-241

(3) IDM Software Reference Manual, Version 1.7, Britton Lee, Inc., Los Gatos, CA

(4) Canaday, R. H., et al. "A Back-end Computer for Database Management", CACM, 17:10 (1974), pp. 575-582

(5) Gray, J. N., et al., "Granularity of Locks and Degrees of Consistency in a Shared Database", in *Modeling in Data Base Management Systems*, G. M. Nijssen, ed., North Holland, Amsterdam, 1976, pp. 365-394. Also IBM Research Report RJ 1706.

RDBM - A Relational Database Machine Based on a Dedicated Multiprocessor System

H.Ch. Zeidler
Institut für Datenverarbeitungsanlagen
Technische Universität Braunschweig
Postfach 3329
D-3300 Braunschweig
West Germany

Abstract

In contrast to the so-called Slotnick-Machines and homogeneous multiprocessor systems the Relational Database Machine (RDBM) implemented at the Technical University of Braunschweig (Germany) is a heterogeneous multiprocessor system with functionalized hardware. Starting with some remarks on the design objectives the overall architecture and the system design of the RDBM as a centrally controlled multiprocessor backend system with purpose-built processors and a commonly shared memory is presented. Details are given with special emphasis on hardware supported functions, whereby the various processor features are discussed.

1. Introduction

The growing number of applications for database systems form an essential component of increasing importance in the wide range of non-numerical data processing. For a long time researchers have been busy in developing dedicated computer systems with purpose-built hardware and software to fulfill the user de-

NATO ASI Series, Vol. F 24
Database Machines. Edited by A. K. Sood and A. H. Qureshi

mands, for example, for comfort, data security and consistency and high-speed access despite of increasing data capacities up to gigabytes. In this way the known disadvantages of using general-purpose computers for DBS, especially with I/O and CPU-load, shall become obsolete.

As known, years ago backend systems with special structures had been developed which especially supported the search operation. In combination with the appearance of cost-effective and efficient hardware these early solutions, the so-called "Slotnick-Machines" or first generation database machines, had been followed by database machines which, in particular as homogeneous multiprocessor systems, supported other important database operations such as sort or join.

The Relational Database Machine RDBM implemented at the Technical University of Braunschweig (Germany), a database machine of the second generation, also had a predecessor, the SURE-system (a search computer), which was completed in 1978 as an experimental project /LSZe 78/. The basic idea involved was to scan data completely and sequentially on-the-fly which means while being read from a disk, using special comparison units. In this way data could be accessed in a content-addressed way from a large associative disk store.

The net positive result of the search processor project was the verification that a special-purpose machine could be built which satisfied the speed requirements for a class of existing search problems. A valuable, but negative, result was that such a machine - although constituting a straightforward general concept - was rather costly in terms of both hardware and software and the scope of suitable applications did not appear wide enough to justify the mass production of a search machine of this type. The conclusion drawn was that it was necessary to revise the technique employed in the search operation, exploiting advances in microprocessor and memory technology, whilst at the same time tackling further database problems (sorting and memory management) using hardware assistance.

The Braunschweig Relational Database Machine is a system of dedicated processors which supports the main subtasks, namely mass data operations (e.g. searching, sorting) and memory management operations, while the user communication, compilation and the overall process control is centrally performed by a general-purpose processor /AHLL 81/. It had been attempted to implement the most significant aspects of a relational DBS with emphasis on the cooperation between the individual components of the system. An experimental machine had been built in order to demonstrate that the concept as a whole is feasible.

After an overview of the RDBM system concept the design of the various components of the system is discussed in detail. The software aspects including performance evaluation and in-depth considerations concerning the implementation of the sort operation are part of the following papers of the RDBM session /Stie 85, Teic 85/.

2. System Concept

2.1. Design Considerations

The primary goal was to implement a complete DBS that supports frequently used and time-consuming functions using appropriate purpose-built hardware components. It is not obvious that the system design has to comprise all the essential DBS components, such as a multiuser environment, checkpointing and recovery, and a functionally powerful user interface, but it is necessary because of the lack of orthogonality in the functional modules of a DBS. Nevertheless, the concentration was laid on certain key points in the actual implementation. These are:

- support of heavily used functions such as data retrieval

- interrecord operations such as the relational join and data aggregation

- consistent processing of concurrent transactions

The system should be capable of being interfaced with arbitrary host computers channel-to-channel as well as via a networking facility, and advanced mass storage devices should be applicable. One of the goals was the exploitation of parallelism in database processing. This included multitasking facilities as well as cooperative execution of operations on the database (e.g. qualification of tuples) by several hardware components in parallel. Moreover, the design of the machine is oriented towards set processing as opposed to single tuple manipulation.

One of the basic decisions was to employ the relational model as the conceptual basis of the database machine which influenced three levels of the system design: the user interface, the operations on data supported by specialized hardware and the structuring of data.

Normalization of relations is a valuable tool for defining the conceptual schema of a database. Normalized relations on the physical level can, however, have a heavy impact on performance. Therefore, internally structured tuples are not normalized: a tuple is a set of attributes, each of which may be simple, multivalued or composed. Whereas a simple attribute may take at most one value in a particular tuple, a multivalued one may have an arbitrary number of individual values. A composed attribute is a sequence of different simple attributes. There may be arbitrary many value sequences for a particular composed attribute in each tuple. Composed attributes are also sometimes called "repeating groups". In order to avoid semantic difficulties, certain relational functions - e.g. the join - are only performed on simple attributes.

A subset of SQL has been chosen as the user interface. The subset comprises the data definition and manipulation facilities, but not integrity constraints. The interface between the database machine and application programs on a host is similar to the program/DBS interface of a conventional database system.

2.2. Overall Architecture and Data Flow

The RDBM system (see Fig. 2.1) may be used in a stand-alone mode (local user), as a specialized node in a computer network by means of a networking interface, or as a backend processor when locally connected to a host computer via a high-speed channel. Its configuration consists of three major components:

- A general-purpose system control processor (DABS) to supervise the different system components and to perform the database operations not supported by specialized hardware, e.g. query analysis

- A mass storage device with its own storage manager and quasi-associative data access facility

- A heterogeneous multiprocessor system consisting of various purpose-built processors with common access to a large main memory. All components communicate via a bus system offering separate paths for data, instruction and status transfers

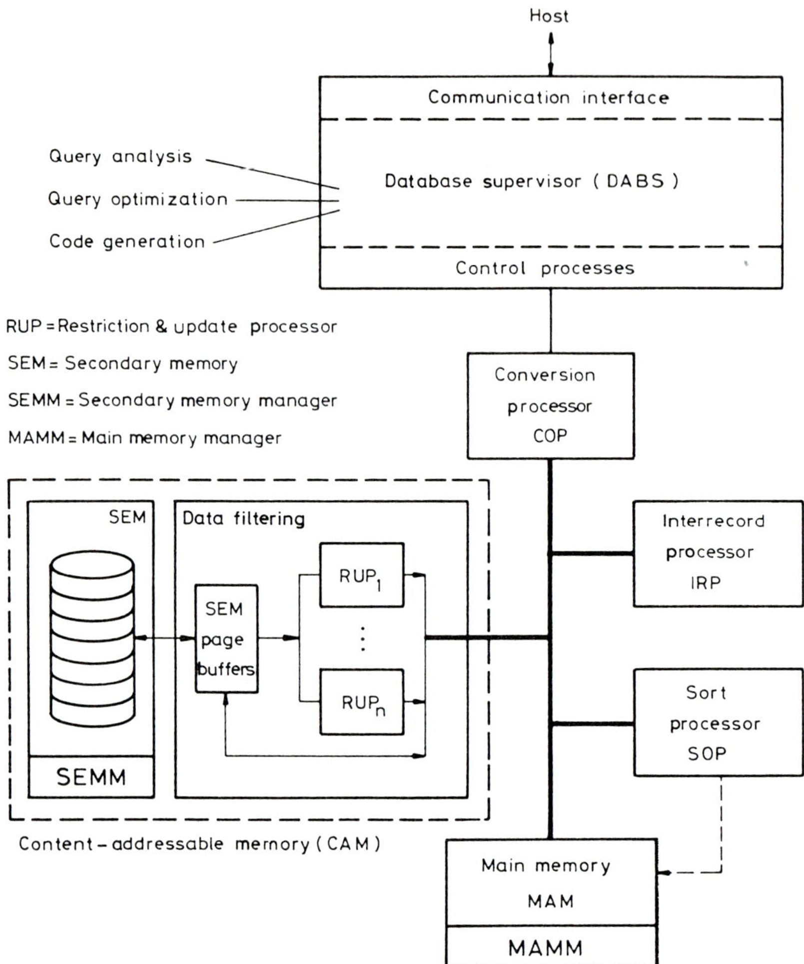

Fig. 2.1: RDBM System Configuration

After reception, a query is decomposed by the control processor software into the elementary operations which are then performed - partially in parallel - by the specialized processors. This includes query preprocessing such as syntax analysis, code optimization taking into account data statistics and the generation of code executable by the hardware components (Note that "query" means all types of user tasks provided by the user interface and not just retrieval operations). The sequence of executable elementary statements is sent to control processes which are responsible for activating the specialized processors as far as possible in parallel during task execution.

Before going into details and discussing the physical layout of the hardware components, at first let us have a look at the data flow between the different components (Fig. 2.2).

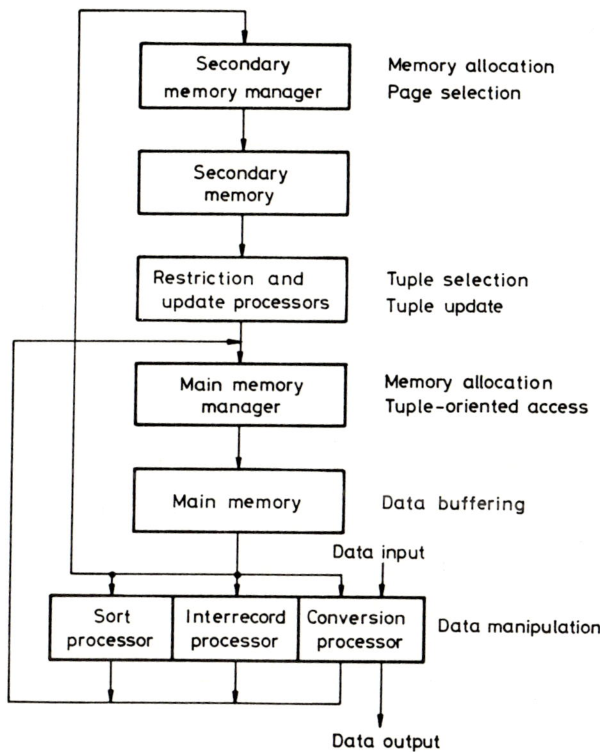

Fig. 2.2: RDBM Data Flow

If a query is to be executed, the secondary memory control process calls for relations or parts of relations relevant to the current query. These accessible data sets (termed segments) are composed of a dynamically alterable number of physical pages residing in the secondary memory. These segments are identified by names, so that the secondary memory manager has to map these names to the physical page addresses. After finding these addresses, the accesses to the storage device are performed and the data is sent to a buffer. The restriction and update processors take these data tuples according to the evaluation program loaded by the database supervisor prior to query execution. If a tuple matches the query, the specified subset of its attributes is selected and then transmitted to the main memory. The main memory is also provided with a logical interface in a manner similar to the secondary memory. The restriction and update processors therefore merely need to specify the name of the target relation in order to allocate its storage space in the main memory. The allocation is dealt with by the main memory manager. A target relation stored in the main memory can be handled in different ways, e.g. it can be returned to the secondary memory and stored there as a new temporary relation if it is only to be used as an intermediate result. Target relations can of course become source relations and then be processed by the database multiprocessor system.

2.3. Purpose-built Processors

The various purpose-built processors of the RDBM comprise specific and standardized hardware (Fig. 2.3) with an 8-bit microprocessor unit /HELL 81/. The processor kernel (AMD 2900 series) consists of an ALU, a sequencer program control unit, an interrupt controller, and a DMA controller. The program memory comprises 8 KB and can be expanded up to 32 KB if required using a special add-on board. The microprogram memory has a capacity of 4K 128-bit words.

The bus interface also constitutes a standardized hardware component of the processors, over which they are connected to the bus system. The hardware of this interface ensures compliance with the various bus protocols and in this way allows considerable simplification of programming and a

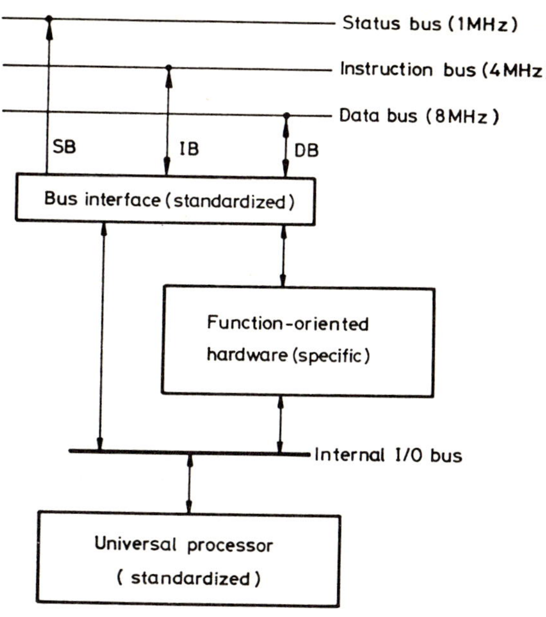

Fig. 2.3: General Structure of the Purpose-built Processors

relaxation of processor timing requirements. It additionally isolates the processor hardware from the bus system.

All these functions cover four double Euroboards. The discussion of the specific hardware is part of Section 3.2 and Section 3.3.

3. Detailed Description of the RDBM Hardware

3.1. The System Control Processor DABS

A NORSK DATA NORD-100 minicomputer with a 1 MB store is employed to provide the overall control of the RDBM system. It is equipped with extensive peripherals to support its additional functions of testing and development. During the development phase, extensive software was being coded at various levels, from the RDBM user interface down to the microprogram code for the individual processors. In addition, it ran programs for the simulation and testing of the various hardware components. As system integration proceeded, an increasing proportion of RDBM control tasks was to be assigned to the NORD-100 running under the existing realtime operating system.

3.2. The Content-Addressable Memory

The mass storage of the RDBM is a content-addressable memory, consisting of a conventional secondary memory (SEM) extended by the SEM page buffers, the secondary memory manager (SEMM) and several restriction and update processors (RUP) for data filtering. The SEM page buffers comprise double buffering each for (swapping) transfer to and from the main memory (main memory page buffer) and for transfer to the RUPs (RUP page buffer).

3.2.1. Secondary Memory SEM

The existing disk from the SURE project was employed as a mass storage. Its capacity of 72 MB and its data rate of 0.8 MB/s do not represent the latest state of the art, but they can be viewed as sufficient for the implementation and evaluation of a prototype system. The HP 2100 minicomputer from the SURE project also serves as a disk controller which provides the data connection to the SEM page buffers. In addition to the disk control program, this minicomputer also contains the emulation of those parts of the secondary memory manager which are currently not implemented in hardware.

3.2.2. Secondary Memory Manager SEMM

The most important function of the secondary memory manager is the conversion of the logical designation of quantities of data into their physical addresses and assembly of the data in the corresponding buffers. Relations, segments and pages can be referred to at a logical level, i.e. by using their names without caring about physical addresses. A relation can be distributed over an arbitrary number of segments, whereby the values of particular attributes can serve as a distribution criterion. A possible algorithm for performing such clustering, termed segmentation, is described in /AhUl 79/. In this way and if these attributes form a search criterion in a request, the data to be scanned by the RUPs can be restricted to one segment. The segmentation therefore represents a very rudimentary access path. The pages of a segment are numbered consecutively, but these numbers only serve to provide the linking between the pages of one segment. It can no longer be guaranteed that a tuple occupies a definite position within a particular segment. The logical interface not only supports the search function, but also simplifies the exchange of pages within the MAM.

The secondary memory manager is a processor executing a constant program code which is interpreting the commands and accompanying parameters received from the other RDBM components. It was, however, designed with such flexibility that it can be adapted to the current application during system generation by the specification of a few parameters (e.g. mean segment size, available secondary memory capacity etc.). The memory management algorithm ensures that the pages of a segment which are frequently accessed in connection with one another are stored in physical proximity on the secondary memory, thereby avoiding large seek movements. This also applies to shadow segments, which are stored in the neighbourhood of the original data to be updated.

The shadow segments are required as part of the transaction-oriented processing of user tasks, the support of which can be seen as the second important function of the secondary memory manager. To be able to perform update operations including system enforced data consistency, the manager allows the setting of locks at page level. It deletes all the shadows generated by a transaction if the transaction is reset. If a transaction is successfully completed, then the manager propagates the shadows of this transaction to the database in a pseudo-atomic operation. Propagating the shadows only requires updates in tables held in the management information buffer which is battery buffered, so that the tables will also survive a power failure. The sequence of updates within the tables is such that after a system crash a repetition of the commitment-command which was not yet completed at crash time within the recovery procedure will result in the desired state of the database. In addition to this, the secondary memory manager provides statistics operations for the investigation of the current state of the data and time measurement functions.

Fig. 3.1 shows the structure of the secondary memory manager. The processor unit is connected via the bus interface with the bus system. Commands arriving from the DABS or the main memory system are deposited in a FIFO buffer, the command waiting queue. If the processor is in a position to process a command then it is extracted from the waiting queue and any necessary address conversion is carried out, using the information stored in the management information buffer. If the required information is not present, it is read using the secondary

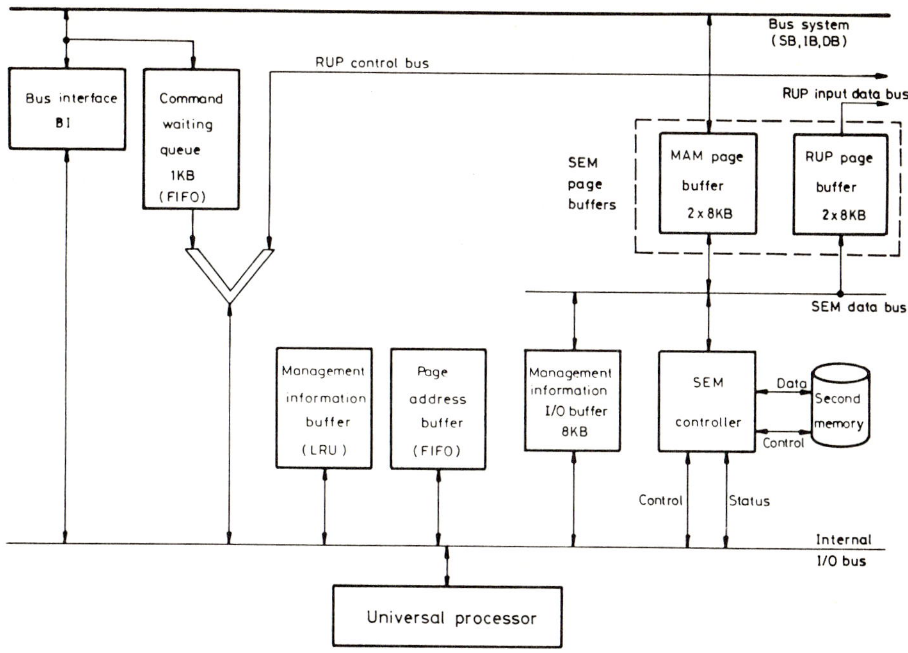

Fig. 3.1: Structure of the Secondary Memory Manager SEMM

memory controller and is then available in the management information I/O buffer. It is then loaded into the buffer store itself, whereby a least-recently-used replacement strategy is employed. If the command embodies the task of making data available to the RUPs, then, as a rule, a series of physical page addresses have to be derived which are deposited in the page address buffer. Whenever the RUP page buffer is free to take more data and the secondary memory controller is available, a page address is removed from its buffer and transferred in an appropriate read command to the controller, whereupon the next page is loaded into the RUP page buffer. However, should a command from the main memory manager (MAMM) arrive, then this can only refer to a particular page. Such a command always has priority over the processing of the page address buffer and is carried out as soon as the main memory page buffer, which contains a page area for each transfer direction, is free and the secondary memory controller is available. Commands from the MAMM must be processed with high priority, as they are frequently connected with page replacement in the main memory (MAM) due to insufficient main storage capacity and are therefore necessary to release deadlock situations blocking the MAM.

Commands which are sent by the RUPs via the RUP control bus are processed with even higher priority. These deal with, for example, locking requests in the context of update operations. The secondary memory manager transmits information over the same bus as to whether the locking request was granted. Fast response to these commands is important, as the data flow to the RUP data buffer is blocked during this processing interval.

3.2.3. Restriction and Update Processor RUP

One of the basic operations in a database is that of searching for (individual) data items among more or less structured quantities of data held in the secondary memory. In each case there are large amounts of data, which have to be filtered to give the relevant information. In addition to various possible access path strategies, this can also be achieved directly by quasi-associative access, using linear search based on simple comparison operations. This search process can be performed in two possible ways: either synchronized with the data stream read from a sequential memory device (e.g. a disk), i.e. on-the-fly, or fully decoupled via intermediate data buffers (for details see /ZeAu 85/). Whereas in the search processor (SURE) the on-the-fly scan was employed for reasons of cost - semiconductor stores were comparatively expensive in the mid 70's - the data comparisons in the RDBM are made asynchronously via a buffer store.

In the RDBM, relevant tuples are selected by applying qualifying conditions. The tuple qualifications on a relation are directly interpreted by the restriction and update processors in the form of qualifications on attributes, these being the smallest addressable components of a tuple.

A search operation requires the cooperation of three independent hardware components: the secondary memory manager, the restriction and update processors and the main memory manager. Initially, the main memory manager is activated. A name for the relation forming the results of the restriction operation is inserted into the main memory directory and free storage may be allocated if necessary. Now it is ready to receive tuples from the restriction and update processors.

In a next step the secondary memory manager which handles allocation and management of the secondary memory is activated. This activation involves the reading of the segments relevant to a query and thus of the corresponding pages. After determining the addresses of the physical pages in the secondary memory, these are read page-by-page into the RUP page buffer using the mentioned double-buffering technique.

Finally, the restriction and update processors must be supplied with the qualification expression itself. A set of standard elementary qualification predicates has been implemented, including tests on attributes involving arithmetic computations. When all RUPs have finished execution, successful completion is in turn notified to the search execution module.

All restriction and update processors execute the same program on different tuples, whereby one program may contain several queries. Thus, if the workload on each individual RUP becomes small, the total throughput of the RUPs will become large, only being limited by the rate at which data can be extracted from the secondary memory. The system will thus always be able to achieve the best response time attainable with the installed hardware. By changing the number of RUPs, the database machine can be tailored to the desired performance ratio. It is the intention of the concept that the overall throughput should reach the speed of the secondary memory (the prototype is geared to 8 MB/s).

After the initial loading of the query program into the RUP, the data is extracted tuple by tuple from the RUP page buffer into an input store using the principle of task quoting. During the loading of a tuple a pointer table is set up automatically which allows direct access to the different attributes of the current tuple. In this way, a RUP is not restricted to process the attributes consecutively but can rather use an optimized sequence, starting with the most significant qualifications. The processing of a tuple can often be terminated after testing only a few bytes if these suffice to determine that this tuple does not match the query.

If a tuple matches a query the specified attribute subset of the tuple is selected and stored in an output buffer. As a final step its content is transmitted to the main memory. Owing to the logical nature of the interface, merely the specified name of the target relation is needed in order to allocate the storage space in the main memory. This allocation is dealt with by the main memory manager.

Thus another form of parallel processing is possible in the RUP: during data transfer to the main memory the next tuple can be loaded from the page buffer and scanned.

The structure of a RUP (Fig. 3.2) consists of two major parts: the microprogrammed universal processor and individual hardware dedicated to the particular function of the processor. This individual hardware essentially comprises a memory to store unqualified data input from the secondary memory (tuple buffer), enhanced by a pointer table for attribute addresses, an output buffer for collecting selected attributes of

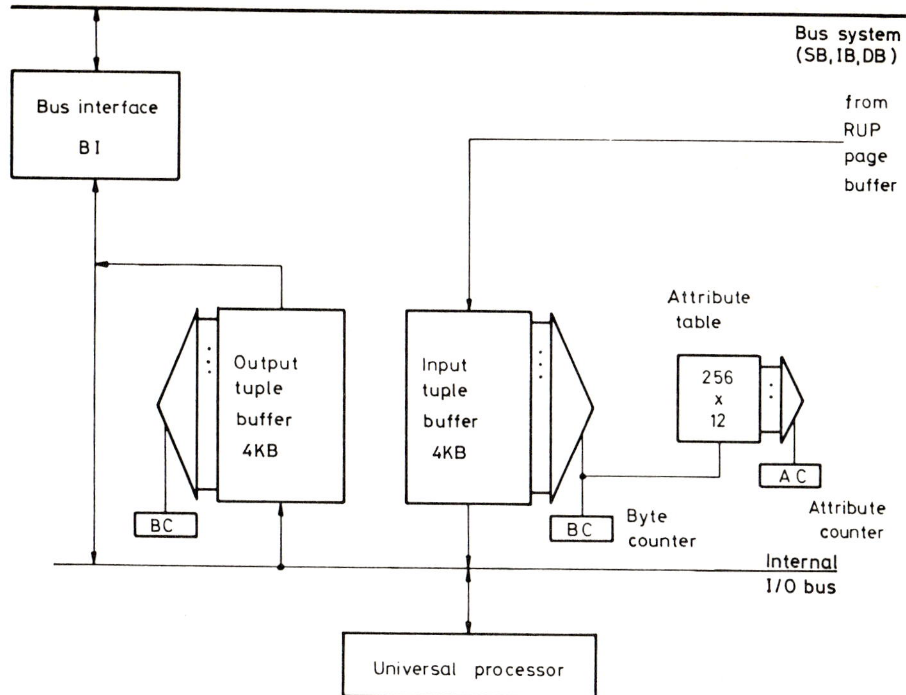

Fig. 3.2: Structure of the Restriction and Update Processor RUP

qualified tuples ready for transfer to the main memory and additional logic which interfaces the RUP to the secondary memory.

3.3. The Heterogeneous Multiprocessor System

The central part of the RDBM is the multiprocessor system with the main memory and its manager and various purpose-built processors representing frequently used database operations. All components are connected via a bus system, which is divided into three separate paths. The data bus (DB) transfers data between the main memory and the processors or the secondary memory, whilst the instruction bus (IB) enables programs to be loaded into different processors by the control processor DABS. During program execution, the processors send their data requests to the main memory manager also via this bus. Via the status bus (SB) information regarding the current processor state or even complete traces can be transmitted to the control processor. Each bus has several transmitters connected to it. An arbiter therefore has to decide which unit should receive permissions to use the bus. The related bus contollers carry out this function for the instruction and data buses. The control of the data bus is incorporated in the main memory manager. This functional assignment makes sense as the main memory is either the transmitter or the receiver during a transfer over the data bus.

3.3.1. Main Memory MAM and its Manager MAMM

The RDBM processors make use of a shared main memory to exchange data, so that this memory must contain shared address spaces. To guarantee a correct data flow between the processors, an appropriate mechanism must ensure that a shared address space may only be accessed by a reading processor after this space has been released by any currently writing processor. This requirement can be met by synchronizing the processors, for example, by logical addressing of the main memory which also allows a considerable better utilization of the memory space (avoidance of fragmentation). The synchronization by means of logical addressing automatically guarantees optimal data flow between the processors, as the main memory data segments employed for data exchange act as FIFO buffers and thus enable good processor utilization and a correspondingly high throughput.

Therefore the main memory is provided with its own attendant main memory manager which permits the processors to address logical data areas (segments) in the memory. The address space of such a data area is thereby not limited by the physical address space of the main memory, as a replacement algorithm is implemented. In addition, the tuples within a segment are not accessed via physical addresses but rather using operations such as GET.NEXT or PUT.NEXT. All processors required to execute a database function (e.g. restriction, join etc.) can be activated jointly by the control software running on the DABS. At least one processor deposits its result data in the target segment specified for it which then in turn forms the source segment for the next processor, from which this processor extracts its input data (Fig. 2.2). If the data required by a processor are not available then the management process returns the corresponding read instruction to the instruction waiting queue. Provided that the various segment names have been correctly allocated, the memory manager automatically ensures that the desired flow of data occurs between the processors. The synchronization can be made optionally at segment level (a segment can only be read after the writing processor has released it) or at tuple level (as soon as a tuple has been written, it can then be read). The second technique allows a further enhancement of throughput.

The core of the Main Memory (MAM) system is formed by a large data memory with a net capacity of 1 MB. To keep costs low, relatively slow dynamic memory chips are employed. Word-oriented operation (four bytes in parallel) enables the required interface data rate of 8 MB/s to be achieved. The large word width also reduces the proportion of memory capacity used to provide error correction redundancy.

The main memory manager processor employs the same board assemblies as the other RDBM processors, whereby the internal instruction set is of course matched to the specific task by special microcode.

A command directed to the main memory manager initially arrives via the instruction bus in a command waiting queue (Fig. 3.3) which is realized as a buffer memory having FIFO

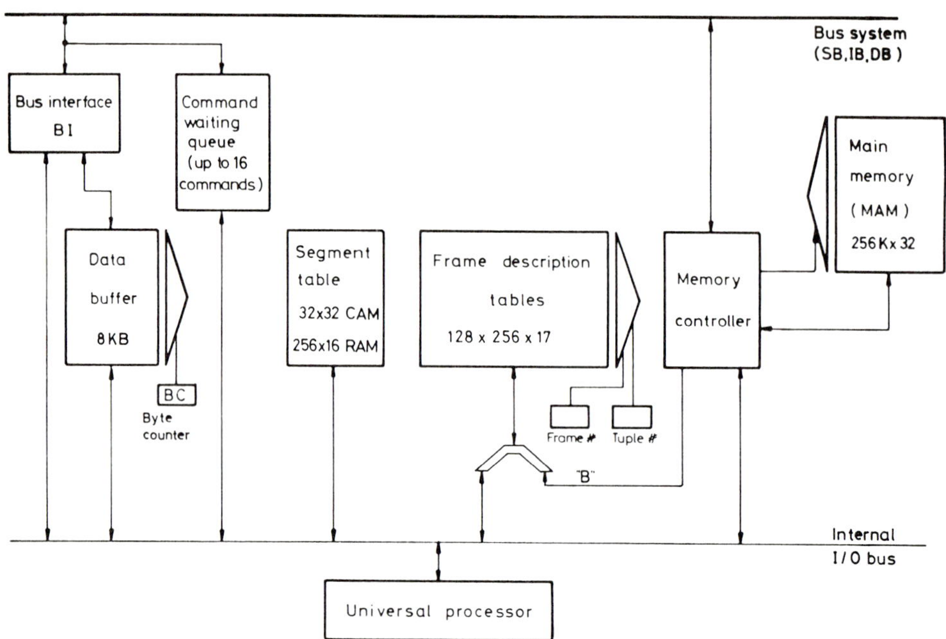

Fig. 3.3: Structure of the Main Memory Manager MAMM

characteristics. If the current command is not executable at that moment, it is again attached to the waiting queue by the processor. As the logical address space is not to be limited by physical memory size, a page swapping technique must be implemented which allows exchanges of pages between the main and secondary memories. Instructions which are concerned with page swapping are routed straight to the processor, by-passing the waiting queue in order to prevent deadlocks.

If the processor encounters an executable data transfer command then the logical address must be transformed into a physical one. To achieve this, the memory manager uses intelligent stores holding the appropriate information, whereby the segment table contains all information appertaining to segments, whereas the frame description tables contain the necessary information on the pages currently occupying the individual frames, e.g. the start addresses of the tuples within a page.

To prevent a deterioration of the throughput by the necessity to perform address transformation, the time required for this must not exceed the average time needed for data transfer. To achieve this, the segment and frame description tables do not consist purely of RAMs but have processing units which, after receiving corresponding operation codes and the accompanying parameters, are able to perform autonomously the required read, write and search operations.

The memory controller synchronizes with the memory the processor which sent the current command to the main memory manager in accordance with the protocol of the data bus, over which it then autonomously performs the data transfer. Any necessary error correction is carried out during read operations. By virtue of the data paths specially adapted to the respective operations and the use of special hardware components (e.g. fast comparators, quasi-associative access using hardware-implemented hash coding), the operations can be performed considerably faster than would be possible for the processor solely under program or microprogram control via the general-purpose processor I/O ports.

The bus interface enables the loading of the processor's program store, whereby this function is actually unnecessary, as the manager is a permanently interpretative processor. The program code is nonetheless held in a RAM so as to allow other algorithms to be tested or time measurement functions to be incorporated, without having to make alterations to the hardware (e.g. replacement of a set of ROMs). Furthermore, the bus interface allows the processor to output commands (in this case directed to the secondary memory manager during the handling of page swapping) and status reports (to the DABS). The DABS also has the facility via the bus interface of interrupting and aborting the processing of current programs by means of privileged commands. Finally, all data to and from the data bus pass through the bus interface.

The data buffer allows the manager processor to perform operations on the data itself, whereby the manager is treated by the main memory control as being the same as the other processors. An example of an operation on the data itself is the generation of the physical sorting of the tuples within a segment. To this effect, the sort processor (SOP) supplies the tuple start addresses in the correct order, whereby tuples with duplicate keys are marked.

In this way the main memory manager provides the DABS with an interface via which it can create and delete segments, unload particular data or influence the page replacement strategy at the segment level. In addition, statistics operations are available. The processors are offered a logical interface with automatic synchronization, whereby essentially sequential tuple-by-tuple accesses are supported. The adopted page swapping process with look-ahead techniques ensures short access times. Specific processor requirements are also catered for, such as data access in loops (interrecord processor IRP during join), the construction of shadow segments (restriction and update processor RUP during update) etc.

3.3.2. Sort Processor SOP

The implementation of all relational interrecord operations can be effectively based on sorting. A sort processor SOP has therefore been designed which is able to support both the internal and external sort operations. It essentially consists of special-purpose hardware, controlled by its own internal microprogram unit which autonomously carries out the various phases of the sort. Overall control of the sort process is provided by macro commands issued by the built-in universal bit-slice microprocessor unit responsible for overall control of a sort task.

Sorting for itself is a wide field of ideas and solutions. Therefore a special paper on this topic is part of the RDBM session. In this context only three characteristics should be mentioned:

- In contrast to numerous other proposals, sorting is not done in a data flow manner, where at the one side raw data are loaded into the device, while on the other side data in a sorted order can be read. The sort procedure is achieved in an interactive communication process between the main memory and the sort processor

- A 4-way merge sort is implemented in hardware

- Not the tuples for themselves but the addresses of the tuples are sorted supported by special hardware

For further details see /Teic 85/.

3.3.3. Interrecord Processor IRP

All intrarecord operations, such as the comparison of attribute values or the calculation of arithmetic expressions involving the attributes within one tuple, are performed in the RUP's, that is in conjunction with I/O to the secondary memory. If more than one tuple simultaneously form the arguments of an operation, this is performed in a separate processor. There are two processing units in the RDBM which handle with multi-argument operations: the sort processor (SOP) and the interrecord processor (IRP) which performs all interrecord operations other than sorting.

The main functions offered by the IRP are the joining of relations, the evaluation of aggregate functions (e.g.

calculating of the average of an attribute, maximum, minimum, sum) and the evaluation of the set comparison operations of SQL (which are used to perform the relational division and evaluate universally quantified expressions). In contrast to the RUP's, the main assumption concerning the data to be processed by the IRP is as follows: all data have to be accessible via the main memory manager. This implies that before an interrecord operation may be commenced, an intermediate relation has to be created in the main memory. This is, however, the typical manner, in which interrecord operations are scheduled, e.g. a restriction of relations will in general precede the join. The IRP reads tuples from relations via the logical main memory interface (in particular: GET.TUPLE(rel), SET.CURSOR(rel), READ.CURSOR(rel), PUT.TUPLE (rel)). As already discussed, this kind of object-oriented addressing allows for a data flow implementation of several sequences of operations. A simple example is given below:

Let R1 be an "order entry" relation:

R1 = orders (cust^-, part^-, quantity,...)

We are looking for a list of all orders of a particular part ("xyz") and the total quantity ordered. Whilst the RUP's are evaluating R2 according to the qualification part="xyz", the IRP already begins calculating the total of the "quantity" attribute. As soon as an intermediate tuple (cust, part) has passed the qualification and been stored in the main memory, a get-tuple request from the IRP will be performed. Since the secondary memory I/O is slower than access to the main memory and the activity of the IRP-CPU, the result relation and the aggregated attribute value will be available shortly after the scan of R1 by the RUP's is complete. This example is very simple but nonetheless serves to demonstrate the principle. Most interrecord operations may be executed by employing this kind of concurrency.

As with the other dedicated processors in the RDBM system, the interrecord processor also includes the universal microprocessor with specific hardware. The additional IRP hardware particulary supports data transfer to/from the main memory. Its structure is less specialized than the sorter, for example, and therefore facilitating later enhancements to the number of functions it can perform. The specific hardware (Fig. 3.4) contains two 8 KB data input buffers and a 4 KB data output buffer. To accelerate logical random access to the individual tuples, an internal attribute pointer address table is also provided for each input buffer which is filled during reading into the buffer. In this way it is possible, particularly in the context of the join operation, to employ double-buffered access to each relation involved. After processing, the result tuples are assembled in the output buffer for sequential transfer to the main memory.

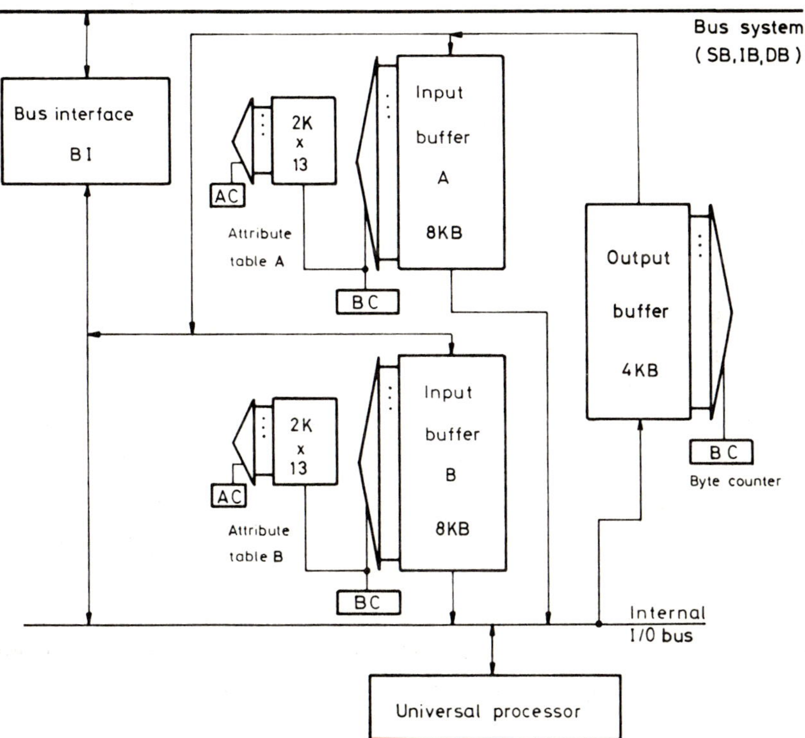

Fig. 3.4: Structure of the Interrecord Processor IRP

3.3.4. Conversion Processor COP

There is another dedicated processor, also forming part of the multiprocessor system which provides the data input/output conversion to the system (Fig. 2.1). This conversion processor (COP) interfaces the system data bus with the control processor (DABS). It is controlled by its own internal program initially loaded via the system instruction bus and by short commands also received via this bus. Feedback reports to the DABS in the form of status information are sent over the status bus.

In addition to its originally conceived task of buffering only to provide an interface between the different data rates of data bus and DABS, the conversion processor also fulfills other functions at a logically higher level:

- Conversion of data from external to internal system data format and vice versa

- Data conversion into predefined codes

- Elimination and alteration of attribute ordering within a tuple for output generation.

Segments of data are transferred between the MAM and the COP either as tuples or as pages of the main memory, whilst data is transferred between the COP and DABS in tuples. The internal COP processing is performed sequentially tuple by tuple. The instructions at a task level each encompass one attribute, the smallest processing unit being one byte.

All data partitions are of variable length. Data length keys are provided external to the RDBM system. These keys which refer to tuples, attributes, values and subvalues are inserted in front of the respective data as a pair of additional bytes.

The individual tuples, attributes and other partitions are

separated internally by special delimiters, whose bit combinations do not occur as normal byte coding. Internal non-numeric data are represented in ASCII-code. On the other hand, numeric data are represented as floating point numbers (BCD-encoded) in compact form, i.e. two symbols per byte. A maximum of seven bytes is allowed for the mantissa.

External to the system, non-numeric data can be represented either in ASCII- code or in EBCDIC-code which must be specified for each task. The following data representations are possible for numeric data:

- Binary integers in two's complement form with a fixed length of 16 or 32 bits (including sign bit)

- floating point numbers with a fixed length of 32 or 48 bits

- Decimal numbers in packed or unpacked form. Packed form indicates two BCD numbers per byte, unpacked one number per byte (right half byte)

As for the other dedicated processors in the RDBM system, the COP comprises the universal microcomputer plus additional hardware to support the individual operations (Fig. 3.5). It essentially contains two 8 KB buffers (RDBM- and DMA-buffer) for data transfers between the main memory and the DABS, together with firmwired tables to support the conversion of data. To speed up logical random access to the tuple stored in the RDBM-buffer an attribute address table is provided to store on-line generated attribute pointers.

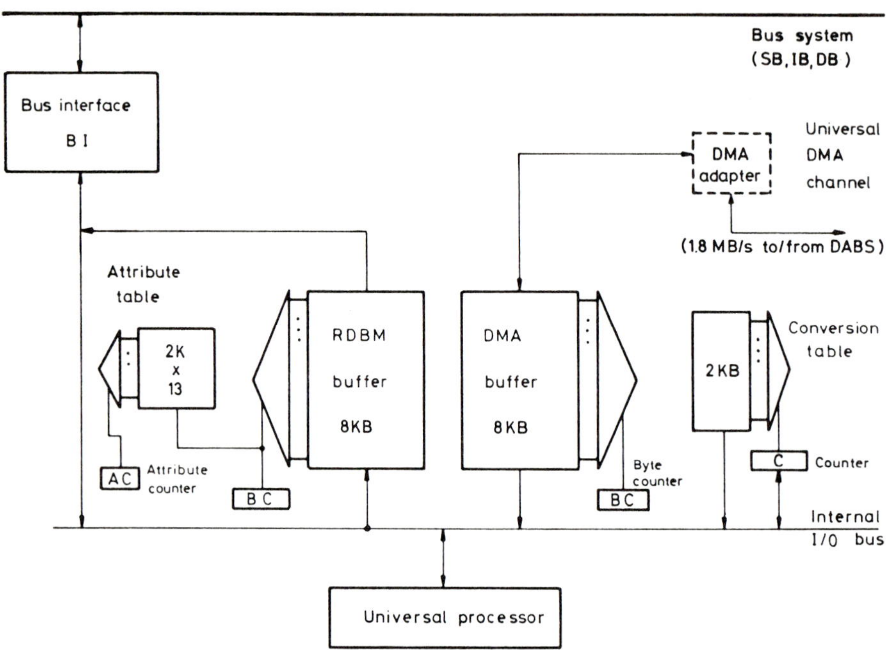

Fig.3.5: Structure of the Conversion Processor COP

4. State of Implementation and Further Project Activities

Funding the implementation of the RDBM by government had been finished by end of June 1985. At this time the overall system had been realized in hardware and software and was ready for running in a first version.

It is planned for the next future up to the end of 1985 to complete some details in hard- and software and optimize and stabilize the running of the system. After that the team will start a detailed evaluation of the database machine which includes the comparison with other systems and an in-depth internal measurement and optimization of the various components of the system.

5. Acknowledgements

The author gratefully acknowledge the contributions by all the members of the RDBM project team. Thanks are due to John Thornton for his help in the preparation of the paper.

The RDBM research project initially supported by the Fraunhofer Society was funded by the German Ministry for Research and Technology.

6. References

/AHLL 81/ Auer, H.; Hell, W.; Leilich, H.-O.; Lie, J.S.; Schweppe, H.; Seehusen, S.; Stiege, G.; Teich, W.; Zeidler, H.Ch.: RDBM - A Relational Database Machine Information Systems 6(2), 1981

/AhUl 79/ Aho, A.V.; Ullmann, J.D.: Optimal partial-match Retrieval when Fields are independently specified ACM Tods Vol. 4(2), June 1979

/CLSu 73/ Copeland, G.P.; Lipovski, G.J.; Su, S.Y.: The Architecture of CASSM: A Cellular System for Non-numeric Processing, Proc. 1. Ann. Symp. Comp. Arch., 1973

/Hell 81/ Hell, W.: RDBM - A Relational Database Machine, Architecture and Hardware Design, Proc. 6th Workshop on Comp. Arch. for Non-numerical Processing, Hyeres, 9.-11.6.1981

/ICL 79/ CAFS 800, (A short overview of the CAFS system) ICL World Headquarters, Putney, London

/LSZe 78/ Leilich, H.-O.; Stiege, G.; Zeidler, H.Ch.: A Search Processor for Database Management Systems, Proc. VLDB 1978

/OSSm 75/ Ozkarahan, E.A.; Schuster, S.A.; Smith, K.C.: RAP - An Associative Processor for Database Management, AFIPS conff. proc., Vol.44, 1975

/Stie 85/ Stiege, G.: "RDBM - Software Considerations and Performance Evaluation" this volume

/SZHL 83/ Schweppe, H.; Zeidler, H.Ch.; Hell, W.; Leilich, H.-O.; Stiege, G.; Teich, W.: "RDBM - A Dedicated Multiprocessor System for Database Management", in Advanced Database Machine Architecture (ed.: Hsiao, D.), Prentice Hall Inc., 1983

/Teic 85/ Teich, Wolfgang: "RDBM - Special Hardware Design for Sorting" this volume

/TeZe 83/ Teich, W.; Zeidler, H.Ch.: "Data Handling and Dedicated Hardware for the Sort Problem", in Database Machines (ed. H.-O. Leilich, M. Missikoff) Springer Verlag Berlin, 1983 (Proc. IWDM-83)

/ZeiAu 85/ Zeidler, H.Ch.; Auer, H.: "On the Development of Dedicated Hardware for Searching", Proc. 4. Int. Workshop on Database Machines, Grand Bahama Island, March 1985

RDBM - Special Hardware Design for Sorting

W. Teich

Institut für Datenverarbeitungsanlagen
Technische Universität Braunschweig
Postfach 3329
D-3300 Braunschweig
West Germany

Abstract

A classification of several possibilities for the generation and representation of sort orders for internal sort operations is presented. A short overview gives some examples of possible structures for parallel sorting machines. The components of a centralized processing unit for a serial merge algorithm using an address table list sort are depicted and a detailed functional description is given. The effects of design parameters and their resulting run time characteristics are discussed. The described implementation forms part of a dedicated multiprocessor system, known as the Braunschweig Relational Database Machine (RDBM).

1. Introduction

The significance of the sort operation in the context of data processing is emphasized by numerous proposals for optimized software routines /Knut 73/. The desire to obtain increased performance in this important area has led, especially in recent years, to the development and application of "sorting

NATO ASI Series, Vol. F 24
Database Machines. Edited by A. K. Sood and A. H. Qureshi

machines". Dependent on the inherent sort algorithm, a number of different hardware structures worthy of mention had been proposed.

Chapter 2 gives a summary of several means of generating and representating sort orders, this forming one of the basic elements of a sort procedure.

Chapter 3 presents the topology of some typical and representative proposals for sort devices, using parallel sort algorithms in 1D/2D array structures and tree configurations. The acceleration of run time is thereby achieved by allocating the sort task to a set of processor elements working in parallel.

Following the example of a concrete implementation within the Relational Database Machine (RDBM) of the Technical University of Braunschweig, in Chapter 4 the functional principle of a serial 4-way merge list procedure is discussed in detail. The described unit performs a microprogrammed sort operation on different data types in close co-operation with the main memory of the RDBM multiprocessor system /AHLL 81, SZHL 83/. An external sort facility by means of a merge run on internally presorted data blocks is supported by the same hardware device. In addition to a description of the processor structure and the sort sequence, comparative run time results are discussed. The effect of selected design parameters on the time characteristics gives some indication as to the best adaption of the presented structure to its environment and special sort requirements.

2. Generation and Representation of Sort Orders

The process of generation of a sort order in a random access memory (internal sort) can be considered independently of the sorting algorithm itself /TeZe 83/. The most natural procedure is that of producing a physical sort order in the data area through continual physical movements of the data entries D_i ("Physical Sort", Fig. 2.1).

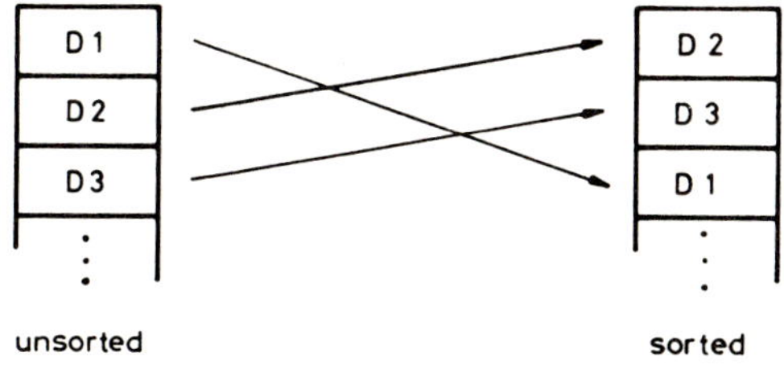

Action: Physical movement of the data entries D_i

Result: Physical sort order in the data area

Fig. 2.1 : Physical Sort

This method may be inappropriate if an unreasonable amount of "satellite information", irrelevant to the sorting operation itself (i.e. bytes not forming part of the sort key), continually has to be moved as well.

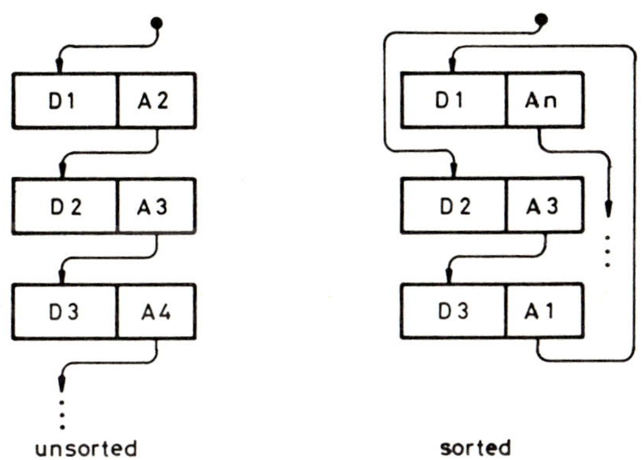

Action: Variation of the address pointer entries A_i

Result: Sort order represented by chain of address pointers

Fig. 2.2 : List Sort

A second possibility is that of linking the data via address pointer entries which are appended to the respective data elements and whose contents are varied during the sort procedure so as to indicate the final sorted order on completion. The

transformation of this linking into a physical ordering requires, however, an additional read access to the address pointer of each data entry. This technique is known as "List Sort" (Fig. 2.2). For variable length data elements, the problem may arise as to how to access the appended address pointer entry.
Secondly, there remains the disadvantage of address information storage in the relatively extensive -and perhaps not very fast- data memory.

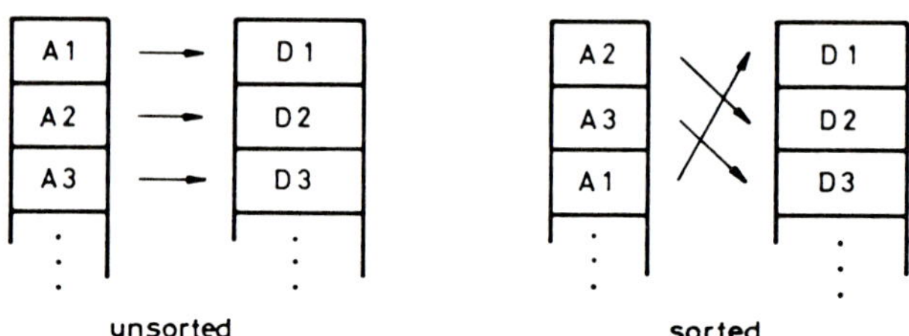

Action: Physical movement of the address pointer entries A_i

Result: Sort order represented by address table

Fig. 2.3: Address Table Sort

If the address pointer entry is no longer viewed as an appendage to the data, but held in a separate area of memory or even in a special memory then the sorted order can be represented by arranging this "address table" in the physical sort order. This order is of course governed by the values of the corresponding data elements. The ultimate sort result in the data area can then be generated by sequential processing of this address table. This "Address Table Sort" (Fig. 2.3) is a favourable configuration for the processing of freely formatted data or data with satellite information. An address table has a fixed format and is normally limited in extent as to allow fast RAM chips to be used. Combining the techniques from the Fig. 2.2 and 2.3 leads to an address table which is no longer physically rearranged. Instead of this, an internal link pointer is appended to each address. Starting from a leading address (anchor) the sort order is represented by the linked address table ("Address Table List Sort", Fig. 2.4). In this configu-

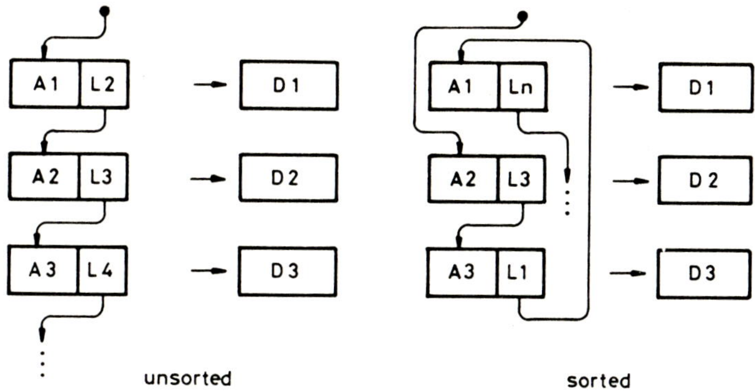

Action: Variation of the link pointer entries L_i

Result: Sort order represented by linked address table

Fig. 2.4: Address Table List Sort

ration, it is possible to process the relative addresses with reduced length and all internal intermediate status registers of the sort device only need to be dimensioned for this size which may represent a valuable increase in performance. However, in addition to the natural limit of data storage in the main memory both address table techniques impose a further limit on the extent of any internal sort procedure: the size of the address table.

3. Some Examples of Sort Hardware Topology

The considerable efforts made to implement sorting algorithm in specialized hardware led very early on to fundamental investigations of networks capable of delivering unsorted input data in sorted form at the outputs after a certain delay /Batc 68/. The simplest network of this form is is constituted by a comparator element with two inputs (bit-serial or bit-parallel) which delivers the minimum or maximum in the same form at the outputs (Fig. 3.1a). The elementary sort functions "compare" and "exchange" are clearly evident here.

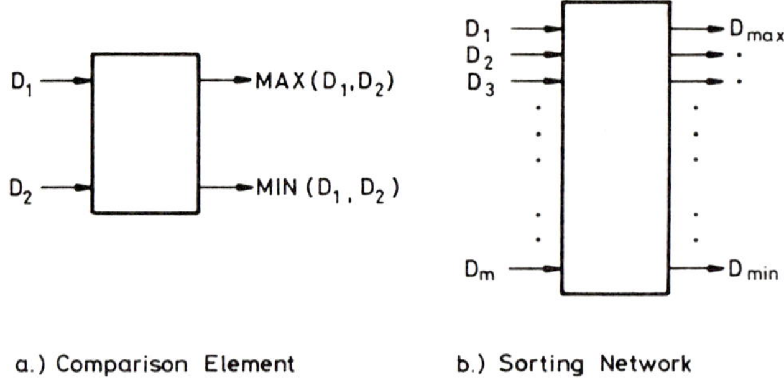

a.) Comparison Element b.) Sorting Network

Fig. 3.1: Network Approach

There are numerous examples in the literature of the cascading of such elements to form networks with minimal processing delay and/or minimal hardware costs, whereby recent developments in VLSI implementation have led to a discussion of the need for fault tolerance in such arrangements. If such a network as shown in Fig. 3.1b is connected with storage elements and, if necessary, feedback paths then particular sorting algorithms can be realized directly in hardware. These in part irregular structures represent a stepping stone towards the implementation of parallel sorting algorithms in regular cell structures. In the following, a one-dimensional (1D), a two-dimensional (2D) and a tree structure are presented. Further 3D (cube, torus) or k-dimensional arrangements have also been proposed.

3.1. 2D-Structures

A network of $n=m^2$ identical processors (Fig. 3.2) contains, per processor and for minimal implementation, the components necessary to compare its own local memory contents (registers) with those of all its neighbours (comparator element) and, if necessary, to exchange them (data path).

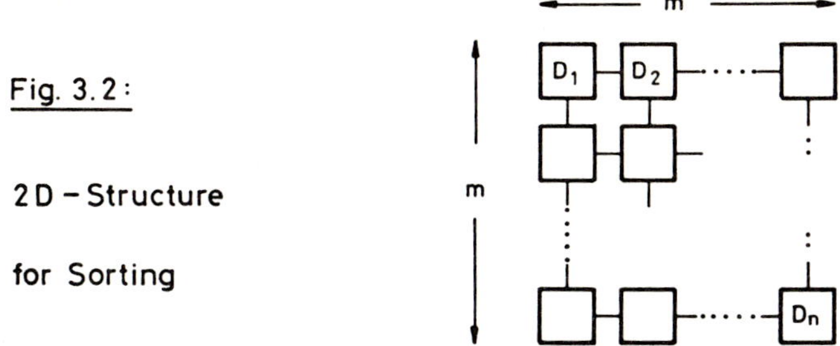

Fig. 3.2: 2D-Structure for Sorting

For control purposes, a subsiduary control unit per cell is necessary, whereby overall coordination can be controlled centrally and synchronously. In /ThKu 77/, various algorithms with processing time O(n) are proposed for this arrangement with a hardware outlay of O(n). After <u>loading</u> the matrix with unordered values, <u>sorting</u> can be performed as desired so as to produce various arrangements (indexings) of the sorted data set. Multidimensional arrangements of the type described here do, however, exhibit problems regarding their interconnection to form larger functional units, for example with reference to the necessary large chip pin number.

3.2. 1D-Structures

A linear chain of m cells with central control and data paths as well as inter-cell interconnections provides an example of the realization of the "Parallel Enumeration Sort" (Fig. 3.3) /YaTY 82/. For an outlay of n=k.m cells which can be connected in series in a simple fashion as k VLSI circuits with m=20...30 (state of the art in 1982), the processing time is O(n). The sort result for the data stream, shifted from left to right and input simultaneously at the input bus, comprises, however, only the output of the relative serial number of each element, thus allowing this method to be classified as an address table technique.

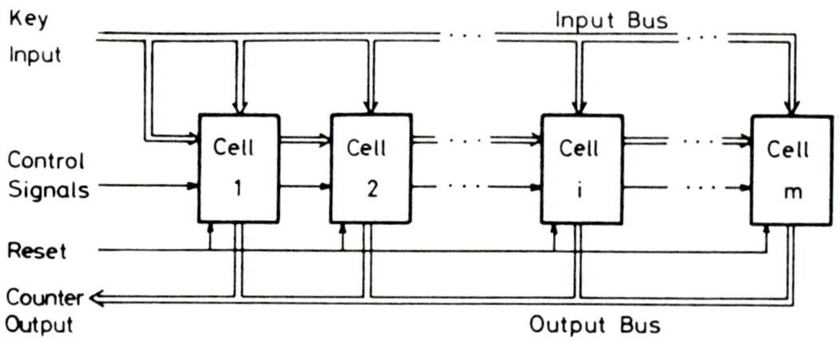

Fig.3.3: 1D-Structure for Sorting

3.3. Tree Structures

Fig. 3.4 shows a tree structure consisting of 2-way merge components.

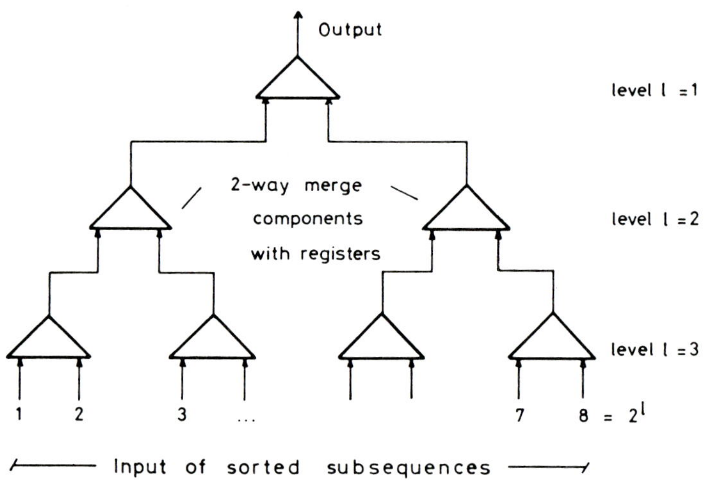

Fig. 3.4: Tree Structure

A continuous input at each of the $m = 2^l$ input branches with $k=n/m$ presorted input elements apiece leads via the l sorting levels to a continuous output stream in sorted order. However, parallel operations only occur once per level, so that for 2^l-1 merge elements a sorting time of O(n.log(n)) results. In /DOSM 82/, a corresponding implementation is presented, whose performance can be enhanced further by additional preconnected, parallel, presorting operations at the lowest tree level together with special data compression. This "Tree Selection" sorting method belongs to the class of physical sorting techniques. A similar arrangement of level circuits with attached memory banks is proposed in /Tana 83/ and uses a "Heap Sort" algorithm to process streams of sort keys.

4. The RDBM Centralized Merge Sort Component

4.1. System Requirements

Within the scope of the development of the Relational Database Machine (RDBM), it has been an essential part of the design of the multiprocessor system to include purpose-built sort hardware. After extensive studies, a decision was made (based on the state-of-the-art technology from the year 1980) to develop a centralized merge sort component using an address table list procedure (see Chapter 2). The most important requirements towards the RDBM system were as follows:

- The data to be sorted are available in a main memory and are transferred via an 8 MB/s data bus.

- The start addresses of the sort keys (tuples) are stored in the main memory within a separate address table.

- The tuples have variable lengths ($\leq$ 4 KB) and up to 256 attributes each one with variable length and data type (string, number) which should be sorted individually in increasing or decreasing order.

- The relational projection and join operations have to be supported by the elimination or marking of duplicates.

- The merge operation on presorted subrelations should be adopted by the same hardware device.

4.2. Algorithm and Data Handling

A serial multiway merge sort algorithm requires accesses to the data to be sorted of the order O(n) for each pass, whereby a quantity of n unsorted keys is processed in log(n)/log(p) passes if a p-way merger is employed. Thus the total number of accesses is of the order O(n.log(n)/log(p)).

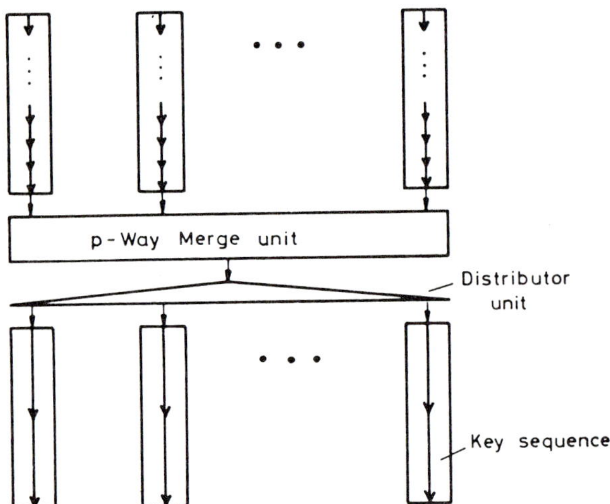

Fig.4.1: Functional Principle of a p-Way Merger with Shift Registers

A possible implementation of the algorithm in a hardware structure is shown in Fig. 4.1. The sort keys held in input shift registers are processed by the merge unit and distributed to output shift registers. The output strings may now form the input for the next merge pass generating new subsequences which are again larger by a factor of p.

The concatenation of a number of merge/distributor/memory units leads to the pipeline merge sort solution /Todd 78/, implemented within the Japanese projects GRACE and DELTA.

For the Braunschweig RDBM the basic idea of only one centralized sorting unit using the multiway merge principle was developed further to an address table technique with link pointers as shown in Fig. 4.2 /Leil 77/.

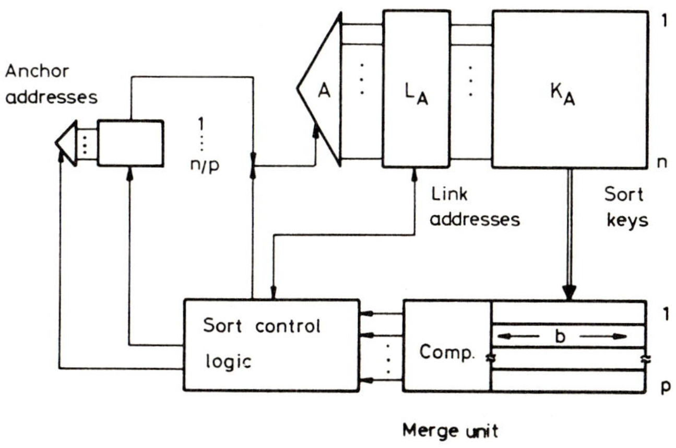

Fig. 4.2: p-Way Merging with Random Access and Address Table

Each sort key K(A) is provided with a link field L(A). In the first pass, sequential stepping through the addresses A allows groups of p keys K(A) to be processed by the merge unit whose ultimate result is the linking of these p keys in sorted order via L(A) to form a string. The anchors of each string thus formed are held in an "anchor memory" for the next pass. After the formation of n/p string subsequences, groups of p anchor addresses are then used to initialize the second pass, leading this time to n/p^2 strings, each of which then contains p^2 sort keys.

The system environment, discussed in Section 4.1, requires read access to data in a separate memory. Fig. 4.3 shows the extension of the hardware components to allow data access to a main memory MA, whereby the address table MA(A) and the link field L(A) form the structure necessary to represent the sorted order for the "address table list sort".

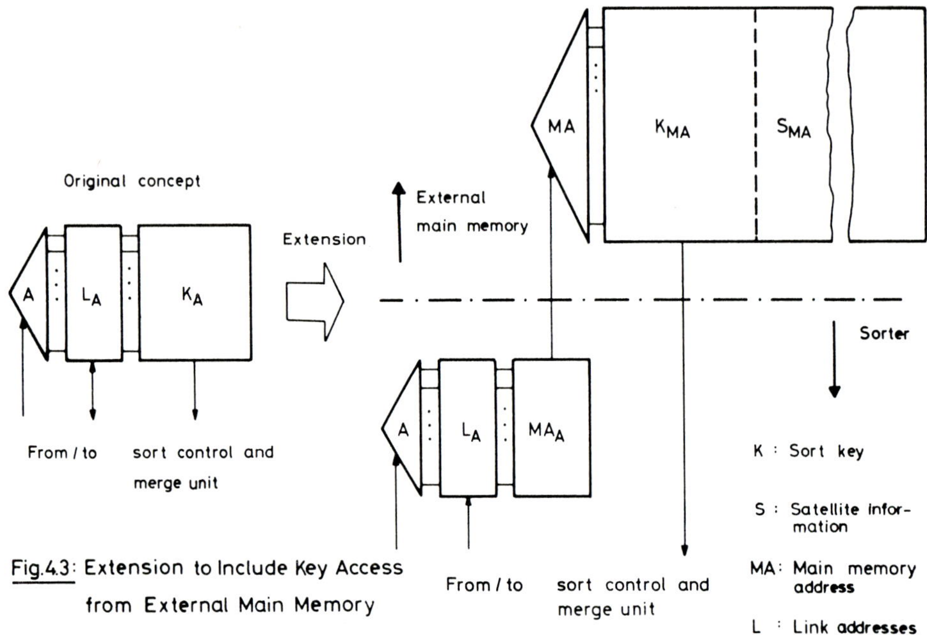

Fig.4.3: Extension to Include Key Access from External Main Memory

The maximum number of entries which can be stored in the address table determines the upper limit to the number of sort keys which can be sorted during an internal sort. The access to the sort keys in the external main memory is sequential during the first pass, whereas random memory access is necessary during all subsequent passes. The data are fed to a high-speed merge unit consisting of a network of fast comparators. A sort control logic unit monitors the course of the linking algorithm.

4.3. Hardware Structure and Functional Description

The actual design of the sort processor /Teic 81/ was derived from the aspects discussed above. The need to establish an efficient procedure required that the processor be provided with its own internal address table. The elements of this address table contain addresses pointing to begin markers of the tuples to be sorted in main memory . These addresses cover the full range of the 1MB main memory MAM. The decision to use direct, physical addresses ensures maximum speed whilst demanding minimum address translation overheads from the main memory manager MAMM. With the aid of a parallel address bus, the addresses concerned can be directly multiplexed into the memory address system (Fig. 4.4).

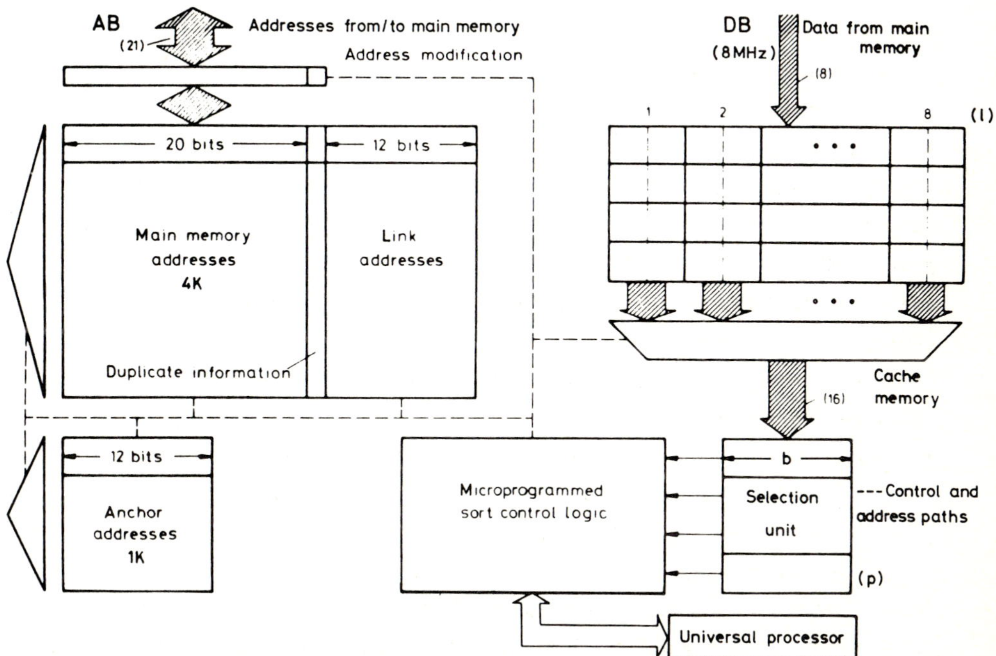

Fig.4.4: Main Components of the Sort Processor SOP

The address table is able to store up to 4K 20-bit addresses. Each address is equipped with a 12-bit link address entry, pointing to the successor within the current sorted sequence.

Each sort operation has to be preceded by a transfer of main memory addresses. This is, however, again supported by the parallel address bus.

In performing a 4-way merge, the first pass is used to form groups of four presorted tuples - or, more exactly, to link the addresses of the respective tuples. A description of the elementary loops of the first pass will demonstrate the function of the various purpose-built hardware units.

After handing over of the address of a desired tuple via the address bus (AB), the corresponding data bytes are received by the sort processor on the RDBM data bus (DB) input. Since the sort key is situated at the beginning of the tuple, the first bytes of the sort key are then stored in a <u>cache memory</u>. The structure of the stored keys has not been changed, as the special characters, forming the boundaries of the attributes, are still contained in the byte string. After four loading cycles are complete, the four sort key entries in the cache memory provide the input data for the merge comparison procedure. This operation can be considered as a selection operation performed by a high-speed <u>selection unit</u>, using a comparison window of 2 bytes. Depending on the specified sort order of the current attribute that is being processed, the selection unit determines either the greatest or the smallest element (the "winner") among the current keys. A specific modification of the type "number" attribute bytes ensures the correct treatment of the represented values of mantissa and exponent before they are processed by the selection unit.

The first winnner forms the "anchor" of the sequence of the four sort keys. Its relative address within the address table is stored in an <u>anchor table</u> and the corresponding index in the selection unit is blocked during the next selection steps. The blocking operation allows a further winner to be found from the other three and its address in the address table can be entered into the link field of its predecessor's address and so on.

When the selection unit is exhausted, it is refilled with the next group of sort keys, which leads to a new anchor as well as a new linked sequence. The execution of the first pass generates up to 1K anchor addresses depending on the original number of keys, each corresponding to a sequence of four or less keys. The first four of these addresses now can be used for the start of the second pass, in which up to 256 anchor addresses are produced. Four chains each of four presorted keys are now merged. Whenever a sort key turns out to be a winner, the corresponding position (index) within the selection unit is not blocked. Instead of this, the winnner key's successor, referred to by the content of the link field, is loaded into the sort processor. Only if an input chain is exhausted and there is no successor can the blocking operation be performed. Each pass of this procedure will further reduce the number of anchor addresses by a factor of 4, whereby the linking within the presorted subsequences is increased. The hardware is able to recognize the last tuple of a linked sequence with the aid of a particular bit which forms part of the link field of the address table.

The merge procedure is finished when the processor detects that only a single chain remains at the end of the pass, with its corresponding anchor address in the first position of the anchor address table. Using the contents of the link field, the original addresses of the main memory entries of the tuples can now be sent back to the main memory manager MAMM via the address bus, but in the correct order. As the main memory uses this address sequence to generate the physical sort order, this is performed by a handshake mechanism. An additional part of each address is the single bit of information as to whether a tuple represents a <u>duplicate</u> of its predecessor. If the sort task had specified "duplicate elimination", then the sort processor would have skipped over the addresses so marked when outputting the sorted address sequence.

After this outline description of the principle operation of the sort processor, some further details of the actual implementation are given. First the operation of the cache memory should be examined, if the selection unit fails to determine that one particular sort key is the winner after a 4-way comparison. In this case, the active positions within the selection unit, which clearly contained duplicate information up to this point, can be rapidly supplied with further bytes read out of the cache memory (first level reload). The positions of the sort keys which have already been eliminated from the comparison are blocked. Each time an attribute boundary is traversed, an examination of the "sort task" information gives the sort order to be observed by the selection unit in comparing the next attribute. On reaching either the end mark of the sort task or the end mark of the tuple, it can be said that the keys which are still active in the selection unit are duplicates. These duplicates are then marked and the lowest numbered active position in the selection unit is declared the winner (stable sort).

It is quite possible that the length of a sort key can exceed that of the cache memory, making a higher level of reload of the cache memory necessary. This requires an access to the main memory, using an address which has been so modified that the next "cache window" of the sort key is read into the cache memory.

In addition to the principal hardware elements described above, a set of fast registers and various logic networks help to deal with the processing and bookkeeping of the sort procedure.

The overall control of the most elementary cycles is performed by the microprogrammed sort control logic (512 x 128 bit), which activates the operations within an elementary sorting loop, such as read/write access to the address tables, loading the selection unit and updating the linking fields. By using fairly fast logic where possible, the memories and registers can be clocked at 8 MHz. The selection unit is constructed with a parallel comparator network in Schottky TTL technology. The overall management of the sort processor itself resides in an attached general-purpose universal processor, to be found in each of the other processors of the RDBM system /Zeid 85/. Its main jobs are to load the sort tasks, to initialize the transfer of main memory addresses and to issue macro commands to the microprogrammed sort control logic.

After the description of the internal sort operation, the external sort feature of the sort processor has to be described. The external sort is similar to the situation immediately before the last pass of an internal sort is about to commence. Two, three or four chains of address links have been generated and the last merge operation lies ahead. This is essentially the situation before the merge pass of an external sort operation. Given that a number of (internally) presorted sequences of tuples are situated on segments within the secondary memory, it is then possible to store two, three or four of them sequentially in the main memory, for instance in portions of up to 2 x 2048 or 4 x 1024 tuples (Fig. 4.5). The sort task is specified on the assumption that the addresses transferred into the sort processor are already chained. The address table can then be filled with two, three or four groups of addresses, each of which are internally chained by links pointing to the respective successor addresses. The similarity to the last merge pass of an internal sort operation was pointed out above. However, for a merge pass of an external sort the exhaustion of the portion of an address chain in the address table does not lead to a blocking of the corresponding input due to exhaustion of the chain, but rather to a request to provide the next portion of the segment in that chain. Before this portion can be loaded in the address table, the linked addresses currently occupying the segment must be output and appended to the part of the merged chain already output. This is achieved by outputting the whole of the linked address sequence in the address table, starting with the anchor address, up to the end of the

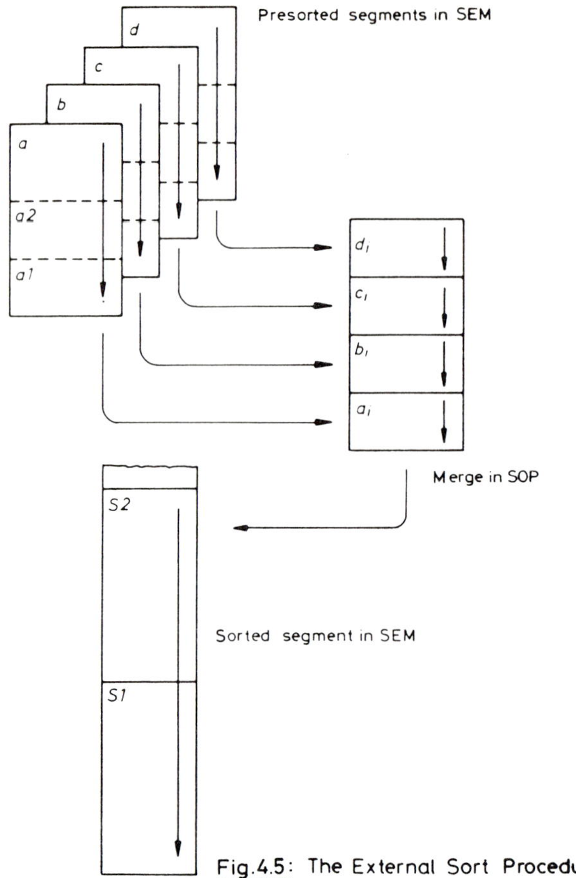

Fig.4.5: The External Sort Procedure

exhausted segment. The main memory then rearranges the corresponding tuples in the correct order and appends them to a target segment in secondary memory. After this, the main memory fetches the next portion of the exhausted chain and transfers the corresponding addresses to the appropriate part within the sort processor's address table. By using a suitable merge strategy comprising many merge passes, an external sort can be performed without any limitations on the size or number of the presorted sequences. The data base administrator system (DABS) retains overall responsibility for the management of the entire sort procedure.

4.4. Time and Design Parameter Considerations

The sort operation of the described hardware structure can be split down into three parts: acceptance of the unsorted address sequence, sorting, and return of the sorted address sequence. In discussing the time dependencies, only the sorting phase is considered here, it being of prime interest. For the p-way merge process, this leads in principle to a sorting time of O(n.log(n)/log(p)). The 4-way merge technique implemented in the RDBM sort processor comprises the following sorting time components:

Sort time: $T_s = (T_{ka} + T_{kp}).N.\log(N)/\log(p)$ (1)

Key access time: $T_{ka} = T_{ma} + l_t.T_t$ (2)

Key processing time: $T_{kp} = T_b(l_s) + l_s.T_k$ (3)

System constants:

T_{ma} = 2.000 μs (Memory access time in MAM)
T_t = 0.125 μs (Transfer time per byte MAM-->SOP)
T_b = 4.250 μs (Basic processing time ($1 \leq l_s \leq 16$)
T_k = 1.050 μs (Processing time per byte)
p = 4

l_t = Transferred key length in bytes
l_s = Significant key length in bytes on an average

The data staging cache with its system parameters (read-out speed, capacity) has an effect on the various time components. The RDBM sort processor was measured and tabulated for various key set sizes ($2 \leq N \leq 4096$) and key lengths ($1 \leq l \leq 4096$ bytes).

Concrete Example

For N=4096 sort keys with a width of $l_s = l_t = 16$ bytes which differ only in their last bytes, we then have from (1) to (3):

$T_{ka} = 4.00\ \mu s$
$T_{kp} = 21.05\ \mu s$
$T_s = 0.5\ (4 + 21.05)\ .\ 4096\ .\ 12\ \mu s = \underline{616}\ ms$

Fig. 4.6 shows the dependency of the sorting time T_s on the necessary penetration depth l_s of the keys to be sorted, if the cache capacity is singly or multiply exceeded. This exceeding leads to reload processes which necessitate a new memory access.

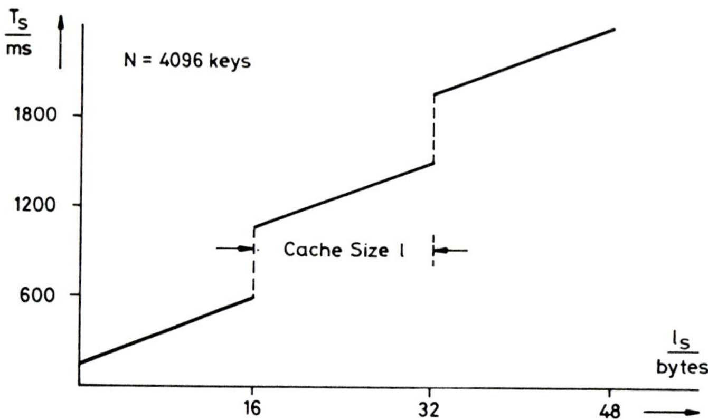

Fig. 4.6: Example of RDBM Sorting Time

A flexible adaption of the key bytes l_t, transferred at each memory access to the cache, to the average penetration depth l_s for as large as possible values for the cache width l is desirable for algorithm optimization.

The central hardware of the sort processor is formed by the multiway comparator. Its essential design parameters are determined by the comparison window b and the number of compared keys p.
As regards p, it should be noted from (1) that it only affects the sorting time through the factor log(p) and that doubling of the hardware outlay only brings real dividends for the enhancement from p=2 to p=4. Simulations also showed that the

processing of duplicates led to unfavourable hardware utilization for larger values of p. An enhancement of the comparison window b would allow faster processing of the cache contents, especially for larger values of l_s. In the implemented sort processor, b was restricted to 2 bytes owing to the byte-oriented tuple structure with embedded special characters, such as attribute boundary markers, in order to keep the number of tuple structure permutations to be examined within reasonable limits.

5. Summary and Future Developments

After the discussion of certain basic principles and structures of specialized hardware for sorting, a concrete implementation within the Relational Database Machine RDBM was presented. The processor described, together with its data and control paths and performance characteristics, was matched to the given system environment and put into operation on seven Double Europe boards in the middle of 1984.

The implementation on the basis of the technology at the beginning of the 1980s led to a centralized processing unit, capable of performing the complex sorting requirements (attribute-dependent sort ordering, type-dependent key handling) using tailored hardware within a respectable time by comparison with software solutions on standard processors. The implemented system parameters can definitely be upgraded from the viewpoint of the current state of the art, whereby an internal sorting of 64K or 256K keys with a considerably enhanced cache could be implemented for only slight extra hardware outlay. There is also good room for improvement in the connection to the data memory, as the byte-oriented access represents a bottleneck for the innermost sorting loop. A very close coupling to the main memory would be conceivable which would render the transfer of address sequences unnecessary and coalesce the sort processor with the main memory manager.

6. Acknowledgements

The author gratefully acknowledges J. Thornton for his help in the preparation of this paper.
The research project was funded by the Federal German Ministry for Research and Technology.

7. References

/AHLL 81/ Auer, Hell, Leilich, Lie, et al.: "RDBM- a Relational Data Base Machine", Inf.Syst., Vol.6, 1981, No.2, pp.91-100

/Batc 68/ Batcher, K.E.: "Sorting Networks and their Applications", Spring Joint Computer Conference, San Francisco, Cal., USA, Apr. 68, AFIPS Conf. Proc. 32, 1968, pp.307-314

/DoSM 82/ Dohi, Y.; Suzuki, A.; Matsui, N.: "Hardware Sorter and Its Application to Data Base Machines", Dep. of Comp. Engineering, Yokohama National University, Japan, 1982

/Knut 73/ Knuth, D.E.: "The Art of Computer Programming", Vol.3, Addison Wesley, Reading, Mass. 1973

/Leil 77/ Leilich, H.-O.: "Eine Sortiermaschine", Internal Report DA-77/10, Institut für DV-Anlagen, TU Braunschweig, W. Germany, 1977

/SZHL 83/ Schweppe, H.; Zeidler, H.Ch.; Hell, W.; Leilich, H.-O.; Stiege, G.; Teich, W.: "RDBM - A Dedicated Multiprocessor System for Database Management", in Advanced Database Machine Architecture (ed.: Hsiao, D.), Prentice Hall Inc., 1983, pp.36-86

/Tana 83/ Tanaka, Y.: "A Data-stream Database Machine with Large Capacity", in Advanced Database Machine Architecture (ed.: Hsiao, D.), Prentice Hall Inc., 1983, pp.168-202

/Teic 81/ Teich, W.:
"The Sort Processor of the RDBM"
Proceedings, 6. Workshop on Computer Architecture for Non Numerical Processing, Hyeres, France, June 1981

/TeZe 83/ Teich, W.; Zeidler, H.Ch.:
"Data Handling and Dedicated Hardware for the Sort Problem", in Database Machines (ed.: Leilich, H.-O.; Missikoff, M.), Proceedings IWDM-83, Springer Verlag Berlin, 1983, pp.205-226

/ThKu 77/ Thompson, C.D.; Kung, H.T.:
"Sorting on a Mesh-Connected Parallel Computer", Communications of the ACM, Vol. 20, No.4, Apr. 77, pp.263-271

/Todd 78/ Todd, S.:
"Algorithm and Hardware for a Merge Sort Using Multiple Processors", IBM J. Res. Develop., Vol.22, No.5, Sept. 78, pp.509-517

/YaTY 82/ Yasuura, H.; Takagi, N.; Yajima S.:
"The Parallel Enumeration Sorting Scheme for VLSI", IEEE Transactions on Computers, Vol. C-31, No.12, Dec. 1982, pp.1192-1201

/Zeid 85/ Zeidler, H.Ch.:
"RDBM - A Relational Database Machine Based on a Dedicated Multiprocessor System", this volume

RDBM - Software Considerations and Performance Evaluation

Günther Stiege

Institut für Theoretische und Praktische Informatik
Abteilung für Betriebssysteme und Rechnerverbund
Postfach 3329
D-3300 Braunschweig
West Germany

Abstract

The core of the RDBM software is the control software running on the control processor (DABS). It has been implemented as a system of cooperating parallel processes which use a common pool of subroutines. The control software is organized in 3 layers: communication layer, translation layer, and execution layer.

The necessity and usefulness of a continuous performance modeling and evaluating activity during the whole planning and construction period became clear only in the later phase of the project. Thus performance modeling and evaluation reduce mainly to 'a posteriori' activities planned for a continuation of the RDBM project.

Remark: This paper is complementary to /Zeid 85/ which should be read first.

NATO ASI Series, Vol. F 24
Database Machines. Edited by A. K. Sood and A. H. Qureshi

1. RDBM Software

1.1. Introduction and General Overview

The core of the RDBM software system is the control software running on the Database Supervisor (DABS), a NORD-100 minicomputer system (see fig. 2.1. of /Zeid 85/). The control software (see figure 1.1.) has been implemented as a system of cooperating parallel processes which use a common pool of subroutines and common memory regions for tables and other data structures. The control software is organized in 3 layers: the communication layer (interface to the outside world), translation layer (translation of database commands into an intermediate language of database functions calls), and execution layer (execution of database functions). A more detailed description of the control software is given in the following subchapters. See also /vKHi 84/ and /SZHL 83/.

An at least equal amount of software has been developed for construction tools and utilities which run also on DABS. About 95% of the control and additional software has been written in PEARL /FuPE 77/. Some critical routines of the control software have been written in assembler for efficency reasons; a small number of the additional software programs are in FORTRAN 77.

In addition, a large amount of code is necessary to operate the special processors. These programs are written in assembler, and from the RDBM implementation view belong to the 'hardware'. The assembler itself is one of the addional programs mentioned above. Even more 'hardware' are the microcode routines which implement the machine instruction set of the special processors and, for specific special processors, certain time-critical routines ('vertical migration'). A microcode-assembler running on a separate minicomputer (HP 2100 A) was used to program these routines.

1.2. The Communication Layer

This layer consists of several parallel processes (rectangles in fig. 1.1.) and interacts with the outside world. Four

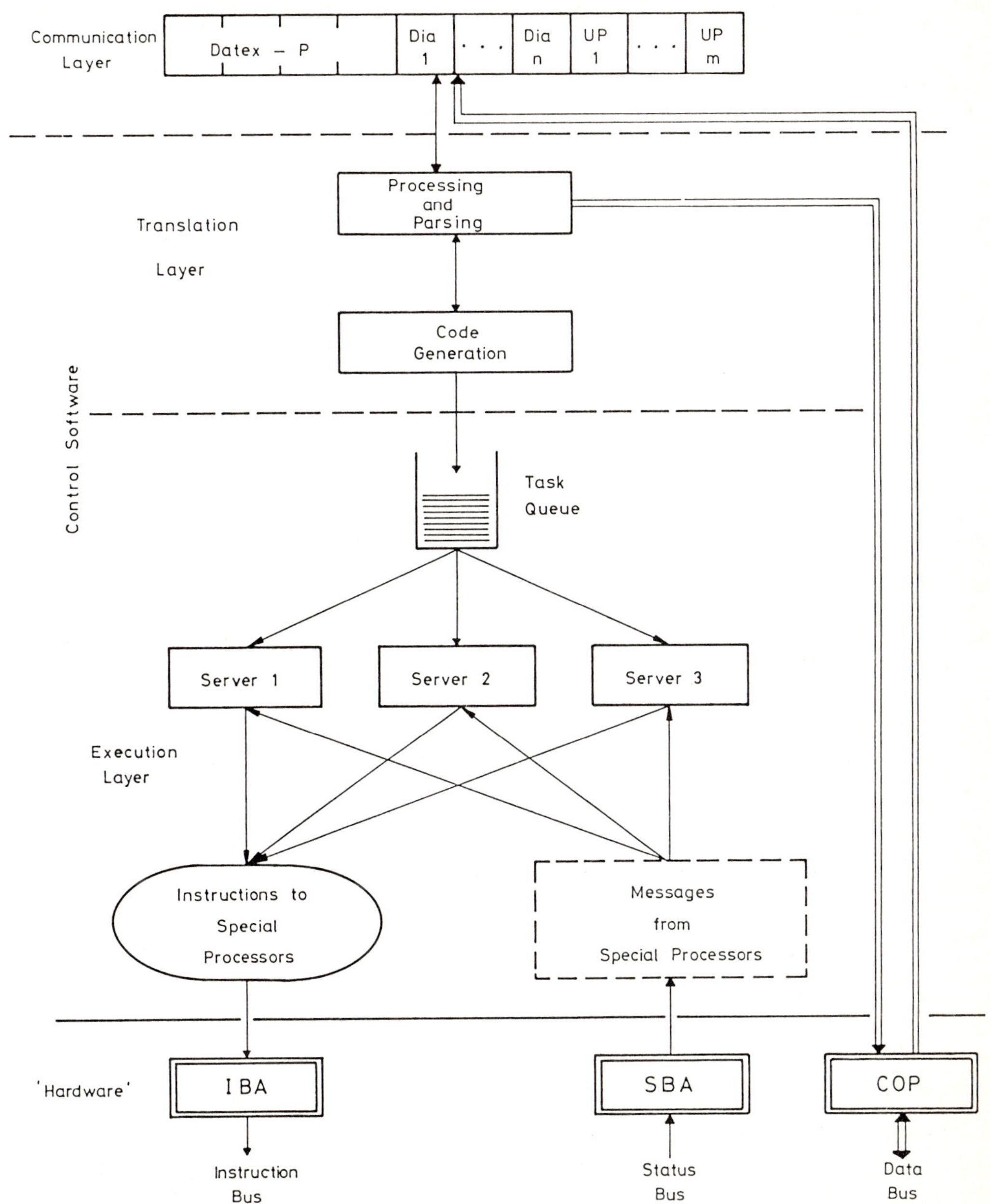

Figure 1.1.
General Structure of the Control Software

processes are used to establish an interface to user programs which run on host computers. These programs communicate with the database machine via the communication network Datex-P, a X.25-based open network operated by the German Mail. Several user programs running on one or more hosts may call on RDBM services in parallel.

A variable number of interactive processes ('Dia' in fig. 1.1.) run on DABS and allow for direct input of database commands including operator commands. The database manipulation language is a dialect of SEQUEL .

An also variable number of user processes ('UP' in fig. 1.1.) may also run on DABS und user programs within these processes are allowed to send database commands to the control software of RDBM.

1.3. The Translation Layer

The translation layer consists of two processes. Preprocessing and parsing of database tasks is done in the first process. A data base task is a sequence of data base commands submitted for execution by a user or a user program. Preprocessing means that all functions which do not have to access the database itself - for instance LOGIN, LOGOUT, queries on schema information, etc. - are executed at this point. All other commands are parsed and sent to the code generating process. There they are translated into a sequence of so called database functions calls and this sequence is put into the task queue of the execution layer.

Although there are two processes in the translation layer they do not work in parallel. The software is divided into two processes mainly for address space reasons. A database task is processed completely by both processes before the next database task is begun by the translation layer.

1.4. The Execution Layer

Three parallel and identical processes act as database servers.

Each server takes a database task from the queue and executes it by calling the corresponding database functions one after the other. The database functions are called as subroutines within the same process. In the same way, they call themselves directly and indirectly several subroutines until the necessary instructions have been sent via the instruction bus adapter (IBA in fig. 1.1.), a hardware board connected to a DMA port of DABS. See lower left side of fig. 1.1. and fig. 1.2. After having sent the instructions to the different special processors involved, the database function suspends the server process and waits for reactions.

After terminating the actual instructions, each special processor sends a status message via the status bus and the status bus adapter (SBA in fig. 1.1.) to the control software. There, all messages are received by a specific process, the status bus adapter driver. This process forwards the message to the driver process which corresponds to the special processor. This process, in turn, sends the message to the database function. Once all initiated activities of special processors are terminated, the database function leaves the suspend status and returns to the server's main program. There, the next database function or the next database task from the queue is initiated. See also right lower side of fig. 1.1. and fig. 1.3.

The flow of information described above corresponds to commands and status information. The flow of data items is different, as shown in figure 1.1. For input, record updates are treated the same way as queries and no special data flow paths are necessary. Insertions are allowed for single records only. In this case, the input data are stored in a buffer in the translation layer. The COP driver process sets up a DMA transfer between this buffer and the COP and controls this transfer. In the same way output, data is directly transferred from the COP to specific buffers in the communication layer. Mass data input is not allowed during normal database mode. A special mass data input mode has to be set up which uses other software than the control software.

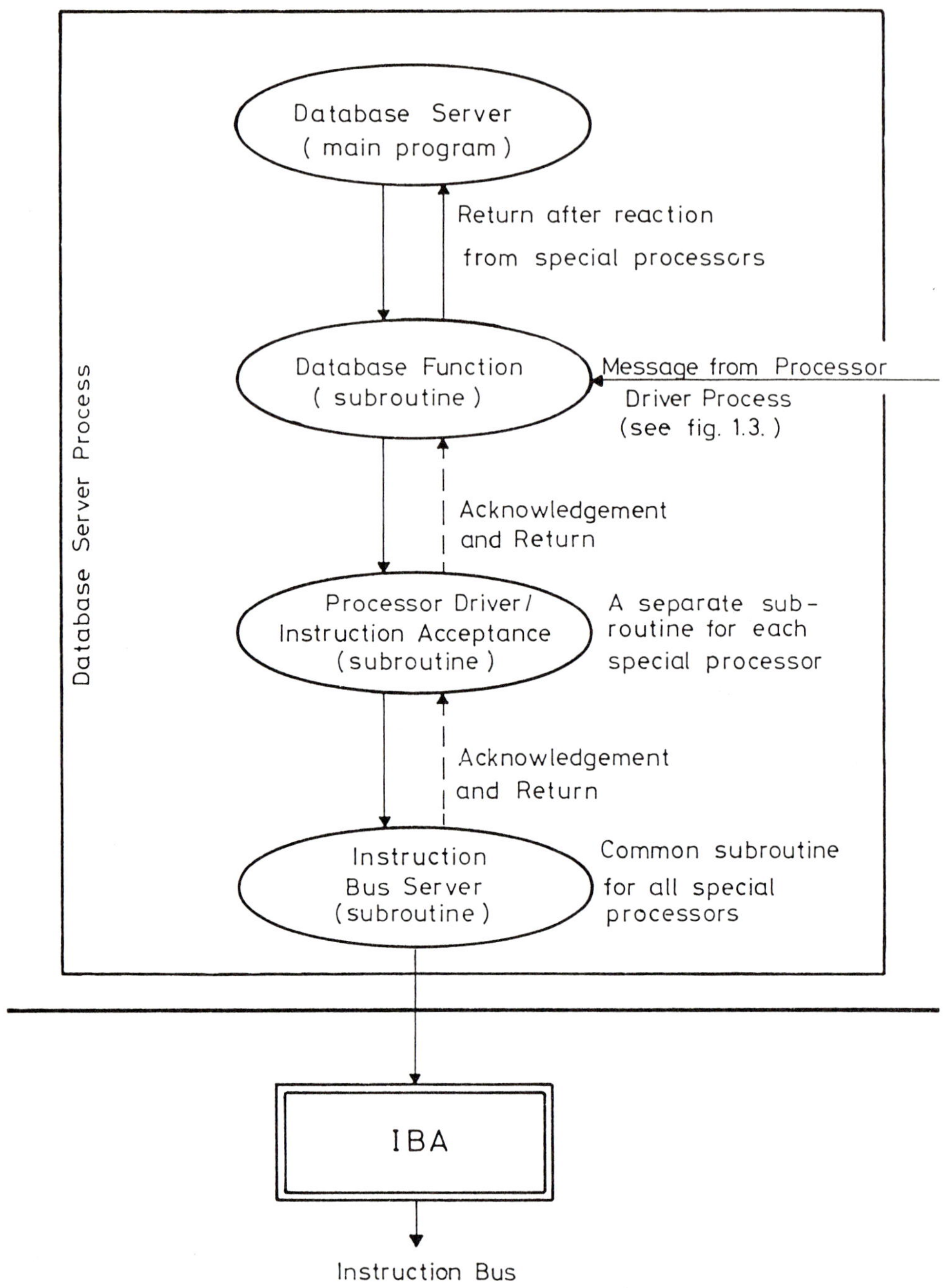

Figure 1.2.

Sending Instructions to Special Processors

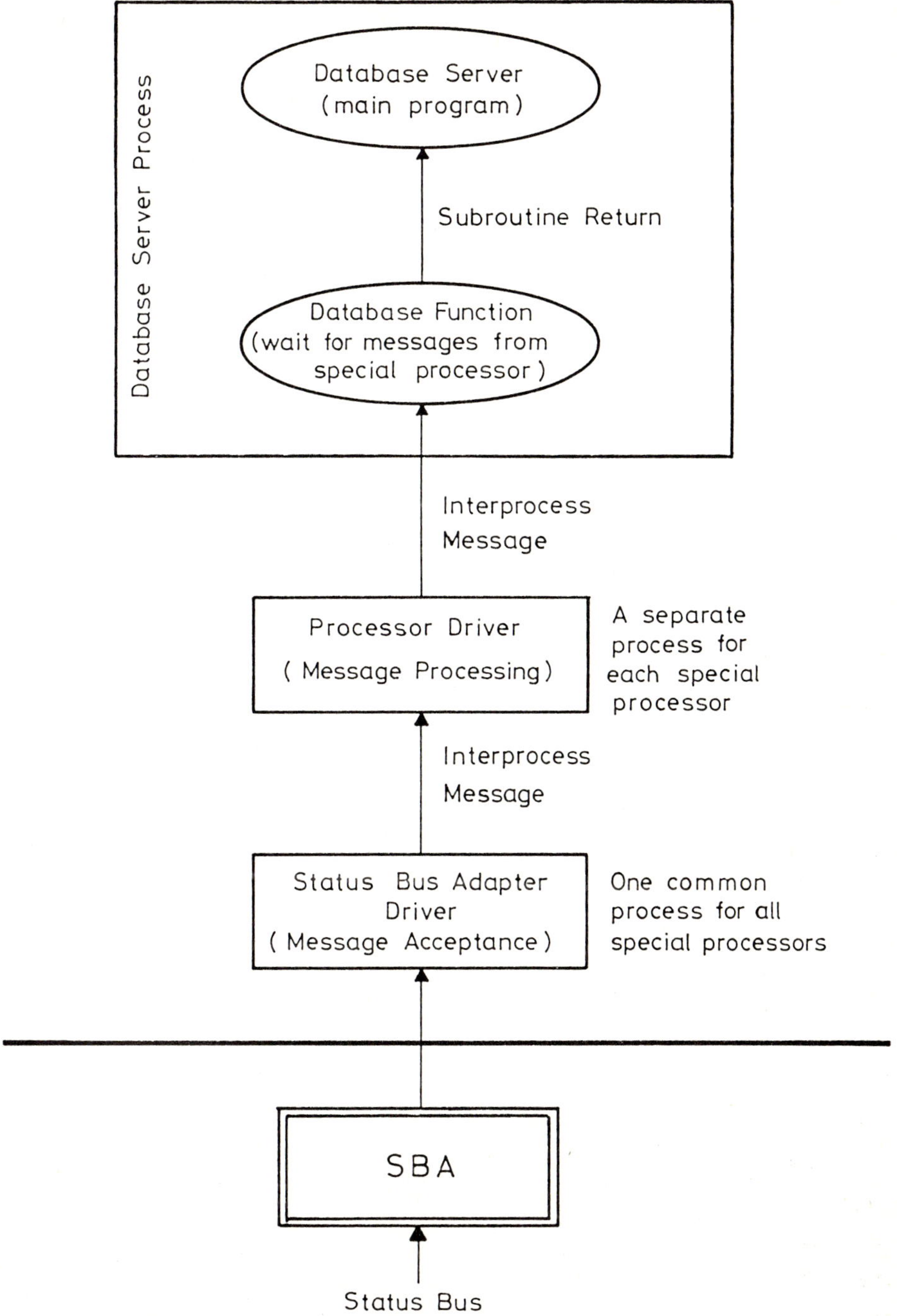

Figure 1.3.

Reception of Messages from Special Processors

1.5. Concurrency

Concurrency is achieved by

A. Concurrency between database tasks

B. Concurrency within a database task.

Concurrency between database tasks is just multiuser mode of operation. In general, each of the 3 database servers executes a database function. If these functions need disjoint special processors, execution in parallel is possible. Bottlenecks are, of course, the special processors, if simultaniously needed by more than one database function, and the control processor DABS itself.

Concurrency within a database task is sometimes possible when a complex database function uses more than one special processor. As an example, consider the database function, which selects subsets of two relations and then equijoins theses subsets over two corresponding attributes. The first step is selection from the first relation. This is done by the RUPs and the result is stored in MAM. The second step is selection from the second relation and storing the result also in MAM. Concurrently to this second step, the first result set is sorted (using SOP) in MAM. After termination of both, selecting from the second relation and sorting the selected subset of the first relation, the result of the second relation is sorted. Following this, both sorted subrelations are joined using IRP and MAM in the final step.

1.6. Experiences

The RDBM project has been succesfully ended. It has shown that ambitious and complex development of new hardware and software structures for database systems is possible. It has also shown that projects of this size come very close to what is feasible in an university environment.

As far as the architecture of the control software is concerned, it can be said that it was well chosen. It was clear enough to make the complex implementation feasible and offered flexibility for changes and expansions which became necessary. By way of contrast, the choice of PEARL as the implementation language turned out to be a severe mistake, not so much for deficencies of the language itself but for the very poor compiler and run time system supplied by Norsk Data.

2. Performance Evaluation

2.1. General Remarks

The necessity and usefulness of continuously monitoring the design and construction process of the system by systematic performance modeling and evaluating activities has become clear to us only in a later phase of the project. For this reason, most of the simulation programs we wrote were aimed at functional validity. One rather large simulation program (/Arlt 82/, Sche 84/) was used in the design phase to obtain rough performance estimates of the entire system. Most of the estimates turned out to be too optimistic.

The primary goal of database machines like RDBM being the passing of database workload from a host system to the backend, a simulation study of the influence of communication between them was made /DrSc 83/. As result, the decision wether to use and eventually upgrade a host-only system or to use a database backend needs a careful analysis of the existing workload including the fraction of non DB-tasks to run on the host. Communication overhead has a much stronger influence than transmission rate on the performance of the host/backend system. For simple database transactions beckends will only occasionally perform better, whereas they are better in general for workload characterized by complex queries.

As a continuation to the RDBM project, a project to develop appropriate measuring and modeling tools for database machines of the RDBM type is planned. As a first step, one study has been carried out and two more are under way. The first study was the development of a complete analytic model of RDBM as a queueing network /Ocke 85/. In the next subchapter a rough

description of this work is given.
The second study is being carried out by Marlis Brunk /Brun 85/ and is aimed to come up with a design plan for measurements in the RDBM control software as well as in the operating software of the special processors. Measurements are planned in single user mode and in multiuser mode. In single user mode, measurement data will be gathered on three different levels. On the level of the special processors the effective execution speed of these is of interest as well as checking the consistent embedding in the general architecture. For instance, the speed of the preprocessing and the postprocessing operations of sorting should be consistent with the speed of the central sorting procedure. By measurements on the level of the database functions we will obtain the time percentage used by a database function for communication and coordination overhead. Measurements on the level of the database tasks will identify typical database function sequences for a user profile. Finally, measurements in multiuser mode will allow quantifying the net effects of paralellism between database tasks. All kinds of measurements will be used to validate the existing simulation and analytic models.
The third study aims at the design and implementation of a hardware monitor system to measure bus traffic and to use the measured data to evaluate the performance of the special processors /MeZe 85/.

2.2. Analytic Model of RDBM

The model was developed by Hilko Ockenga in his master thesis /Ocke 85/. Here, only a short description of the main ideas will be given. Complete details will be published later.
A two level modeling technique is chosen. Starting from the general structure of the RDBM control software (see fig. 1.1.) the main model is set up as a tandem queueing system as shown in figure 1.4. The communication layer is considered to be the source of database tasks. Considering the number of user programs which communicate with RDBM, an infinite source with

Poisson arrivals can be assumed. As in the real system, the database tasks are processed in FCFS order by a single server, the translation layer. The service time is assumed to be negativ exponentially distributed; mainly because a Poisson input to the second system is needed for analytic tractability.

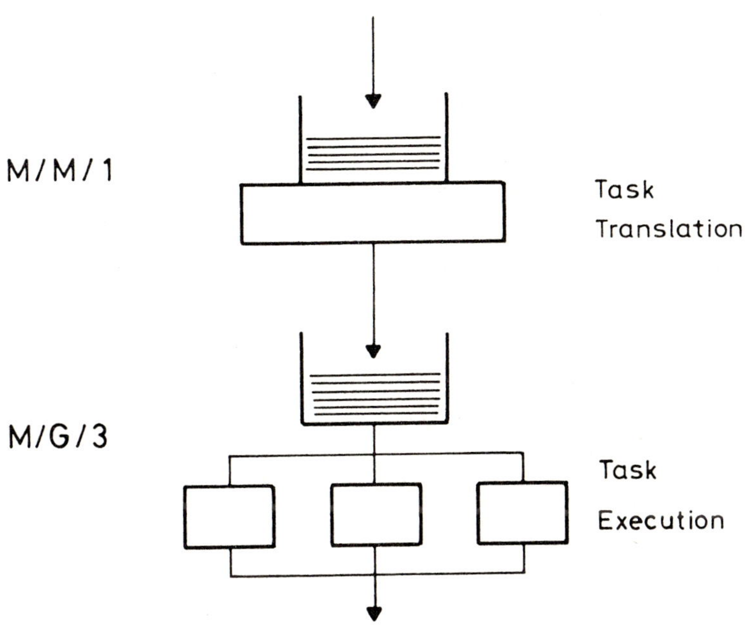

Figure 1.4.
Main Model of RDBM

The second service station models the execution layer as a M/G/3 queueing system, where the servers of the model correspond to the database server processes of the real system. The service order is again FCFS. Now, the hard problem is to determine the service time distribution for a database task in the second service station. Through a careful analysis of the implementation details, Ockenga is able to reduce the service time of a given database task to a function of the execution time of the database functions used in that database task. So the problem reduces to find the execution time distribution of each of the database functions. To solve this problem, again the implementation is analyzed and each database function modeled as a queueing network of instruction calls to special processors. As an example, the queueing network correspondig to database function no.1 will be explained (see figure 1.5.). This database function is "Get Segment with Selection and then Sort", where a segment is a subset of a relation (see /Zeid 85/). In the real system, this database function starts with a call to the main memory manager (MAMM), to reserve an entry in the segment table. In the model (fig. 1.5.) this is shown as the first service node in the network.

Then, the secondary memory manager (SEMM) is called to fill the FIFO buffer with the pages of the segment and the restriction and update processors (RUPs) are instructed to fetch the tuples from the FIFO buffers, perform the selection test and send the qualified tuples to main memory. Since reading pages from secondary memory into the FIFO buffers and reading tuples from the FIFO buffers into the RUPs and processing them there occurs in parallel and takes approximately the same total time, only the RUPs are modeled as service nodes in the network. They form a subnetwork consisting of a 3-way alternative followed by a single service node. Only the single node models the active RUP-time of the database function. The 3 alternatives which precede this node represent blocking situations and waiting times for which fixed branching probabilties are assumed. The branch containing two service nodes represent the case that the two other database server processes will use the RUPs before

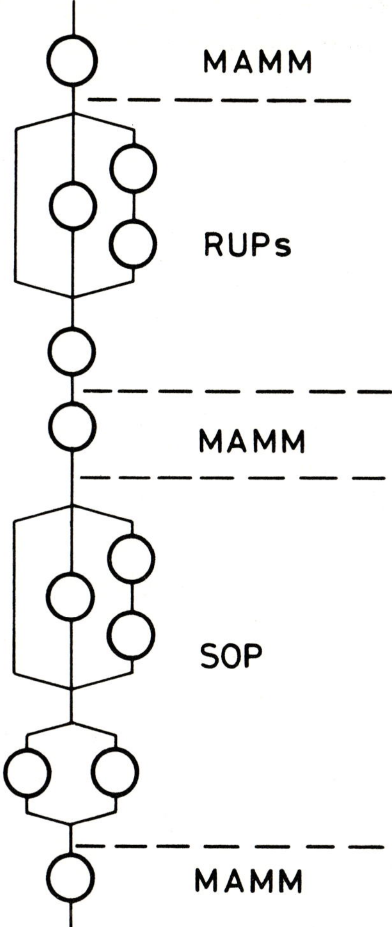

Figure 1.5.

Submodel of a Database Function

the actual server process will get control over them. In the same way the other two branches represent the cases where the actual server process will have to wait for one, respectively none other server process.
In the real system the next step is the call of the main memory manager to reserve a segment table entry and a corresponding node is shown in the queueing network.
Next comes the sorting of the relation. It is implemented by several steps in the real system, which are combined to one in the model. The sorting step of the model is a subnetwork consting of a 3-way alternative to model blocking and waiting times as above and a 2-way alternative for the active sorting procedure. In the 2-way alternative, the branches have fixed probabilities and correspond to internal and external sorting times.For details of sorting see /Teic 85/.
The final step of the database function is a call to the main memory manager to free the segment table entries.
As all individual service times of the special processors are assumed to be negativ exponentially distributed, a first approximation of the M/G/3 system by a M/M/3 system is possible. With this approximation, Ockenga obtains a number of formulae to describe the system.

3. References

Arlt 82 Arlt, V.
"Simulationssystem zur Leistungsmessung und -bewertung des RDBM-Multiprozessorsystems"
Diplomarbeit 1982
Technische Universität Braunschweig
Abteilung für Betriebssysteme und Rechnerverbund

Brun 85 Brunk, M.
"Bewertung des RDBM-Multiprozessorsystems anhand interner Messungen"
to appear as Diplomarbeit
Technische Universität Braunschweig
Abteilung für Betriebssysteme und Rechnerverbund

DrSc 83 Drawin,M.; Schweppe,H.
"A Performance Study on Host-Backend Communication"
in Database Machines
(eds: Leilich,H.-O.; Missikoff,M.)
Springer-Verlag; 1983

FuPE 77 "Full PEARL Language Description"
Gesellschaft für Kernforschung GmbH,
Karlsruhe
PDV-Bericht KFK-PDV130; 1977

MeZe 85 Mertinatsch,P.; Zeidler,H.Ch.
"Development of a Measurement Methodology for Database Machines"
Informatik-Bericht 8503, 1985
Technische Universität Braunschweig
Institut für Datenverarbeitungsanlagen

Ocke 85 Ockenga,H.
"Modellierung des Softwaresystems der Relationalen Datenbankmaschine (RDBM)"
Diplomarbeit 1985
Technische Universität Braunschweig
Abteilung für Betriebssysteme und Rechnerverbund

Sche 84 Scheller, T.
"Messungen am Simulationssystem zu Leistungmessung und -bewertung des RDBM-Multiprozessorsystem"
Studienarbeit 1984
Technische Universität Braunschweig
Abteilung für Betriebssysteme und Rechnerverbund

SZHL 83 Schweppe, H.; Zeidler, H.Ch.; Hell, W.; Leilich, H.-O.; Stiege, G.; Teich, W.
"RDBM - A Dedicated Multiprocessor System for Database Management"
in Advanced Database Machine Architecture (ed: Hsiao, D.), Prentice Hall Inc., 1983

Teic 85 Teich, W.
"RDBM - Special Hardware Design for Sorting"
This volume

vKHi 84 von Kleist-Retzow, H.; Hildebrandt, F.
"Steuerung einer relationalen Datenbankmaschine mit PEARL"
in PEARL-Tagung '84, PEARL-Verein e.V., Pfaffenwaldring 47, D-7000 Stuttgart 80

Zeid 85 Zeidler, H.Ch.
"RDBM - A Relational Database Machine Based on a Dedicated Multiprocessor System"
This volume

DBMAC: A PARALLEL RELATIONAL DATABASE MACHINE

M.Missikoff, S.Salza, M.Terranova
IASI - CNR
Viale Manzoni,30 - 00185 Roma (Italy)

ABSTRACT

This paper presents the database machine DBMAC, a multiprocessor arrchitecture specialized to manage relational databases. DBMAC has been conceived to operate as back-end to a main frame or as a node in a network.

Several are the significant issues of DBMAC. First the physical organization of data, that implements the relational model using a partitioned structure to enhance the parallel processing of the database. Second the logical architecture that presents a high degree of modularity and ample possibility of configuration for the software system distributed over the multiprocessor architecture. Third the physical architecture based essentially on standard off-the-shelf hardware, highly modular and configurable, that allows to build cost effective version of DBMAC for a given application.

Special devices can be (optionally) included in the architecture for a significant gain of performances in the operations of low level database processing.

NATO ASI Series, Vol. F 24
Database Machines. Edited by A. K. Sood and A. H. Qureshi

INTRODUCTION

At the beginning of the seventies the diffusion of large applications using an increasing quantity of data started to showed the limits of current technology.

Complexity and inefficiency were the two major drawbacks of application systems operating on large databases.

The two problems are related. Complexity refers both to the software that implements a DBMS and the interface which is presented to the user, be him the application programmer or the end user, which interacts with the system using a query langage.

Inefficiency was caused primarely by the clumsiness of the interaction with the lower levels of the operating system and by the difficulty in the tune-up uf the DBMS, having a large number of parameters often in conflict one to the other. The latter point is related to the overall complexity of the DBMS.

The beginning of the seventies saw significant efforts both on the methodological and the technological side, aimed to overcome these problems.

At methodological level the major result has been the introduction of the relational model [CODD:70], that brought in the field a clear and manageable data model, and the related interface methods (i.e. query languages based on relational algebra and calculus).

At a technological level the most significant event of the period has been the advent of the microprocessor and, more in general, the advances in the technology of Integrated Circuits. This point brought in the idea that the time were ready to start to conceive multiprocessor architectures capable of processing a large amount of data in parallel.

A typical characteristic of data intensive applications is the repetition of the same, relatively simple, operations on a large amount of data. Therefore an architecture endowed with a number of simple processors, each devoted to process a reletively small fragment of the entire database, was considered a viable and promising solution to increase the performances of database applications. This approach led to the first type of database machines, often referred as cellular architectures (as RARES [LINS76,SMIT79], CASSM [HEAL72,SULI75], DIRECT [DEWI79]).

In the meanwhile the progressive achievement of the relational model was helping the field in dealing with the other historical problem: the complexity of the DBMS.

A better understanding of the functionalities showed that the idea of seeing simple repetitive functions for a database system was true only for low level data management. If you consider the comlete set of functions related to the transaction management, the concurrent access, security and privacy, concistency checking and maintenance, you end up with a great variety of functions, not very simple and not repetitive.

Having this in mind a different approach has been proposed, that conceives multiprocessor architectures where the processors are devoted to perform different funtions, and all together cooperate to implement the set of functions that are usually required in a real world DBMS. This approach led to the architectures often referred as funtionally specialized (as DBC [HSIA77,BANE78], RDBM [SCHW83], VERSO [BANC83], SABRE [GARD83]).

Later appeared that the two approaches, cellular and functional specialization ones, are complementary. In fact it is possible to see the set of functions of a database system partitioned in two: a first part is concerned essentially with functions related to the management of transactions, scarcely repetitive and relatively complex; a second part is devoted to data processing, with functions suitable for the cellular approach.

Following this idea we conceived the database machine DBMAC that integrates the two main approaches developed within the field. It adopts the functional specialization approach in the section of the system facing towards the external world, that we refer as High System, devoted to transaction processing, and a cellular approach in the section of the system dealing with mass memory management, that we refer as Low System.

1 - OVERVIEW OF DBMAC.

The main characteristics of DBMAC, besides the integrated use of the above mentioned approaches, are three: the physical data organization, the flexible multiprocessor/multitask phylosophy, the architecture based on standard off-the-shelf hardware.

DBMAC implements the relational model of data, at a logical level. At a physical level the relations are implemented using a totally inverted data structure: the Data Pool. Each data pool contains the data of a domain (e.g. name, address or department of an employee relation), a database is therefore a collection of data pools. The data pool contains data values jointly with control information necessary to keep track of tuple and relation to which a value belongs. In essence a data pool can be viewed as an inverted file that allow a fast associative access to data; moreover since the relations that have one attribute in common (join attribute) are implemented using the same domain (for that attribute) the data pool represents also a prejoined structure, that allows the join operation to be performed accessing the common data pool within a linear time. The main drawback of this structure is represented by the necessity to reconstruct a relation accessing several different files, one for each domain on which the relation is defined.

The set of interconnected (software) modules that implement the functions of DBMAC are referred as Logical Architecture. We allow a great freedom when configuring a system; since the system is a multiprocessor architecture the first choice refers to the modules allocation. Each processing unit can host several modules, therefore it is important to choose the modules that cohabit on the same processing unit in order to minimize the cost of intermodule communication. In addition it is possible to generate more than one copy of the same module (the number of copies is referred as the multiplicity of the module), whenever the function that it implements appears to be a bottleneck, for a given application.

The physical architecture is implemented using a standard Multibus (TM:Intel) interconnection structure. It is composed of a set of Processing Units (PU), connected through a global bus (G-Bus) and a set of Mass Storage Units (MSU) capable of intelligently manage the database; the MSUs are connected to the PUs via the MS-Bus.

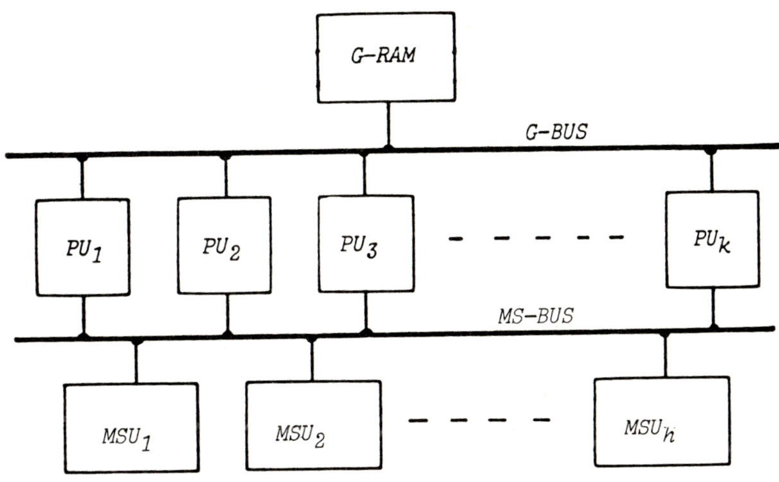

The Physical Architecture of DBMAC

Fig. 1.1

This structure appears flexible and cost effective. It allows to choose the number of processing unit most suitable for a given application (currently: 2 to 16), in order to avoid a scarce usage of processing power (when the hardware is oversized) or long response times (if the number of processing units is undersized). In addition two special purpose devices have been developed: the Intelligent Disk Controller (IDC) that allows a preprocessing of data coming from the disk, and a VLSI device for fast lists intersection (CID: Continuous Intersection Device). The two special purpose devices are conceived to speed up the operations of data processing, but architecturally are not essential, it means that there is the possibility of a configuration of DBMAC without those devices.

The project DBMAC started in 1979 as part of a vast national program for distributed databases. The physiscal architecture of DBMAC has been implemented partially in the laboratories of IASI in Rome (Low System) and at University of Florence (High System), a complete simulation of the machine has been achieved supplying significant results.

1.1 - The Functional Characteristics of DBMAC.

The DBMAC system can be considered as a database utility [HSIA77], in the sense that it is capable to perform a complete set of database management functions. It can be connected as a back-end system to a host computer or as a specialized node in a computer network. In the first case it offloads the host from all tasks inherent to the database transaction processing. In the second case it represents a sophisticated resource at disposal of any host computer whishing to connect to it.

The main characteristics of DBMAC are:

- Functional completeness: the system can manage transactions of the following types: data definition, data manipulation, data retrieval and service (transactions for the administration of the database).

- Security: DBMAC maintains a list of users and their access rights to the system in terms of type of transactions allowable and data access capabilities. Moreover, in the context of a network, it maintains a list of nodes that are eligible to connect and use the services of

DBMAC.

- Multitransaction: the system can manage concurrently different transactions of different users. It provides the concurrency control necessary in such parallel activities.

- Precompiled Transactions: To ease repetitive interactions required by some categories of users, DBMAC maintains a library of precompiled transactions (PCT) that can be activated by simply specifying the identifier of the PCT and the actual parameters.

- Multilevel parallel processing: the philosophy of the multiprocessor/multibus architecture allows a high degree of parallelism at different levels of operation granularity:

  (i) intertransaction, as specified above;
  (ii) intratransaction, allowing different db primitives of the same transaction to be executed in parallel;
  (iii) intraprimitive, allowing different processors to cooperate for the parallel execution of a single db primitive.

For what concerns the performances of DBMAC the key issue is represented by the high level of parallelism. This is enhanced by the partitioning of the physical data organization.

1.2 - A Domain Based Storage Organization.

The internal schema of DBMAC has been devised to exploit at a maximum degree the multiprocessor capability of the architecture and, at the same time, to overcome the two main problems common to most existing database machines (DBM).

- The degree of parallelism of many DBMs, and therefore their processing power, can not be fully exploited because of the conflicts that occur when different transactions try to access large data sets implementing the relations of the database (db).

- The join operation, even when a parallel architecture is used, remains the most complex and time consuming relational operation.

These considerations highlight the principal limitations that a DBM must face independently from the power of its architecture. To overcome these limitations DBMAC has adopted a physical data organization (i.e. internal schema) based on:

(i) a total attribute partitioning of the relations, thus increasing the overall system capacity of parallel processing of the db;

(ii) a pre-joined structure that implements the domains of the db; it contains, enbedded in the structure, the information regarding common values of different relations on join domains.

In the proposed internal schema the unique data aggregation is the domain, the database is represented by the set of domains on which all the attributes are defined; the relations of the conceptual schema are represented by means of control information. The data set, which contains the values of a domain and the control information, is called Data Pool (DP).

The figure 1.2 sketches a DP based database having three relations on four domains.

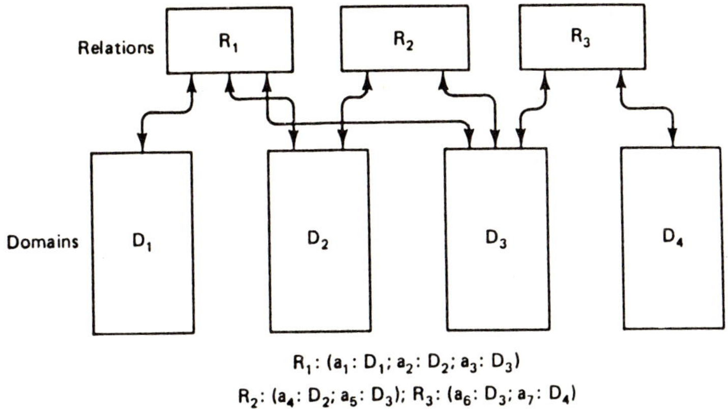

Fig. 1.2 - Structure of a DP based database.

The control information indicates, for each domain value, the relation(s) and the tuple(s) to which that value belongs. Since the DP contains only atomic, non-duplicate values, it is likely that a value belongs to more than one relation, in the case of shared domains, and to more than one tuple, in the most general case.

It can be shown that a DP internal schema, as proposed in [MISS82], leads always to a saving of space in storing the db, compared to a flat file organization (i.e. internal schema which implements the relations by means of flat files).

Values and control information are maintained in the DP using a hierarchical structure called domain tree (DT). The domain tree has constant hight 4; the root (level 0) contains the name of the domain d, at the other three levels we have:

level 1 : node v - contains a value of the domain
level 2 : node r - contains a relation identifier (RID)
level 3 : node t - contains a tuple identifier (TID)

Each path from the root to the leaf:

p(d,v,r,t,)

identifies an istance of an attribute. In the figure 2 we represent a domain tree:

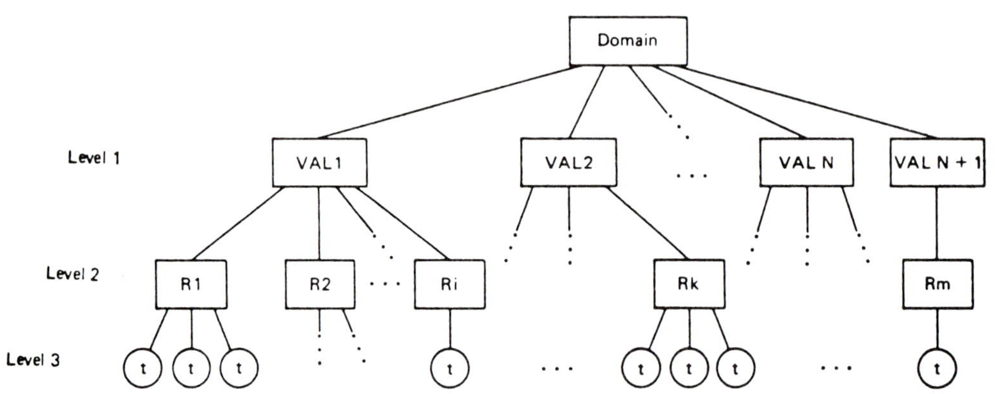

Fig. 1.3 - The domain tree.

There have been different proposals for the implementation of the DP [MISS78,MISS81,PINZ80]. In any case a search on a DP produces an intermediate result (temporary relation called TIDAR) formed by an array of TIDs. In Section 2 we introduce some operations characteristic of DP.

2 - THE LOGICAL ARCHITECTURE.

During the first steps of the design of the functional architecture a great attention has been payed to identify functional areas highly independent (i.e. with clear interfaces) one another. At first we can distinguish two basic sections of the system referred as high system (HS) and low system (LS). The first (HS) is basically devoted to the management of the transactions, i.e. to receive, validate and prepare the transactions for execution. The second (LS) is devoted to the actual execution of the transactions; in particular it executes the db primitives which act on the physical database without being concerned with the transactions they belong to: it is the task of the HS to keep track of the progress of each active transaction during the execution of the db primitives.

At a first level of refinement we can draw the system structured in four functional layers (see figure 2.1).

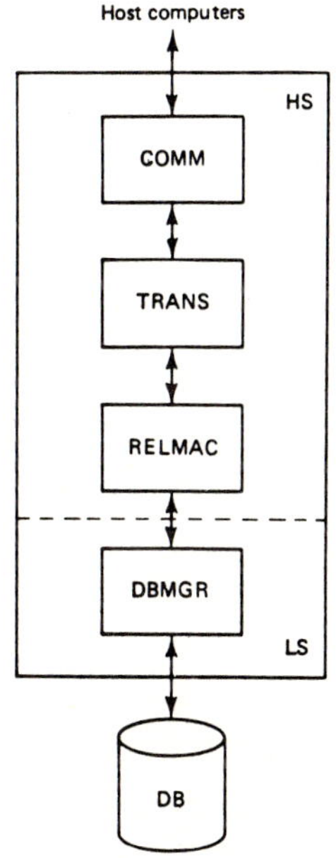

Fig. 2.1 - Overall LARC structure.

The first three layers (components of HS), that manage the transactions, deal only with the conceptual schema. They do not refer to the extention of the db which is dealt completely by the fourth layer.

The COMM layer manages the communication with the outside world sending and receiving messages; it can be reconfigured for different protocols both for local and remote links (respectively acting as back-end to a host or as node in a computer network).

The TRANS layer receives the transactions in external format and encodes them in internal format. It verifies the validity of operands and operators with respect to the active schema; it fills a transaction skeleton with the actual parameters when a PCT is submitted; it provides a first level of scheduling deciding which will be the next transaction to be activated, i.e. to be forward to the next layer.

The RELMAC layer receives the transactions in internal format but still having their structure referring to the relational entities of the conceptual schema. Its task is to map them onto a set of operations defined on the internal schema of the db. In doing so it builds a graph which represents the best way of executing the given transaction on the DBMAC internal data structures: the Data Pools. The executive graph (EG) represents explicitly all the parallel computation achievable in a given transaction. The nodes of EG are the db primitives defined on the DP internal schema. The second major task of RELMAC is to visit in parallel the EG. Actually it follows, for each active EG, all the independent paths and, for each node it encounters, the correspondent DP primitive is activated on the underlying DBMGR layer.

In the above three layers we have a progressive increment of semantics, concerning the objects that are manipulated. The first layer deals with messages without being concerned with their content. The second deals with the syntax of the transactions operating a format change that does not alter the structure. The third layer modifies significantly the transaction touching the structure, operations and operands: this is the only level of the HS that is concerned with the internal schema organization. This layered organization of HS allows a high modular design of the logical architecture and, consequently, of the software that implements it.

The fourth layer, DBMGR, implements all the procedures necessary to manage the physical data structures which implement permanent and temporary relations. The primitives of DBMGR are the only able to access the DP both for search or update. The service primitives allow to restructure the DP, acting on the logical and/or physical schema and on the db itself.

In the next paragraphs we present at a greater level of detail the logical architecture of DBMAC with its processes and system data structures (SDS). This description is divided in two parts, one for HS and one for LS.

2.1 The Logical High System.

The High System of the Logical Architecture will be described as a graph where the nodes represent processes and data structure, and the arcs represent the access rights of the formers on the latters.

The system data structures contain control information necessary to the HS to store the transactions entered in the system and to keep track of their progress.

The SDS are of two types: the first type consists of general information (e.g. on users, sites, db schema, etc.) mostly consulted by the processes; the second type holds the transactions, in their different states, and is used mainly for communication between processes. The SDSs are organized as tables in the first case and as queues in the second: the choice of queueing the messages between the processes is aimed to render more asynchronous the operations of the whole logical architecture.

The processing elements, at this level of representation, are the System Process Families (SPF). Each SPF belongs to a given layer and is devoted to a class of well specified functions. It communicates with others SPF always through one or more SDSs. In a further step of refinement, not reported in the paper, the SPFs are decomposed into the final processes.

The Logical Architecture HS is presented in fig. 2.2. Table 2.1 contains the list of the SDS with a brief description. Table 2.2 contains the specification of the SPFs.

TABLE 2.1 : System Data Structures

PRETR - Library of precompiled transactions.

SCHEMA - Schema of the actual db.

SITAB - Table of the sites from where a user can connect to DBMAC.

SYSIND - Table of system workload indicators.

MSGQUE - Queue of arriving messages.

PREQUE - Queue of precompiled transactions.

QDEF1, QMAN1, QRET1, QSER1 - Queues of internally formatted transactions waiting to be activated (divided on the basis of the type: data definition, manipulation, retrieval and service respectively).

QDEF2, QMAN2, QRET2, QSER2 - Queues of transactions ready to be mapped onto the Data Pool format for the execution.

DPDEF, DPMAN, DPRET, DPSER - Sets of active transactions presently executing in the system.

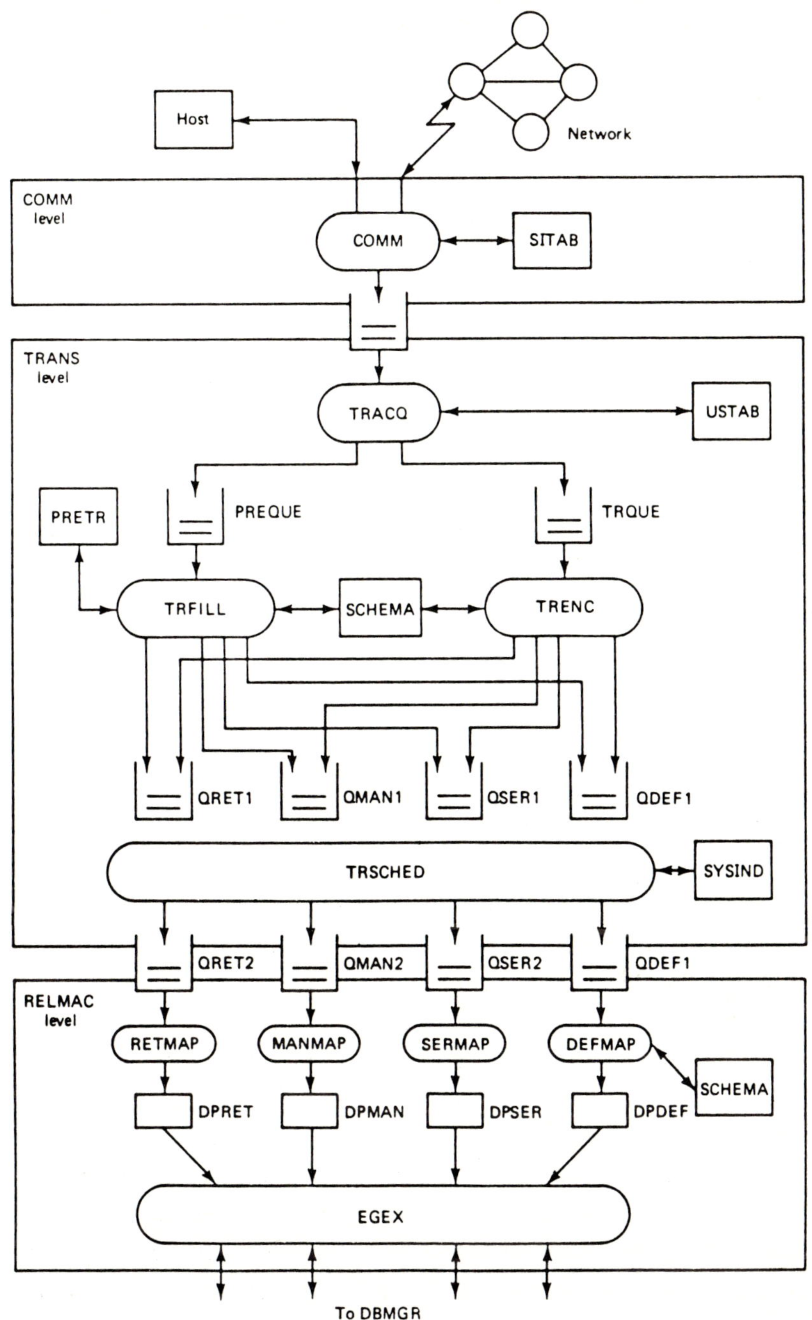

Fig. 2.2 - The Logical Architecture High System.

TABLE 2.2 : System Process Families

TRACQ - Transaction acquisition, user validation, transaction type selection.

TRENC - Transaction validation and encoding into internal format.

TRFILL - Precompiled transaction validation and parameters substitution.

TRSCHED - Transaction scheduling; first level of concurrency control.

DEFMAP, MANMAP, RETMAP, SERMAP - Mapping of ready transactions from internal format to DP format (i.e. in the form of Executive Graph:EG).

EGEX - Execution of active transactions visiting the corresponding EGs.

2.3 - The Logical Low System.

The Low System has a different structure from the HS. It is characterized by a parallel structure and a multiple interconnection with the upper layer.

The figure 2.3 represents, at a first level of detail, the four process families that are in charge of physical db management.

The two queue sets show the fact that each activation of a process of LS is followed by an answer that permits to EGEX to trace continuously the progress of the transactions.

The DP primitives operate on the basis of a complete scan of the DPs. The result produced by a primitive is represented by an array of TIDs (called TIDAR). There are three types of DP primitives:

1. Primitives which operate on a given DP;

2. Primitives which receive a TIDAR and uses it to access a DP;

3. Primitives which receive two TIDARs and operates on both jointly.

These primitives are implemented using two elementary actions:

a) selective scan to check a condition on a value and/or RID;
b) intersection of two sets of TID.

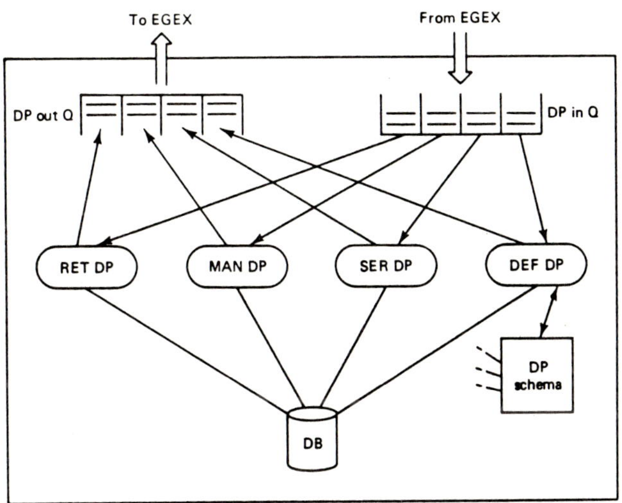

Fig. 2.3 - Low System structure.

The selective scan is performed "on the fly" during a read operation on the DP. The intersection can be performed differently depending on the size of the operands and the degree of parallelism the system can carry out at a given moment (generally this depends on the number of PUs that can be dedicated to an operation). Another operation DBMGR is in charge of is the sort. It can be required as a preliminary step when performing an intersection.

In general the answer to a query is represented by means of a TIDAR. A final step to associate values to TID is then necessary in order to send back to the user the result in the form of a flat file.

The evaluation of the LS is heavily dependent on the db, its schema and size, and the algorithms adopted to execute each DP primitive. An evaluation of the behaviour of the DP primitives is given in [MISS82].

3 - ARCHITECTURE AND SPECIAL DEVICES IN DBMAC

In section 1 we briefly described the physical architecture of DBMAC and introduced its main components, here we will give a closer look, focusing the attention on the special hardware designed for the system. In fact, although DBMAC mainly utilizes standard hardware, some particular solutions and special devices are adopted to improve system responsiveness.

The first subsection illustrates the physical architecture with the same division introduced earlier in high system, devoted to the transaction management, and low system, dedicated to the data management. There we define the main requirements for the system hardware.

The second subsection deals with the system hardware and gives a short description of the Processing Unit (PU), the Mass Storage Unit (MSU) and the Mass Storage Bus (MSB). The attention is focused on the MSU and MSB that exploit a special design to avoid the typical bottleneck of the database machines in the disk i/o.

The last subsection presents CID (Continuous Intersection Device), a VLSI device designed to speed up the operation of intersecating TID lists representing the intermediate results of the queries.

3.1 - The DBMAC physical architecture

The physical architecture of DBMAC reflects the difference beetwen the SPFs and SDSs involved in the transaction processing, performed by the HS, and transaction execution, performed by the LS. The first one requires the exchange of small packets (transaction descriptions) and the access to tables held in main memory, on the contrary the second involves large amount of data stored on disks.

From the characteristics of Logical Architecture (see sect. 2) we can draw some considerations concerning the processing requirements of the Physical High System (PHS):

a) The processing power required by a given SPF can vary greatly according to the type of application (i.e. mix of transactions).
b) The SDS usage, that represents almost the totality of interprocess communication volume, presents a certain degree of locality, that is for a given SDS a limited number of SPFs are responsible for most of the accesses.

To meet these requirements the PHS have to support the following facilities:

1. Number of PUs selectable according to the global processing power required by the application.
2. Process replication on different PU in order to avoid the bottleneck due to an overloaded SPF.
3. SDS-SPF clustering on the same PU in order to reduce the communication beetwen different PUs.
4. Separate allocation of non-clustered SDS to avoid umbalanced access time from different PUs.

According to the above considerations we chose for the PHS the bus architecture shown in Fig. 3.1.

The main characteristic of this architecture is the organization of the main memory into three levels:

1. private : internal to each PU and only internally accessible, stores the programs.
2. public : internal to each PU but accessible also from the G-Bus, contains the clustered SDS that are often accessed locally and seldom externally.
3. global : external to the PUs holds the unclustered SDSs.

In this way the processes implementing the DBMS operates most of the time on the data stored into the internal memory, reducing both the interference among the PUs and the bandwidth requirements for the bus.

The G-Bus (Global Bus) is an high speed parallel bus devoted to inter-PU process communication and shared SDSs access. It has to support multi-master access and is implemented by means of the IEEE 796 standard bus.

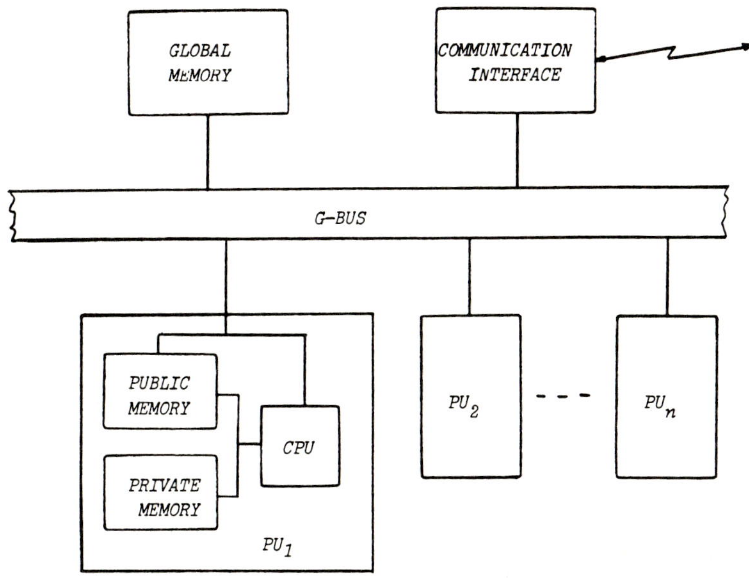

Fig. 3.1 - The Physical High System.

The Global Memory is a medium sized (256 KByte) memory that, besides of the unclustered SDSs, stores data structures of the distributed operating system EXEMAC [MITE80] that are shared among all the PUs.

The Communication Interface is a single board computer dedicated to communication protocol management. It can be configured either for local or network interconnection.

The main task of the HS is to translate the sequence of relational operations implied by a transaction into a sequence of DP primitives that are executed by the LS. The PLS performs three kinds of operations: selection, integer intersection and sorting that operate on large amount of data. In some cases a parallel processing of the same data stream is required, in other cases parallel processing of different data streams for different instructions is also required.

To meet these different requirements we must allow any group of processors to connect to a desired MSU. Thus we selected a bus architecture (see Fig. 3.2) also for the PLS, but special care was taken to avoid the interconnection becoming the system bottleneck.

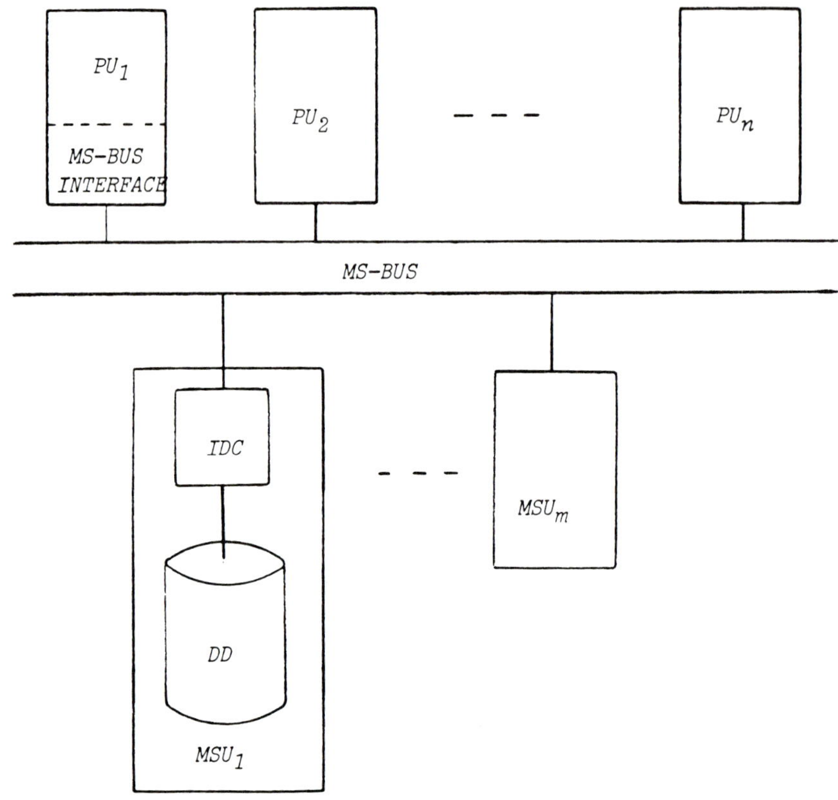

Fig. 3.2 - The Physical Low System.

The MS-Bus architecture will be discussed in the next subsection but it results from the following considerations:

1. Data base applications are characterized by high data block traffic and a unique bus can be saturated when the number of disks increases.
2. Control messages (command and status) generates a very little fraction (0.1% ..0.01%) of the PUs-DDs traffic;
3. Serial connections can be replicated at a small cost if

arbitration problems can be avoided.

4. The throughput of a standard disk storage unit can be supported by an high speed serial connection.

As shown in the figure, the MSU contains two main components: the Disk Device (DD), that is a standard high capacity winchester disk, and the Intelligent Disk Controller (IDC), that is in charge of all the operations involved by the data access including disk access optimization, data caching and data filtering (see 3.2).

Data are stored in 10K pages. To perform a page read a PU sends a read command to the appropriate MSU through the MS-Bus. The IDC of the addressed MSU queues and schedules the request and, when the page is available into its internal buffer, sends the command acknowledge to the PU. Finally the data are transferred via the MS-Bus. A similar procedure applies to write operations.

3.2 - The DBMAC hardware

Most of the DBMAC hardware is standard, in fact the G-Bus has been implemented through the IEEE 796 bus and both the Global Memory and the Host Interface are standard board. The PU also is nearly standard and its prototipe has been realized by means of a 8086 single board computer [MITE82] expanded with a custom piggy-back interface toward the MS-Bus [FRAN85].

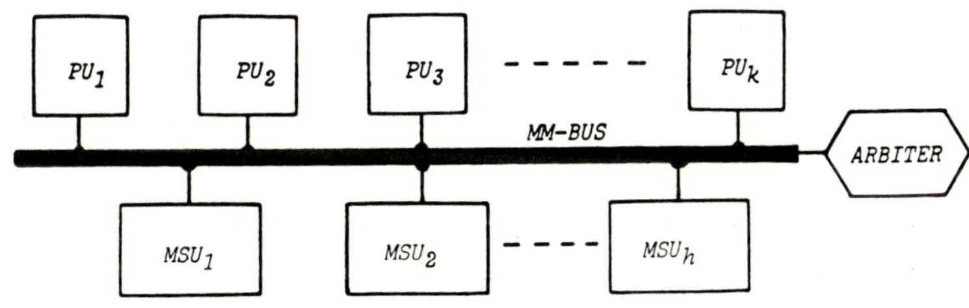

Fig.3.3 - The Single Bus interconnection

A special effort has been payed in MS-Bus design and two different architectures has been considered: the first one, called Single-Bus (SB) and shown in Fig. 3.3, uses a fast parallel bus (again the IEEE 796) and is suitable for small system configuration (see section 4), the other, called Multiple-Bus (MB), is much more complex and allows the MS-Bus throughput to grow according to the configuration.

The MB architecture (Fig. 3.4) provides each MSU with a dedicated bus for data transfer (Data Bus), while an additional shared bus (Control Bus) is devoted to the control messages exchange. Each PU can connect itself to each MSU by selecting the appropriate Data Bus through a multiplexor. All the buses are implemented by high speed serial lines.

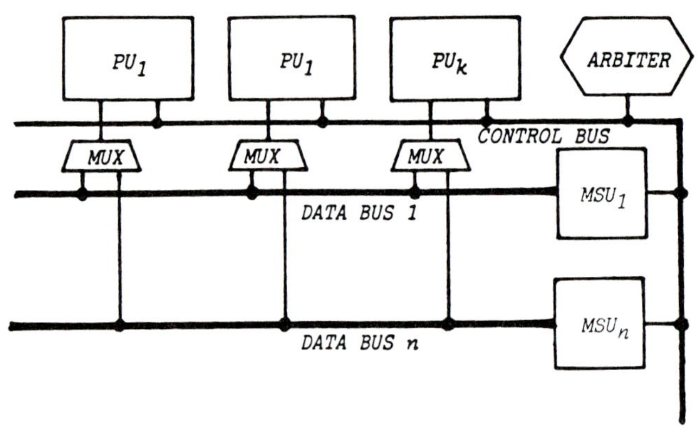

Fig. 3.4 - The Multiple Bus interconnection

A disk access through the MB is performed by delivering the request and the acknowledge messages to the Control Bus. As soon as the PU receives the acknowledge, it establishes the connection with the Data Bus of the MSU and the data are transferred.

The MB architecture allows to perform in parallel as many data transfers as MSU are in the system, thus reaching the highest degree of parallelism on disk data streams. Moreover it supports also data broadcasting from the MSU so that a given data stream can be received by multiple PUs. The arbitration is required only for the Control Bus and can be realized using well known tecniques proposed for multi-master buses [BART79]. Dedication of each Data Bus to a unique MSU avoids line contention and simplifies handshaking, thus allowing a three wire connection [RAIM84] that can be replicated at an acceptable cost.

The main component of the MSU is the IDC that, in the basic configuration for MB, has the architecture shown in Fig. 3.5. It contains a Control CPU, a single board computer that supervises the IDC operation, and a medium sized buffer (1 MByte), implemented by means of a dual port RAM memory, that temporarily stores the data transferred through the Disk Controller and the Data Communication Interface. The speed and the word width (16 bit) of the memory are selected to allow interleaved operation of both the interfaces toward the DD and MS-Bus.

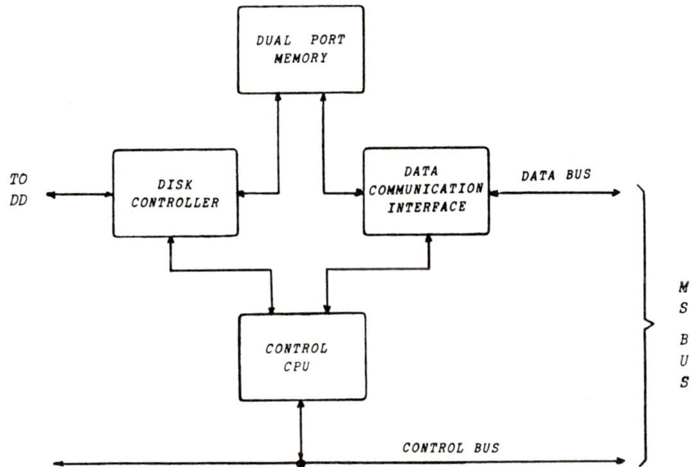

Fig. 3.5 - The Intelligent Disk Device

The purpose of the buffer is to increase the MSU throughput by overlapping the data transfer from/to the PUs with the data transfer from/to the DD. Moreover, because of the particular physical data organization (see section 1.2), a simple prepaging technique based on the reading of several consecutive pages when a page read is actually performed and a shrewd page replacement policy allow to reduce the data access time.

The IDC design can also accomodate an hardware filter to perform some data preprocessing at the MSU level. In this case the architecture is modified as shown in Fig. 3.6. A third port is added to the buffer (Main Buffer) to allow the filter to fetch the data stream to be filtered and an auxiliary dual port buffer, the Filter Buffer, stores the outcoming data. The read and write operation are performed as before using the Main Buffer. The "read and filter" operation involves an additional step in which the filter processes the data page stored in the Main Buffer producing a data block (with size different from the page size) in the Filter Buffer. The data block is then sent to the PU through the Data Communication Interface that can access both the buffers. The filter can be both a standard microprocessor and a special hardware device as the TID list intersector described in the following subsection.

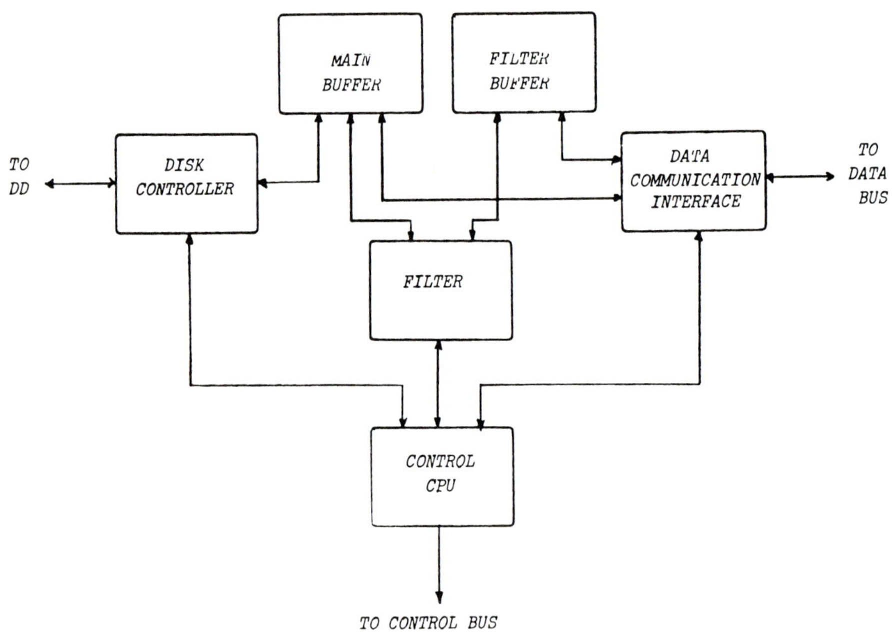

Fig. 3.6 - The IDC with filter

3.3 - The Continuous Intersection Device: CID

The DBMAC data organization requires to intersecate two TID lists representing intermediate results of a query. To speed up this operation we have designed CID, a VLSI device performing the intersection of two set of integers, that exceed the performance of the Array Processor [KULE80] and the Tree Machine [BEKU79,SONG81], the other architectures proposed for this operation [BEMT83]. The better perfomance is due to the elimination of the necessity to perform the operation through several steps when the size of the operands is larger than the number of available processors and to the ability of reusing a processor as soon as it finishes the current operation.

The CID architecture, shown in Fig. 3.7, consists of two sections: the Comparison Section (CS), containing a chain of processors that actually performs the comparison beetwen each element t of the "target" list T and all the elements r of the "rotating" list R, and the Supply Section (SS), that routes each t to the first comparitor that became available.

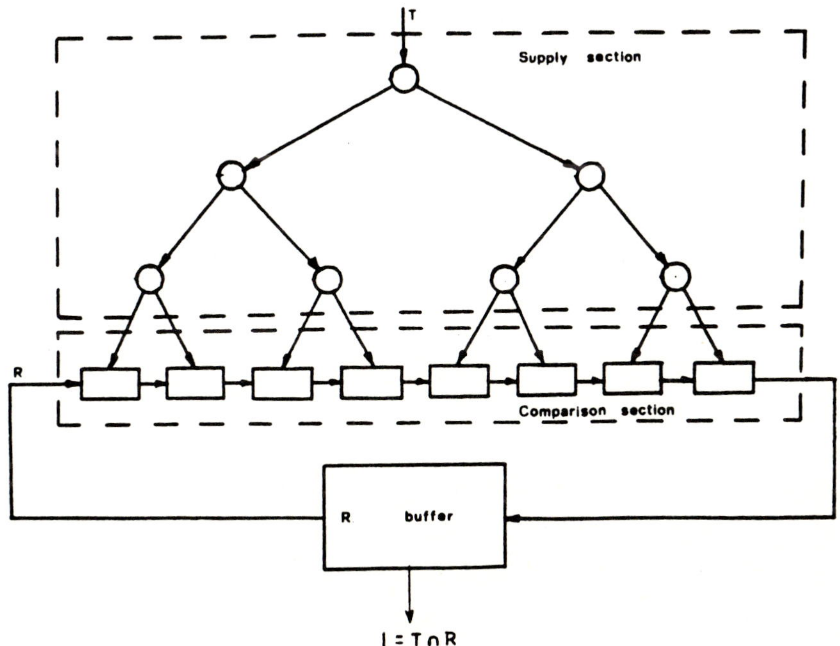

Fig. 3.7 - The CID architecture

External to CID there is the R Buffer that stores the still unmatched elements of R and continuously supplies them to the input end of the comparitors chain. The output of the chain returns to the R buffer that sends a matched r to the result output and eliminates it from the list. In this way the R list (replicated when its cardinality is smaller than the number of processors) seems to rotate through the CS.

Since the number of elements contained into the R buffer decreases during the operation the rotating list is prefixed with a special mark (SOL: Start Of List) that carries the number of elements actually contained in the list (DRC: Dynamic R Cardinality).

The Comparison Section operation can be described with the following algorithm:

```
Begin
  repeat
    fetch t from the SS;
    match <- false;
    count <- 0;
    repeat
      fetch r from the predecessor;
      if r = SOL
        then load DRC
        else
         if r is not marked
           then
             if r = t
               then begin
                      mark r;
                      match <- true
                    end
               else count <- count + 1
    until match or count = DRC
  until elements t are finished
end.
```

The preceeding algorithm assumes that as soon as a processor get rid of t it can fetch a new element from the SS. This is not always true. In fact the Supply Section has a binary tree structure with 2 P - 1 cells (if P is the number of processor in the CS). When a comparison cell needs a new element t the SS cells on the path connecting the processor (leaf) to the input (root) behave as a shift register scaling down its contents. If two comparison processors issue a request simultaneously, a complete shift (from the root to the leaf) will be allowed only for one path (primary path). In this case a lacuna will be generated in the cell of the secondary path that is the son of the root of smallest subtree containing both processors. The lacuna will be filled up with a partial shift from the input to the empty cell in the next cycle.

The Fig. 3.8 shows an example of lacuna generation and filling. When the cells C_1 and C_4 require a new t the path (1,2,4,8) will form the primary path and a complete shift to feed C_1 will occur, while the path to feed C_4, (1,2,5,11) will be broken in 2 and a lacuna will be generated in 5. In the next step a shift through (1,2,5) will fill up the lacuna. In a more general case it is possible to have in the SS many lacunas; at each step without matches the number of lacunas reduces of one, at each step with K matches it increases of k - 1.

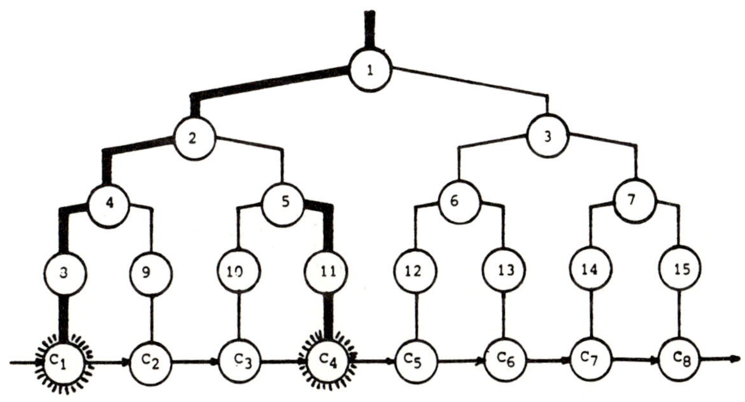

Fig. 3.8 Contention in the SS.

The CID performance in absence of lacunas has been proved to be better than the Array Processor and Tree Machine performance [BEMT83]. The Fig. 3.9 summarizes the result of the simulation of CID performed taking into account the lacunas fenomenon [BATZ85], that is not negligible at the end of the operation, when no more t elements are available and the comparitor utilization sharply decreases. In the figure mean value of the number of step (clock cycles) necessary to perform the operation as a function of the cardinalinalities of the operands R and T and of the result I is given for CID (with and without lacunas), Array Processor and Tree Machine. The size of the device is chosen equal to 32 and the R cardinality is 256 but similar results has been obtained for different values.

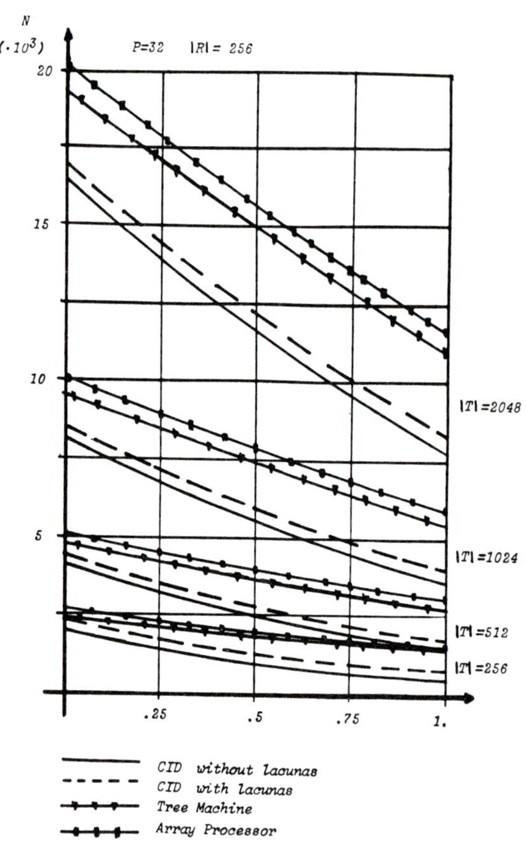

Fig. 3.9 CID performance

4 - THE DBMAC PERFORMANCE EVALUATION

4.1 - Motivations

The performance analysis had an important role in the DBMAC project. In fact the modeling activity was considered as an integral part of the design and began since the early stages of the project. This proved to be a wise choice, since provided a very useful feedback that allowed to verify and correct some of the architectural choices.

The main attention was given to the evaluation of the interconnection architecture, i.e. the Mass Storage Bus that allows the communication between the Processing units and the Mass Storage Bus. This is in fact a potential bottlenek and may eventually affect the overall performace of the system.

More precisely we compared the two interconnection architectures presented in sect. 3.2. The first one, the SB architecture (Fig. 3.3), provides a high speed parallel bus , and sends the data pages partitioned in packets to reduce the waiting time for the control messages. The other solution , the MB architecture (Fig. 3.4), provides a dedicated bus for every MSU, and then a transfer capability that grows with the number of MSUs.

The performance analysis had the following goals:

1. Compare the two architectures on a quantitative basis, to determine the expansion limit of the simpler solution, i.e the maximum number of PUs that the SB can support.

2. Derive general criteria based on the balance of the utilisations of the system resources, to select the right configuration (i.e. number of PUs and MSUs) for given workload characteristics.

3. Provide computationally simple mathematical models to predict both local and global performance indices for given System configuration and workload profile.

We summarize in the following sections both the methodological aspects and the main numerical results. Readers interested in more details should refer to [SATV83].

4.2 - Modeling methodology and basic assumptions

As far as the modeling methodology is concerned the choice was to utilize analytical queueing network models. This has several advantages. First of all these models have a low computational cost and a fairly short setup time, at least when compared to the more complex and time consuming simulation models, that require the use of specialized languages and/or a large programming effort. Furthermore their simpler structure makes possible the extensive parametric analysis required to compare the two architectures for different system configurations and workload profiles.

In our case, due to the complex structure of the system, we adopted a two level hierarchical model. At the lower level (inner model) the DBM operation is analyzed in a stationary condition, i.e. with fixed load and multiprogramming level at the PUs. This allows to establish how the performance depends on the device characteristics and on the system configuration.

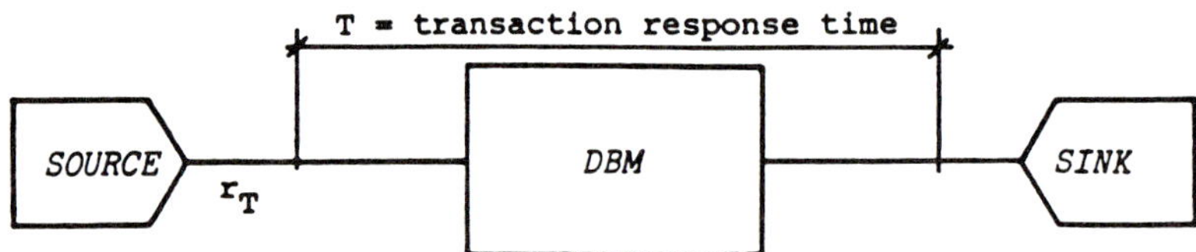

Figure 4.1 - The transaction flow

A higher level model (aggregate model) is then considered to include the external world (front-end or local network) where the transactions originate (Fig 4.1). At this level the whole Database Machine is represented as a single service facility having, for a given workload and configuration, the service rates computed during the solution of the inner model.

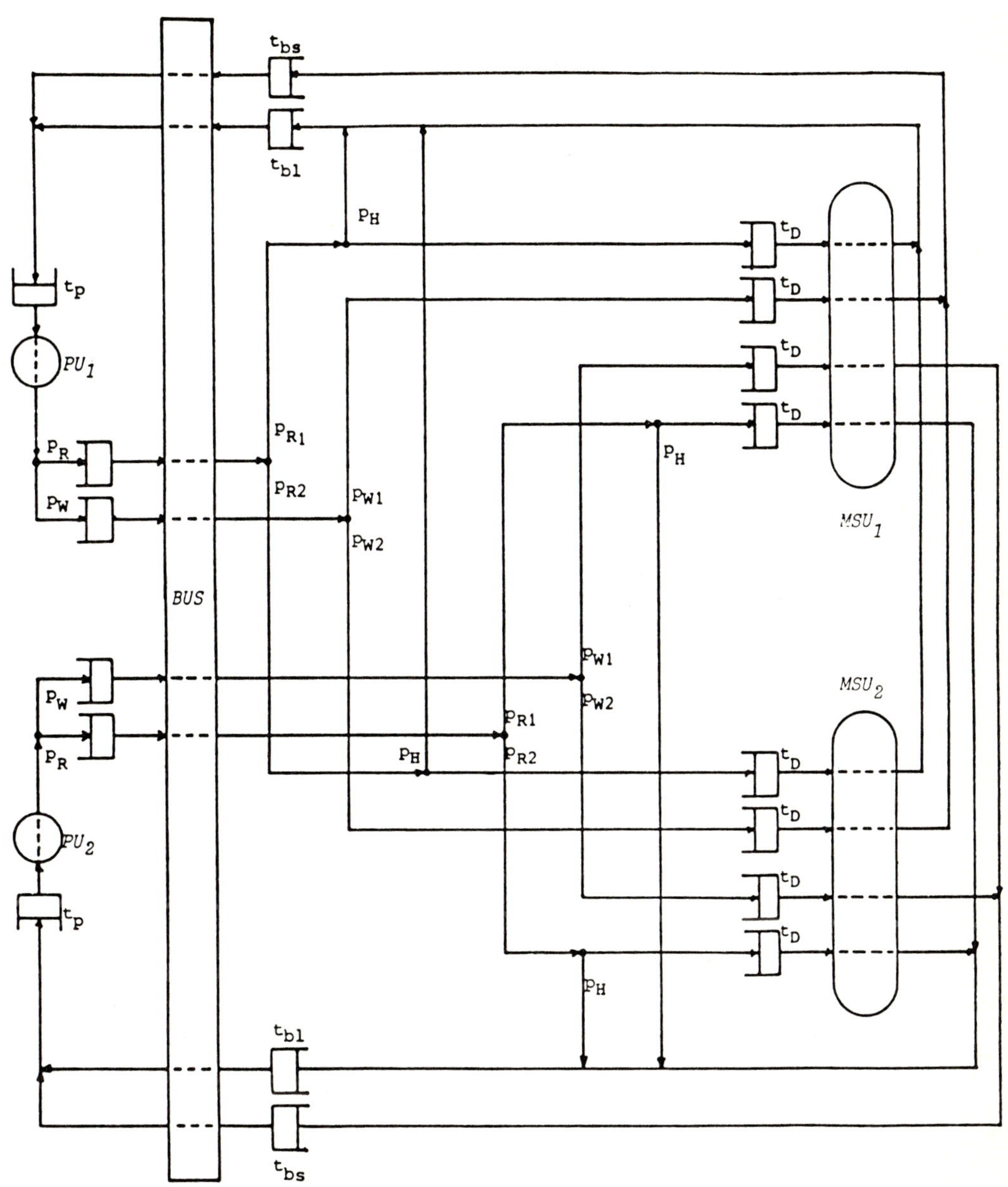

Figure 4.2 - Queueing network model for SB

Both the inner and the aggregate models are simple product form networks [BCMP75], for which very efficient solution algorithm are available [RESA82].

An important point is also the workload model. We made for this the basic assumption that the whole system load could be represented by an appropriate set of transactions $Z=\{z_k, k=1,..,M\}$ that arrive to the system at an overral rate r_T. More precisely identical instances of transaction z_k arrive at a rate $r_k=r_T p_k$ where $\{p_k, k=1,..,M\}$ are the relative frequeces.

Furthermore, according to the DBMAC physical data organisation (see sect. 1.2), every transaction is executed by activating, possibly on different PUs, several parallel _elementary processes_, each operating on a single data page, and then requiring a page transfer from/to the MSUs.

A simple workload analysis technique (see [SATV83]) allows then to summarize the characteristics of the whole transaction mix in an _average elementary process_. This is charaterized by a weighted average processing time t_p and by a set of disk read and write access probabilities $\{p_{Ri}, p_{Wi}, k=1,..,M\}$ defined for all the MSUs in the system, that take into account the allocation of the database files. The average disk service time t_D for the fixed length pages is then computed from the device characteristics.

Finally the processing requirements of every transac-tion are expressed in terms of number of average elementary processes it requires to execute $\{N_k, k=1,..,M\}$.

4.3 - The inner model

At this level the DBM is analyzed in a stationary condition, i.e. working on a fixed population of average elementary processes. Actually a process disappears as soon as its execution terminates, but it is replaced immediately by another with statistically identical characteristics.

The queueing network in Fig. 4.2 represents the model of the SB architecture for the simple case of two PUs and two MSUs. A queue is provided for every system resource, i.e. the

PUs, the MSUs and the Bus which is represented by a queue with Processor Sharing discipline and different service requests for the control and data messages. The service times are those computed in the previous section.

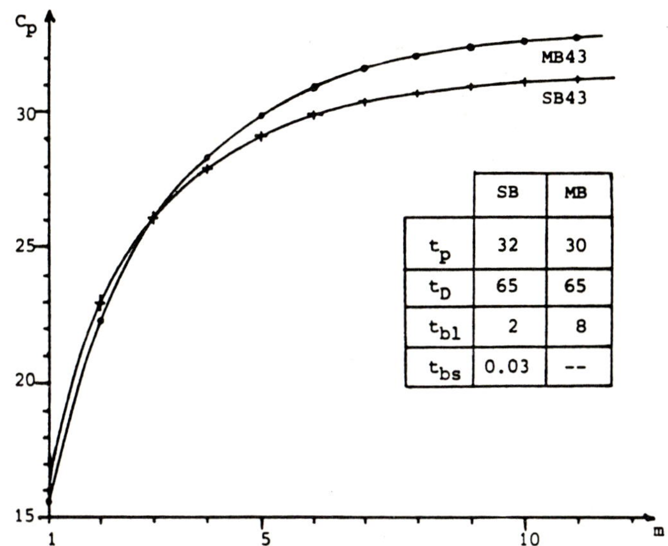

Figure 4.3 - PU throughput vs. multiprogramming level

The customers are organized in routing chains. Each chain represents the set of processes that are currently executed on the same PU, i.e. the multiprogramming set. The routing is probabilistic, based on the disk read/write access probabilities computed in the previous section. Furthermore the probability p_H takes into accont the effect of the prepaging policy (see Sect. 3.2), i.e. expresses the probability that a read access finds the page in the IDC buffer.

A similar model is used for the MB architecture (see [SATV83]). In this case a private bus, and then a separate queue is provided for every MSU.

The PU throughput c_p (average elementary processes executed per unit of time), is shown in Fig. 4.3 for a configuration with 4 PUs and 3 MSUs. The values of c_p are given for both architectures and for various values of the multiprogramming level m. These results allow to select an adequate level as a tradeoff between the throughput and the PU private memory size (which grows with m). For the case considered a reasonable value would range between 4 and 7.

n_p \ n_d	1	2	3	4	6	8
2	54.0	60.0	61.4	61.8	62.0	62.0
4	54.5	99.2	116.0	119.2	121.2	121.6
6	54.7	112.2	152.4	169.2	175.8	177.0
8	54.7	112.8	163.2	201.6	228.0	232.8

t_p = 32ms t_D = 65ms t_{bc} = 2ms t_{bd} = .03ms m = 5 p_H = .7

Table 1 - System throughput

The analysis was performed for a variety of configurations, and the comparison between the results of the two architectures showed that, for the service times considered in Fig. 4.3 and with an adequate number of MSUs, the bus becomes the system bottleneck when the number of PUs is larger than 15. This is indeed a theoretical limit. A more reasonable upper limit on the number of PUs could be 6, with a bus utilizationof of about 30% and a PU utilization around 90%.

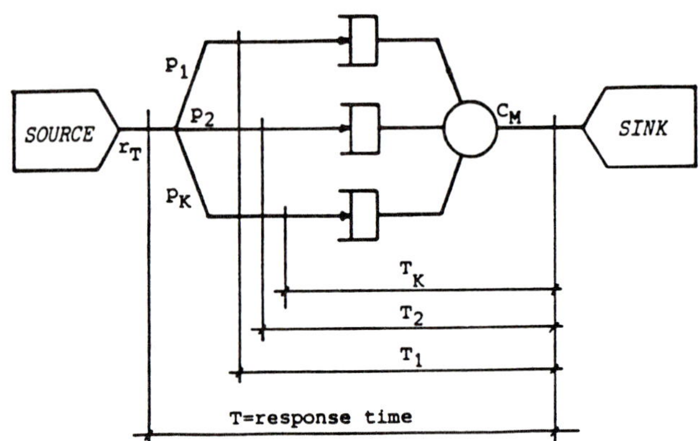

Figure 4.4 - The aggregate model

Values for the system throughput $C=n_p\ c_p$, for the SB

architecture and various system configurations are reported in Table 4.1, and can be used to select a balanced configuration of the system.

4.4 - The aggregate model

The higher level model is shown in Fig. 4.4. It is assumed that a Poisson stream of transactions arrive to the DBM at a rate r_T with relative frequency p_k for every transaction in the set Z. The DBM is represented as a single server having a rate equal to the system throughput C computed in the previous section.

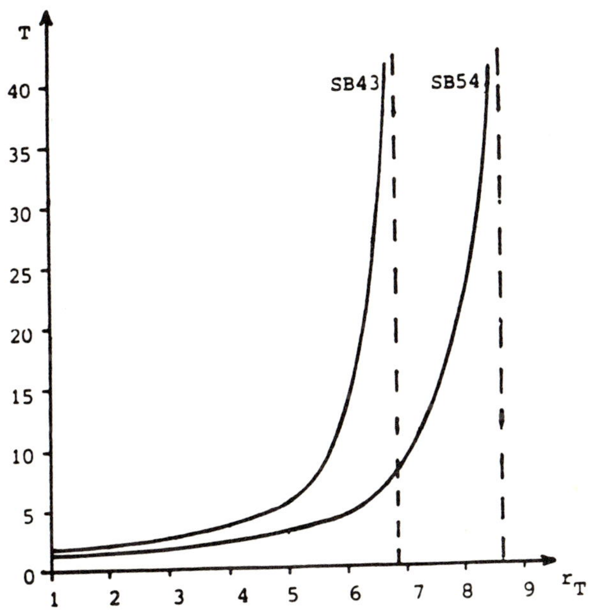

Figure 4.5 - Expected transaction response time

Every arriving transaction z_k requires a service consisting in the execution of N_k elementary processes. According to this and the internal resource allocation policy of DBMAC, we may assume a single queue with different customer classes (the transactions in the set Z) and Processor Sharing discipline. The queue can be easily solved to get the response time both for every transaction z_k and for the whole set.

In Fig.4.5 the average transaction response time is plotted versus the transaction arrival rate r_T for two configurations of the SB architecture. The asymptotes represent the system capacity, i.e. the maximum arrival rate that a given configuration can handle. Finally Table 4.2 shows, for a given workload and multiprogramming level, the influence of the system configuration on the response time.

n_p \ n_d	2	3	4	6	8
4	5.56	1.67	1.47	1.37	1.35
6	1.98	0.66	0.52	0.48	0.47
8	1.92	0.56	0.36	0.29	0.28

$t_p = 32ms$ $t_D = 65ms$ $t_{bc} = 2ms$ $t_{bd} = .03ms$

$m = 5$ $p_H = .7$ $r_T = 2.3$ $N = 40$

Table 4.2 - Response time and system configuration

REFERENCES

[BANC83] F. Bancilhon et Al.; "VERSO: a Relational Backend Database Machine"; in [HSIA83].

[BANE78] J.' Banerjee, R.I. Baum, D.K. Hsiao; "Concepts and Capabilities of a Database Computer" ACM TODS, vol. 3, Dec. 78.

[BART79] J. Barthmaier; " Intel MULTIBUS interfacing"; Intel Corp. Application Note 28A.

[BATZ85] P. Batzella, "Dispositivo VLSI per macchina per basi di dati", Ms Thesis, Università degli Studi di Roma "La Sapienza", 1985.

[BCMP75] Babb E., "Implementing a Relational Database by means of a Specialized Hardware", ACM TODS, vol.4 n.1, March 1979.

[BEKU79] J.L.Bentley, H.T.Kung, "A Tree Machine for Searching Problems", Proceedings of 1979 Int.Conf. on Parallel Processing IEEE, August 1979.

[BEMT83] P. Bertolazzi, M. Missikoff, M. Terranova, "CID: A VLSI Device for Lists Intersection", in [LEMI83].

[CODD70] E.F. Codd; "A Relational Model for Large Shared Data Bank", CACM, Vol. 13, n. 6, 1970.

[DEWI79] D.J. De Witt; "DIRECT - a Multiprocessor Organizatoin for Supporting relational Database Management System"; IEEE Trans. on Computer, vol. C28, n. 6.

[FRAN85] S. Francola, "Interfaccia di accesso a bus multiplo per single board computer 8086 e relativo arbitro", Ms Thesis, Università degli Studi di Roma "La Sapienza", 1985.

[GARD83] G. Gardarin et Al.; "SABRE: a Relational Database System for a Multimicroprocessor Machine"; in [HSIA83].

[HEAL72] L.D. Healy, G.J. Lipowski, K.L. Doty; "The Architecture of a Context addressed Segment Sequential Storage"; 1972 NCC, AFIPS Conf. Proc., vol. 41.

[HSIA77] D.K. Hsiao, S.E. Madnik; "Database Machine Architecture in the Context of Information Technology Evolution"; 1977 VLDB.

[HSIA83] D.K. Hsiao (Ed.); "Advanced Database Machine Architectures"; Prentice Hall, 1983.

[KULE80] H.T.Kung, P.L.Lehman, "Systolic (VLSI) Arrays for Relational Data Base", 1980 ACM/SIGMOD Int. Conf. on Management of Data, Los Angeles, May 1980.

[LEMI83] H.O. Leilich, M. Missikoff (Eds.), "Database Machines", Springer-Verlag, 1983.

[LINS76] C.S. Lin, D.C.P. Smith, J.M. Smith; "The Design of a Rotating Associative Memory for Relational Database Application"; ACM TODS, vol. 1, n. 1.

[MISS78] M. Missikoff; "RELOB: a Relational Storage System"; 1978 ACM - ICMOD Conference.

[MISS81] M. Missikoff, M. Terranova; "An Overview of the Project DBMAC for a Relational Database Machine"; VI Workshop on Computer Architecture for Non-Numerical Processing, June 1981

[MISS82] M. Missikoff; "A Domain Based Internal Schema for Relational Database Machines"; 1982 ACM - SIGMOD

Conference.

[MITE80] Missikoff M., Terranova M., "EXEMAC: un sistema esecutivo per Database Machines", Proc. AICA 80 annual conf., Bologna, Oct. 1980, (in Italian).

[MITE82] Missikoff M., Terranova M., "DBMAC - una multi-processor database machine: l'architettura di base", Progetto Finalizzato Informatica, Sottoprogetto DATANET/DBMAC, Tech. Rep. 3, (in Italian).

[PINZ80] R. Pinzani, F. Pippolini; "Organizzazione fisica dei dati su una macchina per basi di dati"; 1980 AICA Annual Congress.

[RAIM84] F. Raimondi, "Governo avanzato per memorie a disco", Ms Thesis, Università degli Studi di Roma "La Sapienza", 1984.

[RESA78] Reiser M., Sauer C.H., "Queueing Networks Models: Methods of Solution and their Program Implementation", in Chandy K.M. and Yen R.T. eds "Current Trends in Programming Methodology", vol.3, Prentice-Hall, Englewood Cliff, NJ 1982.

[SATV83] S. Salza, M. Terranova, P. Velardi; "Performance Modeling of the DBMAC Architecture"; in [LEMI83].

[SCHW83] H. Schweppe at Al.; "RDBM - A Dedicated Multiprocessor System for Database Management"; in [HSAIA83].

[SMIT79] D.C.P. Smith,J.M. Smith; "Relational Data Base Machines"; Computer, March 1979.

[SONG81] S.W.Song, "On High Performance VLSI Solution to Database Problems". Technical Report n. CMU-CS-81-130, Carnegie Mellon University, 1981.

[SULI75] S.Y.W. Su, G.J. Lipovski; "CASSM: a Cellular System for Very Large Data Bases"; 1975 VLDB.

MASSIVE PARALLEL DATABASE COMPUTER MPDC
AND
ITS CONTROL SCHEMES FOR MASSIVELY PARALLEL PROCESSING

Y. Tanaka
Department of Electrical Engineering
Hokkaido University
Sapporo, 060 JAPAN

1. TOWARDS A MASSIVE PARALLEL DATABASE COMPUTER

1.1 Problems and Required Technologies

High-volume processing of databases requires frequent references to a very large storage space, which makes it inevitable to frequently access mechanically-accessed secondary memory devices like moving head disk units.

Historically, this kind of problems has been repetitively encountered, and resolved through the combination of two technologies. A buffer memory placed between a primary memory and a secondary memory does not only increase access speed but also decreases secondary memory access frequency, while data clustering into segments increases access locality, and does not only decrease segment references but also enhances the buffer effect by increasing a chance of repetitive references to a small set of segments.

These two techniques necessarily introduce a secondary memory access unit called a segment. Segmentation divides database processing into two processing levels, i.e., segment search and segment processing. For a given transaction, segment search searches file directories to generate a set of segment processing commands with one or two segment locations as operands. Segment processing, on the other hand, executes, for each segment command, a basic database operation on one or two operand segments. It requires to fetch operand segments from disks to a work space if they are not there yet. Decomposition of a given transaction into segment processing commands must be controlled by a well-defined concurrency control scheme to maintain database integrity.

NATO ASI Series, Vol. F 24
Database Machines. Edited by A. K. Sood and A. H. Qureshi

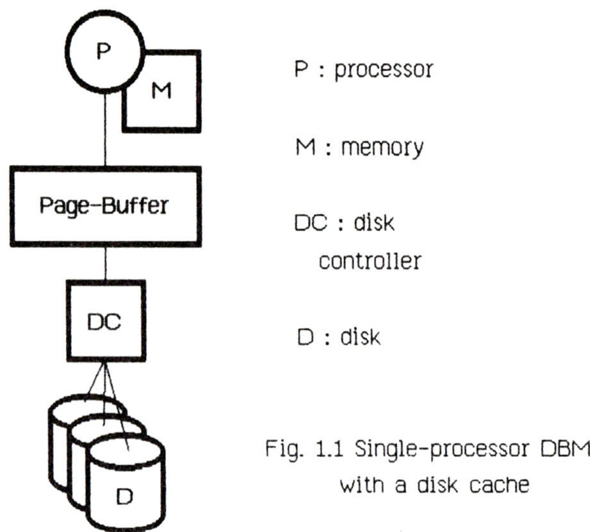

Fig. 1.1 Single-processor DBM with a disk cache

Introduction of a buffer memory between a primary memory and a secondary memory is attemted in recent computer systems to improve database system performance (Fig. 1.1). Such a buffer is sometimes referred to by a disk cache memory. It is a semiconductor memory placed between a primary memory and disk units. Segments, when they are accessed from disk units, are also written on some pages in this buffer and be kept there as long as possible. For each segment access request, if the segment is kept in the buffer, it is read out from the buffer and no disk access is performed. This will reduce disk accesses and increase the data transfer rate. If the buffer overflows, the least recently used page in the buffer is assigned for a new segment. The performance improvement effects of such a buffer are observed in relational database management systems by some main framers. Unfortunately, however, exact figures of the improvement are not publicized due to their confidentiality. It may well be assumed that the introduction of such a buffer memory to massive parallel database machines will also bring the same effect. It is desirable, however, that this buffer memory is a multiport memory shared by a bunch of processors and a set of secondary memory devices. Otherwise, access conflicts are inevitable and its connections to processors and secondary memory devices must be frequently changed and hence it requires explicit control of interconnection networks.

Introduction of parallelism into a single-processor database system as shown in Fig. 1.1 will change it to a configuration as shown in Fig. 1.2.

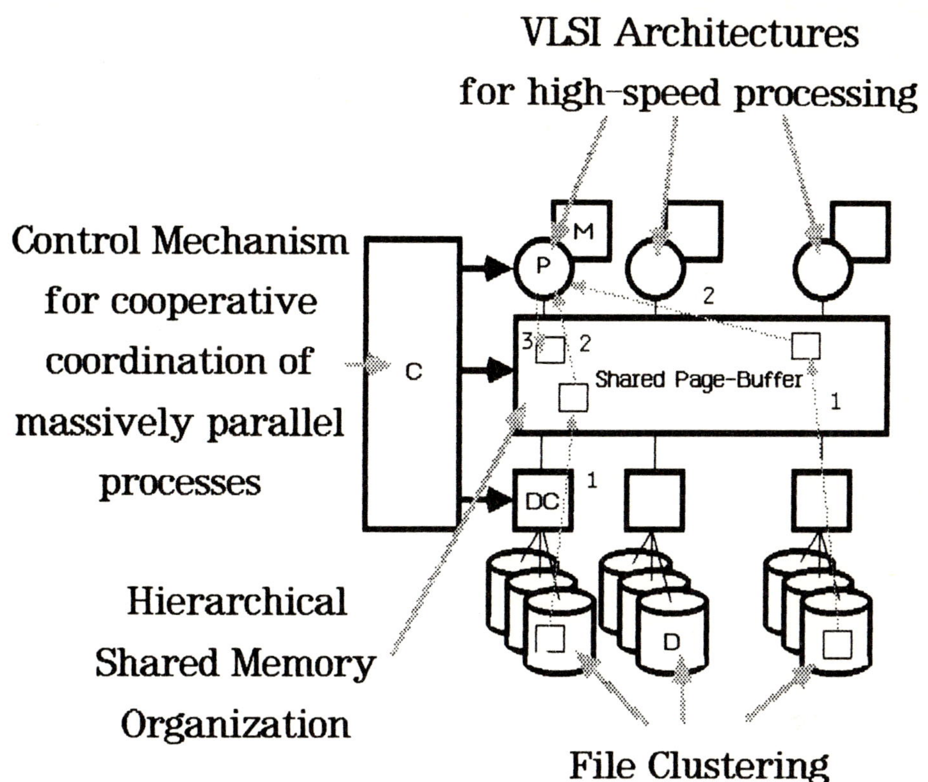

Fig. 1.2 Required Innovations.

It consists of a bunch of processors, a shared page buffer, a set of disk subsystems, and a controller. Each file is assumed to be segmented into a page size. Each access unit is called a segment. The shared page buffer is also segmented into pages. Each transaction is decomposed into a sequence of segment processing commands by the controller. The controller has to interleave these sequences of different transactions to maximize the concurrency of execution. Each segment processing command is decomposed into its operand segment fetch commands and a page processing command that activates the processing of the fetched pages in the shared page buffer. If the operand segment is already kept in the shared page buffer, its fetch command is not generated. Segment fetch command is sent by the controller to a disk subsystem that stores the operand segment. The disk subsystem accesses this segment and sends it to the specified page in the shared page buffer. Each page processing command can be executed by any processor, since the bunch of processors is homogeneous and every processor can access any page in the shared page buffer. Each page processing command is sent to one of the idle processors and be executed there.

Implementation of this abstract model of massive parallel database processing requires technological innovations as shown in Fig. 1.2. The first required technology is a multiport page memory. More than $10^2 \sim 10^3$ ports are necessary to connect a bunch of processors and a set of disk subsystems. Most multiport memories available today have no more than two ports. The second problem to solve is how to segment multiattribute files in order to reduce disk accesses necessary for various retrieval and update operations to databases. The third problem to solve is how to maximize concurrency of segment processing tasks. To cope with multiple user environment, the machine should be capable of concurrently executing multiple transactions. Each transaction should be further decomposed into segment processing tasks to increase concurrency. The controller must be capable of maximizing the concurrency by interleaving segment processing task sets of different transactions without loosing the correctness of transaction execution and database integrity. Besides, the overhead of this control should be hidden by the concurrent execution of segment processing tasks. The fourth problem to solve. is the speed-up of segment processing. Pipeline processing of fundamental database operations and its VLSI implementation are required.

1.2. MPDC Solutions to the Required Innovations

MPDC is a massive parallel database computer architecture that was first proposed in 1984 (Tanaka 1984). It consists of two subsystems, i.e., **Data Subsystem** and **Control Subsystem** (Fig. 1.3). Data Subsystem is in charge of segment accesses and segment processing, while Control Subsystem is responsible to Data Subsystem for decomposing query transactions into concurrently executable segment processing commands. Two types of parallelism are distinguished. Parallelism in each basic segment processing is referred to by **microparallelism,** while parallelism that is found in concurrent processing of segment accesses and segment processing in interleaved execution of multiple transactions is called **macroparallelism.**

MPDC architecture has given technological breakthroughs to the four required innovations for massive database computer. As to microparallel

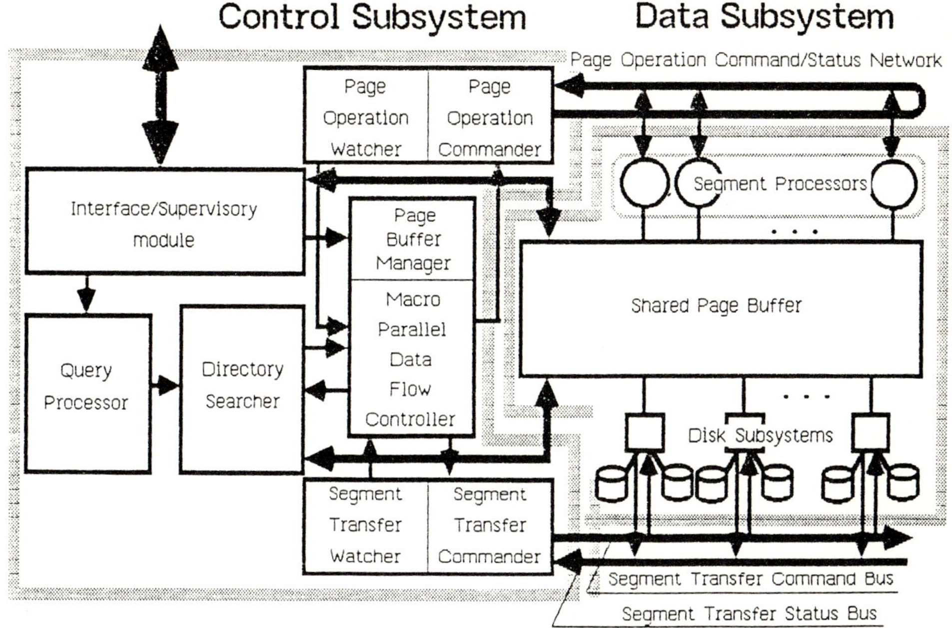

Fig. 1.3 Hardware Configuration of MPDC.

architectures for segment processing, two VLSI algorithms respectively for batch search and sort was proposed in 1980 (Tanaka et al. 1980). These are known as Search Engine and Sort Engine. These are fixed-wordlength modules. Bit-sliced versions of these engines were proposed in 1984 to solve this problem (Tanaka 1984a). These bit-sliced technique made the design specification of the VLSI wordlength independent from the actual requirement on the wordlength. Recently, Sort Engine was extended to cope with the sorting of variable-length character strings (Tanaka 1985).

Multiport page-memory architecture was proposed in 1984 (Tanaka 1984b). It allows each port to access an arbitrary page at an arbitrary time without any conflict with other ports. A page memory with this architecture works as a page buffer that is placed between a bunch of processors and a set of disk storage systems to reduce repetitive disk accesses to a same portion of a file, as well as to enhance the concurrency among disk accesses and also between disk accesses and processor operations. This architecture allows a single page memory space to be shared by $10^3 \sim 10^4$ ports. It allows random accesses of pages from each port, although it can not cope with random accesses of words.

Two multiattribute segmentation schemes was proposed in 1983 (Tanaka 1983b). They respectively minimize average and maximum file access costs for selection operations.

Massive macroparallelism requires highly concurrent execution of segment read and segment write operations. Besides, high reliability requires a sound recovery mechanism that does not seriously lower system performance during its execution. The multiversion model of databases simultaneously satisfies these requirements. Existence of old versions enables us to bring the system back to its old state before a failed update operation. In segmented file organization, each segment independently has arbitrary number of its versions. Version control of segments requires directory handling and concurrency control of segment processing. Therefore, these three functions, version control, file directory handling, and concurrency control should be integrated into a unified control mechanism. Since our multiattribute segmetation schemes use a tree structured file clustering, our concurrency control scheme must be applicable to hierarchically organized files. Control mechanisms for cooperative coordination of massively parallel segment processing tasks were proposed in 1984 (Tanaka 1984c). It is a multiversion concurrency control scheme that is applicable to hierarchically organized directories.

The integration of the independent technologies into a massive parallel database computer architecture MPDC was outlined in (Tanaka 1984c).

This paper will describe the macroparallel architecture of MPDC, i.e., its control schemes for massive parallel processing. The hierarchical multiversion concurrency control and the data flow control of both segment processing and segment accesses will be detailed in this paper.

2. FILE STRUCTURE AND MULTIVERSION HIERARCHICAL CONCURRENCY CONTROL

2.1. Colored Binary Trie Schemes for File Segmenttion

As a multiattribute file segmentation scheme, two types of segmentation schemes were proposed for MPDC to minimize respectively the average number and the maximum number of file segment accesses. They use a tree-structured file directory structure called a colored binary trie. Suppose for example that we have a relation R(A, B) with two attributes A and B. A possible pair of A and B values is represented by a point in the two dimensional area shown in Fig. 2.1 (a). The relation R is considered as a set of points

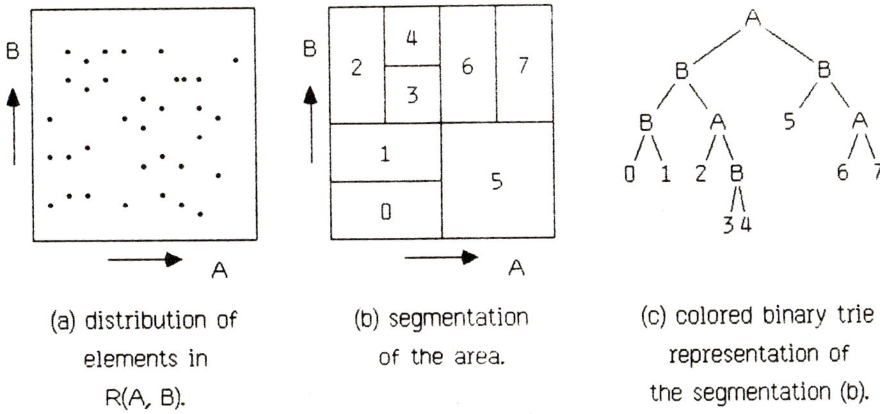

(a) distribution of elements in R(A, B).

(b) segmentation of the area.

(c) colored binary trie representation of the segmentation (b).

Fig. 2.1 Segmentation of a multiattribute file R(A, B).

scattered over this area. A segmentation of R is a segmentation of this area. Initially, when the number of the scattered points that represent tuples of R is not larger than the size of one segment, the area need not be segmented, i.e., the relation R needs no segmentation. However, updates on R may make R too large to be stored in one segment. When this occurs, the original area is divided into two subareas, each of which is stored in a dedicated segment. The simplest way of splitting an area is to select either A or B and to divide the area into two halves by a line perpendicular to the selected coordinate axis. An example segmentation obtained after several applications of splitting is shown in Fig. 2.1 (b). In Fig. 2.1 (c), the same segmentation is represented by a binary tree. An attribute name labeled at each internal node of this tree indicates the attribute used for the splitting at the corresponding stage. This tree is called a colored binary trie. The leaf nodes of this tree labeled by integers denote segments. Suppose for simplicity that attributes A and B take 4 bit values. Then the retrieval of all the tuples satisfying A='0000' requires accesses to three segments 0, 1, and 3. No further accesses are necessary. If the condition is replaced with B='0000', only two segments 0 and 5 need to be accessed.

Let $\rho(A, \alpha)$ denote the number of nodes that are labeled with A along the path from the root to a leaf α. The access cost for an equiselection operation A='v' is defined as the number of segment accesses necessary for this operation. The average access cost of a segmentation represented by a trie T is defined as the average of the access cost over all the possible equiselection operations. Best average segmentation scheme selects, for the splitting of an overflowing segment α, an attribute A that minimizes the average access cost of the resultant trie. It was proved in (Tanaka 1983b) that such an attribute also minimizes $\rho(A, \alpha)$ and vice versa. An alternative segmentation algorithm that minimizes the maximum access cost was also proposed in (Tanaka 1983b).

In Colored binary trie schemes, a search of the directory for N segments and its local rewriting need only O(log N) time on an average for large N. Especially, if the values of the secondary keys are independently and uniformly distributed, these operations need no more than O(log N) time for large N. The best average scheme makes the average number of segment accesses necessary for the processing of a relational selection operation no more than $O(N^{(n-1)/n})$, where N and n are respectively the number of relational records and the number of secondary key attributes. On the other hand, it is proved that, if the record values are uniformly distributed, no segmentation scheme can make this file access cost less than $O(N^{(n-1)/n})$. In the processing of a relational restriction operation, the number of necessary segment accesses is approximately same as in the case of a selection operation.

In the proposed schemes, any full equi-join of two relations each of which has O(N) segments and n secondary key attributes requires no more than $O(N^{2-(1/n)})$ joins of two segments. Otherwise, its maximum time complexity is $O(N^2)$. Besides, in our schemes, if $O(N^{(n-1)/n})$ size buffer is provided, any full equi-join of them requires no more than O(N) disk accesses. Otherwise, O(N) size buffer is necessary to achieve O(N) access complexity. In MPDC, if $O(^{(n-1)/n})$ segment processors and $O(N^{(n-1)/n})$ pages in Shared Page Buffer are available, any full equi-join of them requires no more than O(N) time. This time includes disk access time. No database machines other than MPDC have ever achieved theoretically proved O(N) time processing of any full equi-join.

2.2 Unified Approach to File Organization, Recovery, and Concurrency Control

In a multiversion model of databases, a file is not necessarily provided with a new version of the whole file whenever it is updated. Otherwise, multiversion database systems are impractical. In segmented file organizations, it is sufficient to provide new segment versions only for modified segments. If files are clustered into segments to increase access locality, the number of modified segments in each update operation does not become large. Each segment can be revised independently. Version control of segments requires directory handling and concurrency control of segment processing. Therefore, these three functions should be integrated into unified control mechanism. Since MPDC uses colored binary trie schemes as its segmentation schemes, uses a multiversion concurrency control mechanism for colored binary trie schemes. Actually, the concurrency control described in this chapter is applicable to databases with a tree structured directory, which is not necessarily a colored binary trie scheme. Therefore, it will be formalized in its most general form.

The idea of using multiple versions of data items was first adopted in the Honeywell file system (Honeywell 1973), and the concurrency control of multiversion databases was first theoretically studied in (Sterns et al. 1976). A lot of multiversion concurrency control schemes have stemmmed from their studies. Among them are (Bayer et al. 1980a), (Bayer and Schlichtiger 1984), (Kessels 1980), (Papadimitriou and Kanellakis 1984). There are still some other schemes proposed for distributed database environments (Bayer et al. 1980b, Bernstein and Goodman 1983). These schemes assume no structure among data items in a file.

Some researchers noticed that a hierarchical structure among data items, if it exists as in the case of hierarchically organized files, might simplify the concurrency control. Among them, Silberschatz and Kedem proposed for tree-structured file of data items a locking protocol called the tree protocol (Silberschatz and Kedem 1980), which was further generallyzed by them (Kedem and Silberschatz 1980). In tree protocol, except for the first item locked (which need not be the root), no item can be locked unless a lock is currently held on its parent item. Besides, no item is ever locked twice by one transaction. Some researchers developed the tree protocol algorithm for the special case of concurrent accesses to B-trees (Bayer and Schkolnick 1977, Ellis 1977, Lehman and Yao 1981). However, these are schemes for single version databases.

While concurrency control schemes for multiversion databases and those for hierarchically organized databases have been extensively studied independently, no attempt has been made to integrate these two kinds of schemes. Concurrency control schemes for hierarchically organized multiversion databases, which are the most practical case, especially in MPDC, have never been sufficiently studied yet. Besides, as will be shown in this chapter, such a scheme can not be obtained by just combining two kinds of existing schemes. The new scheme that was first proposed in (Tanaka 1984c) and will be detailed in this chapter adopts lock operations as well as time stamps. In this scheme, read locks need not observe the tree protocol, and a write lock may share a same data item with read locks. Hence, the concurrency is much improved in this scheme.

2.3 Models of Transactions and File Organization

Transactions are classified into two categories, i.e., read transactions and write transactions. Transactions with no update operations are read transactions, while others are write transactions. A whole database is considered as a tree structured set of objects. The root object of this tree may be interpreted as a relation directory that stores, for each relation, the physical location of its segment directory. A son of the root may be interpreted as the entry of the corresponding segment directory. A subtree with a root's son as its root corresponds to a hierarchically organized segment directory of a relation. A colored binary trie is an example. Each leaf node represents a segment, or more precisely, a segment address. In a multiversion directory, every node is allowed to have arbitrary number versions of the corresponding object. Therefore, each segment may have arbitrary number of segment versions. For simplicity, in other chapters, segment versions are simply called segments. Versions should be preserved while they are possibly referred to. Unnecessary versions should be deleted to decrease total number of storage segments.

Objects are lock units. Old versions for each object allow read transactions to read them while a write transaction is producing a new version of the same object. An object is modeled as a finite sequence of values of a same type, i.e.,

$$O = (v_0, v_1, \ldots, v_{n-1}),$$

where n is the number of versions of O and be denoted by n(O). A value v_i is called the i+1st version of the object O, and be denoted by O(i). The index i is called the version number of v_i. We call the first version O(0) the new version, O(1) the current version, and every remaining version an old version. Every new version is usually nil. It takes a non-nil value only while the object is being modified by a write transaction. When the update ends succesfully with a commit command having been issued by the transaction, the object is modified as

$$O \leftarrow (nil, O(0), O(1), \ldots, O(n(0))). \quad (2.1)$$

This operation changes the version number of each version. Actually, versions that will not be further referred to are deleted and the remaining versions are compressed during this assignment. For the present. however, we assume that the number of versions is allowed to increase monotonically. This simplified model will be modified later in this chapter.

A set of correct transactions is considered to produce a correct result if they are executed without any intervention, or in other words, if they are executed one after another. Therefore, the execution of the correct transactions T_1, T_2, ... , T_n will be correct if it produces the same effect as some arbitrary serial execution ($T_{P(1)}$, $T_{P(2)}$, $T_{P(3)}$, ... , $T_{P(n)}$), where P is a permutation function. This condition is referred to as serializability. To achieve the correct execution of the concurrent transactions, they must be synchronized in some way. Usually, this is managed by various locking protocols. Here, we will propose a locking protocol for the above described new model.

2.4 Lock Protocol and Lock Mechanism

Our protocol provides six kinds of lock operations for object locking. They are r-lock (read lock), w-lock (write lock), r-unlock (read unlock), w-unlock (write unlock), commit (commit operation), and roll-back (roll-back operation). Although lock operation names are similar to those in well-known theories, their semantics are quite different.

A read lock, when it is set on an object, keeps its current version value at this time, and ensures the readability of this value untill the lock is released by a corresponding read unlock operation. This current version value may change its version number during the execution, i.e., it may become an old version.

A write lock enables following update operations in the same transaction to exclusively possess the new version while they produce a new value on it. A write lock also ensures the readability of the current version value and prohibits its revision. If all update operations in a transaction have finished normally, a commit command is used to release all write locks. Each new version value produced by the transaction replaces the old current version value if the update operations have actually changed this new version value from nil. In this case, all values of an updated object O will be shifted to the past by the assignment statement (2.1). If no actual update has been done on this object, i.e., if O(0) remains nil, then no operation is performed. If the update operations have not finished normally, write unlock commands are used to release write locks. A single roll-back command can also nullify all update operations in the failed transaction. In these case, versions will not be revised and modified new versions are reset to nil.

In our protocol, neither w-lock, w-unlock nor roll-back is allowed to be used in read transactions, while neither r-lock nor r-unlock is allowed in write transactions. This restriction does not reduce concurrency, because multiversion systems allow simultaneous setting of r-locks and a w-lock on a shared object. Each write transaction is allowed to issue no more than one commit command.

Transactions are assumed to have their identification number. For each object O, the set of transactions that have set a lock on the i+1st version of O is denoted by L(O(i)). The set L(O(0)) is either empty or a sigleton with one write transaction number. For each i, L(O(i)) is either empty or a set with only read transactions.

Each object version represents an object value during a certain time period. To clarify this time period, it is necessary to introduce a logical clock LC. It is a counter that is initially reset to zero and has sufficiently many bits. It is incremented by one whenever a write transaction issues a commit command. The value of LC defines a nonlinear monotonic function of the actual time. It is called the logical time. A new version value becomes referable, i.e., its version number becomes positive, when the modifying transaction issues a commit command. Therefore, the time stamp of a version is defined as the logical time when this version value became referable, i.e., when a commit command made it a current version. For $i \geq 1$, let ts(O(i)) denote the time stamp of a version O(i). In logical time, a version value of O(i) was the current value of the object O during a time period [ts(O(i)), ts(O(i-1))), where $[t_1, t_2)$ denotes a set of real numbers that are greater than or equal to t_1 and less than t_2. For i=1, ts(O(i-1)) is assumed to be the current value of LC.

Now, let us define two macro operations on an object.

```
procedure revise(O, ts);
  begin
    O←(nil, O(0), O(1), ... , O(n(O)));
    n(O)←n(O)+1;
```

```
      for i=n(O) to 1 step -1 do
         L(O(i))←L(O(i-1));
      for i=n(O) to 2 step -1 do
         ts(O(i))←ts(O(i-1));
      L(O(0))←∅;
      ts(O(1))←ts;
   end;

procedure roll-back(O);
   begin
      O←(nil, O(1), ... , O(n(O)));
      L(O(0))←∅;
   end;
```

Lock operations are defined as follows. Associated with each read transaction T is a semi-open interval $[t_1, t_2)$ that is initially set to [0, +), where + denotes the positive infinity. This interval will be called temporal requirement, and be denoted by tr(T). Associated with each transaction T is a finite object set obj(T) that stores names of objects with a lock by this transaction. In the following definitions, T denotes the subject transaction. Locking procedures are defined as follows.

```
procedure r-lock(O);
   begin
      find the minimum i≥1 s.t.
         tr(T)∩[ts(O(i)), ts(O(i-1)))≠∅;
      L(O(i))←L(O(i))∪{T};
      tr(T)←tr(T)∩[ts(O(i)), ts(O(i-1)));
      obj(T)←obj(T)∪{O};
   end;

procedure w-lock(O);
   begin
      if L(O(0))≠∅
         then reject the request
         else
           begin
              L(O(0))←{T};
```

```
          obj(T)←obj(T)∪{O};
        end;
  end;

procedure r-unlock(O);
  begin
     for i=1 to n(O) do
        L(O(i))←L(O(i))-{T};
     obj(T)←obj(T)-{O};
  end;

procedure w-unlock(O);
  begin
     roll-back(O);
     obj(T)←obj(T)-{O};
 end;

procedure commit;
  begin
     if T is a read transaction
        then
          for each O in obj(T) do r-unlock(O)
        else
          begin
            ts←LC;
            LC←ts+1;
            for each O in obj(T) do
              if O(O)≠nil then revise(O, ts)
                            else roll-back(O);
          end;
     obj(T)←∅;
  end;

procedure roll-back;
  begin
     for each O in obj(T) do
        roll-back(O);
     obj(T)←∅;
```

end;

The multiversion hierarchical lock protocol that uses the above lock procedures is described as follows.

<<Protocol>>

1. A write transaction can not refer to nor modify an object without setting a write lock on this object, while a read transaction can not refer to an object without setting a read lock on it.
2. Read transactions do not use w-lock nor w-unlock, while write transactions do not use r-lock nor r-unlock.
3. Each transaction locks an object no more than once.
4. Before locking an object, a write transaction must lock its parent object if it has one. A write transaction should not release a write lock on an object O before it has set all the necessary locks on the son objects of O. If it has locked all necessary son objects, and if it has never modified O and will not modify nor read O, then it may release the write lock on O by using w-unlock. Otherwise, it can release the lock after it has finished all update operations.
5. Each transaction must release all the locks it has set before its exit.
6. Each write transaction can issue no more than one commit command and any number of roll-back commands.

Any interleaved execution that follows this protocol is deadlock-free and serializable. Besides, a roll-back command can roll back any failed updates before exit from the transaction. These properties were proved in (Tanaka 1984c).

The above discussion has assumed a simplified object model that allows monotonically increasing versions. Actually, an old version may be deleted if it is not subject to further references. For each read transaction T, let t(T) denote the LC value at the time when this transaction first set a read lock. Let tR denote the minimum t(T) value among any read transactions that are still being executed. Then, the execution of a commit command may delete all versions whose time stamp is less than tR, remaining only the latest of such versions for each object. It is obvious that these deletable versions are not subject to further references. This method keeps the maximum number of object versions within a reasonable range. The concurrency control of the processing in MPDC is performed by Directory Searcher in Control Subsystem.

3. MACROPARALLEL ARCHITECTURE OF MPDC

3.1 Microparallelism & Macroparallelism

Since microparallelism concerns parallelism in each basic operation, it has a definite structure that can be apriori described. Macroparallelism, on the other hand, concerns parallelism among tasks each of which represents a segment operation. Therefore, the structure of macroparallelism depends on less definitely describable factors like the status of concurrently executed transactions and the status of each computer resource. Macroparallelism requires much flexibility in parallel processing control. No control architectures other than data flow control may have the required extent of flexibility.

MPDC has a configuration as shown in Fig. 1.3. It consists of two subsystems, i.e., Control Subsystem for segment search and Data Subsystem for segment processing. Control Subsystem receives user queries, analyzes and decomposes them into segment processing operations through directory searches, and generates concurrently executable segment commands, while Data Subsystem receives generated segment commands from Control Subsystem, executes segment commands concurrently, and sends back a completion token to Control Subsystem immediately after the completion of each command execution.

3.2. Data Subsystem

Data Subsystem consists of a homogeneous set of segment processors, a set of disk subsystems, and a shared page buffer between these two sets of devices. Shared Page Buffer is a page-access memory that is shared by the set of processors and the set of disk subsystems. It is divided into equal-sized pages. Each page can store one segment of a file and has a unique page address. Shared Page Buffer allows all devices connected to it to concurrently access arbitrary pages without causing any access conflict nor any access wait.

Segment commands in MPDC are classified into two categories, i.e., segment transfer commands and page operation commands. Examples of segment transfer commands are get and put commands. They have two operands, i.e., a segment address and a page address. Each segment in disk subsystems has a unique segment address, which uniquely determines the disk unit that stores this segment. This unit is called the home disk of this segment, while the disk subsystem with the home disk is called the home disk subsystem. A get command requests Data Subsystem to read out its operand segment from the home disk to its operand page in Shared Page Buffer, while a put command requests Data Subsystem to save its operand page value stored in Shared Page Buffer into the operand segment in its home disk.

A page operation command, on the other hand, requests Data Subsystem to execute a relational database operation on its one or two operand pages, and to write one or more pages of result in Shared Page Buffer location specified by its destination operand. These source operand pages must be already loaded either with some segments by get commands or with intermediate result by another page operation command.

Each segment transfer command is sent by Segment Transfer Commander to its operand segment's home disk subsystem through Segment Transfer Command Bus. Its home disk subsystem, when it has received the command, accesses the home disk and transfers one page of information to or from Shared Page Buffer. When a transfer has finished, the home disk subsystem writes a completion status code in its status port, and sends a one bit signal to Segment Transfer Watcher, which always watches segment transfer completion signals and, when one of them is set, gets the associated completion status code through Segment Transfer Status Bus. This completion status code is used as a token by Control Subsystem to activate next executable commands.

Each page operation command may be executed by any processor in the large pool of segment processors. It is put on the ring network (called Page Operation Command/Status Network) by Page Operation Commander and is circulated among segment processors. The first encountered idle segment processor takes out this command from the ring network to execute it. In execution of a three operand page operation command, for example, the allocated segment processor reads out two pages from Shared Page Buffer one after another, executes the operation, and stores the result into the destination operand page in Shared Page Buffer. If a page is not full, the segment processor is not required to read the full page. Actually, each page in Shared Page Buffer is divided into equal-sized tracks (Tanaka 1984b). Segment processors need not read unnecessary tracks, but it must read all words in a necessary track. When the segment processor has finished its execution, it sends out its completion status code into the next empty packet circulating on Page Operation Command/Status Network. Page Operation Watcher always watches circulating packets on the network. Immediately upon receiving a completion status code, it sends this as a token to the data flow control mechanism in Control Subsystem.

Segment processors perform high speed processing of relational operations on one or two pages of relational files staged in Shared Page Buffer. Page processing requires sequential data transfer of pages between a segment processor and Shared Page Buffer. Large delay caused by sequential transfer is inevitable. To overcome this problem, the segment processor architecture should make much use of transfer time for page processing by overlapping processing with transfer. The overlapped execution of basic functions in database processing with sequential data transfer was first introduced by us in 1980 (Tanaka et al 1980, Tanaka 1982, 1983a). Such a mode of execution was called data stream processing.

Segment processor has an architecture consisting of a high performance microprocessor with more than 4 page storage space besides its progrm space, and two engines, respectively for batch search and sort, that have enough capacity to process two pages of data. These engines work as subprocessors of the main microprocessor and they are capable of block data transfer to and from the main processor memory.

Most page operation commands that segment processors receive and execute have either of the following formats;

$$PA^* \leftarrow BO\ (Q_1(PA_1),\ Q_2(PA_2)),$$

$$(Q_i \text{ may be nil,})$$

$$PA^* \leftarrow UO\ (Q(PA)),$$

$$(\text{either UO or Q may be nil,})$$

$$PA^* \leftarrow \text{condense}(PA_1{}^*,\ PA_2{}^*,\ \ldots,\ PA_n{}^*).$$

Here, PA is a page address allocated to a single page variable, and PA^* is a page address allocated to a single page variable or to a multiple page variable. If it has been allocated to a multiple page variable as the first page, it is marked with a multiple page indicator $\Diamond$. Q_i denotes selection and/or restriction operations. BO is a binary operation such as intersection, union, difference, join, and division. UO is a unary operation such as projection, sort, count, sum, average, maximum, and minimum.

A command with the first format requests execution of a binary operation. The segment processor reads out each source operand page from

Shared Page Buffer. During the page transfer, it selects only those tuples that satisfy the qualification condition of Q_i and stores them in its local memory. It performs the binary operation using dedicated engines, and write down the result in the destination operand page.

A command with the second format requests unary operation execution on a single page. The segment processor reads out the page from Shared Page Buffer and selects tuples satisfying the qualification condition of Q during the page transfer. Then it performs the unary operation. The result is saved in the same way as mentioned above.

The third format command requests a special operation. Pages are not always fully loaded. It is sometimes desirable to condense a set of pages into a smaller set of pages. It will decrease page references. The third format command requests this operation. It is the only command that allows a multiple-page operand in a source operand position. The source page list is sent to the segment processor via one page of Shared Page Buffer by Macroparallel Data Flow Controller. The segment processor first reads out this page storing the page list. It repeatedly reads out the pages in this list, condenses them and saves the result in the same way as other format commands save their result.

Each segment processor begins to search for a next task whenever it finishes a task. It continues to probe Page Operation Command/Status Network untill it gets a task.

3.3. Control Subsystem

The increase of concurrently executable segment commands is essential in performance enhancement. This is concerned by Control Subsystem. Control Subsystem consists of five major modules, i.e., Interface/ Supervisory Module, Query Processor, Directory Searcher, Macroparallel Data Flow Controller, and Page Buffer Manager.

Interface/Supervisory Module and Query Processor require no innovative architectural technologies. They are necessary to provide a host computer with a high level interface to MPDC. Their software systems will not become much different from corresponding software modules of current relational database management systems. Interface/Supervisory Module is a super minicomputer that communicates queries and set of data with external systems. It is directly connected to one port of Shared Page Buffer so that it can directly access arbitrary pages in the buffer. Through this path, it can get result pages or initially store a database into MPDC. It works as a service processor to initially store databases in MPDC or to periodically save a dump copy of databases and transaction logs. Besides, it manages transaction statuses.

Query Processor is a minicomputer that transforms a given transaction into an optimized program that searches segment directories and generates segment processing commands. The execution of this program is performed by Directory Searcher. Each segment processing command has one or two source operands s_1, s_2 and the destination operand s_3. Each operand is either a segment of a relational file or a variable. Each variable may be either a single page variable with one page capacity or a multiple page variable with a size of arbitrary number pages. A segment command

$s_3 \leftarrow$ <relational operation> s_1 $(,s_2)$

requests both execution of a relational operation on s_1 (and s_2) and the saving of the result in s_3. Programs transformed from queries by Query Processor have lock statements to control interleaved execution correctly.

Directory Searcher is a super minicomputer that receives transformed programs from Query Processor. It executes the programs to search segment directories and to generate segment processing commands. Generated segment processing commands are sent to Macroparallel Data Flow Controller. Directory Searcher has a sufficiently large primary memory and an external low speed semiconductor memory that is large enough to store all segment directories. This external memory is backed up by the disk subsystems in Data Subsystem through a direct connection to one port of Shared Page Buffer.

Suppose that we have two segment directories, as shown in Fig. 3.1, respectively for R(A, B, C) and S(D, E). These directories are based on colored binary trie schemes. For simplicity, each directory node is assumed to have only its current version. These example directories are much smaller than practical directories. For simplicity, attribute values are assumed to be 4 bit long. Some example query translations into segment processing commands are given below. They are performed by traversing the directories.

<<update>>

Select tuples in R satisfying A=1000, C=0000, and change their B values to 1000.

$X_1 \leftarrow$[A=1000 and C=0000](R_4);

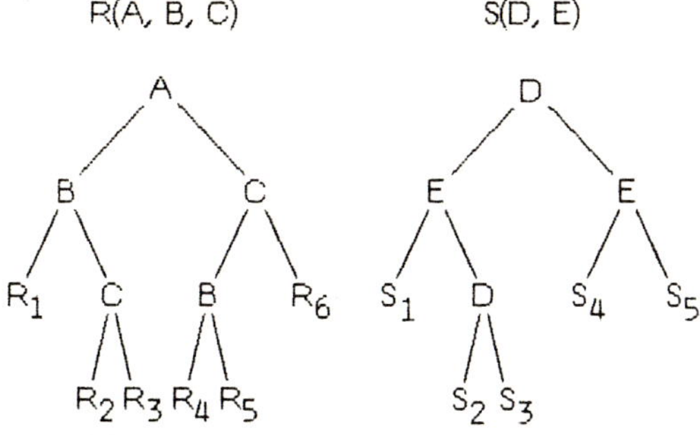

(a) colored trie directory examples.

R	A	B	C
R_1	0***	0***	****
R_2	0***	1***	0***
R_3	0***	1***	1***
R_4	1***	0***	0***
R_5	1***	1***	0***
R_6	1***	****	1***

S	D	E
S_1	0***	0***
S_2	00**	1***
S_3	01**	1***
S_4	1***	0***
S_5	1***	1***

(b) tuples that characterize segments.

Fig. 3.1 Example directories in MPDC.

```
X2←[A=1000 and C=0000](R5);
X3←R4-X1;
X4←R5-X2;
◇X5←[B←1000]X1∪R5;
◇X6←[B←1000]X1∪◇X5;
R4←put X2;
if ◇X6 consists of one page
 then R5←put ◇X6
 else
   begin
    segment-split(R5, attr, seg1, seg2);
    page-split(◇X6, attr, X7, X8);
    seg1←put X7;
    seg2←put X8;
   end;
```

The procedure segment-split(R_5, attr, seg_1, seg_2) will be executed by Directory Searcher during the execution of this program. Given an overflowing segment address, it returns the splitting attribute and two new segment addresses seg_1 and seg_2. The procedure page-split($\Diamond X_6$, attr, X_7, X_8) will be executed by a segment processor. It will distribute tuples in $\Diamond X_3$ into two single page variables X_4 and X_5, depending on the splitting attribute's values.

<<join>>

(R[B=0000])[A=D]S

$X_1 \leftarrow (R_1[B=0000])[A=D]S_1;$

$X_2 \leftarrow (R_1[B=0000])[A=D]S_2;$

$X_3 \leftarrow (R_1[B=0000])[A=D]S_3;$

$X_4 \leftarrow (R_4[B=0000])[A=D]S_4;$

$X_5 \leftarrow (R_4[B=0000])[A=D]S_5;$

$X_6 \leftarrow (R_6[B=0000])[A=D]S_4;$

$X_7 \leftarrow (R_6[B=0000])[A=D]S_5;$

$\Diamond X_8 \leftarrow condense(X_1, X_2, X_3, X_4, X_5, X_6, X_7);$

Actually, directory nodes have multiple versions. However, it does not much complicate directory search and generation of segment processing commands. The update example above, for example, changes the directory as shown in Fig. 3.2 if it causes an overflow. An underflow of a segment is recovered only by merging it with its brother segment if any. Therefore, some underflows are not recovered. However, our theory ensures that it does not cause serious problems. If an underflow occurs in O_7 and the merge of O_7

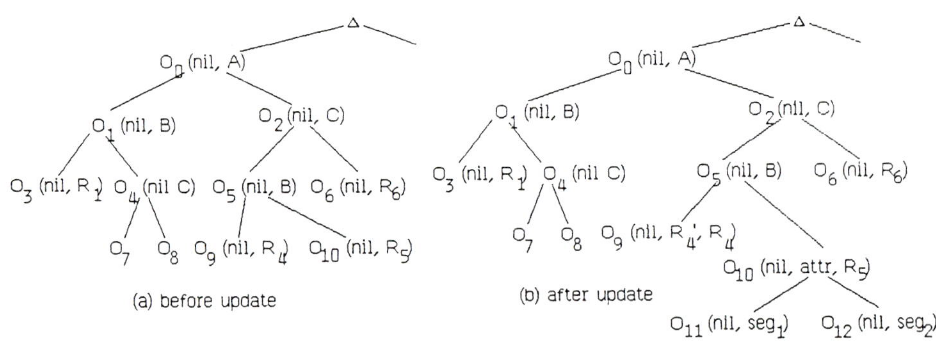

Fig. 3.2 Change of the directory by the execution of the example write transaction.

and O_8 can be stored in a single segment, then they will be merged into a new segment O_{78}, and O_4 will become (nil, O_{78}, C).

Directory Searcher is also in charge of concurrency control. Locks are set on objects in directories, following the protocol in Section 2.4. A read lock set on a segment is released when all commands that refer to this segment in the same transaction complete their execution and their completion tokens are all received from Data Subsystem by Macroparallel Data Flow Controller. A write lock on a segment is released in either of the following cases. If no command in the transaction actually changes this segment, it is released by a w-unlock command after all commands in the transaction that refer to this segment complete their execution. If a command changes this segment, it is released by a commit command after all updates and references in this transaction complete their execution. In a recovery routine of the transaction, a roll-back command is used to nullifies its failed execution.

3.4 Macroparallel Data Flow Controller

Macroparallel Data Flow Controller receives segment processing commands, dynamically constructs data flow programs of segment commands consisting of segment transfers and page operations, sends active segment commands to Data Subsystem through the two commanders, receives completion tokens from Data Subsystem through the two watchers, and transfers activation tokens to next executable commands in data flow programs. To perform these operations, it has five tables, Transaction Table, Command Table, Segment Table, Page Variable Table, and Multipage Variable Table.

Macroparallel data flow programs in Macroparallel Data Flow Controller require each segment to be assigned to a page variable prior to any operation on it. When a segment value is once assigned to a page variable, further references to this segment value refer to this variable. In dynamic construction of data flow programs, segment processing commands sent from Directory Searcher are modified to satisfy this rule. This translation uses a table called Segment Table, which stores information about the assignment of a variable to each segment that has appeared as a source operand (Fig. 3.3). A hash function is used to locate each segment in this table. The table is sequentially searched for the segment from the address determined by the hashing of this segment address.

When Macroparallel Data Flow Controller receives a segment processing

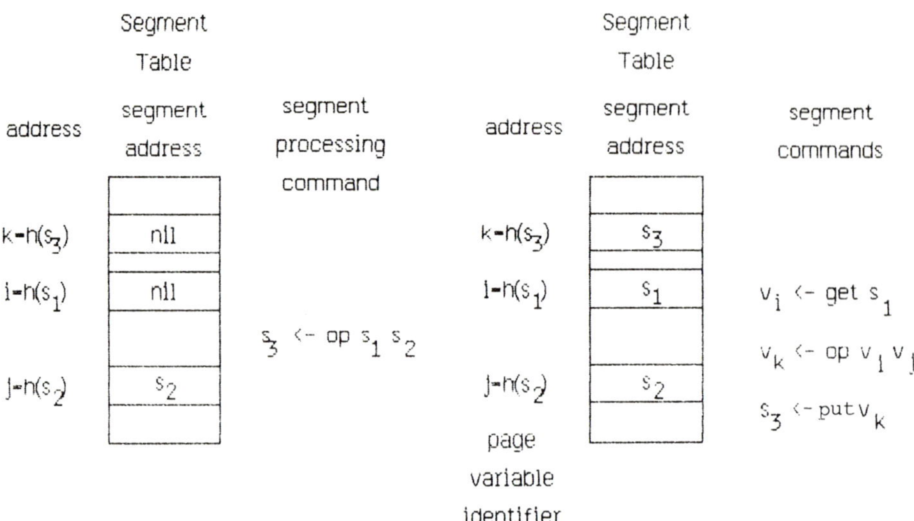

Fig. 3.3 Segment Table and the translation of each segment processing command to segment commands.

command from Directory Searcher, it examines if the command has any operand segments that are not yet registered in Segment Table. If it has any, the controller assigns each of them a new page variable, and stores this assignment in Segment Table. Such a page variable is called a segment page variable. Operand segments in the original command are replaced with their corresponding page variables. A command thus obtained is called a page operation command. If a source segment s of a sement processing command sent from Directory Searcher has not been registered in Segment Table, Macroparallel Data Flow Controller generates a page variable v and generates a get command

$$v \leftarrow \text{get } s$$

before this command. This get command requests transfer of this segment to the assigned page variable. The reference to s in the original command is replaced by the reference to v. Further references to s are all replaced by references to v. A segment processing command that has a segment s as a destination operand is an update command. Such a command is divided into two segment commands, i.e., one for the assignment of the operation result to a temporary page variable v, and a put command

$$s \leftarrow \text{put } v.$$

Put and get commands are called segment transfer commands.

The destination operand page variable of each command is allocated a free page in Shared Page Buffer when it is sent to Data Subsystem for its exexcution. Page Variable Table stores, for each operand page variable, its status, its allocated page address, a pointer to its reference list, and its reference count (Fig. 3.4). The status field shows if the page value is already computed. Each page variable appears no more than once as a destination operand.

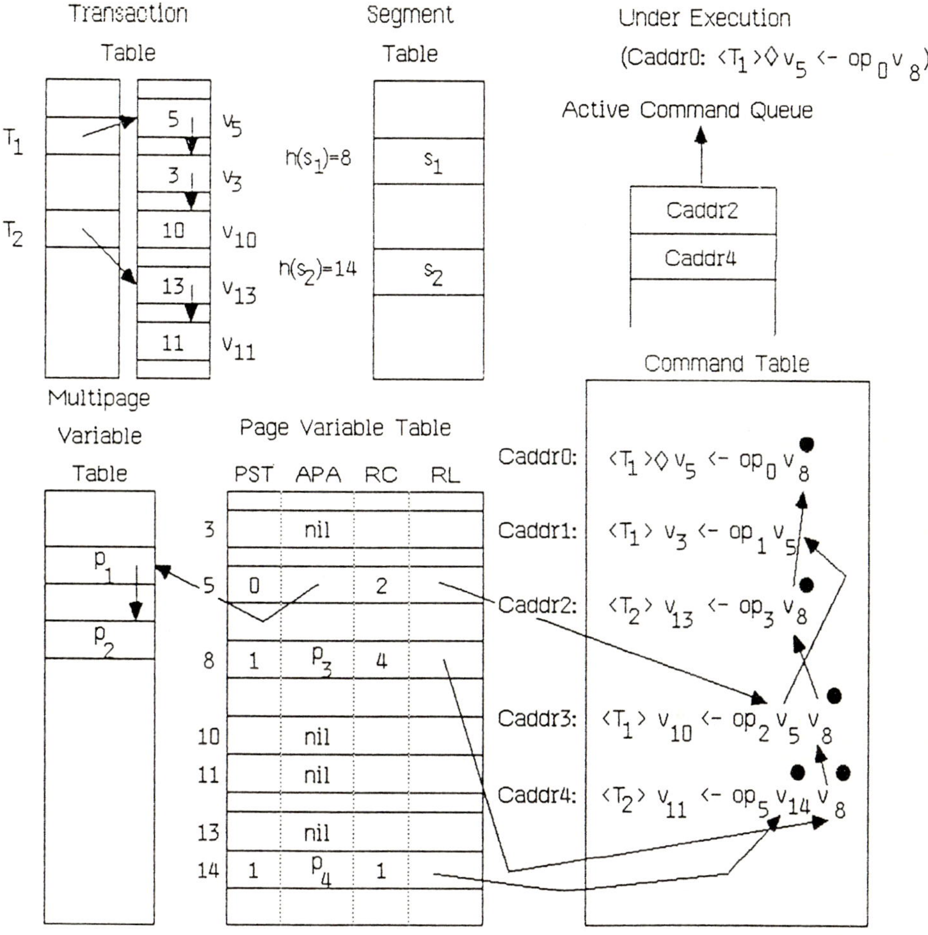

PST : page status, APA : allocated page address, RC : reference count, RL : reference list

Fig. 3.4 Tables in Macroparallel Data Flow Controller.

Data flow programs can be easily dynamically constructed by renaming variables in the original sequences of segment processing commands to satisfy the single assignment rule, i.e., each variable should not appear more than once as a destination operand. Data dependencies of operand page variables among segment commands are managed by Page Variable Table. For each page variable, this table has an entry that points to a list of page operation and segment transfer commands that refer to this variable as a source operand. The number of elements of this list is stored in the reference count field of the table entry associated with this variable.

When all operand segments in a command received from Directory Searcher are replaced with page variables, Macroparallel Data Flow Controller makes a new entry in Page Variable Table for the destination operand page variable. It also searches this table for its source operand page variables, which have been already registered in this table. It stores this command in Command Table with its subject transaction number and links this command to the reference lists associated with the source operand page variables' entries in Page Variable Table. The reference count of these entries are incremented by one. Their page allocation fields are set to nil.

Each command list linked to Page Variable Table is used to move activation tokens to next executable commands when the associated variable has been given a page value. Each segment command, whether it may be a segment transfer command or a page operation command, becomes active whenever it has got tokens for all of its source operands. Each active segment command is sent to Data Subsystem after a page of Shared Page Buffer is allocated to its destination page variable. The destination page variable and its allocated page are registered in Page Variable Table.

Command Table is a waiting room for generated segment transfer commands and page operation commands (Fig. 3.4). It stores a waiting command with its subject transaction number and as many token bits as this command's source operands. Associated with Command Table is the active command queue that stores addresses of the commands in this table that are ready for execution (Fig. 3.4). When a command is stored in Command Table, the controller also examines its source operand page variables' statuses stored in Page Variable Table. If a page variable value is already computed, its corresponding token bit is set to one. Otherwise, it is set to zero. If all token bits of the command are set to one, this command is added at the end of the active command queue. Get commands are always added at the head of the queue immediately after they are generated. Each command becomes active when all of its source operand page variable values are already prepared in

Shared Page Buffer, in other words, when all token bits of the command become one. When a command becomes active, it is added to the active command queue. Active commands are sent to Data Subsystem with their locations in Command Table. Before they are sent, their operand page variables are replaced with physical page addresses in Shared Page Buffer. Their source operand page variables must have been already assigned page addresses because of the single assignment rule and the activation mechanism. Macroparallel Data Flow Controller replaces the source operand page variables with their corresponding page addresses by searching Page Variable Table. If a command has a page variable destination operand, the controller asks Page Buffer Manager to allocate one free page in Shared Page Buffer to this destination operand page variable.

The allocation of a page of Shared Page Buffer to a page variable requires page management of Shared Page Buffer. Page Buffer Manager has a list of free page addresses in Shared Page Buffer. When it is asked for allocation of a free page either by Macroparallel Data Flow Controller or by one of the segment processors, it selects the first element of this free page list, removes it from the list, and returns its address to the requesting module.

If a command is sent to Data Subsystem, it is removed from the active command queue. When Data Subsystem finishes execution of a segment command, it sends back a completion status code to Macroparallel Data Flow Controller either through Segment Transfer Watcher or through Page Operation Watcher. The completion status code includes the command address in Command Table. If the status code shows normal completion of execution, Macroparallel Data Flow Controller reads out the command address from the status code, gets its destination page variable from Command Table, searches Page Variable Table for this variable, and sets the corresponding token bits of all the commands that are chained from the reference list pointer field of this variable's entry in Page Variable Table. During this marking process, if the controller finds out a command whose all token bits become one, it adds this command to the active command queue. For each completed command, the controller also updates Page Variable Table entries associated with its source page variables. It decrements the reference count by one, and removes this command from the reference list. For each transaction, Transaction Table has a pointer that points to a chain of this transaction's variables, except segment page variables, in Page Variable Table (Fig. 3.4). When a transaction finishes its execution, page allocation to the variables in the list linked from this transaction's entry in Transaction Table are all released, and these variables are deleted from page Variable Table.

Some segment commands may require more than one page to save its result. Such a command uses a multiple-page variable as its destination operand. A reference to a multiple-page variable is preceded by an ◇ mark for distinction. Since such multiple page result may become a source operand of another command, multiple-page variables should be allowed to use not only as destination operands but also as source operands.

Macroparallel Data Flow Controller has a table called Multipage Variable Table (Fig. 3.4). When a multiple-page variable is used as a destination operand, a single page is initially allocated to it. A list consisting of only this allocated page address is stored in Multipage Variable Table and a pointer that points to this list is stored in page Variable Table. This command is sent to Data Subsystem and is executed by one of the segment processors. If the execution has spent allocated pages and requires more to save the result, the segment processor dynamically asks Page Buffer Manager for one more page through Page Operation Watcher and Macroparallel Data Flow Controller. An allocated page address is sent to the segment processor through Macroparallel Data Flow Controller and Page Operation Commander. It is also registered in the list of allocated pages that is linked from the corresponding page variable entry in Page Variable Table. Multipage Variable Table remembers the list of pages allocated to a multipage variable when the execution has finished.

If a multiple-page variable appears as a source operand of a segment command, Macroparallel Data Flow Controller decomposes this command into a set of commands without multiple-page variables as source operands. The only exception is a 'condence' page operation command.

When all pages in Shared Page Buffer are spent for page allocations, Page Buffer Manager can not allocate a new page to a new variable without releasing one page allocation. Its selection is based on the LRU algorithm. For this purpose, Page Buffer Manager has a queue of used page addresses. When a page is referenced, its address is put at the end of this queue. The head of this queue is always the address of the least recently used page. Suppose that the selected page is a segment page. If the transaction that requested the preparation of this page is already finished, the page allocation is released and this variable and the read out segment are deleted respectively from Page Variable Table and Segment Table. If the transaction that prepared this page is not finished or if the selected page is not a segment page, then this page value is saved into a work disk storage space provided by the disk subsystems. The destination address in the disk storage space is written in the page address field of Page Variable Table with a mark indicating disk storage space allocation. If an active command that is to be sent to Data Subsystem has a source page variable whose allocated page address is in the disk storage space, the controller asks Page Buffer Manager to allocate this variable a new page, sends a get command to Data Subsystem and put the object command at the end of the active command queue.

Macroparallel Data Flow Controller controls the activation of sufficiently large macro operations such as segment transfer or page processing. Therefore, the control overhead will be hiden by the concurrent execution of macro operations by Data Subsystem. An appropriate selection of segment size is required.

4. CONCLUSION

The massive parallel database computer architecture MPDC is a relational database machine architecture for very large databases. It provides both fundamental technological breakthroughs in the performance enhancement and the capacity enlargement of database processing and a unified way of integrating these technologies into a database computer. MPDC has decomposed database processing into two levels, i.e., directory search and segment processing. Every relation is divided into equal-sized segments. Corresponding to this two-level decomposition, MPDC consists of two subsystems, i.e., Data Subsystem and Control Subsystem. Data Subsystem is in charge of segment accesses and segment processing, while Control Subsystem is responsible to Data Subsystem for decomposing query transactions into concurrently executable segment processing commands. MPDC uses two types of parallelism to speed up database processing. Parallelism in segment search is referred to by macroparallelism, while parallelism in segment processing is called microparallelism. These two types of parallelism are inherently different. The main concern of microparallelism is the high-speed processing of each basic operation on one or two segments. Macroparallelism, on the other hand, aimes at massively parallel processing of concurrently executable segment operations. It must cope with transaction decomposition, concurrency control of interleaved transaction execution, and segment command generation. In transaction decomposition, each operation on one or two relations is decomposed into a set of segment processing commands by Directory Searcher, which uses segment directories represented as colored binary tries. Colored binary tries are data structures that were proposed for adaptive multiattribute segmentation schemes. Control Subsystem uses a unified control algorithm that does not only manage adaptive segmentation but also efficiently and correctly control highly reliable interleaved execution of transactions. Massive parallel execution of segment tasks requires highly concurrent execution of segment read and segment write operations. Besides, high reliability requires a sound recovery mechanism that does not seriously lower system performance during its execution. Control Subsystem uses a multiversion concurrency control mechanism based on the colored binary trie schemes as a unified solution to segment management, concurrency control, and recovery. Concurrency control is managed by Directory Searcher. No deadlock occurs in our concurrency control scheme. The scheme satisfies serializability, i.e., the condition for correct interleaved execution of correct transactions.

Activation of segment access commands and segment processing commands are controlled by a dataflow controller, which automatically controls disk subsystems to transfer segments to Shared Page Buffer prior to their processing. Each active command is sent to Data Subsystem and be executed either by a segment processor or by a disk subsystem.

REFERENCES

Bayer and McCreight 1972

Bayer, R. and E. McCreight, 'Organization and Maintenance of Large Unordered Indices,' Acta Informatica, vol.1 fasc.3, pp.173-189, 1972.

Bayer et al. 1980a

Bayer, R., Heller, H., and Reiser, A., 'Parallelism and Recovery in Database Systems,' ACM Trans. Database Systems, vol.5 no.2, pp.139-156, 1980.

Bayer et al. 1980b

Bayer, R., Elhardt, K., Heller, H., and Reiser, A., 'Distributed Concurrency Control in Database Systems,' Proc. 6th VLDB, pp.275-284, 1980.

Bayer and Schkolnick 1977

Bayer, R. and Schkolnick, M., 'Concurrency of Operating on B-Trees,' Acta Informatica, vol.9 no.1, pp.1-21, 1977.

Bayer and Schlichtiger 1984

Bayer, R. and Schlichtiger, P., 'Data Management Support for Database

Management,' Acta Informatica, vol.21 fasc.1, pp.1-28, 1984.

Bernstein and Goodman 1983

Bernstein, P.A. and Goodman, N., 'Multiversion Concurrency Control - Theory and Algorithms,' ACM Trans. Database Systems, vol.8 no.4, pp.465-483, 1983.

Ellis 1977

Ellis, C.S., 'Concurrent Search and Insertion in 2-3 Trees,' TR-78-05-01, Dept. of Computer Science, Univ. of Washington, Seattle, 1977.

Haneywell 1973

'Haneywell File Management Supervisor,' Order No.DB54, Honeywell Information Systems, Inc., 1973.

Kedem and Siberschatz 1980

Kedem, Z. and Silberschatz, A., 'Non-Two Phase Locking Protocols with Shared and Exclusive Locks,' Proc. VLDB, pp.309-320, 1980.

Kessels 1980

Kessels, J.L.W., 'The Readers and Writers Problem Avoided,' Information Processing Letters, vol.10 no.3, pp.159-162, 1980.

Lehman and Yao 1981

Lehman, P.L. and Yao, S.B., 'Efficient Locking for Concurrent Operations on B-Trees,' ACM Trans. Database Systems, vol.6 no.4, pp.650-670.

Papadimitriou and Kanellakis 1984

Papadimitriou, C.H. and Kanellakis, P.C., 'On Concurrency Control by Multiple Versions,' ACM Trans. Database Systems, vol.9 no.1, pp.89-99, 1984.

Silberschatz and Kedem 1980

Silberschatz, A. and Kedem, Z., 'Consistency in Hierarchical Database Systems,' J.ACM, vol.27 no.1, pp.72-80.

Stearns et al. 1976

Stearns, R.E., Lewis, P.M. II, and Rosenkrantz, D.J., 'Concurrency Control for Database Systems,' Proc. 17th IEEE Symp. Foundations of Computer Science, pp.19-32, 1976.

Tanaka et al. 1980

Tanaka, Y., Nozaka, Y. and Masuyama, A., Pipeline Searching and Sorting Modules as Components of a Data Flow Database Computer,' Proc. IFIP '80, pp.427-432, 1980.

Tanaka 1982

Tanaka, Y., 'A Data Stream Database Computer,' Japan Annual Reviews: Computer Science & Technologies 1982, OHM-North-Holland, pp.265-286, 1982.

Tanaka 1983a

Tanaka, Y., 'A Data-Stream Database Machine with Large Capacity,' Advanced

Database Machine Architecture, Prentice-Hall, Inc., pp.168-202, 1983.

Tanaka 1983b

Tanaka, Y., 'Adaptive Segmentation Schemes for Large Relational Database Machines,' Database Machines, Springer-Verlag, pp.293-318, 1983.

Tanaka 1984a

Tanaka, Y., 'Bit-Sliced VLSI Algorithms for Search and Sort,' Proc.10th VLDB, pp.225-235,1984

Tanaka 1984b

Tanaka, Y., 'A Multiport Page-Memory Architecture and A Multiport Disk-Cache System,' New Generation Computing, vol.2 no.3, pp.241-260, 1984.

Tanaka 1984c

Tanaka, Y., 'MPDC: Massive Parallel Architecture for Very Large Databases,' Proc. Int'l Conf. on Fifth Generation Computer Systems 1984, pp.113-137, 1984.

Tanaka 1985

Tanaka, Y., 'A VLSI Algorithm for Sorting Variable-Length Character Strings,' (to appear in New Generation Computing).

Development of Delta as a First Step to a Knowledge Base Machine

Hiroshi Sakai Kazuhide Iwata Masaaki Abe
Shigeki Shibayama Hidenori Itoh

Toshiba R & D Center ICOT Research Center
Kawasaki Japan Tokyo Japan

ABSTRACT

Delta, a relational database machine is under development at ICOT (Institute for New Generation Computer Technology) to study knowledge base machines (KBMs). This paper focuses on its architecture especially on its specialized processor, RDBE (relational database engine) and also presents our approach to a knowledge base machine.

1 INTRODUCTION

Development of a knowledge base machine (KBM) is one of ICOTS's major themes. By KBM, we mean a backend machine to inference machines, which is able to store and manipulate a large amount and variety of knowledge.

One may regard knowledge information processing in general as a search problem. In this sense, database machines have the advantage of finding all items which match the search condition in a primitive but huge search space, while inference machines have the advantage of finding an arbitrary item in a complicated search space using heuristics in order to avoid combinatorial explosion. The authors think a KBM must have both mechanisms in an integrated manner, since most actual problems seem to need both brute-force search and heuristic search. Since other research groups of ICOT developed inference machines PSI [Taki 84], PIM-R [Onai 84], and PIM-D [Ito 84], the KBM group first focused on the database mechanism and developed Delta [Shibayama 84], a relational database machine. We chose the relational model among others because it seemed to provide a general storage of Prolog facts [Codd 70] [Gallaire 78].

An efficient relational database machine with an intimate interface to logic programming was the prime development objective of Delta. We chose (1) a functionally-distributed architecture, (2) relational database engines (RDBEs) to perform relational database operations, and (3) a large capacity hierarchical memory system.

The current status of the KBM group activities is as follows. Delta is now available to the inference machines and an effort to make the PSI accessible to Delta is being continued. To evaluate Prolog programs on a relational database system, Yokota proposed some methods [Yokota 84] [Yokota 85]. In order to develop a KBM, we have started the discussion about its functions and architecture.

This paper focuses on the development of Delta. In section 2, the overview of Delta and an exemple of query processing are presented. In section 3, the RDBE is described in detail. In section 4, a preliminary performance of some primitive functions is presented. In section 5, current problems of Delta and our efforts to solve them are discussed. In section 6, we will show our informal approach to a KBM.

NATO ASI Series, Vol. F 24
Database Machines. Edited by A.K. Sood and A.H. Qureshi

2 OVERVIEW OF DELTA

2.1 System Configuration

Delta consists of five different kinds of components so that queries from inference machines may be efficiently processed on specialized components. Its architecture is shown in Figure 1.

The components of Delta are as follows:

(1) An interface processor (IP), which serves as a front-end to inference machines via a local area network (LAN).
(2) A control processor (CP), which provides database management functions, such as query language analysis, concurrency control, and dictionary/directory management.
(3) Relational database engines (RDBEs), which are the key components for processing relational database operations.
(4) A maintenance processor (MP), which has an operator console and provides functions for reliability and serviceability.
(5) A hierarchical memory (HM), which provides other units with a common storage.

The rest of this section presents an overview of Delta. Since the Delta system can be easily understood from its memory system, the HM unit is described first.

2.2 Hierarchical Memory Unit

The HM provides a common storage to other units of Delta. It is implemented using a conventional mainframe to achieve large storage and high speed data transfer. It has 128 Mbytes of main memory, 20 Gbytes of secondary memory and four magnetic tape drives. The HM is connected to the IP, CP and MP via block-multiplexer channels (one channel for each unit). As for the RDBEs, the HM has two channels for each so that data may be transferred from HM to RDBE and vice versa simultaneously.

Units other than HM send commands to HM in order to access data in it. That is, the HM may well be regarded as a fast secondary storage. The storage of the HM can be classified into three types as illustrated in Figure 2.

The first type is called Attribute Dataset. It stores ordinary relations. Each relation is split into attributes and each attribute is stored in the secondary storage with an index. The HM software manages it using VSAM (virtual storage access method) and the page size is 4 Kbytes. As for the internal schema, we will discuss its detail later.

This area cannot be accessed directly from other units. In order to access an attribute of a relation, they send a command to make working data from the attribute. When a command has some conditions, the HM selects the data referring to the index as specified by the conditions.

The second type is called RSP Memory. It stores data copied from a relation, data generated by a RDBE and data sent from a host machine via the IP. It consists of 32 Kbyte pages of main memory. A set of pages is assigned to each context of data. For a large amount of data, the HM software stores the overflow portion in the secondary storage without using the virtual storage function of the operating system.

The third type is called RSP Dataset. It stores the directory of Delta. It is segmented into pages of 512 bytes and the HM software manages it using VSAM. The CP manages the contents of each page and the HM is responsible for logging modified pages.

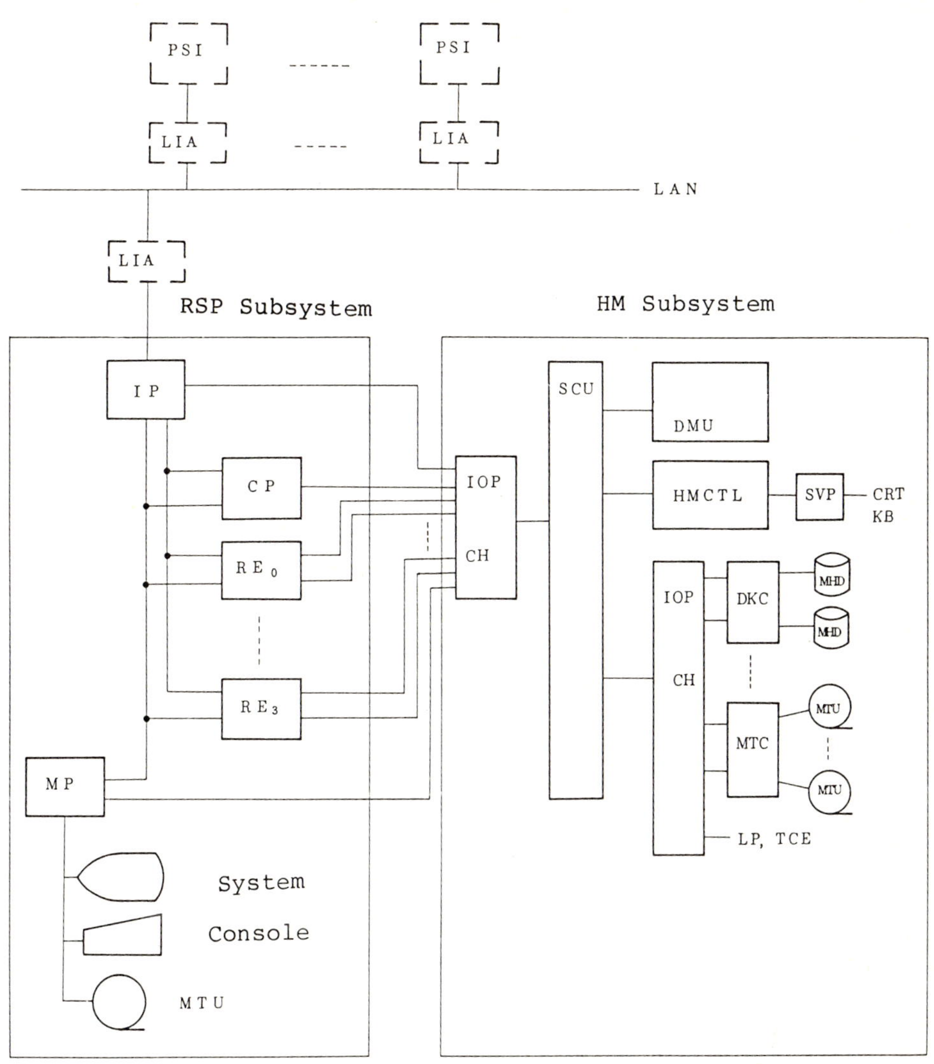

PSI : Personal Sequential Inference Machine
LIA : LAN Interface Adapter
RSP : RDBM Supervisory and Processing Subsystem
IP : Interface Processor
CP : Control Processor
RDBE : Relational Database Engine
MP : Maintenance Processor
HM : Hierarchical Memory Subsystem
HMCTL: HM Controller
DMU : Database Memory Unit
IOP : I/O Processor
SCU : Storage Control Unit
MHD : Moving Head Disk
DKC : Disk Controller
MTC : MT Controller

Figure 1 Delta configuration

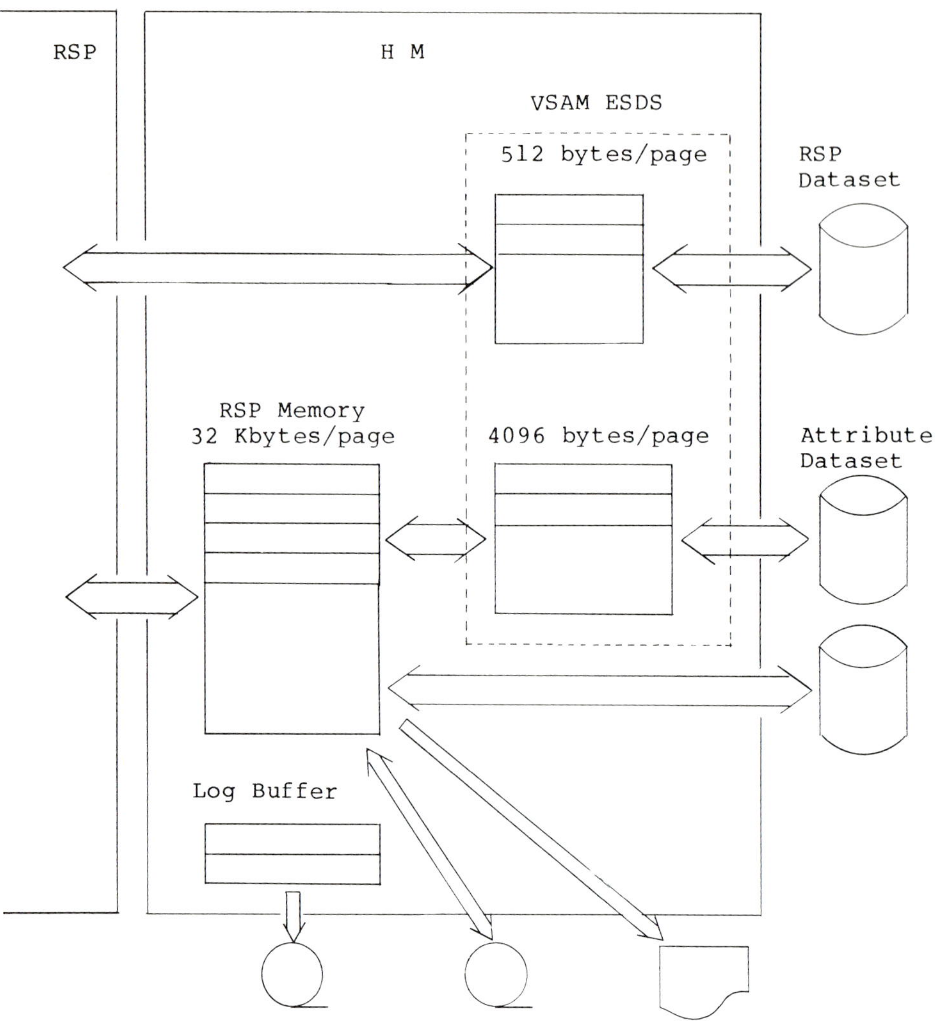

Figure 2 Storage management of the HM

2.3 Internal Schema

Conventional database management systems store a relation as a file in which a tuple is treated as a record and an attribute as a field. Indexing and hashing techniques are applied to rapidly obtain tuples satisfying specific criteria. These methods are useful when the user knows how to use the relation. A DBMS has to scan the entire relation if an indexed or hashed attribute cannot be used as an access path for a given query.

We expect Delta to have unconventional access characteristics because Delta is planned to be used as external storage of Prolog facts for inference machines. Access to the database stored in Delta is predicted to have the following characteristics, based on the usage of Prolog programs:

(1) There are only a few attributes in most relations.
(2) The attributes used as conditions are unpredictable.
(3) The frequency of access to each tuple is relatively uniform.

Delta adopts an attribute-wise schema to efficiently process these kinds of requests. Instead of storing all the attributes of a tuple together, a relation is split into a collection of attributes and stores all occurrences of each attribute together. A TID (tuple identifier) is attached to each attribute value to identify the tuple it belongs to. A two-level indexing method is used for clustering as illustrated in Figure 3.

The merits of the attribute-wise schema are as follows:
(1) Delta can avoid operations for attributes unnecessary for a given request.
(2) Attributes are treated uniformly.

However, there are several demerits as well.
(1) Transformation between the tuple-wise format and attribute-wise format is necessary.
(2) Tuple identifiers occupy additional storage space.
(3) The number of internal commands among the units grows.

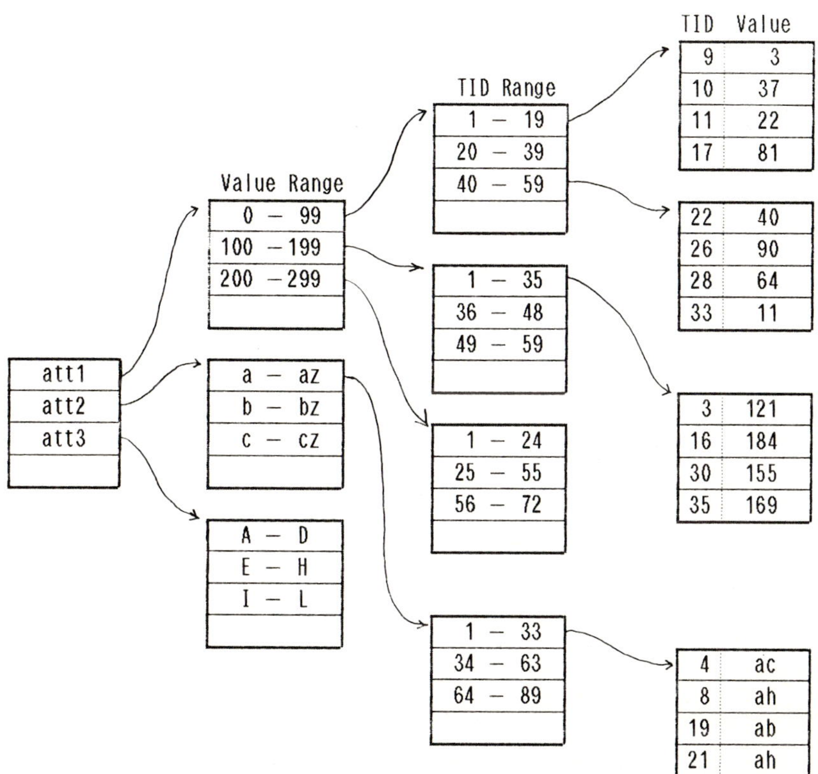

Figure 3 Two-level clustering method of Delta

Command name	Comments
PASS	intratuple operation
JOIN	$=,\neq,<,\leq,>,\geq$,Cartesian product
RESTRICT	$=,\neq$,range
SORT	ascending/descending
AGGREGATE	aggregate operation
UNIQUE	eliminating duplicate tuples
UNION	set operation
INTERSECTION	set operation
DIFFERENCE	set operation
EQUAL	equality test between relations
CONTAIN	inclusion test between relations
COMPARE	compare attributes of each tuple
ZONE-SORT	for clustering
DELETE	for updating

Figure 4 List of RDBE commands

2.4 Relational Database Engine

The relational database engine (RDBE) is a specialized processor to perform various operations on the working data in the HM. Whenever the RDBE performs an operation, data is transferred from the HM to the RDBE and from the RDBE to the HM through channels.

An alternative is to place the RDBE between the HM's main memory and its secondary storage, as in VERSO [Bancilhon 82]. This would reduce data transfer time and improve system throughput. However, we did not choose this alternative because it was difficult to modify the disk controller of the HM.

The RDBE offers various kinds of commands necessary for relational database processing. The list of commands are shown in Figure 4. The RDBE performs these commands using its hardware modules, the sorter and merger, and also using its general-purpose microprocessor. The sorter and merger are designed to perform intertuple commands, i.e. commands which require comparison between records. For ease of implementation, the comparison is limited between a contiguous field of a tuple and a contiguous field of another, i.e. typically an attribute or the entire tuple. Comparison between an attribute value of each tuple and a list of constant values, and comparison between two attribute values of each tuple are also performed by them. The rest of the commands are performed by the microprocessor itself or their combination. The above decision was made according to the frequency expectation of the commands and their processing time, and also the functional flexibility of the RDBE.

The RDBE takes the entire tuple, and not only the key field. An alternative is to make a copy of the key field of each tuple and process it, which would reduce the data transfer between the RDBE and HM, as well as the required RDBE's memory. We did not adopt this alternative because of the following reasons:

(1) The HM would have to process the original tuples according to the result of the RDBE's operation.

(2) Since the set operation requires comparison of the whole tuples, the RDBE must have enough memory either way.

Although Delta adopts the attribute-wise internal schema, there exist working records having several attributes as well, and the RDBE must process them. The internal representation of a record, in general, is illustrated in Figure 5. Each record in a relation has the same length (less than 4 Kbytes) and the same number of fields; corresponding fields over a relation have the same data type and length. A field usually has an extra area called a tag, which indicates whether the value is null. The data types are unsigned integer, signed integer, and single-precision floating point. The length of the first two types must be even and less than 4 Kbytes.

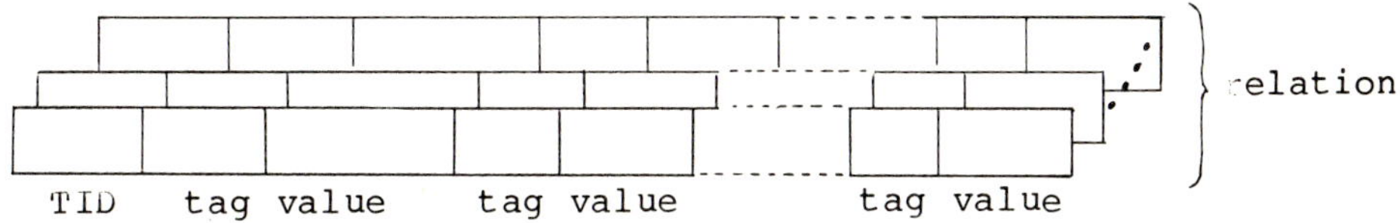

Figure 5 Internal representation of a record

2.4 Query Processing in Delta

This section shows how Delta processes a query using an example. Let us assume the example in Figure 6. A host machine wants to get the names and areas of nations having more than 1,000,000 people. The host machine has to send the sequence of Delta commands based on relational algebra. The IP receives the sequence and sends it to the CP. The CP translates the query into a sequence of internal commands as shown in the figure, each of which is then issued to an RDBE or HM to make them cooperatively perform the specified database operation. After its completion, the IP gets the result from the HM and sends it to the host.

```
—Host Machine—
     SELECT name, area
     FROM nations
     WHERE population > 1,000,000
```

```
—Sequence of Delta Commands—
Selection(nations.population, > 1,000,000, templ)
Projection(templ, [name, area], intl)
Get(intl)
```

```
—Delta—
    CP->HM  : PQB(nations.population, value > 1,000,000, bufl)
    CP->RDBE: RESTRICT(bufl, value > 1,000,000, buf2)
    CP->HM  : PQTB(nations.name, buf2, buf3)
    CP->RDBE: RESTRICT(buf3, TID  buf2.TID, buf4)
    CP->HM  : PQTB(nations.area, buf2, buf5)
    CP->RDBE: RESTRICT(buf5, TID  buf2.TID, buf6)
    CP->RDBE: SORT(buf4, TID, buf7)
    CP->RDBE: SORT(buf6, TID, buf8)
    CP->HM  : TTT([buf7, buf8], buf9)
                 /* from attribute-wise to tuple-wise format */
    IP->HM  : SPI(buf9)
```

Figure 6 Example of query processing in Delta

3 DETAILS OF THE RELATIONAL DATABASE ENGINE

3.1 Basic Idea

The basic idea is that a join operation is performed efficiently by sorting tuples of each relation according to their values and comparing tuples from the relations in a manner resembling a two-way merge operation. This idea is profitable since it can be applied not only to an equi-join operation but also to nonequal join operations and other relational database operations that take two relations. Althogh the idea has also been realized in other database machines, the relational database engine has the following advantages:

(1) The combination of the sorter and merger improves performance as in pipeline processing.

(2) The RDBE can process null values and duplicate values efficiently.

(3) The projection operation is performed during another operation.

(4) Parity check and sorting check mechanisms improve reliability.

(5) Data processing by the RDBE's microprocessor enhances its functional flexibility.

3.2 Configuration

The RDBE configuration is shown in Figure 7. It is designed for high-speed relational database processing by means of pipelined sorting and merge-like operation. The RDBE consists of the following components:

(1) A general-purpose microprocessor, which controls all the hardware modules to perform RDBE commands.

(2) Two HM adapters, which serve as interfaces between the RDBE and HM.

(3) The IN module, which transforms input data into an internal format suitable for the sorter and merger modules. Among these transformations are:

* field ordering, which shifts a key field to the head of the tuple
* data type transformation
* generation of null value bit signals

(4) A sorter, which generates sorted tuples.

(5) A merger, which performs external sorting and relational database operations using a processing algorithm resembling a two-way merge operation.

In Figure 7, DT, PT, NL and DP stand for data lines, parity lines, a null line and a duplication line, respectively. The null line is used to denote that there is a tuple with a null value key on the data lines. The duplication line is used to denote that there is a tuple having the same key value as the subsequent one on the data lines. These modules are controlled to run simultaneously.

Data transfer is performed in the handshake mode between these modules. Each module is designed to achieve a data processing rate as high as the data transfer rate between the RDBE and HM. The main data path is from the HM adapter(IN) to the HM adapter(OUT) through the IN module, sorter, and merger.

If an RDBE operation takes two relations, as in a join operation, the operation is performed in the following way:

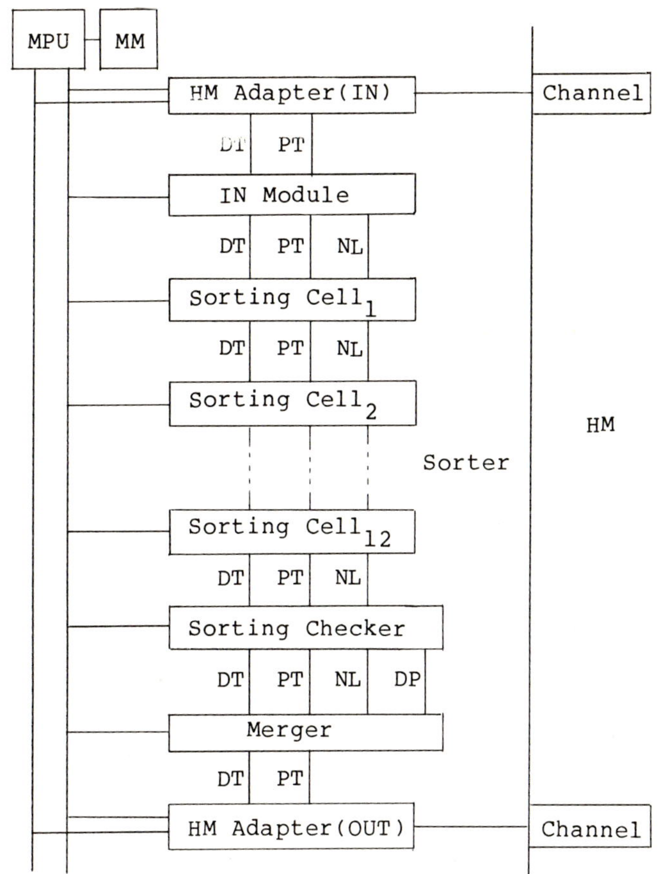

Figure 7 RDBE configuration

The tuples of the first relation, which was originally stored in the HM, pass through the HM adapter(IN), are modifyed by the IN module, sorted by the sorter, and are finally stored into a buffer of the merger. Then the tuples of the second relation pass through the HM adapter(IN), are modified by the IN module, sorted by the sorter, and are stored into another buffer of the merger. While storing the second tuples, the merger also compares these with the previously stored tuples, and generates the results. They are sent to the HM through the HM adapter (OUT).

If the microprocessor itself has to manipulate the data, the result from the merger is sent to its main memory via the HM adapter(OUT). After the microprocessor has finished the operation, the final result is sent to the HM via the HM adapter (OUT).

3.3 Sorter

In order to apply a sorter in the RDBE environment, the following conditions must be satisfied:

(1) It receives the original sequence of tuples from the IN module, and sends the sorted sequence to the merger.
(2) The data transfer rates both at its entrance and at its exit are equal to that between the RDBE and HM.
(3) The delay between the ending of the input data transfer and the beginning of the output data transfer is small.
(4) It is able to sort a small number of tuples at reasonable speed.
(5) It is able to process absolute values of standard binary notation up to 4094 bytes long, possibly with the null value signal on.

Various kinds of sorting algorithms have been studied [Knuth 73], and hardware sorters based on them have been proposed and implemented. Tanaka proposed and implemented a sorter based on the heap sort [Tanaka 80]. Although it satisfies the above four conditions, it is difficult to implement so that it satisfies the last.

Our sorter, based on two-way merge-sort, is similar to Todd's [Todd 78]. It is slightly inferior to Tanaka's for the third condition, but it satisfies the last condition. Our sorter has the following features:
(1) The sorter consists of a linear array of 12 processing elements, called the sorting cell, and one processing element, called the sorting checker; these arrange input data elements in a specified linear order (ascending or descending). Since the data bus consists of 16 lines, the unit size of data, word, is 2 bytes. The sorting operation is performed by pipeline processing.
(2) The sorter performs only the internal sort operation. The maximum number of tuples that the sorter is able to process is shown by the following expression.
      min(2**N, [M/L])
   Here, N is the number of sorting cells (currently 12), M is the memory size of the last sorting cell (currently 64 Kbytes), and L is the tuple length.
(3) The sorting cell has two operation modes: the sort mode and the pass mode. The former merges two sorted sequences of tuples into one. The latter does not merge, but transfers input data directly to the next cell. Let C be the number of tuples to be sorted, then $[\log_2 2(C-1)]$ of the sorting cells become the sort mode, and the others become the pass mode.
   The time required is (2LC + N - 1)T sec, excluding the time which the sorting checker and the control program take, where T is the reciprocal of the data transfer rate (currently 3 Mbyte/sec). For example, 4096 tuples of 16 bytes are sorted in 43 milliseconds. Note that the processing time does not depend on the length of the key field.
(4) The sorter processes null values by recognizing the tag field and locates them at the last part of the sorted sequence.
(5) The sorter performs stable sort operations on equal values, i.e., it keeps the original relative order of the input sequence of tuples having the same values.
(6) The sorting checker compares the key field of each tuple with that of the next one, so that it checks the results to increase the reliability of the sorter. It also generates a

duplicate signal when the values are the same. Since it takes an additional time of LT, the time required is (2LS + L + N)T excluding the software overhead time.

Figure 8 is a block diagram of the sorting cell. It contains two memories, each with a first-in/first-out function (FIFO), a comparator and a control circuit.

The sorting cell operation for every two bytes consists of three cycles. They are memory read cycle, another memory read cycle, and compare-transfer cycle. In the first cycle, the word of the first sorted subsequence is read and stored into the register of the comparator. In the second cycle, the same operation for the other subsequence takes place. In the last cycle, the comparator compares them and the selector outputs the smaller or greater word to the (i+1)th cell, according to the ascending or descending mode. In this cycle, the word sent from the (i-1)th cell is stored into the memory. Each cycle takes 220 nsec, and the two-byte merge operation takes 660 nsec.

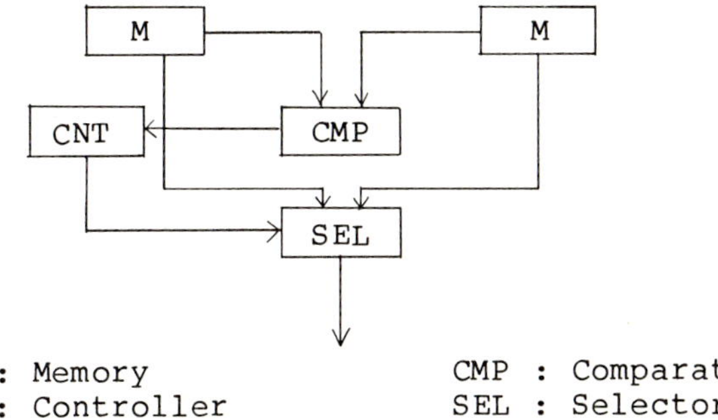

M : Memory
CNT : Controller
CMP : Comparator
SEL : Selector

Figure 8 Block diagram of a sorting cell

3.4 Merger

The merger is the central module of the RDBE, which performs relational algebra operations and other operations using a processing algorithm based on the two-way merge-sort operation. These are called merger commands and are classified into the five types of operations listed in Figure 9. They are characterized by their ability to process null values and duplicate values.

A block diagram of the merger is shown in Figure 10. The merger consists of an operation section and an output control section. The operation section contains a comparator, a control ROM table, and two 64 Kbyte memories (U-memory and L-memory) having a FIFO function. This section performs the following steps:

(1) Store two sorted streams from the sorter into the memories
(2) Read a tuple from each of two memories simultaneously and providing them to the comparator and the tuple memory in the next section
(3) Compare the keys of each tuple and detect output tuples satisfying the conditions of the command

PASS COMMAND	RESTRICT COMMAND
LOAD PASS-1(NOP) PASS-2(UNQ-IN)	REST-NULL REST-NONULL REST-EQ REST-NE REST-RANGE
SORT COMMAND	
SORT-IN SORT-EX UNQ-EX	
COMPARE COMMAND	JOIN COMMAND
COMP-ALL COMP-NULL COMP-NONULL COMP-EQ COMP-NE COMP-LT COMP-GT COMP-LE COMP-GE	JOIN-ALL JOIN-NULL JOIN-NONULL JOIN-EQ JOIN-NE JOIN-LT JOIN-GT JOIN-LE JOIN-GE

NOP : No operation UNQ-IN : Unique-Internal
EX : External NONULL : Not null

Figure 9 List of merger commands

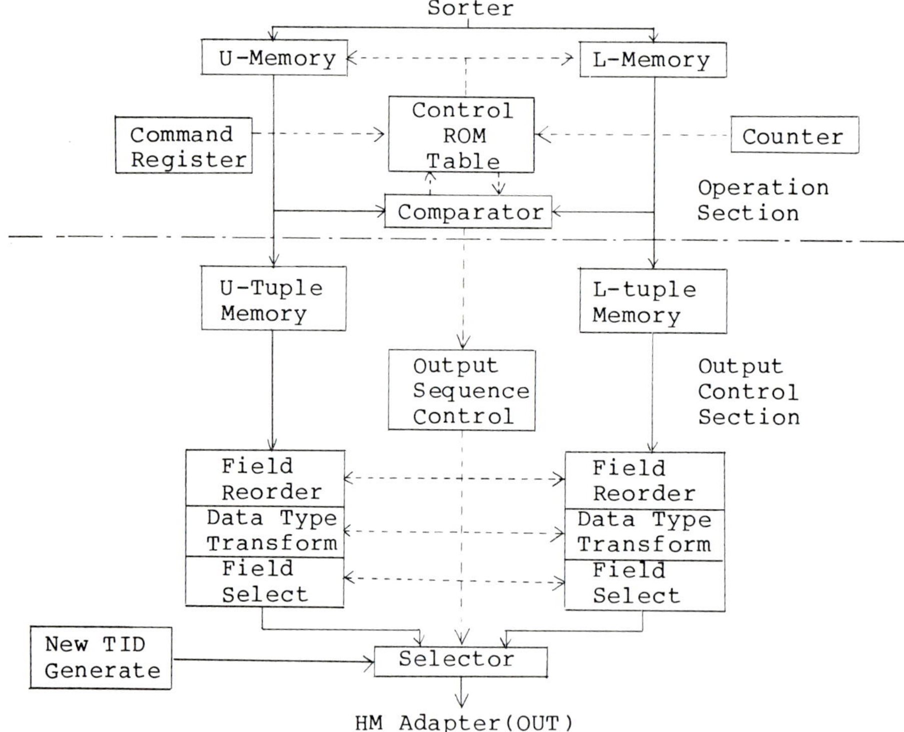

Figure 10 Block diagram of the merger

These functions are executed under the control of a 1-Kword * 10-bit ROM table. The address of the ROM table consists of a null signal, duplication signals, the comparison result flag and so on. The output of the ROM table consists of memory address control signals, tuple-selection signals used for the output control section, and an operation-end signal.

The output control section consists of two 16 Kbyte tuple memories, two field-ordering circuits, two field-selection circuits, two data-type-transformation circuits, a new TID (tuple-identifier) generator, a selector and an output sequence controller. This section performs the following functions under software control:

(1) Reorder the fields of an output tuple
(2) Select fields of an output tuple
(3) Recover the original notation of the key field
(4) Add a new TID to an output tuple

Examples of these functions are shown in Figure 11. Figure 11(a) shows the reordering of the fields of an output tuple. A tuple(1) with five fields (A, B, C, D, E; B is a key field) is rotated to tuple(2) by the IN module, so that the key field is positioned at the head of the tuple, and tuple(2) is rearranged to the original tuple(3) by the merger. The selection of the fields of an output tuple is shown in Figure 11(b). In this figure, tuple(4) is projected to tuple(5) or tuple(6) by the assignment of the two pointers, p_1 and p_2. Figure 11(c) shows the addition of a new TID to an output tuple.

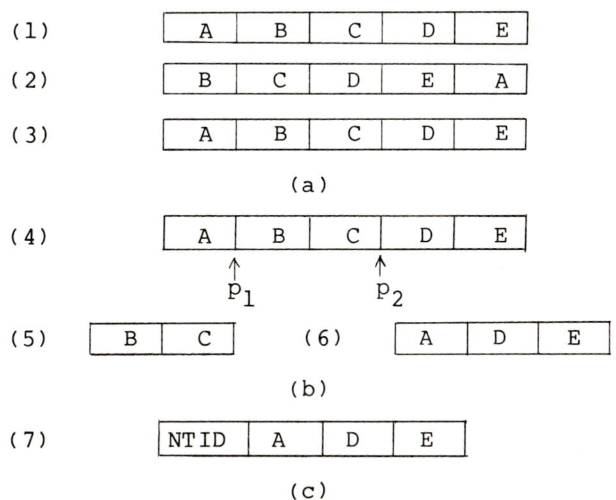

Figure 11 Functions of the output control section

An example of the JOIN-EQ operation is illustrated in Figure 12. JOIN-EQ command is typically used when an equi-join of two relations is performed. Figure 12(a) shows two input streams (S1 and S2) sorted in ascending key-order (A1 and B1); these are stored in the U- and L-memories, respectively. UADR and LADR provide sequence numbers, explaining the address control scheme for each memory.

Figure 12(b) shows the output tuples and Figure 12(c) illustrates the execution process. The processing algorithm of the JOIN-EQ command is as follows:

```
If A1 > B1 then LADR := LADR + 1;
if A1 < B1 then UADR := UADR + 1;
If A1 = B1 then
      output a matched tuple pair
      if the DP of A1 and the DP of B1 are on,
         then LADR := LADR + 1;
      if the DP of A1 is on and the DP of B1 is off,
         then UADR := UADR + 1;  LADR := LADR*
      if the DP of A1 is off and the DP of B1 is on,
         then LADR := LADR + 1;
      if the DP of A1 and the DP of B1 are off,
         then UADR := UADR + 1;  LADR := LADR + 1;
```

Here, DP stands for the duplication line and LADR* points to the first tuple of those which have the same values. Adopting this algorithm, the merger is able to perform the JOIN-EQ command on the attributes having duplicate values efficiently.

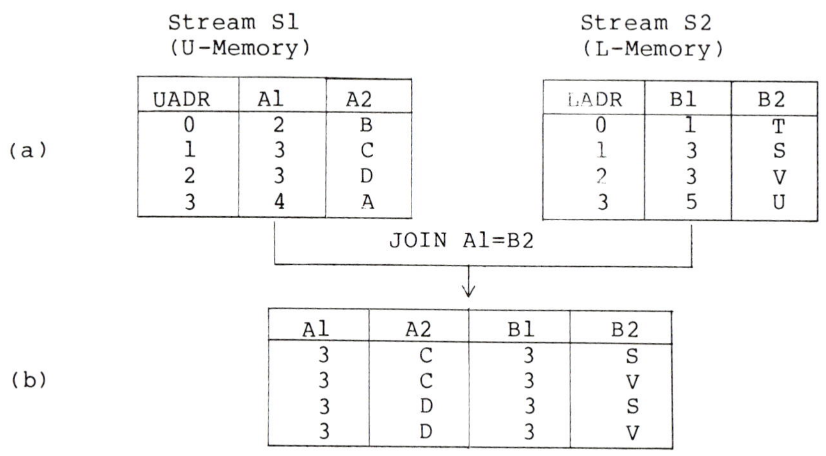

(a)

Stream S1 (U-Memory)

UADR	A1	A2
0	2	B
1	3	C
2	3	D
3	4	A

Stream S2 (L-Memory)

LADR	B1	B2
0	1	T
1	3	S
2	3	V
3	5	U

JOIN A1=B2

(b)

A1	A2	B1	B2
3	C	3	S
3	C	3	V
3	D	3	S
3	D	3	V

(c)

UADR	LADR	U-Tuple	L-Tuple	Result	Output
0	0	2 B	1 T	>	
0	1	2 B	3 S	<	
1	1	3 C	3 S	=	3 C 3 S
1	2	3 C	3 V	=	3 C 3 V
2	1	3 D	3 S	=	3 D 3 S
2	2	3 D	3 V	=	3 D 3 V
3	3	4 A	5 U	<	
END	3				

Figure 12 Example of processing JOIN-EQ command

The operation of the merger is divided into three cycles. These are the four-byte read cycle, compare-transfer cycle and the ROM table read cycle. Each cycle takes 220 ns and is synchronized with the sorter.

3.5 Data Processing by the Microprocessor

Since the operations performed by the sorter and merger are limited to the intertuple comparison concerning one field (typically one attribute) for each relation, the other operations must be performed by its microprocessor. These are as follows:

(1) Selection under complex conditions
(2) Arithmetic operations
(3) Aggregate operations

In order to improve the performance, the RDBE has a compiler which generates the native machine instructions into the main memory. The instructions are executed on the tuples generated by the merger and stored in its main memory by the HM adapter(OUT). The final result is sent to the HM through the HM adapter(OUT).

Since data processing using its microprocessor can be overlapped with the sorter and merger operation, a combined operation is able to be performed in one shot. The following is an exemplified query;

```
SELECT *
FROM A, B
WHERE al = bl AND a2 > b2
```

a join operation with a conjunctive condition. The RDBE is able to perform the join operation in one shot; the equal condition, using the sorter and merger, and the other, using its microprocessor.

3.6 Control Mechanisms

The RDBE's control mechanisms of the modules, in order to perform a RDBE command are described in this section. Since the sorter and merger have limited capacity; i.e. the maximum amount of data which the sorter and merger are able to process in one scan, the microprocessor controls the modules in a different way. This depends on the category of the RDBE command and the amount of data. They are as follows:

(1) Unary intratuple operation;

Arithmetic operations and selection are involved in this category. When the amount of data is so huge that the modules (including the capacity of the main memory) is not able to process it in one shot, the microprocessor controls the modules for each nonintersecting portion (called a substream) of the original data repeatedly.

(2) Sort type operation;

When the amount of data is small enough for the sorter to process in one shot, the microprocessor indicates the sorter to sort it and merger to pass it.

When the data is not greater than twice the sorter's capacity, the microprocessor first indicates the sorter to sort one half of it and the merger to store it into its U-memory. Then it indicates the sorter to sort the rest and the merger to merge them.

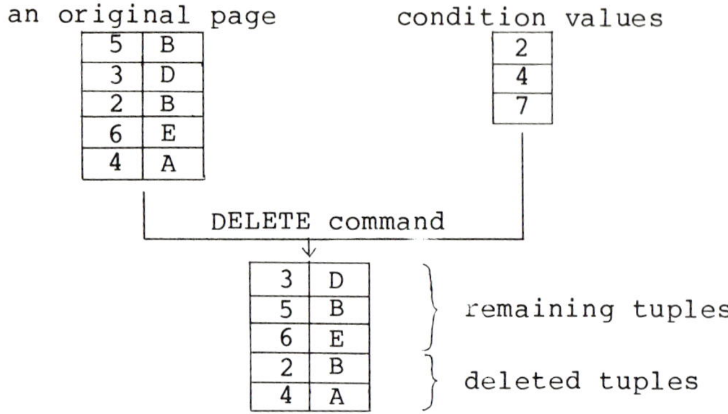

Figure 13 Example of the DELETE command

Otherwise, the microprocessor first controls the modules as in the second case, to generate two partially sorted sequences. Then the microprocessor indicates the merger to merge them repeatedly. Since each step is based on a two-way merge operation, it becomes inefficient when the amount of data becomes large, in comparison with the multi-way merger [Dohi 83].

(3) Binary operation (type 1)

In a join-like operation, the microprocessor controls the modules to perform the operation for each combination of the substreams of the relations repeatedly. An alternative is to sort each tuple first and to process the JOIN command on them. However, this is not adopted for two reasons; (1) it takes more time when the amount of data is not eight times greater than the sorter's capacity, and (2) It does not work well when a large number of tuples have the same value.

(4) Binary operation (type 2)

In a difference-like operation, the microprocessor controls the modules as follows. Let Ra and Rb be the original relations, and the operation be to get (Ra - Rb). It first indicates the sorter to sort the first substream of Rb (say Rb1) and the merger to store it into its U-memory. Then it indicates the sorter to sort each substream of Ra and the merger to perform the RESRICT-NE operation between each substream of Ra and Rb1 repeatedly.

Since the operations described above generates a temporary result of (Ra - Rb1), The microprocessor repeats the same operations to generate the final result.

Besides the control mechanisms described above, the microprocessor controls the merger to perform different operations on the same data. This is useful in the DELETE command. In the DELETE operation, the RDBE deletes those tuples the key of which match any of the condition values. First, the microprocessor controls the sorter and merger to store the condition values into the merger's U-memory. Then, for each page, It controls the sorter and merger in two steps; (1) store all tuples into the merger's L-memory and at the same time, output tuples which unmatch any of the condition values, (2) output tuples in the L-memory which match one of the condition values, Figure 13 illustrates an example. It helps the HM check whether the contents of each page are modified or not.

3.7 Increasing Reliability

The RDBE has the following features to gain reliability. A parity check mechanism and the sorting checker detect hardware errors with very little increase in processing time.

When an error occurs, the microprocessor resets the modules and then controls the HM adapters to inform HM to retry the data transfer. The HM only has to treat it as an ordinary I/O error.

During the power-up sequence, the microprocessor performs RDBE operations on certain test data. The test data in the main memory is provided to the IN module through the HM adapter(IN). The result is stored in the main memory via the HM adapter(OUT) and is checked by the microprocessor.

4 Performance of Primitive Operations

This section presents the performance of some primitive operations of the HM and RDBE. We have a plan for thorough performance evaluation of Delta after finishing its refinement task, which will continue till the end of this year.

As for the HM, performance should be evaluated for each type of storage, since its storage is classified into three types. However, we have only obtained till now the performance of the RSP Memory which stores working data and behave as a fast common secondary storage. The access time and the transfer rate are as follows:

Access Time	8 msec (Typ.)
Transfer Rate (to IP/CP/MP)	1 Mbyte/sec
Transfer Rate (to RDBE)	3 Mbyte/sec

As for the RDBE, we have obtained the performance of its representative commands JOIN (equi-join) and SORT. We will first discuss the theoretical performance estimation of the JOIN operation. Then we will compare it with actual performance.

Since every RDBE module, except the merger, proceeds in a deterministic way, the time required to perform an RDBE operation can be estimated. The activity of the merger, however, depends on the distribution of values in the input tuples, so we present the worst-case estimation. The following list sums up the parameters necessary to estimate performance:

N : number of sorting cells
M : merger's U- and L-memory capacity
Cn : tuple count of the n-th relation
Ln : tuple length of the n-th relation
Fn : number of substreams; equal to [(Cn-1)/min(2N,M/Ln]+1
Snj: j-th substream of the n-th relation
R : tuple count of the result
T : time required to transfer one byte

In a join operation, the microprocessor controls the modules in the following way:

```
send a request to HM through the HM adapter(IN)
while the first stream is not exhausted
begin
 ┌──────────────────────────────────────────┐
 │get a substream from HM                   │
 │modify it in the IN module                │            A
 │sort it in the sorter                     │
 │store it into the U-buffer of the merger  │
 └──────────────────────────────────────────┘
  send a request to HM through the HM adapter(IN)
  while the second stream is not exhausted
  begin
 ┌───────────────────────────────────────────────────────────┐
 │  get a substream from HM                                  │
 │  modify it in the IN module                               │   B
 │  sort it in the sorter                                    │
 │  compare it with the previous one to generate the result  │
 └───────────────────────────────────────────────────────────┘
  end
end
```

Here, the statements enclosed are executed in parallel. Figure 14 shows the time chart of the activities of the modules while executing section A. The total time taken in this section is calculated as follows:

The sorter, including the sorting checker, takes

(2SliLl + N - 1 + L)T

for the i-th substream of the first relation. The IN module takes an extra time of L_1T and the merger takes an extra time of T. The total time is equal to the following expression.

(2SliLl + N + 2Ll) = 2ClLl + Fl(N + 2Ll)

In section B, the merger takes an extra time of

((Sli + S2j)max(Ll+L2) - S2jL2)T

for scanning the i-th substream of the first relation and the j-th substream of the second relation. In addition, generating a record as a result takes (Ll + L2)T.

After all, the JOIN command takes the following time:

(2ClLl + Fl(N + 2Ll))T +
Fl(C2L2 + (Cl + C2)max(Ll + L2) + F2(N + 2L2))T +
R(Ll + L2)T

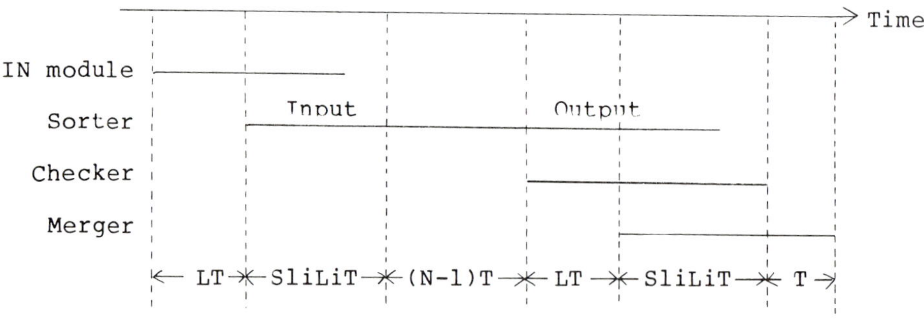

Figure 14 Time table of the activities of the RDBE modules

When C1 and C2 are equal to 4096, and L1 and L2 are equal to 16 bytes, and the resulting tuples are small, the RDBE takes approximately 128 milliseconds. Note that the processing time does not depend on the key size.

Figure 15 shows the theoretical performance estimation and the actual values for JOIN and SORT commands. Here, record size is always 16 bytes. The result shows that the RDBE, cooperating with the HM, achieves the expected performance.

(a) JOIN command

IN1	IN2	OUT	T	A
1	1	1		31
4096	4096	4096	107	150
8192	4096	4096	215	279
16384	4096	4096	301	377
32768	4096	4096	559	660
65536	4096	4096	1075	1345
131072	4096	4096	2107	2366
262144	4096	4096	4171	4793
524288	4096	4096	8299	10856

(b) SORT command

IN	OUT	T	A
1	1		21
4096	4096	43	64
8192	8192	107	136
16384	16384	349	445
32768	32768	961	1299
65536	65536	2446	3139
131072	131072	5940	7356
262144	262144	13978	17127
524288	524288	32148	42292

IN : number of records in the source relation
OUT : number of generated records
T : theoretically estimated processing time (msec)
A : actual processing time (msec)

Figure 15 Performance of the RDBE

5 PROBLEMS OF DELTA

Several problems concerning the performance of the Delta system have been disclosed, although we have not made thorough evaluation. We are refining Delta, especially concerning the internal commands among units and the basic software in order to improve efficiency.

Several crucial problems are derived from the configuration of Delta, especially the separation of the CP and HM. We think that they should be integrated into a single unit and the integrated unit should use the RDBEs as I/O devices because of the following reasons:

(1) The number of internal commands would be reduced approximately by 80%. The integration of the CP and HM would directly make the internal commands between them unnecessary. It would reduce the number approximately by 40%. If the integrated unit would use the RDBEs as I/O devices, then the internal commands between the RDBE and HM would become unnecessary. It would reduce the number by additional 40%.

(2) Since a query compilation, which the CP does now, requires several pages of the directory to be read and modified, the directory should be accessed by the CP as its main memory, and not as its secondary memory.

(3) The scheduling of the query execution, which the CP does now, should be related to the considerations of the HM resources. In order to realize it, the integration of the CP and HM is necessary.

(4) Currently, the RDBE receives an internal command (e.g. JOIN) from the CP and then the RDBE sends several internal commands which require data transfers to the HM. When the RDBE executes an external sort operation on a large amount of data, it is a significant problem on performance that the HM does not know the operation of the RDBE and it cannot predict the RDBE's requirement.

(5) Currently, staging a relation from the HM's moving head disk to its main memory occurs by an internal command sent from the CP. After its completion, the RDBE can perform some relational database operation on it. So the staging phase and the execution phase are not overlapped.

Other problems are derived from the attribute-wise schema of the relations. It needs several times more internal commands than in the case a tuple-wise schema would be adopted. The conversion from attribute-wise data to tuple-wise ones and vice versa requires much resources when the data size is large. The two level clustering, in which each attribute is clustered by the value first and then is clustered by the TID, is not easy to maintain and results in dull selectivity.

Figure 16 shows an example of a preferable internal schema for Delta. The attributes having a fixed length should be gathered together and one of them should be treated as a primary key. The other attributes (e.g. image data or explanations of a dictionary) should be stored separately.

Some more problems are derived from the operating system of the IP and CP. Since they have a modified version of a time-sharing operating system, they are not able to respond internal commands quickly because of the following reasons:

(1) Although Delta is required to support a multi-transaction environment, its operating system need not necessarily support a multi-task environment. Such a powerful operating system consumes non-negligible time for context switching and concurrency control. A monitor of an event-driven type seems best for the IP and CP.

(2) The control program of a special-purpose machine, such as Delta, should be allocated at a certain address during its start-up sequence. An ordinary time-sharing operating system, however, does not allow the static memory allocation for a user program.

(3) Since specific communication requires certain protocol handling, the device handler has to support it in order to achieve quick interrupt handling. Most general-purpose operating systems, however, have only physical-level handlers and it is a user program that must handle the protocol.

TID	name	area

TID	characteristics

TID	map

Figure 16 Example of a preferable internal schema

We plan to improve the efficiency of these units by exchanging the operating system to a realtime monitor of our own. Several times improvement of the systems throughput is expected and also the whole software of the IP and CP will be reduced much in size.

6 Toward a Knowledge Base Machine

In this section, we will present our ideas concerning the KBM. Since we have just started the discussion and various approaches are being proposed and discussed, the contents of this section are still informal and indefinite.

As for the functions of a KBM, we think that operations concerning knowledge (i.e. inference and pattern matching) should be added in order to realize both an intelligent database management system (DBMS) and knowledge manipulation.

We think a conventional DBMS has the following problems:

(1) In a conventional retrieval system using keywords as a search condition, the keywords must be originally registerd by the users.

(2) In a query system with a natural language interface, a conventional DBMS cannot make an incomplete query accurate for the lack of the common sense and knowledge about the contents of the database.

(3) The more a database grows in size, the more important its integrity check becomes. Generally the user must direct the condition timely.

(4) In a conventional database system, the user must choose a suitable file organization for each relation in order to achieve high performance. It needs skill and the choice becomes inadequate when the usage or the size varies.

(5) A conventional DBMS can process a query only when the database has the immediate answer.

We think that these problems should be investigated in the course of our KBM research.

Delta can handle knowledge of tabular form, which, in Prolog, corresponds to facts with constants as arguments. One may well regard a query processing on Delta as a breadth-first evaluation of a Prolog goal. It is a natural idea that a KBM should handle more generalized knowledge than Delta. The following are our fundamental ideas:

(1) Conventional database can only process knowledge as data. That is, it is impossible that the database recognizes the contents of knowledge or executes specific operations (e.g. matching and inference).

(2) In Prolog, knowledge is represented as facts and rules. It is well known that there can exist many facts with the same predicate name. However, it is said that the number of rules with the same predicate name is almost always less than ten. So the Delta architecture which is designed to handle only facts seems insufficient to a KBM. We have an idea of developing a specialized processor called inference engine to perform a breadth-first evaluation of Prolog programs.

(3) We think a KBM should also treat several kinds of knowledge representations other than Horn clauses, (e.g. semantic nets, frames, relations) directly for the sake of efficiency and

ease of understanding. Specialized mechanisms will be required for each knowledge representation and for the conversion between them. Delta-like RDBM should be regarded as a special component for tabular knowledge.

(4) We expect that a KBM must have considerable size of main memory. While the development of semiconductor technology will reduce the cost of memory, the bottle-neck between the processor and the memory will remain. According to such considerations, we have an idea of an intelligent memory system which stores knowledge. Its detail will be presented at a succeeding paper.

7 Conclusions

Delta is a relational database machine developed at ICOT research center as a first step to a KBM. In order to achieve efficiency, we adopted (1) a functionally-distributed architecture, (2) relational database engines (RDBEs) to perform relational database operations, and (3) a large capacity hierarchical memory system. Although the RDBEs, cooperating with the hierarchical memory system, achieved expected performance, the Delta system as a wohle had several problems and we are trying to solve them now.

As for a real KBM, we plan to develop a new machine which can treat several kinds of knowledge representations. The Delta is regarded as its compnent for tabular knowledge.

ACKNOWLEDGMENTS

The present research effort is part of a major research and development project of the fifth generation computer, conducted under a program set up by the Ministry of International Trade and Industry.

We would like to express our sincere appreciation to the members of the ICOT KBM group for their valuable discussions, and to Dr. K. Mori, director of the TOSHIBA Information Systems Laboratory, who provided the opportunity to conduct the present research. Special thanks to Mr. F. Umibe for polishing our English.

REFERENCES

[Bancilhon 82] Bancilhon, F., et al. VERSO: A Relational Back-End Data Base Machine, Proc. of Int'l Workshop on Database Machines, Aug., 1982.

[Boral 82] Boral, H., et al Implementation of the Database Machine DIRECT, IEEE Trans., Software Eng., Vol. SE-8, No.6, Nov., 1982.

[Codd 70] Codd, E.F. A Relational Model of Data for Large Shared Data Banks, CACM, Vol.13, No.6, June, 1970.

[Dohi 83] Dohi, Y., et al. Sorter Using PSC Linear Array, International Symposium on VLSI Technology, Systems and Applications, 1983, pp.255-259.

[Gallaire 78] Gallaire, H., and Minker, J. (eds) Logic and Data Bases, Plenum Press, 1978.

[Hell 1981] Hell, W. RDBM-A Relational Database Machine Architecture and Hardware Design, Proc. 6th Workshop on Comp. Arch. for Non-Numerical Processing, Hyeres, France, June, 1981.

[Ito 84] Ito, N., et al. Parallel Inference Machine Based on the Data Flow Model, Proc. of Int'l Workshop on High-Level Computer Architecture 84, 1984.

[Kakuta 85] Kakuta, T., et al. The Design and Implementation of Relational Database Machine Delta, Proc. IWDM'85, (1985)

[Knuth 73] Knuth, D.E. The Art of Computer Programming, Vol. 3/ Sorting and Searching, Addition-Wesley, 1973.

[Onai 84] Onai, R., et al. Parallel Inference Machine Based on Reduction Mechanisms - Its Architecture and Software Simulation, ICOT Technical Report TR-077, 1984.

[Shibayama 84] Shibayama, S., et al. A Relational Database Machine with Large Semiconductor Disk and Hardware Relational Algebra Processor, ICOT Technical Report, TR-055, 1984.

[Taki 84] Taki, K., et al. Hardware Design and Implementation of the Personal Sequential Inference Machine (PSI), Proc. of International Conference on FGCS '84, Nov., 1984, pp.398-409.

[Tanaka 80] Tanaka, Y., et al. Pipeline Searching and Sorting Modules as Components of a Data Flow Database Computer, IFIP80, pp.427-432, 1980.

[Todd 78] Todd, S. Algorithm and Hardware for a Merge Sort Using Multiple Processors, IBM J. RES. DEVELOP., Vol.22, No.5, Sept., 1978.

[Yokota 84] Yokota, H., et al An Enhanced Inference Mechanisms for Generating Relational Algebra Queries, Proc. of the 3rd ACM SIGACT-SIGMOD Symposium on Principles of Database Systems, Waterloo, April, 1984, pp.229-238.

[Yokota 85] Yokota, H., et al Deductive Database System based on Unit Resolution, ICOT Technical Report, TR-123, 1985.

A Relational Database Machine for Very Large Information Retrieval Systems

Ushio Inoue and Seiichi Kawazu

Yokosuka Electrical Communication Laboratories
Nippon Telegraph and Telephone Corporation, Japan

Abstract

An overview is presented of a new advanced relational database machine (ADAM) for very large information retrieval systems. Novel features of ADAM are as follows.

(1) A relation is divided into several parts and stored in general purpose magnetic disks. A parallel access method and a clustering technique based on the extended K-d tree are employed to shorten data transfer time from disks to the main memory.

(2) Selection operations are performed at the time of the data transfer by specialized hardware attached to a disk controller. A table based on the finite state machine is used to perform text search of selection operations.

(3) The three-phase (filtering, sorting and comparing) join method is used to accelerate join operations. Each phase is performed in parallel by specialized hardware.

The performance of ADAM is two orders higher than that of conventional general purpose computers when applied to very large information retrieval systems. The cost performance is also one order of magnitude better.

1. Introduction

Many information retrieval systems storing a variety of databases are now available. Most of these systems provide secondary data which are converted from original data for the purpose of computer retrieval. In document retrieval systems, for example, databases consist of bibliography

NATO ASI Series, Vol. F 24
Database Machines. Edited by A. K. Sood and A. H. Qureshi

lists, abstracts and keywords which are appended to the bibliography lists by specialists. Problems that arise with systems providing secondary rather than original data are the following.

(1) Enormous specialist manpower is needed to convert original data into secondary data. Extracting abstracts and keywords from the original data is an especially painstaking task.

(2) The use of data can change as time passes. Flexible response to the change is difficult when access pathes to the data are restricted by indexed keywords.

(3) Special techniques for specifying keywords are necessary because retrieval results depend on these keywords.

On the other hand, systems which provide original data have the great advantage that the data can be utilized for a variety of purposes. Development of such systems has tended recently to become easier, as the cost of data storage continues to drop dramatically and as efficient devices for inputting or outputting large quantities of data become available. It is presently, however, impossible to develop online systems which provide large amounts of original data, because general purpose computers do not yet have sufficient power to handle original data.

Many relational database machines (RDBM) have been proposed owing to rapid hardware cost reductions with LSI technology (e.g.[1],[2],[3]). The relational database model is suitable for handling original data because of its flexible data manipulation facilities. Conventional RDBMs have, however, been organized to handle databases of small or medium size (on the order of several gigabytes) and have not yet been able to handle very large (on the order of several hundred gigabytes) databases of original data at a reasonable cost. This is because some of them use special content addressable storage devices and some of their main processors are small microprocessors which work alone.

This paper outlines the overall architecture of a new relational database machine (ADAM: Advanced Database Machine) for very large database systems. ADAM includes mechanisms for high speed disk access, high speed searching, and high speed join operations.

ADAM constructed using the state-of-the-art technology can retrieve data from very large databases two orders of magnitude faster than general purpose computers. The cost performance for the system has also been improved by one order of magnitude.

This paper is organized as follows. Problems in developing very large RDBMs are presented next. The solutions of these problems and the architecture features of ADAM are described. Then some topics on the mechanisms of high speed disk access, high speed searching, and high speed join operation are described. The performance and cost of the ADAM system are very roughly estimated. A conclusion follows.

2. Problems in Very Large RDBMs

Problems to be solved to develop RDBMs which can handle very large databases composed mainly of original data are as follows.

(1) High speed disk access

It is difficult, in general, to make efficient use of indexing methods on RDBs mainly composed of original data, because access patterns to data are variable. Especially, if the database is composed of original data such as text or statistical data, then indexing is impossible. In such cases, all tuples of the relation in the database must be examined exhaustively. A high speed disk access mechanism is needed that can read out all tuples in a relation of several hundred megabytes in a few seconds.

(2) High speed searching

In general purpose computers, all tuples are read out of disks, transferred to the main memory, and examined by the CPU. Two problems arise when the database is very large. First, much CPU time is consumed in the searching. Second, the amount of data transferred between disks and the memory becomes very large. To solve these problems, a high speed searching mechanism is needed which reduces the amount of data transfered while the disks are being accessed.

(3) High speed join operations

Join operations are essential to relational database systems. Join operations require two relations, and it is necessary to compare one tuple of one relation with all tuples of the other relation. In general purpose computers the processing time is enormous, because the time complexity of join operations is order O(n*m) or O(n*log m) where n and m are the numbers of tuples in each relation. A high speed join operation mechanism is required to perform them in a time of O(n).

3. Overview of ADAM

3.1 Basic Concepts

RDBM architectur is determined by algorithms that implement operations in relational algebra. The basic ADAM concepts concerned with the algorithms are as follows.

(1) O(n) implementation

The time required to perform the operations requiring two relations or examining a mutual relationship of tuples in a relation, are a time of O(n*n) or O(n*log n) when the operations are implemented using simple algorithms. In such cases, the time becomes enormous when the number of tuples in the relations increases.

If, however, tuples in the relation are sorted on the key attributes then the following process can be performed in a time of O(n). Several kinds of hardware sorter chips which can sort data in a time of O(n) have been proposed (e.g.[4],[5]), and some of them will soon be available. Therefore ADAM uses hardware sorter chips, and performs all relational algebra operations in a time of O(n).

(2) Parallel processing

Operations which work on a single relation can be divided into any number of independent portions, because each tuple of the relation is independent of the other tuples. Operations which work on two relations can be divided into two kinds of sub-operations; one works on a single relation and the other works on the results of the processing on a single relation.

In ADAM every operation or sub-operation which works on a single relation is divided into several portions and these are processed in parallel.

(3) Pipeline processing

Sub-operations which require the results from the others are processed in pipelined fashions by ADAM, because it is expected to take too much cost to process them in parallel.

The data transfer unit size in the pipeline depends on the data transfer method. If the data is transferred through directly connected wires, then the unit should be a tuple, because the maximum advantage of the pipeline is obtained. If the data is transferred through either I/O channels or buses, then the unit should be a block containing a proper number of tuples, because overhead accompanied with the data transfer control is reduced. Therefore ADAM uses two kinds of pipelines which differ in the data transfer unit size.

3.2 Approaches in ADAM

ADAM solves the problems described in the previous section by the following approaches.

(1) High speed disk access

We consider devices which databases are stored in. The device must have enough capacity to store very large databases at a reasonable cost, and it must have enough speed to transfer a large amount of data in the databases to the main memory of a processor. Following three alternatives are considered.

* Semiconductor disks (e.g.[2])
* Track parallel disks (e.g.[6])
* General purpose disks (e.g.[7])

First, semiconductor disks are made of random access memories (RAM), charge-coupled devices (CCD), or magnetic bubble memories. They can achieve very high data transfer speeds, but their cost per bit is still so high that it is unrealistic to store entire databases in them. Second, track parallel disks are special magnetic disks which can read out data from several tracks at the same time. They can also achieve data transfer speeds h times as high as that of general purpose disks where h is the number of the disk heads. It is doubtful, however, whether they can be put to practical use at a reasonable cost in the near future. Finally, general purpose disks, that is moving head magnetic disks, are inexpensive, and their cost per bit is still decreasing as recording density is raised. The data transfer speed can also be increased by accessing several disks simultaneously.

For the above-mentioned reasons, the high speed disk access mechanism of ADAM is decided as follows.

A relation is divided into several parts and stored in separate general purpose magnetic disks. These disks are accessed in parallel in order to shorten the data transfer time from the disks to the memory. Furthermore, a clustering technique based on the extended K-d tree is used in order to reduce the total number of disk pages to be read when the relation is divided.

(2) High speed searching

In ordinary retrievals, it is possible to reduce the relation size in the database by selection operations at the first stage of the processing. Selection operations should be performed at disk controllers while the relation are being read out of disks so that useless data is not transferred to the memory. This operation must also be performed at the speed of the data transfer from the disk. To develop the dedicated processor for selection operations, following two alternatives are considered.

* Multiple microprocessors (e.g.[8])
* Search processors (e.g.[9])

When the dedicated processor is composed of multiple microprocessors, the minimum number N of parallel processors is calculated by the following formula,

$$N = t * s * k / m$$

where t is data transfer speed, s is the number of instructions required to compare a data byte and a key, k is the number of keys specified in the retrieval condition, and m is the MIPS of the microprocessor. Typical values of these parameters are t=3 (MB/sec), s=5 (instructions/byte), k=5, and m=1 (MIPS), this results in an N of 75. It is difficult with the current technology to achieve parallel processing by many processors at a reasonable cost. On the other hand, it is rather easy to design and implement search processors or specialized hardware, because the searching is simple, repetitious procedure.

Therefore the high speed searching mechanism of ADAM is decided as follows.

Selection operations including restriction and text search are performed by the search processors (SHP) which are special hardware attached to disk controllers (DKC). The SHP decides whether the tuple which is read out of the disk matches the search condition or not, and sends the only tuples that have matched the condition. This process is performed while the data is being transfered between the disk and the memory.

(3) High speed join operation

It is difficult for the SHP to perform join operations because the operations require two relations which may be stored in different disk units. Moreover, the relation may be a temporary relation which is generated in the main memory during a process. Therefore the mechanism to perform join operations should be organized separate from the SHP, and it should work on the relation which is either a searched result by the SHP or a temporary relation on the main memory. Two possible algorithms for join operations are as follows.

* Nested loop (e.g.[10])
* Sort merge (e.g.[11])

The time complexity of the nested loop or scan method is O(n*m) where n and m are the number of tuples in each relation. If we want to perform them in time O(n), then parallel processing by (m) processors is necessary. In large database systems m may be a large number, and it is impractical to achieve such highly parallel processing by so many processors.

On the other hand, the time complexity of the sort merge or scan method is O(n*log m), and in this case parallel processing by only (log m) processors is necessary. Furthermore, hardware sorter chips will soon be available. For these reasons, the sort merge method seems to be better, but one problem arises about the capacity of the hardware sorter chips. When the sort merge method is applied, the number of tuples to be sorted can be large and it would probably cost a lot to furnish large capacity hardware sorter chips and to post-process the large amount of sorted data. This problem can be reduced if the data to be sorted are pre-processed and filtered out.

Therefore the high speed join operation mechanism of ADAM is decided as follows.

The join operation process consists of three phases that is filtering, sorting, and comparing phases, and each phase is performed in a pipelined fashion. This method is called the three-phase join method. The data flow with the three-phase join method is illustrated in Fig. 1.

In the filtering phase the filter (FIL), which is special hardware, filters out the tuples of two relations by means of hashed bit arrays. In the sorting phase the sort-merger (SMR), which is other special hardware including sorter chips, sorts the filtered tuples. In the comparing phase, the sorted tuples are compared based on the actual attribute values and joined into result tuples by a control CPU. Each of the three phases works in the time of O(n).

3.3 The ADAM architecture

The ADAM hardware organization is shown in Fig. 2. ADAM is composed of the intelligent disk controllers (IDKC), the database operation accelerating processors (DAP), and a control CPU. Each IDKC includes one SHP and one DKC, and each DAP includes several FILs and SMRs. The control CPU is a general purpose computer, and it performs the functions not performed by either the IDKC or the DAP. The organization of ADAM is very flexible and allows easy installation, because the performance of the control CPU, and the number of the IDKCs and the DAPs may be changed according to application system demands.

4. Topics in ADAM

4.1 Clustering

The word "clustering" is used to mean a tuple-wise partition of a relation according to the values of specified attributes. If a relation is stored in a disk with a clustering technique, and if the same attributes which were used to make the clusters are specified in the retrieval conditions, then the number of disk pages to be searched decreases.

A lot of clustering techniques using multiple attributes have been proposed in connection with file organization schemes (e.g.[12],[13],[14],[15]). The extended K-d tree scheme[14] is chosen from among them for ADAM because of the following reasons.

(1) It can be easily implemented.
(2) It can be effective for range queries in addition to exact match and partial match queries.
(3) It can be tuned to access characteristics of relations.

The values of an attribute may be duplicated in a real database, but this duplication has not been considered in previous research. As a result, the disk page occupancy decreases and the search time increases.

To solve this problem an improved strategy for selecting attributes, which are called discriminators, is used for relation partitioning. The improved strategy is as follows.

(1) Discriminators at each level of the K-d tree are decided as usual by a discriminator function to minimize the expected number of disk page accessed.
(2) A relation is partitioned as usual by the discriminator decided in (1) unless duplicate values of the attribute cause a large imbalance on the tree.
(3) When a large imbalance is caused in (2), the next discriminator at the lower level of the tree is selected.

An example of this process is illustrated in Fig. 3. On the results of a simulation study, the disk page occupancy is improved considerably, while the increase in disk page access is very small. A typical result of a simulation study is shown in Fig. 4.

4.2 Text Search

The word "text search" is used to mean kinds of selection operations that select tuples containing specified sub-strings, which are called search keys, in character strings of specified attributes. Text search have a lot of merits when the relation includes original text data. However they consume enormous amount of CPU time in general purpose computers, because the usual indexing techniques are not effective.

Several text search techniques which aim at searching data stored in disks have been proposed (e.g.[16],[17],[18]). These techniques can be classified into three groups: parallel comparators, cellular comparators, and finite state machines [19]. They are compared in Table 1 from the viewpoint of hardware and flexibility of function. Table driven implementations of the third group seem to be the best because large size tables can be furnished cheaply owing to the dramatical reduction in RAM cost.

A technical problem in the table driven implementation is the algorithm for constructing the table. Various text search conditions must be represented consistently in the table and the table size should be as small as possible so that many long search keys can be stored. An algorithm is developed for ADAM that has the following features.

(1) Any combination of AND, OR, or NOT on search keys is available. The maximum number of search keys is determined by the RAM capacity and the total length of the search keys.
(2) Data for Japanese character, which is represented with 16-bit code, is divided into two equal parts and processed 8 bits at a time.
(3) Search keys which include either fixed-length or variable-length "don't care" are also available.
(4) Different search keys for different attributes can be stored together in the table.

The first function is achieved by means of an arangement where each entry in the table is composed of a next state number and a bit map. The bit map indicates which search keys are found at any point in time. The second function reduces the table size almost to 1/128 of a straight-foward implementation. The hardware structure of a table driven implementation is illustrated in Fig. 5.

4.3 Filtering

In the filtering phase of the three-phase join method, the tuples which have no possibility of being joined are filtered out by means of hashed bit arrays. Several filtering techniques have been proposed (e.g.[9],[20]). Some of these techniques are illustrated in Fig. 6.

The basic technique, called one-side hashing, requires a bit array and a hashing circuit which maps the value of a specified attribute on to a bit address of the bit array. This technique filters either of the two relations to be joined. The number of tuples to be filtered out cannot be forecast, and may differ if the opposite relation is filtered. Therefore, selection of the relation is a very difficult problem in one-side hashing. Another technique, called both-sides serial hashing, requires two bit arrays and a hashing circuits. Both of the relations to be joined are filtered serially but it takes more time than one-side hashing.

The other technique, called both-sides parallel hashing, requires two bit arrays and two hashing circuits. Both of the two relations are filtered in parallel and it takes the same amount of time as one-side hashing. The processing time is dependent on the total size of the relations, while independent of the relation size ratio. The relationship between processing time and relation size ratio is shown in Fig. 7.

ADAM employs the parallel hashing in the filtering phase.

5. Performance and Cost

In this section, the performance and cost of ADAM is very roughly estimated when ADAM is applied to two types of information retrieval model.

(1) Estimation model

The first model (Model A) is a document retrieval system. Each relation containing long text data is retrieved by a text search. The second model (Model B) is a statistical database system. Two relations are joined after selection operations work on each of the relations. The assumed number of tuples and average length of the tuples are shown in Table 2.

(2) Estimation method

The performance of both, the conventional general purpose computer and ADAM, are measured by the total time of CPU time, data transfer time, and the specialized hardware processing time.

The cost of both machines are measured by the CPU cost and the specialized hardware cost, but the other cost common to both are excluded. The following formulas are used for the estimation.

(a) Model A.

general purpose computer	ADAM
T = Tdk	T = Tdk
Tdk = max(Tio, Tcse)	Tdk = Tio
P = Ccpu	P = Ccpu + Ndk * Cshp

(b) Model B.

general purpose computer	ADAM
T = Tdk + Tjo	T = Tdk + Tjo
Tdk = max(Tio, Tcse)	Tdk = max(Tio, Tdin)
Tjo = Tcso + Tcmp	Tjo = Tdso + Tcmp
P = Ccpu	P = Ccpu + Cdap + Ndk * Cshp

where

T	: total time	Ndk	: number of disks
P	: total cost	Tcse	: CPU search
Tdk	: disk time	Tcso	: CPU data sort
Tjo	: join time	Tdso	: DAP data sort
Ccpu	: CPU cost	Tcmp	: CPU compare
Cshp	: SHP cost	Tio	: disk data transfer
Cdap	: DAP cost	Tdin	: DAP data transfer.

(3) Results

Each parameter value is assumed in accordance with current computer technology. The estimated performance and cost is illustrated in Fig. 8.

The text search technique and the three-phase join method used in ADAM led to good results in Model A and Model B, respectively. The performance of ADAM is about two orders higher than that of conventional general purpose computers for both models. The cost performance is also about one order of magnitude better.

6. Conclusion

ADAM is a relational database machine for very large databases mainly composed of original data. ADAM achieves a substantial improvement in performance and cost.

The problems with very large databases and the solutions by ADAM are summarized as follows.

(1) High speed disk access
 * Parallel access to general purpose magnetic disks
 * The clustering technique based on the extended K-d tree

(2) High speed searching
 * The IDKC consisting of a search processor and a disk controller
 * The text search technique based on the finite state machine

(3) High speed join operation
 * The three-phase join method with the DAP consisting of filters and sort-mergers
 * The both-sides parallel hashing technique in the filtering phase

Acknowledgements

The authors wish to express gratitude to Hideaki Takeda for coming up with the three-phase join and the both-sides parallel hashing, and to Ichiroh Itakura for helping us to analyze the property of the extended K-d tree. The authors are also grateful to K. Sato, S. Takamura, A. Hashimoto, K. Ohashi and M. Haihara for their support and encouragement in promoting this research work.

References

[1] G.G.Langdon,Jr. et al., "Special Issue on Database Machines", IEEE Trans. Comput., Vol.C-28 No.6, June 1979

[2] S.Uemura, T.Yuba, A.Kokubu, R.Ohomote and Y.Sugawara, "The Design and Implementation of a Magnetic-Bubble Database Machine", Proc. IFIP 80, Oct. 1980, pp.433-438

[3] R.Epstein and P.Hawthorn, "Design Decisions for the Intelligent Database Machine", Proc. NCC 80, May 1980, pp.237-241

[4] Y.Tanaka, "Bit-Sliced VLSI Algorithms for Search and Sort", Proc. 10th VLDB, Aug. 1984, pp.225-234

[5] G.Miranker, L.Tang and C.K.Wong, "A 'Zero-Time' VLSI Sorter", IBM J. Res. Develop., Vol.27 No.2, Mar. 1983, pp.140-148

[6] K.Kannan, "The Design of a Mass Memory for a Database Computer", Proc. 5th Comp. Arch., Apr. 1978, pp.44-51

[7] T.Lang, E.Nahouraii, K.Kasuga and E.B.Fernandez, "An Architectural Extension for a Large Database System Incorporating a Processor for Disk Search", Proc. 3rd VLDB, Oct. 1977, pp.204-210

[8] H.O.Leilich, G.Stiege and H.Ch.Zeidler, "A Search Processor for Data Base Management Systems", Proc. 4th VLDB, Sept. 1978, pp.280-287

[9] E.Babb, "Implementing a Relational Database by Means of Specialized Hardware", ACM Trans. DB Syst., Vol.4 No.1, Mar. 1979, pp.1-29

[10] H.Boral and D.J.Dewitt, "Processor Allocation Strategies for Multiprocessor Database Machines", ACM Trans. DB Syst., Vol.6 No.2, June 1981, pp.227-254

[11] M.W.Blasgen and K.P.Eswaran, "Storage and Access in Relational Data Bases", IBM Syst. J., Vol.16 No.4, 1977, pp.363-378

[12] R.L.Rivest, "Partial-Match Retrieval Algorithms", SIAM J. Comput., Vol.5 No.1, Mar. 1976, pp.19-50

[13] J.Nievergelt, H.Hinterberger and K.C.Sevcik, "The Grid File: An Adaptable, Symmetric Multikey File Structure", ACM Trans. DB Syst., Vol.9 No.1, Mar. 1984, pp.38-71

[14] J.M.Chang and K.S.Fu, "Extended K-d Tree Database Organization: A Dynamic Multiattribute Clustering Method", IEEE Trans. Soft. Engi., Vol.SE-7 No.3, May 1981, pp.284-290

[15] S.Fushimi, M.Kitsuregawa, H.Tanaka and T.Moto-oka, "Multidimensional Clustering Technique for Large Relational Database Machines", Proc. Foundations of Data Organization, May 1985, pp.226-235

[16] F.J.Burkowski, "A Hardware Hashing Scheme in the Design of a Multiterm String Comparator", IEEE Trans. Comput., Vol.C-31 No.9, Sept. 1982, pp.825-834

[17] A.Mukhopadhyay, "Hardware Algorithms for Nonnumeric Computation", Proc. 5th Comp. Arch., Apr. 1978, pp.8-16

[18] L.A.Hollaar and D.C.Roberts, "Current Research into Specialized Processors for Text Information Retrieval", Proc. 4th VLDB, Sept. 1978, pp.270-279

[19] L.A.Hollaar, "Text Retrieval Computers", Computer, Vol.12 No.3, Mar. 1979, pp.40-50

[20] D.R.McGregor, R.G.Thomson and W.N.Dawson, "High Performance Hardware for Database Systems", in "Systems for Large Data Bases" P.C.Lockemann and E.J.Neuhold(Eds.), North-Holland, 1976, pp.103-116

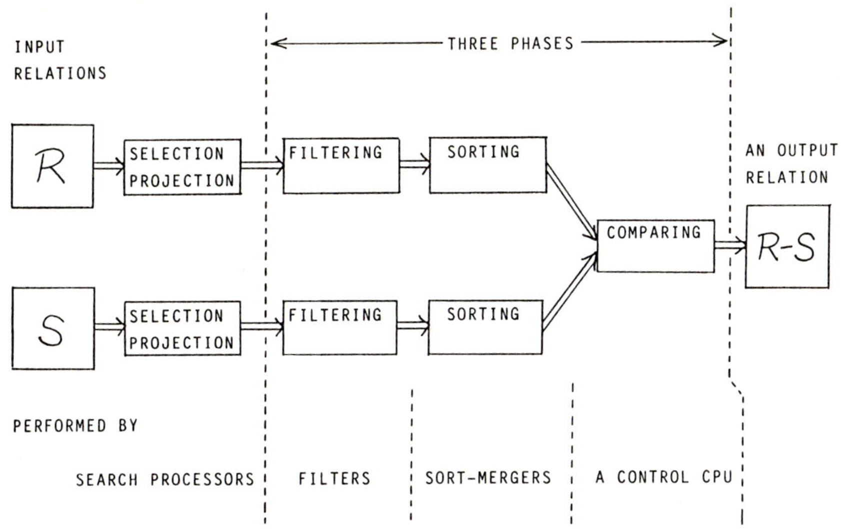

Fig. 1. THE THREE-PHASE JOIN METHOD

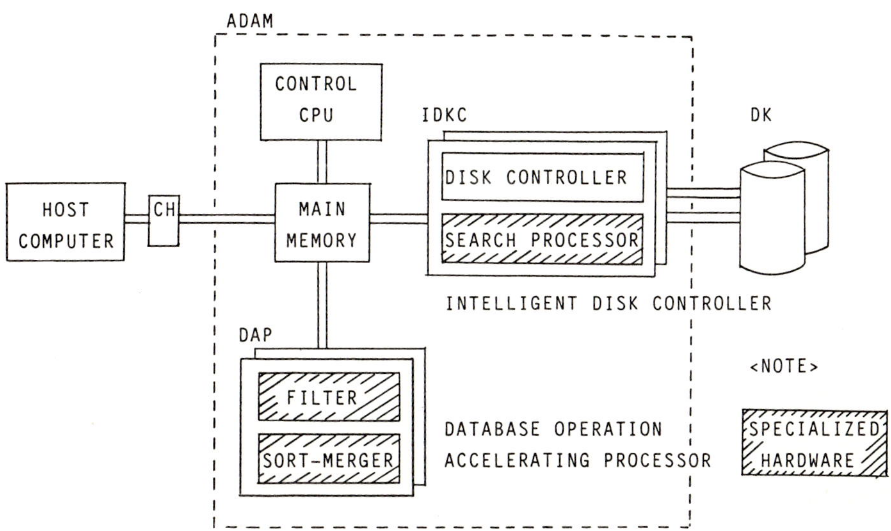

Fig. 2. THE ADAM HARDWARE ORGANIZATION

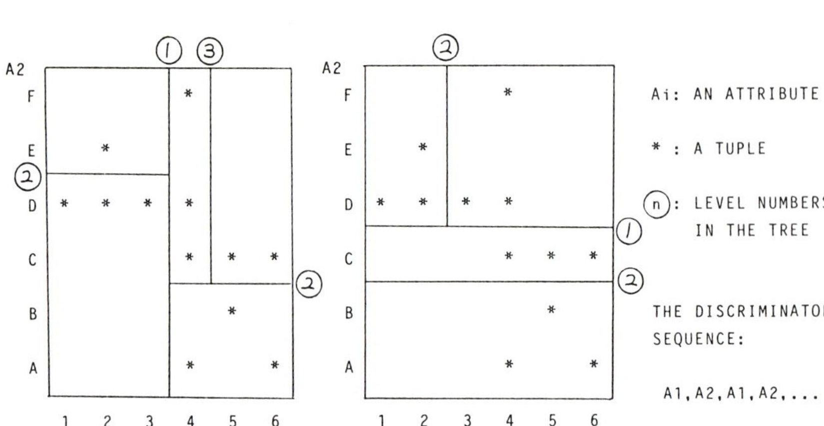

Fig. 3. PARTITIONING PROCESSES WITH THE K-D TREE

(assuming that each cluster cannot have more than three tuples)

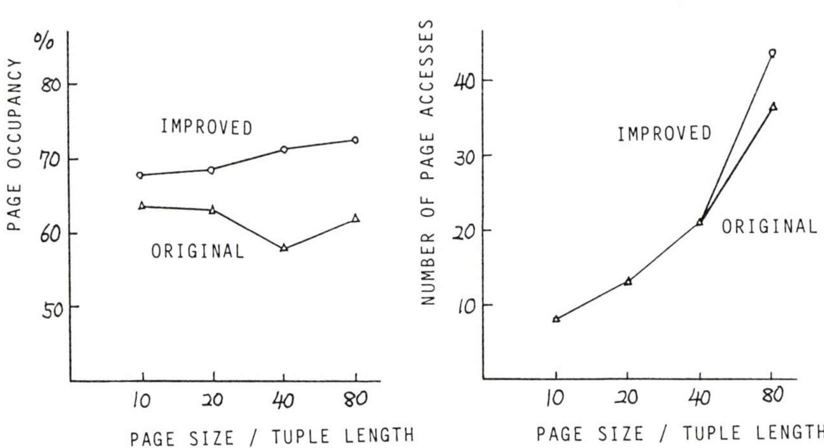

Fig. 4. RESULTS OF THE SIMULATION STUDY

where number of tuples	: 1390
number of attributes	: 4
average numbers of duplicated attribute values	: 1 - 30

Table 1. A COMPARISON OF TEXT SEARCH TECHNIQUES

	PARALLEL COMPARATORS	CELLULAR COMPARATORS	FINITE STATE MACHINES
HARDWARE	A SMALL NUMBER BUT A VARIETY OF CIRCUITS: A SHIFT REGISTER, KEY REGISTERS, COMPARATORS, ETC.	A LARGE NUMBER OF SIMPLE COMPARISON CELLS THAT COMPARE ONE CHARACTER AT A TIME.	A LARGE CAPACITY RAM TO STORE A TABLE AND FEW SIMPLE LOGIC CIRCUITS.
FUNCTIONS	DIFFICULTY IN SUPORTING VARIABLE-LENGTH "DON'T CARE"	DIFFICULTY IN SUPORTING MULTIPLE-KEY SEARCH	DEPENDENT ON TABLE CONSTRUCTION ALGORITHMS
FLEXIBILITY	MAXIMUM NUMBER AND MAXIMUM LENGTH OF SEARCH KEYS DEPEND ON THE HARDWARE STRUCTURE.	DYNAMIC ORGANIZATION OF CONNECTIONS BETWEEN CELLS IS DIFFICULT.	ONLY TOTAL LENGTH OF SEARCH KEYS IS LIMITED BY THE SIZE OF THE TABLE.

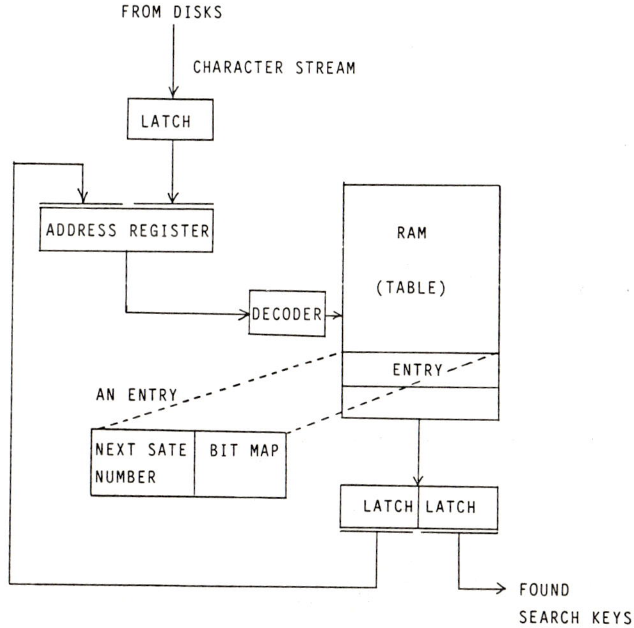

Fig. 5. THE HARDWARE STRUCTURE FOR TEXT SEARCH

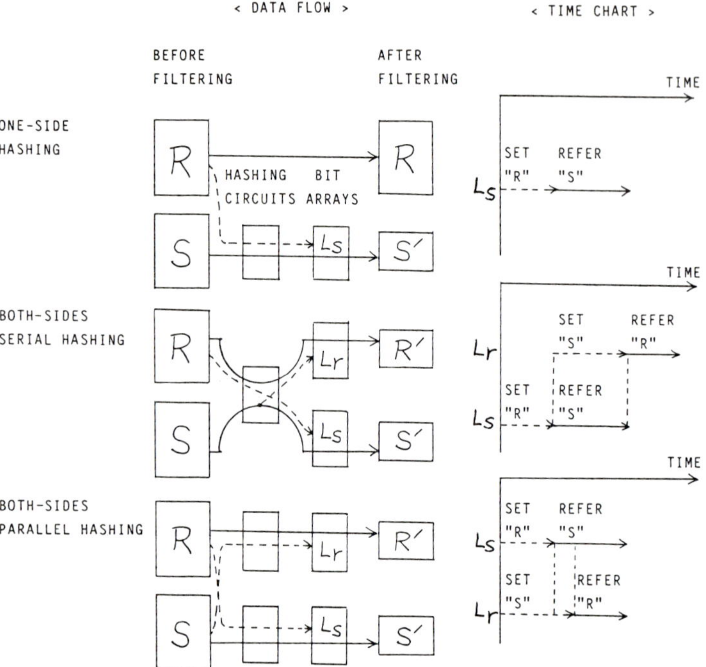

Fig. 6. FILTERING TECHNIQUES

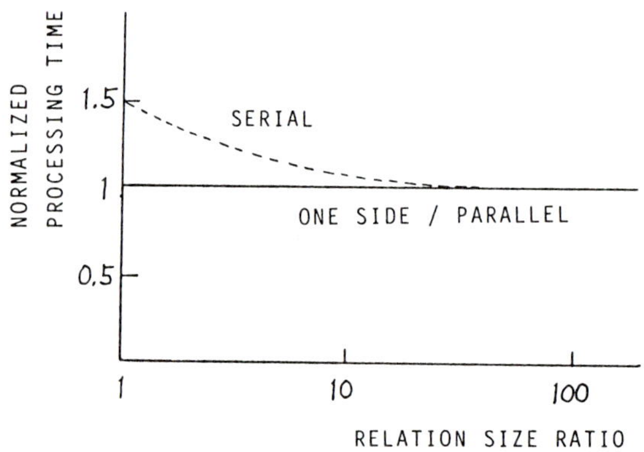

Fig. 7. PROCESSING TIMES WITH FILTERING TECHNIQUES

(where the speed of setting the bit array is equal to the reference speed.)

Table 2. ESTIMATION MODELS

	MODEL A	MODEL B
DESCRIPTION IN A SQL LIKE LANGUAGE	SELECT R.A FROM R WHERE R.B IS LIKE "%xxx%" OR "%yyy%" OR ...	SELECT S.A, T.D FROM S, T WHERE S.B=T.E AND S.C>xxxxx AND T.E>yyyyy
NUMBER OF RELATIONS	1	2
NUMBER OF TUPLES IN EACH RELATION	200,000	1,000,000
AVERAGE TUPLE LENGTH	2000(B)	200(B)
NUMBER OF TUPLES AFTER SELECTION	2,000	100,000
NUMBER OF OUTPUT TUPLES	2,000	10,000

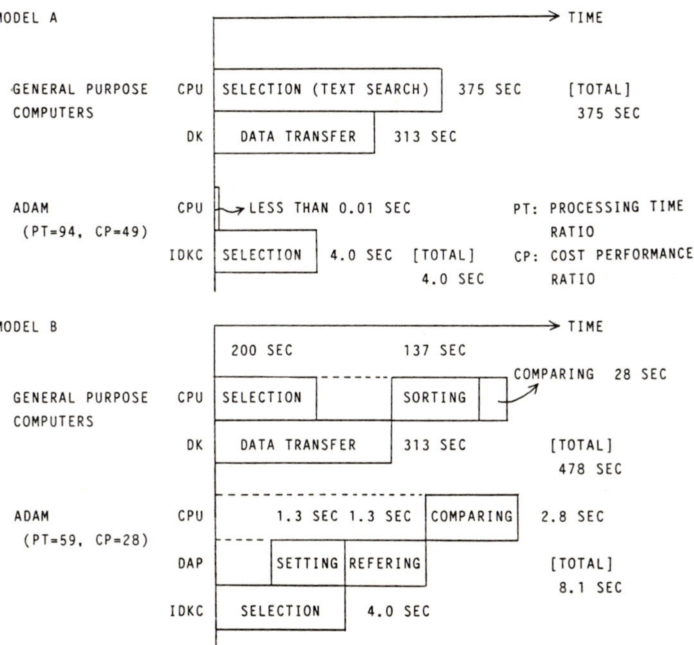

Fig. 8. PERFORMANCE AND COST OF TWO MACHINES

DESIGN AND IMPLEMENTATION OF SABRE
A DEDUCTIVE AND PARALLEL DATABASE MACHINE

Georges Gardarin, Fabrice Pasquer
INRIA and University of PARIS.VI
78153 LE CHESNAY Cedex, FRANCE

ABSTRACT

This paper reports on the design and architecture of the SABRE parallel database machine. It also presents a first design of the rule management functions which are currently being added to SABRE; with such an enhancement, the system will be a fully deductive MIMD knowledge machine offering among others a conversational knowledge manipulation language based on production rules and QUEL or SQL like queries. The main advantages of the system will be the power of the language to express problems, the generality of the approach and the efficiency of the machine.

INTRODUCTION

Most of the relational database systems entail performance problems [Dewitt83]. They are both I/O and CPU bounded. One direction of performance improvement is to use parallelism. Several database machine architectures have been proposed to perform parallelism, including SIMD, MISD and MIMD machines. Sabre intends to be a MIMD machine performing I/O in parallel on several disks and using pipelined specialized processors to share the query processing tasks. In the first part of this paper, we present the evolution and the current state of the Sabre project.

Relational database systems also miss integrated inference capabilities. Several approaches to deductive databases have been studied [Gallaire84]. Most of them are based on a more or less tight coupling of PROLOG to an existing relational DBMS, performing either compilation of Horn clauses into relational queries before execution, or interpretation of the clauses at execution time [Nicolas85]. An other approach [Stonebraker84] consists in extending the QUEL language with recursive commands. In the second part of this paper, we present an intermediate approach based on the addition of a rule definition command to the non procedural data manipulation language of SABRE. The rules are general production rules with variables in which the condition and action parts are expressed in a specific tuple relational calculus. Although the integrated fact and rule manipulation language we propose has some common features with PROLOG, it does not present the drawbacks of PROLOG to access databases and is different in many ways: (i) It is an extension of QUEL with a powerful rule definition command; (ii) it uses tuple variables which are

NATO ASI Series, Vol. F 24
Database Machines. Edited by A.K. Sood and A.H. Qureshi

easier and more efficient to manipulate than domain variables; (iii) it includes the concept of transaction; (iv) production rules inside a rule definition command are not ordered giving the system the ability to find the best order of operations; (v) the input/output of transaction is powerfully managed using forms and report generation; (vi) aggregate functions and more generally complex data type operations are allowed.

In the last part of the paper, we introduce the compilation technique which is currently implemented inside the SABRE system to optimize in a uniform way rule and query execution. This compilation technique is based on predicate transition nets and is presented in more detailled in [Gardarin85].

SABRE : A PARALLEL DATABASE MACHINE

Sabre project objectives

The Sabre project was initiated in 1981 at INRIA, in cooperation with the University of PARIS.VI. At that time, the objectives of the project were the following :

(1) To develop an extendible and portable relational database manager able to run on classical machines and/or on specific database computers.

(2) To improve response time in comparison with classical relational database systems running on similar configurations.

(3) To allow different groups of users to define and query various views of a database containing real or virtual relations.

(4) To guarantee the database integrity when data are updated simultaneously by concurrent transactions or when erroneous updates occur.

Today (May 1985), the objectives (1),(3) and (4) have more or less been achieved [Gardarin84 ,Simon84] while we are still working on objective (2). This second objective, which is probably the most difficult to realize, led us to develop a new access path organization based on predicate trees [Valduriez84] which is currently under evaluation. Also, to achieve this second objective, we are developing a parallel version of Sabre which will, in its first version, encompass two disks or more performing I/O in parallel and two processors or more performing data operations (i.e. selection, join and sort...) in parallel. We envision the parallel version of Sabre for the end of 1986.

Although all the objectives of Sabre have not yet been achieved (e.g. the parallel version of Sabre is still in progress), we are already working on two new objectives :

(5) To enhance the deductive functionalities of Sabre in such a way that it could become a usefull tool for solving decision oriented problems.

(6) To extend the data types offered by the system towards user defined abstract domains.

In our view, these two supplementary objectives with the previous four objectives will lead us towards a fifth generation database management system [GardGel84], that is a DBMS supporting rules and complex data types in an efficient way.

Sabre functional architecture

We distinguish the functional architecture of Sabre which is unique at a time (however, the functional architecture has evolved during the live of the project) from the operational architectures of the various implemented versions of Sabre.

The current functional architecture is composed of three layers of machines, going from the end-users to the disk units:
(1) The interface machine composes the external layer. It is responsible for the dialogue with the end-users and the parsing of the user requests into internal messages constituting an application protocol called the data manipulation protocol. Several types of user interfaces can be offered. For the time being, it includes a flexible relational calculus called FABRE which is a super-set of both QUEL and SQL, a query by form language and also a PASCAL/R like interface. In the case of a database machine configuration, the interface machine is normally implemented on the host computer.
(2) The assertional machine which constitutes the intermediate layer of the system performs the evaluation of relational tuple calculus assertions in terms of an extended relational algebra. This machine also includes integrity, view and security management.
(3) The algebraic machine which is the most internal layer carries out the relational algebra operations as fast as possible. To supply this function, it manages the access path model based on predicate trees, uses a cache memory and implements efficient join [Valduriez83] and filtering algorithms [Gardarin84]. In addition, the algebraic machine performs the physical controls, that is concurrency and reliability controls.

Each machine is divided into functional processors which are generally implemented as software modules. While the interface machine is composed of a unique processor, the assertional machine includes three processors :
(1) The integrity processor performs the integrity control using a specific algorithm [Simon84].
(2) The view and authorization processor carries out the view to database mapping and the access authorization controls.
(3) The request evaluation processor performs an optimized decomposition of each request in a tree of relational algebra operations.
Finally, the algebraic machine is divided into six functional processors :
(1) The relation access processor manages the access paths to a relation, that is the predicate tree associated with each non sequential relation and also clustered indexes.

(2) The join, sort and aggregate processor performs join, sort and compute aggregate functions using specific algorithms [Valduriez83].
(3) The localization and storage processor allocates physical space on disk to store logical subsets of a relation and retrieves these logical subsets on disks from logical addresses.
(4) The concurrency control and recovery processor carries out concurrency control using two phase locking and performs reliability control using shadow page and two phase commit methods.
(5) The filtering processor performs selection, insertion and deletion of tuples in a disk partition which is a fixed size bucket containing tuples stored sequentially.
(6) The cache memory processor is responsible for managing the random-access memory which contains temporary and intermediate results of user operations; this memory is extended to disk if not enough RAM is available.

In summary, the functional architecture of Sabre is portrayed figure 1. Let us point out that the machines and processors defined are virtual in the sense that they correspond to functions; thus in non parallel versions of Sabre, they are all implemented on a unique real processor.

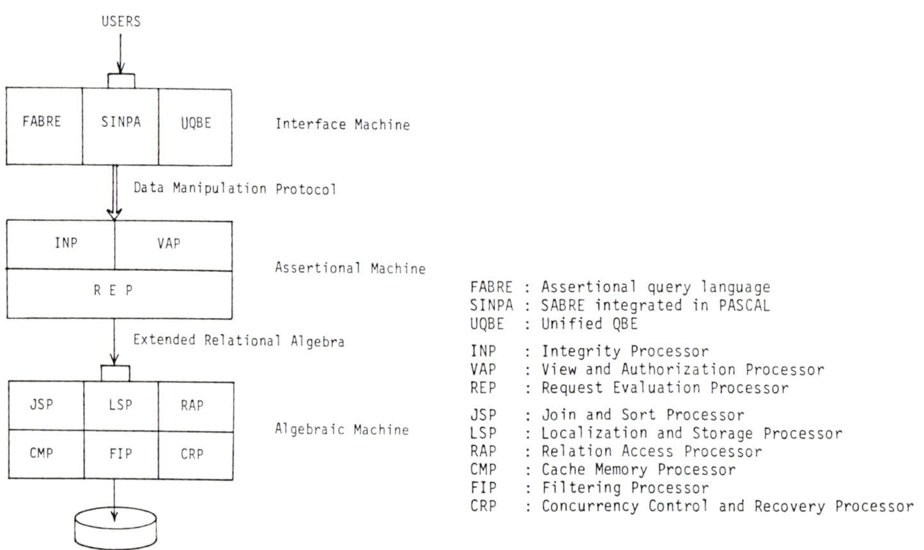

Figure 1 : The functional architecture of Sabre

Sabre non-parallel operational architecture

An operational architecture is associated with each

implemented version of Sabre. The first operational architecture of Sabre was developed on MULTICS. All the functional machines and processors were implemented in PASCAL on a unique real processor. The system was then transported to a French multi-microprocessor called the SM90 and running UNIX. It is currently working on a single 68000 processor, but has been designed to support up to sixteen 68000 processors. The algebraic and assertional machines of Sabre are implemented as a UNIX process while an interface machine is associated with each user process. The two processes communicate through pipes. The Sabre system does not use the UNIX file system, but rather its own way of storing tuples according to predicate trees [Valduriez84]. We are currently experimenting with this prototype and extending it to support several processors working in parallel, as stated below.

The first parallel operational architecture of Sabre

Although we envision a highly parallel version of Sabre [Gardarin83], we restricted the first parallel prototype to three processors and two disks. The physical configuration of the machine supporting this first parallel version is represented in figure 2.

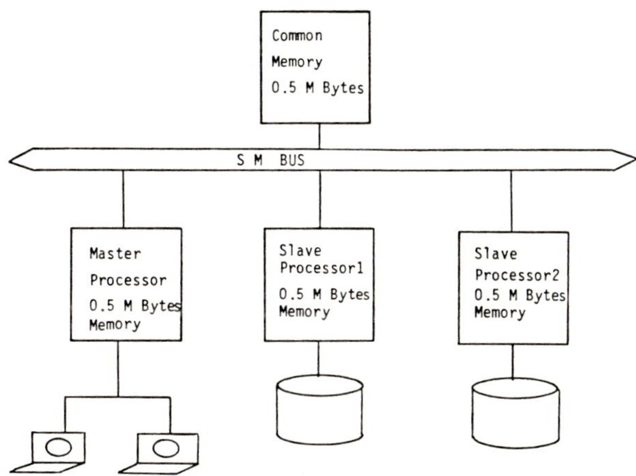

Figure 2 : The Sabre first parallel operational architecture

The master processor executes the UNIX system on top of which runs the assertional machine of Sabre. The two slave processors control a disk unit and run a copy of the algebraic machine of Sabre. The communications between the master and the slaves are performed as I/O.

This first parallel version of Sabre which is currently being developed illustrates two ways of using parallelism [Gardarin83]. On the one hand, vertical parallelism between the master and a slave allows the system to perform inter-request parallelism; it allows the system to execute one request on the master processor while another is performed by the two slaves. Such a parallelism is usefull for different concurrent transactions. On the other hand, horizontal parallelism between the two slaves leads to intra request parallelism; it reduces the I/O time necessary to process a request. Of course, an effective time reduction requires that the data be distributed on the two disks in a uniform way for all queries. For the time being, we plan to use at first a random placement strategy to assign a record to a disk unit.

The implementation of the parallel version of Sabre is currently at the detailled design and evaluation stage. We intend to use the prototype as a test-bed for performance measurements and comparisons of various disk allocation strategies.

The fully parallel operational architecture

Sabre was designed to support a fully MIMD architecture. In that view, the algebraic and the assertional machines would be run by two highly parallel computers. Each logical processor of the functional architecture would be mapped on a class of parallel processors. That would allow us to utilize parallel algorithms for each function of the system; for example, the join algorithms would be run by several cooperating processors of the join class. In addition, the interface machines would be deported on specific personal computers which would communicate with the assertional machine using the data manipulation protocol. The communications between an interface computer and an assertional one would be performed through a local network whereas the communications between an assertional computer and an algebraic one would be through a common memory at very high speed. This fully MIMD architecture is portrayed in figure 3.

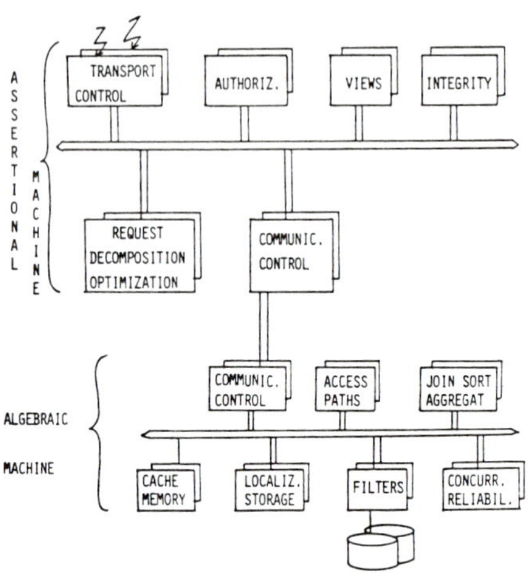

Figure 3 : The fully MIMD architecture of SABRE

THE RULE DEFINITION FACILITIES

Motivations

In its most advanced version, Sabre is a parallel relational database machine running a rather classical (but efficient) relational database management system. As such, it allows the user to store facts in the database and to retrieve them using complex first order logic formulas. A fact is composed of a set of attributes of type integer, real or text. Texts are of variable length but limited to a maximum size of 255 characters.

Looking from a functional point of view, one main limitations of Sabre appears to be the inability of the machine to help in problem solving where some basic inference mechanisms are necessary; the only inference Sabre is able to do is the matching of a formula with a fact using the join or selection operations : it is insufficient to solve most of the decision oriented problems. In the sequel, we intend to introduce basic features to leave out this limitation. These features consist in adding rule management facilities to the system. To motivate and illustrate this new facilities, let us first introduce two problem examples.

The first problem is the very classical ancestor computation problem. We assume here that an implemented relation gives the first generation ascendants of a set of persons :

PARENT(Ascendant, Descendant)

The problem is simply to compute the ancestors of "Toto".

The second problem is a less classical but more difficult electrical circuit problem. Let us assume a relational database composed of a unique relation describing a set of electricity circuits as follows :

CIRCUIT (Name, Wireid, Origin, Extremity, Impedance)

Name is the name of a given circuit; Wireid is a number identifying a given wire in a given circuit; the origin and extremity of that wire are given by the two corresponding attributes while its impedance is defined by the last attribute. For example, <Example,1,A,B,10+5i> is a tuple of the circuit portrayed in figure 4.

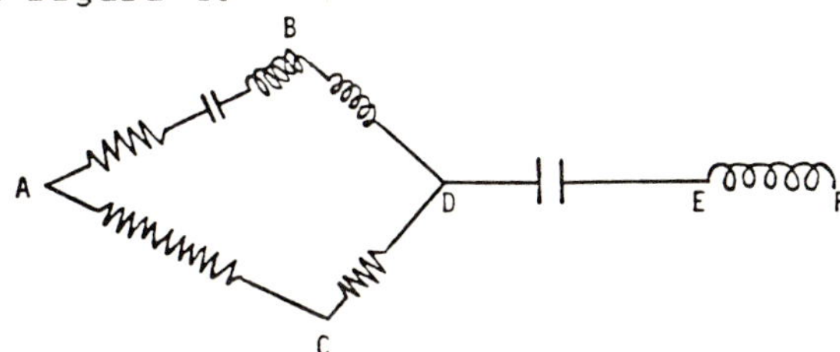

Figure 4 : An example of a circuit

The key of the relation CIRCUIT is the couple of attributes <Name, Wireid>. A typical problem will consist of computing the impedance of a given circuit. For simplicity, we shall assume that only the parallel and serial transformations are sufficient to compute the impedances of all the circuits. Let us recall that these rules consist in replacing two serial wires of impedance Z1 and Z2 by a unique one of impedance Z1 + Z2 and two parallel wires of impedance Z1 and Z2 by a unique one of impedance (Z1*Z2/Z1+Z2).

To supply a useful tool to solve the previous problems, we intend to enrich the present DML of Sabre with a new command allowing the user to declare general knowledge rules. Knowledge will be declared using a set of production rules such as the ancestor generation rules or the serial and parallel transformation rules. The queries (and updates) will be expressed with the current Sabre DML and will refer either to base relation or to derived relation computed using knowledge rules.

Rules could be defined using Horn clauses. However, Horn clauses are often difficult to use and even insufficient to modelize problems as the second one presented above. However, the semantic of non Horn databases is not well understood [Reiter78]. To avoid ambiguity and contradiction with the closed world assumption, we utilize production rules [Nilsson82] of a specific form as defined below.

Tuple relational calculus

The basis of the present Sabre DML is a non function free tuple predicate calculus. We assume here that first order logic is well understood. The syntax of the logic is defined as follows :
(1) A term is defined recursively as a constant, a variable or an n-ary function whose arguments are terms.
(2) An atomic formula is defined as an m-ary predicate whose arguments are terms.
(3) Well-formed formulas (or simply formulas) are defined recursively as follows : atomic formulas are formulas; if F1 and F2 are formulas, then NOT F1, F1 AND F2, F1 OR F2 are formulas; we shall also use formulas of the form F1 -> F2 but only as rules (see below);
For simplicity, we do not use quantifiers : all our formulas are supposed to be in a form where existentially quantified variables have been replaced by Skolem constants or functions and where all remaining variables are implicitly universally quantified.

Some particularities and the interpretation of the logic we utilize are defined below :
(1) A constant is any tuple of finite dimension constructed with integer, real or character strings.
(2) A variable ranges on a finite sorted set of constants having a similar structure, (i.e. an initial or a derived relation).
(3) A predicate is :
- either a relation predicate of the form R(x) which

explicitely defines a variable x onto the tuples of a relation R;
- or a comparison predicate of one of the forms f(x) op g(x), f(x) op constante, where x is a variable, f and g are functions and op is a logical comparator chosen among {=, <, <=, >, >=, <>}.
(4) Functions are chosen among the following set :
(a) Any attribute A defined a function denoted x.A when applied to variable x (i.e projection).
(b) Any arithmetic operator is a function.
(c) There exists a tuple construction function which allows us to build up constants (i.e. tuples) by concatenation; this function is simply denoted c1,c2 to built a new constant by concatenation of c1 and c2.
(d) There exists a set of built in functions count(x), sum(x), min(x), max(x), avg(x) which respectively give the count, the sum , the minimum, the maximum and the average of constants x satisfying the formula in which the function appears.

Rule definition command

Let us first define precisely what type of rules are allowed. A rule is a formula of the form :

Positive formula -> Action formula

where a positive formula is a formula without negative literals and an action formula is a formula without OR and without comparison predicates. Therefore, all accepted rules are of the form (in extended BNF) :
Predicate [{AND/OR} Predicate]... -> [NOT] Relation-predicate [AND [NOT] Relation-predicate]...
Such rules are not ambiguous although not in Horn clause form. The non ambiguous interpretation of a rule is as a production rule which is executed up to saturation for each successive instantiations of the variables by tuples appearing in the database satisfying the positive formula; an execution consists of deleting tuples appearing in the action formula as arguments of negative literals and inserting tuples which appear as arguments of positive literals.

To keep a well understood database semantic , we should restrict ourselves to rules having only one positive litteral in the action formula. Thus, a rule could be replaced by a set of Horn clauses whose semantic is well understood. However, our resolution algorithm will work for general rules as defined.

Let us now give some examples of rules. The following rule defines the Ancestor relation after initializing it with the Parent relation defined above :

```
 Parent(X) and Ancestor(Y) and X.Descendant = Y. Ascendant ->
       Ancestor(X.Ascendant,Y.Descendant)
```

The next rule defines the parallel transformation of an electricity circuit using a wire relation which is a copy of the Circuit relation defined above :

```
Wire(X)  and  Wire(Y) and X.origin = Y.origin and X.Extremity =
Y.Extremity and X.Wireid <> Y.Wireid and X.Name = Y.Name ->
```

NOT Wire(X) and NOT Wire(Y) AND Wire(X.Name, X.Wireid, X.Origin, X.Extremity, (X.Impedance * Y.Impedance) / (X.Impedance + Y.Impedance))

Rules are given to the system using a specific command KNOW whose syntax is :
KNOW rule [,rule]... ;
The full definition of the rules necessary to solve the ancestor problem can be made as follows :

```
KNOW
 Parent(X) -> Ancestor(X),
 Parent(X) AND Ancestor(Y) AND X.Descendant = Y. Ascendant ->
        Ancestor(X.Ascendant,Y.Descendant) ;
```

The full definition of the set of rules necessary to solve the electrical circuit problem is :

```
KNOW
 Circuit(X) -> Wire(X),

Wire(X) AND Wire(Y) AND X.origin = Y.origin AND X.Extremity =
Y.Extremity AND X.Wireid <> Y.Wireid AND X.name = Y.name ->
NOT Wire(X) AND NOT Wire(Y) AND Wire(X.Name, X.Wireid,
X.Origin, X.Extremity, (X.Impedance * Y.Impedance) /
(X.Impedance + Y.Impedance)) ,

Wire(X) AND Wire(Y) AND COUNT(X) = 1 AND COUNT(Y) = 1 AND
X.Extremity = Y.Origin AND X.Name = Y.Name ->
NOT Wire(X) AND NOT Wire(Y) and Wire(X.Name, X.Wireid,
X.Origin, Y.Extremity, X.Impedance+Y.Impedance);
```

Of course, it is not sure that a set of rules is consistent. Also, the effect of a set of rules is a priori not independent of the order in which rules are applied. We shall summarize in the next section a technique to resolve query which will reject inconsistent rules and assertional queries whose answer are rule order dependent. This technique has been developped in more details in [Gardarin85].

<u>Query definition</u>

The query language is the existing query language of SABRE. It is a language based on a flexible syntax [Pasquer85] whose semantic is the tuple relational calculus defined above. For simplicity, we shall use a QUEL like syntax. Therefore, the following queries are expressed as follows :

(Q1) Give the ancestors of Toto :

```
Range of A is Ancestor;
Retrieve A.* where A.descendant = "Toto";
```

(Q2) Give the impedance of the circuit example :

```
Range of W is Wire;
Retrieve W.Impedance where W.Name = "Example";
```

A SUMMARY OF THE INFERENCE TECHNIQUE

Problem

One of the most difficult problem is the compilation of queries involving recursive rules. Several elegant and may be efficient solutions to that problem have been proposed [Chang81, Minker83, MarquePucheu83, Henschen84, Ullman85, Lozinski85]. However, most of the proposed solutions are based on backward chaining interpretation or compilation using conditions to cut the cycles. Moreover, no solution is applicable to non Horn clauses, except may be the capture rule approach of [Ullman85]. Therefore, we need a more general technique to compile our general production rules into a relational algebra extended with fixed point operations, such as transitive closure. This technique which was introduced in [Gardarin85] is summarized in the sequel.

Predicate Transition Net

Our inference technique for solving queries on derived relations is based on predicate transition nets. The notion of predicate transition net (PrTN) derives from the well-known Petri nets [Genrich81]. They have been shown to be a powerful tool for modeling production rules [Giordano85]. The main differences with Petri nets consist of the facts that tokens are structured objects carrying values similar to database tuples, and furthermore, that transition firing can be controlled by imposing conditions on the token values. It is also important to point out that in our view two tokens of equal values which are in the same place are automaticaly merged in a single token, that is double tuples in a same place do not appear when firing transitions . A formal definition of PrTN can be found in [Giordano85].

To construct a PrTN from a set of rules, we use the following method. Any relation P on which a relation- predicate P is defined in the set of rules is modeled by a unique place P. Each rule is modeled by a transition t. An arc connects a place P to a transition t iff a relation-predicate P appears as a premisse (i.e in the left formula) of t; such an arc is labeled by the formal sum of symbols appearing as arguments in the left instance of P (a unique symbol if P appears only once). A positive arc connects a transition t to a place P iff P appears in the conclusion (i.e. the right formula) of t; such an arc is labelled by the sum (+) of the symbols appearing as arguments in each right instance of P. A negative arc connects a transition t to a place P iff NOT P appears in the conclusion (i.e. the right formula) of t; such an arc is labelled by the opposite of the sum (-) of symbols appearing as arguments in each right instance of P. In addition, for each arc going from a place to a transition labelled by x, we add a symetrical arc going from the transition to the place also labelled by x; this displays the fact that in general the firing of a transition which represents the execution of a rule does not remove the tuple from the relation. To simplify net drawing, two reverse arcs with the same label may be portrayed by a unique arc with an arrow in both directions. A transition is controlled by a condition which is the formula composed of the comparison predicates appearing in the premisses of the corresponding rule.

Figure 5 portrays the PrTN which models the ancestor rules while figure 6 portrays the PrTN which models the impedance computation rules.

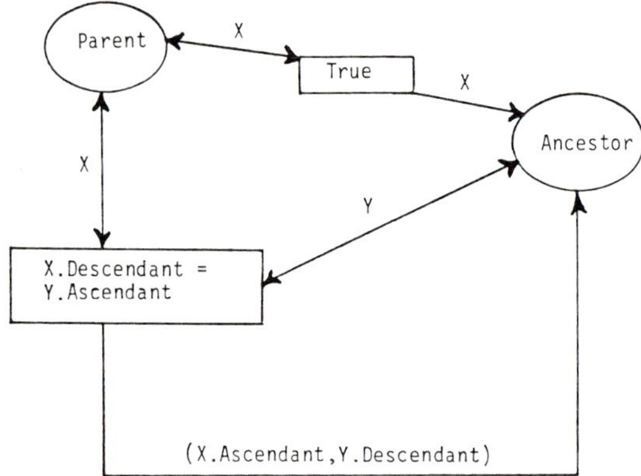

Figure 5 : PrTN for the ancestor rules

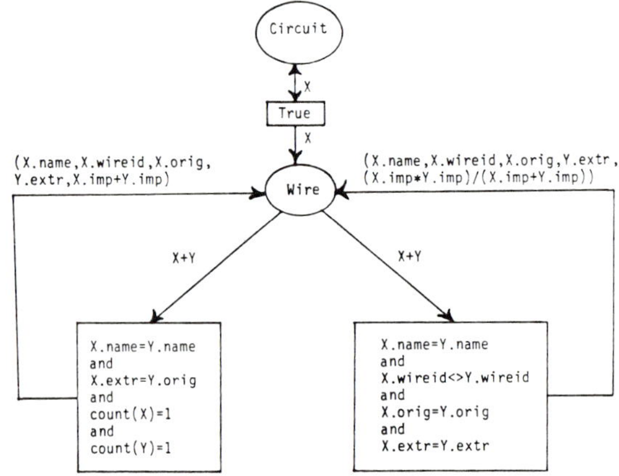

Figure 6 : PrTN for the Impedance computation rules

In our context, an initial marking is generated on a PrTN by puting marks in the base relation places corresponding to these relation tuples. Inference is performed using forward chaining by firing transitions. Inference using backward chaining can be modeled by PrTN transformations as described in [Gardarin85].

Query and rule compilation in SABRE

When the SABRE server(i.e. the assertional machine) receives a query referencing one derived relation (for example, the ancestor relation), it first isolates the set of pertinent rules to evaluate the query. Using this rules, the assertional machine built an internal representation of the predicate transition net which allows the system to ellaborate the query answer using a straightforward forward chaining. This net is checked for consistency using the properties presented in [Gardarin85]. If the net is consistent, we then proceed to the optimization step.

The next step of the compilation is then the optimization of the net. This is performed by a serie of transformations which are defined in [Gardarin85]. The main transformations are the reduction of circuits in the net to loops involving a single node and the move of restriction predicates next to the base relations. These transformations which are only possible under complex conditions give a simple heuristic to get an optimized net in the sense that, when executed, the net will generate a minimum amount of data to get the query answer.

The final step of the query compilation consists in transforming the optimized net in a sequence of extended relational algebra operations. These operations are executed by the algebraic machine of SABRE. Transitions with input arcs coming from one place and output arcs going to another different place are transformed in a selection. Transitions with input arcs coming from two or more places and output arcs going to other places are transformed in join operations. Union and differences are also necessary according to the valuation and the number of arcs going out from transition to places. Finally, loops are transformed in a fixed point operator which is an extension of the well known transitive closure operation. For more details, the reader should refer to [Gardarin85].

CONCLUSION

In this paper, we give an overview of the SABRE parallel and deductive database machine. It is important to see that building such a machine is a huge task that we perform step by step. The first step was the design and implementation of a layered, modular and portable relational DBMS which is now fully operational. The second step is the introduction of parallelism in the system. Although this task is more difficult than expected, it is in good progress. The last step is the support of rules by the machine. The main algorithms have been designed. Their implementation will requires significant enhancement of the assertional machine of SABRE and the adjunction of an efficient fixed point operator to the algebraic machine of SABRE. Finally, SABRE should be an efficient and powerful tool for building management and expert system oriented applications.

REFERENCES

| CHANG 81 | Chang C. L. "On evalutation of queries containing derived relations in a relational data base", Edited by H.Gallaire, H. Minker and J.M Nicolas, Vol.1, Penum Press, New York.

| DEWITT 83 | Dewitt D. , Bitton D., Turbyfill C. "Benchmarking Database Systems : a Systemactic Approach" 9th Very Large Data Bases, Florence Sept. 1083.

| GALLAIRE 84 | Gallaire H., Mincker J., Nicolas J.M. "Logic and database : a deductive approach" ACM Computing Surveys V 16, N 12 June 1984.

| GARDARIN 83 | G. Gardarin, P. Bernadat, N. Temmerman, P. Valduriez, Y. Viemont "Design of a multiprocessor relational database system" IFIP Conference 1983, Paris, September 1983.

| GARDARIN 84 | G.Gardarin, P. Faudemay, P. Valduriez, Y. Viemont "The content adressable page manager of Sabre" Rapport INRIA, ref FMG I 003, Rocquencourt, January 84.

| GARDARIN 85 | G. Gardarin, C. de Maindreville, D. Mermet "Extending a relational DBMS towards a KBMS : a first approach" Knowledge Base Management Systems Workshop, Crête, June 1985.

[GARDGEL 84 | G. Gardarin, E. Gelenbe Ed. "New applications of database" Book, Academic Press, 1984.

| GENRICH 81 | Genrich and Lautenbach "System modelling with high-level Petri nets" Theoretical Comp. Science 13, p. 109-136, 1981.

| GIORDANA 85 | Giordana, Saita "Modelling production rules by means of predicate transition networks", Information Sciences, Vol. 35, Nr 1,1985.

| HENSCHEN 84 | Henschen L., Naqvi S. "On compiling queries in recursive first order database",JACM, Vol. 31, Nr 1, Janvier 1984.

| LOZINSKII 85 | Lozinskii E. "Inference by generating and structuring of deductive data bases" To appear in Proc. of VLDB'85, Stockholm.

|MARQUE PUCHEU 83 | G. Marque-Pucheu, J. Martin-Gallausiaux, G. Jomier "Interfacing Prolog and Relational Data Base Management Systems" in New Applications of Data Bases, G. Gardarin and E. Gelenbe Ed., Academic Press, 1984.

|MINKER 83 | J. Minker "On recursive axioms in deductive data bases", Information Systems 8, 1983.

| NICOLAS 85 | J. M. Nicolas "On deductive Databases" Knowledge Base Management Systems Workshop, Crête, June 1985.

| NILSSON 82| J.N. Nilsson "Principles of artificial intelligence" Book, Spring Verlag,1982.

| PASQUER 85 | Pasquer F. "Conception et réalisation d'un langage de manipulation de données à syntaxe libre", Thèse de 3°cycle, Université de Paris VI.

|REITER 78 | "On closed world databases", in Logic and Data Bases, Gallaire H. and J. Minker, Ed. Plenum, New York.

| SIMON 84 | E. Simon, P. Valduriez "Design and implementation of an extendible integrity subsystem" ACM SIGMOD Conference, Boston, June1984.

| STONEBRAKER 84 | M. Stonebraker "Adding Semantic Knowledge to a Relational Database System", Tutorial, 10 th VLDB 1984, Singapour.

| ULLMAN 85 | J. Ullman "Implementation of logical query languages for databases", ACM-SIGMOD 85, Austin, Texas, to appear in TODS.

| VALDURIEZ 83 | P. Valduriez, G. Gardarin "Join and semi-join algorithms for a multiprocessor Database machine" INRIA Report 1983, Also in ACM Transactions on Database Systems, V9, N1, March 1984, pp. 133-161.

| VALDURIEZ 84 | P. Valduriez, Y. Viemont "A multikey hasching scheme using predicate trees", ACM-SIGMOD, Boston, June 1984, SIGMOD Record Volume 14, N2, p. 107-114.

INTRODUCTION TO

A MATHEMATICAL FOUNDATION FOR SYSTEMS DEVELOPMENT

A Hypermodel Syntax for Precision Modeling of Arbitrarily Complex Systems

D. L. CHILDS
INTEGRATED INFORMATION SYSTEMS
1401 Avondale Avenue, Ann Arbor, MI 48103

ABSTRACT

OBJECTIVE: ***Establish a foundation for system development tools in order to provide reliability and design freedom in future systems architecture.***

PROBLEM: ***Reliability and design freedom are dependent on the ability of designers to control the access, manipulation, transformation and stability of the structural components of the system architecture.***

APPROACH: ***For the specification of development tools, establish a formal environment for modeling structurally dependent components of systems architecture.***

STRUCTURE is defined as having two components: *elements* and the way in which the elements are *organized*. Structures pervade system architectures in: languages, applications, compilers, operating systems, data representations, communications, storage devices, system models, *etc*.. Subtle differences in structural organizations can have a dramatic effect on both the behavior and capabilities of a parent system. Understanding the organization of structures, their differences, similarities and interrelationships, is crucial to the incorporation of reliability and design freedom in system architectures.

The motivation for this paper is to acknowledge and address the growing concern that reliable complex computer systems can not be rigorously analyzed, specified, designed, nor implemented without a more formal means for representing implementation details and a better means for communicating ideas at all levels.

One reason for this concern is that currently available mathematical notation does not adequately capture subtleties of a structure's organization, any more than "3" captures the significance of "π". The second reason is the lack of a formal homogeneous environment for modeling heterogeneous components of a complex system when the components themselves are models. The third, and most important reason, is that there is no uniform cohesive environment that allows general communication between managers at one end of the continuum and implementation detail for designers at the other end of the continuum!

This paper will focus on resolving all three of these issues. The approach is to introduce the concept of a **Function Space Architecture** as a new methodology to system design. The basic *architectural unit* of this new methodology is a **Function Space** which can provide as much or as little detail as a specific instance requires. Coverage will include: the **Function Space** as a unit of architecture for general communication and design detail; **Structure Independent Architectures** as an architectural design guide for reliable and productive systems; the **Hypermodel** to provide the Function Space continuum with explosive resolution; and **Extended Set Notation** to provide generality and rigor to the concept of a Hypermodel.

Though the following paper, by necessity, involves on some arcane syntactic issues of set theory (covered mostly in the Appendix), the reader familiar with Relational concepts should have little difficulty appreciating the thesis that precise control of structural properties is essential to the analysis, specification, design, and implementation of complex systems.

NATO ASI Series, Vol. F 24
Database Machines. Edited by A.K. Sood and A.H. Qureshi

1.0 INTRODUCTION

This paper is designed to lay the foundation for a series of subsequent papers [Ch86a-f], that develop the concept of a *Hypermodel* for the analysis, specification, design and implementation of arbitrarily complex, yet highly reliable, system architectures. Toward that end, this paper has two primary objectives. The first is to establish the justification for the utility of a Hypermodel, and the second is to establish the formal mathematical notation needed to support the requirements of a Hypermodel. The main body of the paper will be directed toward the first objective, while the second is contained in the appendix.

Every computer program, from the simplest to the most complex application, is a modeling of some requirement by a computer-based environment. In order to develop reliable systems we need a modeling environment for precision evaluation of the *requirements*, the *computer-based environment*, and the *mapping* between them. Thus we need a modeling environment for precision evaluation of models, in other words a **Hypermodel**, for evaluating families of program alternatives. Since the entities being modeled by a Hypermodel have structurally dependent components, the utility of a Hypermodel depends directly on its ability to formally capture structure and to provide reliable systems through modeling precision. It may not be immediately obvious, to all readers, why mathematically well-defined structures at the most basic level of system support, are crucial to the reliability and consistency of system design objectives. Hopefully, the presentation that follows will make this position clear. The success of this paper depends solely on how much sense the following sentence makes after the reader has concluded this paper: **To achieve future system design objectives *structure must be captured as a mathematical operand!***

2.0 STRUCTURE

STRUCTURE is defined as having two components: *elements* and the way in which the elements are *organized*. *Structure* includes any organized relationship of: bits, bytes, data, records, files, discs, programs, requirements, applications or any other logical or physical organization of information. Structure, in one form or an other, pervades computer related activities in: languages, applications, compilers, operating systems, data representations, communications, storage devices, system models, *etc.*. Subtle differences in structural organizations can have a dramatic effect on both the behavior and the capabilities of a system:

Structures used in stating problems affect the way the problem is solved.
Structures used in designs affect the way the designs are implemented.
Structures used for data affect the way the data is accessed.
Structures used in programs affect the way the programs behave.
Structures used in secondary storage affect overall system performance.

We either control the structures, or the structures will control us. The key to reliable and productive systems is being able to control, with precision, all structure related activity (access, relocation, modification and transformation) from the initial requirement specification all the way to the final byte of the implementation code. The earlier 'structural flaws' are caught, the less work has to be undone and the more sound is the overall design direction. Pouring concrete is easy, unpouring it is not so easy, and changing its shape after it sets is most difficult.

Understanding the organization of structures, their differences, similarities and interrelationships, is crucial to the incorporation of reliability and flexibility in system architectures.

As in any architecture, the underlying structure provides stability. Software architectures are no different. The reliability or the inconsistency of system behavior is directly attributable to the interaction of the underlying structures. Therefore, a most important concern is structure stability, yet an essential component missing from all current system designs is adequate structure control.

2.1 STRUCTURE MODELING

It has long been recognized by those closest to the subject that reliable, productive software and reliable, productive system architectures can not be achieved without the addition of improved mathematical models. These models must be able to precisely capture all pertinent information regarding the *logical requirement specifications*, the *physical implementation environment*, and the comparison of all *legitimate embeddings* of the requirements into an implementation.

There is a very good, but elusive, reason why these required mathematical models are not currently available. All *useful* mathematics is built from abstraction piled upon abstraction piled upon abstraction. Abstractions have a way of getting rid of the clutter of detail underneath the *real* issues, allowing precision manipulation of complicated relationships with finely chiseled abstract constructs. This procedure has proven to be the most reliable mechanism for the manipulation and modeling of arbitrarily complex environments. Then why does it not work for development of complex computer systems? This paper will point the finger of blame, not at the excellent work done in the computing environment in spite of this modeling handicap, but at *hidden identities* buried in the foundations of mathematics itself.

As unlikely as it may seem, the root cause of software unreliability and restricted capability is hidden deep in the bowels of mathematical foundations. There is a crack in the underlying foundations of mathematical abstractions. It is not a very serious crack, at least not as far as supporting most mathematical interests are concerned. But it is of crucial concern when the layers of abstractions have to be pealed off to reveal their underlying *concrete syntax*, as is required in *strong modeling* of computer systems and architectures. The more the abstractions are pealed away, the more the detail is supposed to be exposed. The problem arises when abstractions are supported by insufficient detail. When the underlying syntax equates as identical two abstract entities that are considered to be distinct, there is a problem! This is exactly the case with two distinct forms of structural organization: *sequences* and *containment*. Details of this problem will be addressed later, for now it is sufficient to recognize that the term *record* in the computing field is intended to represent the concept of *sequence*, not the concept of *containment*, while the term *nesting* is intended to represent the concept of *containment*, not the concept of *sequence*. We now have a problem, for there is no concrete syntax in the foundations of mathematics that supports the separation of the general concept of a record from the general concept of nesting! Without a notation to support a concrete syntax for specific abstract term, then that term is not considered to be *well-defined*. Therefore, without an appropriate syntax, or mathematical notation:

- Records are ***not well-defined!***
- Operations on records are ***not well-defined!***
- Non-binary relations are ***not well-defined!***
- Operations on non-binary relations are ***not well-defined!***
- Data structures are ***not well-defined!***
- Operations on data structures are ***not well-defined!***
- Storage structures are ***not well-defined!***
- Operations on storage structures are ***not well-defined!***
- Mappings between data structures and storage structures are ***not well-defined!***
- Logical requirements are ***not well-defined!***
- Physical environments are ***not well-defined!***
- Implementation mappings between logical requirements and physical environments are ***not well-defined!***

Since records can not be modeled with *concrete* mathematical precision, then neither can collections of records, nor *sequences* of records, nor *nestings* of records! There go all the interesting structures involved in modeling logical requirements, physical environments, and the implementation mappings between them! As will be shown in Section 4 and developed in the Appendix, Extended Set Notation repairs the crack in the mathematical foundations and provides the above terms with a unique concrete syntax, allowing them all to be mathematically well-defined in a common environment.

Though Extended Set Notation **[XSN]** provides the notation for precisely capturing structural distinctions in a mathematical syntax, it does not supply any direct guidance for improving the reliability or capability of future system architectures. For this we need a framework that captures the problem and provides control over the solution. One objective of a Hypermodel is to formalize and control those aspects of system behavior that determine *reliability*. In order to appreciate a solution to the problem of reliable behavior, it is first necessary to further explore the exact nature and scope of the problem itself.

2.2 FORMALIZATION OF THE OBVIOUS

In practice, the term *bug* is used to indicate a discrepancy between an **expected behavior** of a logical requirement system and the **actual behavior** of some reputed implementation embodiment of those same logical requirements. Therefore, a first pass at a definition of *bug-free systems* would be where the expected behavior of the logical system and the actual behavior of the implementation were **identical.** Eliminating 'bugs', or providing reliable 'bug-free', implementations is an elusive objective that has continually evaded all the best efforts of system developers.

The discrepancy between an implementation's actual behavior and requirement specification's expected behavior can be attributed to the lack of formal precision present in the modeling of the embedding of the logical requirements into the physical environment. This lack of modeling precision has the high level advantage of allowing logical requirements to be understood and communicated reasonably accurately in a *smart environment.* But, unfortunately, this lack of precision results in most "unreasonable" behavior when the logical (and reasonable) requirements are transferred to a *dumb environment.* The distinction here between a *smart* and a *dumb* environment is that the *smart* environment thrives on obvious assumptions while the *dumb* environment is a literal environment that chokes on any and all assumptions, especially those that are so *obvious* that they can not even be detected as assumptions in a *smart environment.*

The assumptions that give the most trouble are those that are "so self-evident" that they do not seem to need to be explained nor seem to require their underlying mathematical syntax be examined, as for example the concept of a *record* which we have already encountered.

It is exactly these undetected *obvious assumptions* that trip up the computer giving the unexpected behavior we refer to as a *bug.* If there is ever to be a hope for automated programming and reliable system design, then there must exist a rigorous modeling environment to catch trivial assumptions and insure inherent mathematical integrity.

3.0 MATHEMATICAL MODELING

The concept of mathematical modeling has long been regarded as a rigorous mechanism for capturing details about the behavior of a phenomenon and emulating aspects of that behavior in another (though possibly the same) environment. There are three components to every mathematical model [St77 p. 3, 300]:

- The **phenomenon** to be modeled,
- The **simulation environment** for supporting the modeling,
- The **correspondence** that relates the behavior of the phenomenon to the behavior displayed by the modeling environment.

All three are required for there to be a model, though there are frequent occasions when the modeling, or correspondence itself, is loosely referred to as a model. All computer programs can be considered to be models, or more precisely, modelings.

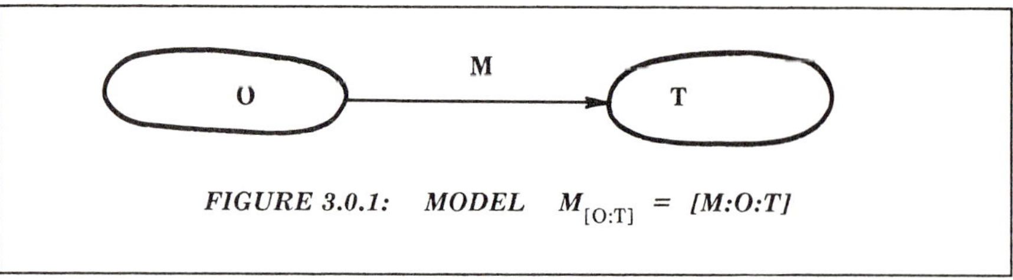

FIGURE 3.0.1: MODEL $M_{[O:T]}$ = *[M:O:T]*

It is sometimes convenient to have a shorthand notation for representing models. Let **O** be the name of the *object* or phenomenon to be modeled, let **T** be the name of the *target* or simulation environment supporting the modeling, and let **M** be the name of the *mapping* or correspondence relating the behavior of the object with the behavior of the target. Then symbolically we can represent the model in Figure 3.0.1 as:

$$\mathbf{M}_{[\mathbf{O:T}]} \quad \text{or as} \quad \mathbf{M: O} \longrightarrow \mathbf{T} \quad \text{or as} \quad \mathbf{[M:O:T]}$$

The value of a model depends on the insight gained by improving the understanding of, or simulating the behavior of, the phenomenon being modeled. Therefore a critical judgement of a model's utility depends on the degree of detail that can be represented by the model. The *resolution* of a model dictates the degree of detail that can be represented by the model. The greater the resolution the more powerful is the model.

3.1 WEAK MODELS vs. STRONG MODELS

Two areas of resolution are associated with a model: function and structure. System architectures demand high resolution in both function and structure. Not all modeling techniques are equally capable in the degrees of resolution which they bestow on the details of structure. For this reason two categories of models need to be distinguished. Since models are generally strong with regard to their ability to capture the details of function, we will distinguish *weak models* from *strong models* by the way a model is able to capture details about structure.

Recall that structure is defined as having two components: *elements* and the way in which the elements are *organized*. It is the modeling of the *organization* details that distinguishes a strong model from a weak one. Informally, the essential distinction between weak and strong models can be stated as follows:

WEAK MODEL: Preserves Functional but not Structural Details
STRONG MODEL: Preserves both Functional and Structural Details

Before giving examples that distinguish the two categories of models, we shall elaborate on the symbolic representation of a model. Since the object to be modeled and the target environment are both comprised of procedures and structures, let $\mathbf{P}_O$ and $\mathbf{S}_O$ represent, respectively, the procedures and structures of the object, **O**. Let $\mathbf{P}_T$ and $\mathbf{S}_T$ represent, respectively, the procedures and structures of the target, **T**. We can then represent the object and target in terms of their procedures and structures as:

$$\mathbf{O} = [\mathbf{P}_O; \mathbf{S}_O] \quad \text{and} \quad \mathbf{T} = [\mathbf{P}_T; \mathbf{S}_T].$$

This notation allows for a more precise definition of *model* in terms of corresponding procedures and structures. [In subsequent formal definitions, the following mathematical shorthand will be used: "∀" means *for all*, "∃" means *there exists*, "ϵ" means *in*, so the expression "$\forall(\mathbf{x})\exists(\mathbf{y})(\mathbf{x} \in \mathbf{y})$" means *For all **x** there exists a **y** such that **x** is in **y**.*]

A MODEL:

GIVEN: $\mathbf{O}=[\mathbf{P}_O; \mathbf{S}_O]$ & $\mathbf{T}=[\mathbf{P}_T; \mathbf{S}_T]$ with $\mathbf{M}: [\mathbf{P}_O; \mathbf{S}_O] \longrightarrow [\mathbf{P}_T; \mathbf{S}_T]$,
IF: $\forall \mathbf{p}_j \in \mathbf{P}_O$ & $\forall \mathbf{s}_i \in \mathbf{S}_O$, $\mathbf{p}_j(\mathbf{s}_i) \in \mathbf{S}_O \rightarrow \mathbf{M}(\mathbf{p}_j(\mathbf{s}_i)) \in \mathbf{S}_T$, and
IF: $\exists \mathbf{s}_m \in \mathbf{S}_T$ & $\exists \mathbf{p}_n \in \mathbf{P}_T$ with $\mathbf{M}(\mathbf{s}_i)=\mathbf{s}_m$, $\mathbf{M}(\mathbf{p}_j)=\mathbf{p}_n$ & $\mathbf{M}(\mathbf{p}_j(\mathbf{s}_i))=\mathbf{p}_n(\mathbf{s}_m)$
THEN: **[M:O:T]** is a **MODEL.**

This effectively says that for every well-defined procedure $\mathbf{p}_j$ in **O** on a well-defined structure $\mathbf{s}_i$ in **O** there is well-defined procedure-structure pair $\mathbf{p}_n$, $\mathbf{s}_m$ in **T** that *behaves* the same way. In order to distinguish between *weak* and *strong* models, the *elements* of a structure and the *organization* of the structure must be separately identifiable with an ability to characterize different organization *TYPES*.

STRONG MODEL:

GIVEN: Any structure **s**,
Let $\gamma(\mathbf{s})$ specify the *elements* of **s**, and
Let $\tau(\mathbf{s})$ specify the *organization type* of **s**,

THEN: **[M:O:T]** is a **strong model** if and only if:
$\forall\, \mathbf{s}_i \in \mathbf{S}_O$ there exists $\mathbf{s}_j \in \mathbf{S}_T$, such that
$\mathbf{M}(\gamma(\mathbf{s}_i))=\gamma(\mathbf{s}_j)$ and $\tau(\mathbf{s}_i)=\tau(\mathbf{s}_j)$.

Since τ is an operator on a structure that specifies the structure's *organization type*, a **strong model** is a model that preserves organization type. As an example of a **weak model**, consider the model $\mathbf{M}_{[O:T]}$ where:

$\mathbf{O} = [\mathbf{P};\mathbf{Q}]$ with $\mathbf{q} \in \mathbf{Q}$ and $\mathbf{q}=\langle\mathbf{a},\mathbf{b},\mathbf{c},\mathbf{d}\rangle$, and with
$\mathbf{P}(1,\mathbf{q}) = \mathbf{a}$, $\mathbf{P}(2,\mathbf{q}) = \mathbf{b}$, $\mathbf{P}(3,\mathbf{q}) = \mathbf{c}$, $\mathbf{P}(4,\mathbf{q}) = \mathbf{d}$, and

$\mathbf{T} = [\mathbf{C}_1,\mathbf{C}_2;\mathbf{S}]$ with $\mathbf{s} \in \mathbf{S}$ and $\mathbf{s}=\langle\langle\mathbf{a},\mathbf{b}\rangle,\langle\mathbf{c},\mathbf{d}\rangle\rangle$, and with
$\mathbf{C}_1(\langle\mathbf{x},\mathbf{y}\rangle) = \mathbf{x}$ and $\mathbf{C}_2(\langle\mathbf{x},\mathbf{y}\rangle) = \mathbf{y}$, and

M is defined by $\mathbf{M}(\mathbf{P}(\mathbf{i},\mathbf{q})) = \mathbf{C}_{m_i}(\mathbf{C}_{n_i}(\mathbf{s}))$ such that
$\mathbf{P}(1,\mathbf{q}) = \mathbf{C}_1(\mathbf{C}_1(\mathbf{s}))$, $\mathbf{P}(2,\mathbf{q}) = \mathbf{C}_2(\mathbf{C}_1(\mathbf{s}))$, $\mathbf{P}(3,\mathbf{q}) = \mathbf{C}_1(\mathbf{C}_2(\mathbf{s}))$, $\mathbf{P}(4,\mathbf{q}) = \mathbf{C}_2(\mathbf{C}_2(\mathbf{s}))$.

Therefore, $\mathbf{M}_{[O:T]}$ is a well-defined model with $\mathbf{M}(\gamma(\mathrm{q})) = \gamma(\mathrm{s})$, but since $\tau(\mathrm{q}) \neq \tau(\mathrm{s})$, **M** is a **weak modeling** of the structure **s**, (*i.e.* **M** does not preserve *organization type*, and therefore, $\mathbf{M}_{[O:T]}$ is a **weak model**!

For an example of a **strong modeling**, consider the model $\mathbf{M}_{[O:V]}$ where **O** is defined as above, but where **V** = **[R;W]** with **w** ϵ **W** and **w** = **<b,c,a,d>** and with:

$$\mathbf{R(1,w) = d}, \quad \mathbf{R(2,w) = a}, \quad \mathbf{R(3,w) = c}, \quad \mathbf{R(4,w) = b}.$$

Then for each of the four cases there exists an **i** and a **j** such that **P(i,q)** = **R(j,w)**. Since **M**(γ(q)) = γ(w) = {**a,b,c,d**}, and since τ(q) = τ(w) = **"4-tuple"** (see Section 4.4), therefore **M** is a **strong modeling** of the structure **q**. If **M** always provides a strong modeling between **O** and **V**, then $\mathbf{M}_{[O:V]}$ is a *strong model.*

3.2 THE HYPERMODEL

A Hypermodel is **a model for modeling models**. Suppose we wanted to define a Hypermodel to model the functional and structural similarities and differences of $\mathbf{M}_{[O:T]}$ and $\mathbf{M}_{[O:V]}$ from the previous section (see Section 6.3). To do so requires an understanding of what is involved in modeling a model.

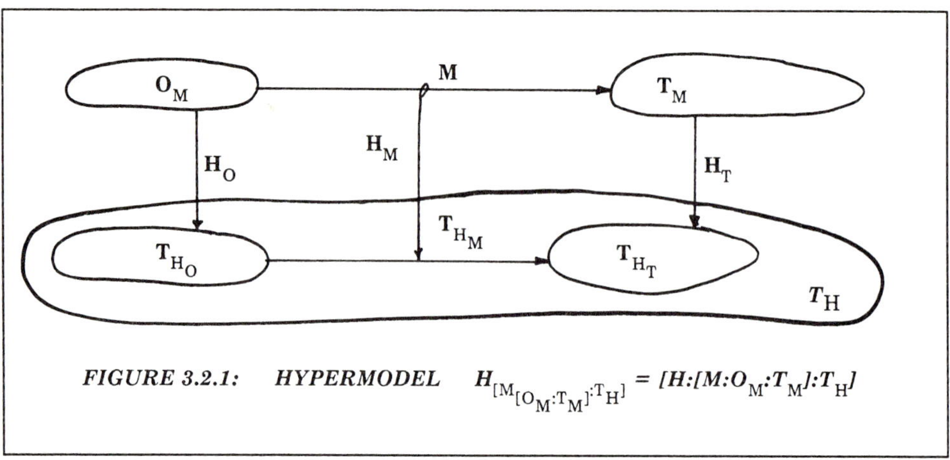

FIGURE 3.2.1: HYPERMODEL $H_{[M_{[O_M:T_M]}:T_H]} = [H:[M:O_M:T_M]:T_H]$

To model just a single model, $\mathbf{M}_{[O_M:T_M]}$, a Hypermodel $\mathbf{H}_{[O_H:T_H]}$ must "capture" the object $\mathbf{O}_M$, the target $\mathbf{T}_M$ and the mapping **M** in the same target environment. This is effectively three(3) distinct strong modelings into $\mathbf{T}_H$, (see Figure 3.2.1):

$$\mathbf{H}_O: \mathbf{O}_M \longrightarrow \mathbf{T}_{H_O}, \quad \mathbf{H}_T: \mathbf{T}_M \longrightarrow \mathbf{T}_{H_T}, \text{ and } \mathbf{H}_M: \mathbf{M} \longrightarrow \mathbf{T}_{H_M}$$

The object $\mathbf{O}_H$ of the Hypermodel $\mathbf{H}_{[O_H:T_H]}$ contains all the procedures and all the structures of both $\mathbf{O}_M$ and $\mathbf{T}_M$, plus all the mappings **M** between $\mathbf{O}_M$ and $\mathbf{T}_M$. The target $\mathbf{T}_H$ of the Hypermodel $\mathbf{H}_{[O_H:T_H]}$ has to include all the procedures and structures necessary to model $\mathbf{O}_H$ to any required resolution. Therefore, an essential requirement of a Hypermodel is that it be a strong model with no less than three(3) mapping components for each model being modeled. Any model of a Hypermodel must itself be a Hypermodel (see Figure 3.2.2 and notice that $[G{:}T_H{:}T_G] = [G{:}[H{:}O_H{:}T_H]{:}T_G]$ and that $[H{:}O_H{:}T_H] = [H{:}[M_1{:}O_1{:}T_1],[M_2{:}O_2{:}T_2]{:}T_H]$).

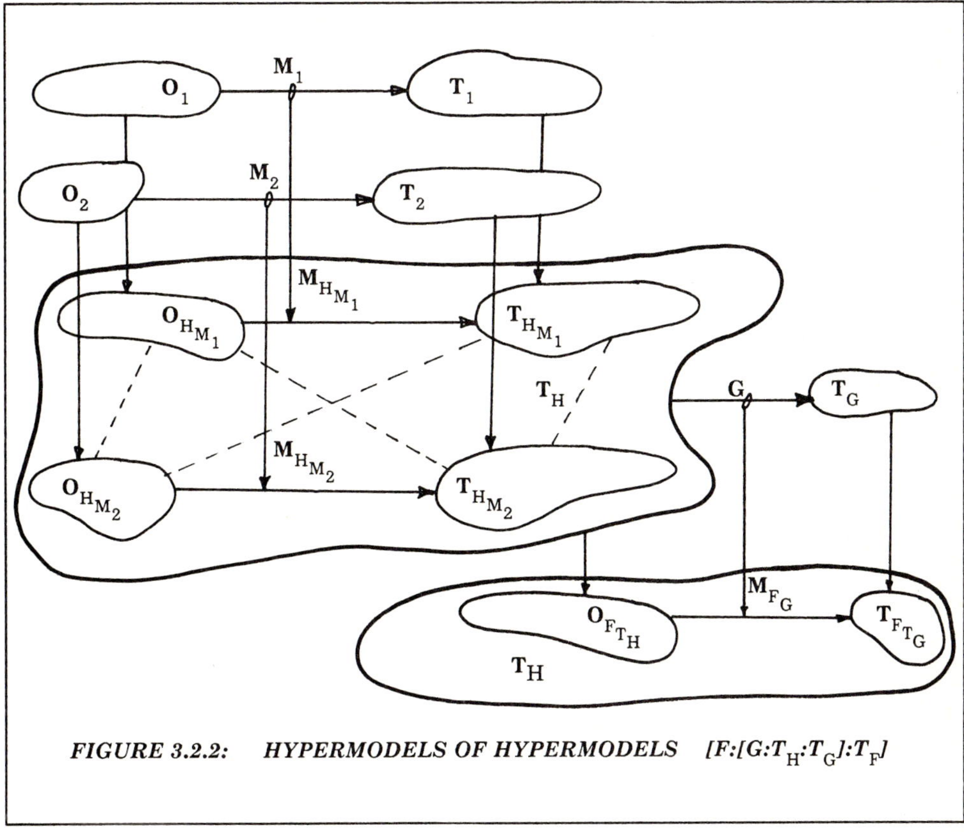

FIGURE 3.2.2: HYPERMODELS OF HYPERMODELS $[F{:}[G{:}T_H{:}T_G]{:}T_F]$

One potentially severe restriction on the utility of the Hypermodel (because of its strong modeling requirements) is the lack of any generally accepted mathematical notation to establish, for all modeling conditions, a Hypermodel as a well-defined mathematical model.

"We can scarcely overestimate the importance of mathematical notation." [Po73 p.134]

The next section introduces Extended Set-theoretic Notation **[XSN]** to support mathematically well-defined Hypermodels.

4.0 EXTENDED SET NOTATION: An Intuitive Perspective

It is assumed that the reader is familiar, to some extent, with the notation of Classical Set Theory (see Appendix for a brief tutorial). Even those familiar with the notation may not be aware of the underlying anomalies involving the conflict between *order* and *nesting*. The concept of *order* is well understood without any mathematical assistance. A sequence of items is a basic concept learned early in life. Every child knows that socks go on the feet before a shoe goes on the sock-covered-foot. Likewise, the concept of *nesting* is well understood without the help of mathematical intervention. The idea of a box inside a box inside a box inside a box is easily understood by a child. Though these concepts are conceptually obvious, they are not very well captured by languages, formal or otherwise! For example if a box contains another box which in turn contains matches, how many would refer to it as "a match-box box"? A more serious problem, which is at the heart of poor computer performance and software unreliability is the lack of set theory to provide a definition to n-tuple (and hence 'record') that has a mathematically well-defined concrete syntax that distinguishes "ordered items" from "nested items" [see Appendix].

> **"An important step in solving a problem is to choose the notation. It should be done carefully. The time we spend now on choosing the notation may be well repaid by the time we save later by avoiding hesitation and confusion. Moreover, choosing the notation carefully, we have to think sharply of the elements of the problem which must be denoted. Thus, choosing a suitable notation may contribute essentially to understanding the problem."** [Po73 p.136]

Since n-tuples are the mathematical mechanism for representing 'records', the precision with which n-tuples can be manipulated mathematically directly affects the precision with which record-dependent systems can be modelled. Since for $n > 2$, n-tuples are ambiguously defined, hence so are n-component records. Therefore, all computer implementations which are heavily involved with record manipulation are ineffectually modeled by Classical Set Theory. (Some authors introduce the deceptive hypothet of a 'sequence' to define n-tuples, which is valid only when underlying refinement is not crucial to their endeavor.)

The objective is to provide a concrete syntax for 'records' using the precepts of set theory and at the same time to extend the usefulness of the set theoretic notation by preserving all conditions where it is useful and eliminating or modifying all situations where it is useless or misleading.

For example, even though n-tuples are defined as sets, no boolean algebra is defined for heterogeneous collections of n-tuples! This is not because there is no need for such an algebra, nor because there is no intuition regarding set operations between n-tuples, but simply because set operations and n-tuple definitions do not behave in the way we would like them to!

By way of illustration, consider the following two ordered pairs:

$$<a,b> \text{ and } <a,c>.$$

They seem to "share an element" in some intuitive sense. In a similar way, so do the pairs:

$$<x,z> \text{ and } <y,z>.$$

In some allied yet different sense 3-tuples may "share an element", e.g.:

$$<a,b,c> \text{ and } <x,b,y>.$$

Yet if we treat these n-tuples as legitimate sets (which they are intended to be), we might get:

$$<a,b> \cap <a,c> \;=\; <a,a>$$
$$<b,z> \cap <c,z> \;=\; \emptyset$$

$$<a,b,c> \cap <x,b,y> \ = \ \emptyset.$$

Even without a formal understanding of 'intersection' or '∩' the above results may seem somewhat counter-intuitive. However, without any explanation of the notation employed in the following, the results may seem intuitively more 'acceptable':

$$<a,b> \cap <a,c> \ = \ \{a^1\}$$
$$<b,z> \cap <c,z> \ = \ \{z^2\}$$
$$<a,b,c> \cap <x,b,y> \ = \ \{b^2\}.$$

For those who are not convinced that the above formulations are not more 'intuitively acceptable' than the first interpretation, let me suggest reviewing the arguments in the Appendix before hardening the judgement.

The intent of the '*superscript*' notation is to capture an additional condition of ***CLAN*** along with the condition of ***MEMBERSHIP***. Since both of these properties are (and will remain) undefined, it makes absolutely no difference what interpretation we place on the notation. Therefore, why not pick a notation that is convenient and an interpretation that is intuitively acceptable?

The only potential drawback with this approach is that notations can not be willed into existence, but must be rigorously derived through accepted mathematical procedures. Since a formal mathematical procedure is delineated in the Appendix, the rest of this paper will concentrate on the application and utility of the notation, and not on its genesis. [If, for some reason, either the term *membership* or the term *clan* is unsuitable or disturbing in any way, the reader is invited to make any uniform substitution they wish, for the following development is impervious to the choice of these *undefined* terms.]

4.1 CLASSICAL SET NOTATION vs. EXTENDED SET NOTATION

In Classical Set Notation **[CSN]** a set **A** is defined soley in terms of the **TRUTH** or **FALSITY** of some given unary function on the variable **x**, $\Gamma(\mathbf{x})$. The function Γ is an interpretation of the undefined condition *membership* of. Thus, if we were to define a set **A** in terms of some Γ, $\Gamma(\mathbf{x})$ would have to be either true or false for every choice of **x**.

That is:

If $\Gamma(\mathbf{x})$ = **TRUE**, then **x** is a *member* of **A**, and

If $\Gamma(\mathbf{x})$ = **FALSE**, then **x** is <u>not</u> a *member* of **A**.

These two assertions can be combined into a single assertion by:

$$\mathbf{A} = \{\mathbf{x}\!: \Gamma(\mathbf{x})\} \quad \textbf{iff} \quad (\forall \mathbf{x})(\mathbf{x} \in \mathbf{A} \leftrightarrow \Gamma(\mathbf{x})).$$

Remember that *membership* is an undefined condition, and just because it may have a reasonable interpretation should not detract from its 'undefinedness'. Now let us assume a second undefined condition represented by (but not defined by) the *clan* of **y**. Given a binary truth-functional $\Gamma(\mathbf{a},\mathbf{b})$, which is either true or false for all instances of **a** and **b**, we can extend the definition of sets, from a dependency on just a single condition, to a dependance on two conditions ***membership*** and ***clan***:

$$\mathbf{A} = \{\mathbf{x}^{\mathbf{y}} : \Gamma(\mathbf{x},\mathbf{y})\} \quad \textbf{iff} \quad (\forall \mathbf{x},\mathbf{y})(\mathbf{x} \in_{\mathbf{y}} \mathbf{A} \leftrightarrow \Gamma(\mathbf{x},\mathbf{y})).$$

This constitutes the truth-functional condition for a set in Extended Set Notation [XSN], and indicates that **A** is a set defined by Γ such that: for all **x** and **y**, **x** is a *member* of **A** under some *clan* represented by **y** if and only if **x** and **y** satisfy the condition $\Gamma(\mathbf{x},\mathbf{y})$. The notation $\mathbf{x} \in_{\mathbf{y}} \mathbf{A}$ is equivalent to the expression **x is a member of A in the clan y**. It will sometimes be convenient to use the Classical Set Notation $\mathbf{x} \in \mathbf{A}$ (where there is no subscript on $\in$) when the *clan* involved is obvious or has specifically been declared as a default. When only one *clan* is involved, distinct choices will give isomorphic results, so the issue of the default *clan* is merely a matter of taste or convenience. Unless otherwise indicated, $\mathbf{x} \in \mathbf{A}$ will be equivalent to $\mathbf{x} \in_{\emptyset} \mathbf{A}$, where the *Null clan* will be assumed as the default.

Thus, somewhat simplistically stated, Extended Set Notation extends Classical Set Notation from a dependency on just one logical condition to a dependency on two logical conditions. It should also be noted that Classical Set Notation is subsumed under Extended Set Notation since every unary truth-functional $\Gamma(\mathbf{x})$, for a **CSN** set definition, can be re-expressed as a binary truth-functional $\Gamma(\mathbf{x},\emptyset)$, for an **XSN** set definition. The following, though possibly bizarre, are legitimate set expressions (see Appendix) using **XSN**:

$$\{\, \mathbf{a}^{\{b^{\{c^{d}\}}\}} \,\}, \quad \{\, \{\mathbf{A}^{z},\{\mathbf{B}^{y},\{\mathbf{C}^{x},\mathbf{D}^{w}\}^{v}\}^{u}\}^{t} \,\}, \quad \{\, \langle \mathbf{a},\langle \mathbf{b}\rangle,\{\mathbf{c},\mathbf{d}\}\rangle^{\langle x,y\rangle},\ \langle\langle \mathbf{e}\rangle\rangle^{\{\{f^{8}\}^{Q}\}} \,\}.$$

Extended Set Notation is purely a syntactical framework for defining consistency of operations on well-defined objects. Any 'meaningful' situation modeled by **XSN** will enjoy the same behavioral consistency, but not because of any inherent 'meaningfulness' in the definitions.

4.2 STRUCTURE MODELING WITH XSN

The primary purpose for introducing **XSN** is to support the strong modeling requirements of a Hypermodel. Some examples will demonstrate how the notation models structure resolution.

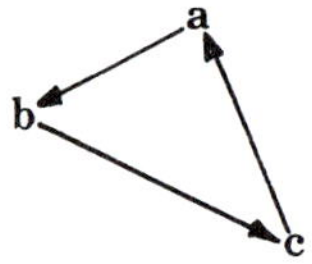

$$\mathbf{A} = \{\, \{\langle a,b\rangle,\langle b,c\rangle,\langle c,a\rangle\}^{C},\ \{c^{1}, b^{2}, a^{3}\}^{Y},\ \{b^{1}, a^{2}, c^{3}\}^{X} \,\}$$

$$\mathbf{B} = \{\, \{\langle a,b\rangle,\langle b,c\rangle,\langle c,a\rangle\}^{C},\ \{c^{1}, b^{1}, a^{2}\}^{Y},\ \{b^{1}, a^{1}, c^{2}\}^{X} \,\}$$

FIGURE 4.2.1: STRUCTURE RESOLUTION

Since the underlying syntax of **XSN** is impervious to the influence of imposed meaning, we may choose any interpretation for *membership* and for *clan* that suits our convenience. For example in Figure 4.2.1, the two graphs **A** and **B** represent the same connectivity of **a** to **b**, **b** to **c**, and **c** to **a**. This *path* can be represented by the set **P**, where the *members are ordered pairs of the the null-clan*:

$$\mathbf{P} = \{ <\mathbf{a},\mathbf{b}>, <\mathbf{b},\mathbf{c}>, <\mathbf{c},\mathbf{a}> \}.$$

If connectivity were the only property of **A** and **B** that we wanted to to capture, then **A** and **B** would be identical under the modeling by **P**. If a spatial orientation were also relevant, then **P** would be inadequate. However, we could distinguish a *Y-AXIS* ordering on **A** by **c** "*comes before*" **b** and **b** "*comes before*" **a** giving:

$$\mathbf{Y}_A = \{ \mathbf{c}^1, \mathbf{b}^2, \mathbf{a}^3 \}$$

Where the *members* of $\mathbf{Y}_A$ are **a**, **b**, and **c** and the *clans* of $\mathbf{Y}_A$ are **1**, **2**, and **3**. The *Y-AXIS* ordering on **B** would give **b** and **c** "*at the same level*" with **a** "*above*" both, giving:

$$\mathbf{Y}_B = \{ \mathbf{b}^1, \mathbf{c}^1, \mathbf{a}^2 \}.$$

The *X-AXIS* orderings of **A** and **B** can be captured by:

$$\mathbf{X}_A = \{ \mathbf{b}^1, \mathbf{a}^2, \mathbf{c}^3 \} \quad \text{and} \quad \mathbf{X}_B = \{ \mathbf{b}^1, \mathbf{a}^1, \mathbf{c}^2 \}.$$

By considering the sets represented by **P**, $\mathbf{Y}_A$, $\mathbf{Y}_B$, $\mathbf{X}_A$, and $\mathbf{X}_B$ as *members* and **C**, **Y**, **X** as *clans*, the graphs **A** and **B** can be written in **XSN** (see Figure 4.2.1) to preserve the structural details of both connectivity and spatial orientation. It should be apparent that this choice of **XSN** representation was quite arbitrary and that many other representations are available. For example if the Cartesian coordinates were known for each of the nodes, then it might be convenient to express the graphs with $\{\mathbf{p}^{<\mathbf{x},\mathbf{y}>} : \Gamma(\mathbf{p},\mathbf{x},\mathbf{y})\}$, where a *member*, **p**, is a node of a graph and a *clan*, **<x,y>**, gives the coordinates of the node.

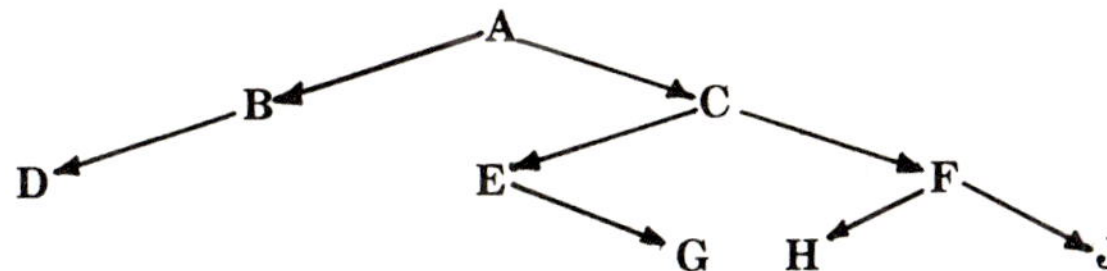

$$\mathbf{H1} = \{ <\mathbf{A},\mathbf{B}>, <\mathbf{A},\mathbf{C}>, <\mathbf{B},\mathbf{D}>, <\mathbf{C},\mathbf{E}>, <\mathbf{C},\mathbf{F}>, <\mathbf{E},\mathbf{G}>, <\mathbf{F},\mathbf{H}>, <\mathbf{H},\mathbf{J}> \}$$

FIGURE 4.2.2: SIMPLE HIERARCHY

The variety of expression of structural detail is limited only by a practitioner's experience and imagination. For example, consider the structure depicted by Figure 4.2.2 and the **CSN** representation of it as a labelled directed graph, or as a simple hierarchy where the nodes themselves are sets.

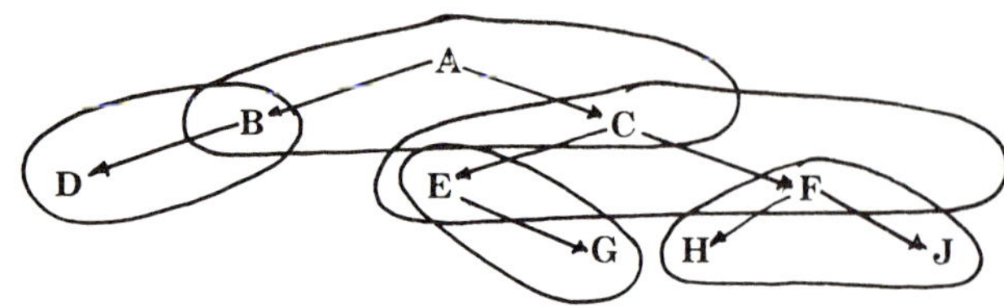

$$H2 = \{ \{A^O, B^L, C^R\}, \{B^O, D^L\}, \{C^O, E^L, F^R\}, \{E^O, G^R\}, \{F^O, H^L, J^R\} \}$$

FIGURE 4.2.3: ACCESS-ORIENTED HIERARCHY

In Figure 4.2.3 the structure is captured as an access-oriented hierarchy where the *clans*, **O**, **L**, and **R** designate the "origin" node, "left" node, and "right" node respectively.

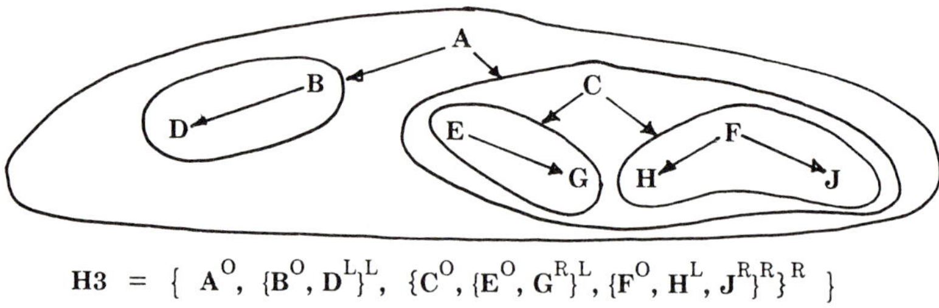

$$H3 = \{ A^O, \{B^O, D^L\}^L, \{C^O, \{E^O, G^R\}^L, \{F^O, H^L, J^R\}^R\}^R \}$$

FIGURE 4.2.4: ACCESS-ORIENTED HIERARCHY OF HIERARCHIES

A more complicated interpretation as an access-oriented hierarchy of hierarchies is given in Figure 4.2.4. Here the *clans* still represent the access orientation of "origin", "left", and "right", but the nodes themselves are now interpreted as access-oriented hierarchies.

Though many further examples of capturing structure resolution in **XSN** could be given (and more will be given in the section on Relational modeling) it is important to remember that the reason for capturing structure in **XSN** in the first place is so that the structure can be treated as a mathematical operand. Capturing the structural resolution in a mathematically well-defined way is only half the job. Operations on structures still have to be defined in order to fulfill the objective.

4.3 EXTENDED SET OPERATIONS

In using **XSN** to define operations, the emphasis will again be on syntax. Just because an operation as no obvious "meaning" or comfortable interpretation in a *real world* environment does not preclude it from being syntactically consistent. Our objective is to build a resource of operations that can later be used to model alternative environments. A few of these operations will be presented here in order to acquaint the reader with **XSN** as it applies to operation definitions, (a more extensive collection of extended set operations appears in the Appendix).

1. UNION: $A \cup B = \{x^i : x \in_i A \text{ or } x \in_i B\}$

2. INTERSECTION: $X \cap Y = \{x^i : x \in_i X \text{ and } x \in_i Y\}$

3. SYMMETRIC DIFFERENCE: $X \triangle Y = \{x^i : (x \in_i X \;\&\; x \notin_i Y) \text{ or } (x \in_i Y \;\&\; x \notin_i X)\}$

4. RELATIVE COMPLEMENT: $X \sim Y = X \triangle (X \cap Y) = \{x^i : x \in_i X \;\&\; x \notin_i Y\}$

5. i-th ELEMENTARY DOMAIN: $D_i(A) = \{x : (\exists v,j)(v \in_j A)(x \in_i v)\}$

6. i-th GENERAL DOMAIN: $\mathcal{D}_i(A) = \{x^j : (\exists v)(v \in_j A)(x \in_i v)\}$

7. SECONDARY CLAN: $\mathcal{C}(A) = \{y^i : (\exists v,x)(v \in_i A)(x \in_y v)\}$

8. RESTRICT: $A|B = \{x^i : (x \in_i A)(\exists b)(b \in B)(x \cap b = b)\}$

9. CONSTITUENT CLANS: $\omega(A) = \{y : (\exists x)(x \in_y A)\}$

10. ELEMENTARY CONSTITUENTS: $\gamma(A) = \{x : (\exists i)\; x \in_i A\}$

11. SUBSET: $X \subset Y \leftrightarrow (\forall x,i)(x \in_i X \rightarrow x \in_i Y)$

12. ORGANIZATION TYPE: $\tau(A) = \{z^y : ((\forall x,i)(x \notin_i A)(z = \emptyset)) \textbf{ or } ((\exists x)(x \in_y A)(z = \tau(x)))\}$

13. BASE STRUCTURE TYPE: $\beta(A) = \{z^{\beta(y)} : ((\forall x,i)(x \notin_i A)(z = \emptyset)) \textbf{ or } ((\exists x)(x \in_y A)(z = \beta(x)))\}$

The following examples use the sets as defined in Section 3.1 and 4.2:

$$\mathbf{A} \cap \mathbf{B} = \{\mathbf{P}^C\} = \{\{<\mathbf{a,b}>, <\mathbf{b,c}>, <\mathbf{c,a}>\}^C\}$$

$$D_O(\mathbf{H2}) = \{\mathbf{A, B, C, E, F}\} \text{ and } \mathbf{H2}|\{\{\mathbf{E}^L\}\} = \{\{\mathbf{C}^o, \mathbf{E}^L, \mathbf{F}^R\}\}$$

$$D_O(\mathbf{H2}) \sim (D_L(\mathbf{H2}) \cup D_R(\mathbf{H2})) = \{\mathbf{A}\}$$

$$\omega(\tau(\mathbf{q})) = \omega(\tau(\mathbf{w})) = \omega(\{\emptyset^1, \emptyset^2, \emptyset^3, \emptyset^4\}) = \{\mathbf{1, 2, 3, 4}\}$$

$$\beta(\mathbf{H2})) = \{\{\emptyset\}\}, \text{ and } \beta(\mathbf{H3}) = \{\emptyset, \{\emptyset\}, \{\emptyset, \{\emptyset\}\}\}$$

4.4 EXTENDED SET NOTATION HAS NO INTRINSIC MEANING

It should be re-emphasized that our concern is purely with syntactical correctness and not on any meanings that may eventually be associated with the notation. In the above, no meaning has been assigned to the phrase *is a member of*, nor to the phrase *in the clan of.* No extended set definitions nor extended set operations depend on any assigned or assumed meaning to the phrase *is a member of* or to the phrase *in the clan of.*

Since *is a member of* is undefined and since *in the clan of* is equally undefined, we are perfectly free to define any consistent syntactical relationships we might care to. If these relationships do indeed happen to model some *real world* situation, then we can be sure we will learn more about the *real world* from the modeling than we will learn about the model from the *real world* situation. This is as it should be! We do not want our modeling to be corrupted by *implicit meaning*.

5.0 MODELING THE RELATIONAL DATA MODEL

Though there is currently a great deal of misunderstanding and confusion regarding E. F. Codd's **Relational Model of Data** [Co70], or Relational Data Model **[RDM]** as it has come to be known, it is certainly regarded (at least by those who understand the implications) as a most seminal contribution to the advancement of information systems technology. One of the most significant, and least recognized, features of the **RDM** is *that it treats structure as a mathematical operand*!

Not only has Codd presented us with a powerful Data Model that treats structure as an operand, but one that, as we shall see shortly, embraces **structure independence**. This is both the **RDM's** strength and its weakness: its strength because convenient, capable, reliable systems require *structure independence* and its weakness because the **RDM** itself gives absolutely no clue as to how this independence should be properly implemented. [This author has had half an aeon of experience in implementing the **RDM** and is biased by experience to assert that no commercially available implementation of a **RDM** system comes close to realizing its latent performance potential.] The **RDM** was never intended to be a design guide for its own implementation, and as long as designers feel that the **RDM** gives them the slightest clue to its own implementation, they are continuing to miss one of the fundamental strengths of the **RDM**, its inherent *structural independence*.

In order to implement the **RDM** to its fullest potential two modelings have to be precisely understood (see Figure 5.0.1): the model, $\mathbf{V}_{[A:D]}$, of the correspondence between the application requirements and the **RDM**, and the model, $\mathbf{X}_{[D:S]}$, of the correspondence between the **RDM** and the supporting environment. Thus the **RDM**, itself, is only one-fifth of the modeling components required to model a complete implementation. In Section 6 the concept of a *Function Space* will be introduced, which when used in conjunction with a Hypermodel, supported by **XSN**, can precisely model the five components required for a *structure independent implementation* of a **RDM** system.

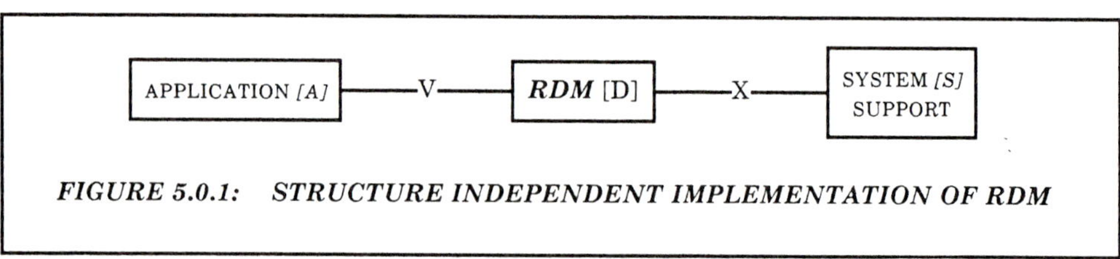

FIGURE 5.0.1: STRUCTURE INDEPENDENT IMPLEMENTATION OF RDM

5.1 RELATIONS AS EXTENDED SETS

The first requirement of a Hypermodel for modeling an implementation of a **RDM** system is a strong model of the **RDM** itself. This means that all the structure types of the **RDM** have to be preserved. Since there is exactly one structure type in the **RDM**, the *relation*, our focus is established. What the **RDM** lacks in quantity of structure types it makes up for in complexity of the structure type. A major reason for the proliferations of inadequate implementation of **RDM** systems is the lack of any well known mathematical formalism to preserve the structural characteristics of a **RDM** *relation.* Though some may believe that this can be achieved with **CSN**, it can not. However it can be achieved with **XSN** as the following will demonstrate.

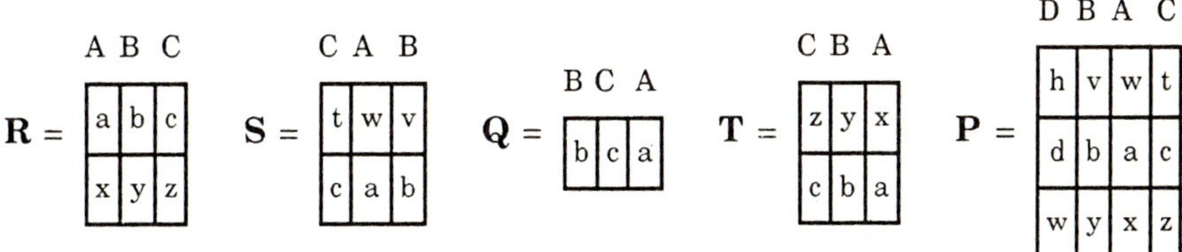

Anyone familiar with the **RDM** will recognize that the above are all relations in the sense of the **RDM**. It will also be clear that **R** and **T** are identical, that the intersection of **R** and **S** is equal to **Q**, that **R** is a sub-relation of **P**, and that **R**, **S**, **Q**, and **T** are domain compatible. All that remains then is to express these observations, both structural and procedural, in an appropriate notation:

$$\mathbf{R}=\{\ \{a^{A},b^{B},c^{C}\},\ \{x^{A},y^{B},z^{C}\}\ \},\quad \mathbf{S}=\{\ \{t^{C},w^{A},v^{B}\},\ \{c^{C},a^{A},b^{B}\}\ \},\quad \mathbf{Q}=\{\ \{b^{B},c^{C},a^{A}\}\ \}$$
$$\mathbf{T}=\{\ \{z^{C},y^{B},x^{A}\},\ \{c^{C},b^{B},a^{A}\}\ \},\quad \mathbf{P}=\{\ \{h^{D},v^{B},w^{A},t^{C}\},\ \{d^{D},b^{B},a^{A},c^{C}\},\ \{w^{D},y^{B},x^{A},z^{C}\}\ \}$$

With these extended set definitions and the extended set operations defined in Section 4.3, the following can be verified:

$\mathbf{R} \hat{\ } \mathbf{T} = \emptyset$ therefore **R** and **T** are identical,

$\mathbf{R} \cap \mathbf{S} = \mathbf{Q}$ therefore **R** and **S** share **Q** as a sub-relation,

$\mathbf{R} \cap \mathbf{P} = \mathbf{R}$ therefore **R** is a sub-relation of **P**,

$\mathcal{C}(\mathbf{R}) = \mathcal{C}(\mathbf{S}) = \mathcal{C}(\mathbf{Q}) = \mathcal{C}(\mathbf{T})$ identical *clans* implies Domain Compatible.

5.2 MODELING EXTENDED RELATIONS

The original work by Codd introduced relations as homogeneous collections that did not allow nestings of relations nor null values. Codd's later works [Co79] indicate a preference for extending the original concepts of a relation. What follows is in no way intended to reflect Codd's endorsement, approval, nor even his preference. It is intended strictly as an exercise in the syntax of **XSN**.

RPG =

H	C	W
a	b,c	d
x	y	w,z

XR1 =

Q	*E*	*D*
c	b	A C D: X | Z | W
z,w	y	x

XR2 =

A	*E*	*M*	*P*
	g		
b	i		q
c		n	r
d	k	o	s
	l		t

$$\mathbf{RPG} = \{\ \{\mathbf{a}^{H},\mathbf{b}^{C},\mathbf{c}^{C},\mathbf{d}^{W}\},\ \{\mathbf{x}^{H},\mathbf{y}^{C},\mathbf{w}^{W},\mathbf{z}^{W}\}\ \}\quad \mathbf{XR1} = \{\ \{\mathbf{c}^{Q},\mathbf{b}^{E},\{\{\mathbf{X}^{A},\mathbf{Z}^{C},\mathbf{W}^{D}\}\}^{D}\},\{\mathbf{z}^{Q},\mathbf{w}^{Q},\mathbf{y}^{E},\mathbf{x}^{D}\}\ \}$$

$$\mathbf{XR2} = \{\ \{\mathbf{b}^{A},\mathbf{g}^{E},\mathbf{n}^{M},\mathbf{q}^{P}\},\ \{\mathbf{c}^{A},\mathbf{i}^{E},\mathbf{o}^{M},\mathbf{r}^{P}\},\ \{\mathbf{d}^{A},\mathbf{s}^{P}\},\ \{\mathbf{k}^{E},\mathbf{t}^{P}\},\ \{\mathbf{l}^{E}\}\ \}$$

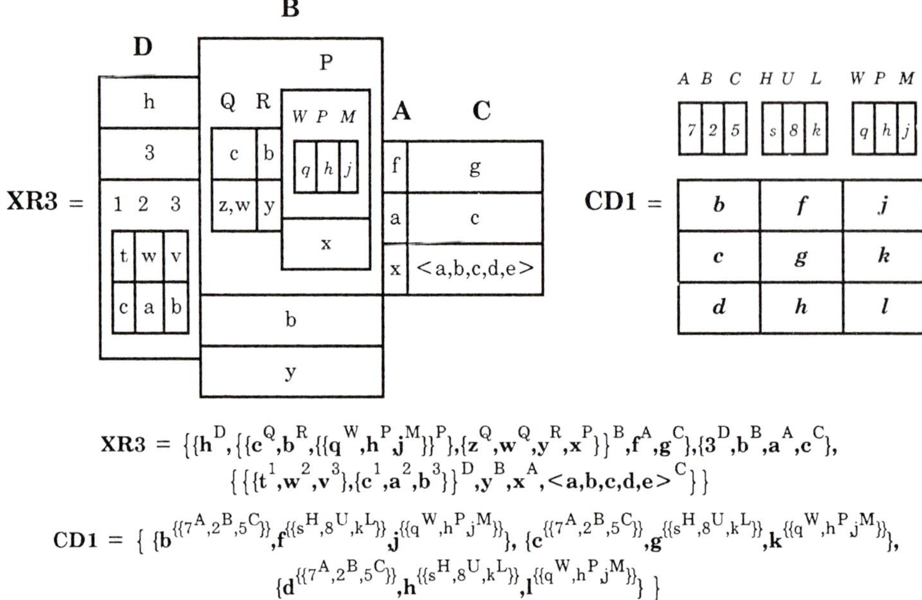

$$\mathbf{XR3} = \{\{\mathbf{h}^D, \{\{\mathbf{c}^Q, \mathbf{b}^R, \{\{\mathbf{q}^W, \mathbf{h}^P, \mathbf{j}^M\}\}^P\}, \{\mathbf{z}^Q, \mathbf{w}^Q, \mathbf{y}^R, \mathbf{x}^P\}\}^B, \mathbf{f}^A, \mathbf{g}^C\}, \{\mathbf{3}^D, \mathbf{b}^B, \mathbf{a}^A, \mathbf{c}^C\},$$
$$\{\{\{\mathbf{t}^1, \mathbf{w}^2, \mathbf{v}^3\}, \{\mathbf{c}^1, \mathbf{a}^2, \mathbf{b}^3\}\}^D, \mathbf{y}^B, \mathbf{x}^A, <\mathbf{a,b,c,d,e}>^C\}\}$$

$$\mathbf{CD1} = \{\ \{\mathbf{b}^{\{\{7^A,2^B,5^C\}\}}, \mathbf{f}^{\{\{s^H,8^U,k^L\}\}}, \mathbf{j}^{\{\{q^W,h^P,j^M\}\}}\}, \{\mathbf{c}^{\{\{7^A,2^B,5^C\}\}}, \mathbf{g}^{\{\{s^H,8^U,k^L\}\}}, \mathbf{k}^{\{\{q^W,h^P,j^M\}\}}\},$$
$$\{\mathbf{d}^{\{\{7^A,2^B,5^C\}\}}, \mathbf{h}^{\{\{s^H,8^U,k^L\}\}}, \mathbf{l}^{\{\{q^W,h^P,j^M\}\}}\}\ \}$$

The purpose of introducing these structural and operational extensions to the **RDM** is solely to demonstrate, on hopefully familiar ground for most readers, an appreciation of the modeling scope provided by the concept of a Hypermodel as supported by **XSN**. The two significant characteristics of an extended set-theoretic Hypermodel **[XSHM]** are the reliability of the design resulting from the employment of an **XSHM** and the scope of applicability. An **XSHM** is not restricted to a specific choice of system that it can model, nor does it provide any guidance to the choice of behavior that a system will provide, other than that it will be reliable. As in any established engineering discipline, the tools provide precision, but not direction. The direction is provided by an independent analysis that utilizes the tool, as opposed to being directed by it. Codd provided both a tool, the **RDM**, and a direction, *data independence* for the users application. For general reliable implementations we have the tool, the **XSHM**, now all we need is the direction that provides general data independence, *i.e.* **structural independence**. As will be shown in the next section, data independence is is achieved *everywhere* in a **structure independent architecture.**

6.0 FUNCTION SPACES and STRUCTURE INDEPENDENT ARCHITECTURES

Recognizing that structure is heavily involved with most computer related activities does not require a great deal of sophisticated insight. Recognizing how to make systems independent of structural dependencies is quite a different matter. The objective is to be able to design systems that allow us to control the structures instead of the structures controlling us. We will call this kind of architecture a **structure independent architecture.** This form of architecture requires that we isolate and control structural dependencies that relate to the behavior of our proposed implementation. The intuition for introducing the concept of a *Function Space* as a building block for structure independent architectures relates directly to the inherent nature of digital computers.

Every implementation on a digital computer consists of a collection of operations on a collection of structures such that the behavior of the implementation is deterministic. This holds for all implementations and for all digital computer configurations – past, present, and future. Though the behavior of every such implementation is deterministic, it may not always be well understood and certainly not always predictable.

In order to more fully understand the nature of computer implementations, let a **FUNCTION SPACE** be any collection of operations defined over a collection of structures, such that closure is preserved. Preservation of closure insures that the behavior of a Function Space is well-defined. Not only is every computer implementation a Function Space, but also an interaction of sub-function spaces.

Since all computer implementations consist of interacting Function Spaces, these implementations can be better understood through a better understanding of how Function Spaces interact. Existing implementations can be analyzed for improved behavior, and future implementations can be designed to provide expanded functionality with a better understanding of performance considerations.

6.1 FUNCTION SPACES

It should be noted that every functional component of any architecture consists of two equally important components: the data organization and operations defined on those organizations. This simple observation is critical to understanding the relationship of current computer system designs relative to potential computer system designs. Since everything that follows next depends on a crisp understanding of the interaction of these operations and structures, a formal definition of Function Space is required.

FUNCTION SPACE:

GIVEN: Any collection of well-defined operators, **P**, and any collection of well-defined operands, **S**:

IF: 1) **f** is an operator, or a collection of operators, in **P**, and
2) **a** is an operand, or a collection of operands, in **S**, such that
3) **f** and **a** are well-defined relative to each other (*i.e.* type compatible), and
4) **f(a)** is a well-defined operand in **S**,

THEN: **A = [P;S]** is a **FUNCTION SPACE.**

Notice that procedures in a Function Space are not restricted to, but certainly intended to include, functions in the *not one-to-many* sense. More generally, the procedures may be any well-defined operator including *one-to-many*. Structures in a Function Space are not restricted to *static organizations*, but may themselves be procedures or Function Spaces. The only criteria for an entity to be a structure in a Function Space is that it qualify as a well-defined operand. The following is a more intuitive definition of a Function Space.

> ***A FUNCTION SPACE is any collection of well−defined structures, along with any collection of well−defined operations on those structures that preserves closure.***

The idea behind a Function Space is to provide a general, well-defined building block unit for modeling *objects*, *targets* and *correspondences* of system architectures. The correlation between Function Spaces and models is anything but an accident. A well-defined model can be expressed as a Function Space of procedures **M** operating on the structure **<O,T>**, giving: $\mathbf{M}_{[O:T]}$ = **[M:O:T]** = **[M;<O,T>]**.

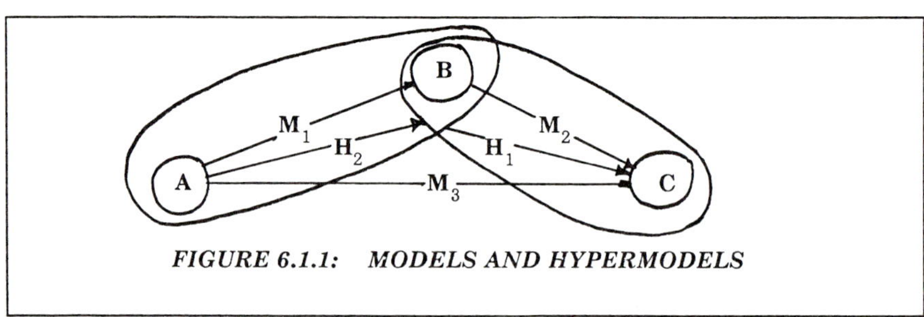

FIGURE 6.1.1: MODELS AND HYPERMODELS

In Figure 6.1.1 there are five modelings represented, two of which are modelings of models. These can now be expressed precisely as Function Spaces:

$[\mathbf{M}_1\mathbf{:<A,B>}]$, $[\mathbf{M}_2\mathbf{:<B,C>}]$, $[\mathbf{M}_3\mathbf{:<A,C>}]$, $[\mathbf{H}_1\mathbf{:<[M}_1\mathbf{:<A,B>],C>}]$, $[\mathbf{H}_2\mathbf{:<A,[M}_2\mathbf{:<B,C>]>}]$

6.2 FUNCTION SPACES AS EXTENDED SETS

There must exist at least one formal mechanism for capturing a Function Space or there will be no mapping, or correspondence, to support the concept of a Hypermodel, (*i.e.* $\mathbf{H}_O$, $\mathbf{H}_M$, and $\mathbf{H}_T$ in Figure 3.2.1). Though a fuller, more formal development of Function Spaces expressed in **XSN** will be given in [Ch86a-f], at least one mapping, **H**, will be given now for a general Function Space, **A** = **[P;S]**:

$$\text{DEFINE: } \mathbf{H}_{[A:XSN]} = \mathbf{[H:[P;S]:XSN]} = \mathbf{H}\text{: [P;S]} \longrightarrow \{\mathbf{x^y}: \mathbf{x} \in \mathbf{S} \text{ and } \mathbf{y} \in \mathbf{P}\}$$

It should be stressed that this is only one of may possibilities for expressing Function Spaces in **XSN**. Depending on the characteristics of the Function Spaces under modeling consideration, the notational formulations could get quite complex. The above definition is one of the simplest formulations that still allows productive modeling, including Hypermodels of Hypermodels. Notice that the mapping $\mathbf{H}_{[A:XSN]}$ can be expressed as $[\mathbf{H};<\mathbf{A},\mathbf{XSN}>]$ which is a Function Space, which can be mapped to **XSN** by **H** which in turn can be expressed as $[\mathbf{H};<[\mathbf{H};<\mathbf{A},\mathbf{XSN}>],\mathbf{XSN}>]$ which is a Function Space which in turn can *etc.*

Using this **XSN** we now compare the two models of Section 3.1. To do so, consider a Function Space **A**, and a Function Space **B** such that $\mathbf{B} \subset \mathbf{A}$, then **B** is a **Sub-Function Space.** Now to compare aspects of the models, let $\mathbf{B}_T \subset [\mathbf{M}_T:<\mathbf{O},\mathbf{T}>]$ and let $\mathbf{B}_V \subset [\mathbf{M}_V:<\mathbf{O},\mathbf{V}>]$, where:

$$\mathbf{B}_T = \{<\{\mathbf{a}^{P(1,q)}\},\{\mathbf{a}^{C_1(C_1(s))}\}>,<\{\mathbf{b}^{P(2,q)}\},\{\mathbf{b}^{C_2(C_1(s))}\}>,<\{\mathbf{c}^{P(3,q)}\},\{\mathbf{c}^{C_2(C_1(s))}\}>,$$
$$<\{\mathbf{d}^{P(4,q)}\},\{\mathbf{d}^{C_2(C_2(s))}\}>\}$$

$$\mathbf{B}_V = \{<\{\mathbf{a}^{P(1,q)}\},\{\mathbf{a}^{R(2,w)}\}>,<\{\mathbf{b}^{P(2,q)}\},\{\mathbf{b}^{R(4,w)}\}>,<\{\mathbf{c}^{P(3,q)}\},\{\mathbf{c}^{R(3,w)}\}>,<\{\mathbf{d}^{P(4,q)}\},\{\mathbf{d}^{R(1,w)}\}>\}$$

An important objective has been achieved. The Function Spaces, $\mathbf{B}_T$ and $\mathbf{B}_V$, are now well defined operands, they are sets, thought this is not the only **XSN** formulation that could have been chosen. Another *functionally equivalent* form is: $\{\mathbf{x}^{<P(i,q),C_j(C_k(s))>} : \Gamma(\mathbf{x},\mathbf{P},\mathbf{C})\ \}$. Now that Function Spaces have been defined as sets, the only remaining definition needed to complete the introduction of Structure Independent Architectures is that of *Structure Independence.*

6.3 STRUCTURE INDEPENDENCE

Two very important concepts for future systems development and performance are the concept of *STRUCTURE DEPENDENCE* and the concept of *STRUCTURE INDEPENDENCE.* As one might suspect, one precludes the other, so it does not matter which one we define first, for the other will be defined as not *it.*

Informally, if a Function Space **Q** is a Sub-Function Space of **A** and **A** contains *information* about a procedure in **Q**, but that *information is hidden* from **Q**, then **Q** is *structure dependent* on **A**. A **structure dependent** Function Space will be defined as a Function Space that contains at least one **structure dependent operator** that is not under its control.

STRUCTURE DEPENDENT FUNCTION SPACE:

GIVEN: $\mathbf{A}=[\mathbf{P}_A;\mathbf{S}_A]$ and $\mathbf{Q}=[\mathbf{P}_Q;\mathbf{S}_Q]$ such that $\mathbf{Q} \subset \mathbf{A}$ and $\mathbf{S}_A \sim \mathbf{S}_Q \neq \emptyset$, then
FOR: $\mathbf{B} \in (\mathbf{S}_A \sim \mathbf{S}_Q)$,
IF: $\exists(\mathbf{x},\mathbf{y}) \in \mathbf{B}$, and $\mathbf{f}$ with $\mathbf{f}_x, \mathbf{f}_y \in \mathbf{P}_Q$, such that
$\exists(\mathbf{a} \in \mathbf{S}_Q)$ and $\mathbf{f}_x(\mathbf{a}) \neq \mathbf{f}_y(\mathbf{a})$,
THEN: **Q is structure dependent on A.**

In the above definition **Q** is a Sub-Function Space of **A** and **f** is a **structure dependent operator** whose *behavior* in **Q** depends on a structure in **A** which is *unknown* to **Q**. Though **f** is well-defined in both **Q** and **A**, and **f** is well behaved in **A**, **f** is not well behaved in **Q**. Therefore, **f** is a structure dependent operator under the control of **B**. Any Function Space containing **f** without **B** would be a Structure Dependent Function Space. A **Structure Independent** Function Space is a Function Space that contains no structure dependent procedures. The ubiquitous **GET NEXT** is an example of a structure dependent operator that renders most Database Management systems structure dependent. The one notable exception is the **RDM**. It can be shown, [Ch86b], that the **RDM** shares no structure type with any physical machine environment. Therefore, no Sub-Function Space of the **RDM** can be a Sub-Function Space of <u>any</u> machine environment, (*i.e.* $\mathbf{D} \cap \mathbf{S} = \emptyset$ in Figure 5.0.1). Therefore, the **RDM** is inherently structure independent of every machine environment, (which Codd has always claimed, few have believed, and none have implemented).

6.4 FUNCTION SPACE ARCHITECTURE or CONNECTED FUNCTION SPACES

In order to define a network of Function Spaces, all that remains is to define how Function Spaces are connected. Two Function Spaces, **A** and **B**, are **connected by** $\mathbf{M}_1$ and $\mathbf{M}_2$, if there exist Function Spaces **O** and **Q** such that:

$$\mathbf{O} \subset \mathbf{A} \text{ with } \mathbf{M}_1 : \mathbf{O} \longrightarrow \mathbf{B}, \quad \text{and} \quad \mathbf{Q} \subset \mathbf{B} \text{ with } \mathbf{M}_2 : \mathbf{Q} \longrightarrow \mathbf{A}.$$

Notice a **connection** is a Function Space: $\mathbf{M}_{[A:B]} = [\mathbf{M}_1;<\mathbf{O},\mathbf{B}>] \cup [\mathbf{M}_2;<\mathbf{Q},\mathbf{A}>]$.

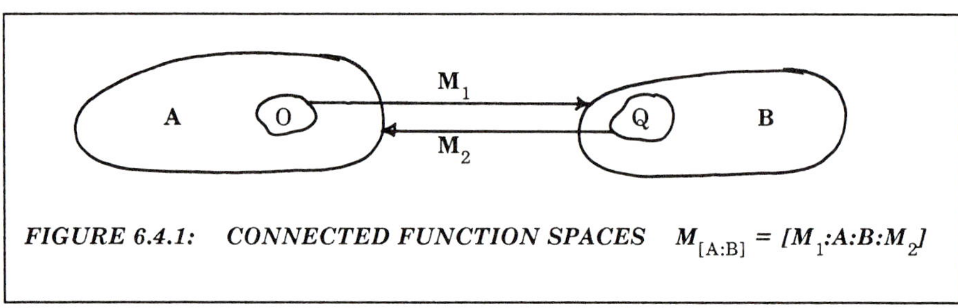

FIGURE 6.4.1: CONNECTED FUNCTION SPACES $M_{[A:B]} = [M_1:A:B:M_2]$

A **Function Space Architecture [FSA]** is a Function Space defined over connected Function Spaces. For **A**, **B**, and $\mathbf{M}_{[A:B]}$ above, $\mathbf{K} = [\mathbf{M}_{[A:B]};\mathbf{A},\mathbf{B}]$ is a Function Space Architecture. The structures of a Function Space Architecture are Function Spaces, and the procedures of a Function Space Architectures are also Function Spaces.

A <u>FUNCTION</u> <u>SPACE</u> <u>ARCHITECTURE</u> is a Function Space of connected Function Spaces!

Of particular interest is a Function Space Architecture with no structure dependent connectors, in other words, a Function Space whose procedures are all Structure Independent Function Spaces, *i.e.* a **Structure Independent Architecture [SIA]**. If $\mathbf{M}_{[A:B]}$ above is a Structure Independent Function Space, then **K** is a **SIA**.

It should be carefully understood that structures of a Structure Independent Function Space could be Structure Dependent Function Spaces as long as no procedure is a structure dependent operator. This is exactly the situation that we want to model with a **SIA**: a structurally independent network of structurally dependent objects!

6.5 STRUCTURE INDEPENDENT ARCHITECTURES

Any computing system environment limited to a rigid, structure dependent architecture is, by design, a performance cripple. Yet to date, every commercially available computer system product relies on a rigid, structure dependent architecture. All computer systems can be characterized by the degree of structural independence existing between the *functional* components of the underlying architecture. In a *Structure Independent Architecture* all components are functionally specific and structurally disjoint components. In brief, the purpose of a **SIA** is to address the problems of performance by allowing organizational control over all structure dependent components, while at the same time preserving the logical structurings as perceived by the applications. The underlying concept of a **SIA** is deceptively simple, yet dramatically different from the current trends in system design.

A STRUCTURE INDEPENDENT ARCHITECTURE is a Function Space of Function Spaces, connected by structurally independent Function Spaces!

A **SIA** is a design guide for directing the employment of Hypermodels. A **SIA** requires structure independent interfaces between all structure dependent components. This enforced structure independence permits *intelligence* to be built into individual components. Since only *functionality* between components need be preserved, separate components can be upgraded or modified without modifying or changing other components in the system. One of the many consequences of this architectural approach is that the life of software application programs can be extended indefinitely, even though the supporting Database Management modules or underlying storage environments may be continually enhanced, or even radically changed or replaced.

It should be emphasized that a **SIA** is not a Data Model, but rather an implementation strategy that relies on Function Space Architectures with extended set operators and extended set operands to preserve the capability and independence of distinct functional components. Since all Data Models are inherently Function Spaces, each can be expressed in **XSN** to any desired degree of resolution, including all logical and physical behavioral characteristics. The modeling can be precise enough to predict operational times and storage requirements before any code has been written. Most Data Models dwell on a specific storage organization with a restricted collection of appropriate operations, while a **SIA** can support structures of arbitrary complexity with a small kernel of generic extended set operations.

It is the structural completeness of **XSN** that allows the **SIA** to embrace all possible Data Models and storage data organizations in a mathematically consistent framework. Though the capability and convenience is a function of the Data Model, the performance of any Database Management System ultimately depends on how data is organized in secondary storage. A **SIA** is an ideal means to design and control secondary storage environments, independent of the Data Model used, in particular the **RDM**.

The **RDM** has an undeserved reputation for having poor performance. This is a fact of history and not because of any inherent property of the **RDM**. Quite the contrary, because of the **RDM's** inherent structure independence it is properly independent of the underlying support that affects the performance and is, therefore, capable of being the *best* performing system. No commercial vender has implemented the **RDM** properly so as to preserve its inherent structure independence.

6.6 STRUCTURALLY INDEPENDENT RDM ARCHITECTURE

As was indicated earlier, every **RDM** system architecture has five components that require modeling: the application, the **RDM**, the machine (or *physical*) environment, and the two correspondences between these three components. From the bias in the previous sections, it should come as no surprise that the way to achieve a structurally independent **RDM** system is to capture all five components as Function Spaces in an **XSHM**.

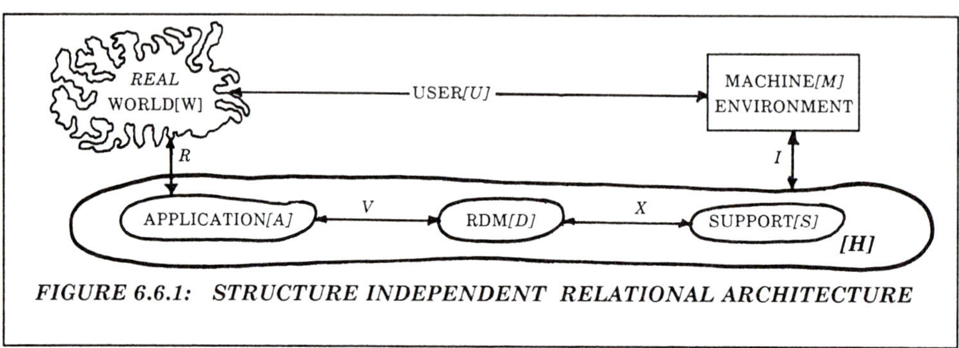

FIGURE 6.6.1: STRUCTURE INDEPENDENT RELATIONAL ARCHITECTURE

As can be seen from Figure 6.6.1 the five components (**A**, **V**, **D**, **X**, **S**) of a **RDM** system architecture, **H**, are related to an operational environment by five other components (**W**, **U**, **M**, **R**, **I**) as follows:

U: W<——>M User connects *Real World* with Machine Environment

R: W<——>A Requirements connect Real World with Application

I: H<——>M Implementation connects Hypermodel with Machine Environment

V: A<——>D View connects Application with Data Model

X: D<——>S Extended Interface connects Data Model with Support

Of the five **connections** involved, only the last two, **V** and **X**, can be formalized in an **XSHM**. Though the above example was directed at an implementation of the **RDM**, the **connections** involved are characteristic of all system architectures. **U** never will be completely understood though opinions will never be in short supply. **R** and **I** have received extensive consideration. But these efforts are far from delivering adequate development tools needed to meet future system requirements. The reason for this is primarily due to an inability to formally synthesize *structural control* into a cohesive design methodology. **I** in particular is the chief cause of system *bugs* or *unexpected behavior.* Eventually, **I** can be automated, but only after **H** is well-defined. These five modelings are to be the subject of intense focus in [Ch86a-f].

7.0 CONCLUSION

As was indicated in the introduction, this paper was designed to lay the mathematical foundation and instigate interest for a series of more extensive papers on the application of the Hypermodel to a wide range of computer related issues that impinge on the restrictions caused by structure dependencies.

The first step in building a mathematical foundation for any discipline is to establish a *pregnant* notation [Po73] suitable for the subject. Since computer systems can not avoid being concerned with structures and their structurings, any suitable notation for supporting a mathematical foundation to systems development must accommodate structures and structurings!

- Systems problems can not be precisely defined, therefore reliable solutions can not be derived!
- A reliable solution is a solution that *fits* the problem.
- To verify that a particular solution actually *fits* a particular problem, requires a precise formulation of both the solution and the problem!
- No problem involving *structures* and *structurings* can be precisely formulated without a precise formulation of *structure* and *structurings*!
- Since most of the problems concerning computer systems development involve *structurings*, most of the problems concerning computer systems development have solutions that do not *fit*!
- Most of today's system solutions are just "speculative solutions", they are neither derivable nor verifiable!
- We need tools to design reliable systems that are more complex than current conceptual schemata will allow.

The key to system reliability and capability is structure control. The most reliable form of structure control is mathematically well-defined structure operations on mathematically well-defined structures. For over eighteen years the development and utilization of such mathematically defined structure operations has been rigorously pursued. The resulting collection of structure operations has been very successfully applied to the design, implementation, and control of some very complex *real world* situations, including: high performance implementations of the Relational Data Model, host-transparent secondary storage networks, text processing applications, and 'mathematical blueprinting' of logical requirement specifications for *bug-free* software.

All behavioral characteristics, both logical and physical, of every computer system are inherently set theoretic. Though Classical Set Notation cannot express some of the needed set structures, required at the physical level of computer system implementations, Extended Set Notation can! **XSN** is general enough to validate any computer system design, for all logical and physical behavior parameters.

Unfortunately, some who should know better, take the position that Graph Theory, Topology, or some other existing body of mathematics can capture the properties of general structures and structurings with sufficient resolution to allow precision formulation of today's systems problems and solutions. This is tantamount to advocating the integer "3" as a precision replacement for "π". Instead of recognizing the need for new tools, some have even taken the position that "if the only tool you have is a hammer, then treat all problems as *nails*." When the problem is to remove a screw, they seem puzzled when their approach makes the problem worse. New tools are sometimes mandatory when current tools just do not work! Software Engineering and the computer industry at large is in dire need of new tools for the analysis, specification, design, and implementation of future system architectures.

Three design criteria are necessary for any well-defined computer system implementation: Functional Capability, Flexible Implementation, and Modeling Validation. A Structure Independent Architecture combines the implementation flexibility with modeling generality and validation. Any well–defined Data Model, or models, providing the desired functional design objectives can then be combined with a **SIA** to yield an implementation that can maximize the potential of the chosen design in the chosen hardware environment. Every level of system design and implementation can benefit from the inclusion of comprehensive structure modeling!

7.1 SUMMARY

To minimize any potential confusion with the role of Extended Set Notation [**XSN**] and the applicability of the Extended Set-theoretic Hypermodel [**XSHM**], in the real world of practical computer systems, the following is a delineation of certain conclusions essential to an understanding of the role of set theory for the modeling of existing or future systems, and as an architectural aid for the implementation of high performance, user friendly systems of tomorrow.

- Set theory is a **mathematical discipline**, not an unproven hypothetical doctrine.
- Every implementation of a computer system is mathematically equivalent to some **XSN** modeling. Therefore, a specific knowledge of the underlying set-theoretic relationships in a

computer system implementation can greatly assist in the maintenance, tuning, and modification of the existing implementations.

- IMS, ADABAS, IDMS, TOTAL, DATACOM, MODEL 204, etc. all have an underlying set-theoretic foundation, even though this foundation is generally unknown to both the users and designers of the systems. However, if this underlying set-theoretic foundation were exposed to the database and system designers of such systems, they could then take advantage of many mathematical understandings, which would otherwise remain obscure. For example: taking advantage of distributive, associative, and commutative properties of operation sequences to optimize performance and reduce overhead. The alternative is to assume that database and system designers have already achieved the most efficacious systems by inadvertently taking advantage of all the underlying mathematical benefits.

- The power of an **XSHM** resides purely in the notation of set theory. The very nomenclature of set theory forces a precision on computer system operations and structures that cannot be captured nor communicated with current computer system vocabularies.

- A crucial concept in **XSN** is that all sets are <u>unordered</u>, though <u>any</u> ordered structure can be expressed. This structural opulence of **XSN** provides a complete variety of both logical and physical structures required in computer systems, including: inverted files, hierarchies, networks, repeating groups, rings, discs, tapes, associative memories, text data, picture data, and, in fact, any discrete collection of discrete objects. Since all these structures are sets, all operations on and between them can also be expressed in the notation of set theory.

- **XSHM** provides database and system designers with the ability to express, in a precise notation, <u>all</u> the structures, operations, and interrelationships relevant to database management systems. Thus, **XSHM** can be used as a rigorous design aid in implementing high performance computer systems.

- Current computer system architectures are grossly inadequate to handle future requirements of information processing supported by very large, distributed secondary storage systems. The reason for this is quite simple. Current computer systems are still based on antiquated design philosophies that focused more on user perceptions than system performance. Future computer system performance will ultimately depend on the structural independence of secondary storage organization. Yet even today, no commercial system provides structurally independent, intelligent management of secondary storage environments.

- Unfortunately, all currently available commercial systems have structurally entwined the architectural components by their implementations, thus restricting user capability, increasing system overhead and precluding intelligent secondary storage management. Though these have, to date, not been perceived as serious drawbacks, they are absolutely disastrous for the requirements of very large distributed databases of tomorrow.

- A Structure Independent Architecture [**SIA**] is any system design that provides structural independence between architectural components. Such a system design allows all the advantages that are usually attributed to the term 'data independence'. This much abused, little understood term has become a desirable computer system feature, so naturally everybody claims to have it – they don't. If systems were literally 'data independent', they would be independent of the data and hence would not work at all. The term should more correctly be 'data representation independent' which is just a cumbersome way of saying 'structurally independent', which is what a **SIA** design provides.

The mixing and manipulation of structurally independent design techniques for obtaining optimum cost/performance and user convenience is an essential contribution of Structure Independent Architectures to future information systems. In order for high performance to become a reality, it is necessary for Structure Independent Architectures to eventually permeate every aspect of future information systems: Distributed Front-end Intelligent Terminals, Host Resident Application Support, Operating Systems, Generalized Database Management Systems, Back-End Database Machines, Distributed Databases and Processing, Storage Device Controllers, Satellite Communications, Very Small To Very Large Secondary Storage Systems, Expert Systems, etc.

The above synopsis, though admittedly terse, should provide additional insight to why set theory is more than just "a little different" notation than is currently available to database and system designers. Set theory is not just a taxonomy for cataloging 'wish lists', but an efficient way of transforming 'wish lists' into economic implementations. No matter how brilliant a designer's ideas might be, for competing with future computer systems, their integration and implementation would certainly be enhanced with a firm understanding of set-theoretic principles. In order to design systems that meet the demands of future requirements, and in order to discern a system's true capabilities, both designers and purchasers of future computer systems must be knowledgeable in set theoretic and function space concepts.

Experience has shown that these concepts are easily assimilated by most system designers in a very short, but intense, training period, especially when the training is oriented toward an ongoing corporate project. Particular success has been achieved with a focus on relaxing the binding constraints dictated by current database design philosophies, thereby allowing developments that relieve current application backlogs while making the system more flexible, more easily managed, more capable, more reliable, and, most importantly, more productive.

8.0 ACKNOWLEDGEMENT

Dr. Arun K. Sood of Wayne State University initiated the interest in this paper, encouraged its development, and provided for its publication. I greatly appreciate the opportunity he provided for delineated some ideas and their relationships that had been developing intuitively for some time, but that had never been reduced to a formal clarification.

APPENDIX: Set-Theoretic Notation

A1.0 CLASSICAL SET-THEORETIC NOTATION

Since the notation and operations of Classical Set Theory are only vaguely familiar to many people, the stress in this tutorial will not be placed on the more abstract mathematical consequences of set theory, but rather on the 'vocabulary' and basic fundamental concepts that will allow the expression of database management related ideas to be clearly expressed and understood in terms of a set-theoretic 'vocabulary'. Though there is considerable difference between an axiomatic development and an intuitive presentation of the set theoretic concepts, the underlying concepts are the same in both. Therefore, an intuitive presentation of the concepts will be emphasized with an introduction to the formalities only after the basic concepts have been established.

A1.1 MEMBERSHIP & SETS

The singularly most important concept in set theory is that of *membership*. Sets, nested sets, ordered sets, and all operations in set theory are defined in terms of membership. The concept of membership is extremely simple, perhaps too simple. More capabilities are attributed to membership than actually exist. For clarification, we will describe what membership is and what it is not.

Membership is an assertion about the existence of a specific entity 'x' relative to another entity 'y', which takes the form:

1) x is a member of y

or

2) x is not a member of y.

One and only one of these statements can be true for any instance of 'x' and any instance of 'y'. If (1) is true, then x is said to be an element of the set y. If (2) is true, then x is not an element of y and it is not even known if y is a set. Membership is the criteria for defining sets.

The intuitive notion of a set is that of a collection or aggregate of items. The specification of exactly which items belong to a particular set is given by a membership condition. Thus the means for specifying well defined membership conditions is crucial to specifying well defined sets. Some simple examples are:

1) Let A be the collection of even integers greater than one and less than ten.

2) Let B be the set containing the elements: a, b, c, d.

3) Let C be the set containing the set in (1) **and** containing the set in (2).

Notice that set C is not the set containing all the elements of the set A along with all the elements in set B. Rather, the set C contains the set A and the set B as its only two elements. Set C demonstrates the important concept of *nesting*. A set may contain other sets as members. As an example, consider a box of matches. The members of the box are matches. Place several of these boxes of matches in a bowl. The members of the bowl are match-boxes, which is distinctly different than a bowl of matches. Therefore, the bowl containing match-boxes as members does not contain matches as members even though there are matches inside the match-boxes. Replacing the bowl with a box, gives a match-box-box containing match-boxes but not matches. Adding a handful of matches to the match-box-box would now allow its members to be both matches and match-boxes.

The precision of a symbolic notation is generally preferred to English prose when defining sets. However, a given notation defines a set only if the notation unambiguously delineates the membership for the set. The most common notation for set theory consists of 'proper combinations' of set brackets, '{...}', commas, and alpha/numeric symbols. For example, the sets A, B, and C from above can be respecified as follows:

$A = \{2, 4, 6, 8\}$
$B = \{a, b, c, d\}$
$C = \{ \{2,4,6,8\},\{a,b,c,d\} \} = \{ A, B \}$

This notation has to be carefully understood in order not to imbue the concept of membership with unintentional characteristics. For example, the notation:

$D = \{a, a, a, b, b \}$

seems to indicate a set D with three instances of item 'a' and two instances of item 'b'; or in the case of set B above, the notation may seem to indicate an ordering preference of 'a' before 'b' before 'c' before 'd'. Neither of these interpretations is correct; they are characteristics of the notation and not characteristics of the concept of membership. Membership simply asserts the existence of an element within a set. Membership does not indicate frequency of occurrence nor order of occurrence. An element is either in a set once or not at all.

The symbol 'ϵ' is a substitute for the expression **'is a member of'** therefore,

$x \epsilon Y$

states that 'x is a member of Y'. The symbol '$\notin$' means **'is not a member of'**, so the expression 'x is not a member of Y' would be expressed as:

$x \notin Y.$

The following are all true statements:

$a \ \epsilon \{ a, \{b\} \}$
$b \notin \{ a, \{b\} \}$
$\{a\} \notin \{ a, \{b\} \}$
$\{b\} \epsilon \{ a, \{b\} \}$

The symbol 'Γ' is used to express the conditions of membership: $\Gamma(x)$ is a truth-functional (that is, it only has values *TRUE* or *FALSE*) for all x. By using these symbolic equivalents along with '$\exists x$' in place of **'there exists an x'**, '$\forall x$' in place of **'for all x'** and '$\leftrightarrow$' (or **'iff'**) for **'if and only if'**, a precise statement of the set notation may be expressed.

SCHEMA FOR A SET

$Y=\{x:\Gamma(x)\} \leftrightarrow [(\forall x)(x \ \epsilon \ Y \ \leftrightarrow \Gamma(x))]$

This states: "Y is the set containing all x such that $\Gamma(x)$ is true if and only if for all x, x is an element of Y if and only if $\Gamma(x)$ is true". Both sides of the statement say the same thing: x is a member of Y if and only if the condition Γ is true for x. Following are some examples to help clarify the use of this notation:

$\{a,b\} = \{x: x=a \text{ or } x=b \}$
$\{x: x \text{ is an even integer}, 1 \leq x \leq 10 \}$
$\emptyset = \{x: x \neq x \}$

This last set has very special significance in set theory. '$\emptyset$' is called the null set. It is the set which has no elements. There are many ways of describing the conditions of the null set. For example, the set of all elephants indigenous to Greenland is the same as the set of all ten year old neurosurgeons, is the same as the set whose elements are unequal to themselves, is the same as the set containing no elements. Notice that the following statement is always true for all x:

$x \notin \emptyset$

The importance of the null set will be discussed later. The primary concern at this point is to understand the correct interpretation of the set theoretic notation. The set D, given above, has exactly two elements: a and b.

$D = \{x: x=a \text{ or } x=b \}$

In the set B defined earlier [B={a,b,c,d}], the notation may seem to imply an ordering on the four elements, yet no ordering is implied. Set B can be written any of twenty four different yet equivalent ways. Here are a few:

$$\{a,c,b,d\} = \{c,b,d,a\} = \{c,d,a,b\} = \{b,d,a,c\} = \{d,a,b,c\}$$

If an element is in a set with other elements, there is no order distinction among the elements inherently supported by the membership of that set. The truth functional can only assert the binary condition of 'in' or 'out'. Though frequency of occurrence and order of occurrence are meaningful concepts, they require more set-theoretic construction in order to be properly established. To establish a notation that properly expresses the concept of order without interfering with the expression of the concept of nesting is a problem of some difficulty. This problem will be addressed more fully later in this paper after a familiarity with set operations and relations has been achieved.

A2.0 EXTENDED SET-THEORETIC NOTATION

Most mathematical endeavors involving set theory are of high enough abstraction to be impervious to the specific underlying syntax mechanism whereby ordered pairs and ordered n-tuples are defined. Yet ordered pairs and n-tuple definitions have long been an unresolved issue in the foundations of mathematics. Skolem [Sk57] concluded his article with "It is still a problem how the ordered n-tuple can be defined in the most suitable way." Rosser [Ro53, p.281] states (in regard to his adoption of Quine's [Qu45] definition of ordered pair) that "We know no way to construct a less artificial ordered pair, and until someone shows how to construct a less artificial one, we shall use ours to do all the things that an ordered pair is expected to do."

The objective here is not to suggest that foundation issues should be a concern of all higher level mathematical endeavors, but to present a new formalism for defining ordered pairs and ordered n-tuples as sets without encumbering potentially spurious complications in areas where the underlying syntax is critical. In addition the definitions presented will satisfy a strong "nesting-order" separation criteria, not currently satisfied by any existing formulation of order. This new formalism also provides a base for broader set theoretic modeling capabilities with new operations and structures not previously found in existing set theories.

In order to fully appreciate the solution presented in this section, the nature of the problem and previously proposed remedies will be presented first. For every familiar definition of ordered n-tuple there is at least one consequence for which the definition is not completely satisfactory. The areas affected by these consequences are generally considered to be "uninteresting" by those not directly affected by the spurious side effects. One objective of this paper is to present a single definition of ordered n-tuple general enough to cover all areas of interest, no matter how narrow or how broad. However, since all the difficulties surrounding the various definitions of ordered n-tuples may not be immediately recallable, a short synopsis of these definitions and their deficiencies seems requisite.

For an axiomatic development of set theory, two primitives may be assumed: membership, $\in$, and the null set, $\emptyset$. (Of course, some set theories may define $\emptyset$ in terms of $\in$, though this is not always desirable, especially when "individuals" are required (see Weiner [Wi14]).) All other set theoretic notions can then be derived from these. To accommodate sets of ordered n-tuples, either the ordered n-tuple must be introduced as an independent notion (which is generally unacceptable and leads to some complications) or for each n, the ordered n-tuple must be defined.

In 1914 Wiener [Wi14] defined the notion of ordered pair in terms of nested sets (thereby reducing the theory of relations to the theory of sets). His definition is:

$$\langle a,b\rangle = \{ \{\emptyset,\{a\}\}, \{\{b\}\} \}.$$

Then in 1921 Kuratowski [Ku21] gave the definition most often used today:

$$<a,b> \;=\; \{\, \{a\}, \{a,b\} \,\}.$$

Other definitions using the notion of nested sets are:

$$<a,b> \;=\; \{\, \{a,\emptyset\}, \{b,\{\emptyset\}\} \,\}$$
$$<a,b> \;=\; \{\, \{a\}, \{b,\emptyset\} \,\}.$$

All of these definitions have the undesirable property that the nesting level (or 'type', in the sense of Russell) is raised by two or three when a pair is defined.

However, the most serious difficulty with these definitions is that they do not preserve the distinction between the notion of nesting and the notion of order. Certain nested sets are "tied up" to serve as ordered pairs. The consequences of this may be quite serious when the notation does not reflect the distinction between these notions. Using the Kuratowski definition as representative, let the set K be defined as follows:

$$K \;=\; \{\, <a,b>, \{\{a\},\{a,b\}\} \,\}.$$

The set K contains only one member not two as the notation would indicate. For occasions where it is necessary to distinguish between the notion of order and the notion of nesting, the above definitions of ordered pair are inadequate.

Another complication concerns the meaningfulness of legitimate set operations between legitimate sets giving non-intuitive results. For example, again using the Kuratowski definition:

$$<a,b> \cap <a,c> \;=\; <a,a>$$
$$<a,b> \cap <c,b> \;=\; \emptyset.$$

These concerns are compounded when the notion of ordered n-tuple is extended to $n>2$, (see Skolem [Sk57]). If S is defined as:

$$S \;=\; <a,b,c> \cap <a,b,d>$$

then what are the members of S?

Assuming the Kuratowski definition of ordered pair, the usual definition for a 3-tuple is one of the following:

$$<a,b,c> \;=\; <a,<b,c>>$$
$$<a,b,c> \;=\; <<a,b>,c>$$
$$<a,b,c> \;=\; \{\, <a,1>, <b,2>, <c,3> \,\}.$$

For any of these, the set

$$V = \{\, <a,b,c>, <a,<b,c>>, <<a,b>,c>, \{<a,1>,<b,2>,<c,3>\} \,\}$$

has cardinality only three, and not four as the notation would seem to indicate. Assuming the Kuratowski definition for ordered pair, it may not be immediately obvious that the above set V is identical to the following set R:

$$\begin{aligned} R = \{\, & <a,b,c>, \\ & \{\{a\},\{a,\{\{b\},\{b,c\}\}\}\}, \{\{\{\{a\},\{a,b\}\}\},\{\{\{a\},\{a,b\}\},c\}\}, \\ & \{\{\{a\},\{a,1\}\}, \{\{b\},\{b,2\}\}, \{\{c\},\{c,3\}\}\} \,\}. \end{aligned}$$

If the notation preserved the distinction between nesting and order, then a casual scan of V and R would indicate that they were unequal and that $V \cup R$ should have cardinality 7 while $V \cap R$ should have cardinality 1.

Not all difficulties are purely notational, some membership anomalies arise from trying to extend the notion of Cartesian product to accommodate n-ary relations. The Cartesian product of Y with itself is:

$$Y^2 = Y \times Y = \{<x_1,x_2>: x_1,x_2 \in Y\}.$$

The temptation is to write Y^n for the product set YxYx...xY taken to n terms, for example:

$$Y^3 = Y \times Y \times Y.$$

A difficulty arises since the Cartesian product is not associative, therefore:

$$(Y \times Y) \times Y \neq Y \times (Y \times Y).$$

For $n>2$, Y^n is not a well defined set. Y^n really represents a class of membership conditions and for most mathematical endeavors they behave identically, so there is no need to distinguish one from the other. When a membership distinction is essential, some canonical pairing of the Cartesian product is required. This forces all n-ary relations to become binary relations. Some modeling environments require this finer resolution to Y^n and also need to distinguish between p-ary and q-ary relations. An alternative approach is to use indexing schemes (see Weiner [Wi14]). For example, if the n-tuple, x(n), is defined functionally as:

$$x(n) = <x_1,x_2,..,x_n> = \{<x_1,1>,<x_2,2>,..,<x_n,n>\}$$

and if the concatenation between a set of m-tuples, A, and a set of n-tuples, B, is defined by:

$$A \bullet B = \{<x_1,..,x_m,y_1,..,y_n>: x(m) \in A \ \& \ y(n) \in B\}$$

then if $Y^1=\{<x>: x \in Y\}$, Y^n can be well defined as $Y^1 \bullet Y^1 \bullet ... \bullet Y^1$ taken to n terms, giving:

$$Y^n = \{<x_1,x_2,..,x_n>: x_i \in Y\}.$$

Since concatenation is associative, the following properties hold:

$$Y^3 = (Y^1 \bullet Y^1) \bullet Y^1 = Y^1 \bullet (Y^1 \bullet Y^1)$$

$$Y^{m+n} = Y^m \bullet Y^n = Y^n \bullet Y^m.$$

However, since the n-tuple was originally defined as a function, every n-ary relation is just a set of binary relations. In addition, this use of notation does not distinguish the difference between the ordered pair and the ordered 2-tuple, giving:

$$<a,b> = \{\{a\},\{a,b\}\}$$

and $$<a,b> = \{<a,1>,<b,2>\}$$

though $$\{\{a\},\{a,b\}\} \neq \{<a,1>,<b,2>\}$$

and $$Y \times Y \neq Y^1 \bullet Y^1.$$

In either case there is still a problem with elevated type. The intuitive notion of the n-tuple, $<x_1,x_2,x_3,..,x_n>$, is easily understood to be an extension of the ordered pair $<x_1,x_2>$; yet as Skolem concluded a suitable definition for n-tuples is difficult to achieve satisfactorily.

The definition of ordered pair proposed by Hausdorff [Ha49]:

$$<a,b> = \{\{a,1^*\}, \{b,2^*\}\}$$

where 1* and 2* are special objects kept distinct from a and b, preserves the notions of nesting and order over collections disjoint from the collection of special objects. The extension of this definition to n-tuples is restricted by the necessity of having to keep the ordered individuals apart from the ordering individuals, otherwise:

$$\text{for} \quad \langle a,b,c \rangle = \{\{a,1^*\},\{b,2^*\},\{c,3^*\}\}$$

$$\langle 3^*,1^*,2^* \rangle = \langle 2^*,3^*,1^* \rangle$$

The inherent difficulty in all these definitions lies in trying to define ordered sequences in terms of nested sets or by introducing additional undefined primitives. Neither approach is acceptable.

Alternative approaches to the ordered pair and n-tuple construction have met with varying degrees of success. Goodman's [Go41] definition reduces the type difference to one, while Quine's [Qu45] definition reduces the type difference to zero. Though this last result is most desirable, the definition forces all sets to be binary relations. Even though these definitions, along with Schwabhauser's [Sc54], have complicated definitions and restrictions, their primary disadvantage is the failure to preserve the distinction between the notions of nesting and order.

The following asserts a condition for the separation of 'order' from 'nesting', which no previous definition of ordered pair satisfies.

SEPARATION CRITERIA:
Let the type, or rank, of a set Y be expressed by $\rho(Y)=n$, where n is a non-negative integer: $\rho(Y)=0 \rightarrow \neg(\exists x)(x \in Y)$, and assuming a definition for ordered pair that allows for a meaningful definition of Cartesian product:

Let: $\S^1(A) = \{x: x \text{ is a subset of } A\} \cup A$

$\S^{n+1}(A) = \{x: x \text{ is a subset of } \S^n(A)\} \cup \S^n(A)$

then, $(\forall B)(\forall n)\big(\rho(B)=1 \rightarrow (B \times B) \cap \S^n(B) = \emptyset\big)$.

This may be broadened to any set of uniform type, $(\exists n)(\forall x)(x \in B \rightarrow \rho(x)=n)$.

EXTENDED MEMBERSHIP PREDICATE FOR SET THEORIES

An extended membership predicate is now introduced to allow definitions of nested sets and ordered sets that accommodate this separation criteria.

GIVEN (as primitives):
The null structure, $\emptyset$, and a binary predicate, ξ.

ξ-STRUCTURE DEFINITION:
Y is a ξ-structure $\leftrightarrow (\exists x)(x \xi Y)$ or $Y=\emptyset$

SCHEMA FOR AN ξ-STRUCTURE:
$[x:\gamma(x)]=Y \leftrightarrow (\forall x)(x \xi Y \leftrightarrow \gamma(x))$
for example: $[x,y] \equiv [z: z=x \text{ or } z=y]$

MEMBERSHIP DEFINITION:

$$x\epsilon_s Y \leftrightarrow (\forall a)(a \xi Y \rightarrow (\exists b,c)(a=[[b],[c,\emptyset]])) \ \& \ [[x],[s,\emptyset]] \ \xi \ Y$$

SET DEFINITION:

Y is a set iff $(\exists x,s)(x\epsilon_s Y)$ or $Y=\emptyset$

SCHEMA FOR A SET:

$$Y=\{x^s: \Gamma(x,s)\} \leftrightarrow (\forall x,s)(x\epsilon_s Y \leftrightarrow \Gamma(x,s))$$

for example: $\{x^a,y^b\} \equiv \{z^v: (z=x \ \& \ v=a) \text{ or } (z=y \ \& \ v=b)\}$

SCOPE:

For every set, Y, there exists a unique **SCOPE SET**, W,
such that
$(\forall y,s)(y\epsilon_s Y \rightarrow s\epsilon_\emptyset W) \ \& \ (\forall s)(\exists x)(s\epsilon_\emptyset W \rightarrow x\epsilon_s Y)$.

Proper selection for W allows a variety of different properties to become integral to the membership condition (see Fraenkel [Fr66] for multiple ordering possibilities). For any given ω, if W is chosen to be $\{\omega^\emptyset\}$, then the membership reduces to the familiar classical membership condition:

$$\{x:\Gamma(x)\} \equiv \{x^w:\Gamma(x,\omega)\} \quad \text{gives} \quad \{a,b,c\} \equiv \{a^w,b^w,c^w\}.$$

The convenience of the familiar set notation is preserved since it can be subsumed under the new notation with an understanding that: $a\epsilon A \equiv a\epsilon_\emptyset A$.

No further use is intended for ξ-structures other than to define sets. For an intuitive clarification, let $\langle\!\langle a,b \rangle\!\rangle \equiv [[a],[b,\emptyset]]$, the membership conditional may now be expressed more simply as:

$$x\epsilon_s Y \leftrightarrow (\forall a)\big(a\xi Y \rightarrow (\exists b,c)(a=\langle\!\langle b,c\rangle\!\rangle)\big) \ \& \ \langle\!\langle x,s\rangle\!\rangle \xi Y$$

Since the scope of every set is determined by a set, at least one set must be a scope set for itself. The following trivial theorem asserts the uniqueness of such a set.

THEOREM:

For any set Q, if Q is a scope set for Q, then $Q=\{\emptyset^\emptyset\}$.

The proof follows immediately since $\{\emptyset^\emptyset\} = [\ [[\emptyset],[\emptyset,\emptyset]]\ ]$ and $a\epsilon_b\{c^d\} \rightarrow w\epsilon_x\{y^z\}$ when $a=b=c=d=w=x=y=z=\emptyset$.

A number of directions can proceed from this point depending on the preference of axioms, the richness of the logic for 'Γ' (see Lyndon [Ly66]), the types of set theoretic objects required (classes, semi-sets, modal-sets, fuzzy sets, etc.), and the purpose or intention for the set theory. In any case this new membership predicate allows definitions which can satisfy the above separation criteria and also avoid the other spurious side effects of previous definitions of ordered pairs and n-tuples. For example, consider the following definitions: $0=\emptyset$, $1=\{\emptyset\}$, $2=\{\emptyset,\{\emptyset\}\}$, $3=\{\emptyset,\{\emptyset\},\{\emptyset,\{\emptyset\}\}\}$, $n+1=\{0,1,..,n\text{-}1,\{n\}\}$ and let $\mathbf{Z}=\{0,1,2,3,...\}$. Sets, whose scope sets are subsets of $\mathbf{Z}$, include all the usual familiar sets, plus the means for defining ordered pairs and n-tuples that satisfy the separation criteria. The nested set $\{\{a\},\{a,b\}\}$ is no longer needed to define $\langle a,b\rangle$, for **ordered pair** can now be defined by:

$$\langle a,b\rangle \equiv \{a^0,b^1\} \quad \text{or by} \quad \langle a,b\rangle \equiv \{a^1,b^2\}.$$

Either case is satisfactory since in both cases $\langle a,b\rangle = \langle x,y\rangle$ implies $a=x$ and $b=y$. This approach may easily be extended to define n-tuples by:

$$\langle x_1,\ldots,x_n\rangle \equiv \{y^v: y=x \;\&\; v=i\}$$

for example:

$$\langle a,b,c,d\rangle \equiv \{a^1,b^2,c^3,d^4\}.$$

Unlike n-tuples, which are well-ordered and without "gaps", the set $\{a^1,b^4,c^4,d^7\}$ has partial order and with "gaps", but it is still a legitimate set under the new definition of membership.

As a result of the extended membership predicate, the difficulties with previously cited tuple constructions now disappear. No additional primitives are required and no special ordering objects are introduced. The set $\{\langle a,b\rangle,\{\{a\},\{a,b\}\}\}$ does not reduce to a one-element set since $\langle a,b\rangle$ is no longer defined by $\{\{a\},\{a,b\}\}$.

Note that even though $\{\langle a,b\rangle,\{a^1,b^2\}\} \equiv \{\langle a,b\rangle\} \equiv \{\{a^1,b^2\}\}$, no interpretation is placed on "$\langle a,b\rangle$" that is not also associated with "$\{a^1,b^2\}$". Therefore, no more confusion results here than with $\{a,a\}\equiv\{a\}$. This is obviously not the case when notational distinctions imply separate notions as when "$\langle a,b\rangle$" represents *ORDER* and "$\{\{a\},\{a,b\}\}$" represents *NESTING*.

Let $\#(X)$ represent the cardinality of the set X, then for the previously defined sets [K,S,V & R]: $\#(K)=2$, $\#(S)=2$, $\#(V)=4$, $\#(R)=4$, and $\#(V \cup R)=7$. Order no longer need be defined using <u>any</u> form of nested set equivalence. Binary relations are no longer required to define n-ary relations. Now n-ary relations have an existence independent of ordered pairs or of any other form of nesting.

Unary, binary, and n-ary relations may now be consistent, with ordered pairs and 2-tuples defined identically by:

$$Y^2 = Y \times Y = Y^1 \bullet Y^1.$$

Operations between n-tuples, which gave less than intuitive results, now may behave "intuitively":

INTERSECTION: $A \cap B = \{x^s: (x \in_s A) \;\&\; (x \in_s B)\}$

for example, $\langle a,b\rangle \;\; \langle a,x\rangle = \{a^1\}$

$\langle a,b\rangle \;\; \langle x,b\rangle = \{b^2\}$

$\langle a,b,c,d\rangle \cap \langle x,b,y,d\rangle = \{b^2,d^4\}$

General n-ary relation operations can now be defined compatibly with all other sets and set operations (*i.e.*, there need not be an artificial type distinction between sets and relations). If the type of a set, Y, is expressed as $\rho(Y)$ equaling a non-negative integer, then for all x in Y^n, $\rho(x) \leq \rho(Y)$. Though the separation criteria was initially specified only for the Cartesian product, it may be generalized to include $B^m \cap \mathcal{S}^n(B) = \emptyset$.

Since any set maybe chosen for a scope set, W, let $W=\{<a,b>^{\emptyset}: a,b \in Z\}$, then 'fuzzy sets' (sets with a probability function associated with the condition of membership) and multiple-instance sets can easily be defined by:

$$\{x^{<a,b>}: \Gamma(x,a,b)\}$$

where "a" represents the order and "b" represents either the degree of membership for a fuzzy set or represents the number of multiple occurrences within a set.

The freedom to choose W as any arbitrary set provides a basis for set structures and operations with unusual nested and ordering properties, yet without the difficulties inherent in previous mechanisms which confuse the notions of nesting and order.

A3.0 SELECTED DEFINITIONS OF SOME USEFUL EXTENDED SET OPERATIONS

Notation used in the following definitions:

$\#(A)$ is the **CARDINALITY** of A, '$\forall$' means 'for all', '$\exists$' means 'there exists',
$N = \{ 1,2,3,4,... \}$, $N(n) = \{ 1,2,..,n \}$ Integers up to 'n',
$Z = \{ 0,1,2,3,4,... \}$, $Z(n) = \{ 0,1,2,..,n \}$, and $<x_1,x_2,..,x_n> \equiv \{x_y^y: y \in \{1,2,3,..,n\} \}$.

1. ***UNION:*** $A \cup B = \{x^i: x \in_i A \text{ or } x \in_i B \}$
2. ***INTERSECTION:*** $X \cap Y = \{x^i: x \in_i X \text{ and } x \in_i Y \}$
3. ***SYMMETRIC DIFFERENCE:*** $X \triangle Y = \{x^i: (x \in_i X \ \& \ x \notin_i Y) \text{ or } (x \in_i Y \ \& \ x \notin_i X) \}$
4. ***RELATIVE COMPLEMENT:*** $X \sim Y = X \triangle (X \cap Y) = \{x^i: x \in_i X \ \& \ x \notin_i Y \}$
5. ***i-th ELEMENTARY DOMAIN:*** $D_i(A) = \{x: (\exists v,j)(v \in_j A)(x \in_i v) \}$
6. ***i-th GENERAL DOMAIN:*** $\mathcal{D}_i(A) = \{x^j: (\exists v)(v \in_j A)(x \in_i v) \}$
7. ***SUBSET:*** $X \subset Y \leftrightarrow (\forall x,i)(x \in_i X \rightarrow x \in_i Y)$
8. ***ELEMENTARY INVERSION:*** $\ddot{A} = \{y^x: x \in_y A \}$
9. ***COMPLETE INVERSION:*** $\check{A} = \{ v^w: (\exists x,y)(x \in_y A)(v=\ddot{y})(w=\ddot{x}) \}$
10. ***EXTRACTION:*** $\rho_i(A) = \{x: x \in_i A\}$
11. ***FACTOR:*** $\pi_\theta(A) = \{x^j: (x \in_i A \ \& \ i \in_j \theta) \ \text{ OR } \ (x \in_j A \ \& \ \theta=\emptyset) \}$
12. ***PROJECTION:*** $\Pi_\theta(A) = \{\pi_\theta(x)^i: x \in_i A \}$
13. ***CLAN RESTRICT:*** $A \downarrow I = \{x^i: x \in_i A \ \& \ i \notin I \}$; $A \uparrow I = \{x^i: x \in_i A \ \& \ i \in I \}$
14. ***CONSTITUENT CLANS:*** $\omega(A) = \{y: (\exists x)(x \in_y A) \}$
15. ***ELEMENTARY CONSTITUENTS:*** $\gamma(A) = \{x: (\exists i) \ x \in_i A \}$
16. ***EXTENDED IMAGE:*** $A[B] = \{y^i: (\exists x)(x \in_i A)(\exists b)(b \in_i B)(b \cap x=b)(y=x \sim b) \}$
17. ***TRANSPOSE:*** $A^T = \{ y^j: (\forall x,w,i)(x \in_i A \ \& \ w \in_j x \rightarrow w \in_i y) \}$
18. ***RESTRICT:*** $A|B = \{x^i: (x \in_i A)(\exists b)(b \in B)(x \cap b = b) \}$
19. ***ORGANIZATION TYPE:*** $\tau(A)=\{z^y: \big((\forall x,i)(x \notin_i A)(z=\emptyset)\big) \textbf{or} \big((\exists x)(x \in_y A)(z=\tau(x))\big)\}$
20. ***BASE STRUCTURE TYPE:*** $\beta(A)=\{z^{\beta(y)}: \big((\forall x,i)(x \notin_i A)(z=\emptyset)\big) \textbf{or} \big((\exists x)(x \in_y A)(z=\beta(x))\big)\}$

A4.0 EXAMPLES OF EXTENDED SET OPERATIONS

Using the sets as described in the text, the following are examples of some extended set operations:

$$\mathbf{A}\uparrow\{\mathrm{Y}\} = \{ \{\mathbf{c}^{1}, \mathbf{b}^{2}, \mathbf{a}^{3}\}^{\mathrm{Y}} \}$$

$$\omega(\mathbf{CD1}) = \{ \{\{\mathbf{7}^{A},\mathbf{2}^{B},\mathbf{5}^{C}\}\},\{\{\mathbf{s}^{H},\mathbf{8}^{U},\mathbf{k}^{L}\}\},\{\{\mathbf{q}^{W},\mathbf{h}^{P},\mathbf{j}^{M}\}\} \}$$

$$D_{\mathrm{L}}(\mathbf{H2}) = \{ \mathbf{B}, \mathbf{D}, \mathbf{E}, \mathbf{H} \}$$

$$(\mathbf{A} \sim \mathbf{B})^{\mathrm{T}} = \{ \{c^{Y}, b^{X}\}^{1}, \{b^{Y}, a^{X}\}^{2}, \{a^{Y}, c^{X}\}^{3} \}$$

$$\mathbf{H2}[\{\mathbf{A}^{O}\}] = \{ \mathbf{B}^{L}, \mathbf{C}^{R} \}$$

$$\beta(\mathbf{XR3}) = \{ \{\emptyset,\{\{\emptyset,\{\{\emptyset\}\}\},\{\emptyset\}\}\}, \{\emptyset\}, \{\{\{\emptyset\}\},\emptyset,\{\emptyset\}\} \}$$

A5.0 COMPLEMENT TO EXISTING DISCIPLINES

This brief introduction to extending the membership condition for set theories should indicate, to appropriate readers, areas in other disciplines that could benefit from the inclusion of a formal separation of the concept of *nesting* from the concept of *sequence.* Fuzzy Set Theory [Za68] and Petri Net Theory [Pe81] are being explored by the author, [Cha-f].

REFERENCES

[Al77] Allwood, J.; Anderson, L.; Dahl, O.: Logic In Linguistics, Cambridge University Press, 1977

[Be81] Beckman, F. S.: Mathematical Foundations of Programming, Addison-Wesley Publishing Co., 1981

[Bj82] Bjørner, Dines; Jones Cliff B.: Formal Specification and Software Development, Prentice/Hall International, 1982

[Ch68] Childs, David L.: Feasibility of a Set-Theoretic Data Structure: A General Structure Based on a Reconstituted Definition of Relation, Proc. IFIP Congress 1968

[Ch77] Childs, David L.: Extended Set Theory: A General Model for Very Large, Distributed, Backend Information Systems, Third International Conference On Very Large Databases, Tokyo, Japan, 1977

[Ch86a] Childs, David L.: Function Space Architectures For Structurally Independent Information Systems, [To be available late in 1986]

[Ch86b] Childs, David L.: High Performance Relational Systems For Very Large Distributed Databases, [To be available late in 1986]

[Ch86c] Childs, David L.: Reliable Software Design and Implementation Through Function Space Modules, [To be available late in 1986]

[Ch86d] Childs, David L.: Parallel Processing and Transparent Storage Networks, [To be available late in 1986]

[Ch86e] Childs, David L.: Design Specification and Implementation Control Through Precision Modeling, [To be available late in 1986]

[Ch86f] Childs, David L.: Amorphous Architectures With Synergistic Behavior, [To be available late in 1986]

[Co70] Codd, E. F.: A Relational Model of Data for Large Shared Data Banks, CACM **13**, No. 6 (June) 1970

[Co79] Codd, E. F.: Extending the Database Relational Model to Capture More Meaning ACM TODS, 4, 4, (Dec. 1979) 397–434.

[Fr66] Fraenkel, Abraham: Abstract Set Theory, North-Holland, 1966, p.131.

[Go41] Goodman, Nelson: Sequences, The Journal of Symbolic Logic 6, Number 4 (December 1941), p.150–153.

[Ge86] Gehani, Narain; McGettrick, Andrew: Software Specification Techniques, Addison-Wesley Publishing Co., 1986

[Ha49] Hausdorff, Felix: Gründzuge der Mengenlehre (Veit, Leipzig, 1914), reprinted 1949 (Chelsea, New York).

[Ku21] Kuratowski, Kazimierz: Sur la Notion d'ordre Dans la Théorie des Ensembles, Fundamenta Mathematicae 2 (1921), p.161–171.

[Ly66] Lyndon, R. C.: Notes on Logic, D. Van Nostrand Co. 1966.

[Qu45] Quine, W. V.: On Ordered Pairs, The Journal of Symbolic Logic 10, Number 3 (September 1945), p.95–96.

[Ro53] Rosser, J. Barkley: Logic for Mathematicians, McGraw-Hill, 1953

[Sc54] Schwabhaüser, Wolfram: Zur Definition des Geordneten Paares von Mengen Beliebiger Stufe, Mathematische Nachrichten 11 (1954), p.81–84.

[Sk57] Skolem, Thoralf: Two Remarks on Set Theory, Mathematica Scandia 5 (1957), p.43–46.

[St77] Stant, D. F.; McAllister, D. F.: Discrete Mathematics In Computer Science, Prentice-Hall, Inc., 1977

[Su60] Suppes, Patrick: Axiomatic Set Theory, Van Nostrand, 1960, p.20 & 141.

[Pa83] Parnas, David L.: A Generalized Control Structure and Its Formal Definition, Communications of the ACM, Vol. 26 No. 8, 1983

[Pa85] Parnas, David L.: Software Aspects of Strategic Defense Systems, American Scientist, Volume 73, Sept./Oct. 1985

[Pe81] Peterson, James L.: Petri Net Theory and Modeling of Systems, Prentice-Hall Inc., 1981

[Po73] Polya, G.; How To Solve IT, Princeton University Press, 1973

[Ru79] Rus T.: Data Structures And Operating Systems, John Wiley & Sons, 1979

[Wi14] Wiener, Norbert: A Simplification of the Logic of Relations, Proceedings of the Cambridge Philosophical Society 17(1912–1914), p.387–390.

[Ye78] Yeh, Ray: Current Trends In Programming Methodology, Prentice-Hall Inc., 1978

[Za68] Zadeh, L. A.: Fuzzy Sets, Information and Control 8, 1968

A Comparison of Performance of Similar Queries on Similar Databases on Several Relational Systems—Hardware and Software

Darrel J. Van Buer , Roy O. Gates and Eric O. Lund
System Development Corporation
2500 Colorado Avenue
Santa Monica, CA 90406

1. Introduction

System Development Corporation has performed a number of evaluations of relational database management systems (RDBMS) to determine their capabilities and performance. We have developed a set of databases and queries to use in these evaluations. Among the problems faced have been: how to perform comparable operations on DMBSs with dissimilar capabilities and optimization strategies, blunders in the DBMS internal query optimizers which sometimes cause dramatic sensitivity to the order of presentation of the query, and even a few obscure bugs in some systems.

This paper describes the basic methodology followed in performing our evaluations. These evaluations are based on developing requirements needed by a DBMS application, comparing those requirements to documented features of a DBMS and performing benchmarks to verify capabilities and performance in the intended application. We have studied implementations of the same DBMS for different systems, different DBMSs for the same system and some combinations of both, and a specialized database machine. Section 2 discusses our evaluation methodology. Section 3 presents a capsule summary of what we have learned. Section 4 presents our conclusions. Appendix A contains a sample questionnaire used to catalog the basic characteristics of a DBMS. Appendix B provides a small sample of the set of queries which make up a benchmark.

2. Evaluation methodology

In evaluating a database management system, there are several steps to take. The first step is defining the requirements of the ideal DBMS for the intended application. The second step is gathering as much information as possible about

NATO ASI Series, Vol. F 24
Database Machines. Edited by A. K. Sood and A. H. Qureshi

each of the DBMSs being considered. Many of the DBMSs will be rejected at this step because they simply do not meet critical requirements. The third step is running a series of benchmarks on the remaining systems to ensure that they meet the specifications and to assess their relative merits. The final step is interpreting the results of the prior steps to select the most suitable DBMS.

2.1 Develop Specifications

The evaluation of a DBMS must be done with reference to an intended application; it cannot be done in a vacuum. The first step is to establish a *functional filter*, which is a list of functional characteristics of the (hypothetical) DBMS required for the application, ranked in importance from five (*critical*), to one (*nice to have*). For example, a requirement that the DBMS run on a particular operating system or machine may eliminate some systems entirely. Or a characteristic such as time to first tuple that is absolutely required for one application may be of no consequence to another application. Factors which are frequently important include host hardware and operating system, data model (relational, hierarchical, network or other), query languages and embedded query languages, and special features or unusual limitations. An example of a special feature are systems which address problems in searching free text. As an example of an unusual limitation, some microcomputer DBMSs have severe limits on the size of intermediate results or the number of relations in a single join operation.

Then, a matrix is established with the functional characteristics along one axis and the potential DBMSs along the other axis. Through literature search, vendor interviews and customer interviews, the presence or absence (or shade in between) of each characteristic is established. This usually leads to a quick reduction of the field of candidate DBMSs. Appendix A is an example of such a matrix used in a recent evaluation. In other studies, more factors and greater detail have generated substantially longer questionnaires. Yao [Yao et. al. 84] and [Templeton et. al. 81] provide further insight into, and examples of this process.

There are also nontechnical features which may be relevant, such as price and support. For example, research INGRES costs nothing (if you already have the proper UNIX license), but is unsupported and has a number of problems which may never be fixed. RTI INGRES requires a separate license fee, but comes with support and ongoing product improvement.

2.2 Benchmark design

A DBMS benchmarking design includes the selection of a test database and query set, the availability of suitable hardware, the acquisition of a variety of DBMSs, and the establishment of goals and constraints by which to analyze the results of the benchmark.

As an example, the considerations and details for one of our benchmarks is given below:

Goal: Determine the relative useability of a proposed RTI MicroINGRES on a Burroughs XE 550 distributed processor with UNIX.

Constraints:

1) Use available DBMSs, hardware, and our current set of test queries for the Navy test database.
2) Complete the benchmark within 4 months although the MicroIngres DBMS was not yet available for the XE550 but was available for the Sun microcomputer.
3) Reduce the large set of performance and functional completeness measurements to a small set of statements to be used to assist in making business choices.

Hardware/Operating Systems:

1) Two super minicomputers: VAX 11/780 with UNIX, VAX 11/750 with VMS.
2) One database machine, Britton-Lee IDM-600 attached to the VAX 11/780.
3) Two distributed processors: XE 550 with UNIX, Stratus fault-tolerant system with VOS.
4) Three microcomputers: SUN microcomputers with UNIX, Burroughs B26 with BTOS, IBM PC-AT with PC-DOS.

DBMSs: INGRES and MicroINGRES, IDM-600, Mistress, Oracle, RBASE 6000, DBASE III, and S1032

Database: Navy test database (17 Relations, 88 Fields, heavily indexed, describes ship movement and repair).

Query Test Set: Approximately 50 queries (from simple retrievals to 12-way joins, query nestings and special queries).

The queries represent an important component of the benchmark. The majority of the queries represent a large number of combinations of query complexity, relation size, and number of relations in a join. A relatively small number of queries are designed to probe details of internal operation. About half of the queries access a single relation, a third join two relations and the remainder join three or more relations. The queries are grouped as a series of increasingly complex variants of the same queries. Appendix B is a small selection of typical queries. Note that in most RDBMSs, the OR operation may be difficult to execute efficiently. The special queries check for sensitivity to order of relations in a join, order of clauses in a qualification, order of queries in a session, cost of sorted results and cost of aggregation. Some test the efficiency of the internal optimizations against externally forcing a particular optimization, such as a sort-merge join. The benchmark also includes a few update operations, with emphasis on scope and duration of locking and interaction with the level of indexing on a relation. [DeWitt et. al. 81] and [Hawthorne et. al. 82] provide a great deal of insight into designing a database and a set of queries.

2.3 Benchmark execution

DBMS benchmarks involve three typical activities: database and query set implementation, functional completeness tests and performance runs, and results analysis and evaluation. Note: as DBMSs failed in functional completeness or capacity during our testing, they were dropped from further testing. Some observations made during these activities are given below:

DBMS/Database Implementation observations:

1) All DBMSs accepted columnar, ASCII data and loaded quickly.
2) There was some difficulty in moving large files among various machines.
3) Indexing differed considerably (B-Trees, Hash, Sorted)
4) There are size limitations on microprocessors.

5) We chose to use static databases with no updating.

Query Set Implementation observations:

1) Languages vary considerably (IDL and QUEL are alike, SQL is somewhat similar but S1032 is quite different)
2) Join techniques were crucial, Mistress was unusable because of its join techniques.
3) Some DBMSs use refinement techniques consisting of a large retrieval and then selections of data from the already retrieved data. This impacts the order of presenting queries which share data.

Functional Completeness observations:

1) Most larger DBMSs have more than enough functionality to run all 50 test queries.
2) Microprocessor DBMSs tend to use refinement techniques where a query consisted of several statements.

Performance Runs:

1) Databases were extensively tested to measure equivalence by value counts, unique value counts, and output comparisons.
2) Runs were automated (usually 10 passes of 50 queries each per session, approximately 1/2 to 2 hours) with a script processing program unique to each DBMS. These programs accept as input a script of queries and pauses between queries, and output a set of statistics resulting from the processing of each query. Scenarios were developed using one or more script processing programs simulating the expected user community.
3) Output was gathered and moved to the IDM-600 into a performance database.
4) Timing methods presented the most challenging problem. We measured elapse and CPU times and some disk activities.
5) We made an attempt to normalize the background load on the systems we shared.

Results Analysis:

1) We collected up to 20 sessions per DBMS over a period of several months.
2) We discarded runs that were deemed unsatisfactory or incomplete.

3. Conclusions

The PCs (B26 with BTOS, IBM PC-AT with PC-DOS) and the PC DBMSs (Mistress, RBASE 6000, DBASE III ans S1032) all were dropped because of inability to complete the tests as specified. This left just the VAX/Unix/INGRES, VAX/VMS/INGRES, Sun/Unix/MicroINGRES and VAX/Unix/IDM-600 for full evaluation. Performance of MicroINGRES on the Sun was comparable to INGRES performance on any of the VAX configurations after consideration of their relative CPU performance. As could be expected, no INGRES system was as fast as the VAX/Unix/IDM-600 combination (with VAX host with a backend database machine).

However, the anomalies (about 16%) were quite difficult to explain. The conclusions drawn that most queries will run proportionately faster on an overall higher performing DBMS, does not hold true for those few queries that ran slower. They ran markedly slower. For example, 5 of 50 queries on the IDM-600 performed consistently the worst although the IDM-600 was the best performer overall. No factor (such as communications interface or indexing/sorting method or amount of data retrieved or size of output or concurrent system load) explained the consistency of this result. Discussions with DBMS vendors shed little light on why these performance anomalies occurred but a possible explanation is that the choice of internal buffer assignment could consistently degrade performance for a given data structure. We could test this by changing the content of the database in areas not impacting the data needed for the query response. This should vary the performance of the anomaly queries but that remains unproven.

DBMS benchmarkers should always benchmark for a given application, and should exercise caution in interpreting average performance because we have found that both extremes (the best and the worst) tend to be associated with anomalies.

4. References

[BLI 83] Britton-Lee Inc.; *IDM Software Reference Manual*; Version 1.4; January, 1983.

[DeWitt et. al. 81] DeWitt, D. J., and Hawthorn, P., "Performance Evaluation of Database Machine Architectures," Invited Paper 1981 Very Large Database Conference, Sept 1981.

[Hawthorn et. al. 82] Hawthorn, P., and DeWitt, D. J., "Performance Evaluation of Database Machines,", IEEE Transactions on Sfotware Engineering, Mar 82.

[Hevner et. al. 84] Hevner, A., Yao, S. B., and Romeo, T., "Database System Analysis—A Benchmarking Methodology", National Bureau of Standards Technical Report; Apr, 1984.

[ORACLE 83] ORACLE Database System Manuals, Version 3.1

[Templeton et. al. 81] Templeton, M., Kameny, I., Kogan, D., Lund, E., Brill, D., *Evaluation of Ten Data Management Systems*, System Development Corp. TM-7817/000/00, 1981.

[Yao et.al 84] Yao, S. B., and Hevner, A. R., "An Analysis of Three Database System Architectures Using Benchmarks", National Bureau of Standards Technical Report; Apr, 1984.

[Youssefi 77] Youssefi, K., Ubell, M., Ries, D., Hawthorne, P., Epstein, B., Berman, R. and Allman, E.; *INGRES Reference Manual - Version 6*; Memorandum No. ERL-M579; Engineering Research Lab., College of Engineering, U. California, Berkeley; 14-Apr-77 (revised).

Appendix A. Hypothetical DBMS Evaluation Form

CRITICAL	DBMS0	DBMS1	DBMS2	DBMS3
1. operating system	5	4	3	4
2. capacity	3	4	3	2

3. performance	3	4	3	3
4. security	5	5	5	0
5. fail-safe	4	4	4	4
6. interactive capability	5	5	5	5
7. consistency/integrity	5	4	4	4

LESS CRITICAL	**DBMS0**	**DBMS1**	**DBMS2**	**DBMS3**
8. retrieval flexibility	5	5	5	5
9. user interface	5	4	5	0
10.documentation	4	3	2	5
11.backend capability	5	5	3	5
12.DBA simplicity	5	5	5	n/a

IMPORTANT	**DBMS0**	**DBMS1**	**DBMS2**	**DBMS3**
13.vendor reliability	5	5	2	5
14.prog.lang.interface	4	4	3	0
15.distrib.capability	3	0	0	0
16.load & backup	5	5	3	3
17.structure modif.	4	4	5	4
18.user views	5	5	5	5
19.ret.across records	4	4	5	4
20.data types	5	4	3	1

LESS IMPORTANT	**DBMS0**	**DBMS1**	**DBMS2**	**DBMS3**
21.report generation	5	1	5	0
22.graphics interface	5	0	0	0
23.user defined functions	4	0	0	0
24.screen formatter	5	0	5	0

NICE TO HAVE	**DBMS0**	**DBMS1**	**DBMS2**	**DBMS3**
25.unstructured data	4	4	1	5
26.RAS*-hardware	n/a	5	n/a	4
27.RAS*-software	3	5	1	3

28.language flex.	4	3	2	5
29.product cost	5	1	5	4
30.devel.cost	3	3	3	0

* RAS is Reliability And Servicability

Appendix B. Representative benchmark queries

1. The queries in this section represent a series of increasingly complex queries over a single relation. Several sets of very similar queries are used over a large range of relation sizes and hit ratios.

1.1

```
range of r is RETAIN-DATA
retrieve(r.SSN, r.RET-GRADE, r.RET-PAY-PLAN)
```

1.2

```
range of r is RETAIN-DATA
retrieve(r.SSN, r.RET-GRADE, r.RET-PAY-PLAN)
where r.RET-PAY-PLAN = "WG"
```

1.3

```
range of r is RETAIN-DATA
retrieve(r.SSN, r.RET-GRADE, r.RET-PAY-PLAN)
where (r.RET-PAY-PLAN = "WG"
  or r.RET-PAY-PLAN = "GM")
```

1.4

```
range of r is RETAIN-DATA
retrieve(r.SSN, r.RET-GRADE, r.RET-PAY-PLAN)
where (r.RET-PAY-PLAN = "WG"
  or r.RET-PAY-PLAN = "GM")
 and r.RET-GRADE > "08"
```

1.5

```
range of r is RETAIN-DATA
retrieve(r.SSN, r.RET-GRADE, r.RET-PAY-PLAN)
where (r.RET-PAY-PLAN = "WG"
  or r.RET-PAY-PLAN = "GM")
 and r.RET-GRADE > "08"
 and r.RET-GRADE < "12"
```

1.6
```
range of r is RETAIN-DATA
retrieve(r.SSN, r.RET-GRADE, r.RET-PAY-PLAN)
where ((r.RET-PAY-PLAN = "WG"
  or r.RET-PAY-PLAN = "GM")
 and r.RET-GRADE > "08"
 and r.RET-GRADE < "12")
or  r.RET-GRADE = "07"
```

2. The queries in this section represent a series of increasingly complex queries over a pair of joined relations. Several sets of very similar queries are used over a large range of relation sizes and hit ratios.

2.1
```
range of r is RETAIN-DATA
range of d id JOB-DETAIL
retrieve(r.SSN, r.RET-GRADE, d.BARG-UNIT)
where r.SSN = d.SSN
```

2.2
```
range of r is RETAIN-DATA
range of d id JOB-DETAIL
retrieve(r.SSN, r.RET-GRADE, d.BARG-UNIT)
where r.SSN = d.SSN
and d.PATCO = "T"
```

2.3
```
range of r is RETAIN-DATA
range of d id JOB-DETAIL
retrieve(r.SSN, r.RET-GRADE, d.BARG-UNIT)
where r.SSN = d.SSN
and (d.PATCO = "T" or d.PATCO = "O")
```

2.4
```
range of r is RETAIN-DATA
range of d id JOB-DETAIL
retrieve(r.SSN, r.RET-GRADE, d.BARG-UNIT)
where r.SSN = d.SSN
and ((d.PATCO = "T" or d.PATCO = "O")
and d.BARG-UNIT = "7777"
and r.RET-GRADE < "08")
```

```
or r.RET-PAY-PLAN = "WG"
```

3. Sample query requiring sorting. Query 3.1 is query 1.1 with an added requirement for sorting on a field other than the primary key. Similar transformations are used for all the the queries in groups 1 and 2.

```
3.1    range of r is RETAIN-DATA
       retrieve(r.SSN, r.RET-GRADE, r.RET-PAY-PLAN)
       order by RET-GRADE
```

4. Sample query using aggregation. Query 4.1 is query 1.1 where r.SNN has been replaced by a count of the number of individuals in the same grade and plan. Similar transformations would be applied to the other queries in group 1.

```
4.1    range of r is RETAIN-DATA
       retrieve unique(r.RET-GRADE, r.RET-PAY-PLAN,
              SSN-COUNT = count(r.SSN by r.RET-GRADE, r.RET-PAY-PLAN))
```

5. Sample queries testing special cases. 5.1 and 5.2 are a pair of queries which test sensitivity to the order of the join qualifications in otherwise identical queries. 5.2 and 5.3 are a pair of queries which test for differences in performance between a qualification implied by a join and three explicit qualifications. Note that the first three queries all produce the same answers. 5.4 and 5.5 are a pair of queries which compare join optimization by the DBMS with an explicit sort-based optimization.

```
5.1    range of p is PERS-DATA
       range of e is EDUCATION
       range of m is PERS-MISC
       retrieve(p.SSN, e.EDUC-LEVEL, p.BIRTH-DATE, m.VET-PREF)
       where m.SSN = 57808501
        and p.SSN = e.SSN
        and e.SSN = m.SSN

5.2    range of p is PERS-DATA
       range of e is EDUCATION
       range of m is PERS-MISC
```

```
      retrieve(p.SSN, e.EDUC-LEVEL, p.BIRTH-DATE, m.VET-PREF)
      where p.SSN = e.SSN
        and e.SSN = m.SSN
        and m.SSN = 57808501

5.3   range of p is PERS-DATA
      range of e is EDUCATION
      range of m is PERS-MISC
      retrieve(p.SSN, e.EDUC-LEVEL, p.BIRTH-DATE, m.VET-PREF)
      where m.SSN = 57808501
        and p.SSN = 57808501
        and e.SSN = 57808501

5.4   range of r is RETAIN-DATA
      range of d is JOB-DETAIL
      retrieve(r.SSN, r.RET-GRADE, d.BARG-UNIT)
      where r.SSN = d.SSN
        and (d.PATCO = "T" or d.PATCO = "O")

5.5   range of d is JOB-DETAIL
      retrieve into TEMP1 (d.SSN, d.BARG-UNIT)
      where (d.PATCO = "T" or d.PATCO = "O")
      create index on TEMP1(SSN)

      range of r is RETAIN-DATA
      retrieve into TEMP2(r.SSN, r.RET-GRADE, t.BARG-UNIT)
      create index on TEMP2(SSN)

      range of t is TEMP1
      range of j is TEMP2
      retrieve(t.SSN, j.RET-GRADE, t.BARG-UNIT)
      where t.SSN = j.SSN
```

SOME REMARKS ON THE INTERFACE BETWEEN DATABASE MACHINES AND DATABASE APPLICATIONS IN NETWORK ENVIRONMENTS

H.J. Forker
C. Riechmann
FGAN, Forschungsinstitut
für Funk und Mathematik
Neuenahrer Straße 20, D-5307 Wachtberg, West Germany

Abstract

The integration of the database machines IDM of Britton Lee and RDBM of the Technical University of Braunschweig into a mainframe-hostsystem is the basis for some considerations concerning database machines as database servers in network environments. After the presentation of their integration into a hostsystem the host interface of these two database machines is compared on the basis of the OSI-model (Open Systems Interconnection) of the ISO. This leads to a discussion of a proposal for a database-application protocol to handle the communication of database machines and database applications on the application layer of the network interface.

1. Introduction

Our experiences during the integration of database computers into hostsystems are the basis for some considerations concerning such special purpose machines as database servers in network environments. On the basis of the OSI-model the requirements of such a database-application protocol shall be examined.

At the end of 1982 we started the integration of the IDM of Britton Lee into a SIEMENS-BS2000-hostsystem. On this basis we examined the IDM with respect to the functional range of the user-interface and the performance in some detail.

NATO ASI Series, Vol. F 24
Database Machines. Edited by A. K. Sood and A. H. Qureshi

Similar work will be done with the database machine RDBM (Relational Database Machine) of the Technical University of Braunschweig. The implementation of the hostsoftware which is needed for this integration has been completed.
In chapter 2 of this paper the details of the integration of the IDM and the RDBM into a BS2000-hostsystem are presented.

The range of applications of db-machines must be seen not only in a tight local connection to one or several hosts as db-backends but also in a network environment as db-servers. In this case they serve as database nodes in a network. This can be done only if they are equipped with a set of network interfaces which is oriented at the current state of the network technology. Adding a network interface to db-machines, the OSI-model of layered communication has to be taken into account.

In order to ensure independence of the db-applications in all layers of the interface of special properties of the db-machine a standard db-application protocol would be helpful. This concerns essentially the two upper layers of the OSI-model. Thus it is a high-level protocol which is closely related to the ideas of virtual terminals as well as virtual files.

In order to get an impression, how db-machines like IDM and RDBM could be used in networks, chapter 3 presents how the different functions of their host interfaces are related to the layers of the OSI-model. On this basis some considerations concerning a database-application protocol are presented in chapter 4.

2. Integration of IDM and RDBM into a BS2000-hostsystem

2.1 Objectives and assumptions

Our examination of the IDM and the RDBM on the basis of their integration into a BS2000-hostsystem had the following aspects:

- Integration of db-machines into existing information systems.

- Functional range as database system and its performance compared to a conventional database system.
- Can the relational datamodel compensate narrow-banded communication lines?

The integration of the IDM and the RDBM into our mainframe-host-system was based on the following assumptions:
- The hostsoftware for the connection should be independent of further releases of the operating system.
- Host and backend are connected via narrow-banded communication lines (RS-232-C, X.25).

2.2 Integration of the IDM into a SIEMENS-BS2000-hostsystem

The IDM (Intelligent Database Machine) of Britton Lee, Los Gatos, Ca. was the first commercially available database machine. Since 1983 other database machines like Intel's iDBP -intel Database Processor- or Teradata's DBC/1012 are on the market (/IDBP/, /TERA/).

Since the end of 1982 the IDM has been available on the European market, represented by the German OEM partner of Britton Lee, the GEI, Aachen. This db-backend offers the full service of a db-system to the users of a hostsystem. To test the capacity of this backend machine, we developed a program system on the basis of the operating system BS2000 for SIEMENS-mainframes, which makes the IDM available as a db-backend for BS2000-hosts.

The IDM is a 16-bit machine with conventional architecture. It has no special hardware components like sorting processors or intelligent memory as they are proposed in some research projects /SZHL/. Nevertheless, since the end of 1983 an additional special processor, the accelerator, has been supplied by Britton Lee, but an essential reduction of the processing times has been achieved only for special database tasks.

The communication interface of the IDM prescribes largely the hardware- and software-components which are necessary for a backend-host-connection. The corresponding concepts of our system software for a BS2000-host are presented in this section, as well as problems occurring during the implementation.

2.2.1 Implementation of the hardware connection

The IDM offers two different kinds of connection to one or several hosts:

- the serial interface (RS-232-C) and
- the parallel interface (IEEE488).

We used the serial interface for the connection, because the parallel interface IEEE488 is neither supported by SIEMENS, nor by many other mainframe manufacturers. An implementation on the basis of IEEE488 therefore requires both the usage of hardware interfaces of the hostsystem which were not generally released and a constant need of maintenance for the software which has to be added to the operating system software for the implementation of this kind of connection.

The serial port of the IDM supports a data transfer rate up to 19200 bps, whereas with respect to the mainframe we have up to 9600 bps available. But even this rate cannot be achieved for our data transfer. Although both having RS-232-C interfaces our host and the IDM cannot be connected directly because of incompatibilities of the data transmission protocols. The data transmission procedure of the IDM is context oriented and does not use control characters. It is based on an IDM-specific fixed format followed by a variable length message. This procedure could not be implemented by the data communication software of our host which uses content oriented protocols. The data communication software of the host could not be adapted because of organizational aspects. To interface both protocols we installed and programmed a gateway processor adapting the IDM-protocol to the basic-mode-procedure MSV2 of the data communication processor of the host. Figure 1 (appendix) shows this configuration.

The first version of such a gateway program and the hardware extension of the microcomputer by an additional RS-232-C interface took us 6 manmonths which could have been saved, if the I/O-controller of the IDM could handle commonly used communication protocols like X.25 or BSC. Britton Lee has noticed this gap. It is said that ETHERNET- as well as X.25-protocols will be released this year. In addition, a connection to the IBM-block-multiplex-channel is available.

The numerous stations on the way from the user program to the IDM with communication between several processes and hardware components caused long transfer times for the first version of our implementation. Because the IDM-protocol consists of a frequent exchange of generally short messages the resulting response times were unbearable. To reduce the number of communication steps between the host and the IDM, the first version of the protocol adapter running on the micro was extended. In the actual version the IDM protocol is run between the micro and the IDM and not between the host and the IDM as in the first version. Between the host and the micro a rather logical user-protocol is installed which reduces the number of communication steps between the host and the micro to a minimum.

A new pipelining version of the protocol-adapter-program running on the microcomputer could improve the situation, where block-buffering or block-pipelining is replaced by character buffering. A reduction of the transfer time by a factor of 2 for large sets of data is expected by this modification.

2.2.2 Software-integration of the IDM into the host

The IDM-backend can be used efficiently by an application program within the host only if the IDM-host-connection is supported by a host software system which makes a coordinated communication possible between userprogram and backend. A program system including these functions had to be designed and implemented (cf. figure 1/appendix).

To begin with there is a control-process (IDM-controller) which coordinates the communication of concurrent users with the IDM.

In addition this software system contains a set of subroutines which are called in the user programs. There is a transformation program which brings the database tasks, written in IDL or any other data manipulation language, to an internal form which is accepted by the IDM (parser).
Next, there are communication subroutines with two functions:
- send the parsed database tasks to the IDM-controller and
- request results from the IDM-controller.

Finally, the results coming from the IDM have to be interpreted and translated from IDM- to SIEMENS-format.

In order to make this software system independent as far as possible of future versions of the operating system it has been implemented in a high level programming language. At the beginning of our project no C-compiler was available under the operating system BS2000. So we could not use a parser and some interpretation software, written in C for VAX-machines, supplied by the OEM-partner of Britton Lee in Germany. We decided to use PL/1 for our implementation. Two reasons were crucial for this choice:
- PL/1 supports the SIEMENS-standard for procedure-calls,
- the IDM should be used in an application, implemented in PL/1.

Basis for the implementation was the IDM Software Reference Manual (/ISRM/), which contains a detailed description of the IDM-host interface and gives support for the host integration.

2.2.3 IDM-application programs

On the basis of the subroutines mentioned above several IDM-application programs have been written.

To begin with we wanted to test the use of the IDM in the experimental information system EMFIS which has been designed and implemented at our institute more than ten years ago for the German DOD. Therefore the data structures and modes of access used in this system had to be transformed to that of the IDM. The application programs for certain user tasks had to be newly designed and adapted to the possibilities of access to the IDM-databases. The resulting IDM-tasks are IDM-stored-commands called by the application programs using parameters.

The main function of a second application program was the easy use of the complete range of the IDL (Intelligent Database Language). This program has a rather comfortable user interface, using a screen editor of the hostsystem for the input of the IDL-tasks and the output of the results. This program is used among others for the db-administration of the IDM.

Another IDM-user program has been written, in which the input of the IDL-tasks is based on a formatted screen dialogue, using the format handling system of the host. For each IDL-task of interest a suitable format has to be generated. The end-user has only to fill data into screen formats. Thus he can use the IDM from the host without knowing anything about the IDL or any other database manipulation language.

For the output of the results coming from the IDM a connection to a report generator has been implemented. The layout-specification for the report generator is generated on-line on the basis of the format description sent by the IDM in front of the result tuples.

2.2.4 Experiences with the IDM

2.2.4.1 Hardware and software

Until now we had one hardware problem which was caused by the database machine itself. It was a little bit unsatisfactory that it took four weeks to get the IDM repaired.

The IDM software is generally stable and efficient. However, some software errors and runtime anomalies occurred in former versions in our applications.

From the viewpoint of an IDM-user and an implementor of an IDM-host-software-system there are left further wishes, e.g.:

- functions over the attributes of one tuple,
- more precise classification of run-time errors,
- better aids for the integration of IDM-transactions and those of modern transaction monitors.

2.2.4.2 Remarks on our IDM-applications

The low transfer rate between host and db-backend is the reason why the IDM should not be used in this configuration for applications with a large amount of data transfer between the database and the application. The administration overhead costs about 3-4 seconds per "average" IDL-statement in this configuration. The transfer rate between IDM and host is about 4800 bps. Thus the transfer of 2K-bytes of data takes about 3-4 seconds.

The typical application of the IDM will be a database task with extensive qualifications, arithmetic as well as sorting and grouping operations. For these applications whole parts of conventional application programs can be replaced by one IDM task.

This has been fully confirmed by the application of the IDM in the information system EMFIS mentioned above. However, a reduction of the reponse times could not be verified in general because the file administration system of EMFIS executes the access to external files in a rather efficient manner. However, the IDM has not been optimally integrated into the existing information system, as could have been done if the IDM and the information system had been integrated from scratch.

In order to give a rough idea of the results of the comparison of the IDM with a conventional database system, it can be stated that the functional range of the IDL is very comprehensive compared to the conventional database system concerned. The ratio between the response times of the conventional system and those of the IDM lies around 5 on a mainframe with 2.5 MB main memory and 0.7 MOPS.

2.3 Integration of the RDBM into a SIEMENS-BS2000-host

2.3.1 Hardware connection

The RDBM in Braunschweig is connected with our host via the German DATEX-P-net which is based on X.25.

2.3.2 Software integration

Apart from the communication between host and db-machine there are no significant differences between the IDM- and the RDBM-integration into our host. Again a controller coordinates the multi-user access from the host to the RDBM. However, there is no need for a parser, because the RDBM accepts db-tasks in a SQL-like database language directly. The subroutines for the communication between application program and controller could be taken over essentially unchanged. Some modifications were necessary concerning the interpretation subroutines, especially because in contrast to the IDM the RDBM uses structured tuples.

The db-application programs which had been developed for the IDM can be used for the RDBM essentially unchanged because the db-interface of the application programs remained unchanged. Major modifications were necessary only concerning the controller. This was caused by the differences in the communication interfaces. The results of IDM-tasks have to be requested or accepted explicitely by the host. However the RDBM interface is based on the properties of the X.25 interface, especially the two-way-simultaneous interaction. The RDBM hands over the results to the communication system independently of host-requests. At the destination node the data are buffered by the communication system and accepted by the host corresponding to the speed of operation of the applications. With regard to a continuous flow of data between db-machine and application, the controller buffers the results coming from the database to a certain degree. The second main task of the controller, the coordination of the multi-user access to the database, could be taken over from the IDM-connection without essential modifications.

3. Comparison of the host interface of the IDM and the RDBM on the basis of the OSI-architecture

The major motivation for the development of db-machines is the improvement of the performance of db-systems. Having db-systems on special db-machines it is reasonable to make them part of computer networks, in order to improve the utilization of database resources. Thus a set of heterogeneous database-applications (mainframe-users, mini- and microcomputers) can access a centrally administered database. Therefore db-machines should have a set of network interfaces which is oriented at the current state of the network standards, especially at the layered OSI-architecture of communication networks.

In the following parts of this chapter the host interfaces of the IDM and the RDBM are compared, especially considering the relation of their different functions to the layers of the OSI-architecture.

3.1 Network layer

Both IDM and RDBM have interfaces for the local connection to hostsystems, namely RS-232-C as well as channel interfaces. For the application in computer networks the RDBM has a X.25 interface. For the IDM an X.25 interface as well as an ETHERNET interface are announced but at present not yet available.

3.2 Transport layer

This is the layer of the end-to-end connections. The other important functions of this layer are:

- end-to-end flow control,
- end-to-end sequencing (virtual circuit),
- fragmentation/reassembly.

For the implementation of the end-to-end conncections both IDM and RDBM map the set of transport connections on one network connection. In the host this is the task of the controller.

Fragmentation and reassembly are not necessary, because data units for the communication between application program and database have the same size as those of the network layer.

Concerning flow control there are differences between IDM and RDBM. The RDBM makes use of the flow control mechanisms, which are part of the X.25 communication system. It sends the result data unasked to the host. The host accepts the result data from its X.25 interface according to the operating speed of its users. Measures for the prevention of an overcharge of the network-system are let to the X.25 communication system.

In the actual version of the protocol the IDM sends result data to the host only after having received a request for the data. This strategy is reasonable for a tight connection of host and db-backend, when the communication system is not able to buffer data. In this case the db-backend buffers the result data until it is needed in the host. However, if the communication is based on X.25, this technique is too restrictive, because the flow of data coming from the database machine is permanently interrupted by the requests coming from the host. Both the X.25 communication system and the host execute flow control but independently of each other. This protocol does not take into account that the communication system is able to buffer data to a certain degree. Instead, it is adjusted to a tight channel or RS-232-C connection. For a X.25 connection the transport protocol of the IDM should be properly adjusted.

3.3 Session layer

The concern of this layer is the dialogue of the end-user with the db-machine. They communicate via the controller in the host. With regard to a continuous flow of data between the application program and the database the session protocol is not being operated directly between these two communication partners, using the controller merely as means of transportation. Instead, the end-user session protocol is executed between the end-user and the controller. This protocol is relatively independent of the transport protocol which is used between controller and db-machine. From the viewpoint of the db-machine the session protocol with an end-user is identical with the transport protocol.

The session protocol between end-user and controller is identical for both db-machines. It comprises the following functions:

OPEN session
  WRITE db-tasks
  READ db-results
  CANCEL command(s)
CLOSE session.

It is a strictly two-way-alternate dialogue. After having written db-tasks further db-tasks cannot be written until all results are read. In addition, the IDM allows for cancelling a set of db-tasks as well as single db-tasks, which are under operation. It is not possible to cancel single RDBM-tasks because results are sent asynchronously by the RDBM to the host. However the RDBM allows for cancelling a set of db-tasks under operation.

An important function of the session layer are recovery mechanisms. The session layer has to be able to continue or terminate a session correctly after a failure of the transport connection. The IDM allows for the negotiation of a timeout-period, at the end of which all processes belonging to the host concerned are aborted. If this timeout-mechanism is turned off, user data are stored until the connection is reestablished. Thus the user-session can be continued correctly. The RDBM recovery is based on the flow control of the X.25 communication system.

In addition, both db-machines allow for the control of a host session. The IDM-host session is opened by a special IDENTIFY-message for the negotiation of certain properties of different communication layers:

- presentation layer features:
  - integer representation,
  - character representation (EBCDIC/ASCII),
- data link layer features:
  - error detection: checksum (yes/no),
  - length of the timeout-period.

The IDM-host session is secured by periodical hello-messages which are sent by the host in periods of negotiated length. This feature is adjusted to a tight connection of the database machine and the host. In a network environment such a feature belongs to the data link layer of the communication system. IDM- and RDBM-host sessions are terminated by a special CANCEL-HOST message which can be used as well to abort the host session.

3.4 Presentation layer

The negotiation of the data representation used by the IDM is host-specific. That means at the beginning of the host-session the representations of integers and of characters (EBCDIC,ASCII) have to be fixed by the host. The negotiation of the data representation of the RDBM is user oriented. It allows only for the choice of the character representation. Floating point numbers are not adaptable.

3.5 Application layer

This is the layer of the datamodel together with the database language. Both database machines have a relational user interface. The RDBM has a SQL-like database manipulation language, whereas the IDL has similar properties as the database language QUEL from INGRES. However, the IDM does not accept db-tasks in IDL-syntax. Instead, db-tasks have to be transformed by the host into an internal tree representation. This function should become part of the IDM-software.

4. Requirements on a database-application protocol

The use of db-systems in network environments could be facilitated if a standard for the access to the database nodes would exist, because db-applications would become independent of special properties of the network interface of the db-systems. In the following requirements on a db-application protocol are considered on the basis of the architecture of the OSI-model. The network interface has essentially two aspects: the communication protocol and the application protocol. The bottom five layers of the OSI-architecture up to the session layer may be regarded as the communication system. In the following we deal with the application oriented issues of the interface. These are the subjects of a db-application protocol. This is a high-level protocol on the two upper layers of the OSI-architecture (application and presentation layer) which is closely related to the ideas of virtual files and virtual terminals.

Db-system and db-application are elements of the application layer. The db-application oriented aspects of their communication make up the db-application protocol. This is characterized essentially by two factors:

1. Type, contents and structure of the messages between the database and the db-application. This concerns the contents and the format of the messages for the delivery of db-tasks as well as of result data.

2. Representation of result data coming from the database. The types of the attributes used by the database are generally not available on the node of the application program. Therefore transformations are necessary.

The first item is subject of the next section. The second one is a typical task for the presentation layer of the network interface. This is considered in more detail in the subsequent section.

4.1 Data structures for the transmission of db-tasks and of result data

The basis for the communication of db-application and database system on the application layer must be a standard message for the transfer of db-tasks and result data.

4.1.1 The transmission of db-tasks

Considering the experiences with the IDM and the RDBM a message for the transfer of db-tasks could have the following structure:

```
+------------------------+
| db-tasks token         |
|------------------------|
| message length         |
|------------------------|
| length of db-task-1    |
|------------------------|
| db-task-1              |
|------------------------|
|      .                 |
|      .                 |
|      .                 |
|------------------------|
| length of db-task-n    |
|------------------------|
| db-task-n              |
+------------------------+
```

Db-tasks are transferred as character strings with preceding length. One message may contain a set of db-tasks. The size of the communication units of the session layer should admit the complete transfer of all types of db-tasks. Fragmentation and reassembly should be the task of the transport layer.

The characterization of this message as a set of db-tasks by a preceding token is necessary to make it distinguishable of special control messages like the CANCEL command used to abort sets of db-tasks being under operation. Such a message may consist of just one token.

Special control messages seem to be necessary, in order to ensure that they are processed as soon as they arrive at the database. They must not be added to the queue of db-tasks waiting for the execution which is generally processed in a FIFO-order. Control messages are reasonable only if the interaction between database and db-application is two-way-simultaneous.

End-user sessions are terminated by means of functions of the session layer of the network interface. Therefore a special CANCEL-PROCESS-command is not necessary on the db-application layer. In addition, a failure of one communication partner is communicated to the other via the session layer. Commands for the control of a host session are needed just as little, because the communication between database and db-application is host-transparent on the application layer.

The structure of this type of message is independent of the different datamodels and db-languages. There may be db-applications requiring a uniform view of a set of db-systems based on different data models. In this case a transformation of db-tasks between different datamodels would be necessary. This would be a task of the db-application protocol, too, but this aspect is not considered here in more detail.

4.1.2 The transmission of result data

The transfer of result data should be independent of the different datamodels for the user interface. This is possible because the record is the basic data structure in all known datamodels. Differences concern the use of multiple fields (arrays) as well as repeating groups. A standard which covers the record structures of all existing datamodels would be needed. In each case the results coming from a database consist of a set of one or more equally structured records. Therefore a message for the transfer of result data might have the following structure:

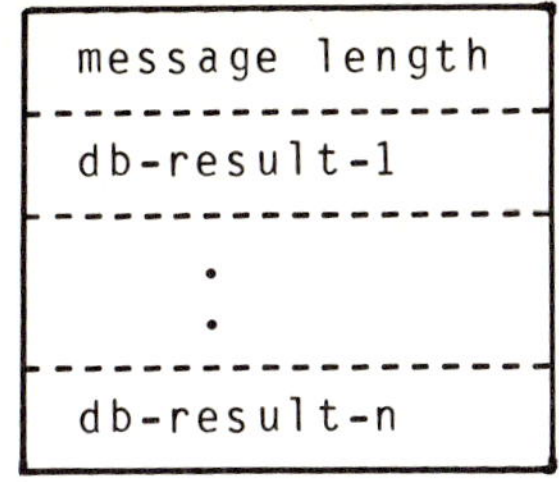

Db-results are of one of the following types: ready message, error message, results of a retrieve statement, acknowledgement of control commands (e.g. CANCEL).
Standards for these types of messages must be fixed. This could be done for example as follows:

Ready message:

[{statistical information unit}]
[number of records involved]
READY token

Result data:

[format description]
[{result record}]
[{statistical information unit}]
[number of records involved]
READY token

Error message:

[{error information unit}]
READY-token

Information units in square brackets may be omitted. To facilitate the interpretation of these messages each information unit of a type with generally variable length may occur a variable number of times. These types of information units are marked with curly brackets. So every information unit is contained completely in a message of the application layer protocol.
In addition, each message should be preceded by a specific token for the identification of the type of the message.

The CANCEL command should make it possible not only to stop the execution of db-tasks but also the transfer of result data. Therefore the CANCEL acknowledgement may occur at least after each information unit.

The receipt of results is completed either by an acknowledgement for a CANCEL command or if all result data have been received for all db-tasks sent to the db-system.

Notice that the db-application protocol is based fundamentally on the virtual connection between db-application and db-system, which ensures the receipt of the messages in the same order they are sent. This is one of the important functions of the transport layer of the OSI-model.

After this discussion of the structure of the result data some remarks seem to be necessary concerning the problems of CODASYL and hierarchical db-systems in network environments. These are based on single record access. By one db-command one record is accessed. Considering the high degree of communication overhead in a network this seems to be impracticable. Therefore the user interface of these types of db-systems must be modified in order to get a set-oriented access to the database. In this case the results have either a relation like structure or they may consist of sets of not equally structured records. In the latter case the different record-structures would have to be supplied with corresponding format descriptions.

4.2 Requirements on the presentation layer

In networks the attribute types of records used by db-systems are generally different from those which are available in the node of the remote db-application. To reduce the amount of transformations it may be reasonable to define a set of virtual attribute types which cover all the attribute types occurring in the different datamodels. Then the attributes used locally have to be mapped to the virtual attributes and vice versa.

This would be a typical task for the presentation layer of the network interface, similar to the transformations in the virtual file concept. Therefore the format description used on the application layer and that used at the interface between application and presentation layer have to be adjusted.

4.3 Conclusions

The db-application protocol has the following two main features:

- application features: contents and structure of the messages for the transfer of db-tasks and of result data,
- presentation features: virtual attributes.

A db-application protocol of this kind is independent of the bottom five layers of the network interface of the OSI-model. Therefore it can be used easily in real networks.

It is important to note that the basic idea of the db-application protocol in network environments is the uniformity of access to db-systems on the application layer. This is based on a standard concerning the data structures used for the transfer of db-tasks and of result data.

In order to be able to use db-machines as well as conventional db-systems as extensively as possible in network environments these systems should be equipped with network-interfaces which cover a wide range of all important existing networks.

Appendix:

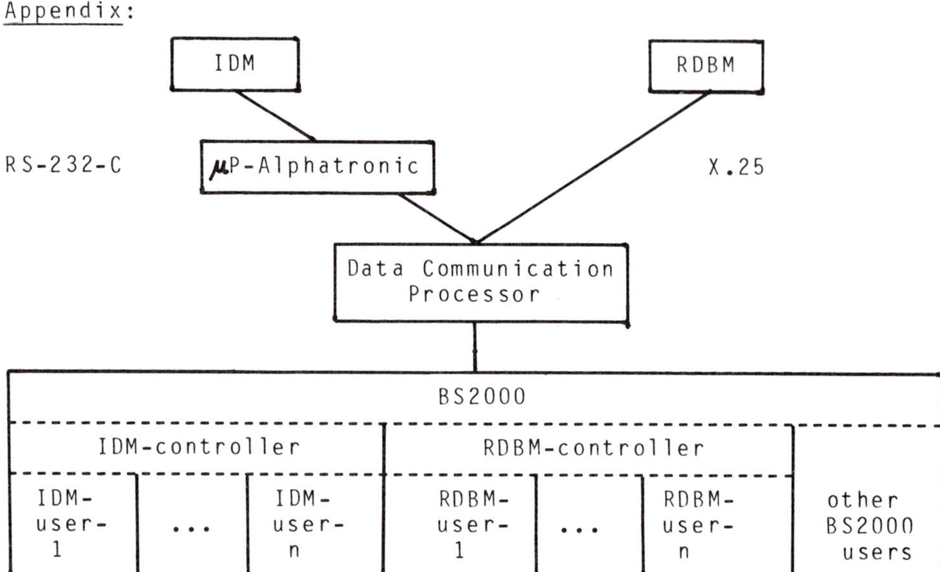

Figure 1

Literature

/IDBP/ Intel Corporation:
"Database Processor (iDBP) 86/440 Technical Summary"
Intel Corporation, Literature Department,
Santa Clara, California, 1983

/ISO/ ISO/TC97/SC16, American National Standards Institute:
"Data Processing - Open Systems Interconnection - Basic Reference Model"
Computer Networks 5(1981), pp 81-118

/ISRM/ Britton Lee, Inc.: "IDM Software Reference Manual"
Version 1.5, June 1983

/KAHN/ R.E. Kahn:
"Special Issue on Packet Communication Networks"
Proc. IEEE, Nov. 1978, Vol 66, No. 11

/SZHL/ Schweppe, Zeidler, Hell, Leilich, et al.:
"RDBM - A Dedicated Multiprocessor System for Data Base Management"
Proc. 2nd.Intern. Workshop on DBM, San Diego, 1982

/TERA/ Teradata Corporation:
"DBC/1012 Database Computer Concepts"
Teradata Corporation, Los Angeles, California, 1983

Sorting and Join Algorithms for Multiprocessor Database Machines

Jai Menon
IBM Research Laboratory
San Jose, California 95193

INTRODUCTION

Several multiprocessor database machines [GARDA81] [BABBE79] [DEWIT79]. have been or are currently being developed. The main objective of these machines is to answer complex queries against very large data bases, with better performance than conventional database systems [CHAMB81] [STONE76].

Two of the most demanding operations that must be performed by such multiprocessor database machines are sorting and join. This paper presents a study of various algorithms for performing these two operations on multiprocessor database machines.

It is not our intent to describe algorithms designed for any one type of multiprocessor. Therefore, we use a rather general model for our multiprocessor. We will describe the architectural assumptions that we make for our multiprocessor in the next section.

The section on sorting is organized as follows. We will begin by considering some new ways to use parallel processors to sort files stored in random access memory (***parallel internal sorting***). In particular, we will show how to use the bitonic merge in order to do parallel internal sorting. Due to memory limitations, sorting of large files cannot be done in memory, and ***external sorting algorithms*** need to be used. Therefore, we turn our attention to such external sorting algorithms. We begin with an odd-even sort. We show the effect on this algorithm of varying buffer size. Then, we show how to improve its performance using pipelining. Finally, we consider the block bitonic sort [BITTO83]. We show how the performance of the block bitonic sort can be improved using the parallel internal sort developed earlier. We conclude that the resulting modified block bitonic sort is a very useful sorting algorithm.

The section on joins is organized as follows. We first present a taxonomy of join algorithms for multiprocessor database machines. Existing multiprocessor join algorithms are classified according to the developed taxonomy. Then, we present and analyze three new join algorithms. One of these is based on the idea of hash parti-

NATO ASI Series, Vol. F 24
Database Machines. Edited by A.K. Sood and A.H. Qureshi

tioning. The other two assume the presence of indexes. We believe that any query optimizer for a multiprocessor database machine will find these three methods to be a valuable complement to other methods for doing joins. In particular, we show that one of the two methods using indexes, which we call the ***merged index scan***, is very promising.

THE ARCHITECTURAL MODEL

In this paper, we are concerned with the parallel execution of sorting and join algorithms on multiprocessor database machines. In particular, we are interested in the class of database machines that do not have any special-purpose hardware for execution of the sorting operation. The class of database machines we are interested in is similar to those which have been used by researchers in the past [BITTO83] [VALDU84]. Such machines will have several general-purpose processors linked through an interconnection network of some sort. Each processor will have its own local memory, and all the processors also share some amount of global memory. The processors exchange data via this shared global memory which may be accessed simultaneously by several processors. The particular method used for interconnecting the various processors is not important as long as it has sufficient bandwidth for the tasks at hand. Our only assumption about the interconnection network is that it does not cause any contention.

The database machines also use conventional disk drives for secondary storage. Relations (files) to be sorted or joined are stored on these disk drives as fixed-size pages. The shared global memory is assumed to be the cache for accesses to secondary store. Then, any page stored in secondary store may be transferred and stored in any page frame in the cache. The local memory of the processors is also assumed to be page-oriented. For a minimum, we will assume that each local memory can at least hold three pages, one for output, and two for input.

Sizes of relations may vary from those that are small enough to fit in the cache, to those that are orders of magnitude larger than the size of the cache.

The general organization of our multiprocessor database machine is shown in Figure 1.

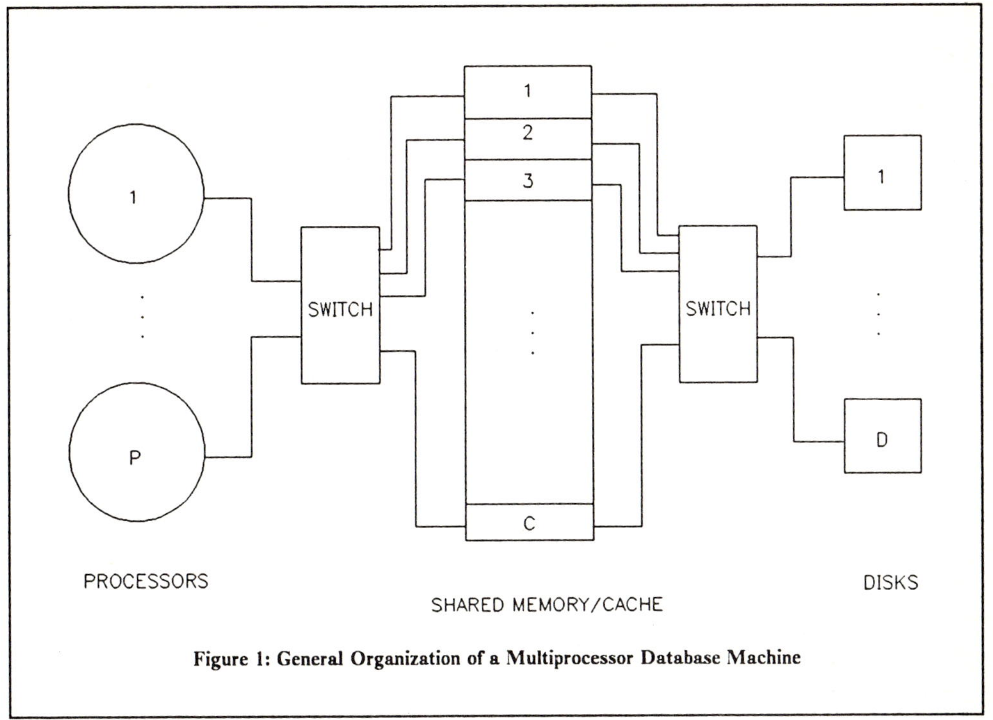

Figure 1: General Organization of a Multiprocessor Database Machine

PARALLEL INTERNAL SORTING ALGORITHMS USING BITONIC MERGE

It is now becoming increasingly feasible to build multiprocessor machines with large amounts of main memory. For instance, we are currently building a multiprocessor with four processors and five megabytes of main memory [MENON85]. It is not inconceivable to think of machines with 16 processors and 64 MB of main memory. Therefore, it becomes interesting to consider algorithms for parallel internal sorting using large amounts of main memory. Such parallel internal algorithms will be the foundation for sorting very large files (using external sorting algorithms) that do not all fit in main memory, and must be brought into main memory in batches and sorted.

Most of the work on sorting using parallel processors [VALIA75] [PREPA78] [MULLE75] [HIRSC78] [THOMP77] [NASSI78] assume that P processors will be used to sort P records. We are more interested in considering methods which can use P processors to sort MP records, where M, which is very large, is the number of records that will fit in the local memory of each one of the P processors (alternatively, the space for MP records may be in the shared global memory).

The algorithms we are interested in proceed as follows. Let us assume that n = MP records are to be sorted using P processors. We distribute the MP records among the P processors so that a set of $M = \frac{n}{P}$ records is stored in each processor's local memory. The processors are labelled $p_1 p_2, ..., p_P$ according to some indexing rule. Then, the processors cooperate to redistribute the records so that

1. The set residing in each processor's memory constitutes a sorted sequence S_i of length M, and

2. The concatenation of these local sequences, $S_1 S_2, ..., S_P$ constitutes a sorted sequence of length n.

The above definition can be easily generalized to the case when the set of MP records to be sorted is stored in the shared cache.

[BAUDE78] was the first paper to consider this problem and present algorithms for sorting MP records using P processors. The class of algorithms presented in their paper was obtained by replacing every comparison-exchange step (in a sorting algorithm consisting of comparison-exchange steps) by a two-way merge. An example of a two-way merge is shown in Figure 2. The merged sequence is split two ways, with the "lower" half sent to one destination processor, and the "upper" half sent to another destination processor.

The problem with the approach taken by [BAUDE78], is that their algorithms require each processor to have 4M memory. Thus, in order to sort MP records using P processors, they use 4MP memory. We present, below, a new class of algorithms that can sort MP records using P processors, with (M + 1)P memory. We also analyze the time complexity of one algorithm in our class of algorithms.

Our class of algorithms, is also obtained from sorting algorithms that do comparison-exchanges. However, rather than replace each comparison-exchange with a two-way merge, we propose that we replace each comparison-exchange with a ***bitonic merge***. An example of a bitonic merge is shown in Figure 3, where we show 2 processors, each with enough local memory to hold five records. The smallest record in P1 is compared with the largest record in P2, the smaller of the two is placed in P1's memory, the larger of the two is placed in P2's memory. Next, the second smallest record in P1's memory is compared with the second largest record in P2's memory. Once again, the smaller record is placed in P1's memory, and the larger record is placed in P2's memory. The process continues until no more exchanging is needed. At the end of these exchanges, the smallest 5 records are in P1 and the largest 5 records are in P2. The bitonic merge is complete, if P1 does a local sort of its memory and P2 does a local sort of its memory in parallel. The fact that the

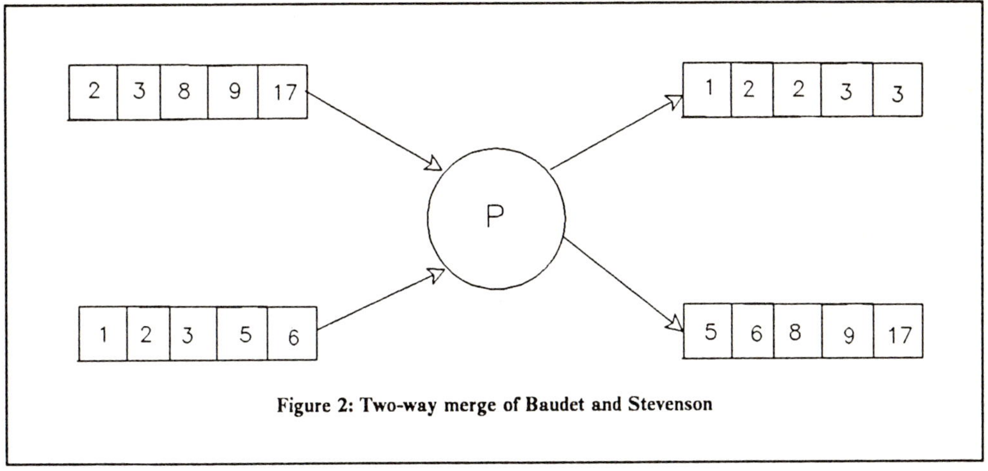

Figure 2: Two-way merge of Baudet and Stevenson

smallest records will be in P1 was proved by Alekseyev [KNUTH73]. He also showed that at the end of the exchanging, the M smallest records in P1 and the M largest records in P2 each form a bitonic sequence (a bitonic sequence is the concatentation of two sorted sequences, one sorted in ascending order, and one sorted in descending order). Clearly, such a bitonic sequence may be sorted by merging the two sorted subsequences from opposite ends.

We note that the above bitonic merge may be performed as follows. P1 sends it smallest record to P2. P2 compares the received record with its largest record. P2 returns the smaller of the two to P1. P1 waits for this returned record. Then, it sends its next smallest record to P2, and so on. In other words, the exchanges and comparisons between the processors can be executed synchronously.

Several reasons make our bitonic merge superior to the two-way merge of [BAUDE78]. First, we only require that each processor have enough memory to hold $M+1$ records, whereas the two-way merge requires each processor to have enough memory to hold 4M records. (In order to ensure that we only need space to hold M records, we must choose a sorting method, such as heap sort, that sorts in place for the final step of the bitonic merge. On the other hand, if we choose to sort the bitonic sequences by using merging, our method will require each processor to have 2M memory.). Second, with the two-way merge, the granularity of processor synchronization is coarser than for the bitonic merge, where the data exchanges are synchronous. Thus, the bitonic merge is more suitable for implementation on parallel computers that require a high degree of synchronization between their processors. Finally, if the data to be sorted resides in a shared cache, and there are more than P processors, additional parallelism may be brought to bear on the problem if a bitonic merge is used. As an example, consider the bitonic merge of two sets S1 and S2, each consisting

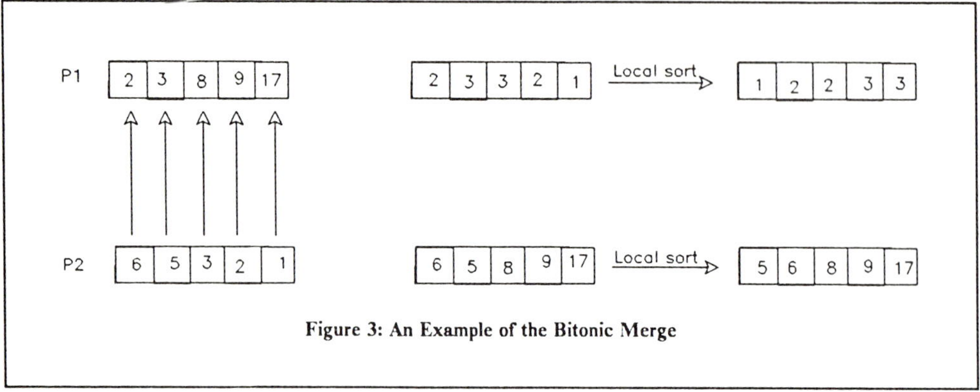

Figure 3: An Example of the Bitonic Merge

of four elements. Also, let there be four processors. Then, P1 may compare and exchange the smallest record in S1 with the largest record in S2, P2 may compare the the second smallest record with the second largest record, and so on, all in parallel.

Parallel Internal Shuffle Sort

A fast and space-efficient parallel internal sort can be derived from Stone's algorithm [STONE71] to sort P elements using P processors in $\log_2 P$ steps, where P must be a power of two. To describe the algorithm, we use the following notation. Let EXCHANGE(i,j) represent the procedure adopted to exchange records between processor i and processor j, so that the smallest M records are in processor i's memory and the largest M records are in processor j's memory. This is done in two steps. First, processor i sorts its records in ascending order, while processor j sorts in descending order. Next, the two processors compare and exchange corresponding records, with the smaller ones being placed in processor i's memory and the larger ones in j's memory.

Also as part of our notation, let us give each processor a binary index. For the case of four processors, processor 0 is '00', processor 1 is '01', ... , processor three is '11'. Then, we define the ***shuffle processor*** for processor k as processor l, if l is k left-circularly shifted. Thus, the shuffle processor for processor 1 ('01') is processor 2 ('10'). Finally, we say that during a ***perfect shuffle***, each processor sends the records in its memory to the memory of its shuffle processor.

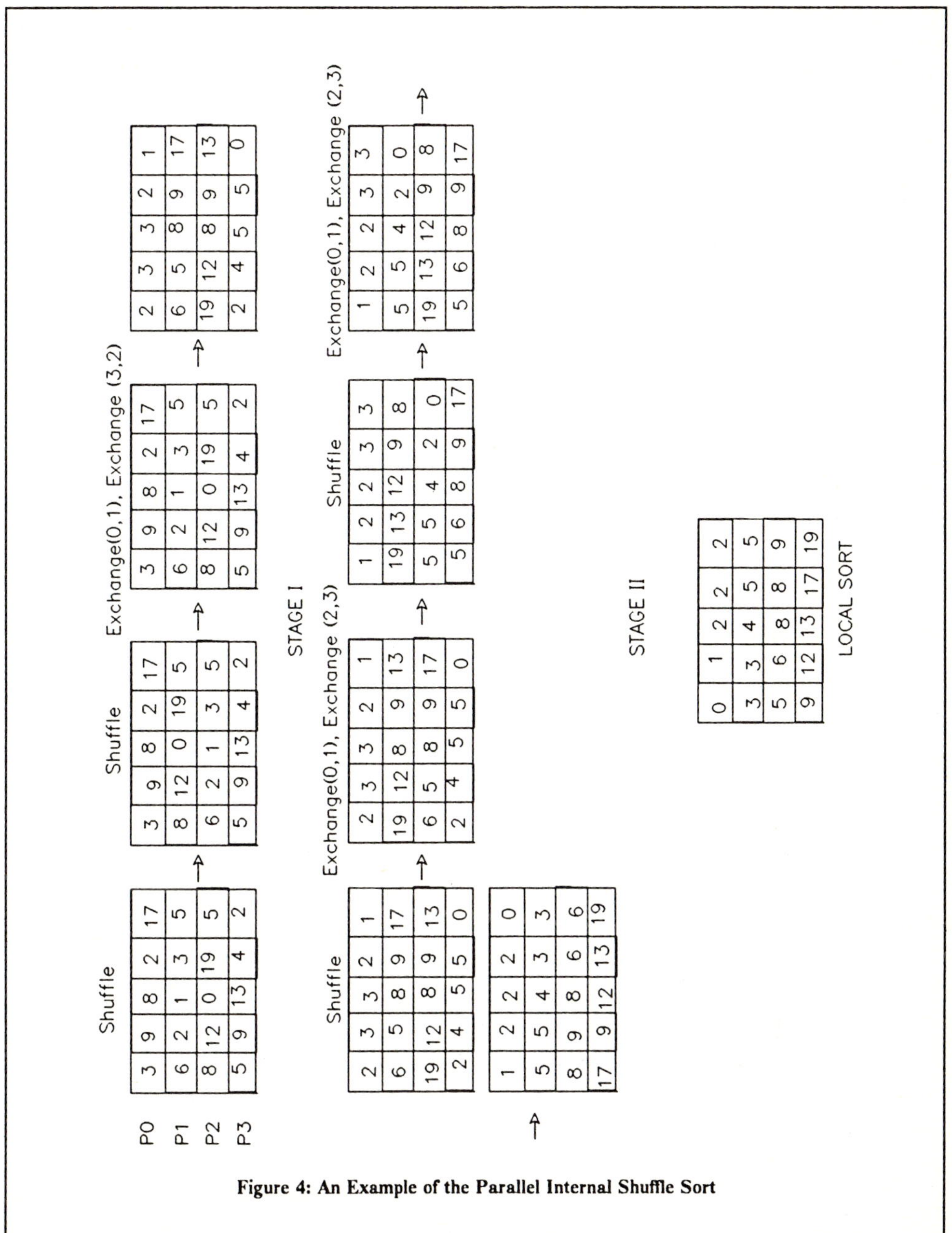

Figure 4: An Example of the Parallel Internal Shuffle Sort

The parallel internal shuffle sort is described below for the case of P=4. Figure 4, shows an example of the parallel internal shuffle sort for P=4 and M=5. In general, the algorithm consists of $\log_2 P$ stages, and each stage has $\log_2 P$ steps.

- STAGE I

  1. Perform the perfect shuffle (each processor sends the records in its memory to the memory of its shuffle processor).

  2. Perform the perfect shuffle. EXCHANGE(0,1),EXCHANGE(3,2) in parallel.

- STAGE II

  1. Perform the perfect shuffle. EXCHANGE(0,1),EXCHANGE(2,3) in parallel.

  2. Perform the perfect shuffle. EXCHANGE(0,1),EXCHANGE(3,2) in parallel.

- FINAL STEP - Do localized sorts.

Analysis of Parallel Internal Shuffle Sort

Let us use the following notation for the analysis.

P	Number of processors
M	Number of records per processor
B	Number of pages per processor local memory
k	Number of records per page, M = Bk
C	Time to do a compare of two keys
V	Time to move a record in memory

We note that the algorithm consists of one exchange step in the first stage, two exchange steps in the second stage, etc., and log P exchange steps in the final stage. Thus, there are a total of

$$(\frac{1}{2})(\log P)(1 + \log P)$$

exchange steps. We also note that there is one final localized sort step.

For our analysis, we will assume that the k tuples inside a page are in sorted order to begin with, though the entire Bk records in each processor's local memory are not in sorted order. Then, for the first exchange, each local processor may sort the Bk records into sorted order by performing a B-way merge of the B sorted pages. (This requires B additional work pages, which we assume exist in the shared global memory). The time for the B-way merge is

$$BkV + Bk(\log_2 B)C$$

In order to complete the first exchange, processors must compare and move Bk corresponding records requiring Bk(C+V) time. Therefore, the total time for the first exchange is:

$$BkV + Bk(\log_2 B)C + Bk(C + V)$$

For each of the remaining

$$\left(\frac{\log_2 P}{2} + \frac{\log_2^2 P}{2} - 1\right)$$

exchanges, the sort step is simpler, since the sequence to be sorted is bitonic and may be sorted by merging from the two ends. The time for each of these exchanges is

$$Bk(C + V) + Bk(C + V)$$

The time for the final sort step is also Bk(C+V). So, the total time for the execution of the algorithm is

$$Bk(C + V)\left[\log_2 P + \log_2^2 P\right] + BkV + Bk(\log_2 B)C$$

PARALLEL EXTERNAL SORTING ALGORITHMS

Let us now turn our attention to parallel external sorting algorithms. These are algorithms which use P processors, each with B pages of memory, to sort N pages, where N is much greater than B (not necessarily much greater than BP). Just as parallel internal sorting algorithms can be derived from sorting algorithms that only do compare and exchange, so also can parallel external algorithms. This fact was pointed out in [BITTO83]. In that paper, a parallel external sorting algorithm called a ***block bitonic sort*** is derived from Batcher's bitonic sort [BATCH68] by replacing each comparison-exchange with a two-way external merge of two runs of size $\frac{N}{2P}$.

Using this same idea for generating parallel external algorithms, we first present an external sorting algorithm based on the odd-even transposition sort [KNUTH73]. Execution of the odd-even external sort for two processors (P = 2) and eight pages (N = 8) is illustrated in Figure 5. The class of algorithms suggested in [BITTO83] can process at most 2P runs with P processors. Therefore, a preprocessing stage is necessary when the number of pages to be sorted exceeds 2P. The function of this preprocessing stage is to produce 2P sorted runs of size $\frac{N}{2P}$ each. Since our external odd-even sort is an algorithm in the class of algorithms suggested in [BITTO83], it will also have a preprocessing stage. In our example, the preprocessing stage will produce four sorted runs of two pages each. Following this preprocessing stage, the odd-even external sort will have 2P more stages (this follows from the odd-even transposition sort), in each stage of which, the processors, in parallel, merge two runs of size $\frac{N}{2P}$.

Analysis of Parallel Odd-Even External Sort

We use the following notation, in addition to those developed for the analysis of the parallel internal sorting algorithms.

Cr Time to read an external page

Cw Time to write an external page

Cm Time to merge two pages = 2k(C + V)

C_P^2 Time to read, merge and write two pages. This is equal to

$$2Cr + 2Cw + 2k(C + V)$$

C_P^B Time to read, merge and write B pages. This is equal to

$$BCr + BCw + BkV + B(\log_2 B)kC$$

As described and analyzed in [BITTO83], the preprocessing stage consists of processors, in parallel, successively merging longer and longer pairs of runs, until the

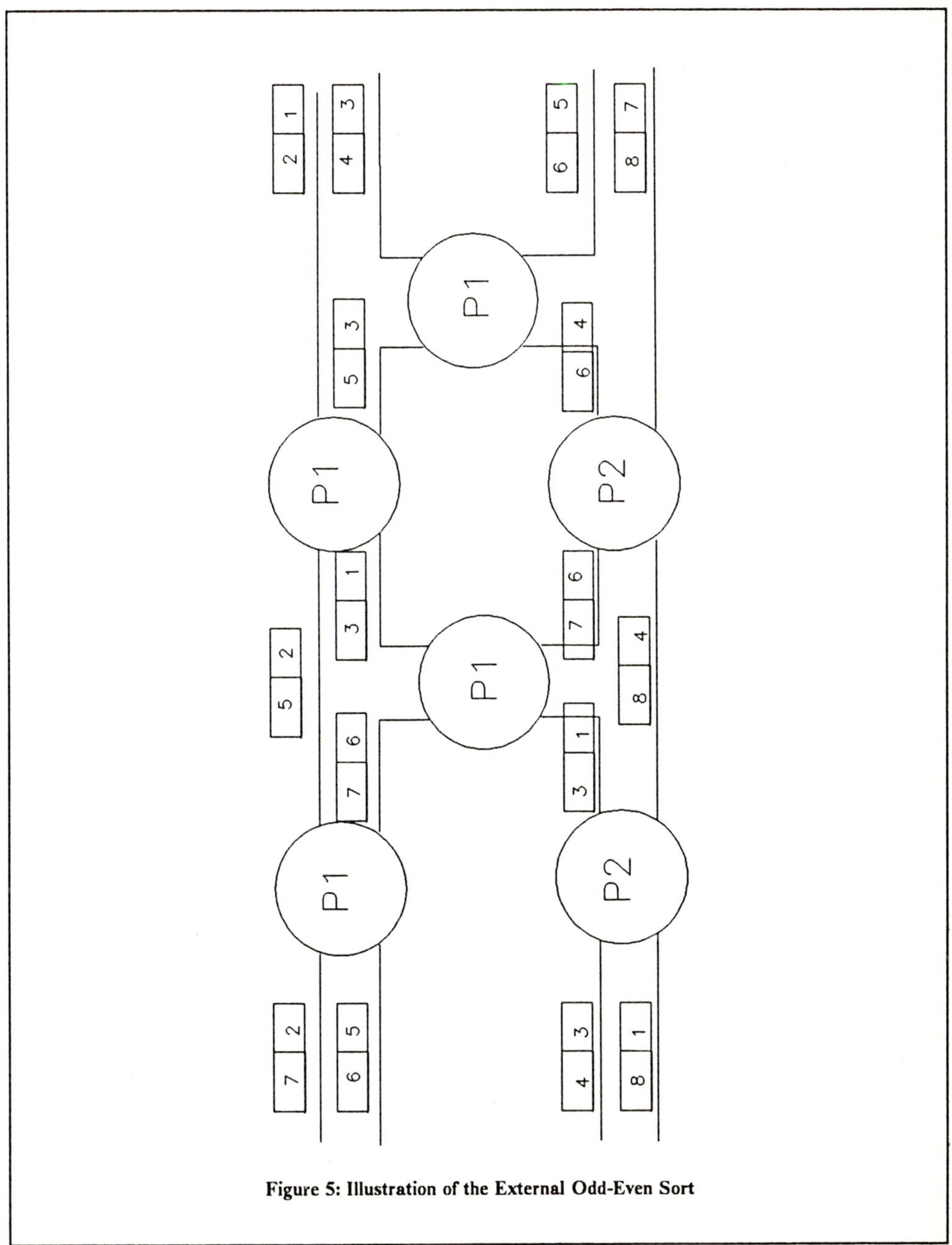

Figure 5: Illustration of the External Odd-Even Sort

number of runs is twice the number of processors. It is the job of each processor to produce two runs of size $\frac{N}{2P}$. This will take

$$(\frac{N}{2P})\log_2(\frac{N}{2P})C_P^2$$

Then, each of the 2P steps of the odd-even external sort requires $(\frac{N}{2P})C_P^2$ steps. Therefore, the total time for the odd-even external sort is

$$((\frac{N}{2P})\log_2(\frac{N}{2P}) + N)C_P^2$$

Parallel B-ary Odd-Even External Sort

We now consider the following refinement. Until now, we had assumed that each processor had enough memory to hold 3 pages, where one page was for output, and the other two pages was to hold the input during a two-way merge. Now, let us assume that each of the processors has more than 3 pages of buffer. Let each processor have B + 1 pages of buffer, so that it may do a B-way merge, rather than a two-way merge. In other words, we are proposing a class of external parallel sorting algorithms that are derived by replacement of each comparison-exchange with a B-way external merge of B runs of size $\frac{N}{BP}$. We illustrate the four-way odd-even external sort in Figure 6.

The preprocessing stage must now produce BP runs of size $\frac{N}{BP}$. This will take

$$(\frac{N}{BP})\log_B(\frac{N}{BP})C_P^B$$

Then, each of the 2P steps of the odd-even external sort requires $(\frac{N}{BP})C_P^B$ steps. Therefore, the total time for the odd-even external sort is

$$((\frac{N}{BP})\log_B(\frac{N}{BP}) + (\frac{2N}{B}))C_P^B$$

Consider the following example.

Example 1. Let N = 4096, P = 16, Cr = 6.4 msecs, Cw = 14.4 msecs, k = 40, C = .01 msecs, V = .20 msecs. Then, C_P^2 is 58.4 msecs and C_P^4 is 118.4 msecs. With these values, the time for the two-way odd-even sort is 291.5 seconds and the

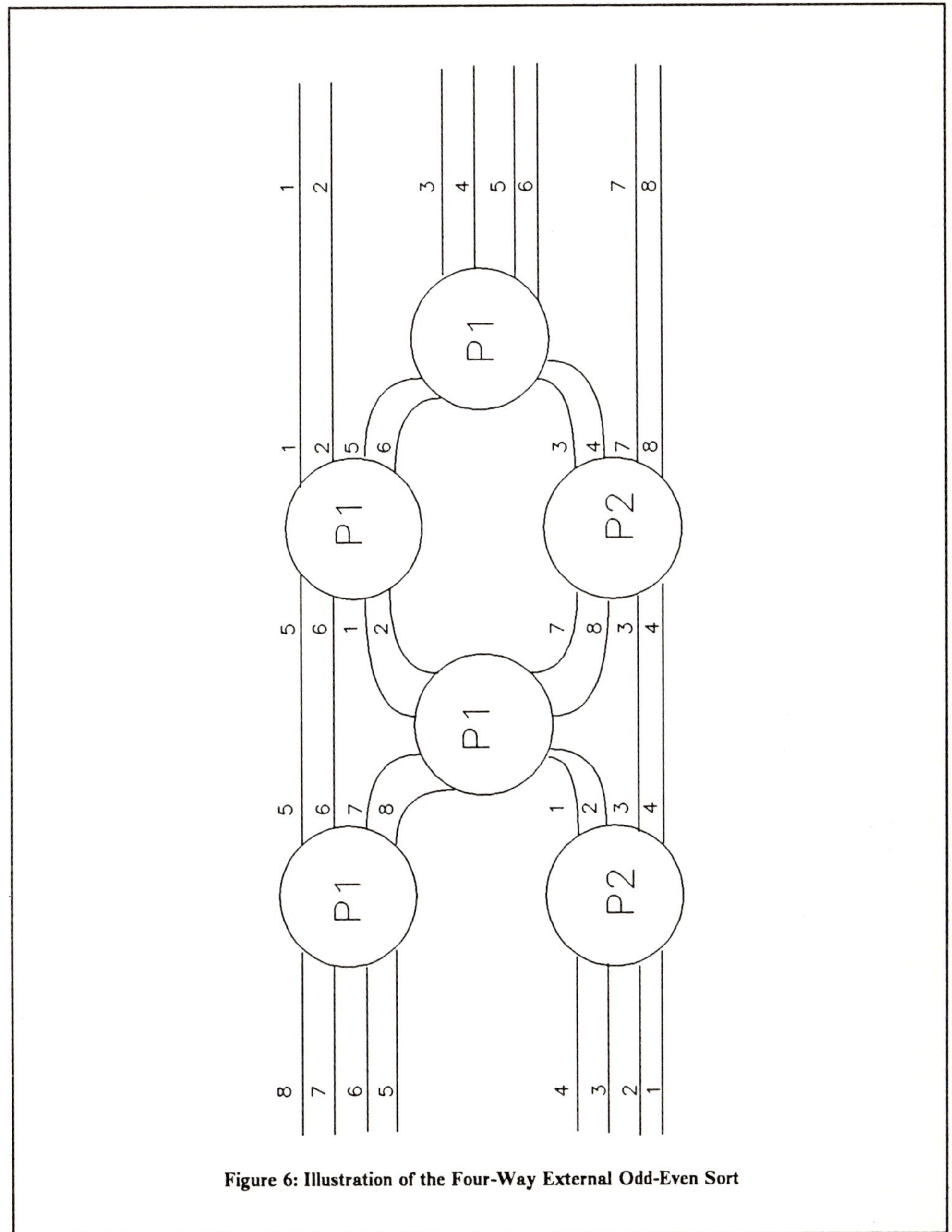

Figure 6: Illustration of the Four-Way External Odd-Even Sort

time for the four-way odd-even sort is 265.2 seconds. Therefore, it is attractive to do a four-way odd-even sort.

The values chosen for Cr, Cw, C and V above are those used in [BITTO83]. In general, increasing B helps to a point. Beyond that critical point, increasing B will actually hurt the performance of the odd-even external sort. The faster the CPU, and the slower the mass storage devices used, the higher the optimal value of B. It is possible to choose different values for these parameters in such a way as to make it unattractive to do four-way merging. Experimenting with different values for Cr, Cw, C and V which will make the four-way odd-even sort unattractive, we found that it would be necessary to reduce Cr and Cw to 1 msec, and to raise C to 1 msec, before four-way merging is unattractive. However, these values for Cr, Cw, and C are quite unreasonable. Therefore, we conclude that the four-way odd-even sort will always be attractive. In fact, as the next example shows, for typical values, the 16-way odd-even sort may turn out to be the most attractive.

In this next example, we choose values for Cr, Cw, C and V, from [BRATS84]. With these new values, we are assuming a slower CPU and slower mass storage devices than was assumed in the first example.

Example 2. Let N = 4096, P = 16, Cr = 17 msecs, Cw = 17.0 msecs, k = 40, C = .25 msecs, V = .10 msecs. Then, C_P^2 is 84.6 msecs and C_P^4 is 173.3 msecs. Also, the time for the two-way odd-even sort is 422.54 seconds, the time for the four-way odd-even sort is 388.16 seconds, the time for an eight-way odd-even sort is 385.78 msecs, the time for a 16-way odd-even sort is 382.88 msecs, the time for a 32-way odd-even sort is 391.33 msecs, and the time for a 64-way odd-even sort is 399.77 msecs. Therefore, for these chosen values, the 16-way odd-even sort is the most optimal.

Pipelined B-ary Odd-Even External Sort

We now consider a further refinement of the odd-even external sort. We wish to reduce the time taken to execute the 2P merge steps in the odd-even sort that follow the preprocessing stage. As it currently stands, the second merge step cannot be executed until the first step completes, the third step cannot be completed until the second step completes, and so on. However, if we had several more processors, then we could assign these extra processors to execute all the 2P steps in a pipelined fashion. Looking back at Figure 5, we see that two processors are used in the first step, one processor is used in the second step, two processors are used in the third step and one processor is used in the final step. Therefore, if we had six processors to do the odd-even sort, we could pipeline between the stages. As soon as the first pages of all the input runs to step 2 were available, step 2 would be started. Then, as soon as the first pages of all the input runs to step 3 were available, it would be started, and so on. This would speed up the algorithm, at the cost of additional processors.

Let us illustrate the difference between the odd-even sort and the pipelined odd-even sort by means of an example. Let P = 6 and B = 2. In the odd-even sort, we will have a preprocessing stage in which we will create 2P or 12 runs of size $\frac{N}{12}$. Then, we will execute 2P or 12 steps in a non-pipelined fashion. In the pipelined odd-even sort, we will have a preprocessing stage in which we will create four runs of size $\frac{N}{4}$. We will then organize the six processors in four steps (two in step 1, one in step 2, two in step 3, one in step 4). Then, we will execute four merge steps in a pipelined fashion.

Clearly, the pipelined odd-even sort takes longer during the preprocessing stage, because it needs to create longer runs. However, it makes up for the longer preprocessing stage by virtue of the fact that it only needs fewer merge steps and because these fewer merge steps can be executed in a pipelined fashion.

Analysis of Pipelined Odd-even Sort

We will do the analysis for B = 2. It is easy to show that with P processors, the pipelined odd-even sort executes the same number of merge steps as a normal odd-even sort with

$$k = \left(\frac{1 + \sqrt{(1 + 8P)}}{4}\right)$$

processors. Thus, for example, with P = 6, the pipelined odd-even sort has the same number of merge steps as a normal odd-even sort with k = 2 processors.

In the first step of the pipelined odd-even sort, we will need to create 2k runs of size $\frac{N}{2k}$, using 2k out of the P processors. It is easy to see that $P \geq 2k$ as long as $P \geq 3$. So, if we only consider P to be three or greater, we can do this first step in

$$(\frac{N}{4k})\log_2(\frac{N}{2k})C_P^2$$

Now, we need to wait until the first pages reach the last step (there are 2k steps) of merging. This takes $(2k-1)C_P^2$ time units. Finally, in the last step, all processors will merge two runs of size $\frac{N}{2K}$, in $(\frac{N}{2k})C_P^2$ steps.

Consider the following example.

Example 3. Let N = 24, P = 6, k = 2. Then, the time for the odd-even sort is 26 time units, whereas the time for the pipelined odd-even sort is 3 log 6 + 9, which is 16.75 time units, and hence, better.

External Block Bitonic Sort

Next, let us consider the Block Bitonic Sort which had been described in [BITTO83]. It is derived from Batcher's bitonic sorter in the same manner as we derived the odd-even external sort from the odd-even transposition sort. The algorithm is illustrated in Figure 7, for P = 2 and N = 8. The preprocessing step is identical to that for the odd-even external sort. However, instead of 2P merge steps, the algorithm only needs

$$(\frac{1}{2})(\log_2 P)(1+\log_2 P)$$

merge steps, so that its total execution time, as analyzed in [BITTO83] is

$$\left[\log_2 N + \frac{\log_2^2 2P}{2} - \frac{\log_2 2P}{2}\right](\frac{N}{2P})C_P^2$$

We begin by improving the performance of this algorithm using B buffers, so that the total execution time now is

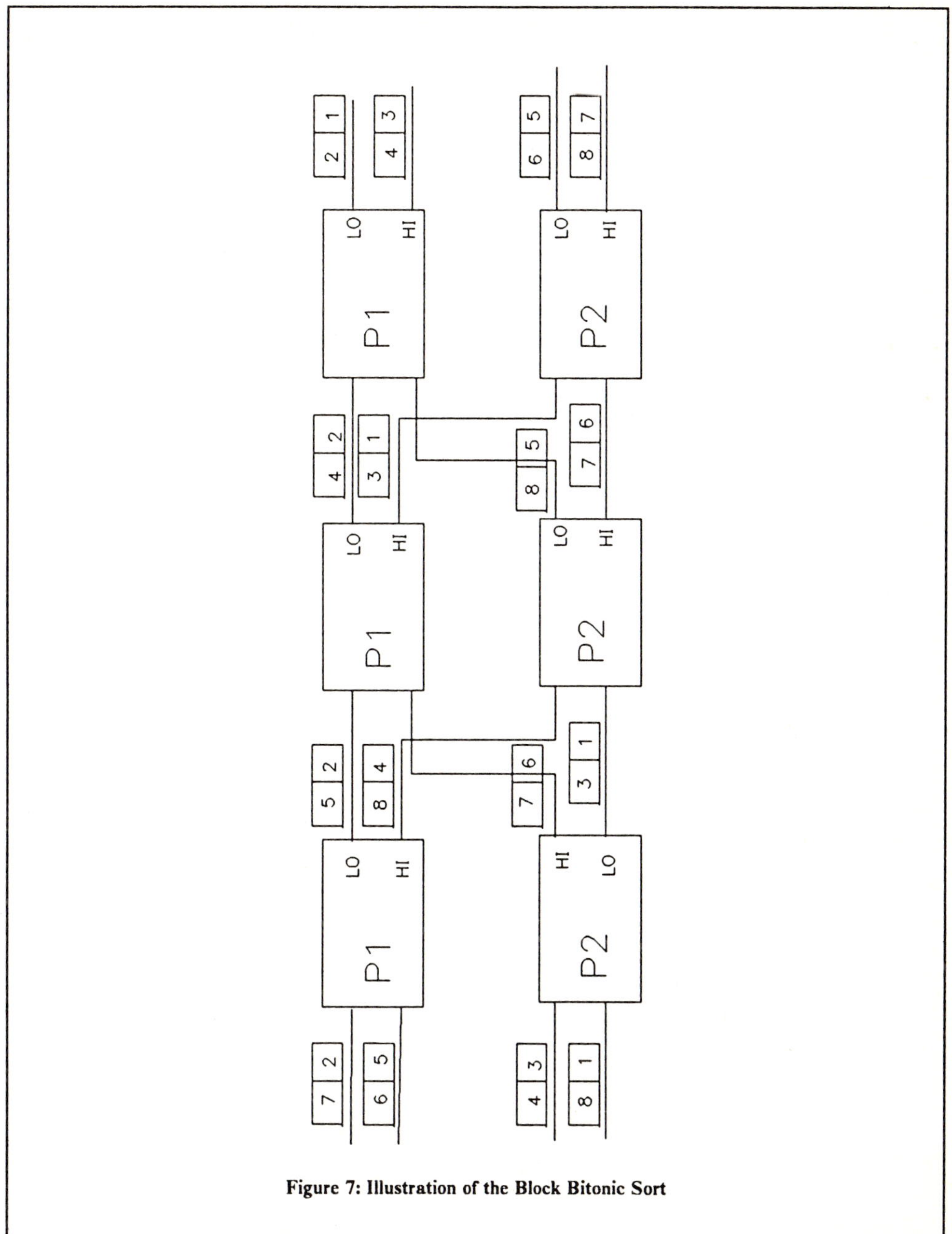

Figure 7: Illustration of the Block Bitonic Sort

$$\left[\log_B(\frac{N}{BP}) + \frac{\log_2^2 2P}{2} + \frac{\log_2 2P}{2} \right] (\frac{N}{BP}) C_P^B$$

Consider the following example.

Example 4. Let N = 512, P = 8, Cr, Cw, k, C and V as in Example 1. Then, the time for the block bitonic sort with B = 2 is 28.8 seconds, whereas the time with B = 8 is 21.12 seconds.

Improving the Performance of the Block Bitonic Sort

There are two possible avenues of attack that may be explored in order to improve the performance of the Block bitonic sort further. As mentioned before, the block bitonic sort consists of a preprocessing step in which BP runs of size $\frac{N}{BP}$ are created. This is followed by

$$(\frac{1}{2})(\log_2 P)(1 + \log_2 P)$$

merge steps. Therefore, in order to improve the performance of the block bitonic sort, we may either improve the performance of the preprocessing stage, or we may try to decrease the number of merge steps needed.

In order to improve the performance of the preprocessing stage, we suggest the use of the parallel internal sort that we developed in the section titled "Parallel Internal Shuffle Sort". Consider the case when N is very large and when $\frac{N}{BP}$ is equal to BP. Then, we may make one pass over the file, bring in BP records at a time, and sort these BP records using the parallel internal sort developed previously. After BP such internal sorts, we have completed the preprocessing stage and created BP runs of size $\frac{N}{BP}$.

Consider the following example.

Example 5. Let N = 4096, P = 16, B = 4, k = 40, Cr = 17 msecs, Cw = 17 msecs, C = 0.01 msecs and V = 0.1 msecs. In this case BP is equal to $\frac{N}{BP}$. Using the method of iterated merging, the preprocessing stage will take 35.33 seconds. This consists of approximately 26.12 seconds of I/O time and 9.21 seconds of CPU time. On the other hand, if use the parallel internal sorts, we can accomplish the preprocessing in 34.3 seconds (25.6 CPU and 8.7 I/O). In other words, the parallel internal sort can be used to improve the performance of the preprocessing stage. The improvement is achieved by trading off CPU time for I/O time.

The example above was chosen rather deliberately so that the two methods for preprocessing took approximately the same time. If the CPU is any faster than the CPU of the example, or the disks are any slower than the disks of the example, the use of the internal parallel sort for the preprocessing stage is recommended. On the other hand, if the CPU is any slower, or the disks are any faster, the method of iterated merging remains superior.

We conclude that it is possible to improve the performance of the preprocessing stage by using parallel internal sorts rather than iterated merging, as long as our processors are fairly powerful. The example shown above considered the case when the file to be sorted was larger than BP. We may also consider the case when the file to be sorted is smaller than BP. In that case, the modified bitonic sort would simply read the file into local memory, do a parallel internal sort, and then write the sorted file back to disk. On the other hand, the unmodified block bitonic sort would need to perform

$$(\frac{1}{2})(\log_2 P)(1 + \log_2 P)$$

merge steps.

Consider the following example.

Example 6. Let N = 64, P = 16, B = 4, k = 40, and Cr, Cw, k, C and V as in Example 1. In this case BP is equal to N. Using the unmodified block bitonic sort, requires 7.6032 seconds for the execution to complete. Using the modified block bitonic sort, we would need only .52 seconds. Therefore, the modified block bitonic sort can be an order of magnitude faster than the ummodified block bitonic sort. We conclude that there are situations where, even with a slow CPU and fast disks, the modified bitonic sort is still the preferred algorithm.

PARALLEL JOIN ALGORITHMS FOR MULTIPROCESSORS

Parallel algorithms for the execution of join have been presented in [MENON81] [BITTO83] and in [VALDU84]. The algorithms presented in [MENON81] and in [VALDU84] are meant for execution on a particular type of multiprocessor database machine. The algorithms presented in [BITTO83], do not, in general, assume a specific underlying architecture. Instead, they use a very general architecture model and develop algorithms for this very general architecture model. It is our intention to follow the example of that paper.

Two algorithms were presented in that paper. One was a parallel version of the ***nested-loops algorithm***, and the other was a parallel version of the ***sort-merge algorithm***. In [VALDU84], two other algorithms were presented - one was called a ***hashing join***, and the other a ***hashing join using semijoin***. These two hashing algorithms were not compared against each other, though they were compared against the nested-loops and the sort-merge algorithms. These join algorithms are essentially parallel versions of the idea of using hashing for filtering out non-candidate records [BABBE79]. [GOODM81] also explores several parallel join algorithms. The most interesting of these are the ***hashing on join fields*** and the ***hash on join index*** parallel algorithms. The hashing on join fields algorithm of [GOODM81] assumes a tree architecture of processors, and also assumes that the result relations are small enough to be stored in the buffers of the processors. If we invalidate the latter assumption, and try to recast the algorithm for our general architectural model with a shared cache, that algorithm becomes similar to the hashing join algorithm of [VALDU84]. However, there still remain some subtle differences between the two algorithms.

Therefore, there are a total of six interesting algorithms that have been proposed for multiprocessor database machines. These may be classified as shown in Figure 8. We first classify algorithms based on whether they use indexes are not. Within each classification, we have four sub-classes - nested-loops, sort-merge, hash filtering and hash partitioning. Of these four sub-classes, only the last one needs any explanation. Parallel versions of algorithms presented in [BRATS84] or in [SHAWD80] for single processors would fall into that sub-class, where the basic idea is to partition the relations to be joined into key-disjoint buckets, such that records in corresponding buckets need to be joined only with each other and not with records in other buckets. It should be pointed out that our classification is not hard and fast. For instance, algorithms that combine the ideas of hash filtering and hash partitioning are also possible (see [BRATS84] for such uniprocessor algorithms). Thus, the algorithms of [MENON81], and the hashing join algorithm of [VALDU84] may both be considered to be parallel algorithms that combine the ideas of hash filtering and hash partitioning.

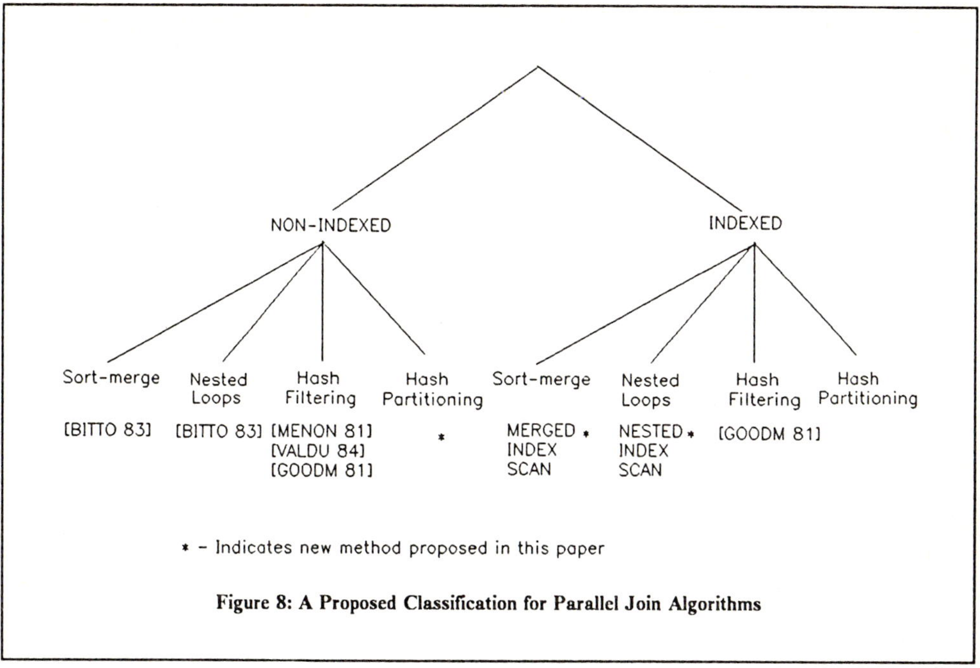

Figure 8: A Proposed Classification for Parallel Join Algorithms

We note, from Figure 8, that the six previously proposed algorithms fall into four of the eight categories developed by us. The hashing on join index algorithm of [GOODM81], is the only algorithm that uses indexes (he also proposes other algorithms using indexes, but they assume a tree of processors, parallel read-out disks, and other assumptions that make them hard to adapt to our general architectural model).

In the following sections, we propose and analyze three new algorithms for doing joins on multiprocessor database machines. The ***nested index scan*** and the ***merged index scan*** consider the use of indexes for doing joins. The third algorithm, called the ***hash partitioning algorithm*** is a parallel version of the algorithm presented in [BRATS84].

The rest of the sections are organized as follows. We shall describe and analyze the three new algorithms that we wish to present. We will then analyze the other six algorithms that we considered interesting in a similar manner. This is not too easy, given that each was designed with a different architectural model in mind. It is our desire to analyze the algorithms as the inventors of these algorithms might have thought to execute them on the common architectural model we proposed in the section titled "The Architectural Model".

Finally, we will present the results of our comparative analysis of these nine algorithms in the last section. These results will be presented in graphical form.

Analysis Parameters

Let the join be performed between relations R and S. We use the following notation for all our analyses on joins.

n	number of pages in R
n1	number of tuples in R
m	number of pages in S
m1	number of tuples in S
r	semijoin selectivity for R (size of semijoin (R by S)/n)
q	semijoin selectivity for S (size of semijoin (S by R)/m)
s	overall join selectivity (size of (R join S)/(mn))
P	number of processors
L	number of tuple identifiers (TIDs) in a leaf index page
E	number of tuples in a data page
B	number of buffers per processor - 1
k	Number of records per page
C	Time to do a compare of two keys
V	Time to move a record in memory
C_r	Time to read an external page
C_w	Time to write an external page
Cm	Time to merge two pages = 2k(C+V)

For the storage models of the relations and their indexes, we follow the example of [BLASG77]. Thus, each tuple has a unique identifier called the ***tuple identifier*** or TID. The higher order part of a TID is a page number; so tuples whose TIDs are close are stored on the same data page.

A single column ***index*** on a column A of a relation R is a binary relation consisting of pairs whose first component is a value from column A and the second the TID of a tuple having this value. Thus, the index consists of (KEY, TID) pairs. It is stored as a B-tree in order to provide rapid access to it. Leaf index pages contain the (KEY,TID) pairs in sorted order, and the higher level pages contain pairs consisting of the high key on a lower level page, and a pointer to that page. An index i is termed a ***clustering index*** with respect to relation R, if, in attempting to access all tuples using that index, a page is accessed at most once.

To understand the importance of clustering, suppose we want to retrieve M tuples from R using index I. If I is a clustering index, we will only need to retrieve

$$(\frac{M}{nl})n$$

data pages. If I is a nonclustering index, we will have to retrieve M data pages.

The Nested Index Scan

We will first describe the algorithm assuming that the buffer size per processor is five pages (two for index pages, two for data pages, and one for output tuples). This method assumes that a join index exists on the join column for both R and S. Each processor begins by reading a different page of the index for R. Then, the first page of the index for S is broadcast to all processors. Each processor scans the index page for R and the index page for S, looking for a pair of tuples with the same value. When they are found, these tuples are retrieved and joined. When the scan on the first page of the S index is complete, the next page of the index for S may be broadcast to all the processors. When all the S pages have been broadcast in this way, each processor has joined a different set of L tuples from R with all tuples of S. If there are more than P index pages in R, we must then read the next P index pages of R, one to each processor. Then, we repeat the broadcasting of all the S index pages. We continue this iteration until all the index pages of R have been scanned.

```
for i = 1 to nl/LP
 fetch the ith page of R index
 for j = 1 to ml/L
  fetch the jth page of S index
  scan the tuples in ith page of R index and jth page of S index
  retrieve and join pairs of tuples with same value
 end
end
```

Each processor must read $\frac{nl}{LP}$ pages of the R index and $(\frac{nl}{LP})(\frac{ml}{L})$ pages of the S index. The scan down the two indexes involves $\frac{nl}{P}$ tuples from R and $\frac{ml}{P}$ tuples from S, assuming uniform distribution of values in the two indexes. Then, each processor reads $r\frac{nl}{P}$ tuples of R and $\frac{qml}{P}$-tuples of S. Depending on whether the indexes are clustered or not, the time to read $\frac{rnl}{P}$ tuples of R and $\frac{qml}{P}$ tuples of S is either

$$(\frac{rnl}{P})Cr + (\frac{qml}{P})Cw$$

or

$$(\frac{rnl}{Pk})Cr + (\frac{qml}{Pk})Cw$$

Finally, each processor moves $\frac{smnk}{P}$ result tuples to an output buffer and writes $\frac{smn}{P}$ tuples of the output relation.

The total time for execution is then

$$(\frac{nl}{LP})C_r + (\frac{nlml}{L^2P})C_r + (\frac{nl}{P})C + (\frac{ml}{P})C + (\frac{rnl}{Pk} + \frac{qml}{Pk})C_r + \frac{smnkV}{P} + \frac{smnC_w}{P}$$

if the indexes are clustered, and

$$(\frac{nl}{LP})C_r + (\frac{nlml}{L^2P})C_r + (\frac{nl}{P})C + (\frac{ml}{P})C + (\frac{rnl}{P} + \frac{qml}{P})C_r + \frac{smnkV}{P} + \frac{smnC_w}{P}$$

if the indexes are not clustered. The execution time of this algorithm can be reduced if there are more than five buffers per processor. With B+1 buffers per processor ($B \geq 4$), B-3 buffers may be used for holding the index pages from the R relation. Then, the total time for execution is

$$(\frac{nl}{LP})C_r + (\frac{nlml}{L^2P(B-3)})C_r + (\frac{nl}{P})C + (\frac{ml}{P})C + (\frac{rnl}{Pk} + \frac{qml}{Pk})C_r + \frac{smnkV}{P} + \frac{smnC_w}{P}$$

if the indexes are clustered, and

$$(\frac{nl}{LP})C_r + (\frac{nlml}{L^2P(B-3)})C_r + (\frac{nl}{P})C + (\frac{ml}{P})C + (\frac{rnl}{P} + \frac{qml}{P})C_r + \frac{smnkV}{P} + \frac{smnC_w}{P}$$

if the indexes are not clustered.

The Merged Index Scan

We now propose the following refinement of the nested index scan. We use the fact that the values of the keys as they appear in the leaf pages of the indexes are already sorted. Therefore, it is not really necessary to examine every page of the index on relation S for a page of the index on relation R. Only the relevant pages of the index on relation S need to be examined. We show an example of what we mean in Figure 9. In this example, we show three processors attempting a join between relations R and S. Three leaf index pages exist on the relation R and three leaf index pages exist on the relation S. First, each processor reads a different page of the index on R. Then, each processor reads only the relevant pages of the index on S. The subsequent retrieval of tuples from R and S, their joining and output are as for the nested index scan. We call this method the ***merged index scan***, and analyze its execution time as

$$(\frac{nl}{LP})C_r + (\frac{ml}{LP})C_r + (\frac{nl}{P})C + (\frac{ml}{P})C + (\frac{rnl}{Pk} + \frac{qml}{Pk})C_r + \frac{smnkV}{P} + \frac{smnC_w}{P}$$

if the indexes are clustered, and

$$(\frac{nl}{LP})C_r + (\frac{ml}{LP})C_r + (\frac{nl}{P})C + (\frac{ml}{P})C + (\frac{rnl}{P} + \frac{qml}{P})C_r + \frac{smnkV}{P} + \frac{smnC_w}{P}$$

if the indexes are not clustered.

It is easy to see, from the equations, that the nested index scan will approach the performance of the merged index scan when the buffers are large enough to hold $\frac{nl}{LP}$ pages of the the index for R.

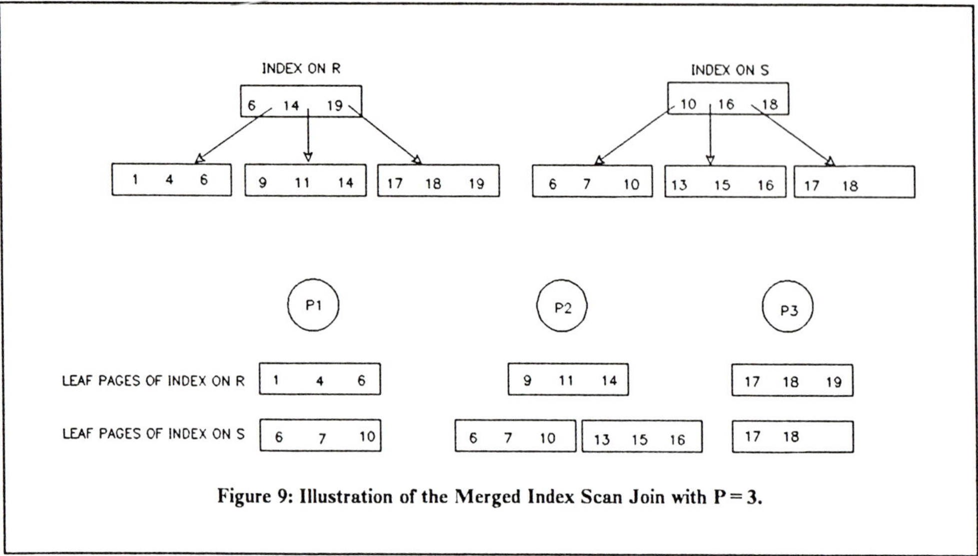

Figure 9: Illustration of the Merged Index Scan Join with P = 3.

Hash Partitioning Join

The method works as follows and consists of two steps. In the first step, we partition each of the relations R and S into P buckets. The bucket into which a tuple falls is determined by the join index value in the tuple. In the second step, each processor does a join of all the tuples from R that fall into a bucket, with all of the tuples from S that fall in the same bucket. With each processor doing the join on a different bucket, all the P processors may join all the P buckets in parallel.

The number of partitions that can be created in each pass is only limited by the number of buffers available. With B + 1 buffers, B partitions can be created in a single pass. If the number of processors exceeds B, we will need multiple passes over the data in order to create the P partitions. [BRATS84] has shown that the number of passes needed in order to create X partitions with B + 1 buffers is 0, if X is 1, is 1 if $X \leq B$ and is approximately $\log_B X$ otherwise.

In each pass over the data, we will read and write every page, and each tuple will be subject to a hash and a move to the appropriate output buffer, depending on the hash value. Thus, each pass over the R relation requires

$$(\frac{1}{P})[C_r n + C_w n + nI(C + V)]$$

and each pass over the S relation requires

$$(\frac{1}{P})\left[C_r m + C_w m + mI(C + V)\right]$$

For step 2, any uniprocessor join algorithm may be used. We suggest the use of a hash partitioning uniprocessor method [BRATS84]. That is, each processor makes one or more passes over the $\frac{n}{P}$ pages of the R relation and the $\frac{m}{P}$ pages of the S relation belonging to the bucket that it was allocated. At the end of these passes, the smaller of these, say $\frac{m}{P}$ has been divided into X partitions, each of size B, where X is $\frac{m}{PB}$. The larger relation has also been divided into X partitions of size $\frac{nB}{m}$. As before, the number of passes needed in order to create X partitions with B + 1 buffers is 0, if X is 1, is 1 if $X \leq B$ and is approximately $\log_B X$ otherwise. The purpose of these passes is to create partitions that will fit in the local buffer memory of a processor. The time to execute each one of these passes is identical to the time to execute each one of the earlier passes.

Now, a nested-loops algorithm may be used to join the corresponding X partitions of the R and S relations. The nested-loops is a good algorithm to use if the sizes of the relations are small and if one of the relations fits in memory as is true in our case.

Using the nested-loops algorithm, we read all of the smaller relation partition into memory. Then, we read the tuples of the larger relation partition, and compare its join value with that of all records from the first relation partition that are stored in memory. When we find a match, the tuples are concatenated and output. The total time for joining all X partitions with nested-loops is

$$C_r\frac{n}{p} + C_r\frac{m}{p} + (\frac{mI}{p})(C + V) + (\frac{nI}{p})(2C) + (\frac{smnk}{p})V + (\frac{smn}{p})C_w$$

Comparative Analysis

Similar analyses of each of the other six methods mentioned in the introduction were made. The analysis is too detailed to present here. So are all the results. A detailed comparison of all the methods is beyond the scope of this paper. We will only show three graphs, one showing the variation in execution time of all methods versus the sizes of the relations being joined (Figure 10), one showing the variation in execution time of all methods versus the number of processors employed (Figure

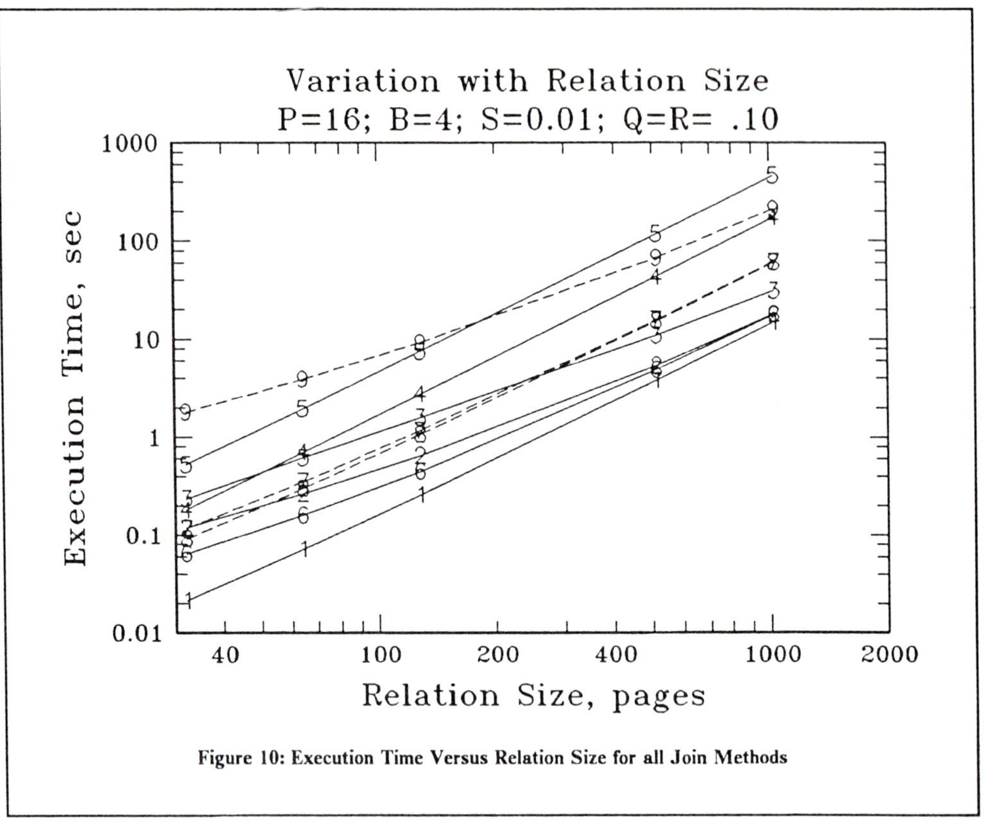

Figure 10: Execution Time Versus Relation Size for all Join Methods

11), and one showing the variation in execution time of all methods versus the number of buffers employed (Figure 12). Our only intention, in this paper, is to show that the merged index scan and the hash partitioning algorithms are worthy candidates for consideration by the query optimizer of a multiprocessor database machine.

In these figures,

1 represents the merged index scan with clustered indexes

2 represents the merged index scan with nonclustered indexes

3 represents the hash partitioning method

4 represents the nested-loops method [BITTO83]

5 represents the hashing join [VALDU84]

6 represents the hashing join using semijoin [VALDU84]

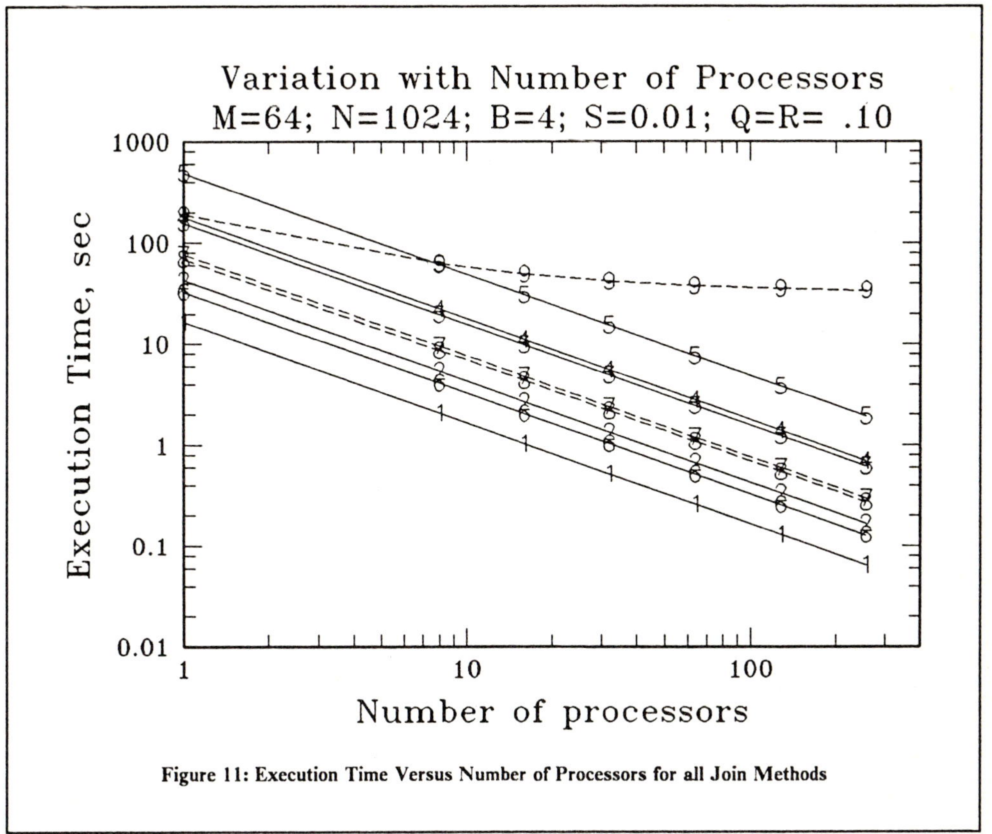

Figure 11: Execution Time Versus Number of Processors for all Join Methods

7 represents the hashing on join fields [GOODM81]

8 represents the hash on join index [GOODM81]

9 represents the sort-merge method [BITTO83]

Figure 10 shows the results for a case where we have assumed 16 processors, 4 buffers per processor, a join selectivity factor of 0.01 and semijoin selectivities of 0.1. ***For this case***, the merged index scan appears to be the best method of all when clustering indexes exist. Without clustering indexes, the merged index scan is third or fourth best for small relation sizes and second best at large relation sizes. The hashing join using semijoin appears to be the best of the non-indexed methods. For the situation shown in the figure, it appears to be the method of choice when no indexes exist, or when the indexes on the join columns are not clustering indexes. The sort-merge join, the nested loop join and the hashing join all have fairly slow execution times for the case considered. The performance of the hashing methods of [GOODM81] and the hash partitioning method proposed by us seem to lie in between

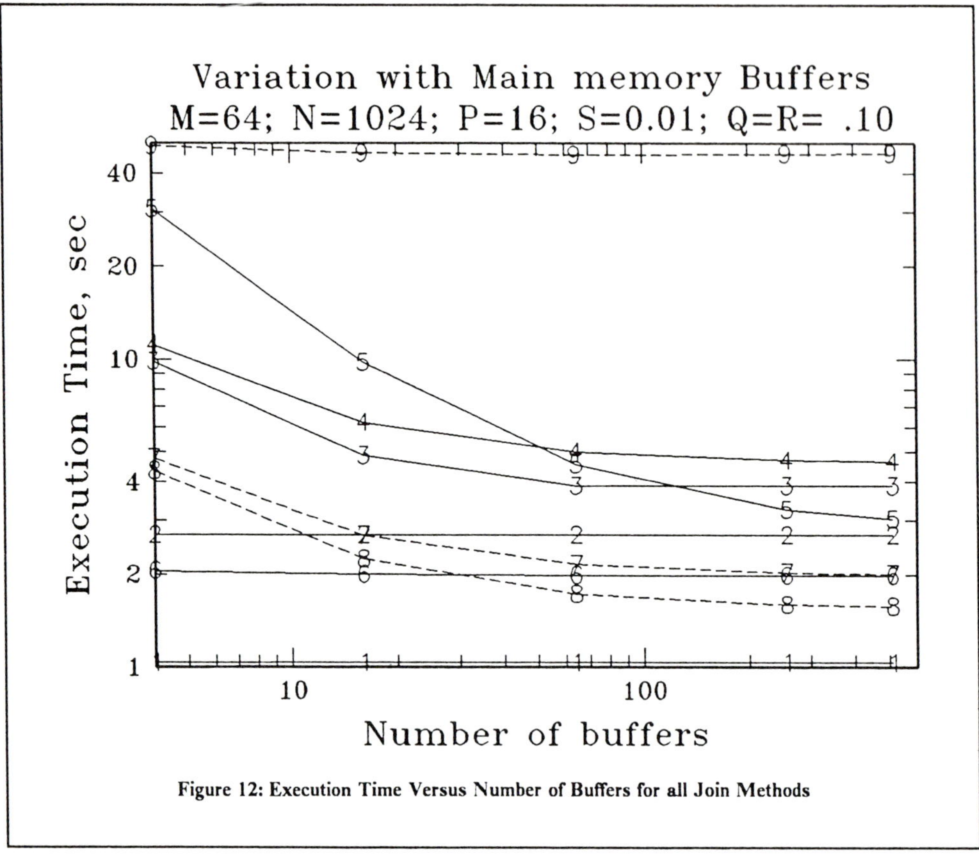

Figure 12: Execution Time Versus Number of Buffers for all Join Methods

the performance of the merged index scan and hashing join using semijoin methods on the one hand and the nested-loops, sort-merge and hashing join methods on the other hand.

Figure 11 shows the variation in execution time with number of processors. All the methods, except for the sort-merge algorithm, make good use of extra processors to reduce execution time. The sort-merge algorithm has a final phase in which the merging is done by a single processor. This accounts for the fact that it does not make as good use of extra processors as some of the other methods (To be fair, [BITTO83] mentions some ways for speeding up the sort-merge by use of pipelining during the join phases and by other ways, and none of these enhancements were considered in the results shown in Figure 11).

Finally, Figure 12 shows the variation in execution time with additional buffers in the processors. The merged index scan, the hashing using semijoin, and the sort-merge make little use of additional buffering capability. All the other methods utilize the extra buffering capability to various degrees. The hashing join, and the methods of [GOODM81] make the best use of extra buffers. In fact, with very large number of buffers, the hashing on join index method described in that reference supplants the hashing join using semijoin as the second-best method.

We would like to emphasize that we have shown only some points in the entire spectrum of possible points that may be used to compare the different methods. Our intention was only to show that such a comparison can be made and that such a comparison must include at least the nine methods considered in this paper. However, a complete and thorough analysis of the different methods can only be presented in a forthcoming paper. As far as this paper is concerned, our main purpose was to introduce several new algorithms and analyze them. We make no claims as to the relative superiority or the inferiority of any of the methods in general.

BIBLIOGRAPHY

[BABBE79] Babb, E., Implementing a Relational Database by Means of Specialized Hardware, *ACM Transactions on Database Systems* **4, No.1** (March 1979) pp. 1-29.

[BATCH68] Batcher, K. E., Sorting Networks and their Applications, *Proceedings of the 1968 Spring Joint Computer Conference* **32** (Atlantic City, N. J., May 1968) pp. 307-314.

[BAUDE78] Baudet, G. and Stevenson, D., Optimal Sorting Algorithms for Parallel Computers, *IEEE-TC* **C-27, No.1** (Jan. 1978).

[BITTO82] Bitton, D., Design, Analysis and Implementation of Parallel External Sorting Algorithms, Ph. D. Dissertation, TR484, Computer Science Department, University of Wisconsin, Madison (Jan. 1982).

[BITTO83] Bitton, D., Boral, H., Dewitt, D. J., and Wilkinson, W. K., Parallel Algorithms for the Execution of Relational Database Operations, *ACM Transactions on Database Systems* **8, No. 3** (Sept 1983).

[BITTO84] Bitton, D., Dewitt, D. J., Hsiao, D. K., and Menon, M. J., A Taxonomy of Parallel Sorting, *Computing Surveys* **16, No.3** (Sep. 1984).

[BLASG77] Blasgen, M. W., and Eswaran, K. P., Storage and Access in Relational Data Bases, *IBM Systems Journal* **16, No.4** (1977).

[BRATS84] Bratsbergsengen, K., Hashing Methods and Relational Algebra Operations, *Proceedings of Tenth International Conference on VLDB* (Singapore, August 1984).

[CHAMB81] Chamberlin, D. D., Gilbert, A. M., and Yost, R. A., A History of System-R and SQL-data system, *Proceedings of Seventh International Conference on VLDB* (Cannes, France, Sept. 1981).

[DEWIT79] Dewitt, D. J., Query Execution in DIRECT, *Proceedings of ACM SIGMOD Conference* (New York, May 1979).

[GARDA81] Gardarin, G., An Introduction to SABRE: a multimicroprocessor database machinc, *Sixth Workshop on Computer Architecture for Non-numeric Processing* (Hyeres, France, June 1981).

[GOODM81] Goodman, J. R., An Investigation of Multiprocessor Architectures and Algorithms for Database Management, Ph. D. Dissertation, UCB/ERL/M81/33, College of Engineering, Berkeley, Ca. (May 1981).

[HIRSC78] Hirschberg, D. S., Fast Parallel Sorting Algorithms, *Communications of the ACM* **21, No.8** (Aug. 1978).

[HSIAO80] Hsiao, D. K., and Menon, M. J., Parallel Record Sorting Methods for Hardware Realization, Technical Report, OSU-CISRC-TR-80-7, Computer and Information Science Department, Ohio State University, Columbus, Ohio (July 1980).

[KNUTH73] Knuth, D. E., *The Art of Computer Programming,* Addison Wesley (Reading, 1973).

[MENON81] Menon, M. J., and Hsiao, D. K., Design and Analysis of Relational Join Operations of a Database Computer (DBC), *Proceedings of Seventh International Conference on VLDB* (Cannes, Sept. 1981).

[MENON85] Menon, M. J., IBM Internal memo.

[MULLE75] Muller, D. E., and Preparata, F. P., Bounds to Complexities of Networks for Sorting and for Switching, *Journal of the ACM* **22, No. 2** (Apr. 1975).

[NASSI78] Nassimi, D., and Sahni, S., Bitonic Sort on a Mesh Connected Parallel Computer, *IEEE Transactions on Computers* **C-27, No. 1** (Jan. 1978).

[PREPA78] Preparata, F. P., New Parallel Sorting Schemes, *IEEE Transactions on Computers* **C-27, No. 7** (July 1978).

[SHAWD80] Shaw, D., A Relational Database Machine Architecture, *Fifth Annual Workshop on Computer Architecture for Non-numeric Processing* (Asilomar, March 1980).

[STONE71] Stone, H. S., Parallel Processing with the Perfect Shuffle, *IEEE Transactions on Computers* **C-20,2** (Feb. 1971).

[STONE76] Stonebraker, M., Wong, E., and Kreps, P., The Design and Implementation of INGRES, *ACM Transactions on Database Systems* **1, 3** (Sept. 1976).

[THOMP77] Thompson, C. D., and Kung, H. T., Sorting on a Mesh-Connected Parallel Computer, *Communications of the ACM* **20, 4** (Apr. 1977).

[VALDU84] Valduriez, P. and Gardarin, G., Join and Semi-Join Algorithms for a Multiprocessor Database Machine, *ACM Transactions on Database Systems* **9, No. 1** (March 1984).

[VALIA75] Valiant, L. G., Parallelism in Comparison Problems, *SIAM Journal of Computing* **3, No. 4** (Sept. 1975).

From Databases to Artificial Intelligence: A Hardware Point of View.

R. Gonzalez-Rubio and J. Rohmer.

BULL. Centre de Recherche.
PC 58A13. 68 Route de Versailles.
78430 Louveciennes B.P.3. FRANCE.
Telex 697030 CIIHB F.
Telephone: 33 (3) 902 42 11.

ABSTRACT.

This paper discusses common ground and similarities between Artificial Intelligence and DataBase systems. The central point is that the same specialized hardware could be used in both domains.

We present first some algorithms and models of computation, then some hardware to build the machines.

This work was partially supported by ESPRIT Project KIMS and ESPRIT Project 415.

---

1. Introduction.

Our experience is that DataBase (DB) hardware is a good basis for the study and development of hardware for Artificial Intelligence (AI). The main reason is that at the heart of these two domains of processing (DB and AI) the data to be manipulated are symbols. Furthermore, both domains require associative access to data (content addressing), and also set-oriented processing.

This paper is divided in two parts, algorithms and architectures.

First, we explain how, in many cases, it is possible to transform complex inference problems of AI into simpler problems of relational algebra. We have proposed the so-called "Alexander Method" to process this transformation.

The advantage of the Alexander Method is that the problems transformed from interface to relational algebra can be processed in parallel, since relational algebra itself can. Selection, joins, etc. could be executed in parallel.

NATO ASI Series, Vol. F 24
Database Machines. Edited by A. K. Sood and A. H. Qureshi

A model of parallel execution based upon these principles is presented.

However, there are some differences between AI and DB. Whereas in DB data are usually flat (records, tuples), AI applications are used to manipulate tree-structureed data, structures which require different implementation techniques.

We propose two different approaches to adapt architectures in order to process trees:

- either we reduce trees to flat relations representing the structure of the tree,

- or we can directly represent trees as raw data, as parenthesized expressions for instance.

We then describe the architecture of a very versatile processor/filter called SCHUSS, a processor that could be used as a fundamental component of a DB machine. It is very well suited to perform algorithms of relational algebra in a serial manner.

DB and AI both require basic algorithms such as tree processing using tagged data as descriptors. Comparisions of the execution of such algorithms on a classical architecture (MC68020) and on a non-classical architectures (SCHUSS) are given.

We finish with a proposal of a MultiSCHUSS architecture.

2. Algorithms from DataBases to Artificial Intelligence.

2.1 The "Alexander Method".

The Alexander Method <ROH 85> is a transformation of inference problems into DB problems.

The following problem is central in the research on deductive DB and more generally in the domain of the relationship between logic and DB.

Given a relational query including virtual relations defined from (possible recursive) axioms (Horn Clauses, with all variables in the conclusion predefined in the hypotheses), how can one translate this query into a relational program, i.e. a set of relational operations concerning only real (non virtual) relations.

Given a very large deductive DB, the objective is to avoid, storing the data as Prolog clauses, since we know that the backtrack mechanism of Prolog performs the operations one tuple at a time, with the worst case for join operations, i.e. nested loops.

The idea is to take advantage of the optimization

techniques developed for DB management systems. We want to use only these techniques to access the data, and not the usual Prolog techniques.

The solution consists in:

1) the initial query is first considered as a goal "à la Prolog", to be solved by backward chaining,

2) this query is translated into a set of clauses which will be processed by forward chaining,

3) this last set of forward clauses is itself translated into pure relational operations.

The problem of recursive axioms of deductive DB is in some sense a "Gordian knot". The naive and classical method of dealing with recursion, i.e. backward chaining with backtrack and several stacks, really looks like a knot.

Forward chaining exhibits many interesting properties of simplicity. A drawback of forward chaining is that it computes all the possible answers to all possible queries, without focussing on the minimal calculus to compute the answer to one particular query.

For instance, if we want to know the ancestors of John, it is useless to compute first all the ancestors of everybody, and then retain just the ancestors of John.

The idea will be, for a given query, to compute a new set of clauses, which, when processed in forward chaining, will saturate only the desired answer.

In some sense, we will use forward chaining to simulate backward chaining.

As Alexander cut the Gordian knot, we shall cut a recursive goal into two pieces.

For instance, the goal Ancestor(John,x) will be cut, giving:

- a problem

- a set of solutions.

The problem is a literal such as PB-Ancestor(John) which can be interpreted as:

"The problem of finding the descendants of John exists"

A solution is a literal such as like SOL-Ancestor(John,Louis) which can be interpreted as:

"Louis is a solution to the problem PB-Ancestor (John)"

To go from backward chaining to forward chaining, we need clauses which will handle PB-Ancestor and SOL-Ancestor literals. For example:

- PB-Ancestor(x) Q --> R

"IF there is the problem of finding the descendants of x, THEN ... "

- A --> SOL.Ancestor(x,y)

"IF A is true THEN y is a solution"

With these intuitive ideas in mind, let us work through an exemple by hand: the goal Ancestor(John,x)

The axioms are:

1) Father(x,y) --> Ancestor(x,y).

2) Father(x,y) Ancestor(y,z) --> Ancestor(x,z).

Rule (1) gives:

(1.1) PB-Ancestor(x) Father(x,y) --> SOL-Ancestor(x,y)

"If there is the problem of finding the descendants of x, and if x is the father of y, then a solution is y"

Rule (2) gives:

PB-Ancestor(x) Father(x,y) Ancestor(y,z) --> SOL.Ancestor(x,z)

"If there exists the problem of finding the descendants of x,
and if x is the father of y,
and if y is the ancestor of z,
then a solution is z"

But this rule itself contains a goal Ancestor(y,z), thus it must be transformed. This goal will itself be cut into two pieces, yielding two new rules: (2.2) and (2.3).

(2.2) PB-Ancestor(x) Father(x,y) --> PB-Ancestor(y)

"If there exists the problem of finding the descendant of x,
and x is the father of y,
then there exists the problem of finding the descendant of y"

This rule generates a new PB-Ancestor, which, by rule (1.1) for instance, will generate a new SOL-Ancestor.

(2.3) SOL-Ancestor(y,z) --> SOL-Ancestor(x,y)

This means that the solutions to the "y" problem are also solutions to the "x" problem.

In fact, this rule (2.3) is not correct, since x appears in the conclusion and not as a hypothesis.

We must transmit the information x between rules (2.2) and (2.3). For that purpose, we create a new literal called context or CONTinuation.

The correct formulation of (2.2) and (2.3) will become:

(2.2') PB-Ancestor(x) Father(x,y) --> PB-Ancestor(y) CONT(y,x)

(2.3') SOL-Ancestor(y,z) CONT(y,x) --> SOL-Ancestor(x,z)

Finally, the transformation results in rules (1.1), (2.2') and (2.3')

Note: In some sense, the CONT literals simulate the mechanism of context saving in a stack, which can be eliminated when treating tail recursion. This simplification could be applied here, and yielding a final version of the program:

PB-Ancestor(x) Father(x,y) --> SOL-Ancestor(y) PB-Ancestor(y)

This has the advantage of elegance!

In a second step, such forward rules can be translated into pure relational programs, as explained below in section execution of logical programs in forward chaining.

2.2. Handling DataBases containing Tree Structures.

Modern DB systems rely upon the relational model, where the basic data are flat tuples. This model has many interesting features, however, it lacks facilities for handling tree structured data, which are ubiquitous not only in the AI literature, but also in real life, e.g. office automation and CAD.

Consider the following tree:

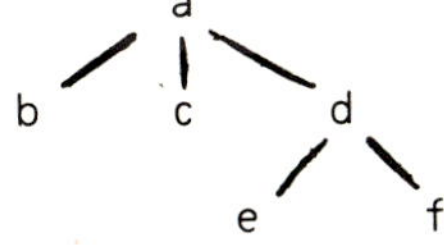

One way to represent and manipulate it in a DB is to use a flat relational model which will describe the graph of the tree.

For instance, the tree could be represented, using two relations:

```
node-name (x,y)
node-son (x,y,z)

node-name (1,a)      the name of node 1 is a
node-name (2,b)                "       2  " b
node-name (3,c)
node-name (4,d)
node-name (5,e)
node-name (6,f)
     .
     .
node-son (1,1,2)
node-son (1,2,3)     the second son of node 1 is node
                     3
node-son (4,1,5)
     .
     .
etc.
```

Any operation on the tree can be specified by expressions using the node-name and the node-son relations.

Example: names of nodes which are grandsons of a node whose name is "a":

Written in relational calculus:

x: node-name(y,"a") node-son(y,z) node-name(z,x)

In this way, all tree-processing can be handled via a relational DB.

For instance, using recursive axioms (as in Alexander Method mentioned above) we can find all the successors of a given node only through accesses to the DB.

This technique is a first solution for handling tree stuctures needed by AI applications. Its execution will indeed require a lot of <u>join</u> operations, which could be executed in parallel on a parallel relational DB machine.

Another solution is not to transform complex data structures (trees) into simpler ones (tables), but to keep complex data and complex basic algorithms to handle them.

For instance, trees can be stored as parenthesized expressions, in our case:

(a b c (d e f))

Then a natural way to manipulate a tree-base is to use pattern-matching primitives:

A pattern will be a tree with constant and variable parts.

Letters at the beginning of the alphabet designate constants, those at the end designate variables.

For example,

(a x c (y e f))

will match the preceding tree, with x=b and y=d

More generally, in AI, we define the unification of two trees, each of which may contain variables, as the attempt to find values for the variables which will make the two trees identical.

Unification can be seen as a super "selection by content" in a DB.

One way to implement unification is to use special-purpose algorithms and/or hardware to compare two strings with parentheses, one coming for instance from a disk, and the other one used as a target pattern.

```
          (a (b..))
Disk ----------------> Filter ---> (a (b .. ))

                                    Result
```

We are developing an implementation of such an operation on the SCHUSS kit, described later in this paper.

This problem is discussed in detail by other authors <Ber 85>.

2.3. Execution of Logical Programs in Forward Chainig.

Here we describe one possible way to implement forward chaining, to execute logical programs translated by the Alexander Method.

In the following we suppose that a logical program is composed of, first, rules of this form:

P(x,y,z)Q(z,x,t)R(l) -> S(z,t)T(y)U(l,x)

in which all variables appearing in the conclusion are present in the hypothesis, and secondly, predicates P(), Q(), etc. in which all variables are instantiated. To run this program is to perform the saturation of the set of predicates on the set of rules, that is, to assert any conclusion that can be logically inferred from the known predicates and the rules, as long as there are new facts belonging to predicates appearing in the hypothesis of any rule. This problem was studied by Pugin <Pug 85>. There are many ways to run such a program on a sequential machine, but basically, if we ignore a number of possible optimizations, the main ones are depth first and breadth first. In a depth first strategie we calculate all that can be inferred from facts belonging to one predicate, then take another; in a breadth first strategy we pass all facts known through all the rules, then do it again and again after adding deductions to the predicates. We define two processes:

- the SQUAREBOX process is associated with the execution of one rule. SQUAREBOX takes any set of new facts belonging to one of the predicates appearing as a hypothesis in the rule, and calculates the reaction of this increment, which we call a delta, on the other predicates.

- the ROUNDBOX process is associated with one predicate named in a rule. ROUNDBOX takes any set of new facts belonging to its predicate and eliminates the duplicates, if any. This process is necessary to avoid running the same facts all the time in some recursive cases, and to check for the end of execution.

The program can be split into as many SQUAREBOXES as it has rules, and as many ROUNDBOXES as there are predicate names in the rules, either in the conclusion or hypotheses. These processes are totally independent. That means they never need to wait for any unknown data to deduce new facts from old.It is easy to see that the process structure corresponding to our logical program is totally asynchronous, and therefore should be able to execute in parallel very efficiently.

Let's see the problems we have to deal with, if we try to achive this in a multiprocessor system.

First, we have a memory problem. All processes have to know the state of the predicates they manipulate. We believe it is necessary to give each processor a private memory which can be either a hard disk memory (for a DB-type process that handles lots of facts for each predicate), or a RAM (for a program-type process that handles many rules and few facts). With the hard disk option a SCHUSS processor could be used. In any case, regardless of the application, important private memory storage is necessary.

Second, there is a communication problem. Each process needs to send the results of its work to all the other processes that need them. ROUNDBOXES have to send the data remaining after the elimination of duplicates to all SQUAREBOXES having the predicate as a hypothesis, and SQUAREBOXES need to send their inferences to the corresponding ROUNDBOXES.

Third, there is a crucial optimization problem. How must our graph of communications be projected onto a real multiprocessor machine? This problem shows that we need a ZERO process able to transform our logical program into instructions to the processors, then to check for the end of the execution. This work could be done by a host, or a user interface, or by one or several of the machine processors (as long as the optimisation algorithms are known).

Let's see now the advantages of our processes structure:

First, there is no need for coordination among processors. Totally asynchronous processes don't need to wait for each other in any way. Information comes when it is available, and the result of the calculation does not depend on the order in which the data arrive. This make our solution very suitable for a multiprocessor.

Second, concerning communications: every processor has its own input memory, a "mail box" from which it takes its mail when it wants to, that is when it is not already working on some new data, or talking to another processor. When an attempt to communicate is unsuccessful, a processor doesn't need to wait to try again, following a predefined procedure. It can go to check its mail box and work again, then try to talk another time, continuing in this way as long as it has something to do. On the other hand, the correspondents may very well never wait for this data, if their own mail boxes are not empty. This too is an incredible "take it easy" multiprocessing feature.

We discuss below an architecture and a simulator that implements this mode of execution (MultiSCHUSS).

3. Architectures, from DataBases to Artificial Intelligence.

3.1. The SCHUSS Filter.

The SCHUSS filter is a processor specialized in filtering, it can process "on the fly" data coming from a disk. SCHUSS can perform searches of reasonable complexity in one pass. Combining searches with other data processing, SCHUSS can execute more complex operations. Examples are semi-joins or joins in relational algebra, again in one pass per file.

The SCHUSS filter has two programming levels. The first is the microprogramming level, at which it is possible to adapt SCHUSS to a given physical data format, or to create new instructions for a specific problem. At the second level the machine language is used. The machine language is a small instruction set specialized in filtering. This machine language is a function of the application. Typically a user query to a database is translated by a compiler into machine instructions.

To take full advantage of this processor requires a well adapted disk controller that sends a data flow (the data to be filtered). This data flow should be as continuous as possible. Other communications between the SCHUSS filter and the host system must be transparent to the controller.

We have built a set of prototypes, each of which we call the <u>SCHUSS</u> <u>kit</u>. It can be seen as a black box containing: a SCHUSS filter and a disk controller. Thus the SCHUSS kit can be seen as a very intelligent disk controller that has the capacity to execute complex searches.

The SCHUSS kit was designed to be integrated as a sub-system for micro computers, personal workstations and perharps some mini computers. The controller has a ST506 interface for 5 1/4" Winchester disks, and a SCSI (Small Computer System Interface) to connect the SCHUSS kit to a host system.

The SCHUSS kit is packaged in a Multibus (Intel) rack with two external interfaces SCSI and RS232.

The SCHUSS kit consists of four Multibus format boards (31 cm x 17 cm):

- the SCHUSS filter processor. Built using bit slice technology, it has a 16 bits address bus, a 16 bits data bus, and a specialized path for data to be filtered.

- the memory and interface. 32K words of 16 bits and an interface to communicate with the disk controller.

- the disk controller.

- RAM for the microprogram. This board is not needed in a kit for a end user.

A typical system using the SCHUSS kit is a host computer with a SCSI interface to which the kit is connected.

Five steps are needed for a filter operation:

1.- a query is compiled into a instruction sequence executable by the SCHUSS filter. This compilation is done by the host processor.

2.- the result of this compilation (the filtering program) is loaded into the filter memory.

3.- the host processor sends a command to the disk controller, indicating which file is to be filtered.

4.- the filter executes its program, processing data coming from the disk <u>"on</u> <u>the</u> <u>fly"</u>.

5.- the filter sends back the results of the filter operation to the host memory.

More sophisticated operations could be implemented e.g. grouping queries in a multi-user environment.

The performance of the SCHUSS kit is limited only by two

factors:

- the data transfer rate of the disk. Currently it is 5 Mbit/s or 625 kB/s due to the disk type used in the kit. Obviously higher performance disks exist and a controller could be built to improve the kit's performance if needed.

- the size of the filter memory, currently 32 K words of 16 bits. The filter stores in this memory the filtering program and the results. Generally the program size is less than a hundred words, but the space occupied by the result depends on the quantity of data to be filtered, and on the filter criterium. If the result fits into memory, the time required for filtering is the time required to read all the data to be filtered. If the result does not fit into memory, the time for filtering is the time needed to read all the data and the time needed to transfer the result, somewhere else in the system, each time that an overflow in the filter memory is detected.

When operations such as joins are performed on two files, a selection is made on the first file, then a second filter criterium for filtering the second file is created within the filter memory, from the result of de previous selection, the second file is then filtered using this criterium. Filtering time is affected if a memory overflow occurs. Once again, when the result of filtering the first file and the filter criterium for the second file do not fit into memory, another algorithm is needed to execute dyadic operations. With a larger memory better performance can therefore be obtained.

3.2. Comparing Instruction Sets.

In this section, we compare the performance of two processors, the Motorola 68020 <Mot 84> and the SCHUSS processor, both executing the same filtering algorithms. A first remark is that there are a few small differences in coding these algorithms because the two processors are different and work in different environments.

The purpose of making this comparison is to show that a general purpose processor as the MC68020 is not as good as a specialized processor, for symbolic treatements. The idea behind this is to propose that a general purpose processor could have a coprocessor for symbolic processing.

Let's explain first the filtering algorithms. We chose to process data with the automata technique. The basic idea is to consider sequential data to be processed, i.e. a file, as a language and queries as a grammar. This technique is very general and allows the treatment of complex data structures (flat, hierarchical) and texts as well as numerical values. Filtering is nothing but making a syntactic analysis of the records, selecting only those in accordance with the grammar.

The inevitable tradeoff when working with automata is

execution time vs. space.

When we began the design of the SCHUSS filter, we considered whether a microprocessor could interpret an automaton fast enough to execute filtering on the fly. There was no processor that could do the job, even for the slow 5" 1/4 Winchester disks (one byte each 2 microseconds), because character comparision is not the only task to be performed while filtering: updating pointers and testing for the presence of data in buffers for exemple, are very time consuming.

Now we consider the architecture of the SCHUSS filter. Externally it has two buses. The first, which has a size of 16 bits for data and 16 bits for addresses, access both a memory and an I/O space, in this memory the filtering program and the results are stored, this memory is both word and byte addressable, in the I/O space a port is used to communicate with the disk controller. The second bus is used to get data to be filtered (8 bits for data and 10 bits for address).

Internally the SCHUSS filter is a microprogrammed processor, with a pipeline register. The cycle time for a microinstruction is 150 ns or 200 ns, selected by microprogram. Of course a instruction is realized by several microistructions. Since many operationts must be performed in parallel, microinstructions have a horizontal format of 112 bits. There are two ALUs of 16 bits each; one is dedicated to processing data (4 x AMD 2903), the other is dedicated to processing addresses (4 x AMD 2901). A counter is used to keep track of the address of the data to be filtered. Instead of using a comparator to process data, the AMD2903 receives two external inputs and use them to execute an operation. All these features allow internal loops of instructions to be executed in very few machine cycles. Typically all of the following operations are done in parallel: a comparision in the data ALU (between the character in the pattern and the character to be filtered), an address calculation in the other ALU, a read or write in memory, an incrementation of the counter of the address to be filtered, a read of the next character to be filtered and a multiple test. Another advantage of using ALUs is that semantic actions are easily microprogrammed.

For the moment we have programmed a filter-oriented instruction set we can execute selections and semi-join operations <Bra 84>. Other operations are under development.

The instructions needed for a selection are:

Semantic instructions:

- Begin_a_filter_operation.
- Begin_a_partition.
- Begin_a_tuple.
- Case (as function of the atribute).
- Skipping_an_attribute.
- Projection.

- End_of_Attribute.
- End.

The filtering instructions are:

- Linear.
- Sequential.
- Indexed.

We have written a compiler that translate a user's query into a set of filter instructions. For the purpose of comparison, we decided to program the same instruction in MC68020 code. In this case the filter istructions are macros.

We have already made some measurements ofthe performance of the kit SCHUSS <Bra 85>. Here we describe only some results and the benchmark environment. The operation is a selection on a 2 MByte file. The result could be stored in filter memory, which is 64 K Bytes less the size of the filtering program (about 200 bytes). The disk is a 10 MByte 5" 1/4 Winchester, the controller allows optimum sequentiallity of a file, e.g. there are no interleaving between sectors, traks and cylinders. About 6 second are required to filter this file. This time is slightly longer than the time to read all file from disk, because there is some communication overhead, among the host, the controller and the filter itself.

What want to emphasize that the performance of the SCHUSS filter is limited only by the disk performance. Most of the time the filter is waiting for data to be filtered. The filter could work even with 3 MB/sec disks.

Two comparisons may be made:

- The performance of the MC68020 in a selection on the same file.

- The speed of each individual filtering instruction.

To perform the selection in the MC68020 environment, the file was in main memory and was reread to simulate a 2 MByte file. This is a very important restriction, because all problems of synchronisation with a disk are ignored. The processor has a clock of 12 MHz (it could work at 16Mhz). The filtering programs were generated by the same compiler. When no work was required for a particular attribute it was skipped, i.e.characters were not read. In SCHUSS all characters are read.

The times obtained were about 8 seconds for filtering the file without the internal cache, and about 7 seconds with the cache enabled.

This result confirms that even now a microprocessor is not able to execute filtering on the fly.

Comparing each individual filter instruction, is very difficult, so we decided to compare the time of the inner most loop of the algorithms.

In general the SCHUSS processor can execute the internal loops in 2 or 3 cycles, i.e. in 300 to 600 ns. The execution of the same loop in the MC68020 could take from 1 to 100 microseconds. It is almost impossible to give a exact number of cycles because many different situations might arise. For example, the first time through an instruction is not in the cache, but if the loop is not very long, the instruction will be in the cache the second through. An internal pipeline could hide the execution time of some instructions, since there is some overlapping almost all the time. The time required for a branch instruction depends on whether or not the branch is taken.

Our point is that a processor like SCHUSS could be used as a coprocessor: when the main processor needs to execute a filtering operation it can call the SCHUSS processor.

We have also made some other comparisons. At present they are not well quantified, but they seem to indicate that for other symbolic operations such as comparing two trees (for unification) the gain in speed using a specialized coprocessor could be even higher.

We want to include tag detection in a symbolic coprocessor.

3.3. A "MultiSCHUSS" Machine.

For the moment we define our "MultiSCHUSS" architecture as a multiprocessor composed of a set of filter cells. A filter cell is composed of a processor/filter, or a processor with a symbolic coprocessor, memory, a disk controller and a disk. We will redesign the filter cell based on our experirence with the SCHUSS kit.

It is clear that, given this architecture, all the relational operations can be executed on the actual SCHUSS kit could be executed more efficiently on the MultiSCHUSS, with the appropiate modifications of the algorithms.

For example, when the SCHUSS filter makes a selection it reads all the data from a file; the response time is slightly longer than the time required to for read the file. With a multiprocessor the operation is split among various filters, all of them working with the same filtering program but acting upon differents parts of the file. In theory the response time would be equal to the time needed to read the whole file using only one filter, divided by the number of filters. For very large data bases this could be an effective technique.

Algorithms to implement other relational operations were

or are under study. Two interconnection nets were proposed to deal with the communications requirements of these algorithms.

We are also studying how the MultiSCHUSS machine could be a deductive database. In this case the machine could be seen as a forward-chaining production system. As explained above, the basic operations are relational mechanisms. We are writing a simulator to study the behaviour of the system and to analyse the impact of new computing requirements on the interprocessor communications, and on the overall structure of the system.

Let's see what the simulator is expected to do, how it runs, and what results it gives.

Specifications: The program is designed to simulate a variety of situations, for it seems really impossible to predict the behaviour of a multiprocessor machine running our logical program. The choice of which architectures to simulate as made with economy and ease of realization in mind. The program is able to simulate the computation and communication of N processors on a single bus, and that of N processors linked by a barrel shifter. In the near future we expect to simulate other networks.

How it works: the simulator is an APL program which executes in three different steps:

- First, it compiles the logical program written in a standard logical syntax into a machine-understandable set of APL functions.

The rule:

father(?x?y)mother(?z?y) -> couple(?x?z)nonorphan(?y)

is compiled in a "true" APL function, this function then "call" the fuctions which performs the relational operations.

- Second, the simulator analyses the program as a graph of communications, and distributes the corresponding processes to the simulated processors, however many there are. The problem of optimisation in the case of a single bus or barrel shifter simulation is fairly easy, but it is a lot harder if we want to simulate other networks, and involves advanced graph theoretic concepts.

- Third, the APL program simulates the parallel action of the processors on the simulated network.

To perform this last task, the simulator manipulates an artificial time calculated with time samples taken on the machine running the program, as a function of the amount of data used by the SQUAREBOX or ROUNDBOX processes and by the transfer function simulating the network. The real machine time alone is not sufficient to calculate the simulated machine time: the volume of data processed must be considered to simulate differents kind of algorithms. For instance, the join algorithm used in our APL program calculates the join in a time proportionnal to the product of the lengths of the files involved, located in the machine memory, whereas the join algorithm executed on the SCHUSS machine takes linear time on data coming straight from a hard disk. It is impossible to determine how long a join would take on a SCHUSS machine by measuring the time it takes in our APL program. The same problem arises when simulating the data transfers on buses. But real machine times have their importance when it comes to simulating actual "inside the processor" actions, such as a buffer checking, or an attempt to talk on the network, where processor speeds can be compared.

The results: the simulator provides statistical information about how long processors remained unoccupied during the simulated time of the parallel execution, how much traffic there was on the network, and how much data the processor's private memories and buffers held during execution. If required, the exact time table can be display, with the names of the data involved in the actions. All this information is designed to help our team decides what architecture is desirable for a logical machine. The simulator allows the study of the effects of economic restrictions (limitations on the size of the input and output buffers, or the private memory) on the execution of the program.

We are studying and defining other aspects of the architecture, for example an interconnection network, communications, modularity, fault tolerance, I/O, components, and custom VLSI to execute special functions.

4. Acknowledgments.

We would like to thank Remi Lescoeur, Laurent Hennoque, Philipe Gast, Isabelle Desfontaine and Didier Terral, who helped us in writing programs to verify many of the ideas expressed in this paper. We also thank Jean-Marie Patry from Motorola, who gave us access to a system to make the measurements.

5. References.

<Bra 84> Bradier A. et Terral D.: Filtre SCHUSS. Manuel d'utilisation. Rapport BULL. 1984.

<Bra 85> Bradier A., Gonzalez-Rubio R., Terral D.:Premières Mesures avec le kit SCHUSS.Journées Base de Données Avancées. St Pierre de Chartereuse. 1985.

<Ber 85> Berger-Sabbatel G., Dang W., Ianeselli J.C.: Stratégie de Recherche et Unification pour la Machine OPALE. AFCET Informatique 85. Paris. 1985.

<Gon 84> Gonzalez Rubio.R, Rohmer.J, Terral.D: The SCHUSS filter : A processor for non-numerical data processing. 11th International Symposium on Computer Architecture. Ann Arbor, Michigan 1984.

<Mot 84> Motorola. MC68020 32 Bit- Microprocessor. User's Manual.1984.

<Pug 85> Pugin J.M. BOUM -An Instantiation of the (PS)2 concept. 5èmes Journnées Internationales Systèmes Experts. Avignon. 1985.

<Roh 85> Rohmer J. and Lescoeur R.: The Alexander Method. A Technique for the processing of recursive axioms in deductive databases. BULL internal Report 1985. (submitted for publication).

HARDWARE IMPLEMENTATION OF RELATIONAL ALGEBRA OPERATIONS

A.K.SOOD, M.ABDELGUERFI, and W.SHU
Department of Electrical and Computer Engineering
Wayne State University
Detroit Michigan 48202

1.INTRODUCTION

The relational database model introduced by Codd in [1,2,3,4,5] has received considerable attention during the last several years. There is an increasing recognition of the relational data model's advantages of simplicity, symmetry of access, and data independence. Another feature of the relational model is that the database may be manipulated by high level, non-procedural data manipulation languages [6,7]. Perhaps the most important feature of the relational database model is that it is based on strong theoretical foundations [8]. This allows for an efficient design of database schemas. In general this is acheived using the normalization theory [5,9].

Because of its strong affinity with logic [10,11,12,13,14,15], the relational database model has been chosen by the Japanese for the Fifth Generation Computer project [16,17,18,19]. Towards this end, several relational database machines are being currently developed in Japan (e.g., SPIRIT.III [20], GRACE [21,22]). These two machines make use of the clustering feature of hashing to improve the processing time of some computationally intensive relational algebra operations such as duplicate removal and join.

Several database machines based on the relational model have been developed. These machines have been traditionally classified as: i) conventional systems, ii) cellular systems, and iii) multiprocessor cache systems.

The first class corresponds to the conventional general purpose processor. In this approach, index tables and pointers are utilized to determine which part of the database is to be moved to main memory. Some of the systems that fit into this category are: IBM's R system [23,24], MULTICS [25], REGIS [26], and INGRES [27]. In general the performance of this type of machine suffers from the mismatch of conventional general purpose computers for non-numeric applications, the existence of many levels of software mapping, and a data transfer bottleneck between mass storage and primary memory.

In cellular systems, "on-the-fly" filtering is utilized to resolve the data transfer bottleneck. This is acheived by performing some relational operations such as selection and projection on tuples of relations without fetching them first into the system main memory. This type of system usually consists of an array of cells driven by a common central controller. The cell

NATO ASI Series, Vol. F 24
Database Machines. Edited by A. K. Sood and A. H. Qureshi

(or filter) can be either microprocessors, special purpose hardware, or both (e.g., the uniprocessor VERSO [28]). Each cell performs its operations directly on a segment of the database. Cellular systems are closely related to the "logic-per-track" concept intoduced by Slotnick in [29]. RAP [30,31], RARES [32], and CASSM [33,34] are typical cellular systems. These systems perform selection and projection very efficiently, but they show poor performance as far as complex relational operations such as join, division, and duplicate removal are concerned.

The third category is characterized by a MIMD architecture and a three-level memory hierarchy (mass storage, cache modules, processor's private memory) [37]. Communication between different processors is done through an interconnection network. In general the interconnection network has a broadcasting capability that allows all the processors to simultaneously read the same data from the cache modules. There are several relational database machines that fall in this category: DIRECT [38], and SABRE [39,40] are typical examples. In [41,42] parallel algorithms to perform relational algebra operations in the context of DIRECT and SABRE are presented. These two systems use an n-ary data structure. Other data structures such as the DBMAC's [43,44] domain based data structure [45,46], the RIS (relational inverted data structure) [47], and the IVH (inverted organization and horizontal separation) [48] have been proposed.

Performance and comparative studies of these three types of machine can be found in [37,49].

Since relational database operations are used as a basis for data manipulation, there have been several attempts to implement this powerful set of operators directly in hardware. CAFS [50], and LEECH [51] are early examples of such a trend. With the rapid advances in VLSI technology, more research is being done in this direction. As a result, several designs aimed towards a VLSI implementation have been proposed in the literature. Kung's systolic array [52] and Yasuura's bus connected cellular array [53], have been used in [54] and [55] respectively to implement several relational database operations. In both designs tuples are input sequentially into the circuit. In [56] a VLSI query processor with bit serial, tuple parallel processing capability [67] is presented. In [57,58,59], odd-even topology [60] is used to perform relational operations in parallel. In this approach (in contrast with [56]) the relational algebra algorithms do not require the relations to be presorted. The design of DBC database machine [61] is aimed towards optimizing the performance of the join operation. The NON-VON machine [62] uses VLSI technology and incorporates a large number of processing elements (over one million) organized in a tree structure. Other VLSI-based proposals include: omnisort [63,64], cellular array [65], and the 2-D join [66].

It is our belief that a good implementation of the relational algebra operations must take into account the following considerations:

(1) Single topology. It is preferable to have a design in which all (or as many as possible) relational operations can be performed utilizing a single network topology.

(2) Static interconnection network. For ease of implementation a static interconnection network between the different processing elements is preferred, as compared to a dynamic interconnection network. This will usually enable better use to be made of the pipelining characteristics of the system.

(3) High throughput. This is usually achieved by the use of parallel and pipelined processing techniques.

(4) Independent of tuple size. In several designs the tuple size affects the number of processing elements [55] or the size of their internal memory [56]. A design independent of the tuple size is more practical.

(5) Independent of number of tuples. This is acheived by developing internal as well as external algorithms.

(6) VLSI implementation. The design must be suitable for VLSI implementation.

In this paper we survey and analyze four different VLSI implementations of relational database operations. These architectures are: bus connected cellular array, systolic array, odd-even network, and query processor [56]. There is general agreement that the analysis of VLSI algorithms must take into consideration the processing time as well as the chip area [68,69]. It is beyond the scope of a single paper to analyze in depth the various VLSI approaches to relational database operations. Our paper does not address the issue of area complexity. Rather we concentrate on the structure as well as the time complexity of algorithms for relational database operations.

The remainder of this paper is organized as follows: In section 2 we define the relational algebra operators as well as some aggregate functions [6,7], and familiarize the reader with the terminology used throughout the paper. In sections 3 and 4 the bus connected cellular array and the systolic approaches are presented. Sections 5 and 6 deal with the odd-even network and query processor [56] approaches respectively. In section 7 the four approaches are compared.

2.Relational Algebra Operators

The discussion of relational algebra operators and aggregate functions requires the review of a few definitions. A *relational scheme* R is a set of attribute names $(X_1,X_2,....,X_N)$. To each attribute name X_i, i=1,...N, corresponds a set D_i (usually finite) called *domain.* A *relation* r defined on the relation scheme R is a subset of the cartesian product D_1 x D_2 x....x D_N. A tuple $T=(x_1,x_2,...,x_N)$ is a mapping from R to $D_1 \cup D_2 ..... \cup D_N$, with the restriction that each x_i, i=1,..,N, must be an element of D_i. A *multirelation* (or multiset) is an extension of the concept of relation (or set) in which duplicate tuples are allowed. An *augmented relation* (or multirelation) r^*

corresponding to a relation (or multirelation) r is formed by attaching two mark bits (M1,M2) and a distinguishing bit (DB) to each tuple of r. It is denoted as $r^* = [M1,M2,DB,r]$. In particular if T(i) and $T^*(i)$ are the i-th tuples of r and r^* respectively, then $T^*(i)=[M1(i),M2(i),DB(i),T(i)]$. Mark bits are used to identify selected tuples, and DB is used to separate different operand relations in some relational operations. The *cardinality* or *arity* of a relation defined on the relation scheme $R(X_1,X_2,...,X_N)$ is N. Throughout this paper, n_i and L_i will denote the number of tuples and the tuple size in relation r_i.

The relational algebra operators as originally defined by Codd can be seen as a collection of operators on relations. Some of these operators are the usual set operators, i.e., *union, intersection, difference.* These operators take two relations as operands, treating each as a set of tuples, and yield a single relation as a result. The operand relations are required to be defined on the same relation scheme. The other operators defined below are: *selection, projection, join,* and *division.*

Selection (σ) is a manodic operator on relations which when applied to a relation r_1, yields a new relation that is a subset of the original one. For example, $\sigma_F(r_1)$ is a relation r_2 whose tuples are those of r for which the formula F is true.

Projection ($\Pi_Y(r)$) of a relation r onto a subset Y of the relation scheme R is a relation obtained by first eliminating attributes of R not in Y, and then removing all duplicate tuples. It is noted that the duplicate removal phase is computationally more complex than the attribute elimination phase.

Natural join ($r_1 \times r_2$) of two relations r_1 and r_2, defined on the relational schemes R_1 and R_2 respectively, is a new relation defined on the scheme ($R_1 \cup R_2$) whose tuples are formed by concatenating tuples of r_1 and r_2 having equal common attributes (common attributes are also known as join attributes). The *theta-join* extends the capability of the natural join to handle comparison between columns having different attribute names but same domains. Further, the comparison is not restricted to equality, but can be: $<, \leq, \geq, >, \neq$.

The *division* operator can be viewed as a counterpart of the universal quantifier [71]. Given two relations r_1 and r_2 defined on schemes R_1 and R_2 respectively, with $R_2 \subseteq R_1$, the division ($r_1 \div r_2$) is a relation r_3 defined on the scheme (R_1-R_2) and whose tuples are such that if T is in $r_3=r_1$-r_2 then:

$$(\forall T_2 \epsilon r_2, \exists T_1 \epsilon r_1 / T_1(R_1-R_2)=T \text{ and } T_1(R_2)=T_2)$$

Expression in which T(X) refers to the projection of the tuple T onto the scheme X. The following example will clarify the above definition. Let r_1 and r_2 be as follows:

r_1(Name	Language)	r_2(Language)
BOB	ENGLISH	ARABIC
MIKE	GERMAN	ENGLISH
BOB	FRENCH	FRENCH
BOB	ARABIC	
MIKE	ENGLISH	
BILL	ENGLISH	

The division can be used to find persons speaking all languages in r_2(Language). In this case the result has just one tuple.

r_1-r_2(Name)
BOB

Division can be expressed in terms of other relational algebra operators [6,7], and therefore does not theoretically extend the expressive power of the relational algebra. However, since division cannot be evaluated efficiently using other operators, we study direct methods of computing division.

In order to provide more flexibility, *aggregate* (built-in) *functions* have been added to relational query languages like QBE [71] and SEQUEL [72]. However, unlike the relational algebra operators, there is no commonly accepted set of aggregate functions. For the purpose of this paper we define three aggregate functions: *Multiple generalized selection*, *Unique generalized selection*, *generalized addition*. Before formally defining these we will illustrate their use through examples on the relation EMP(NAME, SALARY, DEPARTMENT). For ease of presentation, the constructs of SEQUEL have been utilized to formulate the queries.

QUERY1:"List the persons with the lowest salary in each department"

```
SEQUEL: SELECT NAME, MIN(SALARY), DEPARTMENT.
        FROM EMP
        GROUP BY DEPARTMENT
```

QUERY2:"List the lowest salary in each department"

```
SEQUEL: SELECT UNIQUE MIN(SALARY), DEPARTMENT
        FROM EMP
        GROUP BY DEPARTMENT
```

QUERY3:"What is each department's payroll"

```
SEQUEL: SELECT SUM(SALARY), DEPARTMENT
        FROM EMP
        GROUP BY DEPARTMENT
```

In queries 1 and 2, "department" is treated as a "group by" attribute (A_g) and "salary" as a "selection" attribute (A_c). The first query may provide multiple names, while the second yields a single value for each value of the "group by" attribute. The operation needed to execute the first query is referred to as "Multiple generalized selection" and is denoted by Mgsel(A_g,A_c,EMP). The second is referred to as the "Unique generalized selection" and is denoted by Ugsel(A_g,A_c,EMP). In the third query, "salary" is called addition attribute (A_a), and the operation to perform this query is referred to as "generalized addition"(denoted as gadd(A_g,A_a,EMP)).

Definition of generalized selection operation

Let d_i be one of the distinct values of attribute A_g, and assume that T_n, T_{n+1},.....T_{n+m_i} are the only tuples in which A_g takes the value d_i. Further assume that the value of the comparison attribute in T_{n+j} is s_{ij}, and that $s_i = Min(s_{i0}, s_{i1}, \ldots, s_{im_i})$.

(a) In Multiple generalized selection tuple T_{n+j}, $0 \leq j \leq m_i$, will be a qualified tuple only when $s_{ij} = s_i$.

(b) In Unique generalized selection, if $s_{ij} = s_i$ then T_{n+j} is a qualified tuple, and all other tuples with a group by attribute value d_i are rejected.

Definition of generalized addition operation

Let e_{ij} be the value of A_a in tuple T_{n+j}, $0 \leq j \leq m_i$. In the generalized addition operation:

(a) For every group of tuples $T_n, \ldots, T_{n+m_i}$, accept one of the tuples (say n+k) by setting the corresponding mark bit, and clearing the mark bit of the other tuples.

(b) The addition attribute of T_{n+k} becomes $e_i = SUM(e_{i0}, e_{i1}, \ldots, e_{m_i})$.

3.BUS CONNECTED CELLULAR ARRAY

In [55] we proposed algorithms to perform some relational algebra operations on a bus connected cellular array (BCA). The BCA has been used in [53] to perform parallel enumeration sorting. The BCA is similar to Kung's systolic array except that buses permit global communication and dataflow is unidirectional.

We assume that tuples are input serially to an array consisting of n cells. The data is entered into the circuit one tuple at a time. The processed sequence is output serially, each tuple is output with an associated mark bit. The qualified tuples are collected by examining the mark bit. Methods to handle the case in which tuple size is large, or the number of tuples is more than n, are also discussed.

3.1.Duplicate Removal Algorithm

As pointed out in section 2, duplicate removal is the predominant phase in the execution of the projection operation. Duplicate tuples must be removed in order to produce a proper relation. Figure 3.1 shows the data flow in the basic cell utilized in our array. Each cell consists of two q bit registers (R, R'), a comparator (C), a flag (F), and logic circuitry (B.P) for bit processing. In this section it is assumed that each tuple has q or less bits. This condition is relaxed in section 3.3. The algorithm implemented at the i-th cell is :

Procedure dup-rem(T_i,T_j,$M_{j,i}$)

Input:Tuples T_i, T_j, and mark bit $M_{j,i}$ associated with T_j.

Output: Tuple T_j and its new mark bit $M_{j,(i+1)}$.

Step1: Compare T_i and T_j, and compute $M_{j,(i+1)}$ according to the state diagram of Figure 3.2.

Step2: Transfer T_i and $M_{j,(i+1)}$ to output terminals O_D and O_M respectively.

end procedure.

The duplicate removal circuit is composed of n identical cells connected in a linear array (Figure 3.3). Each cell performs the dup-rem algorithm. This array differs from that of [53] in that only one input bus is utilized.

The processing of the n tuples takes 2n time steps, t_1, t_2...,t_{2n}. From t_1 to t_n the tuples T_1, T_2,....,T_n are input serially to the circuit. At time t_i, $1 \leq i \leq n$, the i-th cell flag F_i is cleared and the tuple T_i is input to the first cell with mark bit $M_{i,1}=0$, and is also input to the i-th cell via the input bus. Simultaneously, T_{i-k} and $M_{(i-k),(k+1)}$, $1 \leq k \leq (i-1)$, are shifted from the k-th to the $(k+1)-$th cells. During the interval $(t_{i+(j-1)},t_{i+j})$, $1 \leq j \leq n$, the i-th cell performs dup $-$ rem(T_i,T_j,$M_{j,i}$). At time t_{n+i}, the tuple T_i is output from the n-th cell with a mark bit $M_{i,(n+1)}$. If $M_{i,(n+1)}=1$, then T_i is a qualified tuple, otherwise, T_i is a duplicate. From t_{n+1} to t_{2n}, the sequence $(T_i,M_{i,(n+1)})$, $1 \leq i \leq n$, is output from the circuit. The rejected tuples are removed while outputting the sequence. Figure 3.4 shows an example in which the duplicates of the multirelation $r=(b,a,b,b)$ are removed. Although 2n steps are required to process a sequence of n tuples, at time t_{n+1} we can begin processing a new sequence of tuples. In this way, the I/O time of a sequence is overlapped with the processing time needed by another sequence.

3.2. Applications of the Dup-rem Algorithm

Union. This operation is performed by applying the dup-rem algorithm to the concatenation of the two relations.

Intersection. A slightly modified version of the previous circuit (Figure 3.5) evaluates the intersection relation $P=r_1 \cap r_2$ of two compatible multirelations. Tuples of r_1 and r_2 are input through terminals Input2 and Input1 respectively. The qualified tuples are the elements of P. Figure 3.7 shows the intersection of $r_1=(b,b,a,c)$ and $r_2=(a,a)$.

Difference. The difference $P=r_1- r_2$ of a relation r_1 and a multirelation r_2 is implemented using the circuit of Figure 3.5. Tuples of r_1 and r_2 are input through Input1 and Input2 respectively. The qualified tuples in this case are those that are output with a zero mark bit.

3.3 Processing a Sequence of Tuples Larger Than n

When the number of tuples m exceeds the number of cells n, the sequence cannot be processed directly. However, the sequence can be processed by using two or more circuits. Figure 3.6 shows how two circuits of n cells each can be connected to remove the duplicates of a sequence of 2n tuples $r=(T_1,T_2,...,T_{2n})$. In general $\lceil m/n \rceil$ circuits of n cells are needed to process a sequence of m tuples. The number of steps required to perform the duplicate removal algorithm is still 0(m).

3.4 Processing a Sequence of Large Tuples

The tuple length L is restricted by the cell register length q. In this section we consider the case $L>q$. In the i-th cell, we include an n-bit register $R_i=r_{i1}r_{i2}..r_{in}$, $1 \le i \le n$. Further, each tuple T_i, $1 \le i \le n$, is divided into $e= \lceil L/q \rceil$ subtuples T_{i1}, T_{i2},..., T_{ie}, where each subtuple has q or less bits. In this case, the procedure to remove duplicates is as follows:

Step1: All registers R_i, $1 \le i \le n$, are cleared. From time $t_{(j-1)n+1}$ to t_{jn}, the j-th sequence of subtuples T_{1j}, T_{2j},..., T_{nj}, $1 \le j \le (e-1)$, is input serially to the circuit. In particular at $t_{(j-1)n+i}$, $1 \le i \le n$, T_{ij} is input to the first and i-th cells via the input bus. Simultaneously the subtuples in the array $T_{(i-1)j}$, $T_{(i-2)j}$,.., T_{1j}, $T_{1(j-1)}$,..., $T_{(n-i+1)(j-1)}$, are shifted to the right adjacent cell. During the time interval $(t_{(j-1)n+i+k-1}, t_{(j-1)n+i+k})$, $1 \le k \le n$, the i-th cell performs the following operations: If $T_{ij}=T_{kj}$ then r_{ik} is unchanged, else $r_{ik} := 1$.

Step2: From time $t_{(e-1)n+1}$ to t_{en}, the sequence T_{1e}, T_{2e},..., T_{ne} is input to the array as in step 1 except that at $t_{(e-1)n+k}$, $1 \le k \le n$, F_k is cleared and T_{ke}, is input to the first cell with mark bit $M_{k,1}$ cleared. During the time interval $(t_{(e-1)n+i+k-1}, t_{(e-1)n+i+k})$,the i-th cell performs the following operations: If $r_{ik}=0$ then apply the dup-rem algorithm to $(T_{ie}, T_{ke}, M_{k,i})$ else, set $M_{k,(i+1)} := M_{k,i}$ and transfer T_{ke} and $M_{k,(i+1)}$ to output terminals O_D and O_M respectively.

It is noted that the mark bit $M_{k,(n+1)}$ of tuple T_k is output along with T_{ke} through the n-th cell at time t_{en+k}. In this implementation, in contrast to [54], the number of cells is independent of tuple length.

4.Systolic Array

The systolic architecture has been introduced by Kung and his group at Carnegie-Mellon University. Like the BCA structure of section 3, a systolic array is a set of synchronized special purpose processors with a fixed interconnection structure. Further, both structures are simple and regular, thus suitable for a VLSI implementation. Kung, *et al.* have used the systolic approach to design several special-purpose VLSI chips for various computationally intense problems such as image processing [73] and matrix operations [74]. In [54], this structure has been used to design hardware algorithms for relational algebra operations.

4.1.Duplicate Removal

The array utilized for duplicate removal is shown in Figure 4.1. The multirelation whose duplicates are to be removed is fed into the array from both the top and bottom. Each tuple T_i is divided into e subtuples, $T_i=(T_{i1},T_{i2},\ldots,T_{ie})$. Figure 4.2 shows two consecutive cells. The value of the mark bit M_{ij} corresponding to tuples T_i and T_j is shifted to the right from one cell to another. The algorithm to be performed at cell k, $1 \leq k \leq e$, is described below:

$M_{ij}^{0} := 1$

$M_{ij}^{k+1} := M_{ij}^{k}$ **and** equal(T_{ik},T_{jk})

out1:=T_{ik}

out2:=T_{jk}

where equal(T_{ik},T_{jk}) is 1 if $T_{ik}=T_{jk}$ and 0 otherwise. If $M_{ij}^{e}=1$ $(i \neq j)$, then tuples T_i and T_j are equal. In this case the tuple with the largest index is usually taken as a duplicate. In this approach e(2n-1) cells are required to process a multirelation of n tuples. As discussed in section 3, the above duplicate removal algorithm can also be used to perform the union of two relations.

4.2.Intersection and Difference

The array utilized to perform the intersection $r_1 \cap r_2$ is similar to the duplicate removal array except that an *accumulation column* of unit delay elements is added to the right side of the array (see Figure 4.3). The purpose of the new column is to compute $M_i= \cup_j M_{ij}$, for all $1 \leq i \leq n_1$. A tuple T_i will belong to $r_1 \cap r_2$ only if $M_i=1$. The same array is utilized to perform the difference r_1-r_2. For this operator the qualified tuples are those output with $M_i=0$.

It is noted that in contrast with the BCA approach, the intersection and difference operations cannot be applied directly to multirelations.

5.Odd-Even Network

In [58] a relational algebra machine called BIFRAM (Figure 5.1) has been designed. BIFRAM is constructed using a ROPU (Relational Operation Processing Unit) together with auxilliary modules called MPU (Multiple Processing Unit) and DDU (Detecting and Distributing Unit). Processing elements in MDU perform selection, arithmetic, logic operations, and transact and augment tuples. DDU undertakes distributing and concatenating functions. Using address keys supplied by DDU, the database can be well distributed through a dynamically reconfigurable interconnection network (ICN). For more details the interested reader is referred to [58].

The relational algebra operations are performed in ROPU. ROPU can implement all operations in a tuple parallel bit serial fashion. The architecture of ROPU is based on the odd-even network topology (OEN). The two input, two output processor of Figure 5.2 is the basic unit utilized in the OEN. The iterative design of an OEN is shown in Figure 5.3. A P-input OEN requires $[\frac{P}{4}((\log P))^2 - \log P + 4) - 1]$ processing elements and the longest path goes through $\frac{1}{2}\log P(\log P + 1)$ processors.

5.1.Duplicate Removal

In order to perform duplicate removal, each cell of the OEN performs the following algorithm:

```
procedure dup-rem(M1,M2,T1,T2)

/*Two tuple T1 and T2 with respective mark bits M1 and M2 are

 input to the processor*/
begin

if T1>T2 then/*output tuples in sorted order*/
 begin L←M2,T2; H←M1,T1; end
 else begin

  if T1=T2 then /* manipulate mark bits*/
   begin
     M1:=M1 or M2;
     M2:=0;
   end;
   L←M1,T1;
   H←M2,T2;
  end;
```

13 **end.**/* dup-rem */

Figure 5.4 shows an example in which the duplicates of the multirelation (a,b,c,c,a,a,c,a) are removed. It is noted that tuples are input to the network with their mark bit set. The qualified tuples are those output with a "1" mark bit. Removing duplicates of a multirelation of n tuples on a P-input OEN (n≤P) will require $w=[\frac{1}{2}\log P(\log P+1)+L]$ unit steps. When n>P, the number of steps is (see [58]): $w\lceil 2n/P\rceil \log\lceil 2n/P\rceil$

We note in passing that, unlike the approach of the query processor of [56], mutirelations are not required to be presorted. Further, the OEN approach allows for pipelining of different multirelations.

5.2.Set Operations

The duplicate removal operation can be utilized to perform three set operations.

Union. The duplicate removal algorithm is applied directly to the concatenation of the two operand relations. We note that the two operands can be multirelations.

Intersection. This operation is similar to the union except that the qualified tuples are those output with a mark bit cleared. Again, in this case both operand relations can be multirelations.

Difference. In this case both relations are input simultaneously to the network with different mark bits. For example, if the operation (r_1- r_2) is to be performed then tuples of r_1 are input with mark bit "1" and those of r_2 with "0". The algorithm to be performed by each cell is similar to that of the duplicate removal except for step 7. This step is replaced by "M1:=0". The qualified tuples will belong to the difference. In this operation only r_2 is allowed to be a multirelation.

5.3.Aggregate Functions

To implement multiple and unique generalized selection on an OEN, the group by attribute is used as the major key and the comparison attribute as a minor key. When two input tuples have equal group-by attribute but different comparison attribute, the tuple with the highest comparison attribute will be rejected whereas for two tuples with equal group-by and comparison attribute, both tuples will be rejected if either one has a mark bit already cleared. The algorithm to be implemented by each cell is described below:

procedure gsel(M1,M2,T1,T2,Type)

/*Tuples Ti, i=1,2, with mark bit Mi are input to the cell.

A^i_g and A^i_c are respectively the group-by and

comparison attributes of Ti. This algorithm

performs Mgsel when Type=M, and Ugsel when Type=U.*/

```
begin
  if A_g^1 > A_g^2 then
   begin L ← M2,T2, H ← M1,T1; end
  else if A_g^1 = A_g^2 then
          begin
            if A_c^1 > A_c^2 then M_1:=0 else
              begin
               if A_c^1 = A_c^2 then
                  begin
                    if Type=M
                       begin
                         M1:=M1 and M2;
                         M2:=M1;
                       end;
                     if Type=U
                       begin
                         M1:= M1 or M2;
                         M2:=M1;
                       end;
                  end else M2:=0;
              end;
          L ← M1,T1;
          H ← M2,T2;
end;
```

Figure 5.5 shows an example in which an OEN is used to perform Mgsel on an eight element relation. In this case each processor implements the Mgsel algorithm.

The generalized addition is performed on the OEN as follows: The mark bits are initially set to "1". At each cell, if the tuples have equal group-by attribute values, the corresponding mark bits are manipulated and an addition operation (ADD) is performed on the addition attribute values. The algorithm to be implemented by each cell is:

procedure gadd(M1,M,T1,T2)

/*Mi, A_g^i, and A_a^i are respectively the mark bit, group-by,

and addition attribute of tuple Ti, i=1,2.*/

```
begin
 if A_g^1>A_g^2 then
   begin L←M1,T1; H←M2,T2; end
   else begin
        if A_g^1=A_g^2 then
          begin
            M1:=M1 or M2;
            M2:=0;
            A_a^1=A_a^1 ADD A_a^2
            A_a^2:=0;
          end;
        L←M1,T1;
        H←M2,T2;
      end;
end.
```

5.4.Division

The aggregate functions Mgsel and gadd, and the Dup-rem operation, are used to perform the division over two multirelations r_1(A,B) and r_2(B). As shown in the block diagram of Figure 6.6, the division operation is partitioned into four steps.

Step 1: During this step, r(B) is extended to include the attribute names in A. The A-values of the extended tuples are set to "null". The concatenation c^* of the two extended multirelations $r_1^*=(1,1,1,r_1)$ and $r_2^*=(1,1,0,r_2)$ is then input to the OEN. First, Mgsel(B,DB,c^*) is performed with M1 as a mark bit , followed by Dup-rem using M2 as a mark bit.

Step 2: In this step tuples at the output of the OEN are examined. Tuples with M1=0, M2=1, and DB=1 are collected and the remainder rejected.

Step 3: The B-values of the collected tuples are eliminated, and M1 is initialized to "1". Next, tuples are extended to include an addition attribute A_a. This attribute is initially set to "1". Thereafter the gadd operation is performed on the resulting augmented multirelation.

Step4 : Tuples with M1=1 and $A_a=n_2$ are collected. These tuples belong to $r_1 \div r_2$.

An example of division and resulting tuples after each step is shown in Figure 6.7.

6.Query Processor

In [56] a VLSI parallel and pipelined processor has been proposed. In this processor the relational algebra operations as well as aggregate functions are implemented directly in hardware. Tuples are input in the circuit in bit serial, tuple parallel fashion. The query processor is composed of four different processing circuits (called PIPE's): sorting PIPE, duplicate removal PIPE, join PIPE, and single relational query PIPE. These four PIPE's are shown to be sufficient to perform relational algebra operations as well as aggregate functions.

In this approach the relational algebra operations are performed on presorted relations. Therefore the analysis of the sorting PIPE is necessary for the performance evaluation of the execution time for the operations. Further, the sorting PIPE is not only used for internal sorting but for two-way merge and filtering (squeezing) marked tuples as well. Figure 6.1 shows the basic cell utilized in the sorting circuit. A PxP sorting PIPE can sort a list of P tuples, filter a list of P marked tuples, and merge two sorted lists (runs) of P tuples each. Figure 6.2 shows a 4x4 sorting PIPE. In this figure min and max refer to inputs that are respectively less than or greater than any other inputs.

In general, P(3P-1) cells are needed to design a PxP sorting PIPE. The tuples to be sorted enter the circuit through the vertical input lines. Simultaneously, all the horizontal inputs are set to the min value. The sorted tuples are collected through the horizontal lines. The delay $D_1(n)$ needed to perform internal sorting is given by

$$D_1(n) = (L+2P-1)$$

Merging two ordered lists of n tuples ($n \leq P$) on a PxP is done in the following way: one list is entered through the horizontal inputs, the other through the vertical ones. The list that enters through the horizontal inputs is required to be ordered in descending order from top to bottom. The new ordered list of 2n tuples is collected at the vertical and horizontal output lines. It is noted that the n smallest tuples of the new ordered list are output through the vertical lines. The number of steps required to perform the merge is equal to that of internal sorting.

However, when the number of tuples n in each run is greater than P, several phases are needed. In this case the merging delay is:

$$D_2(n) = (L+2P-1)(2^{\lceil n/P \rceil} - 1)$$

External sorting (i.e., $n > P$) is performed in two steps. During the first step the circuit is used as a sorter; this generates $\lceil n/P \rceil$ runs of P tuples each. During the second step the circuit is used as a two-way merger. The second step requires $\log \lceil n/P \rceil$ phases. During the ith phase, $1 \leq i$

$\leq \log \lceil n/P \rceil$, $(\frac{1}{2})^{i-1} \lceil n/P \rceil$ runs of $2^{i-1}P$ tuples each are converted to $(\frac{1}{2})^{i} \lceil n/P \rceil$ runs of $2^{i}P$ tuples each. The delay introduced by phase i will be:

$$D_3^i(n) = (1-(\frac{1}{2})^i) \lceil n/P \rceil (L+2P-1)$$

The external sorting delay $D_{sort}(n)$ is:

$$D_{sort}(n) = \lceil n/P \rceil (L+2P-1) + \sum_{i=1}^{\log \lceil n/P \rceil} D_3^i(n) \ , \ (n > P)$$

$$= \lceil n/P \rceil (L+2P-1)(\log \lceil n/P \rceil + (\frac{1}{2})^{\log \lceil n/P \rceil}$$

6.1.Duplicate Removal

The duplicate removal is performed in three steps. During the first step the multirelation is sorted. Then the sorted tuples are fed into a duplicate checker (or marker) circuit that marks all duplicate tuples. During the third stage, the marked tuples are filtered out (squeezed).

Figure 6.3 shows a 4-input duplicate marker. In general, a P-input duplicate marker is a two-stage circuit composed of (2P-1) cells. When the number of tuples to be marked is greater than P, several passes are required. During each phase (except the last one) a tuple from the output is fed back to the input. The number of steps required to mark a multirelation of n ($n \geq P$) tuples is:

$$D_{mark}(n) = (1 + \lceil (n-P)/(P-1) \rceil)(L+2) \ , \ n \geq P$$

In the third step, the sorting circuit is utilized to filter out the marked tuples. The filtering delay is:

$$D_{filter}(n) = \lceil n/P \rceil (L+2P-1)$$

6.2.Join

Joining two relations r_1 and r_2 is performed in the following manner: First, a cartesian product of the two relations is performed. This is done by concatenating each tuple of r_1 with each tuple of r_2. At the same time a mark bit is appended to the composite tuples. The value of the mark bit depends on the result of the comparison of the two join attributes. During the second step the marked tuples are filtered out. The concatenation and marking take $O(\frac{n_1 n_2}{P})$ steps. P represents the number of comparators in the join PIPE.

6.3.Set Operations

Union of two relations is performed simply by applying the duplicate removal algorithm to the concatenation of the two relations.

Intersection is treated as a special case of the join operation. In this case the join attribute is the whole tuple.

Difference is performed in the following steps: first, each relation is sorted and its duplicates removed. In order to distinguish between tuples of each relation, the mark bits of tuples of the two relations are set to different values. The two relations are then merged and the resulting relation is fed to the duplicate marker unit. It is noted that in the case of the difference operation the cells of the duplicate marker unit implement a different algorithm.

6.4. Aggregate Functions

In the query processor, aggregate functions are performed in three steps. The relation is sorted and then fed to the aggregation unit. The resulting relation is then sent to the duplicate marker and filter units respectively. The structure of the aggregation unit is the same for all aggregate functions except that the algorithm performed by the cells differs for each function.

The basic unit of the aggregation unit is a two input one output cell. A P-input aggregation unit is composed of logP stages and requires PlogP cells. Figure 6.4 shows a 4-input aggregation unit. The general design of the circuit is as follows: The k-th cell $1 \leq k \leq P$ of the first stage has the k-th and $(k+1)-$th tuples as inputs. In general, in the j-th stage, $2 \leq j \leq \log P$, the inputs of the k-th cell are the output of cells k and $(k+2^{j-1})$ of stage (j-1).

In the case of Ugsel operation, the algorithm performed by each cell is as follows: Two tuples $T_1(A_g^1, A_c^1)$ and $T_2(A_g^2, A_c^2)$ consisting of a group-by attribute (A_g^i), and a comparison attribute A_c^i, $i=1,2$, are input into the cell (see Figure 6.5). It is noted that the input tuples are in sorted order $(A_g^1 \leq A_g^2)$. The output tuple $T(A_g^1, A_c)$ has a comparison attribute A_c such that: $A_c = A_c^1$ if $A_g^1 \neq A_g^2$, or $A_c = \text{minimum}(A_c^1, A_c^2)$ otherwise.

The generalized addition algorithm performed by each cell is similar to that of the Ugsel operation. Except that for the generalized gadd operation the input tuples $T_i(A_g^1; A_a^2)$, $i=1,2$, are composed of a group-by attribute(A_g^i), and an addition attribute (A_a^i). The addition attribute (A_a) of the output tuple $T(A_g^1, A_a)$ is given by: $A_a = A_a^1$ if $A_g^1 \neq A_g^2$, or $A_a = A_a^1 + A_a^2$ otherwise.

The aggregation unit performs other aggregate functions like *count* and *average* over groups. In the case of count operation for example, an extra attribute called *count* attribute (A_c) is needed. This attribute is initially set to 1. The count operation is performed as follows: If the group-by attribute of the input tuples $T_i(A_b^i, A_c^i)$, $i=1,2$, is equal the count attribute of the output tuple $T(A_g^1, A_c)$ is $A_c = A_c^1 + A_c^2$, otherwise $A_c = A_c^1$.

When the number of tuples to be input to the aggregation unit is greater than the number of input lines (P), several phases are needed to process the relation. After each phase an output tuple with the highest group by attribute is fed-back to the input.

6.5.Division

The division $r_1 \div r_2$ of two relations r_1 and r_2 defined on the relation schemes R_1 and $R_2 = R_1 - R_3$ respectively is performed in the following steps: The two relations are sorted and their duplicates removed. For relation r_1, the sorting key is R_3. In the second step each group of tuple of r_1 having equal R_3 attribute is sent along with the tuples of r_2 to the join PIPE. The resulting relation is sent to the aggregate PIPE where the count over group operation is performed. It is noted that for each group only a single tuple is obtained. If the count attribute of each tuple is equal to the cardinality of r_2, then the group-by attribute of this tuple belongs to $r_1 \div r_2$.

7.Comparative Analysis

The four approaches for computing relational algebra operations can be divided into two classes. In the first class are those techniques in which the tuples or parts of the tuple are serially entered into the circuit. The two examples of this type of circuit are BCA (section 3) and Kung and Lehman's 2-D systolic implementation (section 4). In the second class are approaches in which tuples are input in parallel to the circuit. Of course, because of realizability constraints such as the number of pins per chip, the tuples are entered in a tuple parallel bit serial fashion. Two examples of this type of circuit are discussed in this paper: OEN (section 5) and Kim *et al.'s* query processor (section 6). In this section we compare the features of various approaches discussed earlier. However, it is more meaningful to compare each class independently. For this reason we compare features of the BCA with the systolic approach, and OEN with the query processor.

First we compare the serial tuple approaches of section 3 and 4: BCA and 2-D systolic array. Some of the features of the BCA approach are:

(1) The same topology is used for duplicate removal and set operations.

(2) Set operations (except difference) are performed directly on mutirelations.

(3) The design is modular, so that testing and expansion are easy (see section 3.3).

(4) The number of pins is independent of the number of cells.

(5) Unidirectional and regular dataflow are utilized.

(6) Communications are simple and interfacing is easy.

(7) Tuples are output one at a time with their mark bits. Thus rejected tuples can be easily filtered.

(8) The number of cells is independent of tuple size.

(9) The structure is simple and regular, and thus suitable for VLSI implementation.

It is noted that both approaches make use of the mark bit technique to identify undesirable tuples. One of the main differences between the two designs is that in the BCA only one subtuple per relation is input (or output) at a time. This allows for simple global communications, simple filtering of marked tuples, and ease of interfacing. Note that in the systolic approach set operations (except union) cannot be performed directly on multirelations. Further, the number of cells in Kung's approach depends on the tuple size. However, the systolic approach has the advantage that the cells require less memory storage than those of the BCA. Further, in the systolic approach, algorithms have been developed for most of the relational algebra operations, while in the BCA approach only algorithms for duplicate removal and set operations have been developed. It is noted in passing that both approaches make extensive use of pipelining and parallelism. Consequently, both architectures are expected to achieve high throughput. Table 1 summarizes and compares the features of the BCA and systolic approaches. To be specific, we focus attention on duplicate removal, and consider circuits which will simultaneously handle n tuples. In this case for BCA n cells are required, and the 2-D systolic implementation requires $e(2n-1)$ cells. It is recalled that

$$e = \left\lceil \frac{\text{tuple size (L)}}{\text{max. subtuple size handled by each cell } (q)} \right\rceil$$

The number of computation steps required for BCA is $(e+1)n$ and for the 2-D systolic array is $(4n+e-4)$. These estimates are based on the assumption that one subtuple at a time is input to BCA, and k ($\leq \lfloor (e+1)/2 \rfloor$) subtuples are input in the 2-D systolic array case. Consequently, BCA would require q input and output pins, while a direct implementation of the systolic array would require $(e+1)q$ input and output pins. If in the systolic case we restrict the number of input and output pins to q, then the processing delay would be $(e+2)n-2$.

In the OEN and query processor approaches, the bit-serial tuple-parallel approach has been adopted. In the OEN approach a single topology has been utilized to perform relational algebra operations. It is noted that in the OEN architecture internal algorithms (except that of division) require one pass through the network. Consequently, those algorithms have essentially the same time complexity. For the query processor, four different PIPE's are utilized. The time delay associated with each internal algorithm is given in Table 2. The time delay associated with number of processors required for each PIPE is also indicated.

Note (Table 3) that in the query processor the relations need to be presorted before any further processing is possible. For example, the duplicate removal operation is performed in three steps: sort, mark, and filter. It is noted in passing that the sorting and marking steps are performed simultaneously on the OEN network. Further, unlike the query processor approach, most of the algorithms implemented on the OEN network operate directly on multirelations. Finally, in the query processor the complexity of the intersection operation is similar to that of the join operation. Consequently, the intersection operation is performed very inefficiently on the query processor.

Table 1
Comparison of BCA and systolic array
for duplicate removal

Architecture	Number of cells	Number of steps	Number of pins	Number of inputs/relation
BCA	n	$(e+1)$n	indep. of number of cells	1 subtuple
2-D Systolic array	e(2n-1)	4n$+e-$4	depends on number of cells	up to $\lfloor (e+1)/2 \rfloor$ subtuples

Table 2
Hardware units
used by
query processor

Unit	Number of PE's	Delay
Sorting	n(3n-1)	L+2n-1
Marker	2n-1	L+2
Filter	n(3n-1)	L+2n-1
Aggregation	nlogn	(logn)+L
Join	P	$O(\frac{n_1 n_2}{P})$

Table 3
Steps involved in performing relational algebra operations and aggregate functions on the OEN and Query processor

Architecture	Dup-rem Union Difference	Intersection	Aggregate functions	Division
OEN	Mark Filter	Mark Filter	Mark Filter	gsel Dup-rem gadd Filter
Query processor	Sort Mark Filter	Join	Sort Aggregation Mark Filter	Dup-rem Join

REFERENCES

[1] CODD, E.F.,"A Relational Model of Data for Large Shared Data Banks," *Comm. ACM*, June 1970, pp. 377–387.

[2] CODD, E.F.,"A Data Base Sublanguage Founded on Relational Calculus," *PROC. 1971 ACM SIGFIDET Workshop of Data Description, Access and Control.*

[3] CODD, E.F.,"Normalized Data Base Structures: A Brief Tutorial," *Proc. 1971 ACM SIGFIDET Workshop on Data Description, Access and Control.*

[4] CODD, E.F.,"Relational Completness of Data Base Sublanguages;" *Data Base Systems*, Courant Computer Science Symposia 6, Prentice-hall, 1972.

[5] CODD, E.F.,"Further Normalization of the Data Base Relational Model," *Data Base Systems*, Courant Computer Science Symposia 6, Prentice-Hall, 1972.

[6] ULLMAN, J.D.,Principles of Database Systems,Computer Science Press, 1982.

[7] MAIER, D.,The Theory of Relational Databases,Computer Science Press, 1983.

[8] CHAMBERLIN, D.D., *Computing Survey*,VOL.8, No.1, March 1976,

[9] FAGIN, R., "The Decomposition Versus the Synthesis Approach to Relational Database Design," *VLDB III*, Tokyo, Japan,*ACM*, *IEEE*, pp 441–446.

[10] JACOBS, B.E.,"On Database Logic," *Journal of the ACM*, Vol. 29, N0.2, April 1980, pp.310–332.

[11] FAGIN, R.,"Horn Clauses and Database Dependencies," *Journal of the ACM*, Vol.29, No.2, April 1980, pp. 952–985.

[12] MINKER, J.,"Performing Inferences over Relational Databases," *ACM/SIGMOD Int'l Conf. on Management of Data*, San-Jose, Calif., 1975, pp. 79–91.

[13] GALLAIRE, H.,"Impact of Logic on Data Bases," *Proc. 7th Int'l Conf. on Very Large Data Bases*, Cannes, France, 1981, pp. 248–259

[14] SAGIV, Y.,*et al.*,"An Equivalence Between Relational Database Dependencies and a Fragment of Propositional Logic," *Journal of ACM*, VOL.28, No.3, July 1981, pp. 435–453.

[15] FAGIN, R.,"Functional Dependencies in a Relational Database and Propositional Logic," *IBM Journal of Research and Development*, Armonk, N.Y., November 1977, pp. 534–544.

[16] MOTO, T., *et al.*,"Challenge for Knowledge Information Processing Systems," *Fifth Generation Computer Systems*, North-Holland, October 1981, pp. 179–188.

[17] AMAMIYA, M., *et al.*,"New Architecture for Knowledge Base Mechanisms," *Fifth Generation Computer Systems*, North-Holland, October 1981, pp. 3–89.

[18] DAVIS, A.L.,"Tomorrow's Computer-Thc Challenges-Computer Architecture," *IEEE Spectrum*, Vol.20, No.11, November 1983, pp. 94–99.

[19] KAMANOKE, K.,"Current Status and Future Plans of the Fifth Generation Computer Systems Project," *Proceedings of the International Conference on the Fifth Generation Computer Systems*, November 1984, pp. 3–17.

[20] KAMIBAYYA, N.,"SPIRIT-III: an Advanced Relational Machine Introducing a Novel Data Staging Architecture with Tuple Stream Filters to Process Relational Algebra," *AFIPS National Computer Conference*, 1982, pp. 606–610.

[21] KITSUREGAWA, M., *et al.*,"Relational Algebra Machine GRACE," *RIMS Symposia on Software Science and Engineering*, Lecture note in Computer Science, Springer-Verlag, 1983.

[22] KITSUREGAWA, M., *et al.*,"Application of Hash to Data Base Machine and its Architecture," *New Generation Computing* Vol.1, No.1, 1983, pp. 63–74.

[23] ASTRAHAN,M.M., *et al.*,"System R: Relational Approach to Database Management,"*ACM Trans. Database Syst.*, Vol.1, No.2, June 1976, pp. 97–137.

[24] SELINGER, P.G., *et al.*,"Access Path Selection in Relational Systems," *IBM Research Laboratory, RJ2429*, San Jose, CA 95193, January 1979.

[25] DALEY, R.C., DENNIS, J.B.,"Virtual Memory, Processes and Sharing in MULTICS," *ACM Trans. Commun.*, Vol.11, No.5, pp.306–312.

[26] JOYCE, J.D., OLIVER, N.N,"Performance Monitor for a Relational Information System," *Proc. ACM Annual Conf.*, October 1976, pp. 306–312.

[27] STONEBRAKER, M., *et al.*,"The Design and Implementation of INGRES," *ACM Trans. Database Syst.*, Vol.1, No.3, September 1976, pp. 189–222.

[28] BONCILHON, J.D., *et al.*,"VERSO: A Relational Back-end Database Machine," *Advanced Database Machine Architecture*, pp. 1-18, Prentice-Hall, 1983.

[29] SLOTNICK, D.L.,"Logic Per Track Devices," *Advances in Computers*, Vol.10, Academic Press, N.Y, pp. 291-296, 1970.

[30] OZKARAN, E.A., *et al.*,"RAP: An Associative Processor for Database Management," *AFIPS National Conference*, Vol.44, AFIPS Press, pp.379–387.

[31] SHUSTER, S.A., *et al.*,"RAP2: An Associative Processor for Databases," *Proc. of the Fifth Annual Symposium on Computer Architecture*, 1978, pp. 52–59.

[32] LIN,C.S., *et al.*,"The Design of a Rotating Associative Memory for Relational Database Application," *ACM Trans. Database Syst.*, Vol.11, No.1, March 1976, pp. 53–65.

[33] SU, S., LIPOVSKY, G.,"CASSM: A Cellular System for Very Large Databases," *Proc. Conf. on Very Large Databases*, 1975.

[34] LIPOVSKY, G.J.,"Architecture Features of CASSM: a Context Addressed Segment Sequential Memory," *Proc. Fifth Annual Symposium on Computer Architecture*, pp. 31–38, 1978 pp. 255–265.

[35] SMITH, D., *et al.*,"Relational Database Machines," *IEEE Computer*, Vol. 12, May 1979, pp. 27–41.

[36] CHAMPINE, G.A.,"Currrent Trend in Database Systems," *IEEE Computers*, Vol.12, May 1979, pp. 27–41

[37] DEWITT, J.D., HAWTHORN, P.B.,"A Performance Evaluation of Database Machine Architecture," *7-th International Conf. on Very Large Databases*, Cannes, France, Sept. 1981, pp.199–213.

[38] DEWITT, J.D.,"DIRECT- a Multiprocessor Organization for Supporting Relational Database Management Systems," *IEEE Trans. Comput.*, Vol. 28, N0.6, pp.395–406, June 1979.

[39] GARDARIN, G.,"An introduction to SABRE: a Multimicroprocessor Database Machine," *6th Workshop on Computer Architecture for Non-numeric Processing*, Hyere, France, June 1981.

[40] GARDARIN, G., *et al.*,"SABRE: A Relational Database System for a Multimicroprocessor Machine," *Advanced Database Architecture*, pp. 19–36, Prentice-Hall, N.J.,1983.

[41] BITTON, D., *et al.*,"Parallel Algorithms for the Execution of Relational Database Operations," *ACM Trans. on Database Syst.*, Vol. 8, No.3, Sept. 1983, pp. 324–353.

[42] VALDURIEZ, P., GARDARIN, G.,"Join and Semi-Join Algorithms for a Multiprocessor Database Machine," *ACM Trans. Database Syst.*, Vol.9, No.1, March 1984, pp.133–161.

[43] MISSIKOF, M., TERRANOVA, M.,"The Architecture of a Relational Database Computer Known as DBMAC," *Advanced Database Machine Architecture*, pp.83–108, Pentice-Hall, 1983.

[44] MISSIKOF, M.,"Relational Queries in a Domain Based DBMS," *SIGMOD Record*, Vol.3, No.4, 1983.

[45] MISSIKOF, M.,"A Domain Based Internal Schema for Relational Database Machines," *ACM SIGMOD, International conf. on Management of Data*, Orlondo, FL., June 1982, pp.215–223.

[46] MISSIKOF, M., SCHOL, M.,"The Relational Database DBMAC: FSA Filtering on a Fully Invented Physical Organization of Data," *Proc. of the Working Seminar on Databases*, Gressoney, Italy, February 1982.

[47] Tanaka, K., *et al.*,"A File Organization Suitable for Relational Database Operations," *Lecture Notes in Computer Science, Proc. of Int. Conf. on MSIP*, Springer-Verlag, pp. 193-228.

[48] SHU, W., SOOD, A.K.,"Database Systems Using Horizontally Separated and Inverted Data Structure," *Proc. Conf. on Information Science and Systems*, Baltimore, Maryland, March 1983.

[49] HAWTHORN, P.B., DEWITT, D.J.,"Performance Analysis of Alternative Database Machines," *IEEE Trans. on Software Engineering*, Vol. SE-8, No.1, January 1982, pp. 61-75.

[50] BABB, E.,"Implementing a Relational Database by Means of Specialized Hardware," *ACM Trans on Database Syst.*, Vol.4, No.1, March 1979, pp. 1-29.

[51] JOHNSON, R.R., and THOMPSON, W.C.,"A Database Machine for Performing Aggregations," UCRL-87419 Lawrence Livermore National Lab., Calif., 1982.

[52] KUNG, H.T.,"Why Systolic Architectures?," *Computer* Vol.15, No.1, Jan. 1982, pp. 37-46.

[53] YASUURA, H., *et al.*,"The Parallel Enumeration Sorting Scheme for VLSI,",*IEEE Trans. on Comput.*, Vol. c-31, No.12, Dec. 1982, pp. 1192-1201.

[54] KUNG, H.T., LEHMAN, P.L.,"Systolic (VLSI) Arrays for Relational Database Operations," *ACM/SIGMOD International Symposium on Management of Data*, Los- Angeles, 1980, pp. 105-116.

[55] SOOD, A.K., ABDELGUERFI, M.,"Parallel and Pipelined Processing of Some Relational Algebra Operations," *International Journal of Electronics*, Vol. 59, No.4, pp.477-482.

[56] KIM, W., *et al.*,"A Parallel Pipelined Relational Query Processor," *ACM Trans on Database Syst.*, Vol.9, No.2, June 1984, pp. 214-242.

[57] SOOD, A.K., SHU, W.,"Parallel Processor Implementation of Relational Database Operations," *Conference on Vector Parallel Processors in Computing Science II*, Oxford, England, Aug. 1984.

[58] SHU, W.,Parallel Computer Architectures For Relational Databases, Ph.d thesis, Department of Electrical and Computer Engineering, Wayne State University, Jan. 1985.

[59] SOOD, A.K., SHU, W.,"A Relational Algebra Machine for Fifth Generation Computers," *Conf. on Information Sciences and Systems*," Baltimore, Maryland, March 1985.

[60] BATCHER, K.E.,"Sorting Networks and Their Applications," *Proc. AFIPS Spring Joint Computer Conf.*, 1968, pp. 307-314.

[61] MENON, M.J., HSIAO, D.K.,"Design and Analysis of a Relational Join Operation for VLSI," *Proc. 7th Int'L Conf. on Very Large Data Bases* Sep. 1981.

[62] SHAW, D.K., *et al.*,"The NON-VON Database Machine: A Brief Overview," *IEEE Database Engineering*, Vol.1, March 1983, pp. 43–54.

[63] HSIAO, C.C.,Highly Parallel Processing of Relational Databases, Ph.D thesis, Department of Computer Science, Purdue University, Dec. 1982.

[64] HSIAO, C.C.,"Omni-sort: A Versatile Data Processing Operation for VLSI," *IEEE Int'L Conf. on Parallel Processing*, 1980, pp. 222–225.

[65] MURASZKIEWICZ, M.,"Concepts of Sorting and Projection in a Cellular Array," *Proc. 7th. Int'L Conf. on Very Large Data Bases*, Cannes, France, Sep. 1981.

[66] TONG, F., YAO, S.B.,"Performance Analysis of Database Join Processors," *AFIPS, National Conf.*, 1982, pp. 627–638.

[67] BATCHER, K.E.,"Bit Serial Parallel Processing Systems," *IEEE Trans. Comp.*, Vol.31, No.5, May 1982, pp. 377–384.

[68] THOMPSON, C.D.,"Area-Time Complexity for VLSI," *Proc. 11th Annual ACM Symposium on Theory of Computing*, ACM, N.Y., 1979, pp. 81–88.

[69] THOMPSON, C.D.,"A Complexity Theory for VLSI," Ph.D thesis, Department of Computer Science, Carnegie-Mellon University,1980.

[70] MERRET, T.H., OTOO, E.,"Distribution Models of Relations," *Proc. Int'l Conf.on Very Large Data Bases*, Rio de Janeiro, 1979, pp. 418–425.

[71] ZLOOF, M.M,"Query by Examples: A Data Base Language," *IBM Syst. J.*, Vol.16, No.4, 1977.

[72] CHAMBERLIN , D.D., *et al.*,"SEQUEL2: A Unified Approach to Data Definition, Manipulation, and Control," *IBM J. R.D.*

[73] FISHER, A., "Systolic Algoritms for Running Order Statics in Signal and Image Processing," *VLSI Systems and Computations*, pp. 265–272., Oct. 1981.

[74] GENTLEMAN, W.M., KUNG, H.T.,"Matrix Triangularization by Systolic Arrays," *Proc. SPIE Symp.*, Vol.298, Aug. 1981.

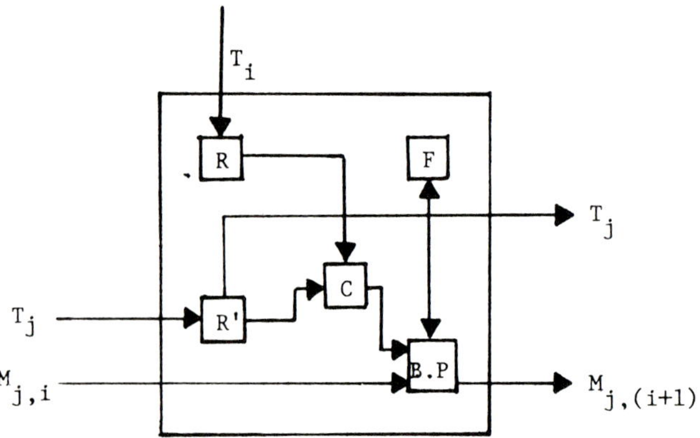

Fig. 3.1 A Typical Cell

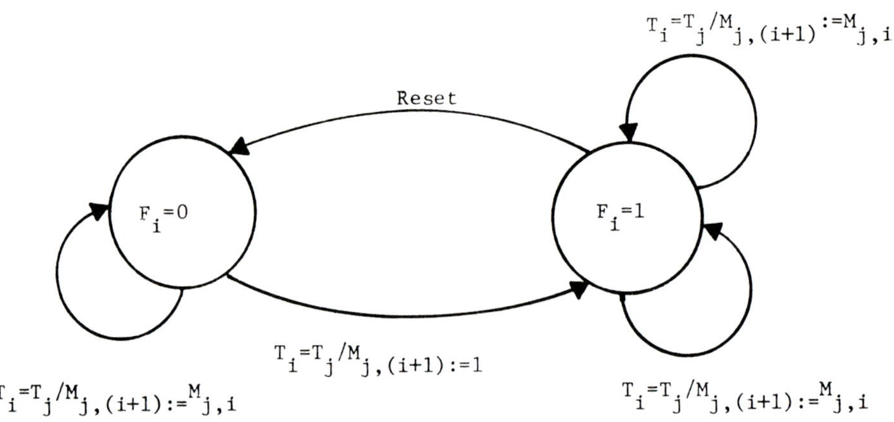

Fig. 3.2 State Diagram

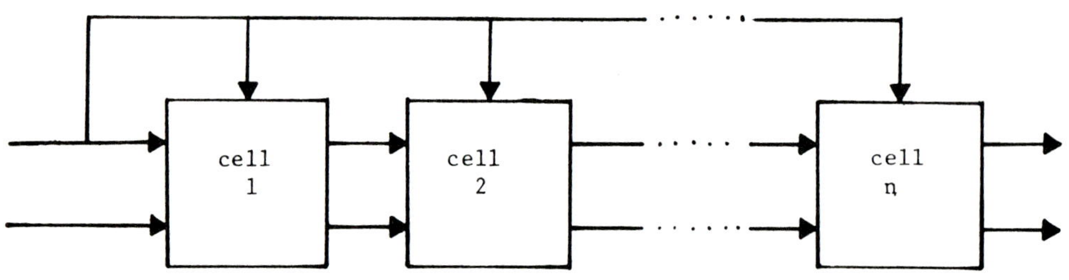

Fig. 3.3 A BCA of n Cells

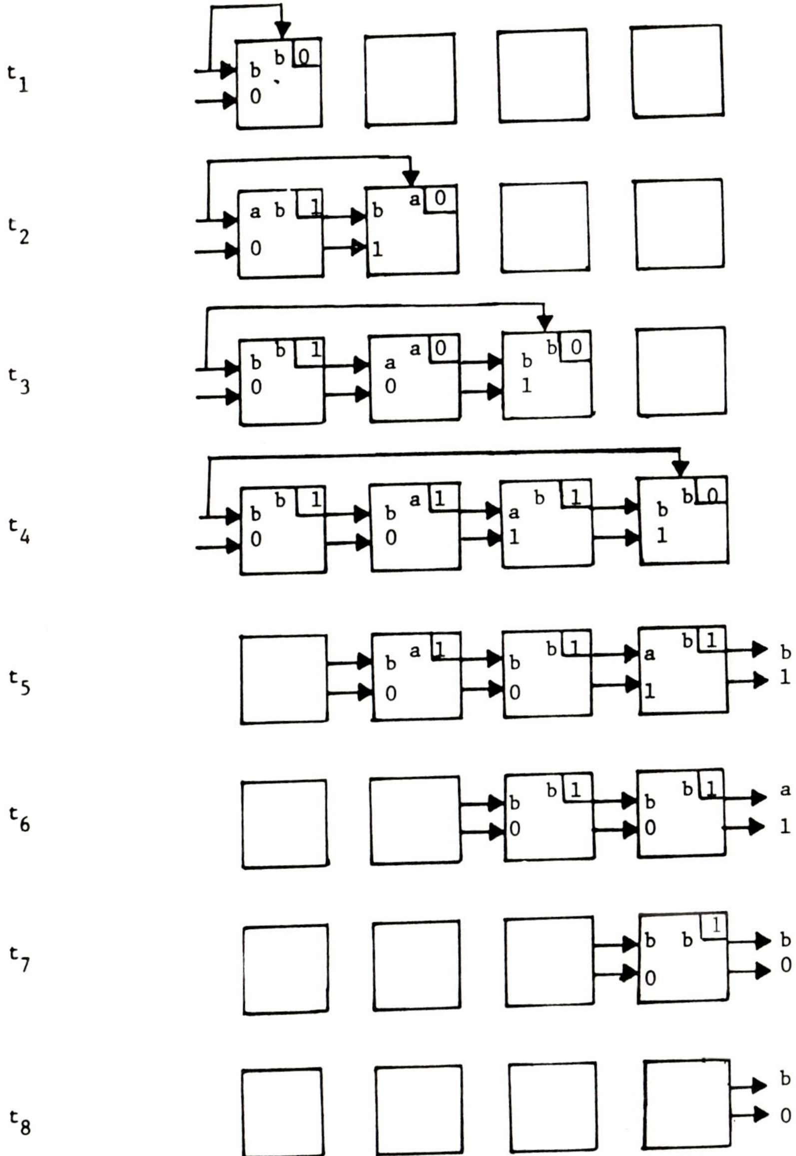

Fig. 3.4 Duplicate Removal of Multirelation r=(b,a,b,b)

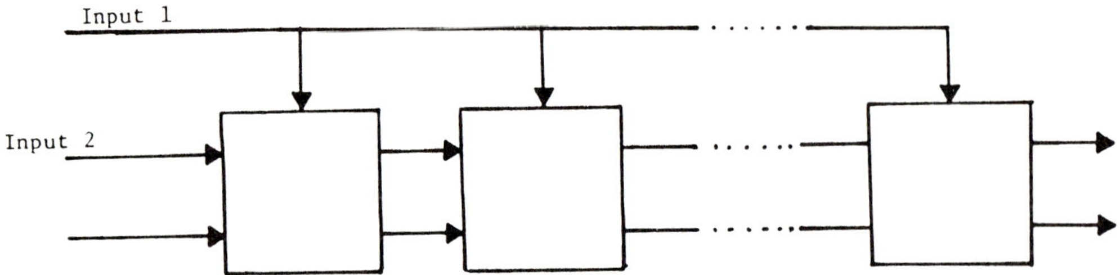

Fig. 3.5 A Modified BCA

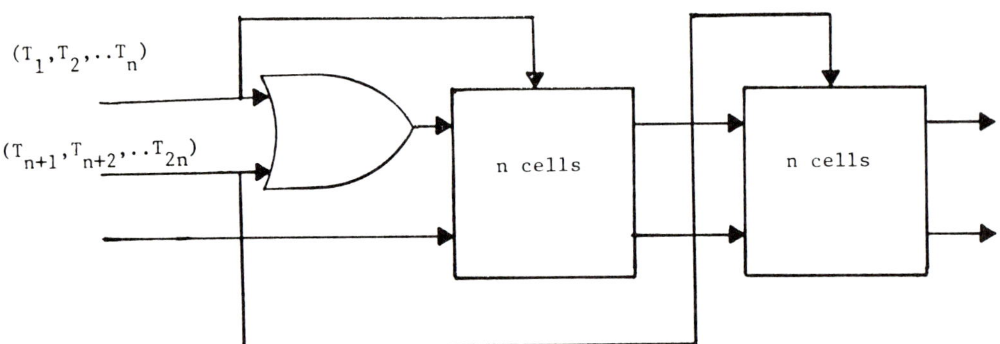

Fig. 3. 6 Processing a sequence of 2n tuples with 2 chips of n cells each

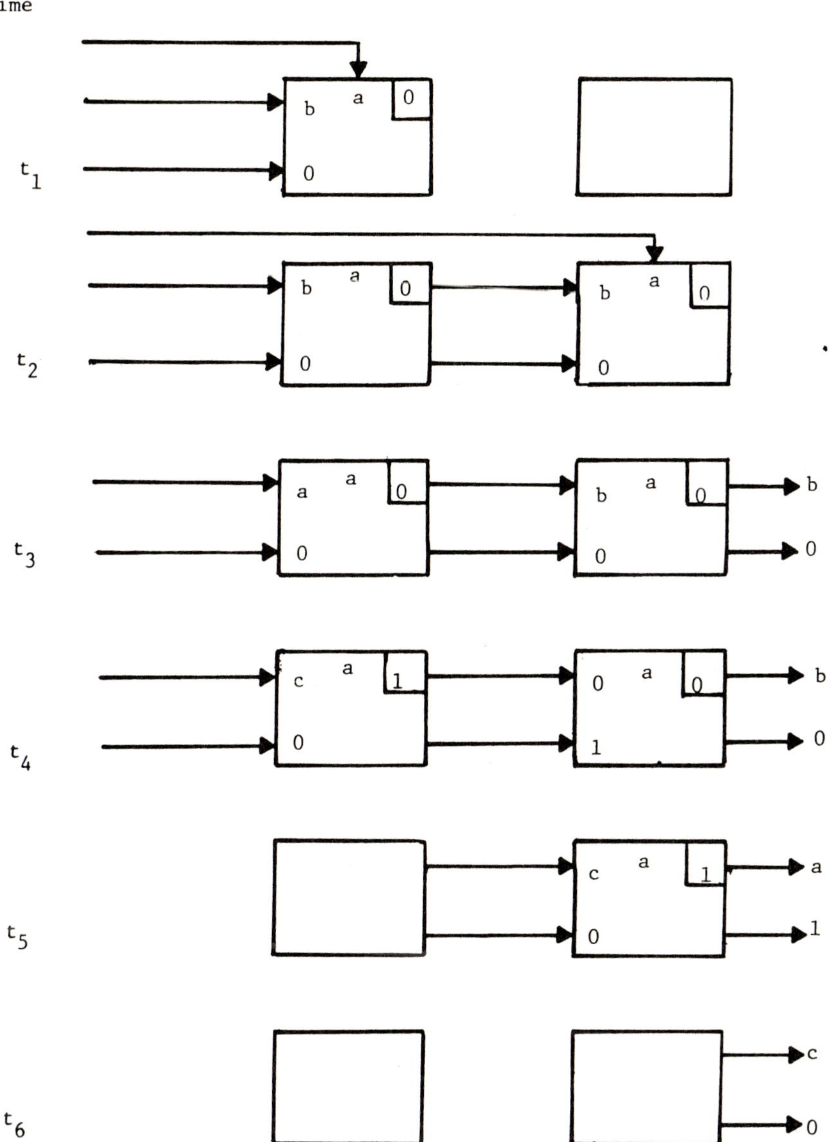

Fig. 3.7 Intersection of Multirelations $r_1=(b,b,a,c)$ and $r_2=(a,a)$

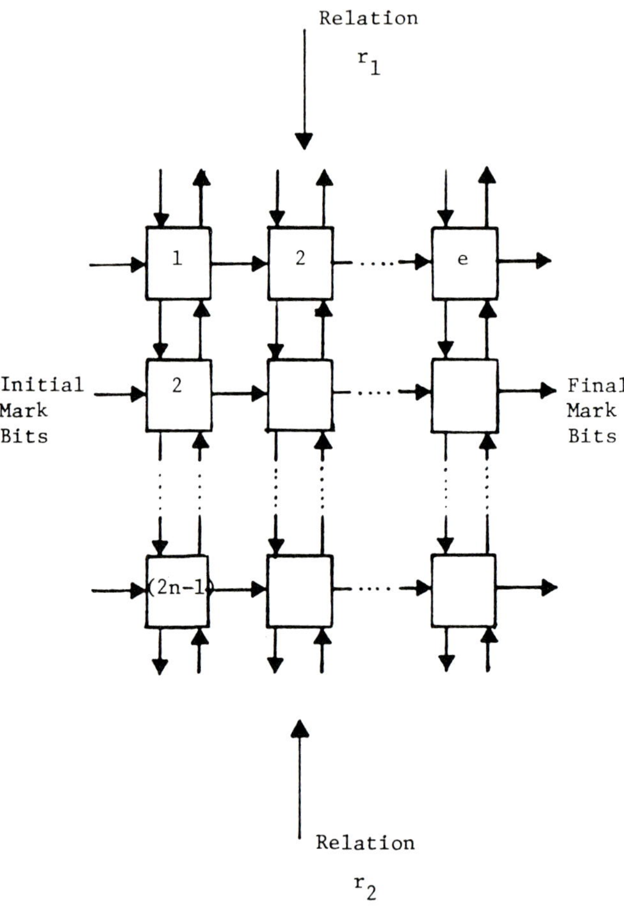

Fig. 4.1 Duplicate Removal Array

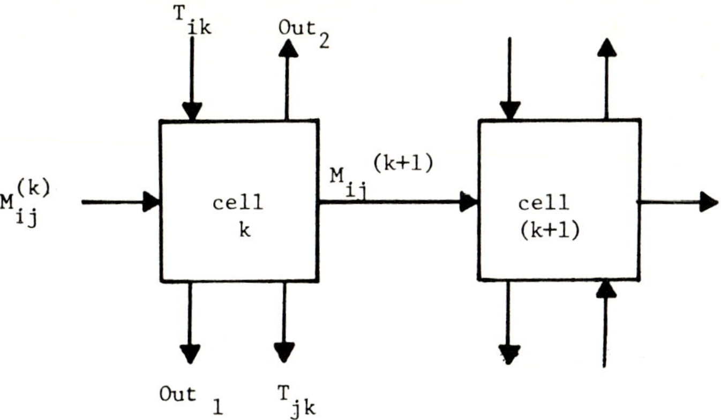

Fig. 4.2 Two Consecutive Cells

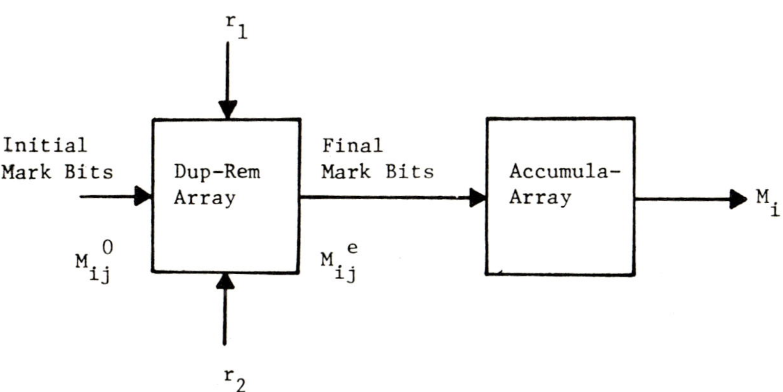

Fig. 4.3 Circuit for Intersection and Difference

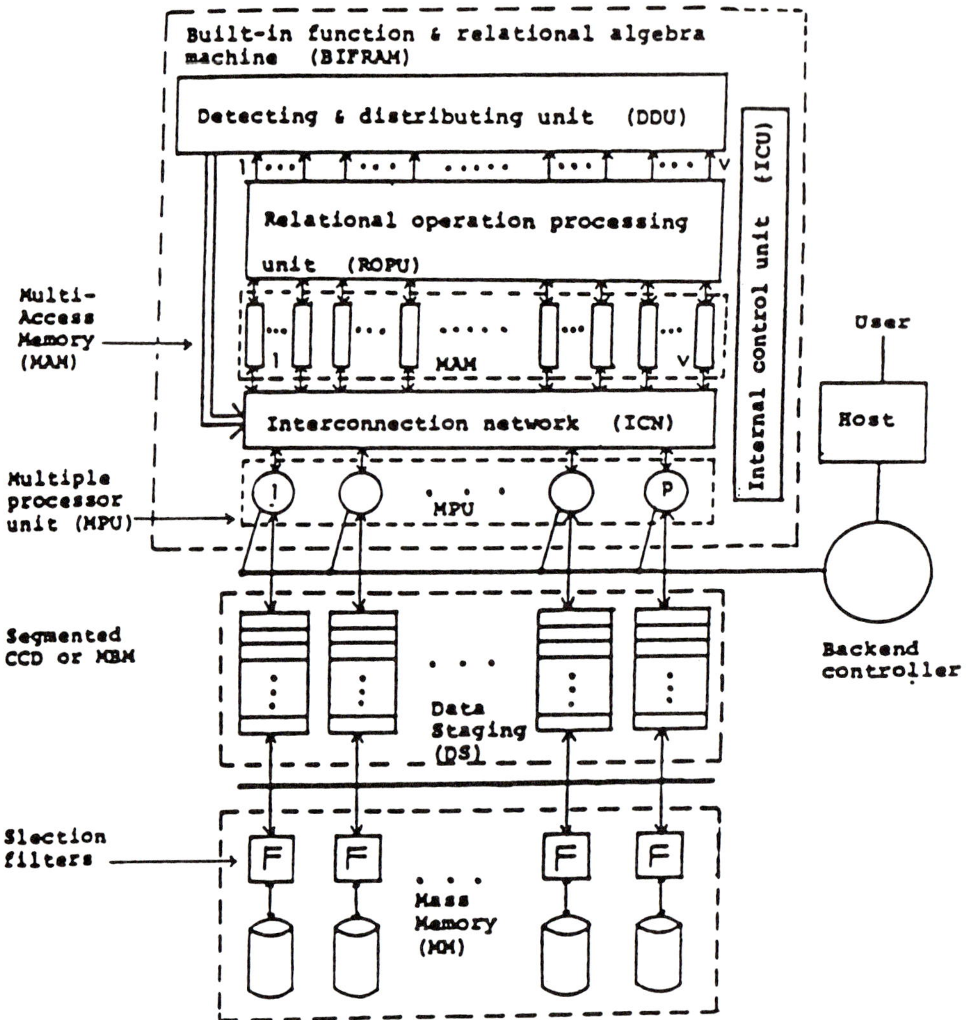

Fig. 5.1 Overall Architecture of BIFRAM Database Machine

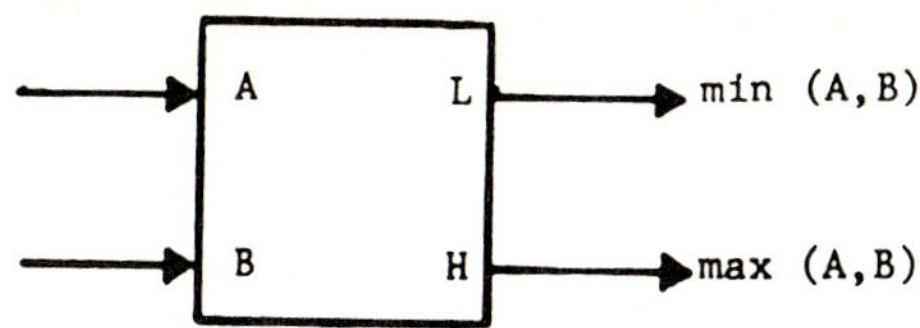

Figure 5.2 Basic Cell of OEN.

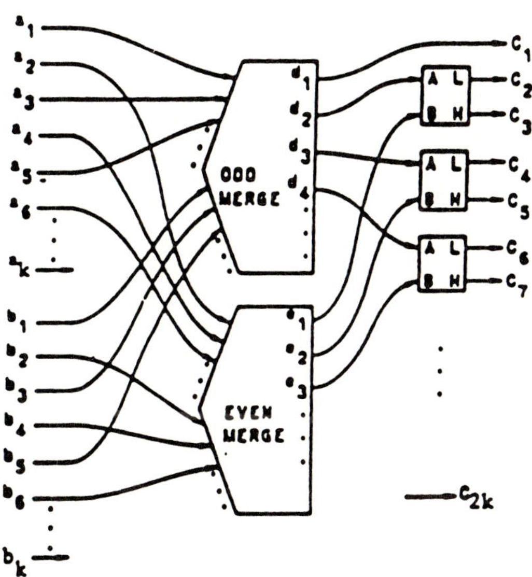

Fig. 5.3 A kxk OEN [60]

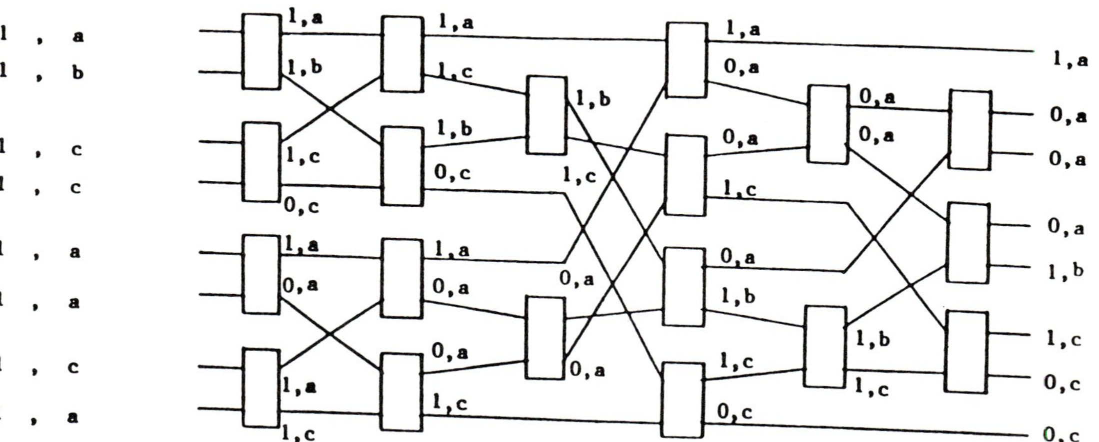

Fig. 5.4 Implementation of Projection on OEN

(a < b < c)

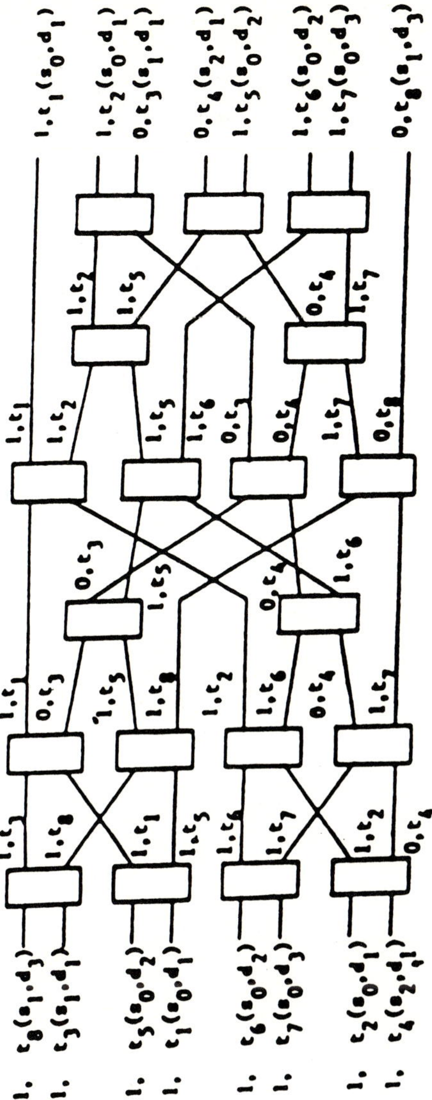

Fig. 5.5 Implementation of Mgsel on OEN

$(d_1 < d_2 < d_3; s_0 < s_1 < s_2)$

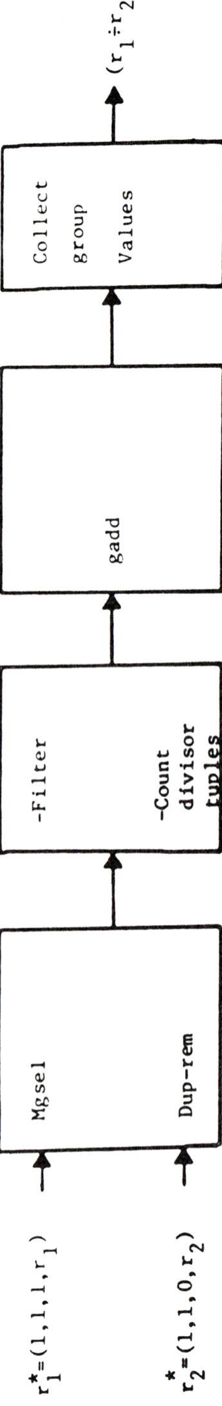

Fig. 5.6 Division over Multirelations

r_1	
b1	a3
b1	a2
b2	a3
b1	a1
b2	a2
b3	a1
b2	a2

r_2
b1
b2
b2

$r_1 \div r_2$
a2
a3

M2	A	M1	DB	B
1	0	1	0	b1
1	a1	0	1	b1
1	a2	0	1	b1
1	a3	0	1	b1
1	0	1	0	b2
0	0	1	0	b2
1	a2	0	1	b2
0	a2	0	1	b2
1	a3	0	1	b2
1	a1	1	1	b3

After step 1

M2	A	M1	DB	B
1	a1	0	1	b1
1	a2	0	1	b1
1	a3	0	1	b1
1	a2	0	1	b2
1	a3	0	1	b2

After step 2

M1	A_d	A
1	1	a1
1	2	a2
0	0	a2
1	2	a3
0	0	a3

After step 3

A
a2
a3

After step 4

Fig. 5.7 An Example of Division over Multirelations

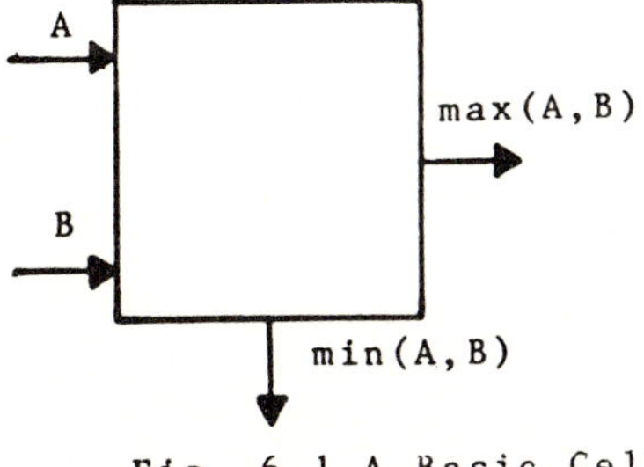

Fig. 6.1 A Basic Cell

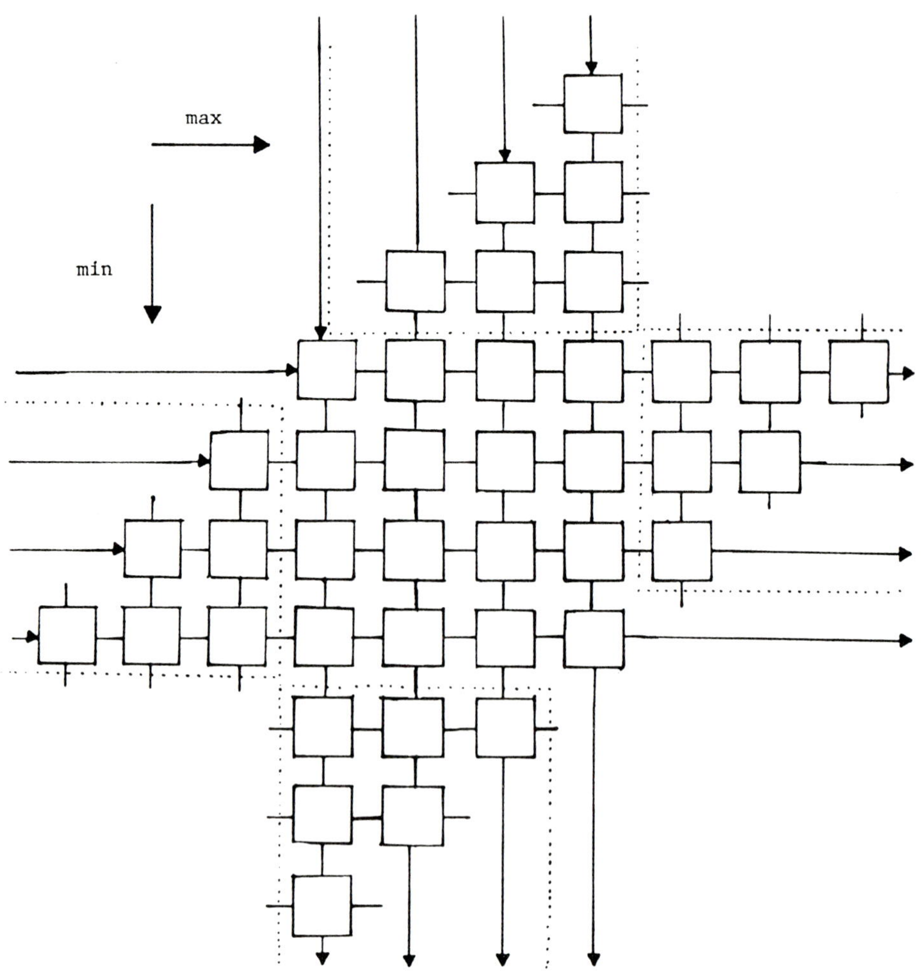

Fig. 6.2 A 4x4 Sorting Circuit

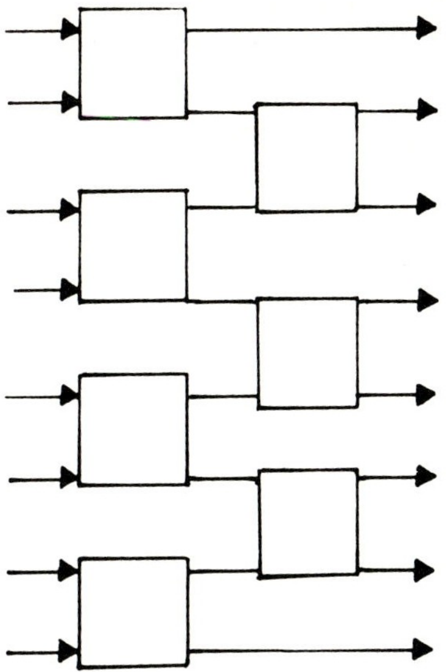

Fig. 6.3 A 4-Input Duplicate Marker

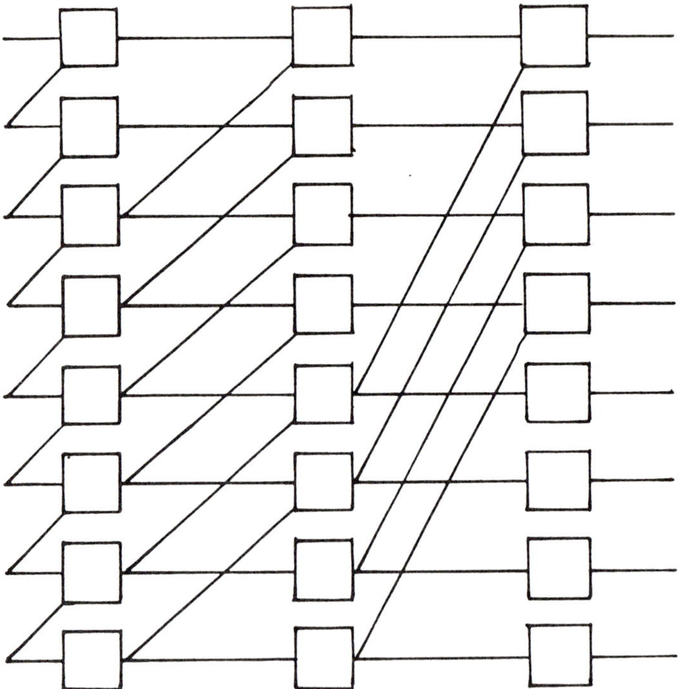

Fig. 6.4 A 4-Input Aggregation Unit

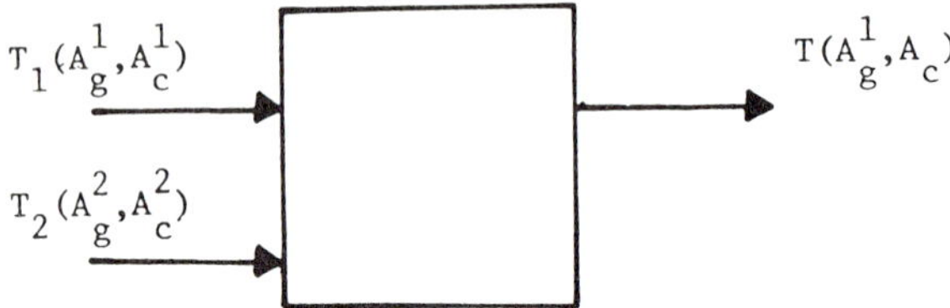

Fig. 6.5 Basic Cell of Aggregate Unit

CAFS-ISP - A UK CONTENT ADDRESSABLE FILE STORE

B.J. Boorman
Defence Technology Centre
ICL
42 Market Place
Reading RG1 2DT
UK

CAFS-ISP is a search engine, or Information Search Processor, exploiting highly parallel hardware techniques to enable information stored on rotating discs to be searched and evaluated at full disc transfer speed. It is intimately associated with conventional disc controllers on ICL's mainframe systems, being an option on 2900 series and fitted as standard equipment on Series 39.

The main elements of the hardware are a Logical Format Unit, which locates significant points in the data stream as it arrives from disc; 16 Key Channels which compare reference values, with optional masks, against actual values in the data; a Search Evaluation Unit which implements boolean logic, or quorum logic, or both types in combination, to determine whether a record qualifies as a 'hit'; a Retrieval Unit which extracts either all fields or a specified subset of fields from hit records; and a Retrieval Processor, capable of executing minor processing functions on hit records, and responsible for controlling their orderly transmission to the host processor.

A File Correlation Unit, which is a published extension to the design and which currently exists in prototype form, facilitates join operations by enabling a representation of the result of any CAFS scan to be created on the fly in a bit-map. The contents of such a bit-map can be associated, by suitable "and, or, not" logic, with any subsequent CAFS scan.

How CAFS works

A process running in the mainframe generates a 'task specification', which instructs the CAFS hardware :

- which part of the disc store is to be searched;
- what conditions identify a 'hit record';
- and which fields are to be retrieved.

The completed task specification is then exported to the CAFS hardware in a single outward transfer, and the elements of the

NATO ASI Series, Vol. F 24
Database Machines. Edited by A.K. Sood and A.H. Qureshi

task are established in the five units of the CAFS engine.

The processes of aligning the read heads with the target cylinder are carried out in the conventional manner. Indeed, it is worth stressing that the disc mechanism itself is completely standard. Data is then streamed off the disc at the full disc transfer speed and onto the byte-wide CAFS highway. Internally the current CAFS engine is capable of searching at up to 3.6 megabytes per second; the effective speed is chiefly determined by the transfer rate of the discs being used.

The Logical Format Unit interprets the data stream as it passes, locating such significant points as the start of a database page, the start of a record, the start of a field to be searched, and the start of a field to be retrieved. When such points are identified, control signals are sent to activate appropriate units in the search and retrieval mechanisms.

The Key Channels compare the reference values provided in the task with the actual values found in the record under consideration. During this process masks may be applied to the actual values, so that insignificant bits are excluded from the comparison. All Key Channels operate independently, so that, depending on the form of the task, all may be looking at different fields or several may be searching for different values in a common field. If a field is repeated, a Key Channel may make and register several comparisons within a single record. Each Key Channel is capable of comparing up to 256 bytes of data. As the data is not buffered, and the comparisons of different fields may take place at different times, a means is needed of registering the result of a comparison until evaluation can take place. For this purpose each Key Channel has an associated comparator latch, in the form of a 3-bit result store.

At the end of each record, the Search Evaluation Unit determines whether or not the record was a 'hit', by an appropriate combination of the results from the Key Channels. This Unit consists of a number of co-operating processors operating in a highly parallel manner, each capable in one step of accepting data from its associated comparator latch, from its own store, and from its neighbour, and capable also both of placing a result in its own store and of passing a result to a neighbour. The most complex evaluation which the unit can be called on to execute can be completed in some 4.5 microseconds, or the time taken for a mere 16 bytes to pass along the highway.

The Retrieval Unit performs the more simple process of extracting required fields from hit records. The machine is able to retrieve either complete records or selected fields. In order to save time, data is received into the store of the Retrieval Unit while the record is still being scanned and evaluated. If the record is not a hit, the data can be discarded; this is much more efficient than any serial process of search followed by evaluation followed by retrieval.

Finally the Retrieval Processor is able to execute certain minor processing functions on the data from hit records. Thus it can identify the maximum and/or minimum value of a field; it can form totals of simple numeric fields; to a limited extent it can perform comparisons between fields in the same hit record. The mechanism is also able to register counts, both of complete hit records and of the number of times particular conditions are satisfied. This unit also returns hit records to the host processor as soon as possible, so that in most cases early hits are available for display or other processing while within CAFS the search is still in progress.

The whole machine thus acts as a very efficient filter, ensuring that the mainframe only sees records which are relevant to the current application process.

The secret of the speed and power of CAFS is that all the searching and evaluating activities are carried out in parallel by special-purpose hardware of ICL design, not by co-operation between conventional microprocessors. This gives it a permanent advantage in serial searching mode over any von Neumann processor.

CAFS records, files, and indexes

Early versions of CAFS required that all the data to be searched should be held in a particular format. But with CAFS-ISP in large scale production this restriction has of course been relaxed, and with some minor exceptions, all normal data and all standard formats are directly CAFS-searchable. Integers, character fields, dates and other simple formats can be searched by a single key channel. More complex formats such as packed decimal and floating point can also be searched, though more than one key channel may be required to cope with them. Fields that do not align to byte boundaries, or that consist of irregular numbers of bits, can be searched with the aid of the standard masking facilities.

Fixed length records are obviously easy : each target field can be located by its offset from the start of the record. Records with a fixed-length root and a variable length trailing component can also be searched, provided that the variable length section is either a single character string, or an array of fixed-length elements repeating a variable number of times, or contains text in self-identifying format.

Most common file organisations are directly accessible through

CAFS: Serial files can be scanned from end to end; index sequential files can either be scanned exhaustively or, more efficiently, can be approached through partial or 'focussed' scans. Databases of Codasyl organisation, either plain IDMS or IDMSX with its indexes on records and sets, are searched one record-type at a time; the extent of each scan is normally one complete area, but can be more finely restricted to the page-range within which the target record-type is stored.

The basic strength of CAFS at serial scanning means that in very many applications a simple full-file scan will provide a perfectly acceptable response time. The speed is so great that there is often no need to engage in the scan-avoiding techniques so common in non-CAFS applications.

However, for systems where faster responses are essential, or where a large population of active users needs to be serviced, the use of indexes to restrict the extent of each scan becomes appropriate. The best example of this is in the use of the primary key on an index sequential file, where a value of the key maps directly onto a particular physical extent of the file. It may be worthwhile to take some care in choosing the primary sequence of such a file, since one needs to identify the most effective clustering key. Preliminary analysis can well be supplemented by observation of the forms of enquiry most commonly employed by typical users. This is quite likely to be much more effective than asking the users themselves what key sequence they would prefer; without prior experience of the benefits of a CAFS enquiry service most users are poor at predicting how they will exploit it. As a simple rule of thumb, if an index sequential file is held in sequence of the record-identifying key it is almost certainly in a sequence unsuitable for efficient CAFS enquiries: a clustering key should define the file sequence, and the record-identifying value should be treated as an alternate key.

Many techniques of secondary indexing have been developed, and several of these may have relevance in a CAFS environment. Conventional methods tend to offer great precision in exactly locating each record, but impose a load in additional complexity which in the case of highly volatile files may be a serious addition to the burden of keeping the file updated. By contrast, a technique of using bit-matrices as simple secondary indexes has been well explored in the CAFS world, and has been found to provide efficient task-focussing with minimal maintenance effort.

This technique relies on the theoretical organisation of the target file in a number of consecutive search 'cells', each corresponding to some small physical section of the file - a block, or a track, or perhaps two tracks. A secondary index is then constructed by establishing, for each value of the indexing variable, a bit-vector having the same number of bits as there are cells in the target file. A setting of '1' in any bit indicates that the corresponding value of the indexing variable occurs at least once in the specified cell. In practice, the value may occur many times within the cell, but a single '1' bit is adequate to locate them all; it is not pointing, as in a conventional inversion, to a particular instance, but indicating that the cell is one which is worth searching by CAFS.

Where more than one secondary index exists, they can very easily be used in combination to establish where CAFS searches should be initiated. Software selects the bit-vectors for the quoted values from each of the available indexes, and combines them by a simple logical 'AND' in the host's store. Any residual '1' bits indicate which cells are worth searching. This process is amazingly simple and efficient when compared with the burden of associating chains of reference values or pointers in conventional inverted lists.

Such indexes are also a great deal easier to update than their conventional analogues. When a new record is added to the file, or when values of indexed fields are altered in an existing record, '1' bits are inserted with logical 'ORs' into the right bit-strings. When a record is deleted, no attempt is made to clear set bits from the indexes. To do so, it would be necessary to confirm that the deleted record was the last one with those values in that cell; establishing this involves a degree of processing which is normally judged unnecessary. As a result, a secondary index on a volatile file may progressively fill up with false bits, causing scans of cells which in fact contain no hits. Clearly this does not produce false results, because hit records are finally selected by CAFS. But if a degradation in performance is observed it is an easy matter to delete the degraded index and regenerate it.

Choosing a suitable cell size depends on such factors as the record size and the distribution of values of the indexing fields. If the cell is set too large, the resulting indexes will be more compact, but may be filled with too high a proportion of '1' bits, with a corresponding diminution in their focussing effectiveness. It is therefore probably wiser to err on the side of small cells, accepting that the indexes will be correspondingly larger; the tiny amount of processing required for both their creation and use makes this quite acceptable.

CAFS software interfaces

Four methods of accessing the CAFS hardware have so far been developed. As will be seen, they provide the means for implementing a very wide range of CAFS-exploiting software.

First, there is a simple CAFS Search Option as one of the facilities of the VME operating system on both Series 39 and

2900 systems. This is intended to allow CAFS to be used to enhance the performance of many existing programs - without such programs having to be edited or re-compiled. It works by invoking a CAFS search, not from within the program itself, but from the System Control Language statements which direct the running of the program. Thus a program which reads a file serially, selecting some records for processing and ignoring others, can easily be given a performance boost: with CAFS it only sees the hit records, and the unwanted records are not even transferred from disc to mainframe.

A Direct CAFS Interface allows programmers operating in any of the normal range of high level languages to exploit all the facilities of the CAFS engine in a wide variety of package and application conditions. Some twenty-five procedures are made available, allowing precise specification of how all the task elements are to be defined and combined. This interface is being used themselves by an increasing number of CAFS users, and is also being exploited by a number of software houses, wherever an existing serial search process is susceptible to CAFS acceleration, and wherever the simplicity of such a search can be usefully substituted for more complex software access mechanisms.

Within the framework of ICL's own Quickbuild and data management products, a Relational CAFS Interface provides even the unskilled COBOL programmer with the ability to write programs which take advantage of the power of CAFS. The programmer does not need to know how the CAFS engine works, not indeed under what conditions it will be used. The interface presents him or her with a view of the required data fields in the form of simple logical records in a simple logical serial file. Below the interface a highly efficient optimiser makes use of whatever access techniques are most appropriate, combining the use of indexes, the following of database pointers, and scans with CAFS.

Also within ICL's own software product range is the general purpose online enquiry language Querymaster, designed for non-technical end-users. This shares the same access optimiser. It also has the advantage of presenting to the user a straight-forward relational view of the stored data, with all the benefits of ease of understanding; underneath, the data is obviously stored in whatever form gives the greatest access efficiency.

CAFS performance

Measurement of the performance of CAFS searches, when they form part of the activity of a machine supporting a mixed workload, is obviously subject to many factors which are not here expounded in full. The crucial factor is the transfer speed of the discs being used. As indicated above, the CAFS engine, even in its present form, is capable of operation at faster speeds than can be supported by any of the discs on which it has yet been implemented.

Successive interactions between the host and the disc controller in which CAFS is incorporated mean that over an extended search the overall scanning rate falls slightly below the basic disc transfer speed. Simple measurements on a variety of discs show that the effective search speed can be from 75% to 85% of the raw disc transfer speed. Thus the discs on 2900 systems deliver just short of 1 megabyte per second of scanning power, while those on Series 39 systems will provide up to approximately 2.5 megabytes per second.

This impressive performance, however, is perhaps less important in itself than in its incidental effects. Chief among these is system simplification. When one has such searching power at one's disposal, there is less need to devise complex structures and sophisticated access techniques. Non-CAFS systems can become heavily dependent on these, as a vital means of avoiding the cost and inefficiency of typical software searching.

Several formal sizing experiments have been conducted to compare the effectiveness of CAFS searches with the same searches carried out by software. In these exercises the systems used have mainly included ICL software and mainframe hardware, but similar comparisons have also been made with searches by well-respected software packages on other manufacturers' hardware systems. The results always show that CAFS provides faster response times and, because the bulk of the searching task is delegated to special purpose hardware, much reduced load on the host mainframe. In summary, the cost effectiveness of a CAFS search is always at least two orders of magnitude greater than the software equivalent.

CAFS application experience

Since March 1984, when the software which exploits CAFS became generally available, well over 400 CAFS engines have been installed on 2900 systems. They can be found in all areas of ICL's customer base - insurance companies, retail firms, manufacturing organisations, as well as government departments, local authorities, public utilities, health authorities, universities, and police and defence establishments. No single type of user predominates, nor is there any particular area of application which overshadows all others. This is well in line with the observation, on which the original development of CAFS was founded, that searching and dealing with ad hoc and unpredictable enquiries form part of the workload of every data processing department.

Users also report that there is no single type of person who benefits most from a CAFS-based enquiry service. Enquirers range from senior executives to ordinary clerical staff. Perhaps the common characteristic of those who are using such services most intensively, among whom are found many senior administrative staff and professionals such as chemists engineers and biologists, is that they already have the most thorough understanding of the stored data and of the extra information that can be derived from it through successive enquiries. But also a CAFS service helps to promote such understanding, since a user can afford to browse among the stored data, asking many questions in succession, because so little machine resource is expended in finding each answer.

The most experienced users of CAFS have all shown a major development in the scope of the enquiry service they provide. Usually some critical file is chosen for the first experiments. When enquiries upon this prove successful, the data processing manager finds that his end users will themselves set the priorities for the spreading of the enquiry facilities to other files. As demand grows, the number of CAFS engines also increases, until a developed system is likely to have CAFS capability on all its disc channels, as well as having more numerous channels than its non-CAFS predecessor.

A further important trend is for the end users to require that not only the current data is made available for interrogation, but also versions of the organisation's data at significant historical points - the end of the last accounting period, the corresponding period of the previous year, and so on - so that enquiries can be made across time. With the prospect of ever larger volumes of data being held online, whether on magnetic or optical media, the management of data across time will demand, in the next few years, the same level of attention as has recently been given to managing the immediate snap-shot state of the database.

CAFS has hitherto been treated mainly as a means of making enquiries on files of data. But its capabilities for searching text are also of great importance. Already the ability to search on such items as product descriptions, names and addresses, delivery instructions, and the like is increasing the value of textual fields where they occur in ordinary data processing files. A number of important applications have also been developed where the ability to search text as it occurs in documents is being exploited with exciting success; this area has certainly a great deal of most interesting potential.

In personnel systems, in market research, in the management of manufacturing inventories, in the control of supplier and customer accounts, many organisations are finding the benefits of allowing their end users to make their own searching enquiries. Online enquiry has become the dominant mode of deriving information from the files of the data processing function, taking the place of many of the printed reports, both regular and ad hoc, which were previously demanded. Consequently, the resources of the data processing department can be more productively deployed in the development of those jobs which have in the past languished in the applications backlog.

Conclusion

Simplification and flexibility are keywords which recur over and over again when users are describing the effect that CAFS has already had on their information handling. They are exploited simultaneously both in the provision of a better information service to end users and in the more productive allocation of skilled system development resource. It is in the confidence that these effects will be both permanent and universal that ICL has now made CAFS not only an optional enhancement to 2900 systems but also an automatic component of all Series 39 systems.

References

1. MALLER, V.A.J. : 'The content addressable file store - CAFS'. ICL Technical Journal, 1979, 3, pp.265-279

2. CARMICHAEL, J.W.S. : 'The application of ICL's content addressable file store to text storage and retrieval'. Proceedings of PROTEXT I, First international conference on text processing systems, Dublin, October 1984

Intelligent Cellular Systems:- A New Direction For Total System Design

by

G. E. Quick

West Glamorgan Institute
of Higher Education
Swansea, U.K.

KEYWORDS

Intelligent Memory, Cellular Computer System, Wafer Scale Integration, Database Machine, Inference Computer

ABSTRACT

With the exception of the INMOS transputer, there has been little advancement in the area of developing the concept of the Intelligent Memory Computer. It seems that researchers have reached an "intellectual brickwall" in the design of these system, although such systems offer many solutions to hardware and software environmental problems associated with Database and Knowledge Applications. In this paper we hope to dismantle some of the intellectual brickwalls by considering a multi-access, or parallel access computer system. In particular we are concerned with engineering a "new wave" machine architecture targeted for fifth generation use, and not rely on the current practice of re-engineering of conventional uni-processor or bounded multi-processor machine architecture. We propose an architecture for Wafer Scale Integration suitable for use in fighting vehicles of various types, as well as in a wider range of application areas.

NATO ASI Series, Vol. F 24
Database Machines. Edited by A. K. Sood and A. H. Qureshi

1. INTRODUCTION

A cellular computing system may be visualised as a homogenious array of intelligent memory cells (Quick 1979), with direct coupling to the outside world, i.e. the users. It is important to visualise this homogenious space as a complete stand-alone system, and not a backend processor as found in many array processors attached to conventional uni-processor systems (Halsall 1984). It is also important to appriciate that these systems will not be constructed from masses of integrated circuits, but will eventually be engineered as wafer based systems (Aubusson 1978, Ueoka 1984, Chesley 1984). This is seen as a first stage in realising three dimensional integrated systems.

The above constraints are important to the computer architect at the start of the design stage of any machine architecture. Failing to observe the techniques of design and development has lead to many proposed architectures being impractical, from the engineering view point, and resulted in them being exercises in computer simulation. More importantly, the design of any new architecture must have a projected life cycle of many years if a computer manufacturer is to develop and retain any confidence in a new architecture. In this case, device integration is a key factor in the organisation of the functional units of the proposed system, as are Computer Aided Design, Manufacture and Testing (CAD/MAT) an economic necessity for future realisation.

2. MOTIVATING FACTORS

The INMOS Transputer (Barron 1983, INMOS 1983, INMOS 1984), see figure 1, is possibly the most innovative architecture currently in the pre-production stage of development. Although the current die size is relatively large; by the process of refinement this architecture is suitable for wafer based cellular systems. As a result of this regular organisation, it is likely that the Transputer will be used in a wide variety of machine architectures ranging from the personal workstation to the mainframe equivalent.

The Transputer's homogenious like architecture leads us into areas that device manufactures welcome, that is, continuous production systems based on a

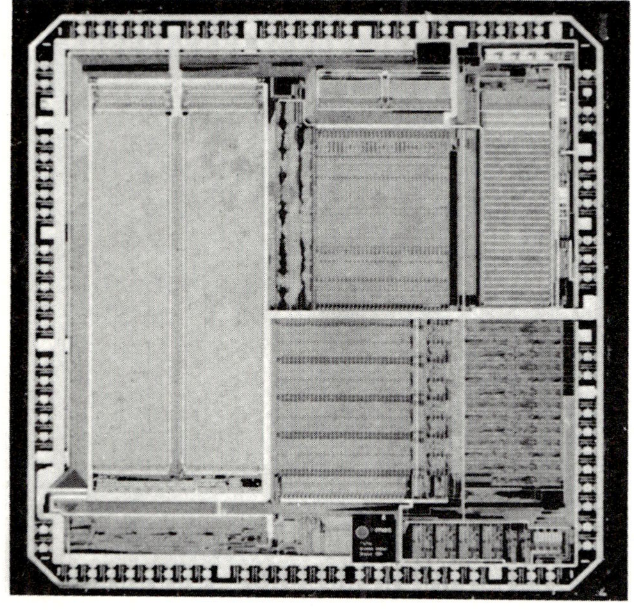

Device Layout

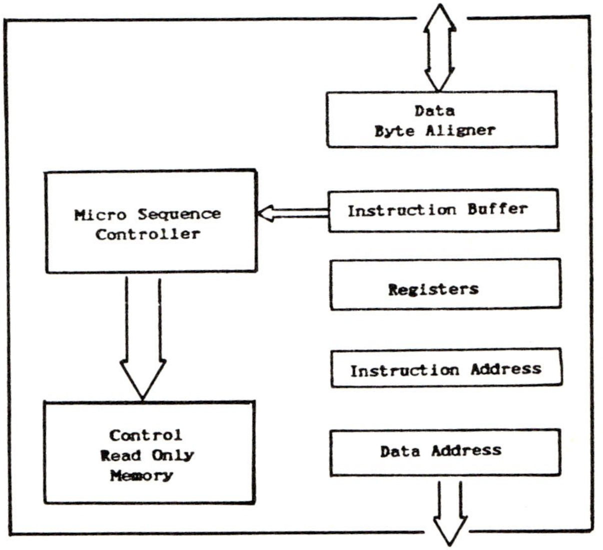

Block Structure

Figure 1 INMOS Transputer

small range of product lines. The motivation for continuous production systems is purely economic; why produce a wide range of devices by batch production methods when cellular systems, such as the Transputer, provide solutions to the ever increasing problems associated with production costs.

The alternative motivation for cellular machine architecture lay in the costs associated with processing vast quantities of data. Whether this data is used in conjunction with database systems, or used processing sensored data in military command and control applications, it must be processed in real-time. When using conventional architectures to effect efficient data processing, we are clearly looking towards super computers of the CRAY type. Alternatively, cellular machine architecture offers a radically different approach to computer architecture by providing potentially faster performance with significantly less production costs. Therefore, if we are to provide a hardware execution environment, suitable for a wide range of intelligent software applications, we must move away from the architecture based on present convention, to an environment based on Intelligent Memory.

3. INTELLIGENT MEMORY SYSTEM

The very basic single user conventional computing architecture has benefited from the careful attention of many throereticians and industrial researchers. They have generated a highly tuned machine which is capable of the fast execution of a wide range of programs. What they have failed to do is to provide an architecture that is truly a general purpose reconfigurble architecture. In this section we will illustrate just one of the attributes of cellular systems configured as intelligent memory, which is increased reliability.

In a true parallel program, the user may define a large number of parallel tasks. These may include the operation to DUPLICATE code to support reliability in addition to more conventional concepts of parallelism. In the operation of highly reliable computing systems of the past, reliability was obtained by the duplication of the hardware (Johnson 1984, I.E.E. 1978). While these systems served their purpose in most application areas, more modern applications require higher degrees of reliability in some tasks than in others. During the execution of highly reliable tasks, voting can take place on the output from each of the duplicated task images, as shown in figure 2,

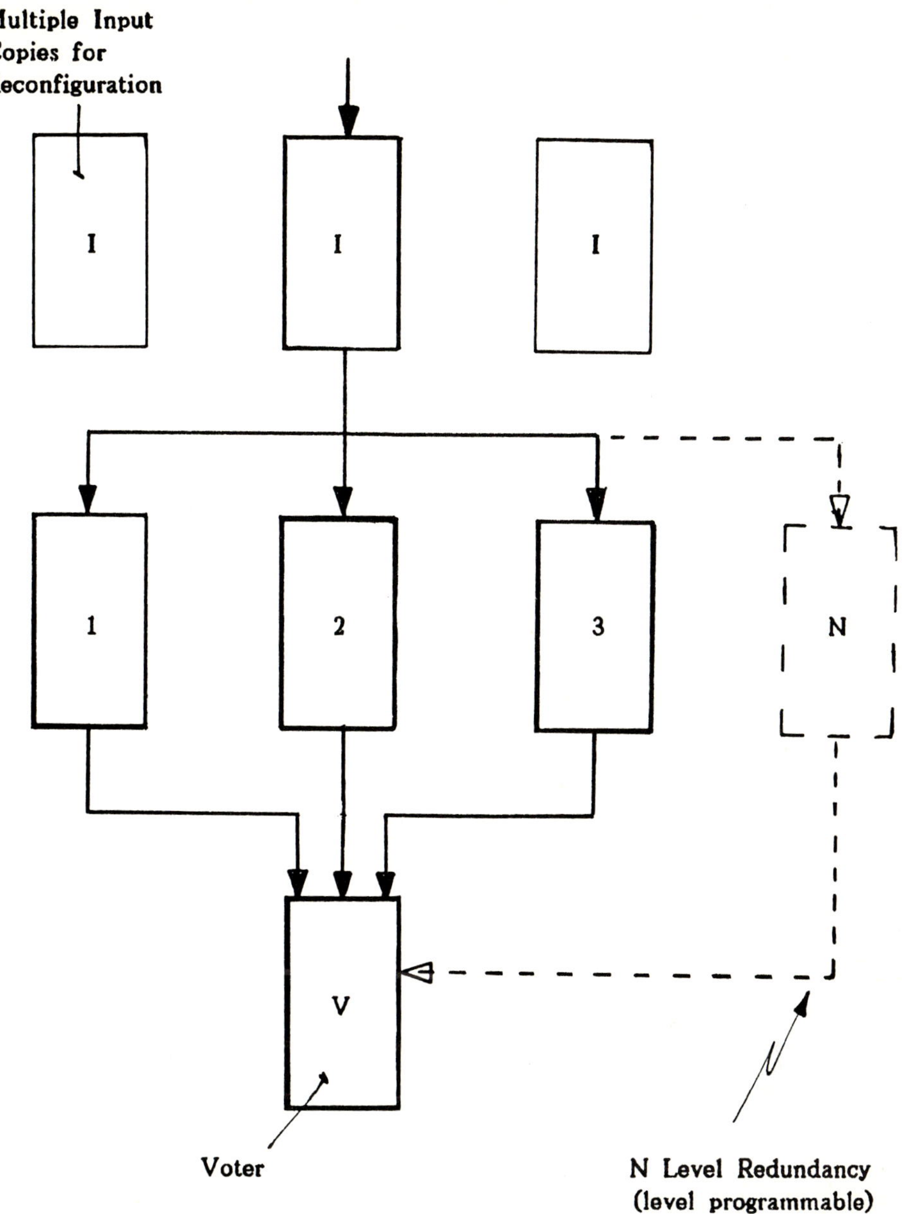

Figure 2 Highly Reliable Structure

with additional input data sets available for system re-configuration. Should an error be detected a majority vote may be defined acceptable or, in highly reliablity mode of operation, error detection may initialise the mapping of the backup tasks into the voting procedure.

Recovery block (Randell 1978) and software duplication can be implemented in a cellular computing system. The recovery block can be viewed as a group of communicating cells, logically coupled to form a sequential process. Duplication of the recovery blocks may be allowed by the specification of the levels of duplication in the software. Highly reliable systems can be configured to incorporate voters at the output stage of the various sections of replicated code. This is shown in figure 2 with the output from the replicated processes 1, 2, 3, to N being compared in the voter process V, each process being located in a seperate cell. Additional voters may be used simply by assigning the number required to perform the task to vacant cells.

The major advantage of the intelligent memory system is the divergence from the hardwired triple redundant systems of the past, to a structure that can be non-redundant in less critical applications, with no voting taking place, to one that can be highly redundant with many active voters. Thus, where high reliability is required, the system can be automatically reconfigured to accommodate the user's needs.

4. GROUP PROCESSOR SYSTEM

In this section we introduce a cellular computer system called the Group Processor System. We shall describe the Group Processor System as cellular computer systems because of its homogenious structure, using an array of programmable components called cells. These cells may be configured as a single user, or multi user parallel access machine environment. The Group Processor System has been designed as a wafer based system that has the capability of being extended to a three dimension system.

The Group Processor concept is not a total system design, but an environment for process execution. The realisation of the architecture for a computing system is based at the highest level, as well as the lowest level, on systems principles. That is, the complete system is built up of sub-systems of common

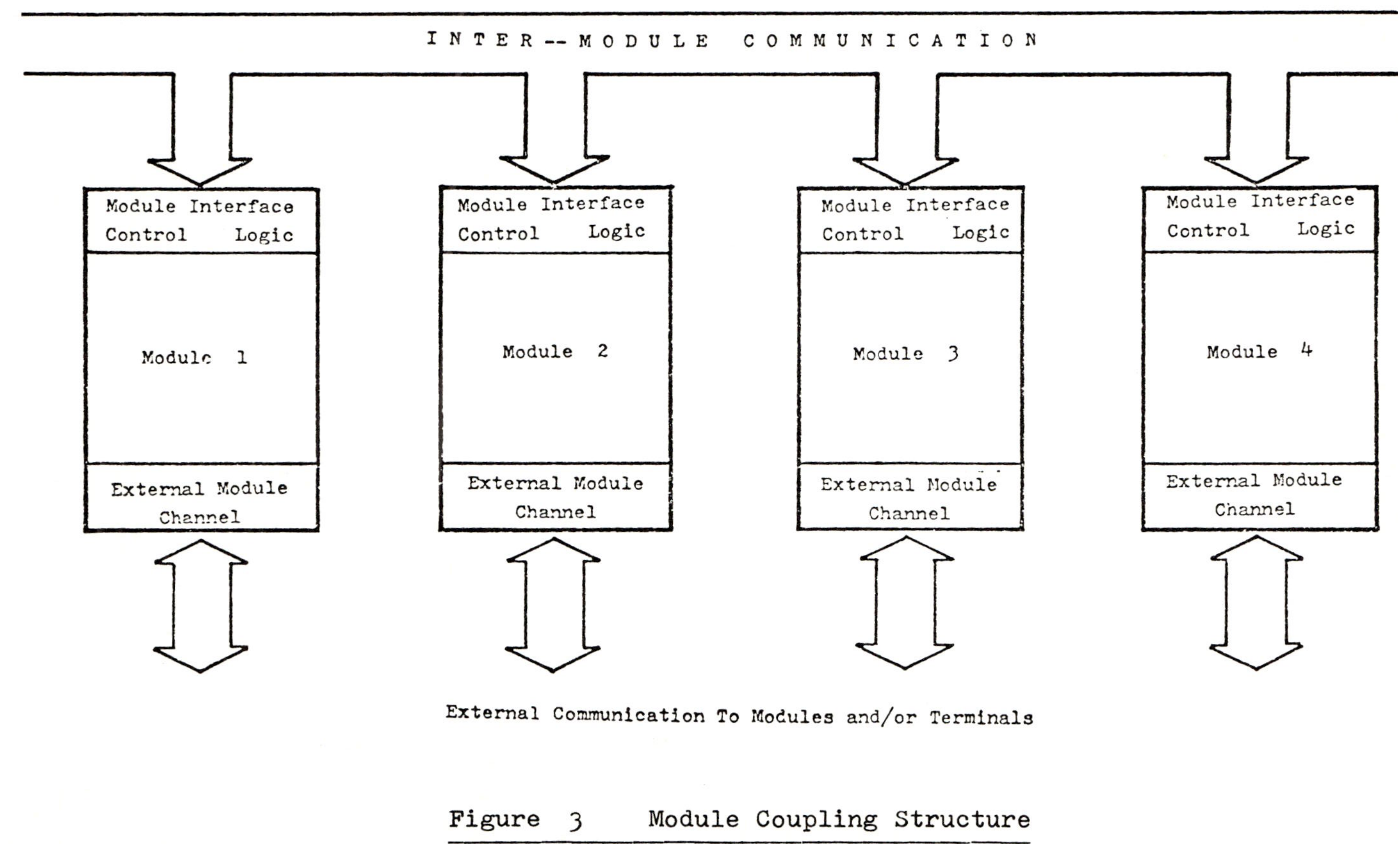

Figure 3 Module Coupling Structure

elements which are cells and modules. Figure 3 shows the functional components of a typical Group Processor System.

The Group Processor concept consists of creating a tightly knit computer sub-system, made up of work-groups of cells with a high degree of group loyalty among the members. To support this degree of stand-alone computing power, each user work space should contain those elements found in conventional computing systems. These elements, such as input/output capability, mass storage, and processing ability, are also contained to some extent with the Group Processor's sub-systems. With processing power available within each cell, we have the ability of providing a high degree of intelligence within the available memory. The sub-systems are engineered as modules and cells. The user work space is made up of cells which are initially held in a pool of resources. Thus, the Group Processor System is a polymorphic architecture because as each program is scheduled for execution, a set of work space cells is allocated to the user. Following successful termination; the user work space set is returned to the common pool of resources. A user has the ability to execute many programs in parallel, providing sufficient work space sets are available.

4.1. High Level System Description

The cellular structure of the Group Processor consists of intelligent memory configured as a complete computing system. This system does not map to the conventional computer architecture but consists of identical assemblies, of one or more cells, and not different assemblies such as processor, memory, and I/O. The support of the individual processes is carried out by the cell structure, as briefly described above. This leads to the distribution of tasks to the individual cells throughout the intelligent memory.

The concepts that underpin the assignment of one or more cells to one process is called Processor Mapping. A real computing system shown in figure 4 provides a modular structure for the support of modular software that demands stand-alone processing power within cells, coupled with the need for system re-configuration. Overall the Group Processor System offers dynamic re-configuration through its highly distributed cellular architecture, and the

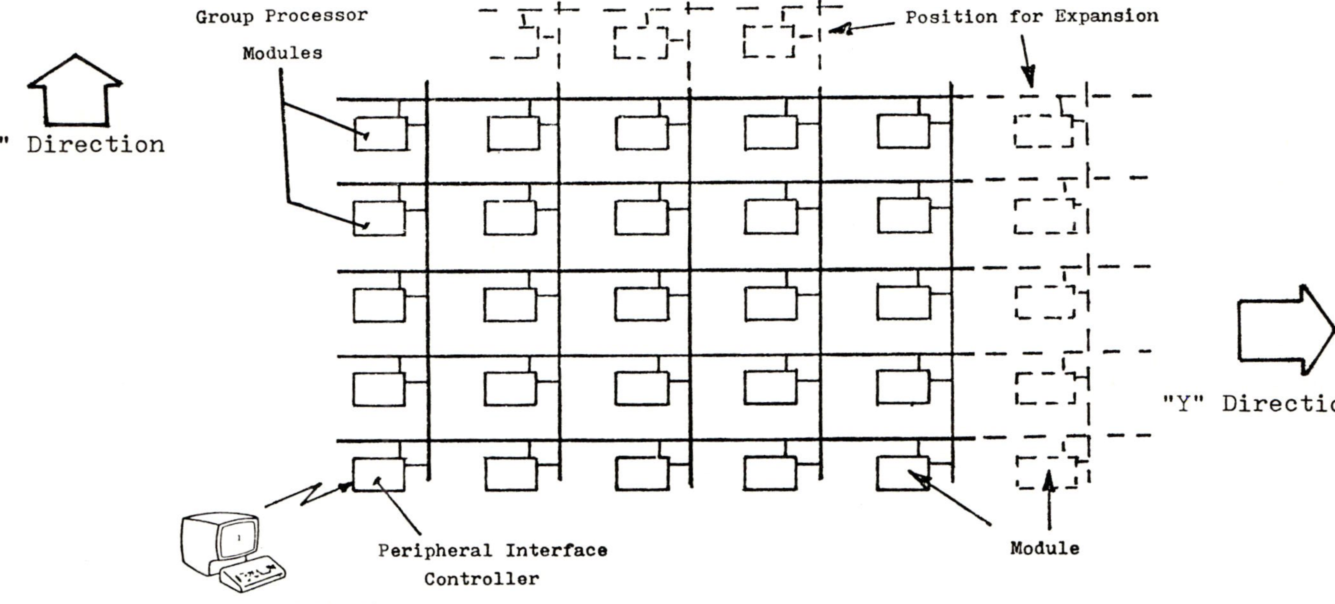

Figure 4 Single User Group Processor System

support of a real closed process environment.

The user interfaces to the Group Processor System through a dedicated software frontend processor. The frontend processor performs many operations on objects (programs and data), e.g. editing and program translation, during the development of user programs. The main software functions that are supported within the frontend processor, termed the peripheral interface environment, is the ability to schedule and transmit the communication between user terminal and the Group Processor modules that make up the remaining Group Processor System.

The peripheral interface environment is constructed from the same module architecture, shown diagrammatically in figure 5, as the main program execution environment. Such a uniform hardware design is a feature of the Group Processor System and has the advantage of minimising the variations of printed circuit board design, which results in lower production and spares cost. The cellular system structure of the module, illustrated in figure 5, executes it's processes within the cells of each module. The only difference between the peripheral interface environment and the main program execution environment is the process definition associated with each cell. As a result, every cell is capable of executing either in a peripheral interface mode or main program execution mode.

4.2. Group Processor Module

The operations performed within the peripheral interface environment or Group Processor environment, which correspond to either a frontend or backend system requirement, are executed by groups of cells configured as work groups. Cooperation between the peripheral interface environment and group processor environment work groups, is achieved by allowing each cell member to communicate with other members via a common bus structure. This bus structure consists of a number of functionally dedicated buses that are made available for use by any cell within the Group Processor System.

Cooperation between work groups is achieved by allowing each member to communicate with other members via the common bus structure. This structure

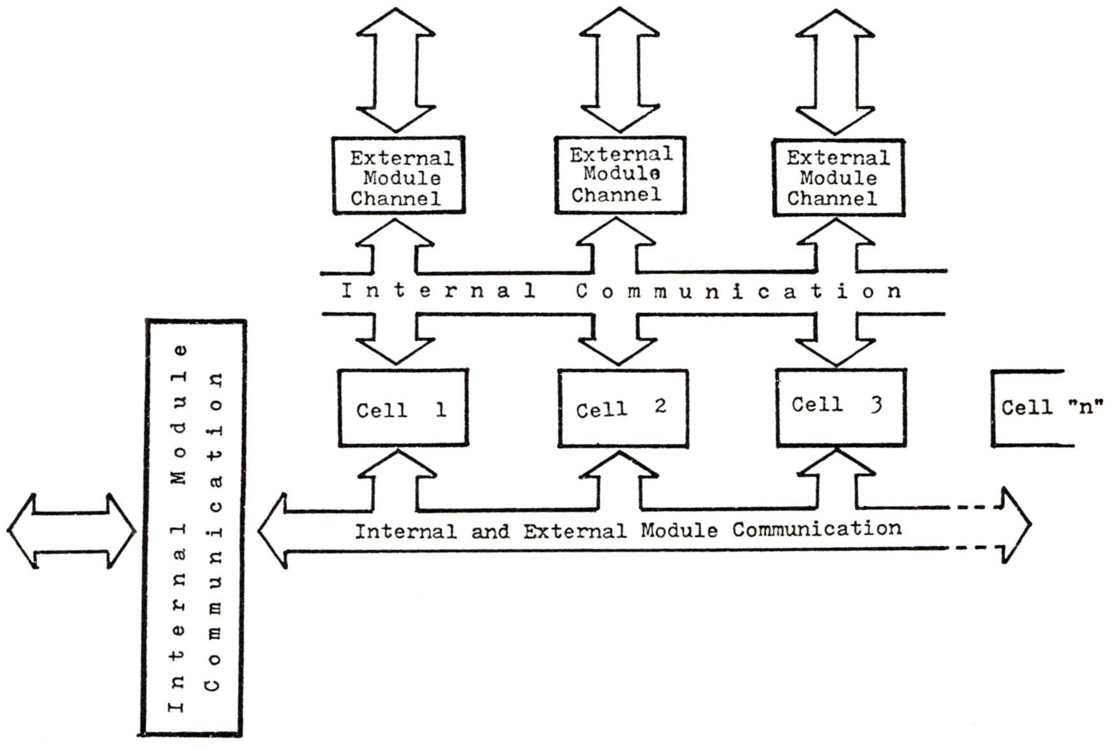

Figure 5 Module's Component Architecture

consists of a number of functionally dedicated buses that are available for use by any cell. These buses are:-

1. Intra module bus
2. Inter module bus
3. Global bus
4. Control bus/lines.

For a minimal system structured on reliability concepts; seven segmented buses are incorporated in the design, although one is required as a minimal system configuration. The control bus is transparent to the user, as it's function is to aid the electronic operation of the system. (The actions of the control bus are described in a paper to be published). The inter module bus structure is "set up" by addressing the module interfaces using the global bus. There are three basic hardware set up structures, which are:-

Distribute
Block
Unique

The basic distribute and block structures enable the hardware to pass data along the bus (distribute), or create separate (segmented) bus structures.

4.3. Module External Input Output

The internal data routing of the inter module bus does not perform any input-output to the system user, as can be seen from figure 5. The system may be configured so as to provide an input output function using dummy modules, which are dirctly linked to the system users. The input output described in this section concentrates on the normal interface between the peripheral interface environment and a typical user terminal.

The architecture of the cell and the module interface enables the various internal systems to communicate via the numerous system buses. The communication to the outside World takes place through an external access port, mounted on the module. This access port is a cell, identical to the other cells on the module, but the three inter module bus ports are dedicated to external module communication with the system users. The Group Processor's input output system has the features required in very modern applications. The need for a Sensory Data Engine and Effector Engine (McPhee 1985) can be mapped into the Group Processor System's distributed input output. The physical nearness of data processing to the input output results in a fast turn around of data processing. The basic data, whether raw or pre-processed, is absorbed into the module through the external module channels and manipulated by the Sensory Data Engine.

Under the control of the Inference Engine, the Knowledge Manipulation Engine processes the output from the Sensory Data Engine and presents it to the Effector Engine for output to the real world. In dedicated systems the Sensory Data Engine, the Inference Engine, the Knowledge Manipulation Engine, and the Effector Engine may be specially designed devices which offer high speed processing, e.g. as needed in fighting vehicles. In a general purpose computing system, the various engines would be software based.

5. CELLULAR OPERATING SYSTEM

The different hardware structure of cellular systems enables a alternative approach to the design of the operating system. Conventional operating system concepts may be mapped onto cellular systems, but in this section an alternative distributed operating system environment is discussed. We hope to provide a insight into how the operation system influences the design of the parallel access machine, and the problems it creates for the bus inter-connection.

5.1. The Environments

The total abandonment of the concept of a processor is important from the

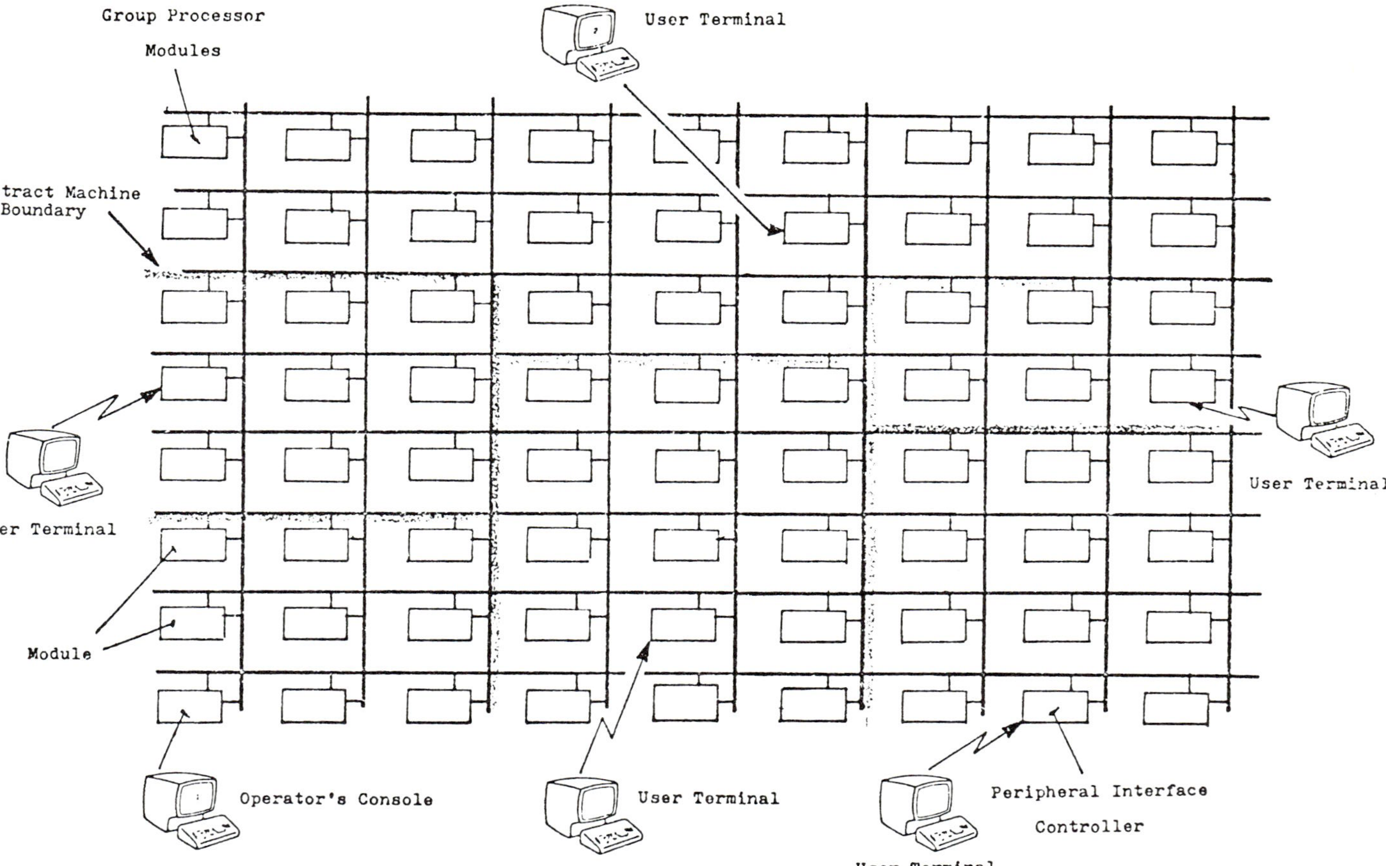

Figure 6 Multi-User Group Processor System

point of removing the verbal contention that surrounds processor architecture and its effects on system performance. The difficulty arises in viewing the functional hardware resources needed by the executing process when no processor exists. How can a systems programmer write code for a processor that does not exist. Indeed, by current definitions of what constitutes a computer system, it may be argued that a computing system without a processor is not a computer. Before we need to re-write the textbooks, we shall (regretably) conform to current terminology and introduce the concept of an abstract processor.

An abstract processor is a group of cells configured so as to execute a given process. These cells are inter-connected by physical, as well as logical, communication paths. Whereas a conventional processor has a clearly defined region which can be identified as the processor, the cellular system has no clearly defined boundaries. There is a motivation for this loose coupling; system reconfiguration for the support of highly reliable applications demands a pool of available resources for the re-configuration process.

We have presented the concept of the abstract processor which enables us to discuss the uses of this concept. The abstract processor is a storage mechanism that is continually executing processes stored within its domain. The domain of the process contains the processor space, that area of the machine which translates the user requests into actions, and the associated data affiliated with the action. We therefore have a sub-division of the machine that contains a single process and data. With many such abstract processors within a machine, the cellular structure can quickly be visualised as inter-connecting abstract processors.

5.2. Logical Images

The abandonment of the processor, together with the need for an abstract processor further reduces the semantic gap. The mapping of the logical process into the abstract processor is intentional as it provides a more structured hardware environment for the support of Logical Images. Images are to cellular systems, as programs are to conventional architecture, and enable software systems to be constructed from groups of abstract processors. Images can be constructed from large software structures or, more importantly the support of the concept of programming in the small (Kernighan 1976). Images are formed by the threading of the executing abstract processor data input and output domain.

5.3. Image Interaction

Image interaction is concerned with the routing of data between abstract processors. This interaction clearly affects system performance, when the routing mechanism within the operating system's abstract processors has to take into account data communication over relatively long data paths. The setting and resetting of data bus switches should be minimised if system performance is to maximised. When we are specific about image interaction we are really concerned with the interaction of many users within the system. The possibility of multi user cellular machines is still in its infancy. However, a multi user cellular machine is the simple extension of the single user environment, with the addition of more input/output channels. Depending on what form these channels will take; system input/output may be complex when there is a high degree of bus contention, or made simple where input/output is local to the abstract processors. Each abstract processor would have a dedicated function, e.g. sensory engine, inference engine, etc.

6. SUMMARY

In this paper we have tried to breakdown some of the intellectual brickwalls that have limited development in designing and implementing cellular computer systems. While some computer architectures claim to present cellular computer systems; a new definition of cellular systems is needed so that a clear exists as to the difference between bounded parallel systems and unbounded parallel systems. We have presented one view of what is a cellular computer system in the context of fifth generation computer systems constructed from identical components.

A multi-access cellular computer system has been re-defined as a parallel access cellular computer system. This change in terminology forces a move from viewing computer systems through the same eyes as with conventional architecture, to viewing systems as functionally distributed integrated software environments. The intelligent memory architecture illustrates how massively parallel system may be designed using the parallel access terminology.

The intelligent memory system has all the attributes of the cellular computer system in many application areas. These application areas cover a wide spectrum of activity from military defence systems to the equivalent of the general purpose computer system. The military application of intelligent memory systems has all the potential of providing massive processing power within a small physical volume. The compact design is possible by the use of three dimensional device integration. The general purpose application of intelligent memory provides the user with a functionally distributed programming environment. This environment has the ability to be extended to a multi user parallel access machine by the simple addition of more interactive terminal devices.

REFERENCES

Aubusson, R.C. and Catt, I. 1978. "Wafer Scale Integration - A Fault Tolerant Procedure". I.E.E.E. Journal Solid State Circuits Vol SC-13. June 1978.

Barron, Iann, et al. 1983. "Transputer does 5 or more MIPS even when not used in parallel". Electronics Nov. 17th. 1983.

Chesley, G. 1984. "Taking a New Look at Wafer Scale Integration". Computer Design May 1984.

Halsall, F. 1984. "Development Aids". In Distributed Computing. Academic Press.

I.E.E. 1978. "Colliquium on: High Available Multiprocessor Systems". Digest of Papers. No. 1978/60.

INMOS. 1983. "IMS T424 Transputer - Advance Information". INMOS, Bristol, U.K. Nov. 1983.

INMOS. 1984. "OCCAM Programming Manual". Prentice-Hall

Johnson, B.W. 1984. "Fault Tolerant Microprocessor - Based Systems". I.E.E.E. Micro. V4,N6. Dec. 1984.

Kernighan, Brian W. and Plauger, P.L. 1978. "Software Tools". Addison-Wesley 1976.

McPhee, D. et al. 1985. "IKBS and Intelligent Machine Interfaces". See this publication.

Quick, G.E. 1978. "Intelligent Memory - A Parallel Processing Concept". ACM SIGARCH V7,N8 1978

Randell, B. et al. 1978. "Reliability Issues In Computing System Design". ACM Computing Surveys V10,N2 June 1978.

Ueoka, Y. et al. 1984. "A Defect Tolerant Design For Full Wafer Memory L.S.I. I.E.E.E. Journal Solid State Circuits Vol. SC-19. June 1984.

Bus Arbitration Concepts For The Fifth Generation Advance

A.K. Roach

Perkin-Elmer Data Systems
European Software Development Group

and

G.E. Quick

West Glamorgan Institute of
Higher Education
U.K.

KEYWORDS

Intelligent Memory, Bus Arbitration, Computer Performance, Cellular Memory

ABSTRACT

Through the use of massive parallelism, Intelligent Memory offers many solutions to software problems. However bus interaction and contention remains a major problem. This paper addresses these problems and highlights possible solutions.

NATO ASI Series, Vol. F 24
Database Machines. Edited by A. K. Sood and A. H. Qureshi

1.0 Background.

The proposed advances in 5th Generation Computing Systems aim to provide an Intelligent Image to the system user. While such images are software based, written in languages such as Prolog and LISP, much of the proposed hardware architecture has lacked innovation and vision. This paper addresses these two important points by providing an insight into modern Bus architectures for multiprocessor systems. In order that unique system architectures may evolve; a hierarchical bus arbitration structure is proposed.

1.1 Introduction

A cloud of uncertainty hangs over the physical image that 5th generation computing systems will adopt. Therefore in this paper, the architecture of a computer system is presented as a functional module structure, together with its operation. This presentation is oriented towards V.L.S.I. realisation of the various modules that will eventually make up a typical 5th Generation computer system. These modules will become sub-system components that will be integrated into an overall system architecture supporting hardware and software extensibility. These separate, but coupled modules, are interconnected by a common bus structure and supervised by the Bus Arbitration Mechanism.

1.2 Current Computer Architecture

In any simple parallel system containing two or more processing cells, e.g. central-processor and I/O processor, a bus controlling mechanism is required to resolve the simultaneous requests for the use of a system resource.[1] A basic requirement of any controller is to allow only one system element or cell, the ability to gain access, i.e. write, to the shared bus. However, systems can be configured for multiple reads on a common data stream, on a common bus system.

The bus arbitration mechanism may be seen as the unifying factor in any multi-processor system architecture, resolving simultaneous bus request conflicts. Alternatively, Bus Arbitration may be conceived as either the system's hub, or the achilles heel, as all communication between intelligent cells are scheduled for bus access by this mechanism.

1.3 Bus Arbitration Objectives

According to Plummer[3] the design of arbiters is somewhat harder than most logic circuits because traditional design approaches are vastly too cumbersome. The usual design assumptions are that inputs are allowed to change only if the circuit is in a stable state and only one input at a time will change. Arbiters violate both of these assumptions.

The basic functional requirement of any integrated bus arbiter must satisfy five basic design operations, which are:-

(1) The operation of mapping one, and only one, output to the corresponding input request must be executed in finite time. That is, the delay in allocation must be seen as transparent to the requesting resource.

(2) The arbiter must be independent of the communication between the communicating cells, during all communication activities. That is, the communicating data should not control the allocation, it should be directed by the system control structure.

(3) The interconnection of arbiters should provide for both equal and priority based arbitration[3]. This allows the operating system to gain control of the system hardware when required.

(4) Mechanisms must be available for the dynamic locking out of an arbiter. This enables a degree of added reliability when arbiter cells become unserviceable.

(5) The maximum number of cells, and system architectures,

should be able to share a common arbiter design. That is, the design should not be tailored to a unique architecture enabling the replication of cells to a high degree.

1.4 Current Arbitration Techniques.

Several methods have been implemented to realise the resolving of bus conflicts. The different control schemes can be roughly classified as being either "Centralised" or "Distributed". If the hardware for passing bus control from one cell to another is largely concentrated in one location, it is called "Centralised", while in a Distributed system, the control logic is spread throughout the cells on the bus. Most arbiters use combinations or modifications of the following three schemes:

1. Daisy Chaining.
2. Polling.
3. Independant Requests.

1.5 Universal Arbiter

The uncertainty that exists in the physical image of 5th generation machines, requires generality in the topology of a 'universal arbiter'. Clearly system bus architectures of various types have to be considered in order that the arbiter be integrated into a single integrated circuit.

By providing a distributed but universal arbiter design, the overall bus arbiter design becomes more complex, as part of the design must cater for a priority based architecture. As an example of this consider an equal priority general design. In reality no such design exists, as a simultaneous demand, e.g. two simultaneous bus requests, are conflicting and hence require arbitration.

The design topology illustrates a hierarchical arbitration structure, Figure-1. Conceptually, each bus request has equal priority, within bus arbiter 1 for example. Similarly, bus arbiter 2 and bus arbiter "n" have equal priority in the centralised, or root arbiter. The centralised arbiter is in effect an overall arbiter to the other arbiters below it in the hierarchy. Although only 24 inputs are shown; the hierarchy is infinitely extendable with seemingly equal priority, by organising the interconnections as a hierarchical tree structure.

<u>Figure-1 Equal Priority Arbitration</u>

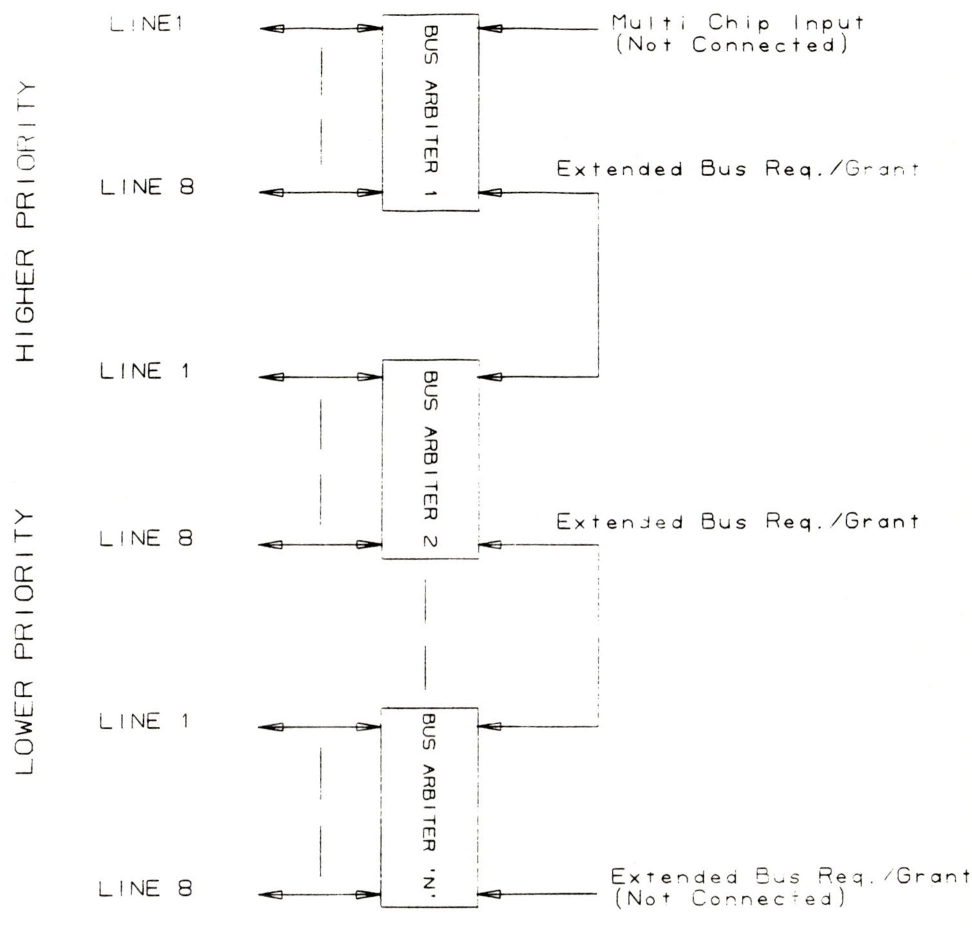

NOTE: All lines are multiplexed.

By comparison, the daisy chain, i.e. semi linear priority scheme of Figure-2 makes line 8, of bus arbiter 1, the lowest priority, and line 1 of bus arbiter "n" the highest priority. It is conceiveable from this topology that in a long daisy chain; the lowest priority may take a long time to get served, due to repeated requests by higher priority requests.

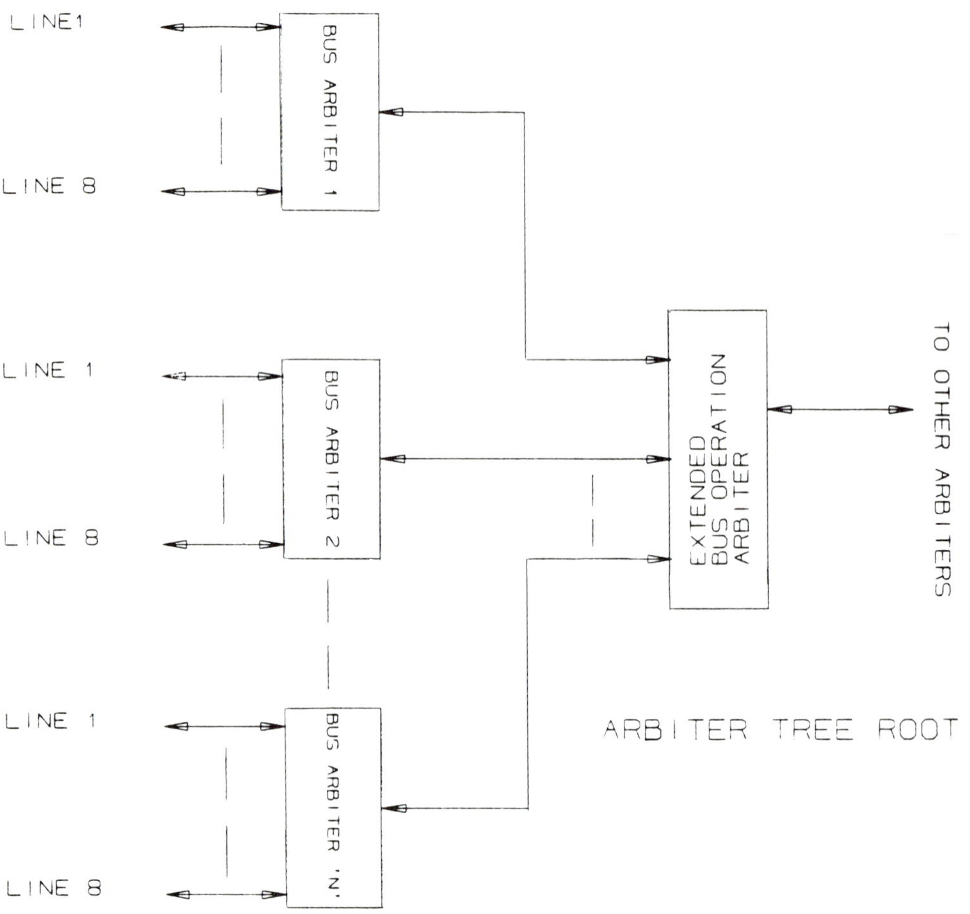

Figure-2 Prioritised Arbitration

In terms of 5th generation multi-processor systems; the daisy chain has certain advantages over an equal priority design. The most important of these is the ability to give a higher priority to the user and the operating system. In reality a totally daisy chained system is impractical as all user oriented modules should have equal priority. In this case a mixture of daisy chaining and equal priority topology may be accepted as providing the degree of operation required, for rapid intervention to the operating system, and equal priority for the user modules. It is also conceivalble, that in 5th generation operating systems, that bus arbitration logic is visualised as shown in Figure-3, where, in conflict conditions, line 1 has a higher priority over line 2 in the system arbiter. Similarly, the nearer to the lower numbered lines a module is connected, the higher the conflict priority.

Figure-3

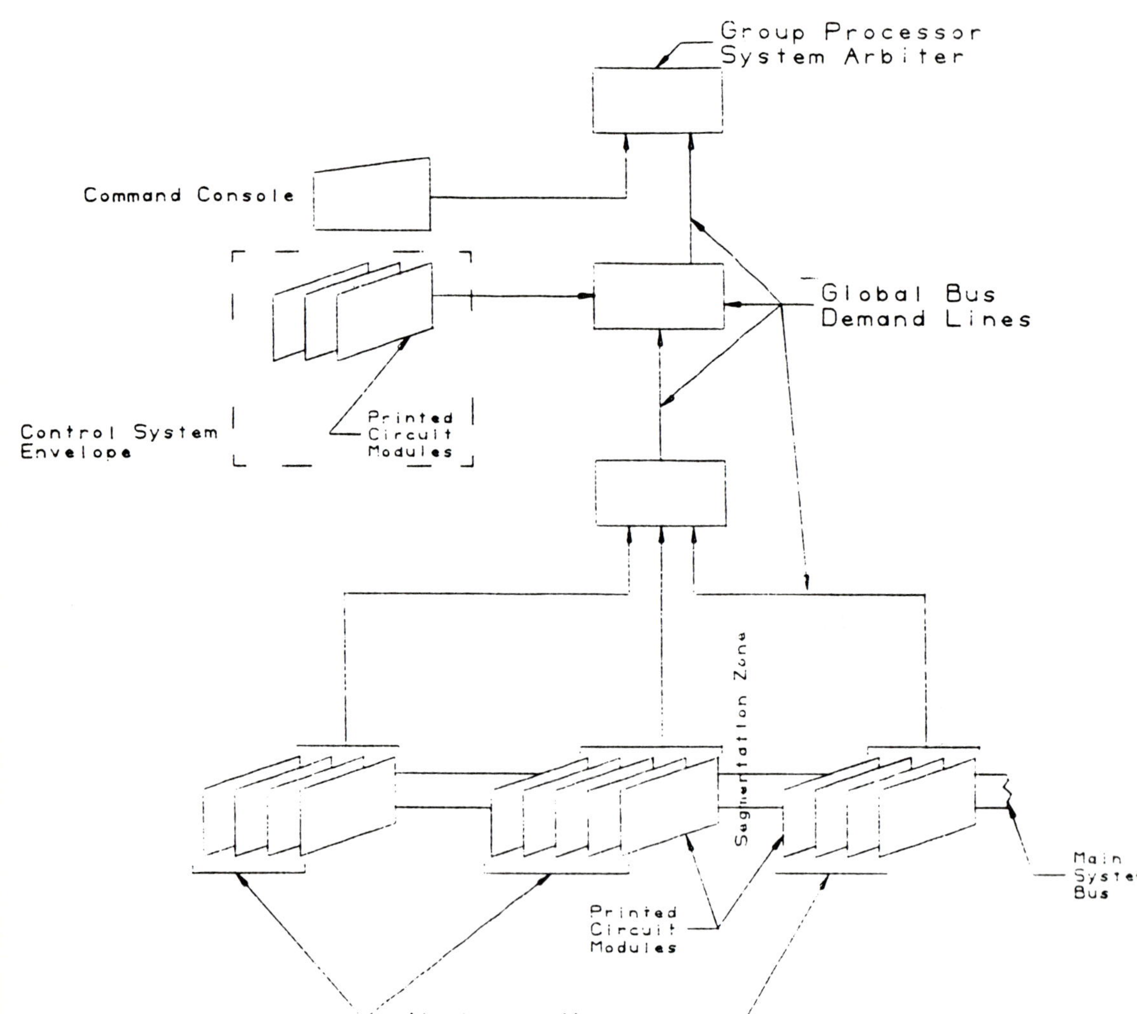
Group Processor
System Arbiter
Command Console
Global Bus
Demand Lines
Control System
Envelope
Printed
Circuit
Modules
Segmentation Zone
Printed
Circuit
Modules
Main
Bus
Abstract Machines

1.6 Summary

In this paper, the architecture of a computer system has been presented as a functional module structure that represents a hardware/software environment for the execution of user programs. This presentation has been orientated toward a true 5th generation machine architecture, though the consideration that machines will be constructed from 100's of thousands of processing cells. These seperate, but coupled cells, need a flexible and extensible bus arbitration network. Such a network has been outlined as a first stage in understanding the complexities that exist when the burden of design and implementation of a 5th generation machine is placed on the computer architect.

When complex bus structures are studied in depth; there is a realisation that long and involved research effort is needed into the wider aspects of bus structures. The interaction of operating systems and the cell design will result in a much closer working attitude between the computer architect and software engineer. Additionally, the practicality of these systems can only be gauged through real design efforts resulting in VLSI cells being produced.

References

1. G.Farber, A Decentralised Fair Bus Arbiter, Euromicro V7 N1 1981

1. J.Nadir & B.McCormick, Bus Arbiter Streamlines Multi-Processor Design, Computer Design V19 N6 1980

1. E.Petriu, N-Channel Asynchronous Arbiters Resolves Resource Allocation Conflicts, Computer Design V19 N8 1972

2. A.B. Kovaleski, High Speed Bus Arbiter for Multi-Processors, I.E.E.E. Proc. V130 N2 1983

3. W.W. Plummer, Asynchronous Arbiters, I.E.E.E. Transactions on Computers V21 N1 1972

IKBS and Intelligent Machine Interfaces

by

D. McPhee, R. D. Stein,
G. E. Quick

West Glamorgan Institute
of Higher Education
Swansea, U.K.

KEYWORDS

Intelligent System, Knowledge Based System, Intelligent Machine Interface, Input/Output Architecture

ABSTRACT

The paper outlines some of the fundamental features of current knowledge based systems. A scenario for future systems of this type is then developed. Special consideration is given to the machine interface since it pervades all aspects of an intelligent system. An alternative input/ouput architecture is proposed that helps to overcome some of the problems associated with the hardware implementation of systems that demand massively parallel input/output.

1. KNOWLEDGE BASED AND EXPERT SYSTEMS

Knowledge based systems are derived from Artificial Intelligence research (Michie 1982 and Fox 1984). They can loosely be described as software that uses specific knowledge of a subject, process, or user to carry out some task, for example, controlling a manufacturing production line, interpreting visual images or controlling a robot. *Expert systems* are knowledge based systems

NATO ASI Series, Vol. F 24
Database Machines. Edited by A.K. Sood and A.H. Qureshi

with some special features notably:

- specialist decision making facilities
- allow highly interactive use.

2. STRUCTURE OF TYPICAL KNOWLEDGE BASED SYSTEMS

The structure of a typical expert system as currently implemented is very straight forward consisting of three main parts (Forsyth 1984) (see figure 1):

- Inference Engine
- Knowledge Base
- User Interface.

The *Inference Engine* solves a problem by interpreting the specific knowledge stored in the Knowledge Base. The system workspace is an area of memory reserved for storing a description of the problem which is constructed for the system from facts supplied by the user or inferred from the Knowledge Base during consultation. A natural or semi-natural language interface exists for communicating with the user and a help subsystem for giving the user some explanation of system interrogation. A *Knowledge Acquisition Unit* is also provided for enlarging the Knowledge Base.

2.1 The Inference Engine

The *Inference Engine* is essentially, a high level interpreter or symbol processor. In knowledge based systems, symbols can represent many types of objects, for example, people, processes, and concepts. Elementary objects, atoms, can be represented by strings of alplanumeric characters. The computer allows an automatic reasoning facility by using string processing operations such as:

- matching character strings
- concatenating character strings
- separating strings
- string substitution.

There are two main reasoning strategies used in inference engines, forward chaining and backward chaining (Bramer 1982). In general, forward chaining involves reasoning from data to hypothesis i.e. the reasoning is data driven, the system attempting to reason forward from the facts to find a solution. This can sometimes result in undirected questioning in dialogue mode. Backward chaining attempts to discover data to prove or disprove a particular hypothesis. This type of inferencing is goal driven, the system working backward from a hypothetical solution in order to find supporting evidence. A specific implementation of a reasoning strategy will depend upon the representation of the knowledge to be manipulated. Some systems use a mixture of both of the above methods, (Naylor 1983) describes a method of 'sideways' chaining known as the Rule Value approach.

3. TECHNIQUES FOR REPRESENTING KNOWLEDGE

3.1 Production Rules

Production rules are two part, the antecedent represents some pattern and the consequent specifies action to be taken when a match is discovered. The antecedent usually consists of a number of clauses linked by logical operators AND and OR. The consequent is made up of one or more verb phrases that specify a course of action. Production rules are good for representing methods of achieving the system objective/goal (Buchanan 1984).

Production rules are the best known technique for representing domain specific problem solving knowledge. The best known example of a system using this type is the medical diagnosis system MYCIN (Shortliffe 1976).

3.2 Semantic Networks

A *Semantic Network* is a method of representing abstract relations among the objects in the system knowledge base (Woods 1975). This could be, for example, membership of a class. It is particulaly useful for representing relationships between objects. The PROSPECTOR expert system (Reboh 1981) developed to assist field geologists and give advice regarding existence and evaluation of mineral deposits and the selection of suitable drilling sites, uses this representation technique.

3.3 Frames

A *Frame* allows an object to be represented by certain standard properties and relations to others (Minsky 1980). A framework system is a semantic network in which objects are represented, not by symbols, but by frames. The framework system usually defines inheritance relationships between objects and the properties of more abstract objects, this will result in an overall saving of memory. A frame may also hold a 'default' value for variable properties that define the system's expectations regarding the particular object considered. Framework systems can store very large amounts of knowledge about relations, objects and their properties.The frame schema has been applied to a number of system design applications. The MOLGEN expert system (Martin 1977) for designing experiments in genetics is probably among the best known example of this method of knowledge representation. Other applications include systems for the comprehension of textual material (Schrank 1977).

3.4 First Order Logic

First Order Logic is a formal way of representing logical propostions and the relationships between them. These rules can be used to derive any fact that logically follows the proposition represented. The programming language Prolog is an example of such an approach. It is seen as an important tool for future systems since it appears to hold more possibilities for parallel processing (Kowalski 1983).

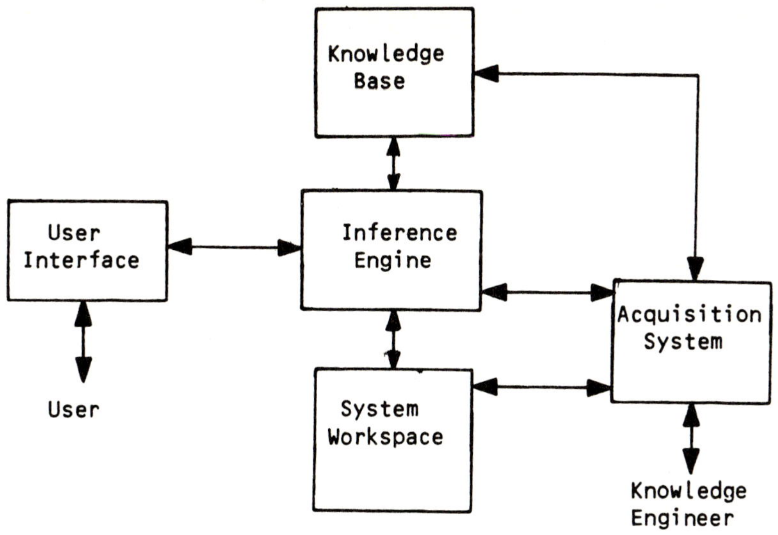

Figure 1 - Typical Knowledge Based System

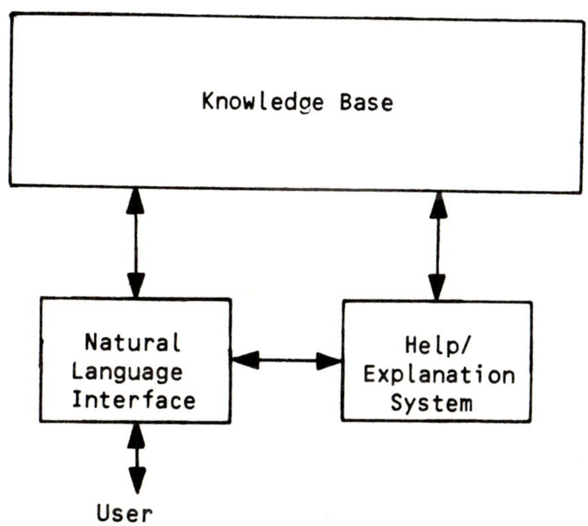

Figure 2 - Intelligent User Interface

4. APPLICATIONS OF KNOWLEDGE BASED SYSTEMS

Knowledged based systems have been developed for many different domains. A large number have been in the field of medical diagnosis but the range of applications has increased rapidly in the last few years as our understanding of what has been termed *knowledge engineering* has developed.

A few of these systems are listed below to show the variety of application:

MYCIN	Medical consulting
DENDRAL	Mass spectroscopy interpretation
PROSPECTOR	Geological exploration
R1	Computer hardware configuration
SACON	Structural Analysis
TAXADVISOR	Estate planning advice
AIRPLAN	Air-traffic movement planning
HASP/SIAP	Sonar surveillance and signal identification

(For further details of these systems see Shortliffe 1976, Lindsay 1980, Hart 1978, McDermott 1981, Bennett 1979, Michaelsen 1984, Feigenbaum 1984 and Nii 1982.)

5. INTELLIGENT MACHINE INTERFACES

Human beings communicate using a wide variety of forms: natural language, both spoken and written, pictures, images and documents. Future systems must be developed to accommodate these forms of natural input/output (Tanaka 1982).

We can identify three fundamental areas of research into intelligent man-machine interfaces:

- natural language processing
- speech processing
- picture and image processing.

Continual research in these areas will provide the foundation for the development of such basic application systems as an intelligent consultation system and a machine translation system.

Natural Language tends to be the preferred form for non-expert users but processing at a truly natural level is still proving to be a very difficult computational task.

Speech Processing is linked to natural language processing in that speech recognition is a two stage process:

(a) acoustic level processing starting with speech analysis and ending with phoneme classification;

(b) language level processing wherein the meaning of the speech is understood using the results of (a).

Picture and Image oriented knowledge is generally composed of structured and spacial features which are described in a symbolic form and/or the image itself in a two dimensional signal form. Examples include:

- line drawing interpretation in CAD/CAM
- aerial and satellite image understanding in remote sensing
- chest X-ray analysis in medical diagnosis.

6. INTELLIGENT SENSOR PROCESSING

Research is currently being carried out to use IKBS to interpret signals produced by sensors (Taylor 1984). For example, analysis of sensor data from radar to analyse air defence situations, multi-sensor data fusion and electronic surveillance. Other work is concerned with passive sonar interpretation and planning.

Modern systems now being installed onboard submarines and other vessels, can generate sonar data at an extremely high rate. Signal equipment has to be configured to process different input and the vessel can also be manoevred to improve the quality of information obtained for processing. Two systems are currently being developed to assist with this task. AURACLE, a static advice system, developed to select a number of pre-stored plans and configure equipment for a specific task. ASDIC is a system designed to correlate information from different sensors and attempts to form contacts, identify noise sources and thus identify vessels.

The structure of this system is similar to HASP, in that it, uses the principle that all signal data on a particular bearing is produced by the same contact, identifies the the type of equipment which best matches this profile, and attempts to classify the signal. The main difference between this system and the HASP/SIAP project is the use of knowledge of what is being looked for, to control the signal processing.

Another project looks at the application of knowledged-based methods to Air Defence Threat Assessment and Resource Allocation. This interprets data from several sources including radar, flight plans and intelligence reports, in order to determine whether any threat is present. The important features of this from a signal processing point of view are:

- the data arrives continuously and is of an asynchronous nature, the KBS has to deal with this data in real time
- the data may contain positional errors
- the data is in different forms, as it comes from various sources
- the data may arrive out of sequence
- reasoning mechanisms to interpret data requires use of the concepts of time and space.

7. THE ROLE OF AN INTELLIGENT INTERFACE

The role which an intelligent interface plays in a system can be varied. It will be affected by the answers to questions like:

- Who takes the initiative, the user or the system?
- Who controls the dialogue?
- Who decides what gets done next?

For example, the system could take the role of an advisor, showing the user what to do. Alternatively, it could act as an intelligent front-end, shielding the user from some other raw system, translating requests into commands for that system, and possibly interpreting it's output.

8. COMMUNICATION WITH THE USER

To be effective the system must have some knowledge of the user. To formulate it's advice and explanations in an understandable way, the system will have to know several things about the user:

- what the user knows about the topic
- what the user currently misbelieves
- what terminology the user is familiar with
- what kinds of explanation the user will find effective.

In effect the system will have to have a *model* of the user, and also, a teaching strategy will be required in order to bring about increased understanding for the user. Most existing systems try to avoid the problem by requiring the user to be familiar with the concepts and terminology of the domain.

Generally an intelligent machine interface system will itself be a kind of knowledge information system, operating in parallel with the 'central' system (see figure 2).

9. KNOWLEDGE ACQUISITION

We can distinguish three methods of knowledge acquisition or elicitation:

- knowledge elicitation from human experts
- knowledge transcription from documentary sources
- knowledge induction from examples.

This area is usually thought of as a bottleneck in the production of knowledge-based or expert systems. The problem, however, may lie with the representation method. For example, if we use a particular expert shell, then we may be forced to use a certain type of production rule to represent the knowledge for that system. We must recognise that even in a single domain of expertise, the knowledge can be of several different kinds (e.g. concepts, relations, procedures, facts, heuristics, classificatory knowledge, etc.) which may, therefore, require different methods to capture it.

10. PARALLEL SYSTEMS IN OPERATION

Future systems which will provide a high level of support and be adaptable to a variety of situations, will require that most of the areas discussed, and which are currently implemented as separate systems, be brought together to work in parallel. The major subsystems which can be identified (see figure 3) are:

- natural language / speech / image processing system
- explanation / help system
- the particular application knowledge system
- learning system
- knowledge acquisition / management system.

The explanation / help system will monitor the current interaction with the user in order to develop a model which can be used to guide any subsequent interaction. A system help feature which can provide a number of different levels of assistance will prove a very useful and, indeed, necessary feature of systems which are to provide a high level of support to the user.

The 'central' knowledge-based system will, in fact, consist of a number of interacting subsystems. For example, it might be possible to have a system monitoring a situation with a set of sensors (e.g. radar) and providing information to a user querying the system. If some critical situation arose it may also be necessary to bring into play various rules and concepts stored in

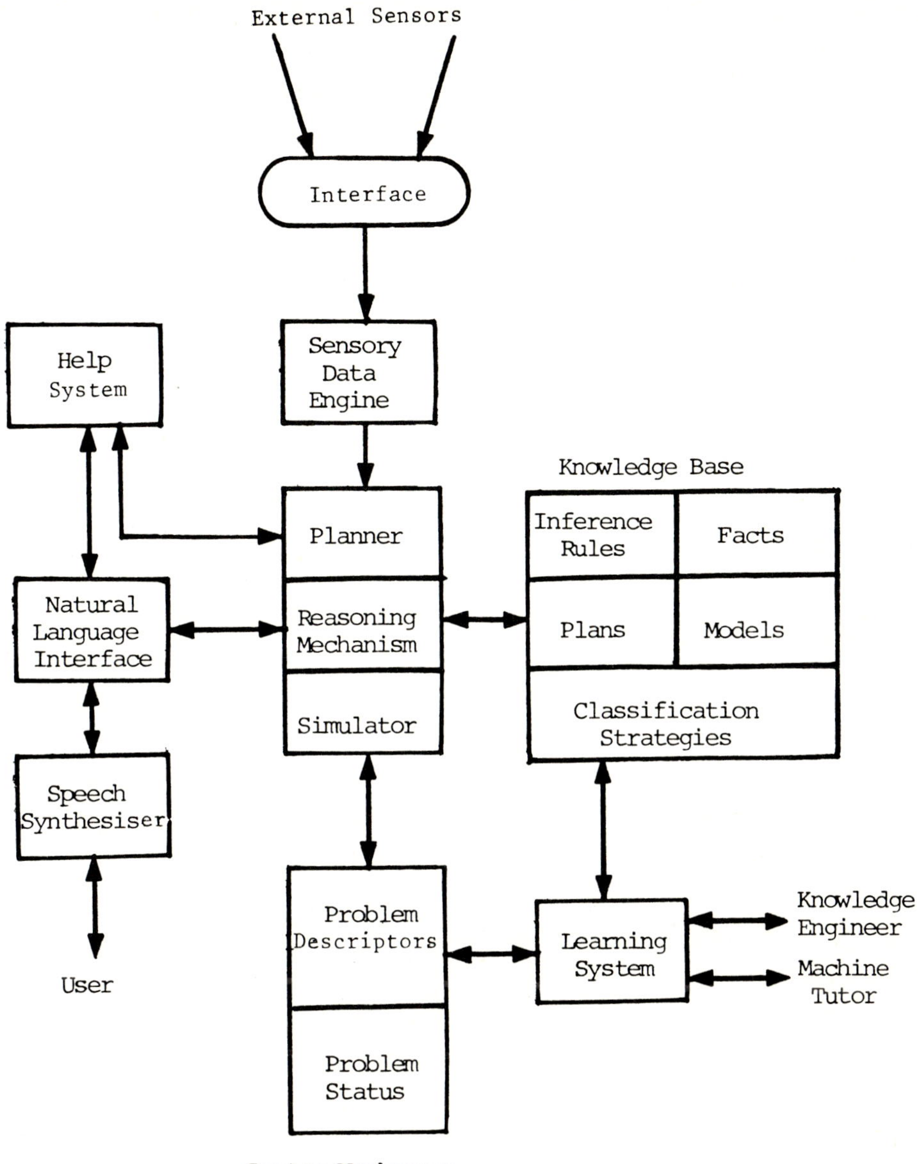

Figure 3 - Future Knowledge Based System

system regarding, say, the implications of various courses of action.

To control the interplay of these various subsystems it is possible to have a further, higher level block of knowledge, *meta-knowledge*, which can guide the system as to how the subsystems are utilised.

The learning system could co-exist with the knowlege base of the application and be constantly in a position to add to the knowledge base as a result of situations which have been monitored and information obtained from the sensor system.

The acquisition of the knowledge requires a *maintenance system* which must be capable of adding to, as well as, allowing alteration to the existing knowledge base, which may have to be 'de-bugged'. Development in this important area of research is required before systems of the type we are discussing can become more generally available.

11. INPUT/OUTPUT ARCHITECTURE

The input/output architecture of computer systems are all too often taken for granted. They tend to be the less fashionable end of the computer science scene. However, we shall give the hardware side of the computer system the full description needed for consideration in IKBS applications. We are not concerned with presenting specific input/output systems, e.g. speech processing (Isard 1983) or image processing (Ballard 1982), but present a *macro* architecture overview of an input/output system for fifth generation use.

The input/output architecture of a computer system provides the communication link between the system and the user. Such communication links in microprocessor based systems utilize both standard and integrated interfaces. Integrated interfaces are provided through the use of input/output ports attached to the bus system, and operated under the direct control of the processor unit. Standard interfaces are more complex in that the processor unit off-loads the input/output function to the input/output interface.

The *intergrated interface* provides a peripheral to processor unit communication link through which programs are transferred to, and interpreted by, peripheral devices. Intelligent and Knowledge Based Military Systems are often executed on computer systems of convention design. Such design either uses pure sequential execution environments at one end of the spectrum, while at the other end bounded multi processor systems offer a potential execution speed up. The integrated interface is too slow for military applications where split second response is essential if the fighting vehicle is to maintain an effective presence. The slow response is the result of the processor unit's multi function role in gathering data and then processing it. The results of using integrated interfaces would be an execution environment that is totally sequential in nature, as the various internal data processing, e.g. accessing the knowledge data base, are executed one after another. Clearly, if faster data processing is required parallel processing within the processor unit and the input/output must be utilised.

Standard interfaces have the advantage of pre-processing input data into a format that is readilly understood by the executing software in the processor unit. Clearly, in many military applications where there may be many hundreds of active sensing devices, standard interfaces offer a speed advantage over the integrated interface as there is a peripheral to processor communication link by which programs and data are transferred to, and interpreted by, a peripheral controller. The use of the standard interface and the peripheral controller relieves the processor unit of the burden of controlling slow peripheral devices. While this is not seen as true parallel processing in the widest context, it does have the advantage of faster user interaction than the pure sequential integrated interface and hence more suited to IKBS.

The use of standard interfaces requires remote processing power in the input/output system. This processor provides the following function:

- executes direct input/output instructions and passes the results to the main processor

- transfers data and input/output programs between memory and device controllers, so that the processor unit may continue to execute other instructions without further intervention.

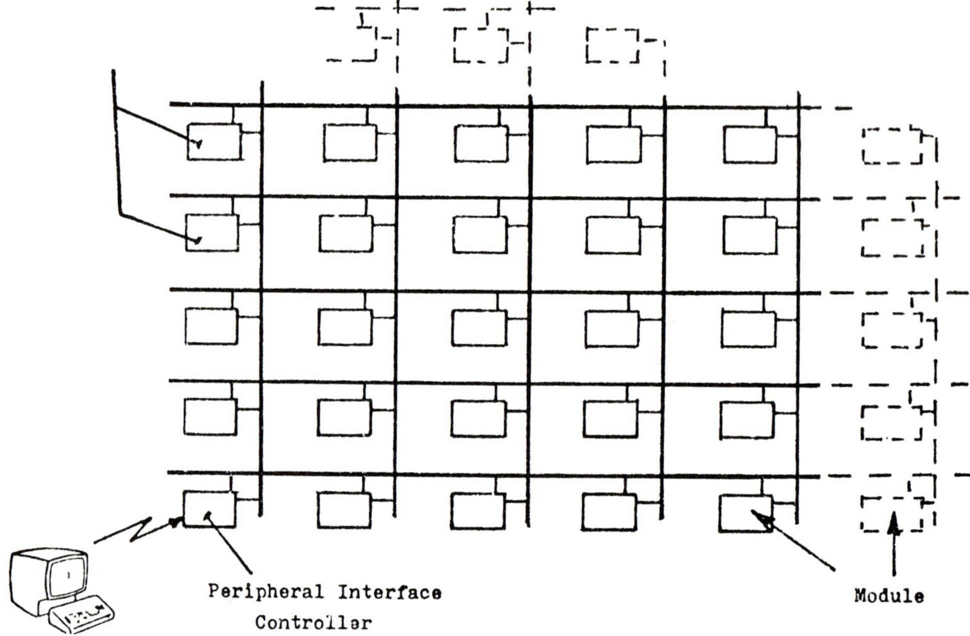

Each Module has an Array of Cells for task execution. With many cells per module, e.g. 128, the cellular system has the resources needed for a fully distributed system. Peripheral Interface Controller is software based for maximum flexibility.

Figure 4 Small Scale Cellular System

12. FIFTH GENERATION INPUT/OUTPUT

Very little research has been carried out in input/output systems for fifth generation use. The exceptions to this are the use of voice and image processing. The wider aspects of integrating many dissimilar input/output systems into an homogenious input/output system has not been considered, particularly in the context of Intelligent and Knowledge Based Systems.

It has been shown that the many applications of Intelligent and Knowledge Based Systems demands a very flexible input/output architecture. Moreover, for economic considerations this architecture must have a high degree of programability in the input/output interface if the architecture is to have a large application base. Figure 4 illustrates a celluar architecture (Quick 1979) that has a highly distributed input/output architecture, see figure 5. This proposed design also decentralises the processing power to many cell like devices that execute the application software. This cellular computing system has an immediate advantage over conventional bounded multi processor systems as it has the processing power to support the numerous execution environments needed in future Intelligent and Knowledge Based Systems.

The cellular input/output system has added flexibility in the input/output domain through the availability of many processing elements. These processing elements are able to be dedicated to a number of functional input/output operations, all executing in parallel. Such cellular input/output systems enable experimentation to take place on a *development basis* on a live system, without any degrade in overall system performance.

12. SUMMARY AND CONCLUSIONS

To build better computer systems for IKBS and Database applications; we need to look long and hard at the overall picture presented by the system user and the available technology. There is a need to match the hardware system to the software system, if future progress is to be maintained. We need to provide system providers with a framework with which massively distributed processing can be supported in a structured fashion. Current architectures do not provide the flexible framework needed as they are based on a bottom up approach to computer system design. A structured design leads us to radically

Nine input/output systems
available on each module

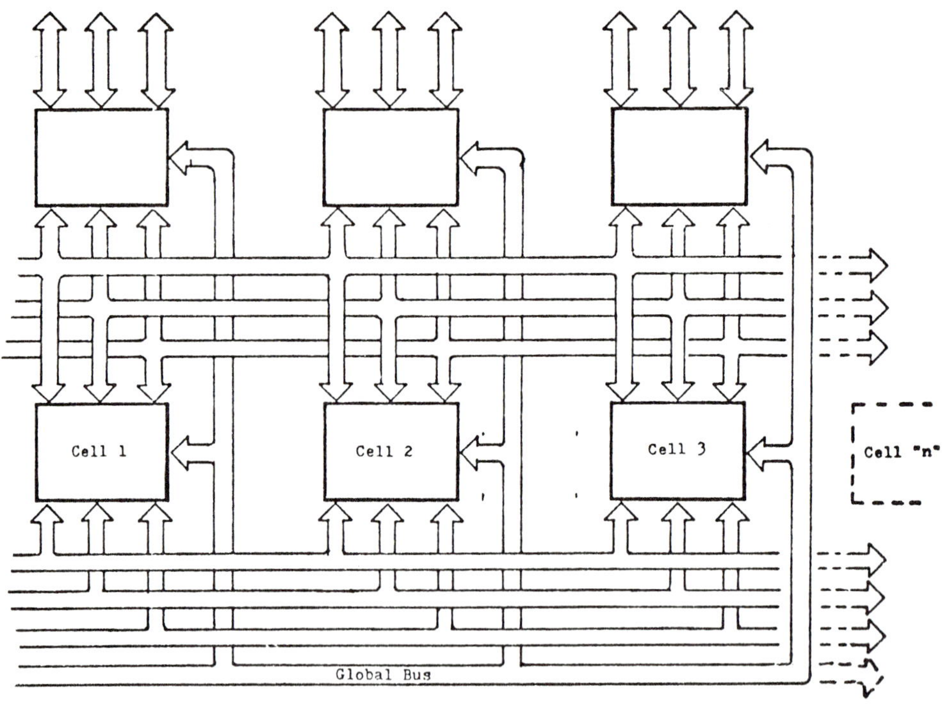

System
Busses

Highly supportive on each module; the module has the ability to massive input/output capability throughout the whole system. Executing software is within a short distance of an input/output channel.

Figure 5 Architecture for Parallel Access Machine

different architecture.

12.1. Intelligent and Knowledge Based Systems

In knowledge based systems implemented on future parallel hardware systems, classification strategies will allow the system to make decisions based on semantics. Simulation of the function of certain systems in order to predict their behaviour will be possible. Such a system will be able to learn from experience by acquiring and analysing information provided either directly from sensors via a 'sensory data engine', which is essentially a vehicle for collecting data from the outside world and converting it into a form that the inference engine can comprehend and process, or other systems of a similar nature. A speech synthesis unit will allow the system to talk to the user and vice versa thus enhancing the user interface interaction process.

12.2. Machine Interface

There has been little advancement in designing communication interfaces for the support of distributed input/output systems. Moreover, what advances that have been made have been disjointed and all to often too remote from the needs of the applications of the future. We have proposed an input/output architecture that aims to get much closer to what is needed by these future applications. The proposed architecture maximises the advantages offered by VLSI technology, namely compact implementation and low power consumption. The architecture also offers a high degree of flexibility in application areas, including configuration as a general purpose computing system.

REFERENCES

Ballard, D.H. and Brown, C.M. (1982). "Computer Vision". Prentice-Hall.

Bennett, J.S. and Engelmore, R.S. (1979). "SACON: a knowledge-based consultant for structural analysis". Proc. Sixth Int'l. Joint Conf. Artificial Intelligence, 1979, pp 47-49.

Bramer, M. (1982). "A survey and critical review of Expert Systems research". In (Michie 1982), pp3-29.

Buchanan, B.G. and Shortliffe,E.H. (1984). "Rule-based expert systems". Addison-Wesley Publishing Co., Reading, MA.

Feigenbaum, E.A. and McCorduck,P. (1984). "The Fifth Generation". Pan Books, London.

Forsyth, R. (1984). "The Architecture of Expert Systems". In Expert Systems, Principles and Case Studies, Chapman and Hall, London.

Fox, J. ed. (1984). "Expert Sytems". Pergamon Infotech Ltd., Maidenhead, Berkshire.

Hart, P.E. et al. (1978). "A Computer-Based Consultation System for Mineral Exploration". Tech. Report, SRI International, Menlo Park, California.

Isard, S.D. (1983). "SPEECH - Recognition and Understanding, Synthesis and Generation". Proc. IKBS Architecture Study Jan 1983.

Kowalski, R. (1983). "Logic as the Fifth Generation computer language". In The Fifth Generation Project, Pergamon Infotech Ltd., Miadenhead, Berkshire.

Lindsay, R.K. et al. (1980). "Applications of Artificial Intelligence for Organic Chemistry: The DENDRAL Project". McGraw-Hill, New York.

Martin, N. et al. (1977). "Knowledge-Base Management for Experiment Planning in Molecular Genetics". Proc. Fifth Int'l. Joint Conf. Artificial Intelligence, 1977, pp 882-887.

McDermott, J. and Steele, B. (1981), "Extending a Knowledge-Based System to Deal with Ad Hoc Constraints". Proc. Seventh Int'l. Conf. Artificial Intelligence, 1981, pp 824-828.

Michaelsen, R.H. (1984). "An Expert System for Federal Tax Planning". In Expert Systems: The International Journal of Knowledge Engineering, Oct.

1984, p149.

Michie, D. ed. (1982). "Introductory Readings in Expert Systems". Gordon and Breach, New York.

Minsky, M.L. (1980). "A framework for representing knowledge". In Mind Design: Philosophy, Psychology and Artificial Intelligence, Bradford Books, Montgomery, VT.

Naylor, C. (1983). "Build Your Own Expert System". Sigma Technical Press, Wilmslow, Cheshire.

Nii, H.P. et al. (1982). "Signal-to-symbol transformation: HASP/SIAP case study". In A.I. Magazine, Spring 1982, pp23-35.

Quick, G. E. (1979). "Intelligent Memory - A Parallel Processing Concept". ACM SIGARCH V7,N12

Reboh, R. (1981) "Knowledge Engineering Techniques and Tools in the PROSPECTOR Environment". Tech. Note No. 243, SRI INternational, Menlo Park, California.

Schrank, R. and Abelson, R. (1977). "Scripts, Plans, Goals and Understanding". Lawrence Erlbaum Associates, Hillsdale, NJ.

Shortliffe, E.H. (1976). "Computer-Based Medical Consultation: MYCIN". Elsevier, New York.

Tanaka, H. et al. (1982). "Intelligent Man-Machine Interface". In Fifth Generation Computer Systems, T. Moto-oka (ed.), JIPDEC, North Holland Publishing Co., Amsterdam, pp147-157.

Taylor, J.M. (1984). "Application Survey: IKBSs in a defence application". In Expert Systems, Pergamon Infotech Ltd., Maidenhead, Berks.

Woods, W.A. (1975). "What's in a link: foundations of semantic networks". In Representation and Understanding: Studies in Cognitive Science, Academic Press, London.

FDE: A System for Experiments in Interfaces Between Logic Programming and Database Systems.

Darrel J. Van Buer, Dan D. Kogan, Donald P. McKay, Lynette Hirschman, Richard Whitney [1] and Rebecca Davis [2]

ABSTRACT

The Flexible Deductive Engine (FDE) was designed to facilitate experimentation with a variety of search strategies to support logic programming as well as knowledge management applications. In addition to supporting various deductive strategies, FDE provides several ways for storing and accessing data. Facts can be represented as assertions and stored in the rule base or they can be represented in the extensions of predicates stored in a database. There is also considerable flexibility in the granularity and timing of access to relational databases. Since FDE contains both an internal relational database management system (DBMS) and interfaces to a number of external relational DBMSs on a local network, such extensional data can reside in the same environment as FDE or be external to it. This paper gives a brief overview of FDE and focuses on its mechanisms for accessing data.

1 Current Address: USC/ISI, 4676 Admiralty Way, Marina del Rey, Ca. 90291
2 Current Address: IntelliCorp, 707 Laurel St., Menlo Park, Ca., 90425-3445

NATO ASI Series, Vol. F 24
Database Machines. Edited by A. K. Sood and A. H. Qureshi

FDE: A System for Experiments in Interfaces Between Logic Programming and Database Systems

Darrel J. Van Buer, Dan D. Kogan, Donald P. McKay, Lynette Hirschman, Richard Whitney [1] and Rebecca Davis [2]
System Development Corporation
2500 Colorado Avenue
Santa Monica, CA 90406

1. Introduction

The flexible deductive engine (FDE) is designed to serve as the deductive core for both logic programming environments and knowledge management systems where database access is a key component. The intent is to create a single system which supports the full functionality of logic programming as well as alternate forms of deduction appropriate for knowledge management applications. Support of both logic programming applications and deductive querying of databases in a single environment is greatly improved by a flexible search strategy that can be tailored to the particular application.

The integration of logic-based deductive mechanisms with searching engines has attracted much attention recently [Dahl 82; Kellogg 84; Kawanobe 84; Vassiliou et. al. 83; Wiederhold 84]. The need for such capabilities arises from two converging application needs. The first is from database applications whose demands *outgrow* existing database technologies and thus require the incorporation of inferential capabilities. The second comes from expert system applications where the number of ground clauses overwhelms the capacity of the deductive environment. Systems which address these applications have been called *Knowledge Information Processing* [Fuchi 82; Ohsuga 82; Suwa et. al. 82], *Knowledge Management* [Kellogg 82] and *Knowledge Base Management* [Wiederhold 84] systems.

---

[1] Current Address: USC/ISI, 4676 Admiralty Way, Marina del Rey, Ca. 90291
[2] Current Address: IntelliCorp, 707 Laurel St., Menlo Park, Ca., 90425-3445

Two such prior systems are DADM [Kellogg et. al. 81] and a Prolog-based front-end to relational databases by Jarke et. al. [Jarke et. al. 84]. Both systems mediate between a deductive component and relational databases to provide expert systems with the ability to access large volumes of data. Deduction control, however, is carried out in a fixed manner by the underlying environment, depth-first in Prolog and heuristically driven in DADM. These strategies, although effective in many cases, may not be suitable for all applications. These systems also differ slightly in their data retrieval behavior. DADM first generates a proof plan, after which all data requests to support it are batched and sent en masse to an underlying database management system. Prolog-based systems, on the other hand, must send their database requests no later than at each backtrack point.

The common feature among both of these prior systems is that they have fixed strategies both for carrying out deduction and for database access. An alternative scheme would be to provide the flexibility in deductive strategy as well as in database access strategy to enable the development of an optimal approach for any given application.

This paper briefly describes the overall structure of the FDE for logic programming and database access. The major emphasis is on the ways in which facts are stored. They may be stored within the FDE in assertions, within an FDE internal DBMS, and in several external databases with an FDE local data dictionary. There is a small example of a query for which every kind of support is used. The paper concludes with a discussion of ongoing research.

2. An Overview of FDE

The goals of the FDE project are to provide an experimental framework where the issues of inference control, database access, and function evaluation are treated as part of a general problem of search control; and to serve as an environment in which to build prototype knowledge management systems. For these reasons, we have designed the core of FDE with a set of well-defined internal interfaces. The developer of a logic system specifies a search strategy by writing a small set of functions, which can be changed to fit the application or class of applications. For example, there exist a set of functions to provide a Prolog-style depth-first search, and another set to provide a Loglisp-style breadth-first search [Robinson & Sibert

80]. Work is in progress to build a set of functions which implement the most sucessful of the DADM heuristics, and to support both the forward and backward chaining of DADM for queries with assumptions. Each set of functions is called a *personality*, since it provides approximately the functionality associated with the named system.

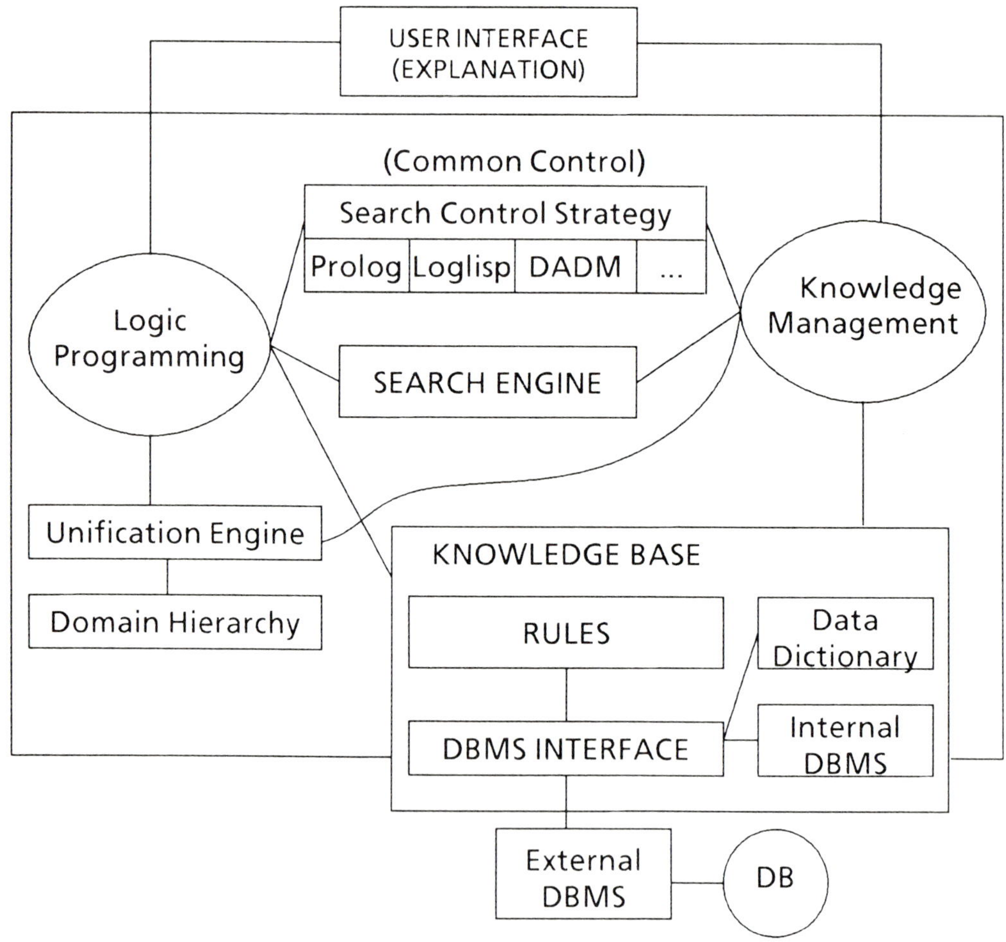

Figure 1. FDE Design

The core of FDE is comprised of five main parts: a knowledge base, a unification engine, a domain hierarchy, a search engine and a search control strategy (see Figure 1). The Knowledge Base consists of a rule base and one or more associated databases. The rule base is used to store general statements about an application domain represented as First Order Predicate Calculus statements. This rule base is stored in a Predicate Connection Graph (PCG) which caches deductive dependencies within rules and between rules [Whitney et. al. 85]. The facts or ground relations are represented in one or more databases. Internal to FDE are a set of relational database management system (DBMS) interfaces and an internal DBMS for storing local facts and staging external database results as they are retrieved. In addition, there may be one or more DBMS's external to the deductive component, possibly implemented in specialized or dedicated hardware. The representation of and access to facts in the FDE is the major focus of this paper and is discussed in the next section.

The Unification Engine is designed to support the binding of logical variables in a (simulated) parallel environment, through the use of contexts and binding environments. The domain hierarchy serves to treat logic variables as part of a multisorted algebra. It has not yet been implemened because experience with the domain hierarchy in DADM has shown that it is not essential to operation of the system. Its most effective use in DADM is as a tool for structuring user interaction with an application, rather than for its effect on unification. The problem space is explored via the Search Engine, which makes use of a set of personality specific functions that describe a Search Control Strategy.

The facilities for creating, modifying, and retaining a knowledge base properly belong to the user interface and not to the core itself, so these facilities are shown in Figure 1 as a box outside the core of the FDE. The ovals depict primary classes of existing applications that FDE will support, namely logic programming (Expert System applications in Prolog or Loglisp) and knowledge management (data base augmentation applications).

A key aspect in the design of the FDE is the notion of a search control strategy [McKay et. al. 85]. The Search Engine provides a framework in which to describe search strategies (personalities) which traverse an AND/OR search tree. The specification and integration of personalities is facilitated by the separation of search strategy-specific information from the Search Engine. For example, when the FDE is using its DADM-like knowledge management personality, a certain set of functions are used to guide the search in a heuristic fashion. To provide a reasonable depth-first system for Prolog-like applications, there is another set of functions which result in a Prolog-style of search.

The FDE draws upon previous research carried out at SDC over the past several years in the general area of Knowledge Management and specifically on the Deductively Augmented Data Management (DADM) system [Kellogg & Travis 81; Kellogg et. al. 78; Klahr 78]. The FDE preserves the general Knowledge Management architecture underlying DADM [Kellogg 84; 83; 82]: it contains an inference engine which accesses a rule base or intensional database and a search engine which accesses a data base of ground clauses (also known as an extensional database). This decomposition of information into intensional and extensional databases has been a central thesis of the DADM architecture as well as other logic-based systems attempting to deal with external DBMS's [Hammer & Zdonik 80; Vassiliou 83; Wiederhold 84].

3. Representation of Facts

As pointed out by Vassiliou in [Vassiliou et. al. 83], a deductive system can access facts in several ways. This section describes the various methods the FDE provides for registering and accessing data. Facts can be represented as assertions, fully instantiated and stored in the Predicate Connection Graph, or they can be represented in the extension of predicates stored in a database. Since the FDE contains both an internal relational database management system (DBMS) and interfaces to external relational DBMS's, such extensional data can reside in the same environment as the FDE or be external to it.

3.1 Assertions

Most simply, facts can be represented as logical assertions. A fully instantiated assertion, one with no variables, such as (HAS-SKILL jones logic-programming) represents the single fact that employee "jones" possesses the skill of logic-programming. A partially instantiated assertion, on the other hand, such as (ASSIGNMENT-PERMITTED 98317 ←EMP) can be interpreted as a collection of fully instantiated assertions matching a particular pattern. A possible interpretation is that the assignment of anyone to project 98317 is permitted so this assertion is equivalent to one fully instantiated assertion for each possible value of ←EMP. Notice that in the internal syntax of the FDE, variables are preceded by a left arrow (←), while constants are conventionally expressed in lower case.

Fully instantiated assertions permit the immediate access to data during the deductive process rather than deferring it for later database requests. Partially instantiated assertions, on the other hand, are useful for describing integrity constraints.

3.2 Internal DBMS

At the next level of sophistication, a generalized database management system can be implemented and can share the same environment as the deductive mechanism. This environment can be Prolog as in [Vassiliou et.al. 83]; [Jarke et. al. 84], or Interlisp-D [Xerox 83] in the case of the FDE.

The database management system internal to the FDE serves two purposes. In the absence of an external DBMS, it can act as the repository of extensional data. If, on the other hand, some of the base relations are stored externally, the internal DBMS acts as an intermediary where the results of queries to the external DBMS's are staged and combined (with each other as well as with results of queries to relations stored internally) to form one resulting relation. In this respect it functions in a manner similar to the *assembly site* in a distributed database environment [Templeton et. al. 83]. Finally, the internal DBMS may complement the external DBMS which may lack some features, such as one of the relational operators or some nonlinear function like great circle distance.

The design of the FDE's internal DBMS is based on several considerations relating mostly to its intended use and the size of the databases it is expected to support: (1) Database or database fragments are expected to be small enough to reside in virtual memory with the rest of the FDE and Interlisp-D, although we are considering changes to premit retrieving results incrementally. (2) The DBMS should be relationally complete, i.e.: at least support the operations of projection, cartesian product and selection. (3) Its performance should be better than that achieved by exporting a search request to and retrieving the results from an external DBMS. (4) Finally, it must provide a set of user-transparent hooks to relations stored in external DBMSs.

The internal DBMS is based on unification for its pattern matching and accepts conjunctive queries. For example given a skills inventory database containing information on employee's skills, skills required by tasks and project breakdowns, a query requesting those employees with the skills needed for a particular project, 98317, would be expressed as:

[(HAS-SKILL ←EMP ←SKILL)
 (SKILL-REQ ←TASK ←SKILL)
 (TASK-PROJ ←TASK 98317)]

It should be noted that the FDE's DBMS currently performs only minor optimization based on query reordering.

3.3 External DBMS

In addition to accessing its own internal DBMS, the FDE can retrieve data stored in external databases. When a search request involves queries to external databases, their results are temporarily stored in the internal database. In order to combine data from the external database with data to be retrieved internally, the internal and external queries are merged and then submitted to the (now augmented) internal database. By separating the logic engine from the database engines, we are able to incorporate quickly any advances in database technology simply by writing a new DBMS query interface to the new systems.

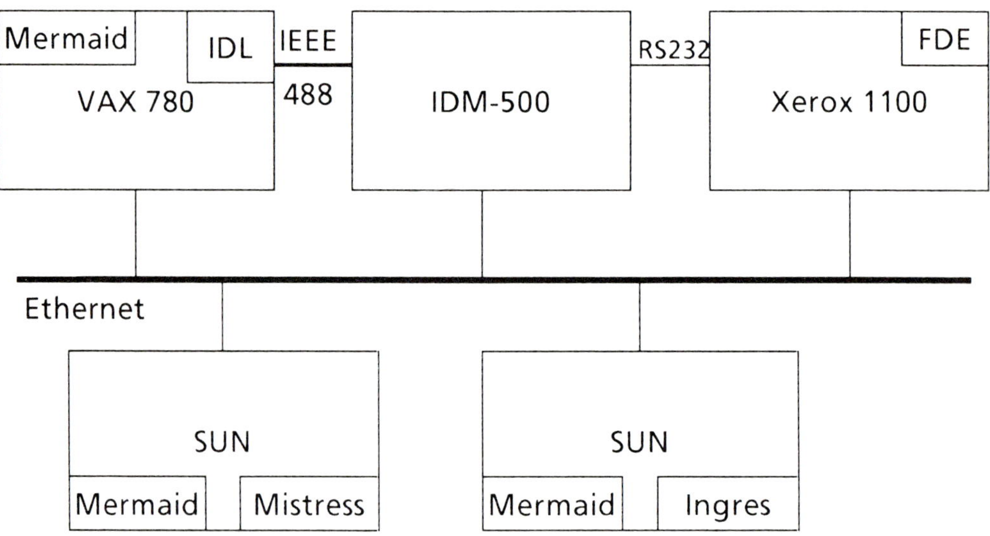

Figure 2 SDC R&D Local Network

In order to establish a connection between an FDE predicate and a relation stored externally, four properties must be specified: the association between attribute names of the external relation with attribute positions of the predicate as it is known to the FDE, the data type of each of the relation's attributes, the name of the relation as it is known to the external DBMS and finally, the interface function to be called for accessing the database where the relation resides. This interface function implicitly specifies the kind of database (e.g. Ingres or Britton Lee), the identity of the remote host and the name of the actual database.

The current internal DBMS supports retrieval of data from several external DBMSs. It contains modules for generating queries in a number of QUEL dialects: Ingres Quel [Youssefi 77], Britton Lee IDL, and Britton Lee internal IDL (as used on the direct hardware interfaces to the Britton Lee) [BLI 83]. It also contains facilities which directly, or in cooperation with external software, retrieve the results generated by Ingres, by the interface software between Unix and a Britton Lee IDM-500 and directly from the IDM via its hardware interfaces. We are also planning an interface to the Mermaid distributed data management system [Templeton et. al. 83]. The FDE operates in the local network environment shown in figure 2.

The algorithm used to convert an internal query into an equivalent one expressed in a QUEL dialect is shown below.

- Each distinct reference to a relation generates one associated range statement.

- The target list is composed of all variables referenced in the internal query.

- Each argument position is translated to the corresponding attribute name.

- References to common variables become join specifications.

- References to constants become restrictions.

- Queries which exceed limits imposed by a particular DBMS query processor are segmented by storing partial results in temporary relations (e.g.: IDL allows at most 15 range statements per query).

The conjunctive query shown previously thus becomes:

```
range of t001 is hasSkill
range of t002 is skillReq
range of t003 is taskProj
retrieve (t001.emp, t001.skill, t002.task)
where
        t001.skill = t002.skill and
        t002.task = t003.task and
        t003.proj = "98317"
```

Only modest modifications are expected when converting to other calculus-based non-procedural languages such as SQL [Chamberlin et. al. 76].

The FDE offers a final degree of freedom in the timing of the issuance of database requests. Alternatives include access before query processing, fully eager (immediate) data base access and fully lazy (deferred) access.

The FDE provides all three options for database access. It operates on the assumption that deferral of data base lookup is controlled by the personality functions, so that a data base node will not be chosen for expansion by the deduction cycle until the personality deems it ready.

Database access before query processing is advantageous when the underlying database management system lacks certain features, when the cost of communications between the deductive processor and the DBMS is high, or the database is not always available to the expert system. For example, the manufacturing database used for configuring some large Burroughs mainframes is not generally available in the sales offices that plan users' computer systems. This problem can be solved by including a snapshot of the database within the internal database of the FDE that is installed in the sales office.

The primary advantage in an early access to the database during deduction is that it may retrieve values which will narrow subsequent deductions by pruning possible deductive paths. Delayed evaluation, on the other hand, enables exploitation of the underlying DBMS's query optimizer.

Another factor in timing is the volatility of the databases. Since the FDE currently makes no effort to lock any of its serving databases during deduction, consistent results for volatile databases are likely only when they are all done at the same time.

4. An Example

A final example of deductive database access with the FDE is shown in Figure 3. The appendix has a description of the schema. Given a project management application, the query asks if there is an employee who can be assigned to a particular project. The database size and schema complexity have been trivialized to highlight the flexibility of data representation and access. Each of the base relations in the example are stored in different places: ASSIGNMENT-PERMITTED is a partially instantiated assertion, TASK-PROJ is kept in the internal database, HAS-SKILL is kept in a database in the Britton-Lee IDM-500 and SKILL-REQ is kept in MicroINGRES on a Sun.

The function ADEDBSEARCH is responsible for generating search requests. As the trace following the query suggests, it is issued twice in the extended Prolog personality used. First it supports the derived predicate QUALIFIED by searching for HAS-SKILL and SKILL-REQ. Since these two relations are stored in two remote databases (MA2 and MA3 respectively as shown in the trace of the functions IDMETHER and QUELSAMVAX), separate binary IDL and Ingres Quel queries are required. ADEDBSEARCH finally returns the combined answers showing the employees whose skills match those required by the existing tasks. The second call to ADEDBSEARCH goes to the local database to test whether or not task 98317A is a part of project 98317. Finally, supporting evidence for the conclusion that employee jones can be assigned to project 98317 is shown graphically at the bottom.

```
PROLOG->  CAN-BE-ASSIGNED(←EMP, 98317)?

ADEDBSEARCH:
SearchReq = (OCC(SKILL-REQ "←T->←T:2" "←S->←S:2")
             OCC(HAS-SKILL "←E->←E:2" "←S->←S:2"))
   QUELSAMVAX:
   SR = ((SKILL-REQ ←T.2 ←S.2))
   COMP = NIL
   VIAHOST = SDCRDCF
   ATHOST = samsun
   ASUSER = darrel
   DBASENAME = MA2
      QUELSUPER:
      SR = ((SKILL-REQ ←T.2 ←S.2))
      DBSTREAM = {STREAM}#56,167000
      QUELSUPER = (←T.2 ←S.2)
   QUELSAMVAX = (((MA2 ←T.2 ←S.2)
                 (98317A prolog)
                 (98317A lisp)
                 (98317B prolog)))
   IDMSERIAL:
   SR = ((HAS-SKILL ←E.2 ←S.2))
   COMP = NIL
   DBASENAME = {CORWIN:}<MA1>
      IDLSUPER:
      SR = ((HAS-SKILL ←E.2 ←S.2))
      DBSTREAM = {STREAM}#61,115404
      IDLSUPER = (←S.2 ←E.2)
   IDMSERIAL = ((({CORWIN:}<MA1> ←S.2 ←E.2)
                (prolog jones)
                (prolog smith)
                (lisp jones)))
ADEDBSEARCH = (("←S->←S:2" "←T->←T:2" "←E->←E:2")
               ((prolog 98317A jones)
                (prolog 98317B jones)
                (prolog 98317A smith)
                (prolog 98317B smith)
                (lisp 98317A jones)))
ADEDBSEARCH:
SearchReq = (OCC(TASK-PROJ 98317A 98317))
ADEDBSEARCH = (NIL T)
```

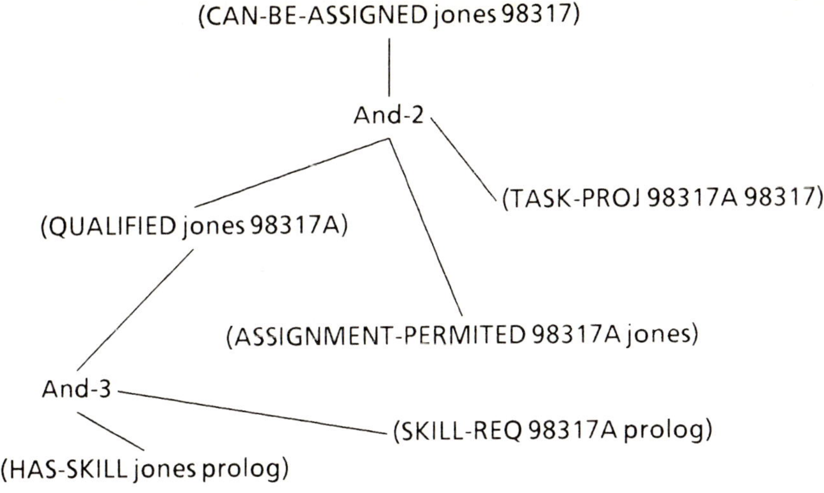

Figure 3. Sample query, trace and result

5. Work in Progress

Although the FDE has been successfully demonstrated, its development is far from complete. A major shortcoming is its current inability to handle evaluable entities, including evaluable predicates, functions and set-valued operators such as aggregation. DADM supports both functional arguments and evaluable predicates, but requires that all arguments be fully instantiated. For example, In (EQUAL (ADD ←X 5) 7), it should be possible to infer that ←X must be 2, but in DADM, ←X must have a value before DADM will evaluate the expression as true or false. A similar limitation made aggregation expensive and left DADM unable to exploit much of the support available in many DBMSs.

The next major step is to overcome these deficiencies possibly following the approach of Maier & Warren [Maier & Warren 81]. In addition a DADM personality will be completed which will complement the Prolog (depth-first) and Loglisp (breadth-first) deductive strategies with a third heuristically-driven scheme.

6. References

[BLI 83] Britton-Lee Inc.; *IDM Software Reference Manual*; Version 1.4; January, 1983.

[Chamberlin 76] Chamberlin, D.D, Astrahan, M.M., Eswaran, K.P., Griffiths, P.P, Lorie, R.A., Mehl, J.W., Reisner, P. and Wade, B.W.; SEQUEL 2: A unified Approach to Data Definition, Manipulation and Control; *IBM Journal of Research and Development*; Vol 20, No. 6; Nov. 1976.

[Dahl 82] Dahl, V.; On Database Systems Development Through Logic; *ACM Transactions on Database Systems*; Vol 7, No. 1, Mar 1982.

[Fuchi 82] Fuchi, K.; Aiming for Knowledge Information Processing Systems; In Proc. *International Conference of 5th. Generation Computer Systems*; Moto-Oka, T., ed.; North-Holland; 1982

[Hammer & Zdonik 80] Hammer, M. and Zdonik, S.B.; Knowledge Based Query Processing; In Proc. *International Conference on Very Large Databases*; 1980.

[Jarke et. al. 84] Jarke, M., Clifford, J. and Vassiliou, Y.; An Optimizing Front-End to a Relational Query System; in Proc. *SIGMOD*; 1984.

[Kawanobe 84] Kawanobe, K.; Current Status and Future Plans of the Fifth Generation Computer Systems Project; In Proc. *International Conference on Fifth Generation Computer Systems*, Tokyo, 1984.

[Kellogg et. al. 78] Kellogg, C., Klahr, P., and Travis, L.; Deductive Planning and Pathfinding for Relational Data Bases; In *Logic and Data Bases*; Gallaire, H. and Minker, J. (eds.); Plenum Press; 1978.

[Kellogg & Travis 81] Kellogg, C. and Travis, L.; Reasoning with Data in a Deductively Augmented Data Management System; In *Advances in Data Base Theory*; Gallaire, H., Minker, J. and Nicholas, J. M. (eds.); Plenum, 1981.

[Kellogg 82] Kellogg, C.; Knowledge Management: a Practical Amalgam of Knowledge and Data Base Technology; In Proc. *National Conference on Artificial Intelligence*; 1982.

[Kellogg 83] Kellogg, C.; Intelligent Assistants for Knowledge and Information Resources Management; In Proc. *International Joint Conference on Artificial Intelligence*; August, 1983.

[Kellogg 84] Kellogg, C.; The Transition from Data Management to Knowledge Management; In Proc *IEEE International Conference on Data Engineering*; April, 1984.

[Klahr 78] Klahr, P.; Planning techniques for rule selection in deductive question-answering; In *Pattern Directed Inference Systems*; Waterman, D. A. and Hayes-Roth, R. (eds.); Academic Press; 1978.

[Kogan 84] Kogan, D.; The Manger's Assistant, an Application of Knowledge Management; In Proc. *IEEE Conference on Data Engineering*; 1984.

[Maier & Warren 81] Maier, D. and Warren, D.S.; Incorporating Computed Relations in Relational Databases; in Proc. *SIGMOD*; 1981;

[McKay et. al. 85] McKay, D.P., Davis, R., Hirschman, L., Van Buer, D.J., Whitney, R. and Kogan, D.; A Flexible Deductive Engine; internal SDC document; 1985.

[Ohsuga 82] Ohsuga, S.; Knowledge Based Systems as a New Interactive Computer System of the Next Generation; *Japan Annual Review in Electronics, Computers and Telecommunications: Computer Science and Technologies*; Kitagawa, T. (ed.); 1982.

[Robinson & Sibert 80] Robinson, J.A. and Sibert, E.E.; *LOGLISP - An Alternative to PROLOG*; Technical Report No. 7-80; Computer and Information Science, Syracuse University; December, 1980.

[Suwa et.al. 82] Suwa, M., Furukawa, K., Makinouchi, A., Mizoguchi, T., Mizoguchi, F. and Yamasaki H.; Knowledge Base Mechanisms; In Proc. *International Conference of 5th. Generation Computer Systems*; Moto-Oka, T., ed.; North-Holland 1982.

[Templeton et. al. 83] Templeton, M., Brill, D., Hwang, A., Kameny, I. and Lund, E.; An Overview of the Mermaid System -- A Frontend to Heterogeneous Databases; In Proc. *16th. Annual Electronics and Aerospace Conference and Exposition*; September, 1983.

[Vassiliou et. al. 83] Vassiliou, Y., Clifford, J., and Jarke, M.; How Does and Expert System Get Its Data?; in Proc. *International Conference on Very Large Databases*; 1983.

[Whitney et. al. 85] Whitney, R., Van Buer, D.J., McKay, D.P., Kogan, D., Hirschman, L., Davis, R.; Predicate Connection Graph Based Logic With Flexible Control; in Proc. *International Joint Conference on Artificial Intelligence*; 1985.

[Wiederhold 84] Wiederhold, G.; Knowledge and Database Management *IEEE Software* Vol 1, No. 1; Jan 1984.

[Xerox 83] Xerox Corporation; *Interlisp Reference Manual*; October, 1983.

[Youssefi 77] Youssefi, K., Ubell, M., Ries, D., Hawthorne, P., Epstein, B., Berman, R. and Allman, E.; *INGRES Reference Manual - Version 6*; Memorandum No. ERL-M579; Engineering Research Lab., College of Engineering, U. California, Berkeley; 14-Apr-77 (revised).

APPENDIX A - Schema

The schema used in the example is a distillation of an experimental decision support system implemented under DADM to aid project managers [Kogan 84]. In this case there are six relations whose names and method of support are:

Relation	Support
CAN-BE-ASSIGNED	Deduced
QUALIFIED	Deduced
ASSIGNMENT-PERMITTED	Predicate Connection Graph
TASK-PROJ	Local Database
SKILL-REQ	External Database MA2 - Sun microINGRES
HAS-SKILL	External Database MA3 - Britton Lee IDM

Figure 4 . Relations and their support

Figure 5a shows the three premises which support the two deduced relations. Each rule is preceded by a unique identifier and is expressed as an implication and written in prefix notation. For example, rule P0055 can be read as "**If** an employee is qualified for a task **and** the employee is allowed to be assigned to the project **and** that task is part of a project, **then** the employee can be assigned to the project." Finally, Figure 5b shows the extension corresponding to the two relations SKILL-REQ and HAS-SKILL, which are stored remotely on the IDM in database MA2 and Sun microINGRES in database MA3 respectively.

```
(P0054 :(ASSIGNMENT-PERMITED 98317A ←E))
(P0055 :(IMP (AND (QUALIFIED ←E ←T)
                  (ASSIGNMENT-PERMITED ←T ←E)
                  (TASK-PROJ ←T ←P))
             (CAN-BE-ASSIGNED ←E ←P)))
(P0056 :(IMP (AND (HAS-SKILL ←E ←S)
                  (SKILL-REQ ←T ←S))
             (QUALIFIED ←E ←T)))
(TASK-PROJ FACTS ((98317A 98317)
                  (98317B 98317)))
```

Figure 5a. Rule base and internal database

```
idl
1) open MA1
2) range of h is hasSkill
Tecnol
3) retrieve(h.all)   go

|emp       |skill     |
|---------------------|
|jones     |prolog    |
|smith     |prolog    |
|jones     |lisp      |
|---------------------|
3 tuples affected
1) exit
```

```
rsh samsun ingres MA2
SUN MicroIngres/Net Version 2.0
Copyright (c) 1984, Relational

* retrieve(skillReq.all)  \go
Executing . . .
|task      |skill     |
|---------------------|
|98317A    |prolog    |
|98317A    |lisp      |
|98317B    |prolog    |
|---------------------|
(3 rows)
* \quit
```

Figure 5b. Distributed databases

TRANSMEDIA MACHINE

Y. Tanaka and K. Takahashi
Department of Electrical Engineering
Hokkaido University
Sapporo, 060 JAPAN

1. INTRODUCTION

While a deluge of publications nowadays is increasing the needs for computerized management of these information, their input to computer systems is becoming much harder than before because of their rapidly growing huge volume. Today, we have two types of systems for the management of voluminous information. Database management systems on a general purpose computer store typed-in information, while electronic filing systems using laser disks store information as images. In the latter system, not only drawings, pictures and photographs, but also text documents are stored as images. Through the technological breakthrough in rewritable image file device technology such as optomagnetic disk devices, recent electronic filing systems have come to allow users to input information through image readers on the spot in their offices. A database management system allows us the text editing of retrieved information. The edited text can be saved into the same database management system. However, it requires us to type in all the information one by one character. An electronic filing system, on the other hand, can input voluminous text documents through an image reader. It requires no typing. However, it offers us only restricted functions to edit retrieved information. These functions are mostly layout change functions implemented by cut-and-paste operations on images. An cut-and-paste operation cuts out an rectangular area in an original image and pastes this area at an arbitrary location in this image. The text-editing functions are not provided by electronic filing systems.

Database management systems and electronic filing systems are complementary. They provide functions that each other needs. However, they can not actually complement each other since they are separate systems using different data structures and different processing algorithms. The text editing of a retrieved document adds a new meaning to this document. In

NATO ASI Series, Vol. F 24
Database Machines. Edited by A. K. Sood and A. H. Qureshi

other words, it yields new meaningful information. Such a kind of works constitutes a major part of our intellectual activities. Therefore, the same information management system should be able to treat edited documents in the same way as it treats original documents. A single management system should be capable of storing, editing, and retrieving both original and edited documents. Besides, it should be able to read original documents without asking users to type them. The manual input of documents through keyboards will inevitably become the most serious bottle neck in building large databases. It requires a large amount of manual labor.

Transmedia Machine is a new document management architecture that has been studied in Hokkaido University since 1983 to satisfy the above mentioned requirements. In a transmedia machine, all the functions of database management systems and electronic filing systems are merged into an integrated system. A transmedia machine will have a configuration as shown in Fig. 1.1. It consists of a transmedia processor, a bit-map display with a keyboard, code file storage devices like magnetic disk storage devices, image file storage devices like laser disk or optomagnetic disk storage devices, an image reader, and an image printer. Its functions will cover most of the office works, i.e., storage, retrieval, edit, word processing, and communication. Each object document may be either a typed-in document, a document read-in as an image, or a mixture of these two types of

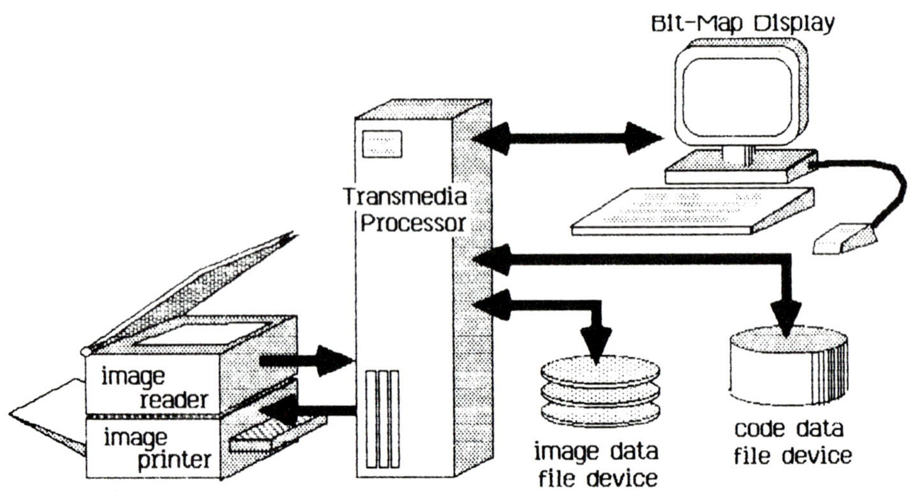

Fig. 1.1 Configuration of a Transmedia Machine.

documents. the difference of these three types of documents is not visible to the users of this system. Users need not distinguish actual representation of documents. They are provided with a single view upon document representations.

Functions of a transmedia machine other than editing and word processing are almost already provided by electronic filing systems, which also provide basic layout editing functions implemented by cut-and-paste operations. Therefore, among the functions of a transmedia machine, text editing and word processing functions are most fundamental and yet most difficult to implement. Implementation of these functions for image documents require fundamental algorithms for text processing on image documents. This paper will show both these algorithms and their emulation on a general purpose conventional computer, and prove the feasibility of transmedia machines.

2. TEXT EDITING BY A TRANSMEDIA MACHINE

If the characters in an image text are recognized and translated into character codes, the text editing of the translated text would be an easy task. However, the pattern recognition of characters is not an easy task, especially if multiple fonts are used for each character. Transmedia machines adopt an alternative approach. They do not recognize characters, but it recognizes text line boundaries, character boundaries, word boundaries, and paragraph boundaries. It recognizes all of these boundaries as rectangles with different sizes and different shapes (Fig. 2.1). After the extraction of these rectangles, each rectangular area of an image can be easily moved to a favorite location in the image using a cut-and-paste operation. With repetitive applications of cut-and-paste operations in a systematic way, you can manually move all the word rectangles in an image text to change the line length of the image text without changing the sentences in it. If you have much more perseverance, you can align the left end and the right end of the text to the respective margines as if you had typed this text with a word processor. This operation can be performed by equally distributing remaining space in each line to all the gaps between neighbouring words in this line. If you have a font table that lists up all the characters printed with the same font used in the object image texts, you can also rewrite the original texts. If you want to delete a character, you can cut off the character rectangle enclosing this character from the

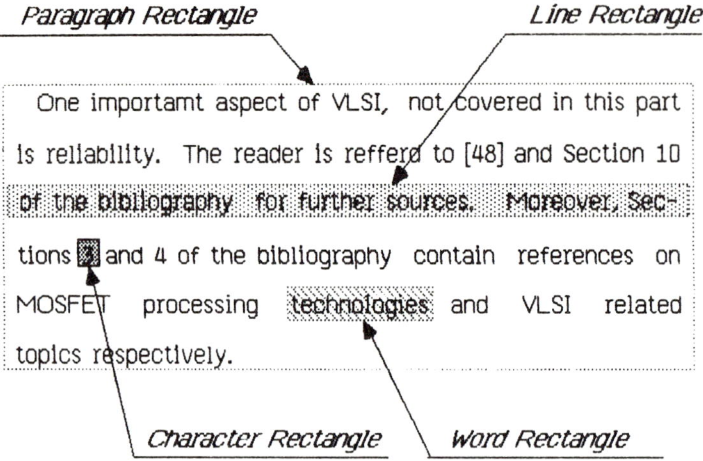

Fig. 2.1 Various Rectangles to be Recognized.

enclosing word rectangle. The word rectangle including this character may be cut into two. These two parts will be sticked together. If you want to insert a character, you can split the enclosing word rectangle at the insertion point to make a room, copy a character rectangle corresponding to this character in the font table, insert this copied rectangle into the split, and stick these three rectangles together to form a single word rectangle. In other words, you can perfom most of the text editing functions even on an image text manually with cut-and-paste and copy-and-paste operations. However, the manual execution of these procedures are too much time consuming and monotonous even for a person with much perseverance to edit several pages of image texts in such a way.

This monotonousness and elaborateness well encourage computer execution of these procedures. Transmedia machines electronically perform the same operations in the same way as the above described manual execution. Besides each original image text, it stores the size and the location of each character rectangle in this text. Image texts are stored in image file strage devices, while the sizes and the locations of character rectangles are stored in code file storage devices such as magnetic disk units. The latter kind of information is obtained by the preprocessing of each image text. It is represented as a stream of character rectangle characteristics with several marks inserted among them (Fig. 2.2). The order of character

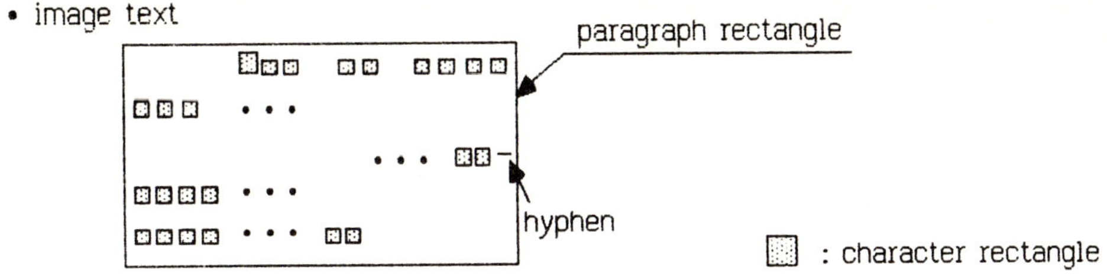

PG ; symbol which represents the biginning of a paragraph
SP ; symbol which splits the stream into words
HY ; symbol which represents a hyphen

Fig. 2.2 Preprocessing of an Image Text.

rectangles in this stream is same as that in the original image text. Inserted marks indicate either the beginning of a paragraph, a word gap space, existence of a hyphen, or an inserted character.

Transmedia machines will provide screen editors, in which a single page of an image text will be displayed on the screen, and the character rectangle at the cursor position repetitively reverses its contrast. The cursor is moved by moving the flickering from one character rectangle to another. Association of the cursor movements with the cursor keys on the keyboard will move the cursor as if we are using a text editor for code texts. From users' point of view, the text editing of an image text by a transmedia machine works in the same way as that of a code text by an ordinary word processor.

3. BASIC ALGORITHMS

New Application of Known Algorithms

The preprocessing of an image text to obtain line rectangles, character rectangles, word rectangles, and paragraph rectangles can be performed by combination of known basic image processing techniques. It requires no innovative algorithm. After the extraction of rectangles, each rectangle area can be easily moved to another location by a simple cut-and-paste operation, which does not require an innovative algorithm either. This section roughly describes an algorithm for each step of the preprocessing.

Line Rectangle Extraction

An image text that is input from an image reader is first transformed into a mesh of binary valued cells. Black cells are represented by '1', while white ones are represented by '0'. The mesh is assumed to cover an image text so that the mesh rows are parallel to the text lines. At the next step, line rectangles are extracted from an image text. This is performed by analyzing a histogram that shows the frequency of black cells for every mesh row. For an example image text in Fig. 3.1, this histogram looks like

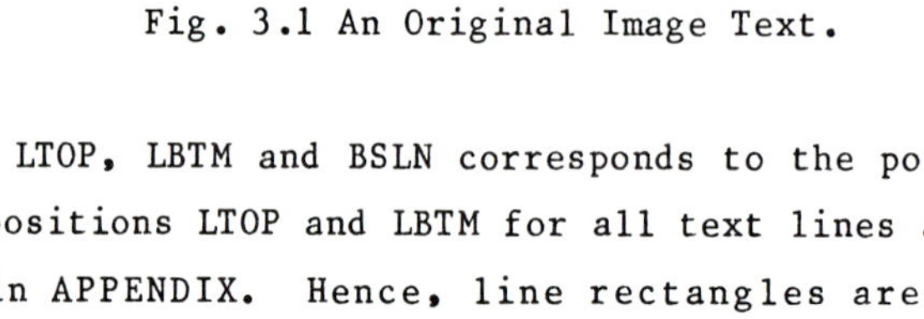

> One important aspect of VLSI, not covered in this Part is reliability. The reader is referred to [48] and Section 10 of the bibliography for further sources. Moreover, Sections 3 and 4 of the bibliography contain references on MOSFET processing technologies and VLSI related topics respectively.

Fig. 3.1 An Original Image Text.

Fig. 3.2, where LTOP, LBTM and BSLN corresponds to the positions defined in Fig. 3.3. The positions LTOP and LBTM for all text lines are obtained by an algorithm A1 in APPENDIX. Hence, line rectangles are extracted. This algorithm automatically discards phantom text lines that may be sometimes yielded by noises between consecutive text lines. The base line position BSLN in each line rectangle is obtained as a characteristic point of the histogram by another algorithm A2 in APPENDIX.

Character Rectangle Extraction

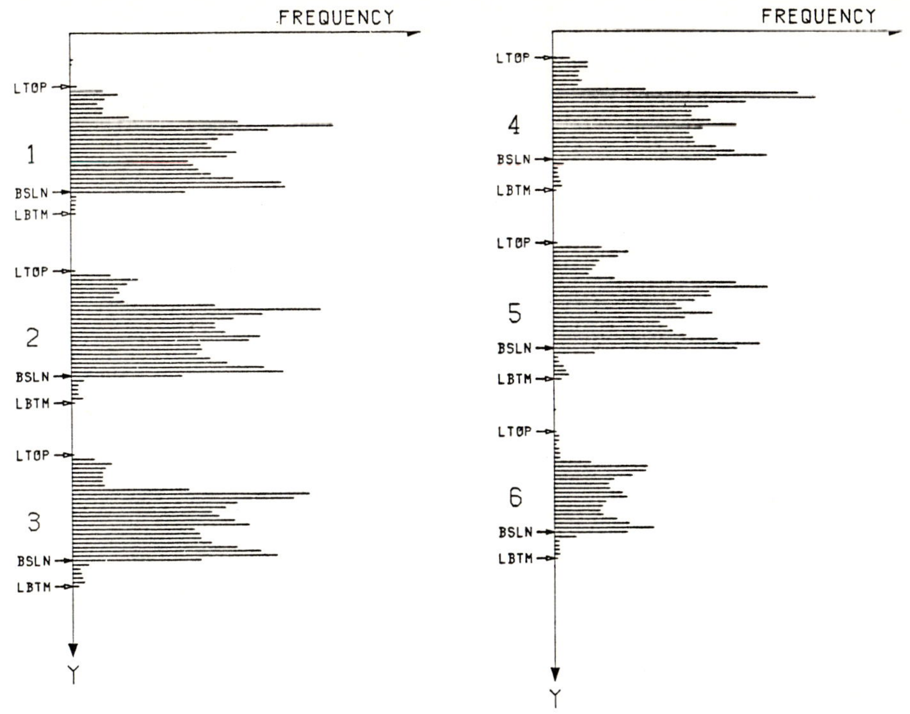

Fig. 3.2 The Histogram of the Frequency of Black Cells in Each Mesh Row of the image text in Fig. 3.2.

LTOP ; Line top vertical position in the text line
LBTM ; Line bottom vertical position in the text line
BSLN ; Base line verticalposition in the text line

Fig. 3.3Three Important Vertical Positions.

At the next step, the system extracts character rectangles in each line rectangle. The vertical projection of black cells in each line rectangle to

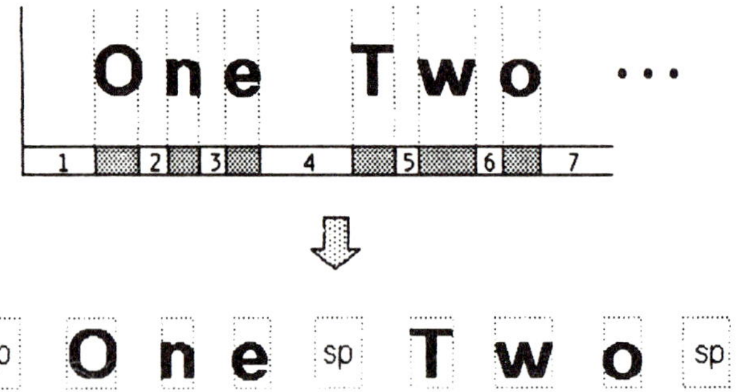

Longer spaces such as 1, 4, and 7 above are spaces between words. Analysis of histogram of space length determines the thleshold that seperates these two classes.

Fig. 3.4 Separation of Word Gap Spaces from Character Gap Spaces.

a horizontal line yields a sequence of alternating black and white runs of mesh cells (Fig. 3.4). Each black run usually corresponds to one character. In proportionally spaced printing, consecutive characters sometimes loose a gap between them. In such case, such a pair of two characters may be considered as a single character. This causes no serious inconvenience. Extraction of character rectangles uses an algorithm A3 in APPENDIX.

White runs correspond to two kinds of spaces, i.e., character gap spaces and word gap spaces. They can be classified by cluster analysis. After the extraction of character rectangles and the separation of word gap spaces from character gap spaces, the system generates an auxiliary code file that stores a sequence of character rectangle characteristics and special marks that indicate either a new paragraph, a word gap, or a hyphen (Fig. 3.4). It stores, for each character rectangle, only its location and size. Character images are not stored in the code file. This file is called the acompanying code file of the binary image text.

Paragraphs are easily extracted by detecting indentations, while a hyphen is detected by a simple template matching technique.

4. LINE LENGTH CHANGE AND REWRITING

In a transmedia machine, an accompanying code file for a given image text plays the same role of a text file produced by a conventional word processor. In an ordinary text file storing a sequence of character codes, the order of character codes defines the order of characters in its printed image, and each character code is used to get its font image from character generator ROMs. In an acompanying code file for an image text, the order of character rectangles defines the order of characters in the printed image of this text, and the location and the size of each character rectangle is used to get its font image by copying this rectangle area of the image text. A word gap space mark in an acompanying code file corresponds to a space code in an ordinary text file. The size of each character rectangle corresponds to the character width in proportionally spaced printing. It is used to determine the change of line and to align the left and the right end of an text to the respective margines.

Deleted characters lose their corresponding rectangles in the acompanying code file. Original image texts are not modified. In acompanying code files, each inserted character is represented by its character code preceded by an insertion mark. This pair of a mark and a character code is inserted at an insertion position in the acompanying code file. If such a character code is encountered in the printing of this file, the system gets the corresponding font image from a preprocessed font table to print this character. An acompanying code file in a transmedia machine may consists of insertion marks and character coodes. Such a file corresponds to a text that is fully typed into the system.

No transmedia machine has been implemented yet. However, a partial emulation program that performs image reading, preprocessing, extraction of various rectangles, generation of an acompanying code file, line length change, left and right alignment to the margines, text rewriting, and printing by a laser printer. The emulation program was written in FORTRAN. An example of a text line length change is shown in Fig. 4.1, where a hyphen at the end of the third line in the original image text is deleted. Its

One important aspect of VLSI, not covered in this Part is reliability. The reader is referred to [48] and Section 10 of the bibliography for further sources. Moreover, Sections 3 and 4 of the bibliography contain references on MOSFET processing technologies and VLSI related topics respectively.

Fig. 4.1 A Change of Text Line Length of the Image Text in Fig. 3.1

A G M S Y e k q w 2 8 = [, ¥ "
B H N T Z f l r x 3 9 <] : # '
C I O U a g m s y 4 + > { ; $ ^
D J P V b h n t z 5 - ( ) ? % |
E K Q W c i o u 0 6 * } . ! & _
F L R X d j p v 1 7 /

Fig. 4.2 A Font Table that is read in as an Image Text.

One important aspect of VLSI, not covered in this Part is reliability. The reader is referred to [48] and Section 10 of the bibliography for further sources. Moreover, Section 15 of the bibliography contain references on MOSFET processing technologies and VLSI related topics respectively.

Fig. 4.3 An Image Text obtained by the rewriting of Fig. 3.1.

original text was shown in Fig. 3.1. Another example that rewrites the original text using a font table in Fig. 4.2 is shown in Fig. 4.3. These examples prove the feasibility of transmedia machines.

5. CONCLUSION

This paper has proposed Transmedia Machine architecture that integrates functions of mutually complementary two kinds of information management systems, i.e., database management systems for coded information and electronic filing systems for image information. It can reads printed documents through an image reader. Printed documents need not be manually typed into the system, which removes the input bottleneck of information management. Besides, this machine provides a screen editor that allows its user to rewrite image texts as if they are typed-in texts. Rewritten texts are also managed by the system. The machine can cope with image texts, rewritten image texts, and typed-in coded texts in a unified way. Its user can not distinguish the difference. Rewritten image texts are internally represented as a mixture of image texts and coded texts.

The algorithms used by the machine to preprocess original image texts are combinations of known image processing algorithms. The machine does not recognize each character in image texts. Instead, it recognizes the

boundary of each character. The fundamental algorithms necessary to implement a screen editor of a transmedia machine have been given in this paper. An emulator that was programmed based on these algorithms has proved the feasibility of this machine.

APPENDIX

A1. Text Line Extraction Algorithm

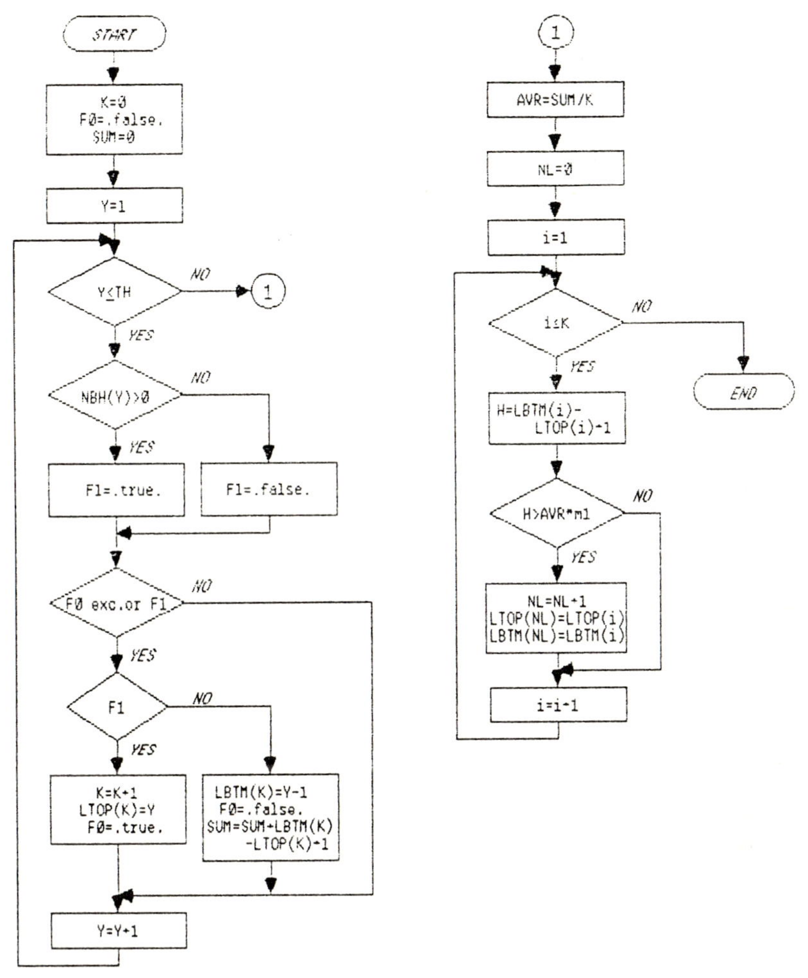

X ; A horizontal position in the text   Y ; A vertical position in the text

TW ; The text width   TH ; The text height

NBH(Y); The number of vertical black mesh cells in the horizontal mesh at a vertical position Y

LTOP(i); The line top vertical position in the text line (i)

LBTM(i); The line bottom vertical position in the text line (i)

NL; The number of text lines

AVR; An average of H over all the text lines

m1 ; Heuristically defined parameter (we set m1=0.5) used to remove phantom text lines

A2. Base Line Extraction Algorithm

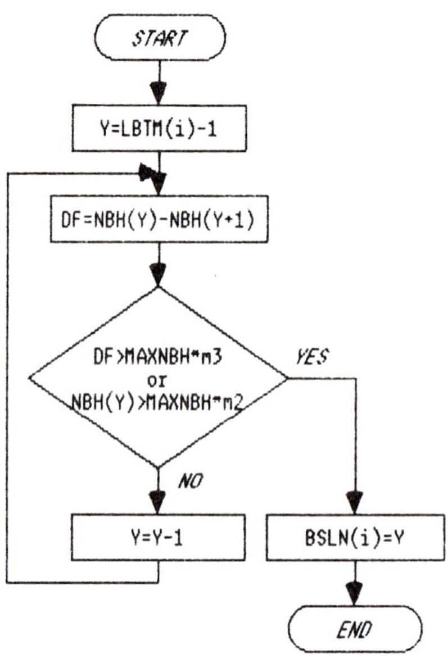

BSLN(i) ; Base line vertical position of the text line (i)
MAXNBH ; Maximum number of black mesh cells in a line among all the mesh lines in the text
m2, m3 ; Heuristically defined parameter (we set m2=0.3 and m3=0.3)

A3. Character Extraction Algorithm

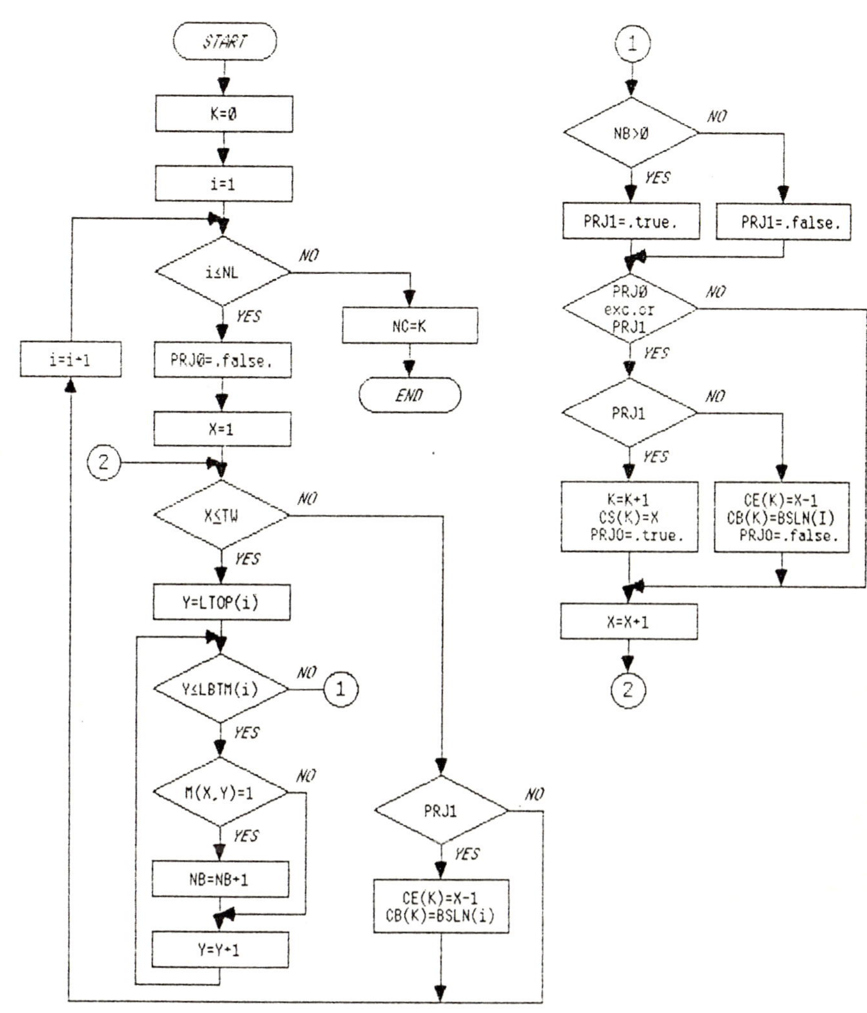

M (X,Y) ; Binary value of the mesh cell at the its location (X,Y)
A black cell is represented by 1.

NB ; Number of black mesh cells
x-coordinate -- X , y-coordinate -- from LTOP to LBTM

CS(k) ; Horizontal start position of the character (k)

CE(k) ; Horizontal end position of the character (k)

CB(k) ; Base line vertical position of the character (k)

NC ; Number of all characters ina whole image text

AN ARCHITECTURE FOR INTEGRATING IMAGES AND TEXT IN A DATABASE ENVIRONMENT

William I. Grosky
Computer Science Department
Wayne State University
Detroit, Michigan 48202

1. INTRODUCTION

Modern textual database management systems are designed to promote the controlled sharing of information. Different users have their own view of the centrally managed data and act as if the system were designed specifically for them. Recently, there has been much interest in various sorts of non-textual database management systems, especially those which handle image data and support retrieval of information by content.

Computer vision, image understanding, and digital image processing are some of the fastest growing areas of computer science. The applications of the above areas in industry, medicine, the military, cartography, geology, biology and other fields, coupled with the progress in computer hardware suggests the continual growth of these areas at ever increasing rates. The concern of most researchers in these areas has been to improve the quality of the images and/or to compute some semantic information contained in them with the aim of understanding their contents.

In many applications a very large number of images, sometimes in the millions, are obtained, and it is desired to store them for later use, perhaps after some processing. In other applications, it is required that a database contain not only alphanumeric data, but images also. Yet other applications require databases containing mostly images along with some information concerning the images. All such applications have encouraged researchers to investigate techniques for image data management and pictorial databases.

Many systems have been proposed to manage image data, but they all have the weakness of a non-integrated approach to handling textual versus non-textual information. There is no notion of a conceptual and external schema for images. All image processing is 'hard-wired' into the system and there is no controlled sharing of these routines.

In the literature there have been two major types of pictorial databases. The first are those which are concerned mainly with images. These are designed to be used by researchers in computer vision and image processing and by people in certain application areas, such as geography and cartography. The textual aspects of these systems are minimal, and consist mostly of textual encodings of pictorial positional information. The second are those systems which resemble a textual database management system but with pictures occurring as part of

NATO ASI Series, Vol. F 24
Database Machines. Edited by A. K. Sood and A. H. Qureshi

a logical record. However, the pictorial information is not treated equally with the textual information. The types of queries which are generally asked are those in which one wants to retrieve textual information concerning all entities having certain properties, as well as pictures of these entities. Queries would be processed as in a textual database to find the appropriate entities but instead of giving the user only the textual fields of the corresponding records, the pictures associated with these records would also be output.

In this paper, we survey previous approaches and introduce the system REMINDS, a completely integrated approach to the management of image and textual data which is an extension of the standard ANSI/SPARC 3-schema architecture of textual database management systems. Our system is completely general in that it may be used as a purely textual dbms, a purely iconic dbms for pattern recognition/image processing applications, a purely graphics dbms for CAD applications, or in any combination of these. It supports conceptual and external schemas for images and their associated procedures, and permits their controlled sharing. We also discuss various query processing strategies and some new index mechanisms which are especially suitable for images.

2. PREVIOUS WORK

Early image database management systems were concerned mainly with file management. They were designed so as to facilitate image processing operations on stored images. Such a system was EIDES (Electrotechnical Laboratory Image Database for Experimental Studies) [TaM77]. This system allowed image entry and retrieval and the examination of various image statistics over defined windows. Each image had a 512 byte header which contained information regarding the division of the image into sub-images as well as more textually oriented information such as who took the picture. Image processing operations were provided via sub-routine calls.

IMDS (Image Database System) [Lie77] provided an interactive query language. As well as storing images, various graphics related transformations could be saved and then used on the images interactively.

MIDAS (Multi-Sensor Image Database System) [McR77] introduced a new approach. Symbolic as well as signal representations of the underlying image were kept. Both utilized the then emerging concept of pyramidal architecture; that is, viewing a concept or an image at different levels of resolution, all the time keeping track of the corresponding entities. Scenes were decomposed hierarchically into various types, each scene type consisting of some particular, physical entities. These in turn were similarly decomposed. The corresponding sub-images were noted and represented via signal pyramids; that is, smaller and smaller images at different levels of resolution. Each pixel at a low order of resolution represented an average of a set of pixels from a higher resolution image.

A similar approach was taken by DIMAP (Distributed Image Management and Projection) [CDM77, LiC80]. Information was represented in terms of physical as well as logical pictures, both in the form of a hierarchy. Each node in the physical picture hierarchy had a corresponding table in the logical picture hierarchy. This system also supported the concept of **zooming**; that is, browsing in the logical picture hierarchy utilizing similarity retrieval.

In ADM (Aggregate Data Manager) [TII79], images are data types, but with only equality/inequality comparisons allowed. The kernel of this system was based on System R.

The system IMAID (Integrated Image Analysis and Image Database Management System) [ChF80] was designed for geographical data. It was very CAD-like, representing geographical entities in terms of points, lines, regions, and their combinations. Routines called **processing packages** were supplied to convert images to maps. A language called **Query-by-Pictorial-Example** was used as a data manipulation language, which supported similarity retrieval.

Finally, the system IDMS (Integrated Database Management System) [Tan81] represented images as attributes. It supported a logical I/O system and had a SEQUEL-based query language.

3. INTEGRATED PICTORIAL DATABASES

The type of database management system we envision would support the following types of queries and updates:

1. Display the address of the employee with identification number 5318.

2. Display the identification numbers and the numbers of children of all employees whose first name is Joseph.

3. Display the managers' names of the departments where employees living on Canal Street work.

4. Display all pictures taken between 3 − 2 − 79 and 5 − 10 − 80 of all employees with three children.

5. Display the name and address of the employee whose picture is given.

6. Display the department number of all employees whose pictures are given.

7. Display the names and addresses of all persons on file who were photographed together with employee Joseph Smith.

8. Display the name, addresses, and most recent pictures of all persons on file who were photographed together with the employee whose portrait is given.

9. Insert the given picture, taken by Susan Jones on 4−8−81, into the database.

10. Insert the given picture as being a picture of the employee with identification number 6577.

Given that employees and departments are individual entities, the eight initial queries above seemingly represent increasingly complex situations. The first three can be processed using the classical relational operators of selection, projection and join. It will be seen that classical-like relational operators can also be used to answer queries #4−#8.

Notice that update #9 doesn't associate the picture with any entity contained in the picture, while update #10 does. The given picture in this latter update could reside in the database already or be an input parameter.

In all of the systems of the previous section, the image processing aspects are all 'hard-wired' in. Thus, the image part of the these systems is treated differently from the textual part. The system closest to overcoming this handicap is IMAID, with its processing packages. However, processing packages don't interact with each other and there is no notion of controlled sharing of image processing routines.

In the next section, we will present a view of an integrated image database system as we feel the user should see it. We will then view such a system from the point of view of the database administrator.

4. A USER'S VIEW[1]

The paper [Tan81] is one of the few papers of which we are aware which concerns the design of an integrated pictorial database from the user's point of view. His design, however, is implicit in the way he organizes iconic and textual data. He never explicitly discusses the advantages and the disadvantages of his approach. As mentioned in a previous section, Tang's approach consists of simply having images treated as another domain over which attributes are defined.

This leads to a number of problems, not the least of which is that an entity cannot have more than one picture for each picture type which is an attribute. For example, if the entity

---

[1]This consists of a survey of our paper [Gro84].

set in question consists of people and we have the iconic attributes **face** and **fingerprints**, then a particular person cannot have more than one face picture or more than one fingerprint picture represented. The reason for this is that we would then have at least two tuples in the relation with the same set of key-domain values, and this is not allowed. We are assuming here, of course, that the iconic domains are not part of the set of key domains. (Repeating groups, of course, are not allowed if the tables are in first normal form.) This is a fair assumption since Tang does not say anything concerning key domains, and if the iconic domains were part of the set of key domains then we would be forced to make the restrictive assumption that every entity must have a picture corresponding to the given attribute. As it is, if an entity does not have a corresponding picture, this entry in the table would have to be null, creating other subtle problems.

Moreover, in Tang's model a picture has to have a corresponding entity; it cannot stand by itself in the database. This is clearly a disadvantage in the many applications where numerous unexamined pictures need to be entered into the database. These unattached pictures could be processed in query operations, if the user so desired, possibly resulting in partial information. Query #8 in the preceding section is an example of this. If the given portrait matched the picture of a person in the database, we could efficiently access all the attached pictures in which this person appeared, look for the other people in these pictures, and then find their names, addresses, and most recent photographs if these latter people's pictures were attached to a person. However, if the given portrait did not match the picture of a person in the database, but did match an unattached picture, we could still proceed, albeit less efficiently. Similarly, it would be less efficient to proceed if any of the latter people's pictures were unattached. The user could be informed along the way of these eventualities and would be able to direct the system in an appropriate manner.

We will now present a way of organizing an image database management system from the user's perspective in the light of the above objections. As in the entity-relationship model of data, we are going to have a table for each entity being represented as well as for each relationship between entities. Since our database utilizes iconic information, let us choose to call an individual picture an entity. To be more precise, we will form three entity sets: one consisting of individual analogue pictures, another consisting of individual digital pictures, and the last consisting of digital subpictures corresponding to the individual subject entities which occur in these pictures. The analogue picture entity set may have such attributes as Date-of-Photograph and Name-of-Photographer, while both of the digital picture entity sets will have no attributes at all. (Various iconic features of the set of digital pictures will be part of the conceptual schema, to be described in the next section.)

We must now choose a set of entity keys for this situation. That is, we must find a group of attributes which stand in 1-1 correspondence with the set of analogue pictures, and similarly for the set of digital pictures. The groups of domains which these attributes map to will then, so to speak, replace the individual entities, and will become the key domains of the tabular representations of the given sets.

For the set of analogue pictures, there may not be such a group of attributes. Thus, we will need a group of unique objects which are in 1-1 correspondence with this set. These objects are called **surrogates**, and when implemented will be system-generated identifiers. Following [Cod79], we will have one unary entity table and various property tables (called, respectively, an E table and P tables) in our database corresponding to the set of analogue pictures. The E table consists of a list of surrogates, one for each individual analogue picture, which is itself not stored in the database. Each P table has as a key the attribute which makes up the given E table, the other attributes being arbitrary yet semantically related. Thus, the properties of each entity are connected to the assertion of its existence by its presence in the E table. Of course, we must specify the necessary integrity rules regarding insertions and deletions so that, for example, an entity mentioned in a P table must appear in the E table. Here, we will have the analogue picture E table **Analogue** as well as the two analogue picture P tables **AnalogueWhenTaken** and **AnalogueTakenBy**.

The sets of digital pictures behave in an ostensibly different fashion. They are entity sets in which the entities themselves are directly represented in the computer and may thus serve as their own key. If we choose to follow this approach, however, we would be using structures akin to surrogates; it would be wasteful to have more than one copy of the digital picture stored and we would thus be using pointers or some other indirect method to refer to a particular digital picture in all relations in which it partakes. Thus, for the sake of consistency, we choose to use surrogates in this case too. We may assume that these surrogates are symbolic addresses of the digital images in secondary memory. The digital picture and digital subpicture will be called **Digital** and **SubDigital**, respectively.

As far as relationships are concerned, we will have a table **AnalogueDigital** connecting an analogue picture to its various digitized images, a table **DigitalSubDigital** connecting digital subpictures to the digital pictures in which they occur, and a table **AppearingIn** connecting a digital subpicture to the subject entity appearing in it.

As an illustration, suppose we have the situation depicted in the following tables. We exhibit here analogue pictures, digital pictures, digital subpictures, and employees, as well as their properties and relationships, using the tables we have previously discussed. Note that the attribute **Sid** represents the surrogate identifier.

Query #7 may then be written as follows,

Analogue

Analogue.Sid

Digital

Digital.Sid

SubDigital

SubDigital.Sid

AnalogueDigital

Analogue.Sid	Digital.Sid

DigitalSubDigital

Digital.Sid	SubDigital.Sid

Employee

Employee.Sid

AppearingIn

SubjectSid	SubDigital.Sid

AnalogueWhenTaken

Analogue.Sid	Date

AnalogueTakenBy

Analogue.Sid	LaboratoryName

EmployeeId

Employee.Sid	IdNumber	Name

EmployeeInformation

Employee.Sid	Address	NumberOfChildren	Salary

```
select Name,Address {Query #7}
from EmployeeId,EmployeeInformation
where Employee.Sid in
    select Subject.Sid
    from AppearingIn
    where SubDigital.Sid in
        select SubDigital.Sid
        from DigitalSubDigital
        where Digital.Sid in
            select Digital.Sid
            from DigitalSubDigital
            where SubDigital.Sid in
                select SubDigital.Sid
                from AppearingIn
                where Subject.Sid in
                    select Employee.Sid
                    from EmployeeId
                    where Name='Joseph Smith'
```

Notice that this query may result in a partial answer, as there may be pictures containing Joseph Smith which are not noted in **AppearingIn.** Even if all pictures containing Joseph Smith are so noted, there may be employees appearing with him in a picture, with these occurrences not being noted in **AppearingIn.** Thus, we note an important fact: a pictorial database management system which can support pictures as entities cannot rely solely on textual indices. We also require some sort of iconic indices. This topic will be elaborated on in the succeeding sections.

As pictorial matching is very time consuming compared to exact textual matching, the use of the pictorial indices will be much more expensive than the use of the textual indices. Thus, their use should be restricted to those times when the user specifically requests it. We now extend our query language to encompass this usage. Consider the following queries Q_1 and Q_2,

```
select Digital.Sid {Q1}
from DigitalSubDigital
where SubDigital.Sid in
    select SubDigital.Sid
    from AppearingIn
    where Subject.Sid in
        select Employee.Sid
        from EmployeeInformation
        where NumberOfChildren=3
```

```
select picture(Digital.Sid) {Q2}
from DigitalSubDigital
where DigitalSubDigital.Sid in
    select DigitalSubDigital.Sid
    from AppearingIn
    where Subject.Sid in
        select DigitalSubDigital.Sid
        from EmployeeInformation
        where NumberOfChildren=3
```

The first query will use the textual indices to first find the surrogate identifier values of all employees having 3 children, then find the surrogate identifier values of all digital subpictures in which these employees are noted as appearing, and finally find the surrogate identifier values of all digital pictures in which these subpictures occur. Thus, this query outputs the surrogate identifier values of each digital picture in which an employee with 3 children has been noted to appear. The second query will output the actual digital pictures instead of their surrogates. These 2 queries illustrate how to retrieve the digital pictures themselves as opposed to just their surrogate identifier values. Pictorial indices will not be used at all in the processing of these queries. In order to use the pictorial indices for the latter query, for example, this query may be written as either Q_3 or Q_4, where CertaintyFactor is a number between 0 and 1, inclusive.

```
select picture(Digital.Sid) {Q3}
from Digital
where picture(Digital.Sid)
contains(CertaintyFactor)
    select picture(DigitalSubDigital.Sid)
    from AppearingIn
    where Subject.Sid in
        select Employee.Sid
        from EmployeeInformation
        where NumberOfChildren=3
```

```
select picture(Digital.Sid) {Q4}
from Digital
where picture(Digital.Sid)
contains(CertaintyFactor)
    select min(DigitalSubDigital.Sid)
    from AppearingIn
    where Subject.Sid in
        select Employee.Sid
        from EmployeeInformation
        where NumberOfChildren=3
    group by Subject.Sid
```

Query Q_3 will use the textual indices, as above, to first retrieve the surrogate identifier values of all employees having 3 children and then retrieve the surrogate identifier values of the digital subpictures in which these employees are noted as appearing. The **picture** function retrieves the actual digital subpictures. It is at this point that the pictorial indices are used.

They determine which digital pictures contain the subject entities which correspond to those appearing in the given digital subpictures. Since the pictorial indices will rely on some best-match criteria, we provide a certainty factor which indicates how strongly we want the resultant match to be.

Query Q_4 is similar to query Q_3 except that only one digital subpicture for each given employee is used in the matching. This digital subpicture is the one with the least surrogate identifier value. This query should be more efficient than query Q_3 and give us similar answers in many cases, such as when each subject entity presents the same 2-D view in all its pictures, except for possible translations and rotations.

The above examples illustrate that only minimal changes to existing textual query languages are needed to support an integrated pictorial database management system.

5. THE DATABASE ADMINISTRATOR'S VIEW

Our approach is model-based. It supports the creation of arbitrary models as part of the database. Related to this is the formulation of an extension to the conceptual schema, the so-called **functional sub-schema**. We utilize the notion of **complex objects**, a way of representing an entity which consists of many components in given relationships to each other. This notion has been gaining popularity in CAD applications and is related to the relational models of [ShH81]. Our use of this notion is novel, however, and motivates the design of both our query processing strategies and one of our index mechanisms.

The conceptual schema of our system consists of 4 parts: the **model-base**, the **model-base instantiation**, the **instantiation-object connection**, and the **object information repository**.

The model-base itself consists of 2 parts: the **generic entity definitions** and the **functional sub-schema**. A generic entity is a complex object: it consists of various components in certain relationships to each other. For example, in a 2-D manufacturing environment, where parts must be recognized as they progress along a conveyor belt, a part might consist of 3 sub-parts connected together in a given fashion. These sub-parts might consist, in turn, of other sub-parts. Elementary, atomic parts would then consist of variously shaped regions, each region defined in terms of its boundary edges, each edge defined in terms of some given boundary pixels. The description of such a part would consist of many tuples structured in a hierarchical fashion. Each tuple in the hierarchy would describe either a complex object consisting of components, these, in turn, described by tuples which are children of the given tuple, or a relationship among various complex objects at many levels. Such relationships will, in general, be defined in terms of simpler relationships on their components. The model for each entity would thus correspond to a hierarchy of tuples. In actuality, we allow a directed acyclic graph (dag) of tuples, as models may share sub-models.

Corresponding to each tuple in the generic entity definitions is a set of procedures, each of which may be used to calculate an instantiation of this tuple in terms of the instantiations of its children tuples. We thus have a dag of sets of processes. This is the **functional sub-schema**. Together, the generic entity definitions and the functional sub-schema will allow us to have the controlled sharing of image descriptions, both declarative and procedural.

The **model-base instantiation** is a dag of tables which is in $1-1$ correspondence with the tuples of the model-base. Information regarding each particular iconic instantiation of a generic entity will reside in a table occupying the same relative position in the dag as that of the given generic entity. In other words, information regarding image data will reside here.

The **instantiation-object connection** is, similarly, a dag of tables which is in $1-1$ correspondence with the tuples of the model-base. Each iconic object corresponds to a real-world object with given semantics, and it is here that the correspondence is defined.

Finally, the **object information repository** consists of normal textual information concerning the real-world objects described by our collection of models.

For query processing in the context of iconic information, different mechanisms will be invoked depending on whether or not specific models for the iconic object are previously known. Once the functional sub-schema has been invoked and the correct model-base instantiation computed, there is still the necessity for entity matching. That is, one must determine whether a similar entity already exists within the database. For this problem, we have a method of matching hierarchically defined entities. It is done at various levels of resolution and relies on the fact that attribute values at one level of the hierarchy may be defined as aggregates of attribute values at lower levels.

Finally, we will introduce an edge-based pictorial index mechanism which will allow for rapid search of particularly shaped regions.

6. AN EDGE-BASED INDEX MECHANISM

Given 2 strings $A = a_1...a_M$ and $B = b_1...b_N$ over a finite vocabulary V, a common problem is to find their **longest common subsequence (LCS)**. This is a string $C = c_1...c_L$ of maximal length which is a subsequence of both A and B. Note that a subsequence need not consist of contiguous symbols. Thus, for V = {a,b,c,d}, A = abcdbb, and B = cbacbaba, the string C = acbb is an LCS.

There exist numerous algorithms for this problem. The best known are those of [Hir77] and [HuS77]. The time complexity of the former is $O(N(L+\log_2 N))$, while that of the latter is

$O((R+N)\log_2 N)$, where R is the total number of ordered pairs of positions from A and B, respectively, at which the 2 sequences match. In this paper, we will concentrate on the latter algorithm, whose worst-case time complexity is $O(NM\log_2 L)$.

Consider the binary image shown in Figure 1, which consists of a single segment. Starting from the segment's northwest corner, we derive a chain-code of A = $2^7 4^4 6^7 0^4$. Upon rotating the segment by 120 degrees, we get the image shown in Figure 2. Its chain-code, starting at the corresponding point is B = $(70)^3 112(34)^3 556$. The LCS of these 2 strings is C = $24^3 6$. Notice, however, that adding 5 mod 8 to each entry of A produces a string A' = $7^7 1^4 3^7 5^4$, whose LCS with B is C' = $7^3 1^2 3^3 5^2$.

FIGURE 1 – A BINARY DIGITAL IMAGE

FIGURE 2 – THE IMAGE OF FIGURE 1 ROTATED 120°

The above example illustrates the process of **generalized pattern-matching**. More formally, for vocabulary V = $\{v_0,\ldots,v_{p-1}\}$, define an operator, Next, from V onto V by $\text{Next}(v_i) = v_{(i+1) \bmod p}$. We extend Next to words $w = v_{i_1 \ldots i_d}$ over V by putting Next(w) = $\text{Next}(v_{i_1})\ldots\text{Next}(v_{i_d})$. We also define $\text{Next}^0(w) = w$, and $\text{Next}^{q+1}(w) = \text{Next}(\text{Next}^q(w))$. Then, if A and B are 2 strings over V, we call C = $c_1 \ldots c_L$ a **longest q-generalized common subsequence (LqGCS)** of A and B is C is a sequence of maximal length such that $\text{Next}^a(C)$ is a subsequence of A and $\text{Next}^b(C)$ is a subsequence of B, for $0 \le a,b \le q \le p-1$. Using the above example, C' is an L3GCS, but not an L2GCS, of A and B. Notice that finding an LCS of strings A and B corresponds to finding their L0GCS.

We would like to formulate an efficient algorithm to find an LqGCS of 2 strings. One might assume that one can use the standard pattern-matching algorithms on the first difference of A and B. While this is the case for the longest common substring problem – a related problem with the extra condition that $Next^a(C)$ and $Next^b(C)$ must be a sequence of contiguous symbols from A and B, respectively – it will not work for our situation. The first differences of A and B are $A' = 0^6 2 0^3 2 0^6 2 0^3$ and $B' = (\bar{7}7)^2 7 1 0 1^3 (\bar{1}1)^2 1 0 1$, for $\bar{i}$ the negative of i, which have an LCS of $C = 0^2$.

We have developed an algorithm for the LqGCS problem with a worst-case time complexity of $O(NM\log_2 L)$, which is independent of $|V|$. Notice that this is the same order of magnitude as the standard pattern-matching algorithm of [HuS77]. This algorithm, however, is not of much use for our application, due to the fact that a chain-code is a description of a closed boundary, and is sensitive to where on the boundary one starts. Indeed, this is one of the reasons stated for not using chain-code matching [Dav79]. We avoided this issue in the previous example by starting in the same relative position each time. Under more realistic circumstances, however, such as in a database environment, choosing the same starting position cannot always be guaranteed.

We thus do the following. Assuming, without loss of generality, that $M \geq N$, we find the set of LqGCS's of B and every length M substring of AA, and take the LqGCS of maximum size as our final answer. This is a particular example of what we call the **shifting window, longest q-generalized common subsequence (SWLqGCS)** of A and B. It is defined for a particular window size W by finding the set of LqGCS's of B and every length W substring of A and taking the LqGCS of maximum size as our result. The algorithm which we have developed for this problem [GrL83, GrL84] is of worst-case time complexity $O(\max((M-W)NL, MN\log_2 L)$, where W is the window size and L is the size of the SWLqGCS.

The index mechanism we describe in this section has aspects of clustering, Hough-based approaches, and generalized pattern-matching. Simply put, we pack our database of boundary-codes into a superstring. The length of this superstring will be much less than the sum of the lengths of the individual strings. Each character in the superstring will have a set of votes for the individual strings to which it belongs. When an incoming string needs to be classified, we find the SWLqGCS of this string with the superstring and use the votes of matching and non-matching characters to find the strength of the matches between this incoming string and each of the database strings.

We will now formally describe our approach. Given p strings $A_1,...,A_p$, their **shortest q-generalized common superstring (SqGCS)** is a string Z of minimal length such that each of $A_1,...,A_p$ is a q-generalized common subsequence of some length $|Z|$ substring of ZZ. For $q=0$, a related problem is NP-complete [GMS80], and we conjecture the same for this problem. However, we have a heuristic technique to find such short superstrings. Given two strings A and B, it finds a string Pack(A,B) such that both A and B are q-generalized common subsequences of some length |Pack(A,B)| substring of Pack(A,B)Pack(A,B). While not of minimal length, it is usually of much shorter length than |A|+|B|.

Without loss of generality, assume that $|A| \geq |B|$. Our technique starts out by finding the SWLqGCS of AA and B with window size A. Suppose the first matching locations are position p_a in AA and position p_b in B. Let A' be the length |A| substring of AA beginning at position p_a and B' the length |B| substring of BB beginning at position p_b. Let A* be $\mathrm{Next}^x(A')$ for that x such that the characters in matching locations of A* and B' are equal. Suppose A* = $a_1 \ldots a_N$, B' = $b_1 \ldots b_M$ and that the matching locations are $i_1,\ldots,i_L$ in A* and $j_1,\ldots,j_L$ in B'. Note that $i_1 = j_1 = 1$ and that $a_{i_k} = b_{j_k}$ for $1 \leq k \leq L$. We then define Pack(A,B) = $c_1 a_2 \ldots a_{i_2-1} b_2 \ldots b_{j_2-1} c_2 a_{i_2+1} \ldots a_{i_3-1} b_{j_2+1} \ldots b_{j_3-1} c_3 \ldots a_{i_{L-1}+1} \ldots a_{i_L-1} b_{j_{L-1}+1} \ldots b_{j_L-1} c_L a_{i_L+1} \ldots a_N b_{j_L+1} \ldots b_M$, where for $1 \leq k \leq L$, $c_k = a_{i_k} = b_{j_k}$.

For example, let q=0, A=abgcd, and B=fchae. Then A'=A=cdabg, B'=chaef, and Pack(A,B)=cdhabgef. Note that the first character 'c' and the fourth character 'a' belong to both strings A and B, while the other characters belong either to string A or string B, but not to both.

Now, for p strings $A_1,\ldots,A_p$, we define Pack$(A_1,\ldots,A_p)$ by Pack(... Pack(Pack$(A_1,A_2),A_3)$, ... $,A_p)$. Given a set of strings, they may be packed together in various ways. For example, for $\{A_1,A_2,A_3,A_4\}$, we may form Pack(Pack(Pack$(A_1,A_2),A_3),A_4)$, Pack(Pack(Pack$(A_3,A_4),A_1),A_2)$, or even Pack(Pack(A_1,A_4),Pack(A_2,A_3)). Each one of these will, no doubt, produce different results. We have found that when the strings are ordered on their lengths such that $|A_1| \geq |A_2| \geq \ldots \geq |A_p|$, then the previous definition produces good results. As an example, see Table 1, which lists |Pack$(A_1,\ldots,A_p)$|, $|A_1|+\ldots+|A_p|$, and their ratio, where $2 \leq p \leq 10$, for 10 boundary-code sequences, 6 of them from the images of Figure 3-8.

We now describe the voting procedure. Associated with Pack$(A_1,\ldots,A_p)$ will be a length |Pack$(A_1,\ldots,A_p)$| sequence of subsets of $\{1,\ldots,p\}$. Informally, each character of Pack$(A_1,\ldots,A_p)$ will 'vote' for a subset of strings from $\{A_1,\ldots,A_p\}$ to which it belongs.

Let A and B be two strings about to be packed and suppose that Vote_A and Vote_B are the sequences of votes associated with A and B, respectively. Define $\mathrm{Vote}_{A'}$ as the length |A| subsequence of $\mathrm{Vote}_A\mathrm{Vote}_A$ beginning at position p_a, and $\mathrm{Vote}_{B'}$ as the length |B| subsequence of $\mathrm{Vote}_B\mathrm{Vote}_B$ beginning at position p_b, where p_a and p_b are defined as before. Then, the sequence of votes $\mathrm{Vote}_{\mathrm{Pack}(A,B)}$ is defined by associating the following votes to each character of Pack(A,B) as previously defined. With c_k, $1 \leq k \leq L$, we associate the set of votes $\mathrm{Vote}_{A'}[i_k]$

Table 1
Length Saved by String Packing

Number of Strings	Sum of Individual Lengths	Length of Packed Superstring	Percentage Saving
2	394	271	31.2
3	581	293	49.6
4	765	330	56.9
5	948	354	62.7
6	1121	363	67.6
7	1287	379	70.6
8	1432	385	73.1
9	1564	389	75.1
10	1677	389	76.8

$\cup$ $Vote_{B'}[j_k]$, with a_d, $d \in \{2, \ldots, i_2-1, i_2+1, \ldots, i_3-1, \ldots, i_{L-1}+1, \ldots, i_L-1, i_L+1, \ldots, N\}$, we associate the set $Vote_{A'}[d]$, while with b_d, $d \in \{2, \ldots, j_2-1, j_2+1, \ldots, j_3-1, \ldots, j_{L-1}+1, \ldots, j_L-1, j_L+1, \ldots, M\}$, we associate the set $Vote_{B'}[d]$. This procedure is iterated in calculating $Vote_{Pack(A_1,\ldots,A_p)}$, for $p>2$.

In our previous example, where $q=0$, A=abgcd, and B=fchae, we have Pack(A,B)=cdgabgef and $Vote_{Pack(A,B)}$ = <{A,B}, {A}, {B}, {A,B}, {A}, {A}, {B}, {B}>.

Now, let S be a superstring and $Vote_S$ its associated sequence of votes. Suppose the votes are over strings $A_1,\ldots,A_p$. To find the strength of the match between an incoming string A and each of $A_1,\ldots,A_p$, we do the following. First we find the SWLqGCS of SS and A with window size $|S|$. For each $1 \le i \le p$, the ith substring A_i is extracted from S via the votes. If one of the characters of S is part of a matching pair and doesn't survive the extraction, that particular match is nullified. The strengths of the resulting matches are then calculated as in the previous section. Note that only a single pattern-match is done, while p separate strengths are calculated.

As an example, suppose $S = s_1 \ldots s_9$, $A = a_1 \ldots a_6$, $Vote_S$ = <$\{A_1,A_3\}$, $\{A_3\}$, $\{A_1,A_2,A_3\}$, $\{A_1,A_3\}$, $\{A_2\}$, $\{A_2\}$, $\{A_2,A_3\}$, $\{A_1,A_3\}$, $\{A_1\}$> for strings A_1, A_2, and A_3, and that a_2 matches with s_7, a_3 with s_8, a_5 with s_1, and a_6 with s_5. Then, the strength of the matches between A and A_1,A_2,A_3 are determined by examining the strings $a_3a_4a_5a_6a_1a_2$ and $s_8s_9s_1s_3s_4$ with matching pairs $\{<a_3,s_8>, <a_5,s_1>\}$, $a_2a_3a_4a_5a_6a_1$ and $s_7s_3s_5s_6$ with matching pairs $\{<a_2,s_7>, <a_6,s_5>\}$, and $a_2a_3a_4a_5a_6a_1$ and $s_7s_8s_1s_2s_3s_4$ with matching pairs $\{<a_2,s_7>, <a_3,s_8>, <a_5,s_1>\}$, respectively.

Rather than computing the strength of the match between an incoming string A and each of the database strings $A_1,\ldots,A_p$, we may cluster these strings together and compute the strength of the match between A and each of the clusters. Letting S and $Votes_S$ be as before, suppose we want to form a set of clusters $C_1,\ldots,C_d$, where for $1 \le i \le d$, C_i consists of strings $A_{j_1},\ldots,A_{j_i}$. Then, the clustered votes, CVote $= <V_1,\ldots,V_{|S|}>$, where for $1 \le k \le |S|$ and $1 \le i \le d$, $C_i \epsilon V_k$ if and only if $\{A_{j_1},\ldots,A_{j_i}\} \cap Votes_S[k] \neq \phi$.

Continuing our example, let cluster C_1 consist of strings A_1 and A_2, while cluster C_2 consists of string A_3. Then, CVote $= <\{C_1,C_2\}, \{C_2\}, \{C_1,C_2\}, \{C_1,C_2\}, \{C_1\}, \{C_1\}, \{C_1,C_2\}, \{C_1,C_2\}, \{C_1\}>$. The strength of the matches between A and C_1,C_2 are then determined by examining the strings $a_2a_3a_4a_5a_6a_1$ and $s_7s_8s_9s_1s_3s_4s_5s_6$ with matching pairs $\{<a_2,s_7>, <a_3,s_8>, <a_5,s_1>, <a_6,s_5>\}$, as well as $a_2a_3a_4a_5a_6a_1$ and $s_7s_8s_1s_2s_3s_4$ with matching pairs $\{<a_2,s_7>, <a_3,s_8>, <a_5,s_1>\}$.

Using appropriate clusters, we may be able to locate the closest match of an incoming string among D database strings in time $O(\log_2 D)$. This is done by dividing the database strings into two clusters, each cluster into two sub-clusters, and so on. The advantage of this approach is that the relatively expensive pattern-matching need be done only once, while the cheaper linear-time calculation of the match strengths are done $O(\log_2 D)$ times.

In our index experiments with clusters, we modified the procedure of calculating the match strength between an incoming string and a particular cluster. The characters in the cluster boundary-code which do not match characters in the incoming string can originate from any of the strings composing the cluster. Thus, including these characters in our match strength calculation may not be to our benefit. (This should not apply to clusters consisting of a single string, however.) We thus calculate the strength of a match using a greedy approach. A particular non-matching cluster character is included in the calculation only if it is locally helpful. More formally, we first transform the cluster via the Next operator so that the matching characters are equal. Now, each matching character of the incoming boundary-code corresponds to a point on the boundary of the segment whose boundary-code this is. Similarly, each matching character of the cluster boundary-code corresponds to a 2-D point. Of course, this latter point should be as close as possible to the corresponding point of the incoming boundary-code. We thus include a particular non-matching cluster character if it brings us closer to this point. When this scheme is used, we will refer to the **optimized match strength.**

We formed the superstring S = Pack(Pack(Pack(Pack(Pack(1,5),3),4),6),2), where i, for $1 \le i \le 6$, denotes SEG[i,0], where SEG[i,j] denotes segment i rotated j degrees. We then formed the clusters (((1) (6)) (((2) (4)) ((3) (5)))) and tried to locate various rotated strings using this clustering. See Table 2 for some of our results on segments rotated 15°, which are quite encouraging. How we arrived at this clustering will be described in a future paper.

Table 2
Cluster Comparisons

Incoming Segment	Cluster	Maximum Match Strength †Optimized
SEG[1,15]	((1) (6))	0.968†
	(((2) (4)) ((3) (5)))	0.954†
	(1)	0.973
	(6)	0.925
SEG[2,15]	((1) (6))	0.964†
	(((2) (4)) ((3) (5)))	0.988†
	((2) (4))	0.970†
	((3) (5))	0.965†
	(2)	0.932, 0.970†
	(4)	0.932, 0.911†
SEG[3,15]	((1) (6))	0.970†
	(((2) (4)) ((3) (5)))	0.982†
	((2) (4))	0.954†
	((3) (5))	0.976†
	(3)	0.944
	(5)	0.928
SEG[4,15]	((1) (6))	0.970†
	(((2) (4)) ((3) (5)))	0.980†
	((2) (4))	0.976†
	((3) (5))	0.974†
	(2)	0.897
	(4)	0.940
SEG[5,15]	((1) (6))	0.949†
	(((2) (4)) ((3) (5)))	0.971†
	((2) (4))	0.915†
	((3) (5))	0.971†
	(3)	0.959
	(5)	0.979
SEG[6,15]	((1) (6))	0.974†
	(((2) (4)) ((3) (5)))	0.968†
	(1)	0.904
	(6)	0.932

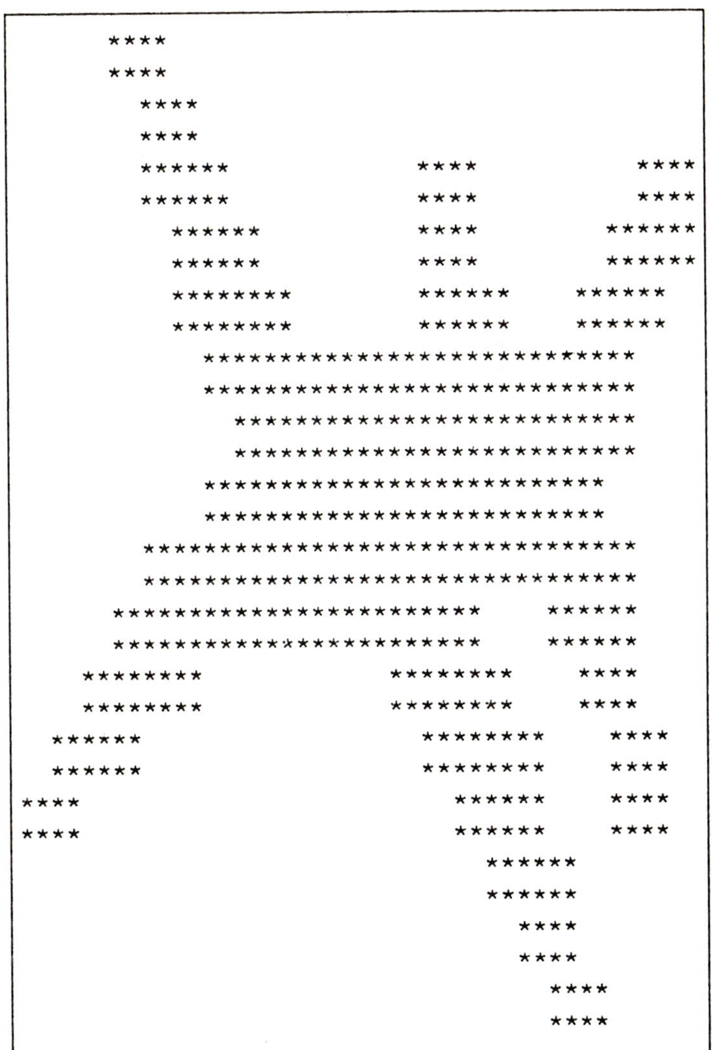

FIGURE 3 – SEGMENT #1

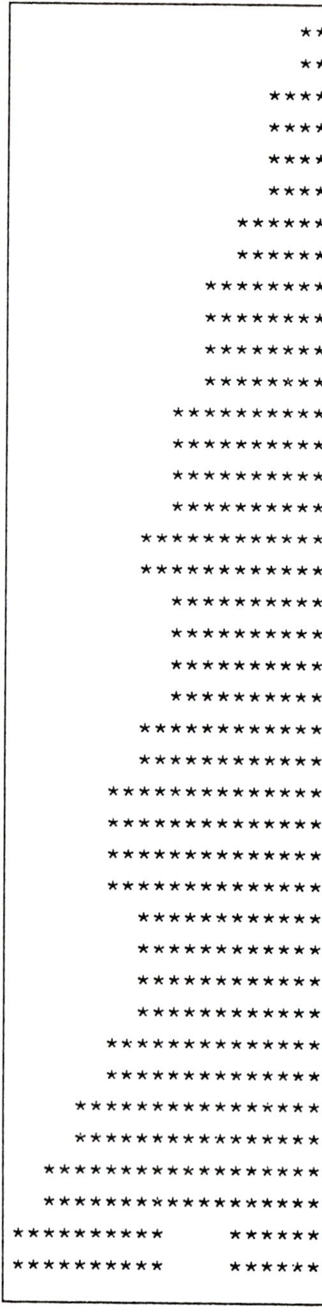

FIGURE 4 – SEGMENT #2

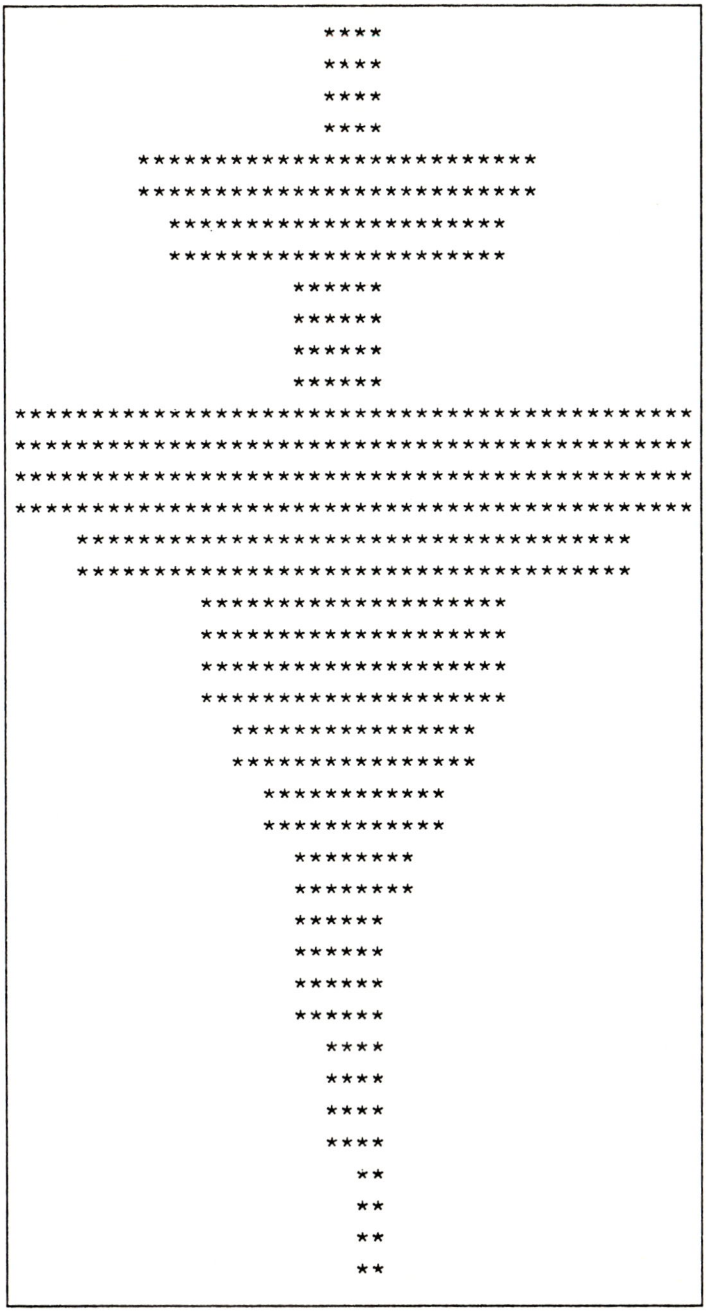

```
                    ****
                    ****
                    ****
                    ****
        **************************
        **************************
          **********************
          **********************
                  ******
                  ******
                  ******
                  ******
********************************************
********************************************
********************************************
********************************************
    ************************************
    ************************************
            ********************
            ********************
            ********************
            ********************
              ****************
              ****************
                ************
                ************
                  ********
                  ********
                  ******
                  ******
                  ******
                  ******
                    ****
                    ****
                    ****
                    ****
                      **
                      **
                      **
                      **
```

FIGURE 5 – SEGMENT #3

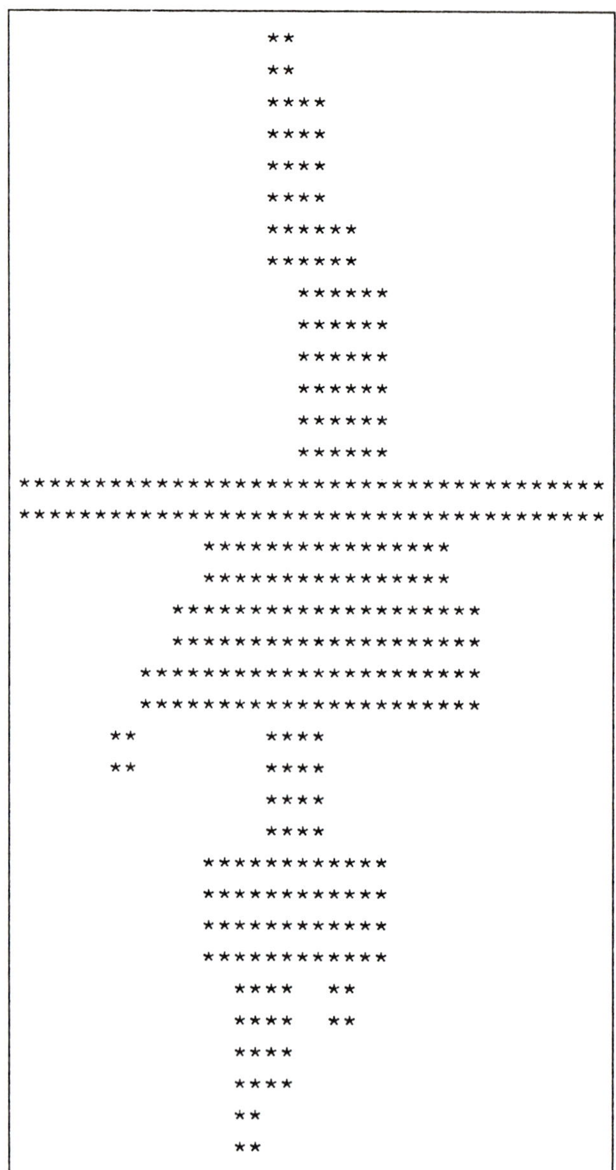

FIGURE 6 – SEGMENT #4

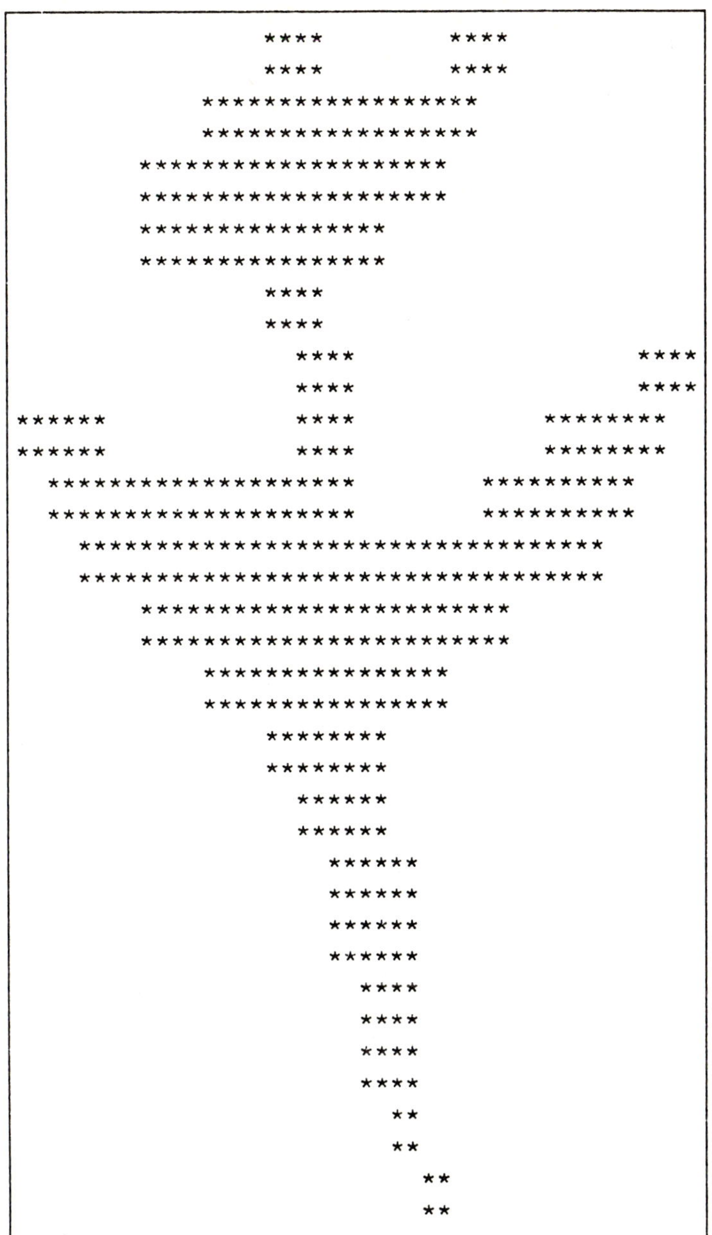

FIGURE 7 – SEGMENT #5

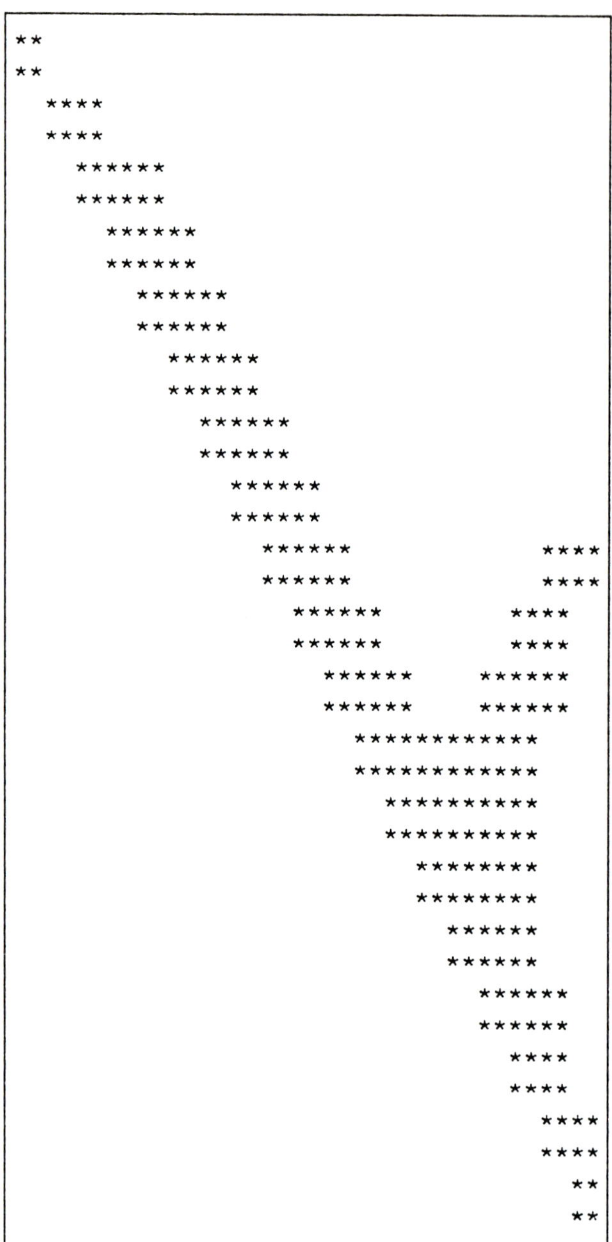

FIGURE 8 – SEGMENT #6

REFERENCES

[CDM77] S.K. Chang, N. Donato, B.H. McCormick, J. Reuss, and R. Rocchetti, 'A Relational Database System for Pictures,' **Proceedings of the IEEE Workshop on Picture Data Description and Management**, April 1977, pp. 142–149

[ChF80] N.S. Chang and K.S. Fu, 'Query-by-Pictorial-Example', **IEEE Transactions on Softwarc Engineering**, Volume SE-6 (1980), pp. 519–524

[Cod79] E.F. Codd, 'Extending the Database Relational Model to Capture More Meaning,' **ACM Transactions on Database Systems**, Volume 4 (1979), pp. 397–434

[Dav79] L.S. Davis, 'Shape Matching Using Relaxation Techniques,' **IEEE Transactions on Pattern Analysis and Machine Intelligence**, Volume PAMI-1 (1979), pp. 60–72

[GMS80] J. Gallant, D. Maier, and J.A. Storer, 'On Finding Minimal Length Superstrings,' **Journal of Computer and System Sciences**, Volume 20 (1980), pp. 50–58

[GrL83] W.I. Grosky and Y. Lu, 'Rotationally Invariant Pattern Matching of Boundary Codes,' **Proceedings of the Third Scandinavian Conference on Image Analysis**, Copenhagen, Denmark, 1983, pp. 109–114

[GrL84] W.I. Grosky and Y. Lu, 'Iconic Indexing Using Generalized Pattern Matching Techniques,' **Proceedings of the Seventh Conference on Pattern Recognition**, Montreal, Canada, 1984, pp. 1168–1170

[Gro84] W.I. Grosky, 'Toward a Data Model for Integrated Pictorial Databases,' **Computer Vision, Graphics and Image Processing**, Volume 25 (1984), pp. 371–382

[Hir77] D.S. Hirschberg, 'Algorithms for the Longest Common Subsequence Problem, **Journal of the ACM**, Volume 24 (1977), pp. 664–675

[HuS77] J.W. Hunt and T.G. Szymanski, 'A Fast Algorithm for Computing Longest Common Subsequences,' **Communications of the ACM**, Volume 20 (1977), pp. 350–353

[LiC80] B.S. Lin and S.K. Chang, 'GRAIN – A Pictorial Database Interface,' **Proceedings of the IEEE Workshop on Picture Data Description and Management**, August 1980, pp. 83–88

[Lie77] Y.E. Lien and D.F. Utter, 'Design of an Image Database,' **Proceedings of the IEEE Workshop on Picture Data Description and Management**, April 1977, pp. 131–136

[McR77] D.M. McKeown and D.R. Reddy, 'A Hierarchical Symbolic Representation for an Image Database,' **Proceedings of the IEEE Workshop on Picture Data Description and Management**, April 1977, pp. 40–44

[ShH81] L.G. Shapiro and R.M. Haralick, 'Structural Descriptions and Inexact Matching,' **IEEE Transactions on Pattern Analysis and Machine Intelligence**, Volume PAMI-3 (1981), pp. 504–519

[TaM77] H. Tamura and S. Mori, 'A Data Management System for Manipulating Large Images,' **Proceedings of the IEEE Workshop on Picture Data Description and Management**, April 1977, pp. 45–54

[Tan81] G.Y. Tang, 'A Management System for an Integrated Database of Pictures and Alphanumerical Data,' **Computer Graphics and Image Processing**, Volume 16 (1981), pp. 270–286

[TII79] Y. Takao, S. Itoh, and J. Iisaka, 'An Image-Oriented Database System,' In **Data Base Techniques for Pictorial Applications**, Edited by A. Blaser, Springer-Verlag, New York, 1979, pp. 527–538

EXPLOSION IN THE AMOUNT OF SATELLITE ACQUIRED IMAGE DATA AND THE REQUIREMENTS FOR NEW IMAGE DATA BASE SYSTEMS

Ergin Ataman
Electronics Division
TÜGAM Marmara Research Institute
Gebze - Kocaeli - Turkey

Digital image processing (IP) is one of the new branches of electrical engineering and computer science that has matured within the last decade or so. Development and widespread application of IP was catalyzed by several other developments in other branches of engineering. They are:

i) Tremendous increase in the performance/cost ratio of digital electronics and computers. Although many of the fundamental techniques of image processing and pattern analysis were suggested about three decades ago, they were not considered as "solutions" and was abandoned as their computational requirements far exceeded what was available then.

ii) Availability of CCD devices and other high quality low cost cameras for image acquisition and high resolution digital image displays and hard copy devices.

iii) Developments in robotics, medical imaging, ultrasonic,radar and infrared imaging, military surveillance satellites.

Another important dimension of the developments in IP is the explosive growth in the amount of available data in picture based information systems. A good example is seen in the area of geographic information systems where satellites are used for acquiring images of the earth.

The amount of data acquired by a satellite depends on the

NATO ASI Series, Vol. F 24
Database Machines. Edited by A. K. Sood and A. H. Qureshi

spatial, spectral and radiometric resolution of the image acquisition system on board and the visiting frequency of the satellite.

The MSS image acquisition system of the LANDSAT satellites has a spatial resolution of 80 m., spectral resolution of 4 bands (2 in the visible and 2 in the near infrared band), and a radiometric resolution of 6 bits/pixel. Each image covers an area of 185x185 km.

The new generation of LANDSAT satellites that is LANDSAT 4 and 5 bears an additional image acquisition system called "Thematic Mapper" (TM) which has spatial, spectral and radiometric resolution of 30 m., 6 bands and 8 bits/pixel respectively. TM also has another band in the thermal infrared with a spatial resolution of 120 m. Other important earth observing satellites are HCMM, SEASAT, NIMBUS and NOAA.

Currently, only two LANDSAT earth stations in Europe, Fucino, Italy and Kiruna, Sweden stations receive 38 Gigabytes of data from LANDSAT 4 and 5 every day. This amounts to 1.14 Terabytes of data/month from only these two satellites and for Europe only.

As the resolution and the number of satellites increase, the amount of geographical data will increase accordingly. In fact, the SPOT satellite that will be launched in late 1985 will bear two imaging systems with spatial resolutions of 10 m and 20 m.

The major algorithms used for processing the satellite images are:

i) Radiometric correction
ii) Geometric correction
iii) Registration
iv) Enhancement
v) Edge detection
vi) Filtering
vii) Clustering
viii) Classification
ix) Compression
x) Signature analysis and image understanding algorithms.
xi) Pattern recognition.

The explosion in the amount of image data requires new computer architectures and software systems for storage, retrieval, processing and analysis of image data. It should be noted that, there are many types of images and each type might require a different type of architecture and algorithms. The images acquired by the satellites are multi gray level and generally multispectral (i.e. color) images. However, the images used in many applications are only binary (or two gray level) images such as graphics.

In multispectral image applications, the emphasis is usually on classification of the images or extraction of some information such as roads or geographic structures etc., whereas the emphasis in the binary image applications is often on identification of patterns out of a known pattern menu.

Pictorial information is used in many areas other than the geographic information systems, e.g. in medical diagnosis, robotics, CAD/CAM, image based text processing systems etc. [1,2]. As the requirements of different application areas might be different, a pictorial data base system developed for one area may not be much use in another area. Moreover, unless information in images can be extracted and represented in the form of alphanumeric strings as attributes of the images, the classical data base systems cannot be used either. However, in general, extraction of the attributes of an image is a very difficult problem even in cases one knows what to look for. Therefore, some new data base systems concepts and architectures are needed to solve this problem. In view of the very large amount of data, one has to look for fast and simple rather than powerful but slow techniques.

REFERENCES

[1] S.K.Chang, "Image Information Systems", Proc. IEEE, Vol.73, No.4, April 1985, pp. 754-763.

[2] S.K.Chang, Ed, IEEE Computer Mag. Special Issue on "Pictorial Information Systems", Vol. 14, No.11, Nov. 1981.

INTEGRATION OF FACT/DOCUMENT RETRIEVAL SYSTEMS INCORPORATING THE SUPPORT OF A DATABASE MACHINE AND A CLUSTERING SCHEME

Fazlı CAN
Department of Electrical & Electronics Engineering
Middle East Technical University
Ankara-Turkey

I. INTRODUCTION

The demands for effective and timely retrieval of facts and documents are constantly increasing. Also, the global information structures of applications are more sophisticated than ever before, requiring representations of complex relationships among facts as well as documents. An efficient and effective retrieval environment should therefore, integrate the mechanisms of both Information Retrieval System (IRS) and Database Management System (DBMS). One cannot merely incorporate some string operations into a DBMS data language or store keywords as an attribute of a formatted database. One cannot implement DBMS functionalities as file programs embedded within an IR system. Such an effort would lack the advantages of DBMS such as data independence, real time response, and ad hoc query formulation capability. On the other hand, the unique features of IR cannot be fitted into the deterministic, non-iterative nature of DBMS data manipulations.

The answer for the proper integration lies in a synthesis that will combine IRS and DBMS by preserving their unique features in such a way that the advantages of both systems can be shared.

In this paper, an experimental system, which aims to synthesize a relational DBMS and an IRS capable of context sensitive full text searches, is presented. -In the text, Information Retrieval (IR), Text Retrieval (TR), and Document Retrieval (DR) phrases will be used interchangeably.- The IR system relies on a clustering subsystem for database partitioning and relation fragmentation. The clustering subsystem uses a seed oriented, partitioning type classification based on the new concept called cover coefficient [2,3,4]. The support architecture for the context sensitive search operations is the RAP.3 database machine. The use of the RAP.3 machine brings all of its capabilities into such an integration [8,9].

NATO ASI Series, Vol. F 24
Database Machines. Edited by A. K. Sood and A. H. Qureshi

In the remainder of the paper, firstly a brief description of the hardware for text retrieval operations is given. This is followed by a model for the integration of DBMS and IRS. Two basic subsystems of the model are a clustering subsystem and a support system for the realization of the context sensitive text retrieval operations. The clustering subsystem uses a seed oriented, partitioning type classification based on the new concept called cover coefficient. The aim of the clustering subsystems is to narrow the data to be searched by the text retrieval hardware to a reasonable size. The support system uses the RAP.3 database machine. In the paper, it is shown that the fundamental unformatted text retrieval problem is solved with the formatted data structure approach without destroying the context dependent nature of the problem. The text retrieval primitives incorporated with RAP.3 and a brief description of the query processing strategy of the integrated system are also given.

2. HARDWARE SOLUTIONS FOR TEXT RETRIEVAL

The hardware organizations specializing in text retrieval operations are called "text retrieval computers". In general, text retrieval computers have the basic architecture presented in Figure 1 [6] and this architecture is especially suitable for free (full) text systems. (In free text systems, all the text of documents are scanned in query processing.)

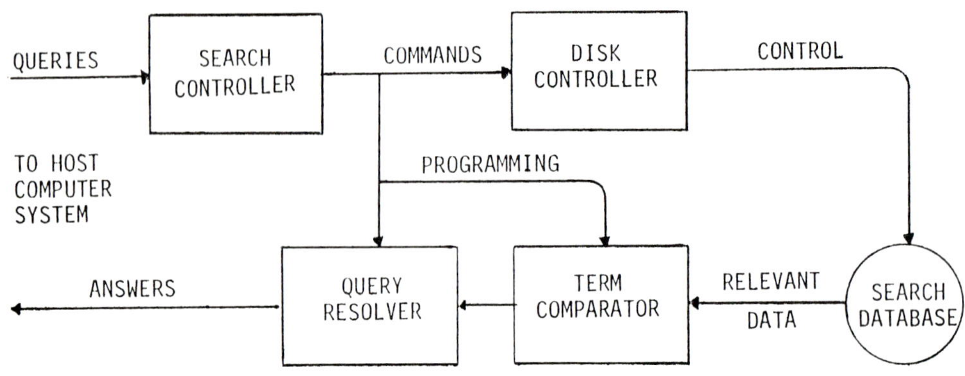

Figure 1. Text retrieval computer.

In this organization, the text retrieval query issued by the user is taken by the "search controller" which controls the overall operation of the system. It sends the programming information to the units called "query resolver" and "term comparator". Search controller also sends some commands to a"disk controller";these commands will fetch relevant data from the search database into the"term comparator unit".The term comparator unit performs a fast matching operation with the terms and phrases specified in the query. Further qualification tests (such as to see if the match occurs in the proper context, i.e., to see if the proximity of the match is proper with respect to a previous match, etc.) on data are done in the query resolver. The fully qualified data items are returned to the host computer as the answers. The answer is usually in the form of whereabouts for the documents which satisfy the query requirments.

In the text retrieval computer architecture, the system bottleneck rest in the term comparator. There are three main approaches to build the term comparator [6] :

a) Cellular Automata;
b) Finite State Automata;
c) Parallel Associative Array.

In (a), the basic building block is a cell element which can match a single character. For complex queries, cascade operation of the cell elements and hardwired query resolution are needed. In (b), an automaton is constructed for each search pattern which appears in the query. For real life problems, large number of cells and their dynamic and flexible interconnections must be constructed for the former, and a large automaton with a large number of states would be necessary for the later. In (c), one can utilize the structure of the RAP.3 database machine to make it also a text retrieval computer [1,4,8,9] . This will be illustrated in section 3.2.

For information retrieval there are some other approaches. For example the proposal on constructing fast index processors to speed inverted list intersection and merge [5] . However, such an architecture is not categorized as a text retrieval computer.

Typical text retrieval operations are listed in the following [6] :

A : Finds any document that contains the word A.

A or B : Finds any document that contains either the word A or B.

(A,B) IN SENT : Finds any document that contains both the word A and word B in the same sentence (specified context).

A B : Finds any document that contains the word A immediately followed by the word B.

A....B : Finds any document that contains the word A (either immediately or after an arbitrary number of words) by the word B.

<A.n.B > : Finds any document that contains the word A folloled by the word B within n words (directed proximity).

<A,B > n : Finds any document that contains the words A and B within n words of each other (undirected proximity).

A???B : Finds any document that contains the word A, followed by fixed length don't care characters, then folloled by the word B.

A * B : Finds any document that contains the word A, followed zero or more characters, then followed by the word B.

3. A MODEL FOR INTEGRATED FACT/DOCUMENT INFORMATION SYSTEMS

In this section, an experimental system, which aims to synthesize a relational DBMS and IRS capable of context sensitive full text searches is presented. The IRS relies on a clustering subsystem. The support architecture for the context sensitive search operations is the RAP.3 database machine.

The integrated database management and information retrieval system, IS, is described by a 6-tuple:

$$IS = < R, D, Q, C, E, T >$$

where R represents a set of relations which contain structured data about the documents or document entities. The nature of the interrelationships among the structured entities will be described by means of the E/R (entity/relationship) conceptual data model. D represents the documents.

Q is a set of user queries. A given query, Q, is defined as

$$Q = \{ Q_T, Q_R \}$$

where Q_T is the part of the query that holds the content sensitive, document search specification.

Q_R is the part of the query that holds search specification on the $\{R, D\}$ set operable by the DBMS instruction set.

C is a hierarchical structure of clusters for D. (In the context of information retrieval, the term cluster indicates a homogeneous group of documents such that the documents within a group are more strongly associated with each other than those in different groups [2].)

E is a mapping function, called the evaluation function, $E: Q \rightarrow 2^D$, used to find the relevant documents to a query [11] . In reality, a subset of the range of this mapping is reached through the complex operations of clustering, building hierarchies of clusters, implementing search functions for these hierarchies, and using feedback. T represents the terms used for the description of documents.

3.1. Clustering Subsystem

The clustering subsystem uses a seed oriented, partitioning type classification based on the new concept called cover coefficient [2,3,4] . The starting point is a document by term (mxn) matrix. This means that m documents $\{d_1, d_2 .... d_m\}$ (i.e., the collection) are defined by n terms $\{t_1, t_2, ..., t_n\}$. Each document-i, $d_i (1 \leq i \leq m)$, is defined by a document (description) vector of size n: $(d_{11}, d_{12}, ... d_{in})$. The vector entries can be either binary (0 or 1) or weighted (non-negative real numbers). The clustering process will produce a cluster partitions: $P=\{C_1, C_2, ... C_{n_c}\}$, where C_i will be a non-empty cluster and $C_i \cap C_j = \Phi$ for $i \neq j$ (i.e., there is no overlapping among clusters.

In the D matrix each document is described by at least one term and each term describes at least one document.

The D matrix is mapped into a cover coeffjcient matrix, C of size mxm [2,4] . The C matrix is obtained by two matrices S and S'. Two matrices S and S' are defined from the D matrix as follows:

$$s_{ij} = d_{ij} / \left(\sum_{k=1}^{n} d_{ik} \right), \quad s'_{ij} = d_{ij} / \left(\sum_{k=1}^{m} d_{kj} \right) \quad \text{for } 1 \leq i \leq m \text{ and } 1 \leq j \leq n.$$

The normalizations can be interpreted as:

s_{ij}: significance of t_j for d_i

s'_{ij}: significance of d_i for t_j

The C matrix is defined as $C = S x S'^{\tau}$ where τ is the matrix transpose operation. An element of C is obtained as

$$c_{ij} = \sum_{k=1}^{n} s_{ik} x s'^{\tau}_{kj} = \sum_{k=1}^{n} (\text{significance of } t_k \text{ in } d_i) x (\text{significance of } d_j \text{ for } t_k)$$

$$= \alpha_i \sum_{k=1}^{n} d_{ik} x \beta_k x d_{jk}$$

where α_i and β_k are the inverse of the sum of row-i and column-k respectively.

Each entry of C, c_{ij}, indicates the extent with which d_i is covered by d_j. The properties of the C matrix are the following: (1) $0 \leq c_{ij} < 1$ for $i \neq j$ and $c_{ii} > 0$: a document may or may not be covered $-c_{ij} \geq 0-$ by other documents, however, it is always covered by itself $-c_{ii} > 0-$;(2) each row sum is equal to 1;(3) $c_{ii} \geq c_{ij}$: a document is covered mostly by itself, others can cover it as much as itself;(4) $c_{ij}=0$ implies $c_{ji}=0$ and $c_{ij} > 0$ implies $c_{ji} > 0$. However, in the latter case, it is generally $c_{ij} \neq c_{ji}$–i.e., coverage is mutual, however generally, not symmetric–. (The properties of the C matrix and the algorithm concepts to be defined are also valid for a weighted D matrix with some minor modifications [4].)

Each diagonal entry of the C matrix, c_{ii}, is the decoupling (uniqueness) coefficient of d_i, δ_i. The sum of the off-diagonal entries of row-i, yields the coupling coefficient, Ψ_i, of d_i.

From the properties of the C matrix: $0 < \delta_i \leq 1$, $\Psi_i = 1 - \delta_i$ and hence $0 \leq \Psi_i < 1$ for $1 \leq i \leq m$. A document that shares a large number of terms with the other documents will have a large Ψ_i but a low δ_i value. If a document d_i does not have any common term with the other documents, i.e., $\sum_{k=1}^{n} d_{ik} x d_{jk} = 0$ for $1 \leq j \leq m$ and $j \neq i$, then its decoupling coefficient (δ_i) will be 1.

Coupling and decoupling can be computed for the entire collection as:

$$\delta = \sum_{i=1}^{m} \delta_i / m \ , \qquad \Psi = 1 - \delta \qquad (0 < \delta \leq 1 \ , \ 0 \leq \Psi < 1)$$

The theoretically implied number of clusters, n_c, needed for the collection is estimated as:

$$n_c = (\text{decoupling coefficient of the collection}) x (\text{number of documents})$$

$$= \delta x m = \sum_{i=1}^{m} \delta_i = \text{trace}(C)$$

The average number of documents per cluster, d_c, is given by $d_c = m/(\delta x m) = 1/\delta$.

The cluster seeds are selected by a new concept called the cluster seed power. The cluster seed power, p_i of d_i is defined as $p_i = \delta_i x \Psi_i x t_i$ where $t_i = \sum_{j=1}^{n} d_{ij}$ is the number of terms in the document description vector of d_i. In p_i, δ_i and Ψ_i contributes the isolation of clusters and compactness among the members of a cluster, respectively; t_i provides normalization.

The documents are assigned to the cluster seeds with respect to either a single-pass or a multi-pass algorithm [2,4]. A brief description of the single-pass algorithm is the following:

1) Determine the first n_c cluster seeds from the first highest p_i.
2) Repetitively do for i=1,m: If d_i is not a cluster seed then find the cluster which maximally covers it, i.e. max (c_{is_j}) where s_j, $1 <= j <= n_c$, is the seed documents.
3) For the remaining unclustered documents, either form a ragbag (common) cluster or compare the documents with the documents of the clusters already formed to find a maximal cover for each document and add the document into the respective cluster.

Implementation of the algorithm does not require the construction of the whole C matrix. The algorithm is independent of the order of documents and has a complexity of 0(mlogm) [2,4] .

After forming the clusters each of them is described by a cluster representation vector (centroid) [2,11] .

The aim of the clustering subsystem is to narrow the data to be searched by the text retrieval hardware to a reasonable size.

Once the clusters are formed, the system can search them by comparing the centroid vectors with that of the user query (it is referred to as Q_s in section 3.3) returning the selected documents for the full text search. If, however, there are a very large number of clusters making the linear (single level) cluster search prohibitive a hierarchy of clusters (tree), HCT, can be constructed for a sublinear search.

In dynamic environments of very large databases where clustering becomes a bottleneck, a sample of documents can be used to constract a HCT of core clusters [11] . The remaining documents can be entered to this HCT by using the same search strategy applied for user queries.

In our case, one can easily compute the theoretically implied number of clusters, n_c, for the collection with a procedure of $0(mn_{avg})$ complexity [2,4] , where n_{avg} is the average number of terms in the documents. (A rough estimation for n_c based on the cover coefficient concept can also be made: $n_c=(mxn)/t$ [3,4]. Where, t is the total number of term assignments in the D matrix, i.e. $t=\sum_{i=1}^{m}\sum_{j=1}^{n} d_{ij}$.)

In the search of the HCT, one may stop at an intermediate node, depending on the search strategy. However, one should get to one of the lowest level (leaf) cluster under that node to add the document being processed. In such cases, one can pick the cluster with the maximum cluster seed power for the seed document [4,9].

3.2. Text Retrieval With The RAP Database Machine

The approach to be presented in this section can be classified as the cellular/parallel associative approach. The current version of RAP, which is RAP.3, emphasizes the utilization of LSI components, inexpensive LSI memories, off-the-shelf microprocessors, and firmware query processing [7,10].

The RAP. 3 database machine uses parallel cells and microprocessors in each cell [7,10]. Each microprocessor executes firmware of query routines implementing DBMS and IR instructions. The entire device memory, which is equal to the union of cell memories, is made to work like an associative memory. The microprocessors of each cell executes query routines on the tuples of the cell memory in parallel. The device memory is a quasi associative memory. In the microprocessor of each cell, efficient string search is performed [1,4,8]. The complexity of this operation is of the order 0(m) character comparisons where m is the length of the literal text attribute in a RAP.3 tuple. The increase in efficiency due to hardware will be by a factor (kxn) where k is the number of parallel microprocessors (subcells) within each cell and n is the number of parallel cells in the device [10].

The multi-microprocessor approach for the cell architecture restructured the RAP cell in yet another array of independently operating subcells. The tuples of a relation are loaded into the memory buffers related with each subcell and a data move strategy is incorporated to allow for parallel processing of consecutive tuples of a "RAP relation" [10]. A RAP relation is a normalized relation augmented with a set of mark attributes. Accordingly, each RAP tuple instance has a set of mark (tag) bits ahead of n-tuple values. A RAP tuple can be seen in Figure 2.

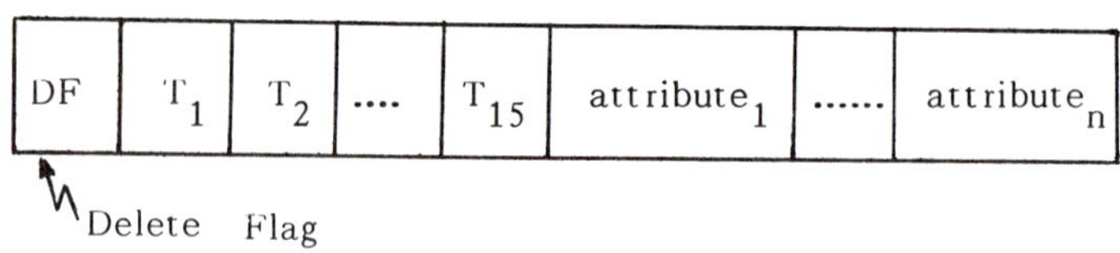

Figure.2. RAP tuple structure.

3.2.1. RAP Assembler Language

The RAP assembler language also known as the RAP DBMS Assembler is relationally complete [10]. The RAP DBMS Assembler has the following general syntax:

< label> < opcode><specification >< qualification > < parameter>

The label is a symbolic instruction address, the opcode is the operation to be performed, and a specification has the following format:

< relation > (< attribute-1 > , < attribute-2 > ,..., <attribute-s >)

A qualification is a Boolean expression (possibly null) of simple conditions Q_i where Q_i is one of the following: (a) MKED (tc) denoting any combination of true (i.e., set) mark bits; (b) UNMKED (tc) denoting any combination of false (i.e., reset) mark bits; (c) <attribute> <comparator > <operand > where comparator is one a relational operator (like > , < ,etc.) and <operand> is a numeric or literal constant, or another attribute name. < parameter> specifies the second operands in arithmetic operations. (For the full explanation of RAP.3 instructions one may refer to [10].)

The operation of each instruction is iterative due to its associative nature. An instruction, directly works on the memory contents, evaluates the qualification stated on the tuple contents, and executes the opcode on the tuple contents if the qualification holds for the tuple contents. A given instruction is terminated after all tuples of the relation are processed in parallel.

3.2.2. How To Support Unformatted Data in Database Architectures

For text retrieval operations with RAP.3 a set of related documents constitutes a relation. The query term matching operation on this relation can be either done on a limited portion of the relation or on its entirety. The limitation of the search will be done by document clustering.

The integration of the text retrieval capability to RAP will give emphasis to the following points:

a) Domain type must support literals;
b) Domain length must be variable for literal types;
c) Efficient string search primitives must be incorporated;
d) Sentence structure and adjacency must be recognized;

e) A way of processing unformatted data with formatted data structures must be found; and,

f) Resolution capability must be added to operations supported in (c) and (d) in order to support text retrieval operations.

The requirement of (a) has already been provided by RAP.3. The change made in RAP allows a literal data type to be as long as a tuple itself. RAP.3 also provides variable length tuple to store the unstructured document attribute. The requirement of (c) will be provided by fast pattern matching algorithms. Text representation within the RAP.3 relation tuples will satisfy the requirements of the items (d) and (e). The (query) resolution requirement of item (f) will be provided by the RAP assembler language.

The following is the format specification for text representation in the RAP.3 relations.

a) Each tuple may contain one (or more) complete sentences.
b) The first tuple of each document starts with a blank.
c) As with standard typing rules, at least one blank should follow a punctuation mark.
d) At the end of a sentence an End of Sentence EOS marker is placed following a period. EOS must be followed with at least one blank.
e) The last tuple of the document terminates with an End of Document (EOD) character.

The following is the layout of a RAP.3 tuple to be used in text retrieval operations:

D F	Mark Bits	D_1 Long text attribute (variable length)	ND_1	ND_2	D_4	.....	D_n

Accordingly, a document file corresponds to a RAP.3 relation. This relation can hold one or more clusters of documents, or for large clusters can also be horizontally split. The associated storage overhead is the same in file representations with the exception of one or two words per tuple reserved for tagging (marking) of data. Complete sentences from the documents are mapped into the D_1 attribute of consecutive tuples.

The ND_1 and ND_2 attributes of the integer domain are needed for the internal use of the context sensitive, text retrieval operations. D_4 is the key attribute, which is a unique document identifier. D_5 through D_n are the attributes reserved for formatted data. That is, in one relation, we can store both the formatted and unformatted data if they are needed for the convenience and efficiency of processing.

3.2.3. RAP.3 DBMS Assembler Commands for Text Retrieval

As can be seen from the RAP.3 text mapping scheme, an important problem of text retrieval is the need to maintain text contiguity both in string searches and context resolutions. This problem has been solved, to a great extent, by the variable length text attribute feature of RAP.3. By this feature, some context resolution problems, such as splitting a text word between tuples (called term overflow) and passing overflow information to subsequent tuples to finalize the search, are inherently solved. However, there still remains the problem of context resolution for the text retrieval operations of the type A...B and < A,B > n. This is because the specified context might not be satisfied within a tuple. The necessary information for context resolution is passed from tuple to tuple by a feature referred to as link passing. The following gives the syntax definition of the new RAP.3 DBMS Assembler commands needed to perform the text search, and link pass operations [1,4,8,9] :

```
MATCH(tc) [ rel(atr1 { ,atr2 { , atr3 }} ):qual ] { [ lit ] }
MATCH-WS(tc) [ rel (atr1 { ,atr2 } ):qual ]{ [ lit] }
MATCH-WWC(tc) [ rel(atr1 { ,atr2 { , atr3} } ):qual ]{ [ lit] } { [int] }
LİNK-PASS(tc1,tc2 ) [ rel( { atr1, } atr2) ]
```

where

$\underline{tc_i}$ combination of tag (mark) bits t_1 through t_{13}.

$\underline{rel}$ is the relation name of the document.

$\underline{atr_i}$ $1 \leq i \leq n$ (maximum tuple length is 1024 bytes) are the attributes of the relation corresponding to $D_1, ND_1, ND_2, D_4, \ldots, D_n$ in the RAP.3 tuple layout shown earlier.

$\underline{qual}$ Boolean qualification expression.

$\underline{int}$ is a positive integer.

{ } indicates options.

$\underline{lit}$ is the literal constant corresponding to the search pattern. Examples of search patterns are: 'AA'?'BB', 'A'??'BB', 'AA'??'BB'3?'C' where an ? correspond to variable length don't care (VLDC) and fixed length don't care (FLDC) character respectively, and int? indicates repetetions of?

The first match instruction searches for the equality of the search pattern, in the text stored in atrl and tc marks all the qualified tuples within the cell storing the document; atr2 gives the beginning search offset within the text string (i.e., atrl). If atr2 is not specified then the search offset is taken as 0. If atr3 is specified, all occurrences of the search pattern within atrl are determined and the total number of occurrences is stored in atr3, within each tuple. The difference of the second match instruction is that the first occurrence of the search pattern is found within the sentence of atrl. The entire match should be contained within a sentence. The third match instruction finds the first occurrence of the search pattern, bypassing at most int number of words of the text. The value of int can be specified explicity, or implicitly by atr3.

During execution of the third match instruction, if the search pattern is not found and the search context specified by the word count is not satisfied within a tuple, then t14 mark bit of that tuple is set. This specific case is called an overflow condition and can occur only during the execution of the MATCH-WWC instruction, since the context of a match is always satisfied in the other types of the match instructions. The LINK-PASS instruction takes one memory cycle to execute and resolve the overflow condition in those tuples marked for overflow. The resolution requires resetting the t14 mark bit (tc2 in the instruction syntax) of the tuples marked for overflow, setting tc1 bits of the subsequent tuples, and passing the unprocessed (i.e., remaining) count values into the predetermined attributes of the subsequent tuples.

In the other use of the LINK-PASS instruction, when the literal attribute atrl is specified, if a tuple is tc2 marked and its atrl attribute does not contain an EOD character then the following tuple(s) of this document will be tc1 marked and their atr2 is set to zero. This feature of the LINK-PASS instruction is used to set the search context of the text retrieval operation A....B.

In the match commands the search pattern can be specified explicity (by lit) or implicitly (if lit is not specified it is available in the RAP register REGU-1).

It is assumed that the don't care character will not match an EOS character. This semantic property of search patterns prevents the occurrence of an overflow during term matching.

In the RAP.3 text retrieval system, a great portion of the context dependent query resolution takes place in the operation of the new text retrieval commands whose basic task is term matching. For example, sentence structure and adjacency are recognized as an integral part of the operations. Such resolution operations constitude a totally separate task in most other text retrieval systems. For the execution of the context sensitive text retrieval operations of the more complex nature (such as (A,B) IN SENT, A....B, < A.n.B > , < A,B > n); however, more sophisticated resolutions are required. The resolutions are embedded in the logic of small RAP.3 programs. To aid the user, each of these programs are made general purpose text retrieval macros running under the macro processor RAPMAC [4,8,9] .

3.3. QUERY PROCESSING IN THE INTEGRATED SYSTEM

In the integrated information system, a user request, Q, such as "Find those documents which are referenced by the papers written by JOHN DOE and by the papers containing the phrase SEMANTIC DATA MODEL and AGGREGATION in the same sentence" would require both DBMS and IR specific operations in an interrelated sequence of processing steps. The subset of Q dealing with DBMS and IRS type activities are referred to as Q_R and Q_T, respectively. Q_T of the above query deals with the context sensitive search SEMANTIC DATA MODEL and AGGREGATION in the same sentence. While Q_T will be preserved for final processing in the RAP.3, a query called the system query Q_s will be derived from Q_T to initiate a search of the relevant clusters in the database. This search is carried out to narrow the search space, before the full text search can be conducted.

A Q_s query will include those terms of the Q_T that are included in the set of index terms of the collection with a possible inclusion of certain other components to increase system effectiveness. Figure 3 shows an abstract view of the query processing environment. With Q_s, a hierachy of clusters will be searched and the corresponding data D_{Q_s} will be returned when the cluster search is optimally terminated by the use of evaluation function E. The two resulting sets of data D_{Q_R} and D_{Q_s}, corresponding to DBMS and IRS operations, respectively, will be jointly processed by the integrated system -f(Q_{SR})- to produce the user's response. The user may ask the system to repeat the operation by providing an indication of the relevant/irrelevant documents. With this feedback, Q_s will be modified and the previous cluster selection will be refined.

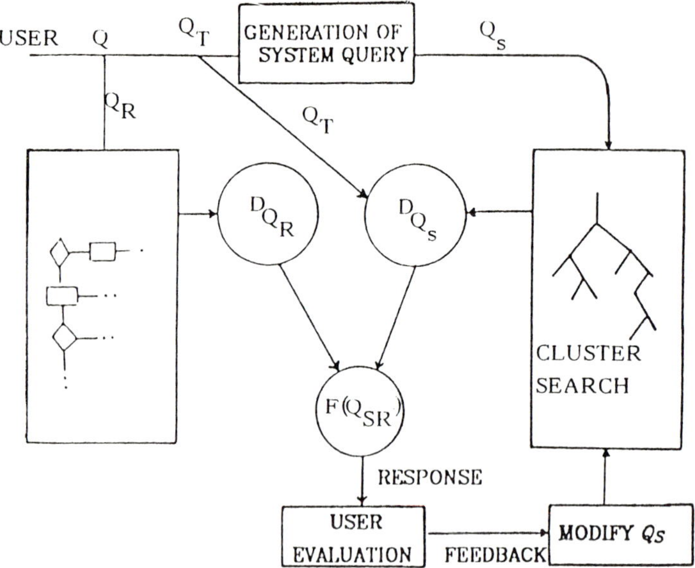

Figure 3. Abstract view of the query processing environment.

4. CONCLUSIONS

In this paper an integration model is proposed for DBMS and IRS. The proposed model relies on a clustering subsystem for database partitioning and relation fragmentation. For the implementation, the concepts of the single-pass algorithm, which is presented in Section 3.1 is proposed. The support architecture for the search operations is the RAP.3 database machine.

The proposed integration is expected to be efficient due to following main features: (a) The IR features are based on the efficient string search operations and the context sensitive full text commands carry out query resolution to a great extent; (b) Clustering is used as an efficient IR index; (c) IR features are integrated with DBMS at the primitive level and the integration of DBMS and IRS at the primitive level results in minimum layers of software which contributes to overall system efficiency; (d) There are no need for a separate computer for query resolution and the necessary communication of term matches since all those functions are handled in the RAP.3 system.

5. REFERENCES

[1] Can,F., Ozkarahan,E.A."Text Retrieval With the RAP Database Machine", Comp.Eng.Dept., Middle East Tech.Univ.,Tech.Rep.ISDB-10;June 1981.

[2] Can,F.,Ozkarahan,E.A."Two Partitioning Type Clustering Algorithms" Journal of the American Society for Information Science. 35(5) :268-276;1984.

[3] Can,F., Ozkarahan,E.A."Concepts of the Cover Coefficient Based Clustering Algorithm" Proc.of the 8th Annual SIGIR Conf.,ACM.Montreal,pp.204-211; June 1985

[4] Can,F.,"A New Clustering Scheme and Its Use in an Information Retrieval System Incorporating the Support of a Database Machine." Ph.D. Dissertation, Middle East Tech.Univ., Ankara, Jan.1985.

[5] Hollaar,L.A.,"Specialized Merge Processor Networks for Combining Sorted Lists." ACM Transactional on Database Systems. 3(3):272-284; 1978.

[6] Hollaar, L.A."Text Retrieval Computers."Computer,12(3):40-50;1979.

[7] Oflazer,K.,Ozkarahan,E.A.,Smith,K.C."RAP.3-A Multi-microprocessor Cell Architecture for the RAP Database Machine." Proc.of Int.Workshop on High Level Language Computer Architecture. pp.108-119;May 1980.

[8] Ozkarahan,E.A.,Can,F.,"Integration of Fact/Document Retrieval Systems Within a Database Machine", Dept.of Computer Science,Tech.Rep.TR-88-02, Arizona State University; Nov.1982.

[9] Ozkarahan, E.A.,Can,F."An Integrated Fact/Document Information System for Office Automation." Information Technology: Research and Development. 3(3):142-156; 1984.

[10] Ozkarahan,E.A. Database Machines and Database Management. Englewood Cliffs, N.J.: Prentice-Hall; 1985.

[11] Van Rijsbergen, C.J. Information Retrieval, 2nd ed. London: Butterworths 1979.

A VLSI processor for concurrent list intersection

D. D. Caviglia, E. Boveri, C. Merlo, E. Di Zitti, G. M. Bisio

Dipartimento di Ingegneria Biofisica ed Elettronica
Universita' di Genova, Italy.

Abstract

The functionality, architecture and design of a VLSI array processor for list intersection is presented. A NMOS implementation on a 5×5 mm^2 chip, with lambda rules using a 2.5 μm line witdth process is considered. The resulting chip, totaling 55,000 transistors, is organized in 16 comparison and 15 supply cells operating cuncurrently. Limits and potentialities of the processor are discussed.

1. Introduction.

VLSI special processors can be designed to perform directly in hardware intersection operations of two or more lists of data belonging to a large database. Different array structures have been proposed for this task [1,2,3]. Among them the **CID** (**C**ontinuous **I**ntersection **D**evice) [3], allowing continuous loading of the different intersecting processors in the array, looks most effective. In this paper some major modifications to the original CID architecture and its complete design are presented.

2. Processor functionality and architecture.

2.1 Generalities.

Let **T** and **R** be two unsorted lists of integers of cardinality $|T|$ and $|R|$ respectively:

$$\mathbf{T} = \{t_i\} \qquad i = 1,2,\ldots,|T|$$

$$\mathbf{R} = \{r_j\} \qquad j = 1,2,\ldots,|R|$$

NATO ASI Series, Vol. F 24
Database Machines. Edited by A. K. Sood and A. H. Qureshi

the output intersected list , **I**, is defined as follows:

$$\mathbf{I} = \mathbf{T} \cap \mathbf{R}$$

The intersection operation requires the comparison of each t_i element with each r_j element. However, if one assumes, as it is often the case, that both lists do not have duplicated elements, the comparison of each t_i element can be interrupted as soon as the match occurs.

Having a chain of P comparators the intersection operation can be performed comparing simultaneously P elements t_i with the entire **R** list which is kept running along the processor chain in a circular fashion, using a RAM buffer . Each element t_i in the intersector chain can be unloaded after being compared with all r_j elements or as soon as a match occurs, leaving its place to a new incoming t_i element (*Continuous Intersection*).

To achieve good performances it is necessary to timely supply a new t_i element each time a comparator needs it . Fig. 1 illustrates the processor architecture, consisting of two sections : *Supply Section* and *Comparison Section*. The leaves of the Supply Section keep a new t_i element close by each comparison cell. In this way the turnaround of t_i elements occurs without any idle time. Each element of the lists is accompanied by a short descriptor field (1-bit for t_i and 2-bit for r_j elements) that indicates what operation are to be performed on it.

2.2 Comparison Section.

The Comparison Section is a linear array of processors with next neighbour connection which are fed by the leaf-cells of the Supply Section. In each processor (see Fig. 2) the intersection operation between t_i and r_j elements proceeds under the control of three signals: the end of operation (for the current t_i) and the descriptors of t_i and r_j elements.

A counter (COUNTER in Fig. 2) records the number of comparisons already performed for the current t_i element. When this number reaches the current value of the **R** list cardinality (DRC, **D**ynamic **R** **C**ardinality) stored in DRCR, a t_i element is requested by the signal *end of operation* (COMP2) from the Supply Section, erasing the old one, and COUNTER is resetted.

The t_i descriptor indicates if the value of the t_i element in the comparator register T is valid or not. If valid the t_i element can be compared with the incoming r_j element, otherwise it has to be substituted by a new t_i.

The r_j descriptor indicates if the content of r_j comparator register RIN is (1) a valid r_j, (2) the new value of DRC, (3) an r_j element already matched in previous cells or (4) a no-operation element (simple propagation). When a match occurs the LOGIC sets the descriptor field of the r_j element to the 3rd configuration, requests a new t_i and resets the COUNTER. This information is used by the RAM buffer (outside the chip) to eliminate the matched r_j elements from the rotating **R** list and to decrease the stored value of DRC. The circulating DRC is periodically updated every time it reaches the buffer.

2.3 Supply Section.

The Supply Section presents a ***binary tree*** structure to feed, according to its request, each comparison cell with a different t_i element. Each supply cell can store a t_i element and needs a simple logic to arbitrate its transfer to the requesting son. In this way the network of the tree cells can dinamically distribute the flow of t_i elements towards the Comparison Section.
The buffering capability of each node allows the Supply Section to satisfy simultaneus requests from the Comparison Section thus achieving concurrence in data comunication as well as in data processing.

3. Physical implementation .

3.1 Generalities.

The list intersector has been designed for a 2.5 μm line width (λ = 1.25 μm) NMOS process. The resulting chip contains 16 comparison cells and 15 supply cells, for a total of about 55,000 transistors occupying an area of 5x5 mm^2. It operates with syncronous, non-overlapping two phase clocking.

The list **T** is inputted after the two signals of request and acknowledge: the former signal indicates that the root of the supply section needs a new element t_i, the latter, coming from outside the chip, that the requested element t_i is ready.

The word lenght of r_i and t_i elements is of 24 bits, the maximum cardinality of **R** is of 256k.

3.2 Floor-plan and Layout.

The floor plan of the comparison cell is shown in Fig. 3. Each cell contains two 26-bit dynamic registers to move in and out the r_j elements, a 25-bit static register to hold the t_i element, a 18-bit static register containing the actual lenght of the **R** list, a 18-bit counter, two circuits comparing t_i with r_i and DRC with counter, a random logic block for the control.

The comparison cell has been constructed to be connected without routing. Its rectangular shape presents a form factor close to 1:2, thus allowing an efficient area organization in 4-cell superblocks arranged in a star structure for the whole chip, as shown in fig. 4.

The supply section finds its place at the center of the whole structure. Each supply cell contains a 25-bit static register and six gates (random logic) managing the communication along the tree, realized following the request/acknowledge protocol described just above.

The cells at even level (leaf cells define odd level) in the supply tree have their input active in the first phase of the clock and their output active in the second one. The I/O timing is reversed for those cells at odd level, thus reducing the supply time of **T** list.

The layout of a leaf supply cell is shown in Fig. 5, that one of a comparison cell in Fig. 6. Both types of cells presents a bit slice structure thus achieving a highly modular architecture.

3.3 Design verification.

System functionality has been verified with KARL simulator [4] in the case of 8 comparison cells of 8-bit elements.

A more detailed verification have been performed with the switch level simulator LOLA [5] for a case of 8 comparison cells of 3-bit elements, while the counter was kept at full 18-bit lenght for considering the proper value of the carry delay. Comparative simulations of critical subcircuits with SPICE [6] suggest that the circuit can run at a 5 MHz clock frequency, which is sufficient to manage present disk data streams.

4. Discussion.

The list intersection processor has been devised [3] for a system configuration in which the **T** list comes directly from the disk storage and the **R** list is loaded by the CPU in the RAM buffer. The processor is operated at a clock frequency high enough to perform "*on the fly*" intersection of t_i elements coming from the disk in the reading phase, and will be idle in the seek phase.

If the cardinality of **R** list is larger than 256k, the intersection operation can be performed on splitted sequences of **R** list. This procedure will require to supply from secondary mass memory the entire **T** list for each splitted sequence.

Technological advances in integration can be exploited on the CID architecture in two ways:

(1) Increasing the word length by 1-bit steps.

(2) Adding some processors to the structure.

Since the comunication logic between nodes support also incomplete subtrees the Comparison Section can have an arbitrary number of processors. Missing nodes in the Supply Section will be regarded as cells that never require a t_i element.

To achieve a higher degree of parallelism it is possible to combine more chips producing a longer chain of intersecting processors, by adding very little extra logic for implementing additional nodes of the supply tree at card level (see Fig. 7).

Acknowledgement.

We would like to thank M. Missikoff and M. Terranova of IASI-CNR in Roma for valuable discussions and ample documentation on the CID.

References

[1] H. T. Kung and P. L. Lehman, "Systolic (VLSI) Arrays for Relational Data Base", 1980 ACM/SIGMOD Int. Conf on Management of Data, Los Angeles, May 1980.

[2] J. L. Bentley and H. T. Kung, "A Tree Machine for Searching Problems", Proc. of 1979 Int. Conf. on Parallel Processing, IEEE August 1979.

[3] P. Bertolazzi, M. Missikoff and M. Terranova, "CID: a VLSI Device for List Intersection", Rept. R. 75, CNR Istituto di Analisi dei Sistemi e Informatica, Rome, November 1983.

[4] R. Hartenstein, P. Liell, "KARL II Language Reference Manual", Kaiserslautern Univ., 1983.

[5] D. D. Caviglia, "Current Source Model for Transistor Level Simulation of Logic MOS Circuits", Tech. Rep. DIBE, Università di Genova, 1985.

[6] L. W. Nagel, "SPICE2 : a Computer Program to Simulate Semiconductor Circuits", Univ. California, Berkeley, ERL Memo ERL-M520, May 1975.

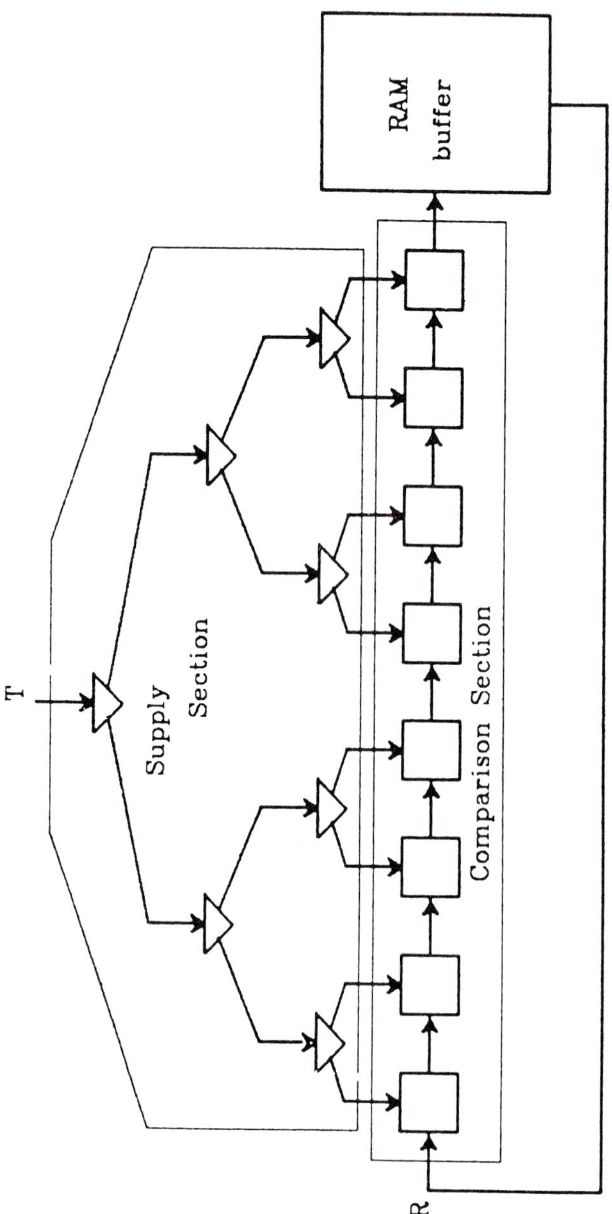

Fig. 1. CID architecture, composed of a Supply Section (binary tree) and a Comparison Section (linear array). The RAM buffer is outside the chip.

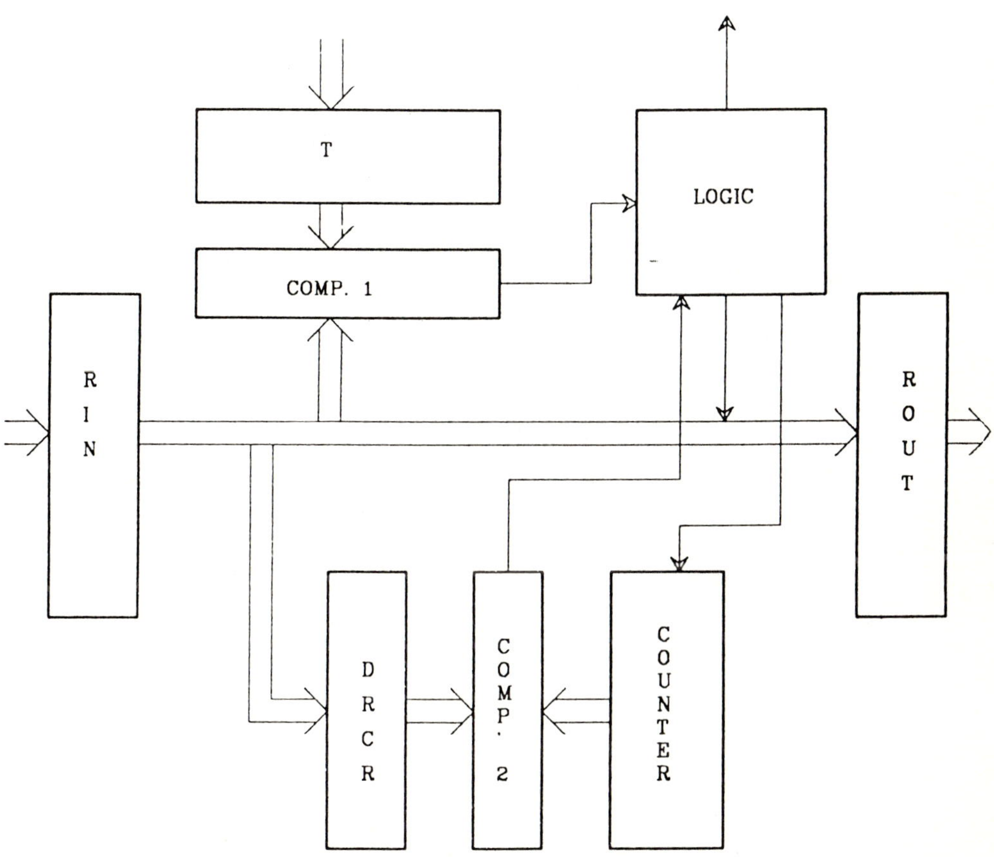

Fig. 2. Block diagram of a Comparison Cell showing datapaths and control signals (thinner lines).

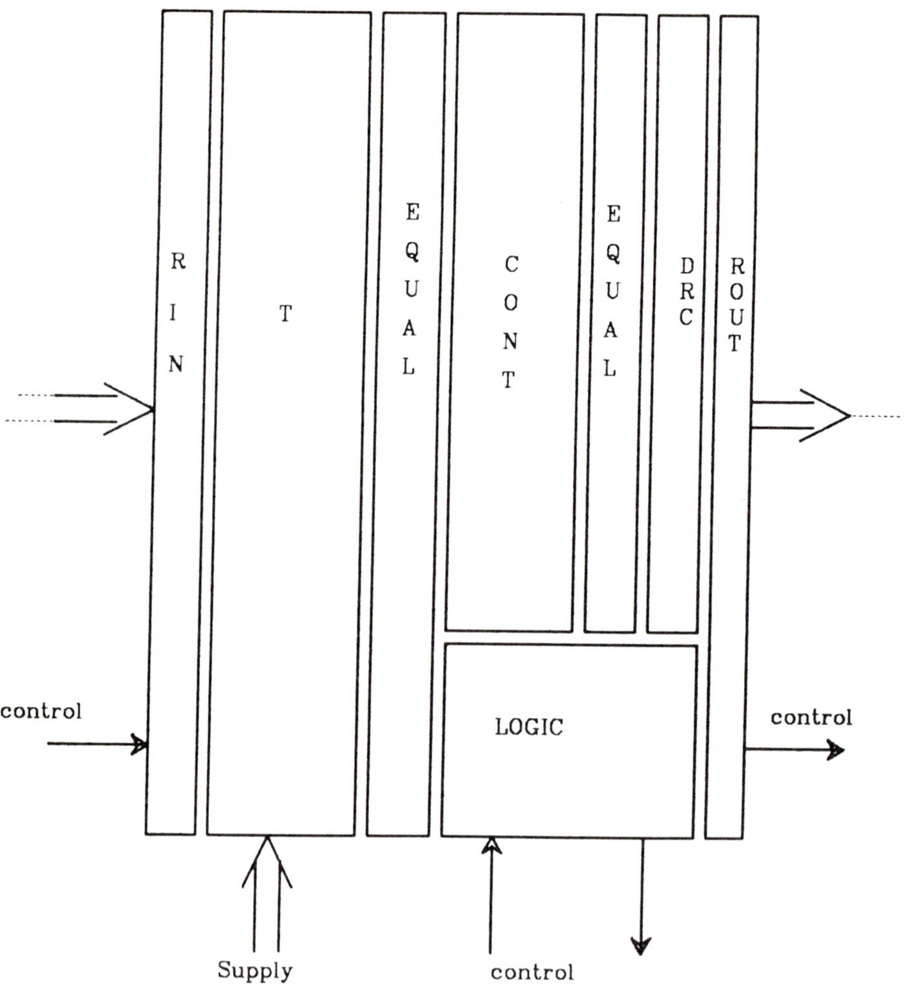

Fig. 3. Floor plan of a comparison cell. The R list datapath is incorporated in the blocks.

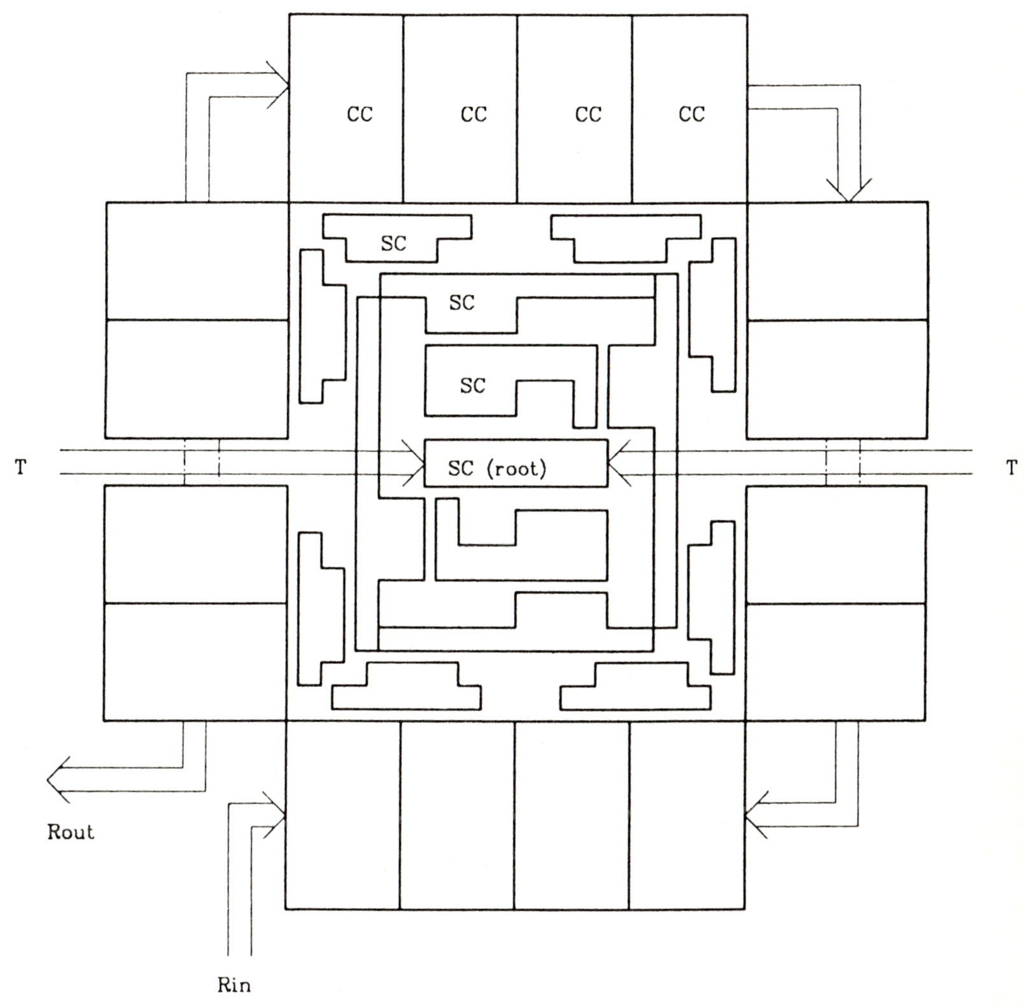

Fig. 4. Floor plan of the whole chip, CC = Comparison Cell, SC = Supply Cell.

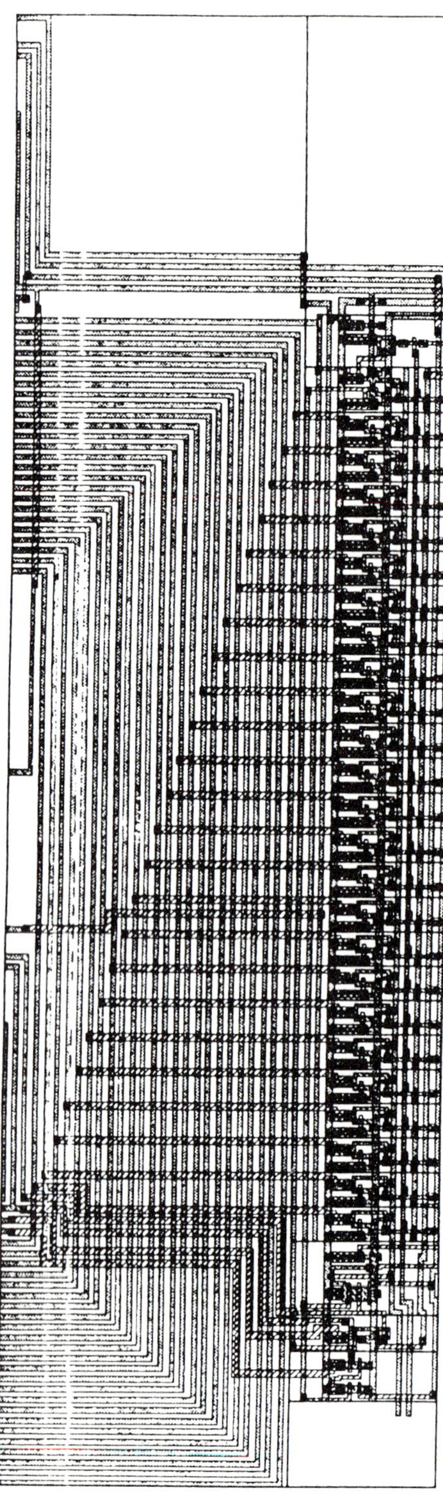

Fig. 5. Layout of a Supply Tree leaf.

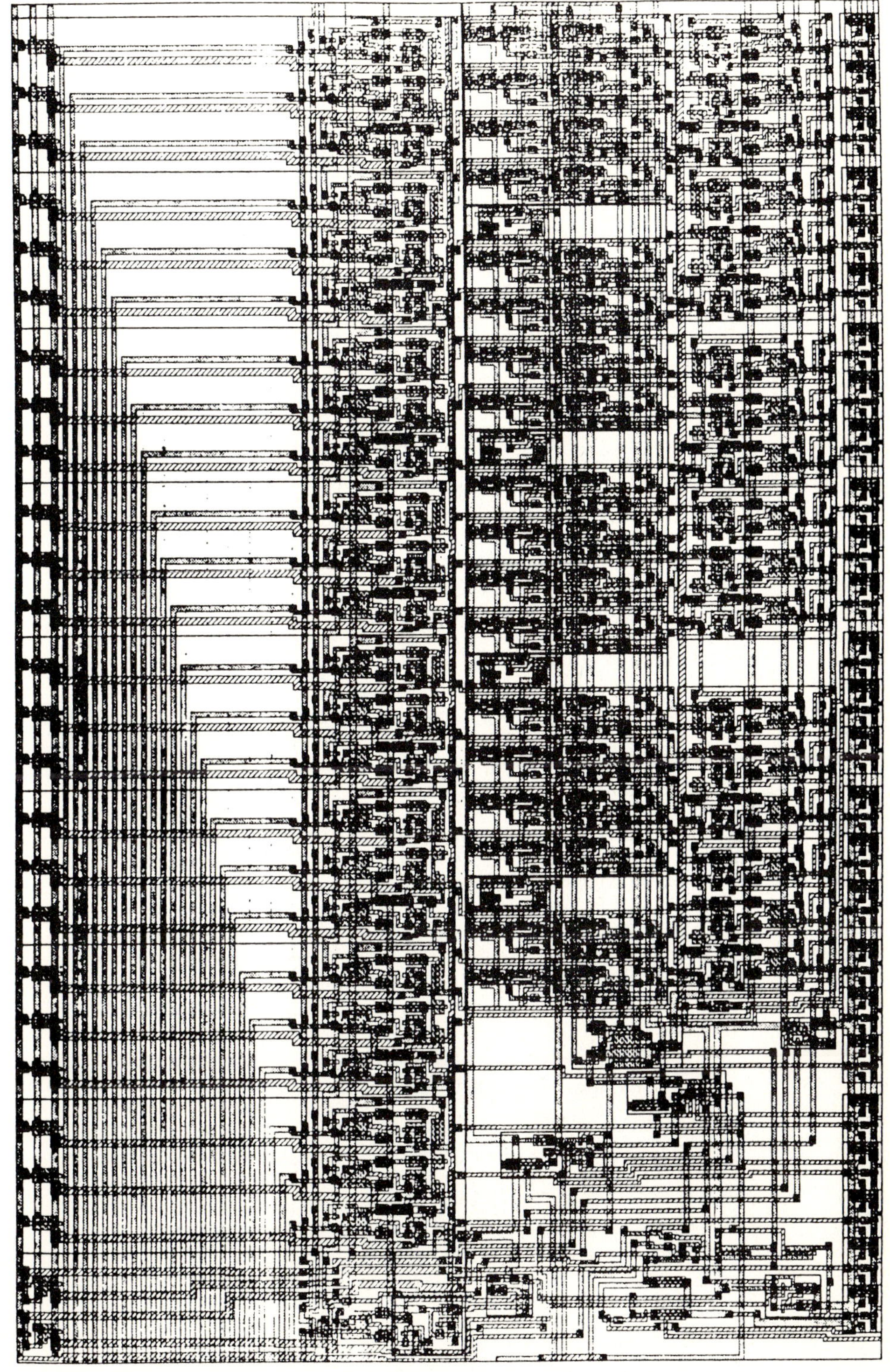

Fig. 6. Layout of a Comparison Cell.

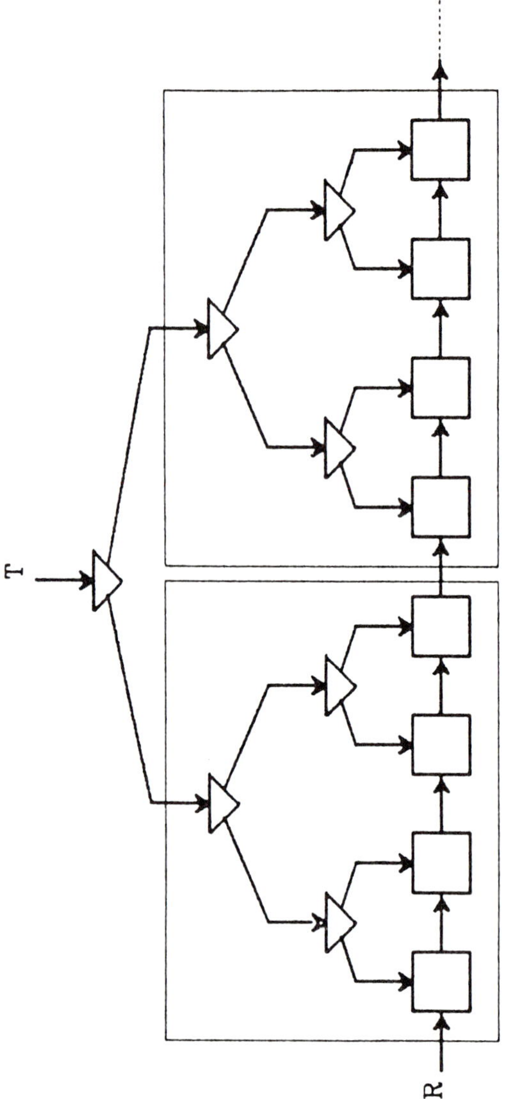

Fig. 7. Chaining of two chips to enhance parallel processing.

METU-GDBMS: A GENERALIZED DBMS FOR THE RAP DATABASE MACHINE

ASUMAN DOGAC
Middle East Technical University
Ankara, Turkey

ABSTRACT

METU-GDBMS is a generalized database management system implemented for the RAP (Relational Associative Processor) database machine.

METU-GDBMS, following the ANSI/SPARC proposal supports the three popular data models (namely, the relational, the network and the hierarchical data models) at the external interfaces along with the associated query languages (namely, SQL, LSL and MRI System 2000 DML). The Entity-Relationship Model is chosen as theconceptual common denominator because of its semantic richness. The RAP DBMS assembler is found to be an efficient facility for supporting METU-GDBMS both structurally and operationally.

INTRODUCTION

METU-GDBMS (Middle East Technical University-Generalized Database Management System) is a generalized DBMS implemented for the RAP database machine |1,2,3,4,5| . Although several prototypes of the RAP database machine exist, the software emulator which is running on IBM 370 model 145 operating under OS/VS1 is used for the implementation |6|.

RAP directly supports relational model of data and has a relationally complete DML which is called RAP assembly language.

However, the need for a generalized DBMS has been extensively discussed in the literature and a multilevel architecture has been proposed in the ANSI/SPARC report |7|. The framework consists of external, conceptual and internal schemas. The universe of discourse is defined in the conceptual schema and different external schemas are generated from this definiton. The conceptual schema is mapped into internal schema which represents the actual physical storage of data.

NATO ASI Series, Vol. F 24
Database Machines. Edited by A. K. Sood and A. H. Qureshi

2. ARCHITECTURE OF THE METU-GDBMS

The architecture of the METU-GDBMS is identical with that of ANSI/SPARC framework.

The relational, the network and the hierarchical data models are supported at the external interfaces.

In order to describe the information at the conceptual common denominator, a data model, as we call it a meta data model (MDM), is necessary.

A survey of existing data models revealed the fact that the Entity/Relationship model |8| would be suitable as a meta data model for our purposes.

The important features of thes model can be summarized as follows:

a) The Entity/Relationship model distinguishes entities from the relationships defined between entities. This results first of all, in relations with clearer meanings.Secondly, it provides ease in generating data models which are explicitly based on relationships between entities. As an example, both the hierarchical data model and the network data model are organized according to the relationships between record types representing entities. The Entity/Relationship model which separates entities from relationships at the very beginning, therefore forms a clear basis from which these data models can be generatid.

b) Attributes of entities and relationships are defined as functions mapping entity sets and relationship sets into value sets. Such a definition in return, prevents the normalization problems to a large extent.

c) Mapping information about the relationships also exists in the model. This piece of information is helpful in deriving other data models.

d) There is no restriction about the relationships. A relationship may be defined on more than two entity sets, or on only one entity set. Also, there may be more than one relationship defined on the given entities.

e) The semantic fact that the existence of an entity depends on the existence of another entity is also clearly expressed in the data model.

This design is based on a database machine with the consideration of recent developments in the area of database machines. It is foreseable that database machines will replace concentional computers in the non-numeric processing area, because of their performance superiority |3|. RAP (Relational Associative Processor) |4,5| is chosen as the database machine since besides being available, it provided great ease and efficiency in the design and implementation.

Figure 1 illustrates the Entity/Relationship model data structure diagram of some entity sets and relationship sets which might be of interest to a manufacturing company |8|. This example will be used throughout the paper.

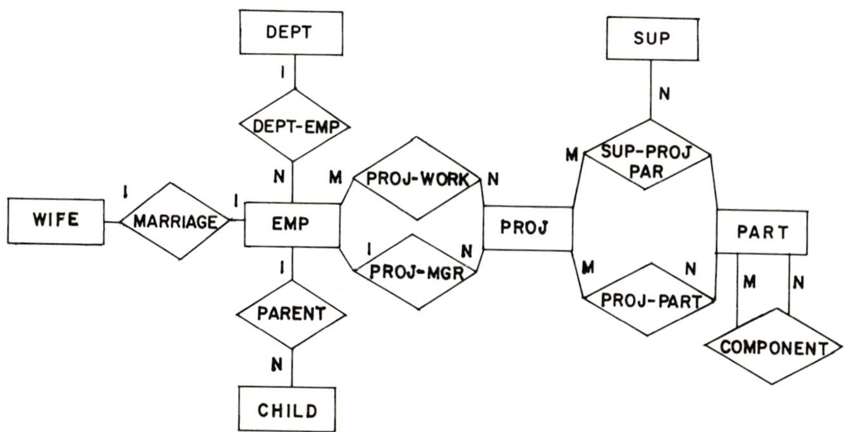

Figure 1. Entity/Relationship diagram of an example database.

In METU-GDBMS, a data definition language is designed and implemented in order to define the database using the concepts of the Entity/Relationship model. During the information analysis phase, the information needed by an enterprise (a universe of discourse) is defined in terms of the Entity/Relationship model. METU-GDBMS then generates the external schemas, according to user requests.

2.1. Data models supported at the external schema

The three data models which have gained wide-spread acceptance, i.e. the hierarchical, the network and the relational model are supported at the external schema.

Once the information is defined through the data definition language of the meta data model, the user, by submitting two key words such as NETWORK VIEW or RELATION VIEW to the system, obtains a display of corresponding external schema definiton in the associated DDL, which are implemented according to the features of the data models supported.

The query languages supported for the external models are as follows:

a) SEQUEL |9| for the relational model
b) LSL |10| for the network model
c) MRI System 2000 |11| query language for the hierarchical data model
d) RAP DBMS assembler at any one of the above interfaces.

2.2. Structural Transformation within METU-GDBMS

There are two levels of structural transformations within METU-GDBMS. The first level is for generating external models from the information defined at the conceptual schema through the ER model. The second level is mapping the ER model into the RAP tabular structures in the internal schema.

2.2.1. E-R model to Relational Model Transformation

As explained in the original paper by Chen |8|, the entity-relationship data model directly maps into the relational model where, there corresponds a relation for each entity and relationship and the relations obtained have better update properties. These relations constitude both the user relational view of the database and the RAP relations in the internal schema.

2.2.2. Entity-Relationship to Network Model Transformation

In the DBTG Network Model, a set type defines a 1:n relationship between the owner and the member record types. Therefore whenever, there is a 1:n relationship between two entity relations in the E-R model, this simply implies a network set type with the appropriate owner and member record types.

In order to express m:n relationships in the network model, a link record type is introduced. Such a record type however already exists in the E-R model, that is, the relationship relation between two entities. In this case, the owner is the record type represented by the entity relation and member is the record type represented by the relationship relation. For k-ary relationships ($k \geqslant 3$), the set types are generated in the same way.

The mapping information and the relationship relations in the E-R model are thus proved to be very useful in conversion to the network model.

2.2.3. The Entity-Relationship Model to Hierarchical Model Transformation

The parent-child relationship in the hierarchical data model represents a 1:n relationship and the records are organized in the form of a tree.

In order to obtain a hierarchical definition of tree from the E-R definition of data the following procedure is used.

1. Create a level 1 tree from each 1:1 and 1:N relationships where determining entity is the root.
2. Create an arbitrary level 1 tree from m:n relationships.
3. Of a leaf is a parent in another tree, combine them to obtain a tree with level increased by one. Continue until no leaf is a parent in another tree.

3. THE LANGUAGE INTERFACES AND OPERATIONAL TRANSFORMATIONS

3.1. Data Definition Languages

3.1.1. Meta data model data definition language

In the following, the features of the MDM data definition language will be highlighted by presenting a partial definition of the information about the company example given earlier.

```
DEFINE ENTITY TABLE DEPT 10
DNO INTEGER 2 KEY , DNAME LITERAL 16;
DEFINE ENTITY TABLE EMP 300
ENO INTEGER 4 KEY , ENAME LITERAL 16
AGE INTEGER 2 RANGE (18:65) , SAL INTEGER 4 RANGE (3000:60000);
DEFINE RELATIONSHIP TABLE DEPT-EMP 300
FROM DEPT/ONE , FROM EMP/N;
DEFINE ENTITY TABLE PART 2000
PNO INTEGER 4 KEY , PNAME LITERAL 10 , WEIGHT INTEGER 2, COLOR LITERAL 8;
DEFINE RELATIONSHIP TABLE COMPONENT 3000
FROM PART/M , FROM PART/N RENAME AS CNO;
DEFINE WEAK RELATION TABLE EMP-DEPN 250
```

FROM EMP/ONE
FROM DEPENDENT/N
EXISTENCE OF DEPENTENT DEPENDS ON
EXISTENCE OF EMP;

Entities are defined through DEFINE ENTITY TABLE keywords. The table name is followed by table size denoting the maximum number of occurences that can be stored in the database. Attribute types can be integer or literal. Literal domains may contain upto 16 characters, whereas integer domain lengths can be halfword or fullword. For numeric domains, range values can also be specified. These are used for integrity checks.

Relationships between entities are defined through DEFINE RELATIONSHIP TABLE keywords. In this definition, the entities participating in the relationships and their mapping information are provided.

Since a relationship can be defined on a single entity, it is necessary to introduce a renaming facility. For example, a relationship COMPONENT is defined on the entity PART, denoting the fact that a component is made up of parts and the component itself is a part. The COMPONENT relation table will contain two attributes both containing the part numbers, but one of them will denote the component number, thus it has to be renamed.

In the Entity/Relationship model, the semantic information about the existence dependency is expressed through weak entity relations and weak relationship relations. In the DDL, this fact is expressed by DEFINE WEAK ENTITY TABLE and DEFINE WEAK RELATION TABLE keywords.

3.1.2. Relational model data definition language

The RAP DDL facility |6| is used in displaying relation definitions to the user. The language features will be depicted with the following example.

```
RELATION < DEPT (10):DNO, INTEGER, 2, KEY
                     DNAME, LITERAL, 16>

RELATION < DEPT-EMP (300): DNO, INTEGER, 2, KEY
                           ENO, INTEGER, 4, KEY>
```

The keyword RELATION identifies a relation definition which includes the table name, maximum expected size of the table in number of tuples and the associated attribute definitions.

3.1.3. Network model data definition language

A data definition language similar to that of LSL is used. The following example related to the previous MDM definition will depict the language features:

```
DEFINE RECORD DEPT
     ATTRIBUTE DNO INTEGER 2 KEY
     ATTRIBUTE DNAME LITERAL 16;
DEFINE RECORD DEPT-EMP
     ATTRIBUTE DNO INTEGER 2 KEY
     ATTRIBUTE ENO INTEGER 4 KEY
DEFINE LINK LNK1
BETWEEN DEPT
AND DEPT-EMP
WHERE DEPT.DNO=DEPT-EMP.DNO;
```

With this data definition language, the user is supplied with the record definitions and associated link definitions of the network model. According to these definitions, the user can code his LSL queries.

3.1.4. Hierarchical model data definition language

The data definition language designed for the hierarchical data model specifies the logical organization and the characteristics of data according to the hierarchical data model. The record dype and data item definitions are also provided.

The characteristics of the language can be observed from the following example database definition which is in accordance with the previous MDM definition:

```
DATABASE DEFINITION NAME MANAGEMENT
RECORD DEPT ROOT
        ATTRIBUTE DNO INTEGER 2
        ATTRIBUTE DNAME LITERAL 16
DESCENTANTS = EMP
RECORD EMP
        ATTRIBUTE ENO INTEGER 4
        ATTRIBUTE ENAME INTEGER 16
        ATTRIBUTE AGE INTEGER 2
```

```
        ATTRIBUTE SAL INTEGER 4
DESCENDANTS = CHILDREN, PROJECT, WIFE
RECORD CHILDREN
        ATTRIBUTE CNAME LITERAL 16
RECORD PROJECT
        ATTRIBUTE PJNO INTEGER 2
RECORD WIFE
        ATTRIBUTE WNAME INTEGER 16;
```

3.2. Data manipulation languages and operational transformations

3.2.1. The relational model data manipulation language: SEQUEL

The query language supported for the relational model is SEQUEL. A compiler coded in FORTRAN IV translates SEQUEL queries and update commands into the RAP assembler language.

The syntax of SEQUEL has been modified to provide ease in implementation and to meet the requirements of the chosen parsing algorithm.

In the following, selected features of the language are demonstrated with the corresponding RAP code using the previous database definition. A brief summary of the RAP language opcodes is provided in Appendix 1.

a) Restriction: This corresponds to RAP's MARK instruction.

Example: For the query "Find the names of employees whole salary are greater than 10,000".

```
SEQUEL: (SELECT ENAME
          FROM EMP
          WHERE SAL>10000);
```

The following RAP code is generated by the SEQUEL complier and executed by the RAP emulator at the physical common denominator.

```
          RAP:MARK (T1)<EMP:SAL GT 10000>
              READ<EMP (ENAME): MKED (T1)>
              EOQ
```

b) Composition: This corresponds to implicit join in RAP and is performed by a CROSS-MARK instruction.

Example: For the query "Find the names of employees who work in department number 12".

```
SEQUEL : (SELECT ENAME
          FROM EMP
          WHERE ENO =
             (SELECT ENO
              FROM DEPT-EMP
              WHERE DNO = 12));
RAP:MARK (T1) < DEPT-EMP : DNO EQ 12>
    CROSS-MARK (T2) < EMP: ENO EQ DEPT-EMP.
                ENO > <  DEPT-EMP.MKED (T1)>
    READ<EMP (ENAME): MKED (T2)>
```

The basic features of SEQUEL such as quantification, GROUP BY clause,basic set operations, free variable clauses as well as update functions have been implemented. The following gives an example of an update query.

Query: "Change the department of JOHN DOE to department number 12".

```
SEQUEL: (UPDATE EMP-DEPT
                 SET DNO =12
                 WHERE ENO =
                      (SELECT ENO
                       FROM EMP
                       WHERE ENAME = 'JOHN DOE'));
RAP: MARK (T1) < EMP: ENAME EQ 'JOHN DOE'>
     CROSS-MARK (T2) < EMP-DEPT: ENO EQ EMP.ENO>
                          < EMP.MKED (T1)>
     REPLACE < EMP-DEPT(DNO):MKED (T2)><12 >
     EOQ
```

As is clear from this example, any SEQUEL query construct may follow the WHERE clause of the UPDATE command.

3.2.2. Network model data manipulation language

For the network model, LSL is implemented as the data manipulation language. There is a differing feature of this language from the original specification, that is, in a selection path, links have to be in a chain. Some examples of the typical language constructs along with the corresponding RAP code will be given in the following.

a) Restriction: For the query "Find the salary of the employee whose employee number is 1055"

```
LSL: SELECT EMP
          WHERE ENO = '1055'
          KEEP SAL;
RAP: MARK (T1) |EMP: ENO EQ 1055|
          READ |EMP(SAL): MKED (T1)||WA|
          EOQ
```

As can be seen from the example above, it is not difficult to map LSL into RAP, especially when linking information is readily available in the definition of set types. If more than one attribute is involved in linking relations, then a CRS-COND-MARK following the first CROSS-MARK would be necessary for each additional attribute.

3.2.3. Hierarchical model data manipulation language

The data definition given in Section 3.1.4. along with the relations at the physical common denominator are adequate to process queries that are specified with a high level hierarchical data language like MRI 2000.

Due to the duplication of a given record type in a database, because of its involvement in diverse relationships, it has been decided to qualify the attribute names used in the queries with the hierarchical record type name. Similar to the previous language examples, some typical data operations and their corresponding RAP code can be given as follows:

a) Restriction: For the query "Find the employees whose salary are greater than 10000".

```
MRI 2000: GET WORK.ENO WHERE SAL GT 10000;
     RAP : MARK (T1) |EMP:SAL GT 10000|
           READ |EMP (ENO): MKED (T1)||WA|
           EOQ
```

b) Upward normalization: For the query "Find the location of the companies which supply parts to project PJ11".

```
MRI 2000: GET SPP.LOC WHERE DJNO EQ 'PJ11";
RAP: MARK (T1) |PROJ:PJNO EQ 'PJ11'|
     CROSS-MARK(T2)|SUP-PROJ-PAR:PJNO EQ PROJ.
                        PJNO||PROJ.MKED(T1)|
```

```
CROSS-MARK(T3) |SUP:COM EQ SUP-PROJ-PAR.COM|
               |SUP-PROJ-PAR.MKED(T2)|
READ |SUP(LOC):MKED(T3) |WA|
EOQ
```

3.2.4. Operational mapping into the RAP language

In all of the language transformations into the RAP assembler from various other languages, it has been observed that the RAP language is complete and efficient for operational mappings. This can be explained in the following ways. First, with RAP, all relational algebra operations can be programmed either explicitly or by RAP's way of short cuts. On top of this, the language allows free variable operations in its cursor mode, value set quantifications, efficient set oriented processing, and all forms of logical access features common to various data models. All these capabilities are sufficient for processing almost all possible operational mappings. In fact, besides few special features, all languages share the same set of operational mapping constructs. The RAP assembler is not only complete in processing the operational mappings, but also efficient in whatever it does. This is because it is a database machine language which does not depend on access paths. Intermediate transformations are minimized in RAP. It has been observed that a complicated query involving restriction, division and several projections translates into a RAP code of about 30 to 40 RAP instructions which are executed directly by the database machine.

Another important point about the METU-GDBMS operational mappings is that they are performed in such a way to preserve database consistency. Two main reasons for this are 1-RAP joins are implicit hence do not create any sort of connection problems and 2-As can be noticed in the operational mappings described for the three models, external schema operations are performed on the common schema by simulated accesses on the link structures rather than doing transformed operations on the transformed structures.

4. SECURITY AND INTEGRITY IN METU-GDBMS

Presently in METU-GDBMS, some user authentication process exists. The user, before submitting his queries in any one of the external interfaces, gives a password. This password is translated into RAP's AUTHORIZE instruction. The emulator then rejects execution of the queries if the password is not a legal one. Also, the requested operations in the query are screened with respect to the capabilities allowed for the user by the DBA who declares them through the RAP RELATION command. The integrity constraints can be defined in two ways:

a) In the DDL of the MDM, range values can be given for numeric domains.

b) Following the DDL of the MDM, some integrity constraints can be given by means of assertions. The following is a valid assertion accepted by the system:

```
ASSERT A1 ON PART: COLOR = 'YELLOW';
```

5. CONCLUSION

The paper presented, the design and implementation of the RAP database machine based GDBMS implementation called the METU-GDBMS. The implementation is in accord with ANSI/SPARC proposal. While the structural transformations are two levelled, operational trahsformations are performed by a single step until they reach the Internal Schema in the METU-GDBMS. Several language translators that generate RAP code are implemented to be used at the external interfaces.

The implementation makes use of the E/R model in its meta data model interface and several DDL features have been implemented for this interface as well as the external schema interfaces generated from it.

With the experiments conducted in the METU-GDBMS environment, it is being observed that database machines, when used in the DBMS architectures will greatly enhance the system efficiency at low costs. This is because they support associative reference and set oriented processing directly by their parallel hardware at great speeds. By doing so, they also eliminate acces paths and excessive intermediate level transformations.

Finally, according to a further performance study made on the RAP database machine systems |12|, the generalized DBMS a structure outperformed the other relatively more primitive DBMS architectures which did not use common conceptual schema and/or common internal schema.

APPENDIX -1

Summary of the instruction set of the RAP DBMS Assembler language selection and retrieval commands: Implement selection and/or data retrieval.

MARK	: Selects and tags
RESET	: Selects and removes tags
READ	: Selects and reads
CROSS-MARK	: Maps between two record types
CRS-COND-MARK	: Maps between two record types
GET-FIRST-MARK	: Cursor and mapping within a record type
GET-FIRST	: Cursor
SAVE	: Selects and saves item in RAP register
Update Commands	: Perform selection and in-place arithmetic and replacement updates.
ADD	: Item1 $\leftarrow$ Item1 + Item2 (or constant)
SUB	: Item1 $\leftarrow$ Item1 - Item2 (or constant)
MUL	: Item1 $\leftarrow$ Item1 * Item2 (or constant)
DIV	: Item1 $\leftarrow$ Item1 / Item2 (or constant)
REPLACE	: Item1 $\leftarrow$ Item2

Insertion and deletion commands: Insert and delete record occurances

DELETE	: Selects and deletes record occurences.
INSERT	: Inserts record occurences into the record type

Data definition commands : Initialize, populate, and delete a record type.

RELATION	: Defines a new relation (record type).
CREATE	: Populates the database for the specified record types which have been defined by the RELATION command.
DESTROY	: Deletes a record type
System commands	:
AUTHORIZE	: Grants access to the user via password
LOCK	: Specified record types are locked against concurrent accesses
RELEASE	: Releases locks
SAVE MARKS	: Current mark bits of specified relations are pushed onto stacks of each tuple

RESTORE-MARKS : Restores marks by poping the saved mark bits

LOCATE : Returns the node address of the relation to the specified site

STATUS : Performs dynamic status checking for branching purposes

READ-MARKS : Same as READ, but output includes also mark bits.

Decision and transfer commands: Control program loops.

TEST : Tests presence of tags within a record type

BC : Branch, conditional and unconditional

EOQ : End-of-query

REFERENCES

1. DOGAC, A., "Generalized Database Management Systems: Concept, Design and Analysis", PhD. Thesis, Department of Computer Science, Middle East Technical University, Ankara, Turkey, September 1980.
2. DOGAC, A., OZKARAHAN, E.A., "A Generalized DBMS Implementation on a Database Machine", Proc. of ACM, SIGMOD, Santa Monica, 1980, pp.133-143.
3. OZKARAHAN, E.A., SCHUSTER, S.A., SEVCIK, K.C., "Performance Evaluation of a Relational Associative Processor", ACM Transactions on Database Systems, Vol. 2, No. 2, June 1977, pp. 175-195.
4. OFLAZER, K., OZKARAHAN, E.A., SMITH,K.Ç., "RAP. 3-A Multi-Microprocessor Cell Architecture for the RAP Database Machine", Proc. of the Intl. Workshop on HLLCA, Florida, May 1980.
5. OZKARAHAN, E.A., "Evolution and Implementations of the RAP Database Machine", New Generation Computing, Vol. 3, No. 3, 1985.
6. UNLU, S., "Design and Implementation of a Software Emulator for the Relational Associative Processor-RAP", M.Sc. Thesis, Dept. of Computer Engineering, METU, August 1979.
7. Interim Report ANSI/X3/SPARC Study Group on Data Base Management Systems, FDT 7 No. 2, ACM, New York, 1975.
8. CHEN, P.P., "The Entity Relationship Model-Toward a Unified View of Data" ACM Transactions on Database Systems, Vol. 1.,No.1, 1976,pp.9-36.
9. BOYCE, R.F., CHAMBERLIN, D.D., "SEQUEL: A Structured English Query Language", Proc. of ACM SIGMOD, 1974, pp. 249-264.

10.TSICHRITZIS, D.C., LOCHOVSKY, F.H., " Data Base Management Systems", Academic Press, 1977.

11.MRI SYSTEMS CORP., "System 2000 Publications: General Information Manual, Basic Reference Manual and Immediate Access Feature", Austin, Texas, 1972.

12.OZKARAHAN, E.A., KAYAKUTLU, G., "Performance Analysis of RAP Database Machine Systems", Dept. of Computer Engineering, Technical Report ISDB. 9, Middle East Technical University, 1979.

ASSOCIATIVE MEMORY AND DATABASE MACHINES - A BRIEF SURVEY AND A DESIGN PROPOSAL USING HARDWARE HASHING

J.G.D. da Silva[1], I. Watson[2] and A.C.D. de Figueiredo[1]

[1]Departamento de Engenharia Electrotécnica, Universidade de Coimbra, 3000 Coimbra, Portugal

[2]Department of Computer Science, Manchester University, Manchester M13 9PL, England

ABSTRACT

An associative database machine could loosely be defined as a database machine which uses an associative memory in conjunction with the relational model. Large truly associative memories are not practical, due to high cost. The solution to implementing large associative memories lies in the use of pseudo associative memory, built from conventional random access memory with additional logic to make it appear associative. Several systems have been proposed in the past, ranging from the "word serial" systems to the "fully parallel" systems. At one extreme these exhibit low performance, while at the other extreme they approach the complexity of truly associative memory. Hardware hashing, used in conjunction with the parallel accessing capabilities of a bank organized conventional memory can bridge the gap between those two extremes, producing a design which can offer access times close to the access time of the conventional memory used, without excessive additional hardware. A design for such a memory is presented. It is inspired on previous work by Ida and Goto in Japan, but by using a different technique for overflow handling, it can offer superior performance with no loss of modularity, and therefore of its capability for expansion. This memory could be used effectively in a database machine.

Index Terms: associative memory, database machines, hashing, relational database machines.

NATO ASI Series, Vol. F 24
Database Machines. Edited by A.K. Sood and A.H. Qureshi

INTRODUCTION

Associative memory techniques and content search operations have been proposed for or used in database machines since their inception. In a comprehensive survey, Berra [1982] identifies content search operations such as 'equal to', 'greater than or equal to', less than or equal to', etc. among the desirable attributes of a database management environment, and considers that work on database machines can be divided in six somewhat overlapping groups, one of which being the Associative Memory/Processor Group. In fact, associative memory/processing techniques can be found in a variety of database machines, some of which are usually identified with a class other than the Associative Memory/Processor Group. One example is CAFS [Maller 1979], classified by Berra [1982] under the Special Purpose Function Architecture Group. Another example is RELACS [Oliver 1979] or DBC [Banerjee et al. 1979], both considered by Berra [1982] as belonging to the Multiple Processor System Group.

The application of associative memory techniques has been limited mainly by the high cost of truly associative memory. Recently available semiconductor CAMs (content addressable memories) had a maximum of 64 bits of storage capacity, while RAMs (random access memories) of 64K are widespread [IC MASTER 1984]. CAMs are inherently complex, due to the need for comparison logic for every bit cell and due to the high pin count that results from the impossibility of encoding addresses on-chip. VLSI techniques can only alleviate, but not solve, these limitations.

Implementation of large capacity associative memory has been resolved by using conventional RAM with additional logic to make it appear associative. Past designs have been classified into "word serial", "bit serial", "block organized" and "fully parallel" [Parhami 1973]. "Word serial" systems are the hardware implementation of a program loop to perform a linear search, and are therefore poor in performance. "Fully parallel" systems associate comparison logic with every bit or group of bits, and are therefore almost as complex as truly associative memory. "Bit serial" systems operate on one bit of every word simultaneously, and therefore a tight limitation is imposed on the number of memory words. "Block organized" systems, commonly based on rotating storage devices, offer large capacities, but with a significant penalty in speed.

Hardware hashing, by limiting the search to a subset of the total number of stored words, can go some way towards bridging the gap between the two extremes of "word serial" and "fully parallel" systems, without the drawbacks and limitations of "bit serial" systems. The superior performance of hashing against other known search techniques is well established in software systems [Knuth 1973]. Hardware hashing has the immediate advantage of faster execution and, coupled with the parallel accessing capabilities of a bank organized conventional memory, can be used to implement efficient searching mechanisms. Ida and Goto [1977] describe a pseudo associative store using hardware hashing which can perform a basic search in a time comparable to single indirect addressing; here, 'basic' refers to 'pure' search, i.e. search not followed by insertion or deletion. Their system comprises a parallel hash table implemented with parallel banks of conventional RAM, a hash address generator and a control unit. Presented with a search word, the hash address generator computes an address which is used to access the memory banks in parallel. Each bank is provided with a comparator; these perform the key comparisons between the search word and the read-out words simultaneously. The control unit does the decision making, based on the results of the key comparisons. Collisions are resolved using the 'open addressing' method. If the first probe is unsuccessful, a second hash address is generated, and the memory banks are re-accessed at the location determined by the new address. The cycle is repeated until an empty position or a matching key is found, or all the memory has been scanned.

The organizational problems of 'open addressing' when deletions occur are well known [Knuth 1973]. Ida and Goto tackle the problem by associating 'conflict counters' with the hash table locations. During an insertion operation the counters are incremented for every probed location with no matching key; during a deletion operation the same counters are decremented for every probed location with no matching key. However, the manipulation of the 'conflict counters' implies that 'composite' operations (search followed by insertion and search followed by deletion) require two passes through the hash table. As a result, a search followed by deletion will take twice the time of the initial search and a search followed by insertion, in itself poorly performant, may have its time significantly increased [da Silva and Watson 1983]. As a consequence, the average execution time for the 'composite' operations becomes of the order of twice the time for single indirect addressing, as confirmed in a later paper by Goto et al. [1978]. The best figures require an hash generator of reasonable complexity, capable of generating as many hash sequences as there are banks. This, in turn, requires one 'conflict counter' for every store location rather than solely for every hash address, and a separate address bus to each bank [Ida and Goto 1977, 1978]. Consequently, the system ceases to be modular and its capability for expansion is seriously impaired.

HARDWARE HASHING WITH SEPARATE OVERFLOW

The known alternative in software systems of using a separate area for overflow handling can solve these limitations while offering average access times for the 'composite' operations in fact comparable to the time of single indirect addressing.

Consider the system depicted in Fig. 1. The Main Storage Area comprises B memory banks of M words each, virtually identical to Ida and Goto's (empty locations are signalled by a single additional bit tag, rather than a reserved word). Entries will not be stored in these banks outside their home area. Overflow entries are, instead, stored in the physically separate Overflow Storage Area. No 'conflict counters' are needed in the Main Storage Area. But their function must be provided for signalling which hash addresses have entries in the Overflow Storage Area, and this can take the form of an additional M-word bank, the Overflow Indicator Bank, accessible in parallel with the B main banks.

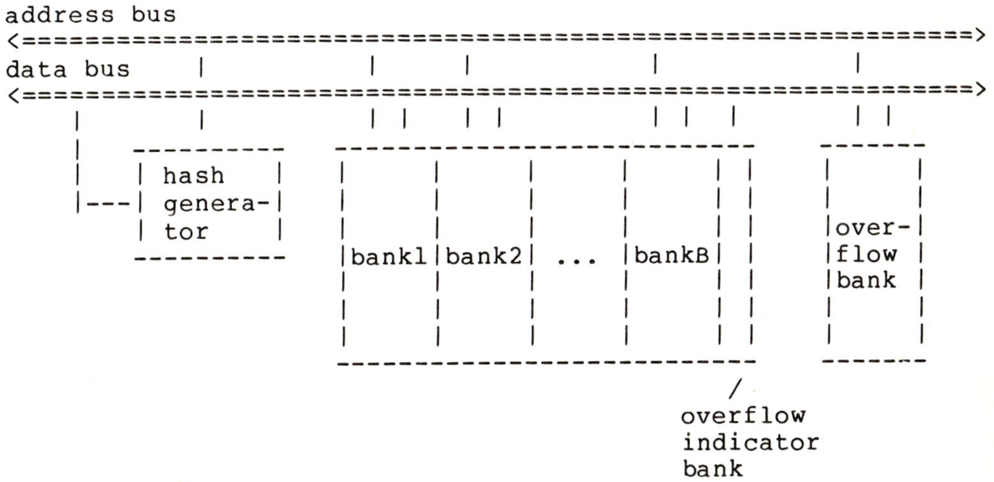

Figure 1: Pseudo associative memory with separate overflow.

The hash generator (whose operation could be pipelined with the main store access) generates an address from the search key, which is used to access the main banks and overflow indicator bank simultaneously. If the search is unsuccessful in the main banks and the overflow indicator access signals the existence of overflow entries, then the overflow bank is searched, possibly under independent control. The system is entirely modular, as the main banks are identical, there is a single address bus for all banks and their controller does not need to differentiate between them [da Silva and Watson 1983].

PERFORMANCE ASSESSMENT

The performance of the system can be easily assessed assuming an ideal hash function, i.e. that for a given data set the distribution of hash addresses is uniform.

The occupancies of the main and overflow areas can then be determined modelling the system by the random placement of balls in cells [Feller 1968]. The model can be simulated using a random number generator with a uniform distribution to produce sequences of R numbers in the range 1 to M [da Silva 1982]. The results are shown in Table 1, where the load factor alpha takes into account a fixed size Overflow Storage Area, for a fairer comparison with schemes that do not use a separate area for overflow.

		alpha						
		0.5	0.6	0.65	0.7	0.75	0.8	0.85
B	4	93.09	89.33	87.20	85.00	82.72	80.43	78.13
	8	98.45	96.52	95.15	93.60	91.84	89.87	87.67
	12	99.56	98.56	97.72	96.59	95.22	93.57	91.68
	16	99.85	99.37	98.85	98.03	96.93	95.52	93.78

Table 1: Relative occupancy of Main Storage Area, fixed Overflow Area Size = M, alpha = R/(MxB+M), M = 2048.

As would be expected, the more banks are used, the higher the percentage of entries in the Main Storage Area. The experiment can also give an indication of the average number of probes for unsuccessful searches, the most often quoted performance figure for search mechanisms. The average number of overflow entries per hash address is given by the ratio of the total number of overflows by the number of different hash addresses. Assuming, solely for the purpose at hand, that the overflow area is organized as a chained hash table and has a cycle equal to the main area cycle, the average number of probes for unsucessful searches will be given by 1 plus the average queue length. The corresponding figures are given in Table 2. From the tabulated results it can be seen that the proposed system does not appear to suffer from the catastrophic symptoms of systems that do not use a separate area for overflow entries when the hash table becomes nearly full.

		alpha						
		0.5	0.6	0.65	0.7	0.75	0.8	0.85
B	4	1.173	1.320	1.416	1.525	1.648	1.783	1.930
	8	1.070	1.188	1.284	1.403	1.551	1.729	1.942
	12	1.029	1.112	1.193	1.310	1.466	1.669	1.920
	16	1.013	1.064	1.127	1.235	1.391	1.610	1.900

Table 2: Average number of probes for unsuccessful search, fixed Overflow Area Size = M, alpha = R/(MxB+M), M = 2048.

'ASSOCIATIVE' DATABASE MACHINE

An 'associative' database machine can be visualized as a database machine using an associative memory and content search operations in conjunction with the relational model.

Inselberg [1983] reports on a comercial system using associative memory that uses non-indexed, parallel data searches and addresses data by contents. The author further refers that the machine uses 8K bytes of associative memory, due to excessive cost.

The proposed scheme, on the other hand, has already been used to implement a 279K byte pseudo associative memory for a prototype dataflow machine [da Silva 1982], which has subsequently been increased to 11M byte [Gurd et al. 1985].

With current technology it is certainly feasible to implement a 2M byte (e.g. 16 bank, with 2Kx256 bits per bank) pseudo associative memory, which could be used as sketched below (Fig. 2) to offer a potential 16-fold speed-up in search operations, leaving ample room for more time consuming operations to be performed within the limits imposed by the disk data transfer rate.

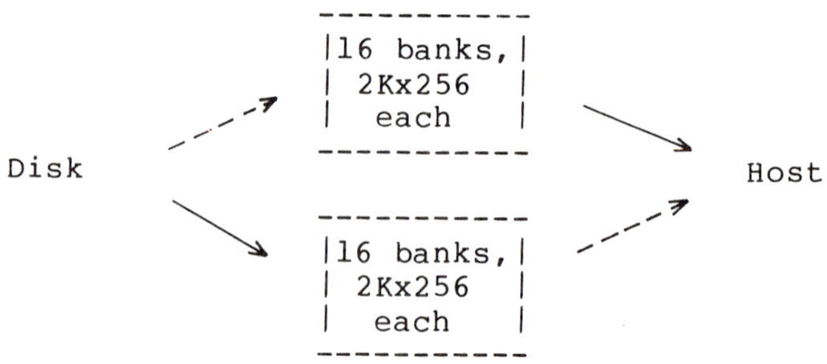

Figure 2: Database machine with pseudo associative memory.

CONCLUSION

The use of associative memories of significant capacity in database machines has been made difficult by the high cost of the required hardware. Truly associative memory is inherently complex, and available semiconductor CAMs have low density and high pin counts.

A large pseudo associative memory, with access times close to the cycle time of the original RAM used, can be built combining hardware hashing with the parallel accessing capabilities of a bank organized memory. Such memory could be used effectively to speed-up content search operations in a database machine.

REFERENCES

Banerjee, J., Hsiao, D.K. and Kannan, K.: "DBC - a Database Computer for Very Large Databases", IEEE Trans. on Computers, C-28, 6, Jun. 1979, pp. 414-430.

Berra, P.B.: "Some Architectures for Database Management", Infotech State of the Art Report on Computer Architecture, 1982, pp. 173-187.

da Silva, J.G.D.: "The Matching Unit of the Manchester Dataflow Computer: a Pseudo-associative Store with Hardware Hashing", Ph.D. Thesis, Depart. Computer Science, Manchester University, 1982.

da Silva, J.G.D. and Watson, I.: "Pseudo-associative Store with Hardware Hashing", IEE Proceedings, 130, Pt. E, 1, Jan. 83, pp. 19-24.

Feller, W: An Introduction to Probability Theory and its Applications (Vol. I), 3rd ed., John Wiley and Sons, Inc., 1968.

Goto, E., Ida, T. e Gunji, T.: "Parallel hashing algorithms", Inf. Proc. Letters, 6, 1, Feb. 1977, pp. 8-13.

Gurd, J.R., Kirkham, C.C. and Watson, I.: "The Manchester Prototype Dataflow Computer", Comm. ACM, 28, 1, Jan. 85, pp. 34-52.

IC MASTER: Hearst Business Communications, Inc./Utp Division, Garden City, NY 11530, 1984.

Ida, T. and Goto, E.: "Performance of a parallel hash hardware with key deletion", IFIP 77, Conf. Proc., North-Holland Pub. Co. 1977, pp. 643-647.

Inselberg, A.: "Database-management Systems", Mini-Micro Systems, XVI, 14, Dec. 83, pp. 193-205.

Knuth, D.E.: The Art of Computer Programming (Vol. 3: Sorting and Searching), Addison-Wesley Pub. Co., 1973.

Maller, V.A.J.: "The Content-Addressable File Store (CAFS) System", ICL Technical J., Nov. 1979.

Oliver, E.: "RELACS, an Associative Computer Architecture to Support a Relational Data Model", Ph.D. Dissertation, Syracuse University, Jun. 1979.

Parahami, B.: "Associative memories: an overview and selected bibliography", Proc. of the IEEE, 61, 6, Jun. 1973, pp. 722-730.

THE DESIGN OF AN ADAPTIVE EXPERT DATABASE INTERFACE

Dr. Robert G. Reynolds
Department of Computer Science
Wayne State University
Detroit Michigan 48202

There have been many attempts to increase a users effectiveness at retrieving data from a database. These attempts frequently focus on enhancing the interface through which the user accesses the system. The use of natural language as a medium in which to express a data retrieval task is an example of such an enhancement [1-4]. This paper examines how expert knowledge about relationships between variables in a database can be used to make inferences concerning items to be retrieved. While the principles used to design an expert interface for information retrieval can be generalized to other datasets, the focus here will be on the design of the interface for a particular dataset. The dataset of interest describes makes of automobiles in terms of 39 variables.

The subsequent sections of this paper detail the basic design of the system. First, the problem to be solved is described in terms of a state-space search. Then, the basic organization of the adaptive retrieval interface expert system (ARIES) is discussed. The overall system consists of two parts. The first part, the on-line inference subsystem, is described in detail, followed by a description of the off-line subsystem. The off-line subsystem updates, in response to changes in the database, the knowledge base used by the on-line system.

One of the main problems in designing this interface has to do with the fact that the composition of the database is continually changing. Values for current variables may change and makes of automobiles may be added and deleted. Thus, the off-line subsystem must be able to adapt to these changes efficiently.

The final section of this paper concerns possible extensions and generalizations of the design principles used in the

NATO ASI Series, Vol. F 24
Database Machines. Edited by A. K. Sood and A. H. Qureshi

ARIES system.

INFORMATION RETRIEVAL AS A STATE-SPACE SEARCH PROBLEM

The overall goal of the system is to infer the range values associated with the set of autos desired by the user. Once a reasonable approximation of these ranges is achieved, the system will retrieve the makes which satisfy these constraints. Further range reductions may be made based upon properties of the retrieved autos, before the final solution set is returned to the user.

Before embarking on a detailed description of the ARIES system, it will be useful to produce a more precise characterization of the problem. As suggested by Rich [5], many problems in artificial intelligence can be described as searches through a space of possible solutions. The problem posed here is no exception.

The state-space description of a problem has the following components:

1. The state variable set contains those variables that describe the current state of the solution process.
2. The state-space set contains those legitimate combinations of state variable values that can occur during the search process.
3. The set of initial states contains those states from which the search process can commence.
4. The set of final states contains those states in which the search process can terminate.
5. The action set represents those changes in state allowed during the search process.

The state variable set will be the currently inferred upper and lower bounds for each of the 39 variables by which the automobiles are described. The state-space set will be the cartesian product of all legitimate combinations of upper and lower bounds for the state variables. The initial state will be the current maximum and minimum values for each variable over all items in the data set. The maximum value for a variable will be the initial upper bound for that variable's range, and the minimum value will be the initial lower bound. These values will be determined by the off-line subsystem in response to dataset updates.

The final state set can be any element in the state-space whose ranges are within those given in the initial state. The job of the inference system will be to reduce the ranges for the variables until they approximate those needed by the user. In the case where the user provides absolutely no information to the system, the initial state and the final state will be the same.

The action set will be the intersection of the newly inferred range values for a variable and its previous range. The result of such an intersection will be the new reduced range. In terms of this action set, backtracking means that the online inference system needs to expand a range that it previously contracted. This can be expressed as the union of the expanded range with the previous one.

The state-space representation can be thought of as corresponding to a directed graph. Each node is a problem state and the search can proceed either by forward resoning from the start state, or backward reasoning from a goal state. For this problem forward reasoning was selected. This is due, in part, to the fact that each combination of ranges can be derived in many different ways. Thus, there are many targets at which to aim the search process.

Also, since there are many ways by which the target set of ranges can be inferred, the central heuristic used by the system will be best first with an agenda. This heuristic is a combination of depth first and breadth first search. The agenda allows the comparison of alternative paths for the inference process.

THE BASIC ORGANIZATION OF THE SYSTEM

The basic organization of the adaptive retrieval interface expert system (ARIES) is given in Figures 1 and 2. Figure 1 describes the on-line portion of the system, while Figure 2 describes the off-line portion. The on-line portion consists

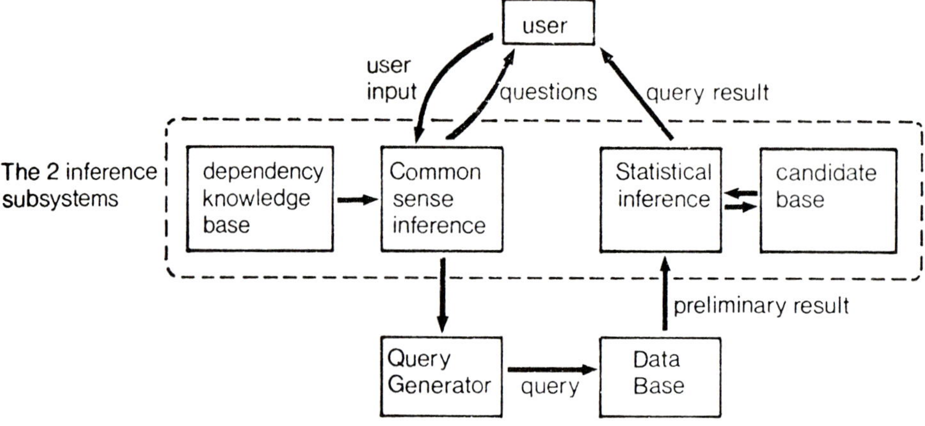

Figure 1. The basic organization of the on-line subsystem.

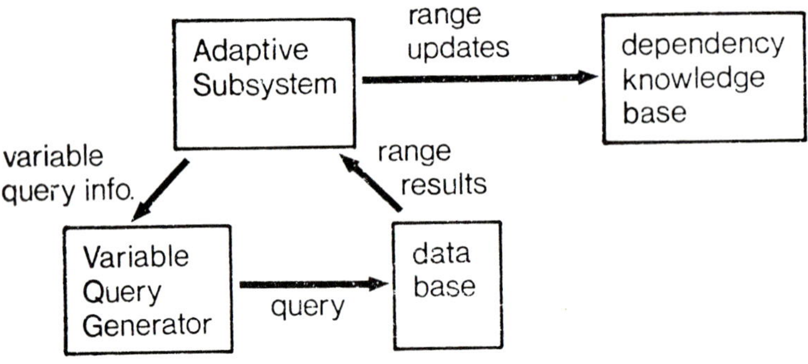

Figure 2. The off-line adaptive subsystem.

of two inference subsystems. The first subsystem is based upon "common sense knowledge" applied to information input by the user regarding the items to be retrieved. The key here is that there are general properties that influence values for groups of related variables in the dataset. For example, in the automobile dataset, there are basic high-level design principles that influence a number of the variables to different degrees. Such principles can relate to performance, fuel economy, and comfortability among others.

The "common sense" inference system is designed to infer general properties about the set of automobiles the user is interested in. These properties are then used to:

1. Restrict the range of values that certain variables can take given that certain properties hold.
2. Use these properties to infer other properties which in turn can be used to further restrict values.

The goal is to use knowledge about a few basic properties to reduce the range of possible values for a large number of variables. The common sense inference subsystem produces a set of range values for variables that limit the solution set to those cars that satisfy the range constraints while requiring the user to specify only a few properties.

When the common sense inference process is completed, the range values for the variables are given to the query generator. It then generates an explicit query in terms of the range values. The preliminary solution set is retrieved and given to the second inference subsystem. This subsystem uses principles of statistical inference to "fine tune" the dataset. Since phase one generates only an approximation of the ranges sought by the user, it is possible that certain outliers might remain. These outliers represent items that were not intended by the user to be in the solution set, and are targeted for removal by the statistical inference system. The goal of this system is to determine if there are records in the candidate set whose values are far enough removed from the rest to be omitted from the solution set. If any items fall into this category they are removed and the final solution set is returned to the user. Information justifying the removal of outliers as well as the inference of properties can be provided to the user upon request.

The off-line portion of the system is described in Figure 2. This adaptive system is designed to update the dependency knowledge base used in phase 1 of the on-line system. Since makes of cars may be added and deleted from the datset and values for variables may be changed, the dependency knowledge base may be affected. In particular, the system may adjust the set of inferences made about the range of values taken by a variable based upon the presence of certain properties. The exact nature of these adjustments will be discussed later, once the contents of the dependency knowledge base have been described in more detail.

THE DESIGN OF THE ON-LINE INFERENCE SYSTEM

A functional description of the first phase of the on-line inference system is given in Figure 3. Figure 3 contains a data flow diagram documenting the basic functions of the common sense inference subsystem. Functions are given as circles; data objects are given as rectangles. Directed arcs represent the flow of information from one function or informational structure to another.

The goal of the common sense inference system is to produce inferences regarding the range of variable values associated with the subset of cars required by the user. These ranges are stored in the state variable range list. They are initialized to the current maximum and minimum for each variable as determined by the off-line adaptive system.

The agenda contains a list of range reduction tasks by variable. Agenda items are rank-ordered based upon two criteria:

1. The extent to which the original range has been reduced so far.
2. The importance and number of properties that determine the range of each variable.

The most highly ranked task is selected by the next task scheduler, and the task is given over to the interpreter for execution.

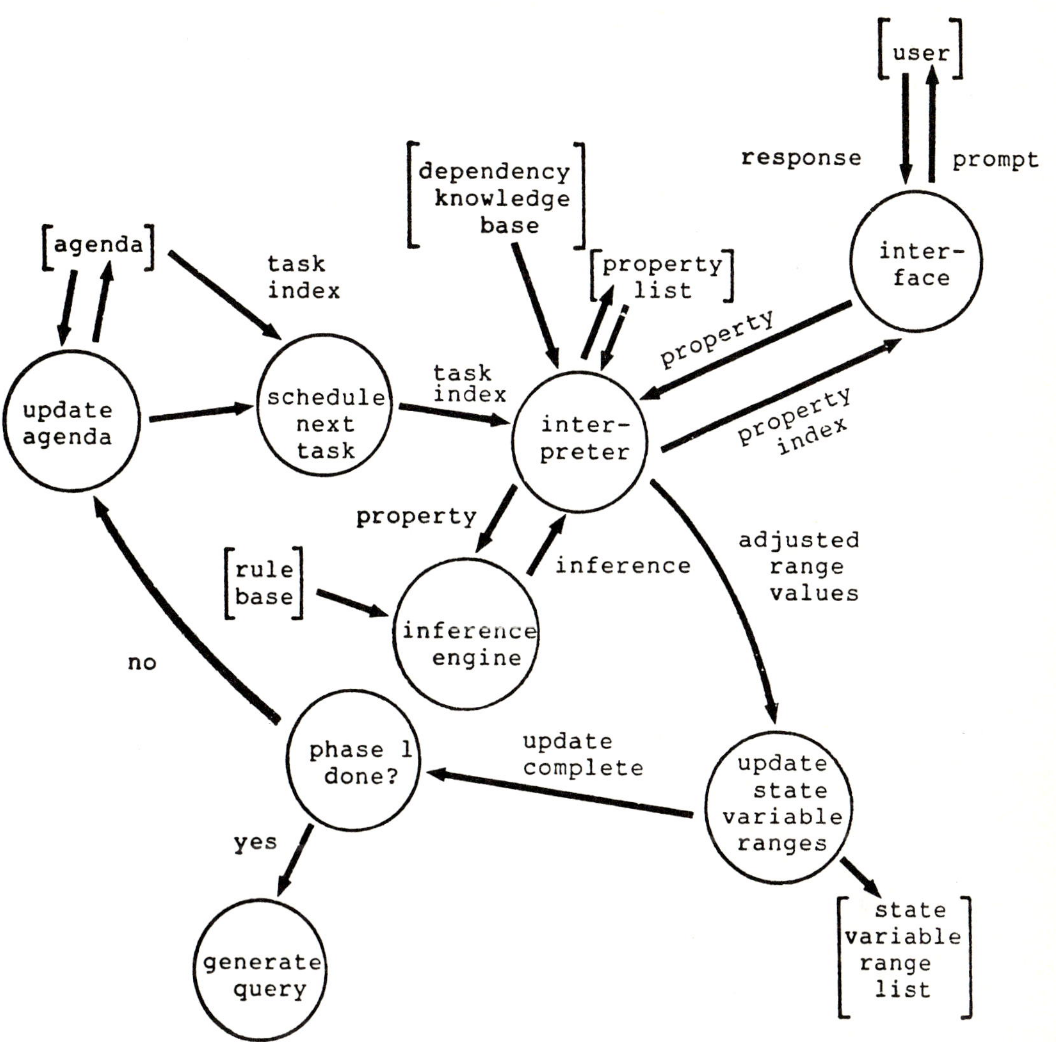

Figure 3. A dataflow diagram of the "common sense inference" portion of the on-line system.

The job of the interpreter is to reduce the range for a given variable. It does so by deriving general properties about the group of automobiles to retrieve and by using these properties to infer new range values for the variable. For the automobile dataset, relevant properties are performance, affordability, size, comfortability, etc. Each of these properties has a set of classes associated with it. The interpreter attempts to determine which of these classes for a property pertain to the current query, and employs this information to reduce the range of a variable. Those classes for each property that have been determined to apply to the current request are stored in the property list.

When the interpreter receives a range reduction request for a variable, it checks the dependency knowledge base to see what properties influence that variable. The knowledge base contains, for each variable, the number of properties that influence it as well as the inferred range for each class of the property. An example of this information for one variable, maximum front leg room, is shown in Figure 4 using a modified semantic net. In the net, length is described as a kind of (ako) size affected, and comfort affected variable. For each property there is a (isa) set of classes. Each class that is relevant to the current query constrains the upper bound (ub) and the lower bound (lb) for the variable. This expert information was provided by a group of 25 automotive engineers at Ford Motor Company.

The interpreter selects a property that influences the range for the target variable and checks the property list to see which classes for the property have been derived previously. If any are present, the range values associated with them are sent to the update state variable range function and the range reduction task is then complete for the variable. If no classes for the property have been determined, the interpreter sends the property index to the inference engine. The job of the interence engine is to infer new property classes based upon the presence of other property classes. Pertinent rules are then fetched from the rule base. As soon as the antecedent for a retrieved rule is satisfied, that inference is performed.

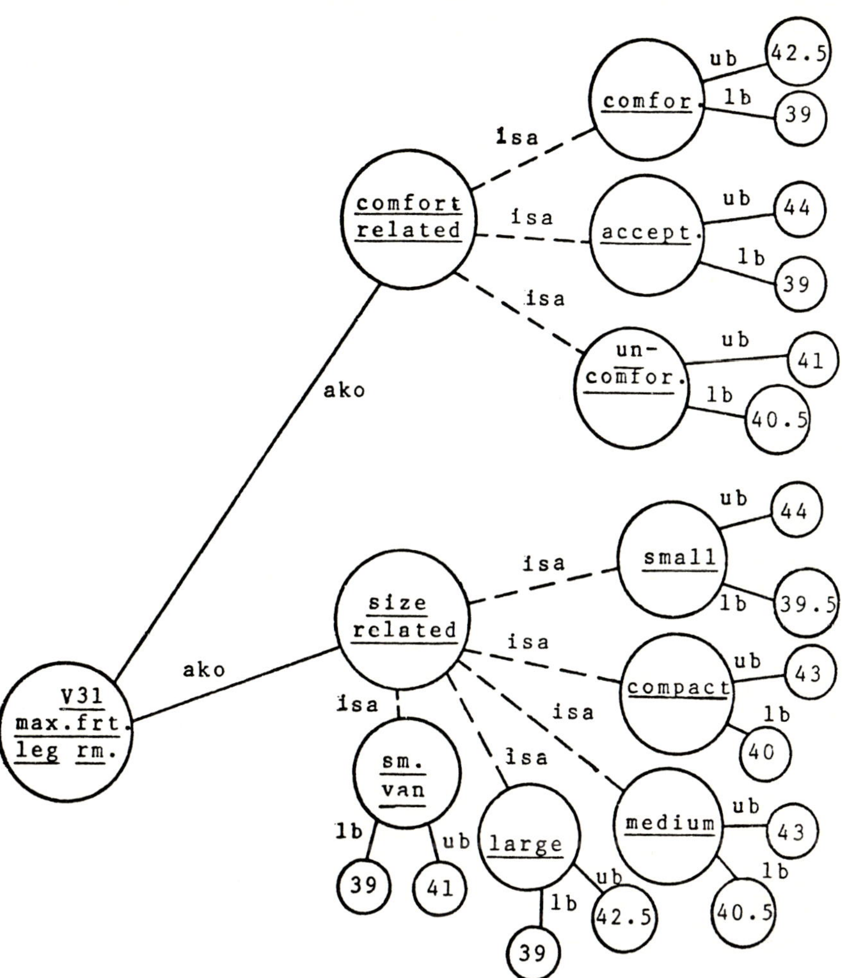

Figure 4. Information in the dependency knowledge base represented as a semantic net.

The basic form for the rules are, if <antecedent> then <consequent> , as discussed in Hayes-Roth [6]. An example of such a rule is the following:

If price:expensive then comfort:very comfortable.

So, if expensive is currently in the property list for the property price, then infer the class of very comfortable cars for the comfort property. The inference is then placed in the property list by the interpreter and that range for the variable updated.

In the situation where no rules can be activated, the interpreter sends the property index to the interface. The interface subsystem then displays a question to the user asking which classes of the property pertain to the current query. The resulting classes are given to the interpreter which places them in the property list, and again sends the appropriate ranges to the range update function.

Once the range reduction task is completed, the agenda is updated and the process repeated with another variable. When the common sense inference process is complete the current set of ranges are used to retrieve those automobiles satisfying the range constraints. The resulting records are placed in the candidate set.

Figure 5 describes the activities of the second phase of the on-line inference system. Since the retrieved items are based upon approximations to desired ranges as inferred by phase 1, the role of phase 2 is to "fine tune" the candidate set by removing cars whose values do not statistically fit with the rest (outliers). By removing makes of automobiles whose values for one or more variables are far removed from those for the remaining makes, the system is reducing the range for variables.

Phase 2 begins by computing the mean and standard deviation for each variable based upon the set of candidate cars. Variable reduction tasks are then ordered in the agenda based upon standard deviation. The larger the standard deviation for a variable the more likely that it will contain outliers. The variable with the largest non-zero standard deviation is selected for reduction. For each make of car, a standardized

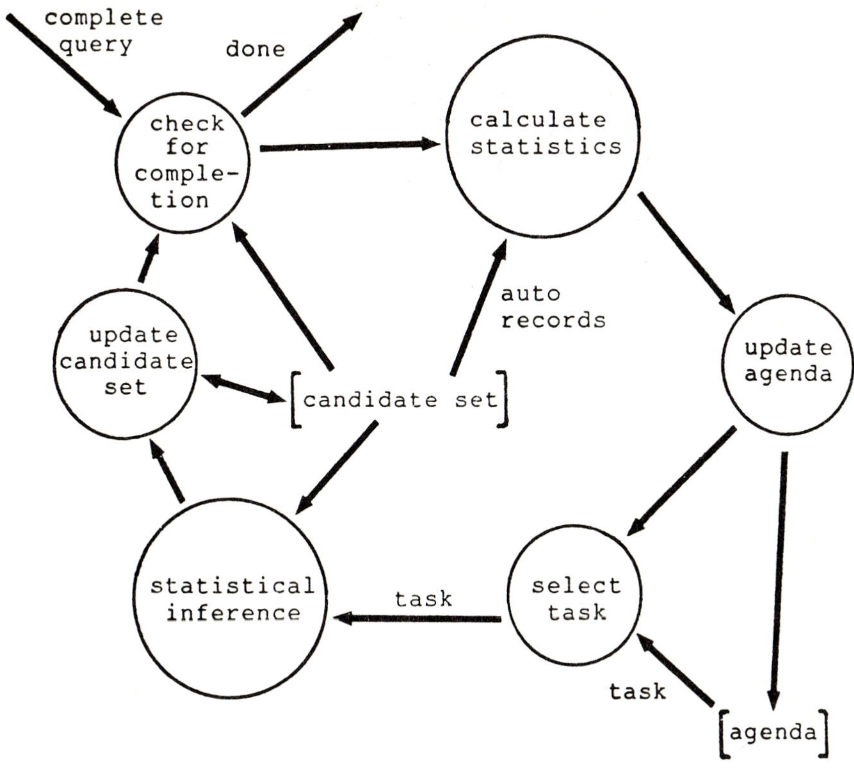

Figure 5. A dataflow diagram of the statistical inference portion of the on-line sybsystem.

Z-score is computed. The Z-score is the difference between the value for the car and the average value, divided by the standard deviation. This gives the deviation from the mean in units of standard deviation. If it is assumed that the underlying distribution of values about the mean is normal, then a likelihood function based upon the Z-scores can be easily established. For example, the likelihood that an observation is more than 3 standard deviations from the mean ($|$Z-score$| > 3.0$) is .0014. Cars that exceed $\pm$ 3.0 will be removed from the candidate set. Once the items are removed, new means and standard deviations are calculated and the agenda updated. This process continues until the standard deviations no longer are large enough to produce new outliers.

The assumption of an underlying normal distribution can be tested for each variable. Also, the user can change the Z-score and the likelihood associated with the removal of items. Once the outliers have been pruned by the inference mechanism, the results are returned to the user.

THE ADAPTIVE OFF-LINE SYSTEM

The on-line system performs three basic types of inferences:

1. Infers range values based upon properties.
2. Infers new properties based upon current properties.
3. Infers outliers based upon statistical properties of remaining cars.

The off-line system focuses on adjusting the first two types of inferences as a result of database updates. The main adjustment for the third type, upper bounds on the Z-scores, is provided by the user.

Update of the dataset may affect the ranges associated with each class of a property. The adaptive system has access to an operationalization table. This table contains those values for variables that are used to delimit the desired classes for a property. Then, for each variable affected by the property, the system generates a query to determine this new upper and lower bound for the variable as a function of the class. These new values are then substituted into the dependency knowledge base.

Type 2 inferences can be updated by observing the frequency with which makes of cars co-occur with each other. That is, how frequently does a car found in one class of a property occur as a member of another class. If the frequency of co-occurrence is above a certain level, then an inference rule can be formed and added to the rule base. Likewise, if the frequency falls below a certain level a rule may be removed.

FUTURE ELABORATIONS

Although the ARIES system deals specifically with a dataset describing of automobiles, the principles underlying the systems design may be applied to other datasets as well. Datasets most amenable to such application will be those where: 1. reasonably large sets of variables are present, and 2. where relationships can be established between variables. This is true for many physical systems, such as automobiles, where physical limitations constrain the choices for a designer, and produce numerous design tradeoffs.

This would also be true of many representations of physical systems. A pictorial database that contains images of physical objects might be easily accessed using the type of expert system interface described here. Given the numerous potential applications, the next step envisioned for ARIES is to generalize the system into a shell such that one need only set up the database and enter the inference rules in order to have a working system.

BIBLIOGRAPHY

1. Waltz, D.
1978
"An English Language Question Answering System for a Large Relational Database," Communication of the ACM, V21, No. 7, pp. 526-539.

2. Stohr, E., Turner, J., Vassiliou, Y., and White, N.
1982
"Research in Natural Language Retrieval Systems," CRIS Working Paper #30, New York Univ.

3. Bates, M., Bobrow, R. J.
1983
"A Transportable Natural Language Interface for Information Retrieval," Proceedings of the 6th Int'l. ACM SIGIR Conf., June, 1983.

4. Artificial Intelligence Corp.
1982
"Intellect Query System," reference manual.

5. Rich, E.
1983
Artificial Intelligence. McGraw-Hill, New York, N.Y.

6. Waterman, D.A. and Hayes-Roth, F.
1983
"An Investigation of Tools for Building Expert Systems," in Building Expert Systems, edited by F. Hayes-Roth, et al., pp. 169-218, Addison-Wesley, Reading, MA.

NATO ASI Series F

Vol. 1: Issues in Acoustic Signal – Image Processing and Recognition. Edited by C. H. Chen. VIII, 333 pages. 1983.

Vol. 2: Image Sequence Processing and Dynamic Scene Analysis. Edited by T. S. Huang. IX, 749 pages. 1983.

Vol. 3: Electronic Systems Effectiveness and Life Cycle Costing. Edited by J. K. Skwirzynski. XVII, 732 pages. 1983.

Vol. 4: Pictorial Data Analysis. Edited by R. M. Haralick. VIII, 468 pages. 1983.

Vol. 5: International Calibration Study of Traffic Conflict Techniques. Edited by E. Asmussen. VII, 229 pages. 1984.

Vol. 6: Information Technology and the Computer Network. Edited by K. G. Beauchamp. VIII, 271 pages. 1984.

Vol. 7: High-Speed Computation. Edited by J. S. Kowalik. IX, 441 pages. 1984.

Vol. 8: Program Transformation and Programming Environments. Report on an Workshop directed by F. L. Bauer and H. Remus. Edited by P. Pepper. XIV, 378 pages. 1984.

Vol. 9: Computer Aided Analysis and Optimization of Mechanical System Dynamics. Edited by E. J. Haug. XXII, 700 pages. 1984.

Vol. 10: Simulation and Model-Based Methodologies: An Integrative View. Edited by T. I. Ören, B. P. Zeigler, M. S. Elzas. XIII, 651 pages. 1984.

Vol. 11: Robotics and Artificial Intelligence. Edited by M. Brady, L. A. Gerhardt, H. F. Davidson. XVII, 693 pages. 1984.

Vol. 12: Combinatorial Algorithms on Words. Edited by A. Apostolico, Z. Galil. VIII, 361 pages. 1985.

Vol. 13: Logics and Models of Concurrent Systems. Edited by K. R. Apt. VIII, 498 pages. 1985.

Vol. 14: Control Flow and Data Flow: Concepts of Distributed Programming. Edited by M. Broy. VIII, 525 pages. 1985.

Vol. 15: Computational Mathematical Programming. Edited by K. Schittkowski. VIII, 451 pages. 1985.

Vol. 16: New Systems and Architectures for Automatic Speech Recognition and Synthesis. Edited by R. De Mori, C.Y. Suen. XIII, 630 pages. 1985.

Vol. 17: Fundamental Algorithms for Computer Graphics. Edited by R.A. Earnshaw. XVI, 1042 pages. 1985.

Vol. 18: Computer Architectures for Spatially Distributed Data. Edited by H. Freeman and G. G. Pieroni. VIII, 391 pages. 1985.

Vol. 19: Pictorial Information Systems in Medicine. Edited by K. H. Höhne. XII, 525 pages. 1986.

Vol. 20: Disordered Systems and Biological Organization. Edited by E. Bienenstock, F. Fogelman Soulié, G. Weisbuch. XXI, 405 pages.1986.

Vol. 21: Intelligent Decision Support in Process Environments. Edited by E. Hollnagel, G. Mancini, D.D. Woods. XV, 524 pages. 1986.

Vol. 22: Software System Design Methods. The Challenge of Advanced Computing Technology. Edited by J.K. Skwirzynski. XIII, 747 pages. 1986.

NATO ASI Series F

Vol. 23: Designing Computer-Based Learning Materials. Edited by H. Weinstock and A. Bork. IX, 285 pages. 1986.

Vol. 24: Database Machines. Modern Trends and Applications. Edited by A.K. Sood and A.H. Qureshi. VIII, 570 pages. 1986.